Woodrow Wilson
A BIBLIOGRAPHY

Photograph of Woodrow Wilson courtesy of Public Policy Papers, Department of Rare Books and Special Collections, Princeton University Libraries.

Woodrow Wilson

A BIBLIOGRAPHY

Compiled by
**JOHN M. MULDER,
ERNEST M. WHITE,
AND ETHEL S. WHITE**

**Bibliographies of the Presidents of the United States,
Number 27**
Mary Ellen McElligott, Series Editor

GREENWOOD PRESS
Westport, Connecticut • London

Library of Congress Cataloging-in-Publication Data

Mulder, John M., 1946–
    Woodrow Wilson : a bibliography / compiled by John M. Mulder,
Ernest M. White, and Ethel S. White.
        p.   cm.—(Bibliographies of the presidents of the United
States, ISSN 1061–6500 ; no 27)
    Includes bibliographical references and index.
    ISBN 0–313–28185–8 (alk. paper)
    1. Wilson, Woodrow, 1856–1924—Bibliography.   I. White, Ernest M.
II. White, Ethel S. III. Title. IV. Series.
Z8976.9.M85   1997
[E766]
016.97391'3092—dc21   97–22554

British Library Cataloguing in Publication Data is available.

Library of Congress Catalog Card Number: 97–22554
ISBN: 0–313–28185–8
ISSN: 1061–6500

First published in 1997

Greenwood Press, 88 Post Road West, Westport, CT 06881
An imprint of Greenwood Publishing Group, Inc.

Printed in the United States of America

The paper used in this book complies with the
Permanent Paper Standard issued by the National
Information Standards Organization (Z39.48–1984).

10 9 8 7 6 5 4 3 2 1

FOR
Mary M. Mulder, Jessie A. White, Galen J. White, Jr.

Contents

Foreword

Nothing in the American constitutional order continues to excite so much scholarly interest, debate, and controversy as the role of the presidency. This remains the case in spite of the complaint, so common in the historical profession a generation ago, about the tyranny of "the presidential synthesis" in the writing of American history.

This complaint had its point. It is true enough that the deep currents in social, economic, and intellectual history, in demography, family structure, and collective mentalities, flow on without regard to presidential administrations. To deal with these underlying trends, the "new history" began, in the 1950s and 1960s, to reach out beyond traditional history to anthropology, sociology, psychology, and statistics. For a season social-science history pushed politics and personalities off the historical stage.

But in time social-science history displayed its limitations. It did not turn out to be, as its apostles had promised, a philosopher's—or historian's—stone. "Most of the great problems of history," wrote Lawrence Stone, himself a distinguished practitioner of the new history, "remains as insoluble as ever, if not more so." In particular, the new history had no interest in public policy—the decisions a nation makes through the political process—and proved impotent to explain it. Yet one can reasonably argue that, at least in a democracy, public policy reveals the true meaning of the past, the moods, preoccupations, values, and dreams of a nation, more clearly and trenchantly than almost anything else.

The tide of historical interest is now turning again—from deep currents to events, from underlying trends to decisions. While the history of public policy requires an accounting of the total culture from which national decisions emerge, such history must center in the end on the decisions themselves and on the people who make (and resist) them. Historians today are returning to the insights of classical history—to the recognition that the state, political authority, military power, elections, statutes, wars, the ideas, ambitions, delusions, and wills of individuals make a difference to history.

This is far from a reversion to "great man" theories. But it is a valuable corrective to the assumption, nourished by social-science history, that public policy is merely a passive reflection of underlying historical forces. For the ultimate fascination of history lies precisely in the interplay between the individual and his environment. "It is true," wrote Tocqueville, "that around every man a fatal circle is traced beyond which he cannot pass; but within the wide verge of that circle he is powerful and free; as it is with man, so with communities."

The *Bibliographies of the Presidents of the United States* series therefore needs no apology. Public policy is a powerful key to an understanding of the past; and in the United States the presidency is the battleground where issues of public policy are fought and resolved. The history of American presidents is far from the total history of America. But American history without the presidents would leave the essential part of the story untold.

Recent years have seen a great expansion in the resources available for students of the presidency. The National Historical Publications Commission has done superb work in stimulating and sponsoring editions, both letterpress and microform, of hitherto inaccessible materials. "Documents," as President Kennedy said in 1963, "are the primary sources of history; they are the means by which later generations draw close to historical events and enter into the thoughts, fears and hopes of the past." He saluted the NHPC program as "this great effort to enable the American people to repossess its historical heritage."

At the same time, there has been a rich outpouring of scholarly monographs on presidents, their associates, their problems, and their times. And the social-science challenge to narrative history has had its impact on presidential scholarship. The interdisciplinary approach has raised new questions, developed new methods and uncovered new sources. It has notably extended the historian's methodological arsenal.

This profuse presidential literature has heretofore lacked a guide. The *Bibliographies of the Presidents of the United States* series thus fills a great lacuna in American scholarship. It provides comprehensive annotated bibliographies, president by president, covering manuscripts and archives, biographies and monographs, articles and dissertations, government documents and oral histories, libraries, museums, and iconographic resources. The editors are all scholars who have mastered their presidents. The series places the study of American presidents on a solid bibliographical foundation.

In so doing, it will demonstrate the wide sweep of approaches to our presidents, from analysis to anecdotage, from hagiography to vilification. It will illustrate the rise and fall of presidential reputations—fluctuations that often throw as much light on historians as on presidents. It will provide evidence for and against Bryce's famous proposition "Why Great Men Are Not Chosen Presidents." It will remind us that superior men have somehow made it to the White House but also that, as the Supreme Court said in *ex parte Milligan*, the republic has "no right to expect that it will always have wise and humane rulers, sincerely attached to the principles of the Constitution. Wicked men, ambitious of power, with hatred of liberty and contempt of law, may fill the place once occupied by Washington and Lincoln."

Above all, it will show how, and to what degree, the American presidency has been the focus of the concerns, apprehensions and aspirations of the people and the times. The history of the presidency is a history of nobility and of pettiness, of courage and of cunning, of forthrightness and of trickery, of quarrel and of consensus. The turmoil perennially swirling around the White House illuminates the heart of American democracy. The literature reflects the turmoil, and the *Bibliographies of the Presidents of the United States* supply at last the light that will enable scholars and citizens to find their way through the literature.

Arthur Schlesinger, Jr.

Editor's Preface

Individuals who rise to the highest elected office offered by the American people hold a special fascination. Their backgrounds, their philosophies over time, the way they "rise" are matters of enduring observation, commentary, and analysis. The Greenwood *Bibliographies of the Presidents of the United States*, splendidly begun by the late Carol Fitzgerald in 1988, provides to both the specialist and generalist a comprehensive guide to every aspect of those unique individuals.

Each volume records the mundane and the critical—from early education, to contemporary news and political analysis, family reminiscences, scholarly analysis and revision, partisan attacks, official papers, personal manuscripts, visual records, and, for administrations of our day, the film and video record.

The Greenwood series offers the possibility of complete access to every instant of the Chief Executive's career or preparation. Taken together, the volumes provide chronological, precise, and detailed accounts of how each President has risen, administered, and withdrawn—and how scholars, pundits, and the American people have weighed that progress.

Mary Ellen McElligott

Introduction

The presidency of Woodrow Wilson (1913–1921) stands out as one of the turning points in American history. Domestically, the Wilson years represent the high point of progressive reform, which laid the foundation for the New Deal of Franklin D. Roosevelt and the modern welfare state. In foreign policy, Wilson articulated the assumptions and implemented programs that have continued to influence the relationship between the United States and the rest of the world throughout the twentieth century.

Wilson has also been perhaps the most controversial president in the history of the United States. Both in his own day and in subsequent historiography, he was the subject of ridicule and scorn as well as effusive praise and extravagant hagiography. Annotating such literature has been a considerable challenge, and we have attempted to summarize arguments without rendering judgments about their quality or validity.

Wilson would have been a major figure in the late nineteenth and early twentieth century even if he had not entered politics. For seventeen years he served successively on the faculties of Bryn Mawr College, Wesleyan University, and Princeton University, earning a reputation as one of the most gifted teachers in higher education. He wrote widely in history, political science, and literature; some of his works, especially *Congressional Government* and "The Study of Administration," continue to attract analysis and debate in the late twentieth century.

From 1902 to 1910 he served as President of Princeton University. During his tenure he transformed Princeton and outlined the vision of what has made it a major institution of higher education in this century.

During the academic years, he travelled and lectured widely, gradually honing his rhetorical skills and acquiring a national reputation. He also yearned for the opportunity to enter politics, and when the opportunity to run for governor of New Jersey came in 1910, he seized it. The press quickly saw Wilson as a progressive Democrat and a strong candidate for the presidency in 1912. From Princeton to Trenton to Washington in three years—it was a dramatic and sudden rise to the highest office of the land. In retrospect, however, it was not surprising. Wilson had been preparing for presidential leadership all his life.

Fortunately, students of Wilson now have an unparalleled resource for the study of his life and presidency—*The Papers of Woodrow Wilson*, edited by Arthur S. Link, David W. Hirst, John E. Little, M

anfred Boemke, Fred Aandahl, et al. This 69–volume series, complete with comprehensive tables of contents and indexes, is the epitome of historical editing. We will probably never have a comparable series for any other president in the twentieth century, partly because of the explosion in the quantity of material and partly because of the expense of publishing.

As the volumes of *The Papers of Woodrow Wilson* appeared, the complexity of his personality and the intricacies of his thought became much more evident. As a result, scholars have been compelled to reassess the often polemical categories in which he had been portrayed and to explore one of the most fascinating individuals ever to occupy the White House. Wilson continues to excite strong judgments, but *The Papers of Woodrow Wilson* now provides a body of evidence on which those verdicts can be rendered more plausibly and persuasively.

In preparing this bibliography, we set a lofty goal: to produce a resource of secondary literature that would complement *The Papers of Woodrow Wilson*. We have tried to be comprehensive, covering literature about Wilson during his lifetime as well as subsequent discussions of his life. We have not been exhaustive, but we believe this bibliography will be the most complete coverage of literature on Wilson published thus far.

A word is in order about some editorial principles we have followed. Citations from *The Papers of Woodrow Wilson* follow the style used by the editors, which includes the date of Wilson's composition or date of first publication. We have not generally included reviews of books about Wilson except when they exceeded ten pages. We have tried to annotate as much of the material as possible, with one exception. The section on Wilson's "Associates" is not annotated because most of the material is only tangentially related to Wilson himself. The "Associates" were determined by examining the frequency with which they appeared in the comprehensive indexes to *The Papers of Woodrow Wilson*. Writings by unknown authors are alphabetized according to their titles. Our cut-off date for the inclusion of new material was 1994.

We have incurred many debts in our research. Milton J. Coalter, Library Director and Professor of Bibliography and Research at Louisville Presbyterian Theological Seminary, was drawn more deeply into this project than either he or we desired. His assistance with bibliographical software was invaluable; his patience has been unwavering. The Louisville Seminary Library staff provided skilled assistance: Elna Amaral, Nancy Elstone, Laura Graham, Angela Morris, Stephen Pillow, Susan Richardson, and Chris Weaver. We are also grateful for the secretarial assistance of Kem Longino, Jean Newman, and Melissa Nebelsick.

We have benefitted from the help of a large number of student assistants: Mark McCullough, Anne Mayo, Kathy Nunamaker, Deborah Prince, Amanda Ragland, Jack Ragland, Judith Williams, and Scott Winnette. Because of their length of service, five assistants have been especially crucial in completing the bibliography in annotating entries and entering information into the computer: Jan Gallagher, Aaron D. Purcell, Miles Spalding, Ingrid Tange, and Galen White III. Each worked on this project for more than a year and devoted themselves to it with energy and good humor. John E. Little, Ellen Rudolph, and L. C. Rudolph loaned their skills in annotation and preparation at many points along the way, and we thank them for locating material inaccessible to us. We are especially grateful to Stan Fedyszyn and Aaron D. Purcell for preparing the indexes.

No project of this type could be completed without the cooperation and support of many libraries. Besides the Ernest Miller White Library of Louisville Seminary, we wish to thank the Boston Public Library, the Library of Congress, and the libraries of Hope College, Indiana University, Princeton Theological Seminary, Princeton University, Southern Baptist Theological Seminary, the University of Kentucky, the University of Louisville, the University of Michigan, the University of Tennessee, Vanderbilt University, and Western Theological Seminary.

We appreciate the guidance and especially the patience of our editors: Carol Fitzgerald, Cynthia Harris, and Mary Ellen McElligott.

Preparing this bibliography has taken ten years. Although collaboration inevitably creates tensions, we remain warm friends and colleagues at the end of a decade of often tedious work. We hope that the fruits of our labor will be widely used by students and scholars seeking to understand Woodrow Wilson and the impact he made on our nation and our world.

Abbreviations

DAB	*Dictionary of American Biography*
DLB	*Dictionary of Literary Biography*
PWW	*The Papers of Woodrow Wilson*
ed.	edition
enl.	enlarged
rev.	revised
supp.	supplement
trans.	translated
vol.	volume

Chronology

1856

December 28. Thomas Woodrow Wilson born in Staunton, Va., the third child of the Rev. Joseph Ruggles Wilson and Janet Woodrow.

1858

Moves to Augusta, Ga.

1867

Enrolls in "Mr. Derry's Classical School" in Augusta. Remains there until 1870.

1870

Fall. The family moves to Columbia, S.C. Woodrow is privately tutored in Latin and Greek by Mrs. Joseph R. Russell.

1873

Enters Davidson College, Davidson, N.C.

1874

The Wilsons move to Wilmington, N.C., where Woodrow remains at home for a year after leaving Davidson.

1875

Fall. Enters Princeton University. Elected an editor of *The Princetonian*. Becomes involved in debating society.

1876

August 16. Publishes "Work-Day Reform" in the Wilmington *North Carolina Presbyterian*.

August 23. Publishes "Christ's Army" in the Wilmington *North Carolina Presbyterian*.

August 30. Publishes "The Bible" in the Wilmington *North Carolina Presbyterian*.

September 5. Publishes "A Christian Statesman" in the Wilmington *North Carolina Presbyterian*.

October 25. Publishes "The Positive in Religion" in the Wilmington *North Carolina Presbyterian*.

December 20. Publishes "Christian Progress" in the Wilmington *North Carolina Presbyterian*.

December 27. Publishes "One Duty of a Son to His Parents" in the Wilmington *North Carolina Presbyterian*.

1877

April. Becomes an editor of *The Princetonian*.

November. "Prince Bismarck" is published in the *Nassau Literary Magazine* under the pseudonym, Atticus.

1878

May. Becomes Managing Editor of *The Princetonian*.

October. Prize essay, "William Earl Chatham," published in *Nassau Literary Magazine*.

1879

June. Graduates from Princeton with an A.B. degree.

August. "Cabinet Government in the United States," written while a senior at Princeton, published in *International Review*.

October. Enters University of Virginia Law School.

1880

Delivers oration before the Jefferson Society of the University of Virginia on John Bright; published in the *University of Virginia Magazine* in March.

Presents before the Jefferson Society the negative side of the debate, "Is the Roman Catholic element in the United States a menace to American institutions?"; published in the *University of Virginia Magazine* in April.

April. Article, "Mr. Gladstone, a Character Sketch," published in *University of Virginia Magazine* under the pseudonym, "Atticus."

August 26, September 7, and September 30. "The Education of the People" is published, without credit, in the Wilmington, N.C. *Morning Star.*

December. Withdraws from the University of Virginia.

1881

Returns home to engage in independent study.

February 16. "Stray Thoughts from the South" is published in the New York *Evening Post.*

1882

Admitted to the Georgia bar and joins Edward I. Renick in the practice of law in Atlanta.

April 26. "New Southern Industries" is published in the New York *Evening Post.*

Fall. Leaves the practice of law and begins doctoral work at Johns Hopkins University.

September 22. Testifies on the tariff issue before the Tariff Commission in Atlanta.

1883

Receives "Historical Fellowship" at Johns Hopkins.

March 7. "Convict Labor in Georgia" is published in the New York *Evening Post*, without an editorial heading.

1884

January. Publishes "Committee or Cabinet Government?" in the *Overland Monthly.*

February 23. "President Eliot's Views" published in the New York *Evening Post.*

March 10. "Johns Hopkins University" published in the New York *Evening Post*, without editorial headings.

April 15. Publishes another newsletter about Johns Hopkins in the New York *Evening Post.*

June 27. "American Universities" is published in the New York *Evening Post.*

1885

January 24. First book, *Congressional Government*, published.

April 29. "Bryn Mawr College" is published in the New York *Commercial Advertiser*.

June 24. Marries Ellen Louise Axson, of Savannah, Ga.

September. Becomes Associate Professor of History and Political Economy at Bryn Mawr College.

1886

Margaret Wilson is born.

Receives Ph.D. from Johns Hopkins. *Congressional Government* fulfills his thesis requirement.

February. "The 'Courtesy of the Senate'" is published in the Boston *Citizen*.

February. Publishes a review of *The Greville Memoirs* in the Chicago *Dial*.

April. Publishes "Responsible Government under the Constitution" in the *Atlantic Monthly*.

September 26. Publishes "Wanted—A Party" in the *Boston Times*, editorial headings and by-line omitted.

1887

Jessie Woodrow Wilson is born.

March. Publishes "Of the Study of Politics" in the *New Princeton Review*.

July. Publishes "The Study of Administration" in the *Political Science Quarterly*.

1888

Accepts Chair of History and Political Economy at Wesleyan University.

"Taxation and Appropriation" is published in Albert Shaw, ed., *The National Revenues*.

April. Janet Woodrow Wilson dies.

September. Publishes "An Old Master" in the *New Princeton Review*.

1889

Eleanor Randolph Wilson is born.

The State: Elements of Historical and Practical Politics is published. Revised and rewritten in 1898.

The State and Federal Governments of the United States: *A Brief Manual for Schools and Colleges* is published, a reprint of chapter eleven of *The State: Elements of Historical and Practical Politics.*

March. Publishes "Bryce's American Commonwealth" in the *Political Science Quarterly.*

October 15. Publishes "Preparatory Work in Roman History" in the *Wesleyan University Bulletin.*

November. "Character of Democracy in the United States" is published in the *Atlantic Monthly.* It is later reprinted, somewhat altered, in *An Old Master and Other Political Essays.*

1890

Accepts chair of Jurisprudence and Politics at Princeton University.

October-January 1891. "The English Constitution" is published in the *Chatauquan* in four installments.

1891

September. Publishes "The Author Himself" in the *Atlantic Monthly.* Reprinted in *Mere Literature and Other Essays* in 1896.

September. "The Study of Politics" is published in the Philadelphia *Book News.*

1892

October 27. Publishes "The True American Spirit" in the Boston *Congregationalist.*

1893

Division and Reunion, 1829–1889 is published.

An Old Master and Other Political Essays is published.

April. Publishes "Mr. Cleveland's Cabinet" in the New York *Review of Reviews.*

August. Publishes "Anti-Slavery History and Biography" in the *Atlantic Monthly.*

October 11. Publishes *An Old Master and Other Political Essays.* (Charles Scribner's Sons, N.Y.)

December. "Mere Literature" is published in the *Atlantic Monthly.* Reprinted in *Mere Literature and Other Essays* in 1896.

December. "Mr. Goldwin Smith's 'Views' on Our Political History" is published in the New York *Forum.*

1894

February. Publishes "A Calendar of Great Americans" in the New York *Forum*. Reprinted in *Mere Literature and Other Essays* in 1896.

September. Publishes "University Training and Citizenship" in the New York *Forum*.

1895

July. Publishes "The Proper Perspective of American History" in the *Forum*.

September. Publishes "On the Writing of History. With a Glance at the Methods of Macauley, Gibbon, Carlyle, and Green" in the *Century Magazine*. Reprinted under the title, "The Truth of the Matter," in *Mere Literature and Other Essays* in 1896.

November. "A Literary Politician" (Walter Bagehot) is published in *Atlantic Monthly*. Reprinted in *Mere Literature and Other Essays* in 1896.

1896

Mere Literature and Other Essays is published.

March. "On an Author's Choice of Company" is published in the *Century Magazine*. Reprinted in *Mere Literature and Other Essays*.

October 21. Makes speech, "Princeton in the Nation's Service," at the University's 150th Anniversary celebration. [Published in *The Forum*, December, 1896.]

1897

George Washington published by Harper & Brothers, New York, having been serialized in *Harper's Magazine* in 1896.

March. Publishes "Mr. Cleveland as President" in the *Atlantic Monthly*.

July. Publishes "The Making of the Nation" in the *Atlantic Monthly*.

September. "On Being Human" is published in the *Atlantic Monthly*.

1898

September. "A Lawyer with a Style" (Sir Henry Maine) is published in the *Atlantic Monthly*.

October. "A Wit and a Seer" (Walter Bagehot) is published in the *Atlantic Monthly*.

1901

Publishes "An Introduction" to *The Autobiography of Benjamin Franklin*.

When a Man Comes to Himself published by Harper & Brothers.

"The Real Idea of Democracy" is published in Seymour Eaton and Frederic W. Speirs's *Problems in Modern Democracy.*

January. Publishes "Editor's Study" in *Harper's Magazine.*

January. Publishes "The Reconstruction of the Southern States" in the *Atlantic Monthly.*

January-May. "Colonies and Nation: A Short History of the People of the United States" is published in *Harper's Magazine.*

March. Publishes "Democracy and Efficiency" in the *Atlantic Monthly.*

September. "Edmund Burke and the French Revolution" is published in *Century Magazine.*

December. "The Coming of Peace" is published in *Harper's Magazine.*

1902

Publishes *A History of the American People*, 5 vols., Harper & Brothers.

His preface, "The Significance of American History," is published in *Harper's Encyclopedia of United States History.*

August 1. Elected President of Princeton University.

October 25. Inaugurated President of Princeton and delivers address, "Princeton for the Nation's Service." Published in the Princeton *Alumni Weekly*, December 13, 1902.

1903

Publishes "Preface" to Andrew F. West's *The Proposed Graduate College of Princeton University.*

January 21. Joseph Ruggles Wilson dies.

June 23. His article, "State Rights," is published in *Cambridge Modern History.*

1905

Publishes "An Introduction" to *The Handbook of Princeton.*

April 28. "The Preceptors" is published in the *Daily Princetonian.*

June 24. Publishes "New Plans for Princeton" in *Harper's Weekly.*

August. Publishes "The Princeton Preceptorial System" in the *Independent.*

1907

March 17. Publishes "Grover Cleveland, Man of Integrity" in the *New York Times*, magazine section.

April 18. Publishes "The Southern Colonist" in *The Youth's Companion*.

September 12. "The Personal Factor in Education" is published in *The Youth's Companion*.

November. "Politics (1857–1907)" is published in the *Atlantic Monthly*.

1908

Constitutional Government in the United States is published.

May. His article, "The States and the Federal Government" is published in the *North American Review*.

1909

October. "The Tariff Make-Believe" is published in the *North American Review*.

November. Publishes "What is a College For?" in *Scribner's Magazine*.

November. Publishes "My Ideal of the True University" in *The Delineator*.

1910

January. "The Democratic Opportunity" is published in the Buffalo, New York *National Monthly*, without an editorial heading.

April 9. "Living Principles of Democracy" is published in *Harper's Weekly*.

May. Publishes "Hide and Seek Politics" in the *North American Review*.

September 15. Receives Democratic nomination for Governor of New Jersey.

October. "Life and Education" is published in the *Nassau Literary Magazine*.

October 23. Resigns as President of Princeton.

November. Elected Governor of New Jersey.

1911

January 17. Delivers Inaugural Address as Governor of New Jersey, favoring corporate regulation, an employer's liability law, a primary election law, a public utilities commission, ballot reform, tax equalization, and a corrupt practices act.

October 4. The New Jersey Democratic Platform is published in the *Newark Evening News*.

1912

January 9. Delivers first annual message to New Jersey legislature.

July 2. Nominated for President of the United States on the forth-sixth ballot at the Democratic National Convention in Baltimore, Md.

August 7. Accepts the presidential nomination in a speech delivered in Sea Girt, N.J.

Fall. Campaigned for the "New Freedom," which called for free competition and the end of business monopolies. Roosevelt's "New Nationalism" welcomed big business but prescribed a strong federal government to regulate it. The two philosophies were closer than campaign rhetoric suggested.

November 4/5. Elected President of the United States with 435 electoral votes, to 88 for Theodore Roosevelt, the Progressive Party candidate, and 8 for the Republican, William Howard Taft. Wilson received 6,286,214 popular votes, while Roosevelt received 4,126,020, and Taft 3,483,922. The Socialist Party candidate was Eugene Debs.

1913

Publishes *The New Freedom: A Call for the Emancipation of the Generous Energies of a People*.

January. *The New Freedom*, a compilation by William B. Hale of Wilsons's campaign speeches, is published.

February 25. The 16th Amendment, permitting an income tax, is ratified.

March 1. Resigns as Governor of New Jersey.

March 4. Inaugurated President of the United States and delivers first Inaugural Address.

March 11. Issues a statement explaining his decision not to recognize the Huerta government in Mexico, thereby departing from traditional American foreign policy, which recognized governments in power. Gen. Victoriano Huerta had overthrown the government of Francisco I. Madero, who, in turn, had overthrown the government of Porfirio Diaz after a 30–year reign.

April 8. Calls Congress into special session and delivers address asking for immediate revision of the Payne-Aldrich Tariff. [Wilson was the first President to deliver a message in person since John Adams.]

April 24. Secretary of State William Jennings Bryan with ministers in Washington submitted arbitration treaties to all nations calling for a "cooling off" period before declaring war. The United States ultimately ratified treaties with 21 nations.

May 3. Over Wilson's objections, California passes law preventing Japanese aliens from owning property, thereby damaging American-Japanese relations.

May 31. The 17th Amendment, calling for the direct election of U.S. Senators, is ratified.

June 23. Delivers address before another joint session of Congress urging legislation which later becomes the Federal Reserve Act.

August 27. Delivers address before Congress on Mexican relations.

October 3. Signs Underwood-Simmons Tariff Act, which lowers tariff rates and imposes the first income tax, after a five-month struggle. Makes a brief address at the White House.

October 27. Delivers address in Mobile, Alabama, promising that the United States would "never again seek one additional foot of territory by conquest."

December 2. Delivers first annual address before a joint session of Congress pressing for, among other things, banking and currency reform, provision for primary elections, and increased rights for people in the territories.

December 23. Signs the Federal Reserve Act which creates a new national banking system with twelve regional banks.

1914

January 20. Delivers address before joint session of Congress asking for antitrust legislation.

February 3. Lifts the arms embargo of Mexico to help Venustiano Carranza, who opposed Huerta.

March 5. Delivers address before Congress on the Panama Canal tolls problem.

April 7. Signs treaty with Colombia agreeing to compensation for loss of Canal Zone. Not ratified by Senate.

April 9. Asks Congress for permission to occupy Tampico, Mexico, and establish a blockade against Huerta after American sailors are arrested there by mistake.

April 20. Delivers address before joint session of Congress calling attention to situation in Mexico.

April 21. Orders seizure of Customs House at Vera Cruz in order to prevent arrival of German arms for Huerta. Huerta severs diplomatic relations with United States, and the two countries are brought close to war.

May 8. Smith-Lever Act provides for agricultural extension work through cooperation between Department of Agriculture and land-grant colleges.

May 20–June 30. Wilson accepts offer of Argentina, Brazil, and Chile to mediate dispute with Mexico, resulting in ABC Conference. Mexico rejects conference's proposal but Huerta feels compelled by it to leave office.

June 4. Delivers address at Arlington in memory of Confederate Dead.

June 11. At Wilson's urging, Congress repeals clause in Panama Tolls Act of 1912 declaring the United States would pay no tolls in Canal. Wilson signs the bill four days later.

August 4. World War I begins in Europe. Issues proclamation of neutrality.

August 6. Death of Ellen Axson Wilson.

August 15. Panama Canal opens.

August 19. Issues proclamation appealing to American citizens to be "neutral in fact as well as in name."

September 4. Makes speech to joint session of Congress requesting a tax increase.

September 26. Federal Trade Commission Act passes at Wilson's recommendation, as part of his program to regulate trusts. Designed to prevent unfair methods of competition in interstate commerce.

October 15. Clayton Antitrust Act passes, supplementing and strengthening Sherman Antitrust Act by defining certain new illegal practices and providing remedies. Wilson Administration brought 92 antitrust suits in eight years.

State Department permits war loans to belligerents.

November 23. United States occupation forces withdraw from Vera Cruz.

December 8. Delivers address at second annual joint session of Congress.

1915

January 28. Returns to House of Representatives, without approval, bill regulating immigration.

February 10. Sends cablegram to Ambassador Gerard in Berlin asking him to warn German government against violating American neutrality on high seas.

May 7. Germans sink British steamship *Lusitania*. Over one hundred American lives are lost.

May 10. Delivers address, "Too Proud to Fight," at naturalization ceremonies of 7,000 foreign-born citizens in Philadelphia.

May 13. Sends first of series of notes to Germany following sinking of *Lusitania* about violations of American neutrality.

June 2. Issues statement to press stating American policy toward Mexico.

June 7. William Jennings Bryan resigns as Secretary of State over Wilson's handling of American neutrality on the high seas. Wilson appoints Robert Lansing in his place.

June 9. Sends second note to German government about sinking of *Lusitania*.

July 21. Sends third note to German government about sinking of *Lusitania*.

July 29. Dispatches marines to Haiti following a series of revolutions there. Treaty ratified February 28, 1916.

September 8. Requests that Austrian government recall Ambassador Dumba because of hostile acts in the United States.

October 7. Announcement of engagement to Edith Bolling Galt.

October 19. Recognizes government of Venustiano Carranza in Mexico.
   Issues proclamation prohibiting exportation of arms to Mexico, with exception of Carranza government.

October 21. Sends letter to Ambassador Page in London declaring illegal British blockade of neutral ports in Norway, Sweden, Denmark, and Holland.

December 4. Requests that German government withdraw Boy-Ed and Von Papen because of hostile acts in the United States.

December 7. Delivers third annual address before joint session of Congress.

December 18. Marries Edith Bolling Galt.

1916

January 27–February 3. Makes series of addresses on national defense.

January 28. Nominates Louis D. Brandeis to United States Supreme Court. Confirmed by Senate.

February 17. McLemore Resolution asking Wilson to prohibit Americans from traveling on armed vessels introduced in Congress. Senator Thomas Gore introduces a similar resolution in Senate. Both resolutions ultimately tabled in face of Wilson's opposition.

February 22. Presents memorandum to Lord Grey declaring his willingness to propose a conference for the purpose of ending war, and suggesting terms.

February 24. Sends note to Senator Stone expressing opposition to Gore and McLemore resolutions, which warned that Americans that traveled on armed merchant ships of combatants did so at their own risk.

March 3. Gore resolution tabled in Senate.

March 7. McLemore resolution tabled in House of Representatives.

March 15. Sends General Pershing and six thousand troops into Mexico in pursuit of Pancho Villa.

April 19. Makes speech to Congress on Sussex Affair.

May 4. German government informs the United States that it has ordered submarine commanders to stop ships only in accordance with principles of visit and search.

May 27. Delivers address before first annual meeting of League to Enforce Peace in Washington, D.C., urging "universal association of nations."

June 3. National Defense Act passes, calling for expansion of army.

June 16. Renominated for President of the United States at National Democratic Convention in St. Louis.

July 11. Signs Federal Highway Act providing federal funds for state roads.

July 17. Signs Federal Farm Loan Act, enabling farmers to secure long-term loans at low interest rates.

August 4. Signs treaty purchasing Virgin Islands from Denmark for $25 million. Ratified in 1917.

August 11. Signs Warehouse Act, which provided farmers with collateral to help finance their crops

August 29. Delivers address before joint session of Congress on impending railroad strike.

Jones Act passed by Congress, promising independence to Philippines and providing for new government.

September 1. Signs Keating-Owen Child Labor Act which excluded from interstate commerce goods manufactured by child labor.

September 2. Makes speech at Shadow Lawn, N.J., accepting renomination for President of the United States.

September 3. Signs Adamson Act, mandating eight-hour day for railroad workers, and authorizing study commission.

September 7. Signs bill creating United States Shipping Board, with power to buy and construct naval and merchant marine ships.

Signs Workmen's Compensation Act which created a plan of compensation for injuries sustained on the job by federal employees.

September 8. Makes speech at Women's Suffrage Convention in Atlantic City.

Signs Emergency Revenue Act increasing the income tax and adding an inheritance tax.

November 7. Reelected President of the United States, receiving 277 electoral votes, against 254 for Charles Evans Hughes.

November 26. Approves American military regime for Dominican Republic after series of revolts there. Occupation lasts until 1924.

December 5. Delivers fourth annual address before joint session of Congress.

December 18. Sends communication to each of the belligerent powers, with copies to all neutral governments, suggesting statement of terms for conclusion of war.

1917

January 22. Makes speech before Senate outlining terms for peace in Europe.

January 29. Sends to House of Representatives second veto of immigration restriction bill. (Bill passed, overriding veto.)

January 31. Germany notifies the United States that submarine activity will resume on February 1.

February 3. Delivers address before joint session of Congress advising that diplomatic relations between the United States and Germany are being severed.

February 5. Vetoes literacy test, which is subsequently overridden by Congress.

February 23. Signs Smith-Hughes Act, providing federal grants-in-aid for vocational education.

February 26. Delivers address before joint session of Congress requesting authority to arm merchant ships.

March 1. "Zimmermann Note," proposing alliance between Germany and Mexico, released by State Department.

March 2. Jones Act passed, making Puerto Rico a United States territory and granting citizenship to its inhabitants.

March 5. Inaugurated President of the United States for second term and delivers second inaugural address.

March 22. Recognizes provisional regime in Russia, after revolution leads to abdication of Czar.

April 2. Delivers address before joint session of Congress asking for declaration of war.

April 4. Senate adopts war resolution by vote of 82 to 6.

April 6. House of Representatives adopts war resolution by vote of 373 to 50. Wilson signs proclamation declaring existence of a state of war.

April 14. Establishes Committee on Public Information to unite public opinion behind war effort.

April 16. Makes address to American people asking them to support war effort.

April 24. Signs Emergency Loan Act (or Liberty Loan Act), authorizing a bond issue and providing for loans to Allies.

May 18. Signs Selective Service Act.

Announces assignment of expeditionary force in France under Major General John J. Pershing.

June 8. Sends message to Russia outlining the United States' purposes in entering war.

June 15. Congress passes Espionage Act, providing penalties for those guilty of aiding enemy or causing disloyalty in armed forces.

July 9. Issues embargo proclamation prohibiting export of certain commodities except under licenses or regulations.

July 28. War Industries Board established by Council of National Defense to coordinate war effort.

August 10. Signs Lever Act (or Food Control Act), which established a Food Administration to control production and fix prices.

August 27. Replies through Robert Lansing to peace proposals of Pope Benedictus XV.

October 3. Signs War Revenue Act, doubling 1916 income tax and levying excise taxes.

October 6. Signs Trading with the Enemy Act, which forbade commerce with enemy nations and permitted censorship of mail.

November 2. Lansing-Ishii Agreement signed, recognizing Japanese rights of propinquity in China and open door and territorial integrity of China.

November 12. Delivers address to American Federation of Labor Convention at Buffalo, N.Y.

November 16. Requires registration of enemy aliens.

December 4. Delivers fifth annual address before joint session of Congress.

December 7. Congress adopts joint resolution declaring existence of state of war with Austria-Hungary.

December 26. Issues proclamation placing railroads under government control.

1918

January 4. Makes speech before joint session of Congress reporting assumption of control of railroads.

January 8. Delivers address before joint session of Congress enunciating Fourteen Points as basis for world peace.

February 11. Delivers address before joint session of Congress on German and Austrian replies to statement of Allied war aims.

April 8. Appoints National War Labor Board to act as court of last resort for labor disputes.

April 10. Signs Webb-Pomerene Act, which enabled exporters to form associations without being subject to antitrust laws.

May 16. Congress passes Sedition Act, amending Espionage Act.

May 20. Signs Overman Act, authorizing President to coordinate and consolidate government agencies.

May 27. Delivers address before joint session of Congress concerning revenue for war.

July 4. Makes speech to Diplomatic Corps at Mount Vernon, describing American purposes in war.

July 22. Issues proclamation placing telephone and telegraph systems under government control.

August 31. Signs amended Selective Service Act.

September 14. Federal court sentences Eugene Debs to 10 years in jail and has his citizenship revoked for interfering with military recruiting. President Harding releases him in 1921, without restoring his citizenship.

September 30. Delivers address before Senate appealing for passage of woman suffrage amendment.

October 6–7. Germany and Austria send peace proposals to Wilson. Series of notes between the three powers follows.

November 4. Allies agree upon draft of armistice.

November 11. Makes announcement of signing of Armistice.
   Delivers address before joint session of Congress announcing signing of armistice.

November 18. Announces that he will attend European peace conference with commission consisting of Col. Edward M. House, Secretary of State Lansing, General Tasker H. Bliss, and Republican Henry White.

December 2. Delivers address before joint session of Congress announcing departure for peace conference in Paris.

December 4. Sails for Europe to attend Paris Peace Conference.

December 14. Arrives in Paris.

December 26. Arrives in London and is guest of King and Queen of England at Buckingham Palace.

1919

January 3. Arrives in Rome and is guest of King and Queen of Italy.
  Delivers address before Italian Parliament on being made citizen of Rome.

January 7. Arrives in Paris.

January 18. Delivers address at opening session of Peace Conference.

January 29. 18th Amendment ratified, prohibiting manufacture, sale, or transportation of alcoholic beverages.

February 3. Delivers address before French Chamber of Deputies in Paris.

February 14. As chairman of League of Nations Commission, presents report of Commission on plan for League of Nations.

February 15. Sails for United States.

February 24. Arrives in Boston.

March 5. Sails to Europe for resumption of Paris Peace Conference.

March 14. Arrives in Paris.

April 28. Presents to Peace Conference revised covenant of League of Nations report.

May 20. Cables message to 66th Congress at beginning of first session, focusing on postwar domestic issues.

June 28. Signs peace treaty with Germany at Versailles.
  Cables American people explaining provisions in peace treaty.

June 29. Sails from France for the United States.

July 8. Arrives in Hoboken, N.J.

July 10. Presents peace treaty to Senate for ratification.

July 29. Sends message to Senate with text of tripartite treaty of guarantee between United States, France, and Great Britain.

August 8. Delivers address before Congress on high cost of living.

August 19. Holds conference at White House with members of Senate Committee on Foreign Relations to discuss peace treaty.

September 3–28. Embarks on nationwide tour, making series of addresses on peace treaty and urging its support.

October 2. Suffers stroke which incapacitates him completely until October 20; holds no Cabinet meetings until April 13, 1920; never fully recovers from paralysis.

October 27. Vetoes Volstead Act prohibiting sale of intoxicating beverages. Congress passes act over President's veto.

November 6. Henry Cabot Lodge, Chairman of Senate Committee on Foreign Relations, proposes fourteen reservations to League Covenant.

November 1. Beginning of bituminous coal strike.

November 19. Senate rejects peace treaty, in two votes.

December 2. Sends seventh annual message to joint session of Congress.

December 24. Issues proclamation relinquishing control of railroads and other property taken in wartime.

1920

January 5. United States Attorney General A. Mitchell Palmer authorizes raids on suspected Communists. Over 4,000 people ultimately are arrested and 556 deported.

January 13. Calls, by cable, first meeting of Council of League of Nations to be held in Paris January 16, 1920.

February 12. Secretary of State Robert Lansing writes letter of resignation, prompted by Wilson's discovery that he had called several Cabinet meetings during Wilson's illness.

February 13. Accepts Lansing's resignation.

February 28. Esch-Cummins Transportation Act returns railroads to private ownership and empowers Interstate Commerce Commission to plan for exemption of railroad groups from antitrust laws. It also fixes minimum and maximum rates and creates Railroad Labor Board to mediate wage disputes.

March 19. Senate rejects Treaty of Versailles a second time with fifteen reservations. Wilson continues to oppose any reservations.

May. Sudden drop in prices is followed by severe recession in 1921. Wilson's postwar policy of balancing budget after wartime deficits, and return of over four million servicemen, are partly responsible.

May 24. Sends message to Congress requesting power to accept mandate over Armenia. Declined by Senate.

May 27. Sends message to House of Representatives vetoing resolution declaring peace with Germany and Austria-Hungary.

June 5. Jones Merchant Marine Act authorizes sale of government ships to private operators. Government loans and other provisions are designed to encourage private shipping.

June 8. Republican Convention meets in Chicago and nominates Senator Warren G. Harding of Ohio for President. Governor Calvin Coolidge of Massachusetts is nominated for Vice President. Platform rejects League of Nations.

June 10. Water Power Act creates Federal Power Commission to license and regulate power plants.

June 28. Democratic Convention meets in San Francisco and nominates Governor James M. Cox of Ohio for President and Assistant Secretary of Navy Franklin D. Roosevelt from New York for Vice President. Platform supports League of Nations.

July 2. By joint resolution Congress terminates war with Germany and Austria-Hungary.

July 15. Issues formal call for first meeting of Assembly of League of Nations on November 15, at Geneva.

August 26. 19th Amendment, calling for woman suffrage, ratified.

October 18. Senate ratifies separate peace treaties with Germany, Austria, and Hungary.

November 2. Harding elected President with 404 electoral votes to 127 for Cox. Eugene Debs, Socialist candidate, receives 3.4% of popular vote but no electoral votes.

November 15. First meeting of Assembly of League of Nations. Cables are sent to and from Wilson.

December 7. Sends eighth annual message to joint session of Congress

December 10. Receives 1920 Nobel Peace Prize.

1921

January 3. Vetoes bill extending term of War Finance Corporation. Congress later passes bill over veto.

February 6. Refuses to submit railway wage controversy to Congress, on grounds that it is within jurisdiction of Interstate Commerce Commission and Railroad Labor Board.

March 3. Sends last message to House of Representatives, enclosing veto of Emergency Tariff Bill, which would impose temporary duties on certain agricultural products.

March 4. Final term as President expires at noon. Leaves White House at 11:00 a.m. and rides with President-elect Harding to Capitol. Signs remaining legislation passed by 66th Congress. Drives to new home at 2340 S Street, N.W. in Washington, D.C.

November 11. Pays tribute to unknown soldier, riding in funeral procession from Capitol to Arlington National Cemetery.

1923

August 8. Accompanies body of President Harding, who has died August 2 in San Francisco from an embolism, from White House to Capitol.

November 10. Delivers last public address, "The Significance of Armistice Day," over radio.

November 11. Large crowd gathers outside Wilson home on Armistice Day, and Wilson delivers short address.

1924

January 16. Receives members of National Democratic Committee at his home.

January 31. Suffers collapse at his home.

February 3. Dies at 11:15 a.m. Crowds of people gather in street outside his residence.

February 6. Is buried in Bethlehem Chapel of Washington Cathedral. Road from his house to Cathedral is filled with thousands of mourners.

Woodrow Wilson

A BIBLIOGRAPHY

1
Manuscript and Archival Sources

A. Unpublished Personal and Administrative Papers

1. Clark, Alexander P. "The Woodrow Wilson Collection: A Survey of Additions [manuscripts] Since 1945." *Princeton University Library Chronicle* 17 (Spring 1956): 173–82. An overview of printed books, rare books, manuscripts, letters, and other material at Princeton by and about Woodrow Wilson.

2. *Diary and Papers of Edward M. House.* Yale University, New Haven, Conn. Collection of unique materials necessary for studying the Wilson presidency.

3. Eaton, Vincent L. "Books and Memorabilia of Woodrow Wilson." *Library of Congress Quarterly Journal of Current Acquisitions* 4 (November 1946): 2–6. Library of Congress acquisitions of Wilson's personal library and other objects.

4. *Index to Woodrow Wilson Papers.* Library of Congress. Manuscript Division. Washington, D.C.: Government Printing Office, 1973. 3 vols. Presidents' Papers Index Series. Guide to the use of either of the collections cited in 7 and 9.

5. "Woodrow Wilson: Catalogue of an Exhibition in the Princeton University Library . . . Commemorating the Centennial of His Birth." *Princeton University Library Chronicle* 17 (Spring 1956): 113–62. Describes Princeton's Woodrow Wilson Collection, which includes letters, manuscripts, articles, addresses, speeches, lecture notes, all of his published writings, as well as other Wilson writings and other Wilson material and memorabilia.

6. *Woodrow Wilson Papers.* Princeton University Library, Princeton, N.J. Includes Wilson's personal correspondence with many of his closest friends and associates.

7. *Woodrow Wilson Papers*, 1786–1961. Library of Congress, Manuscript Division, Washington, D.C. Collection of Wilson manuscript material covering both his personal life and public career.

8. *Woodrow Wilson Papers.* Washington, D.C.: Library of Congress, 1973. The Library of Congress collection on microfilm, 540 reels.

9. *Woodrow Wilson Papers,* 1913–1921. The National Archives, Washington, D.C. Includes many of Wilson's presidential documents scattered through the records of cabinet departments and other government agencies.

B. Published Woodrow Wilson Papers

10. Grantham, Dewey W., Jr. *"The Papers of Woodrow Wilson*: A Preliminary Appraisal." In **1083**, 281–301. A highly favorable review of the series shortly before its completion.

11. Noggle, Burt. "A Note on Historical Editing: The Wilson 'Papers' in Perspective." *Louisiana History* 8, no. 3 (1967): 281–97. Reviews Volume 1 of *PWW* against the historical background of the editing and publishing of historical documents in the United States.

12. Wilson, Woodrow. *The Messages and Papers of Woodrow Wilson.* 2 vols. New York: Doubleday, Doran & Co., 1924. [With editorial notes, an introduction by Albert Shaw, and an analytical index.] Compiles many of Wilson's official addresses, messages, and announcements.

13. ———. *The New Democracy*: *Presidential Messages, Addresses, and Other Papers (1913–1917),* ed. Ray Stannard Baker and William E. Dodd. 2 vols. New York: Harper & Brothers, 1926. Early collection of Wilson's public papers.

14. ———. *The Papers of Woodrow Wilson,* ed. Arthur S. Link, David W. Hirst, John E. Little, Manfred Boemke, Fred Aandahl, et al. 69 vols. Princeton: Princeton University Press, 1966–1994. The most complete edition of the public and personal papers of any President of the United States. Hereafter cited as *PWW*.

15. ———. *President Wilson's State Papers and Addresses.* 2nd ed., ed. Albert Shaw. New York: George H. Doran, 1918. [First issued by the Review of Reviews Co., 1917. For addresses and writings to 1923, see 12.] Contains addresses and writings from March 4, 1913, to April 6, 1918.

16. ———. *Proclamations by the President of the United States.* Washington, D.C.: Government Printing Office, 1915–1923. U.S. Congress, *Statutes at Large,* vols. 38–41. Contains all of Wilson's proclamations issued during his two terms in office.

17. ———. *The Public Papers of Woodrow Wilson.* Authorized ed., ed. Ray Stannard Baker and William Edward Dodd. 6 vols. in 3. New York: Harper and Brothers, 1925–1927. The first major compilation of Wilson's papers by Baker, the authorized biographer, and Dodd.

18. ———. *Selected Literary and Political Papers and Addresses of Woodrow Wilson.* 3 vols. New York: Grosset & Dunlap, 1926–27. [Vols. 1–2 published by arrangement with Harper & Brothers; vol. 3 published by arrangement with Harper & Brothers and Houghton Mifflin Co.] Reprints several of Wilson's literary efforts, longer historical works, literary articles, political papers and addresses, war papers, and documents pertaining to the League of Nations.

C. Contemporary Newspapers and Magazines

For Wilson's presidency, among the most influential newspapers were the *Atlanta Constitution, Atlanta Journal, Baltimore News,* Baltimore *Sun, Boston Daily Globe, Boston Evening Transcript, Boston Herald, Brooklyn Daily Eagle,* Chicago *Daily News, Chicago Daily Tribune, Chicago Herald, Chicago Times, Cleveland Leader, Cleveland Plain Dealer, Dallas Morning News, Denver Rocky Mountain News, Kansas City Star, Los Angeles Times,* Louisville *Courier-Journal, Memphis Commercial Appeal, Milwaukee Journal, Nashville Banner, Nashville Tennessean, New Orleans Picayune, New York American,* New York *Evening Post, New York Herald,* New York *Sun, New York Times, New York Tribune,* New York *World,* Philadelphia *Public Ledger, Philadelphia Record,* Richmond, Va., *Times Dispatch, St. Louis Post Dispatch, Washington Evening Post,* and *Washington Post.*

For his governorship of New Jersey, the principal newspapers were the *Camden Courier,* Jersey City *Jersey Journal, Newark Evening News, Newark Star, Trenton Evening Times, Trenton True American,* as well as the New York and Philadelphia papers cited above.

For coverage of Wilson's years as professor and President of Princeton, see the *Daily Princetonian, Nassau Literary Magazine, New Princeton Review, Princeton Alumni Weekly,* and *Princeton Press.*

Among the most important magazines of his time were the *American Review, American Review of Reviews, Atlantic Monthly, Century Magazine, Collier's Weekly, Dial* (Chicago), *Harper's Magazine, Harper's Weekly, Independent* (New York), *Literary Digest, The Masses* (New York), *Nation* (New York), *New Republic, North American Review, The Outlook, Scribner's Magazine,* and *World's Work.*

2
Writings of Woodrow Wilson

A. Books

19. Wilson, Woodrow. *Congressional Government: A Study in American Politics.* Boston: Houghton Mifflin Co., 1885. [Accepted as his doctoral dissertation in 1886. New inscription to 14th impression, written August 14, 1900, and found in *PWW* 11:572. Introduction by Ray Stannard Baker to the edition of 1925. Preface to the 15th edition written August 15, 1900, and found in *PWW* 11:567–71. For a collection of reviews, see *PWW* 4:236–40, 282–83, 284–86, 309–15, 372–75, 403–9.] Wilson's analysis of Congress, in which he argues that it ought to be reformed along the lines of the British parliamentary system. It appeared in many printings or editions from Houghton Mifflin and was reprinted in 1956 by World Publishing Co. and by Johns Hopkins University Press in 1981.

20. ———. *Constitutional Government in the United States.* Columbia University Lectures. George Blumenthal Foundation, 1907. New York: Columbia University Press, 1908. Wilson's lectures at Columbia University, which reveal his growing recognition of the power of the presidency over Congress in shaping national policies.

21. ———. "Constitutional Government in the United States." In *PWW* 18 (March 24, 1908): 69–216. [The text of **20**. For a collection of reviews, see *PWW* 18:384–85, 446–48, 477–78.]

22. ———. *Division and Reunion, 1829-1889*, Epochs of American History, vol. 3. New York: Longmans, Green, and Co., 1893. [For a collection of reviews, see *PWW* 8:185-92, 195-97, 203–5, 218–19, 222–24, 294–306, 344–46.] Wilson's treatment of the sectional crisis, the Civil War, and Reconstruction. It went through many printings by Longmans, Green, and Co., including two editions with maps and additional chapters by Edward S. Corwin, published in 1921 and 1926.

23. ———. *George Washington.* New York: Harper & Brothers, ca. 1896. [Originally published as six separate articles in *Harper's Magazine*, January-November

1896. For a collection of reviews, see *PWW* 10:64–68, 122–23, 204–10.] A biography written for a mass audience. In it Wilson reveals some of his own hopes and aspirations as he chronicles Washington's career. It went through several editions and revisions and was translated into French and Italian.

24. _____. *A History of the American People.* 5 vols. New York: Harper and Brothers, 1902. [Documentary edition 1918, 10 vols. An alumni edition, a subscription library edition, and a regular trade edition were issued October 28, 1902. In 1910 a popular edition was published. For a collection of reviews, see *PWW* 14:248–52, 280–83, 286–87, 309–13, 338–46, 350–53, 441–45, 309–13.] Wilson's multi-volume survey of American history written for a popular audience.

25. _____. *Leaders of Men*, ed. Thomas Hubbard Vail Motter. Princeton: Princeton University Press, 1952. [Reprinted in *PWW* 6 (June 17, 1890): 644–71. Taken from a December 3, 1889 address, with an extensive editorial introduction.] Asserts that the literary man sways the people by his writing, while an active leader of men enjoys the chance to address the masses in public.

26. _____. *Mere Literature and Other Essays.* Boston: Houghton, Mifflin and Co., 1896. [For a collection of reviews, see *PWW* 10:99–101, 135-37.] Several essays covering the relevance of literature, British history, and American history.

27. _____. *The Minister and the Community.* New York: Student Young Men's Christian Association, 1909. [Originally entitled "The Relation of the Minister to the Community," an address at Hartford Theological Seminary, March 30, 1906. Reprinted in *PWW* 16 (March 30, 1906): 346–51.] Argues that ministers should try to remind people that eternity is a present thing and not something in the future, and that a line connects every transaction of today with eternity.

28. _____. *An Old Master, and Other Political Essays.* New York: Charles Scribner's Sons, 1893. [For a collection of reviews, see *PWW* 8:400–1, 418–20.] Contains articles from the *New Princeton Review* and the *Atlantic Monthly.* Articles listed separately by title.

29. _____. *On Being Human.* New York: Harper & Brothers, 1916. Discusses natural habits exhibited in human behavior.

30. _____. "Princeton in the Nation's Service." Speech on October 21, 1896, at Princeton University's Sesquicentennial Celebration. [Originally appeared in *New York Evening Post* (October 21, 1896), and *Daily Princetonian* (October 22–23, 1896). Complete version reprinted in New York *Forum* 22 (December 1896): 447–66. Also reprinted in *PWW* 10 (October 21, 1896): 11–31.] This became one of Wilson's most important and influential statements on education.

31. _____. *The Road away from Revolution.* Boston: Atlantic Monthly Press, [ca. 1923]. [Reprinted from *Atlantic Monthly* 132 (August 1923): 145-46. Copy of text in *PWW* 68 (April 8, 1923): 322–24.] Wilson's last essay, dictated to his wife during the spring of 1923 in their Washington home. Believes that the world has been made safe for democracy, but democracy has not made the world safe against irrational revolution.

32. _____ . *The State*: *Elements of Historical and Practical Politics*. Boston: D. C. Heath and Co., 1889. [For a collection of reviews, see *PWW* 6:458–62, 550–52.] Wilson's massive textbook on the development of Western political thought and institutions, in which he drew heavily on nineteenth-century German scholarship. It went through many editions and revisions and was translated into Japanese, French, Russian, Italian, Spanish, and German.

B. Articles, Essays, Reviews

33. Wilson, Woodrow. "Abraham Lincoln: A Man of the People." In *PWW* 19 (February 12, 1909): 33–46. [Later published in Nathan William MacChesney, ed. *Abraham Lincoln*: *The Tribute of a Century, 1809–1909*, 14–30. Chicago: A.C. McClurg and Co., 1910.] Centennial address on Lincoln's life explaining the significance of his singular life and character.

34. _____ . "Addresses, 1906–1910." A collection of abstracts given to Princeton University Library by Gilbert F. Close, Wilson's secretary, and called *The Close Connection*.

35. _____ . "The American State." In *PWW* 5 (ca. August 8, 1886): 308–10. An unpublished outline of an elementary text on American government.

36. _____ . "The American State." In *PWW* 5 (ca. August 8, 1886): 310–12. Fragment of a first chapter of a proposed elementary text.

37. _____ . "The American State: Elements of Historical and Practical Politics in the United States. A Textbook for Grammar and High Schools." In *PWW* 6 (ca. May 1 - ca. June 5, 1889): 186–214. Chapters of an unpublished textbook.

38. _____ . "America's Opportunity." In *PWW* 37 (July 30, 1916): 500–1. An unpublished article about America's fitness for leadership and service.

39. _____ . "Anti-Slavery History and Biography." In *PWW* 8 (August 1893): 294–306. [Originally published in the *Atlantic Monthly* 72 (August 1893): 268–77.] A review of John T. Morse's *Abraham Lincoln* (New York: Houghton, Mifflin & Co., 1893); Edward L. Pierce's *Memoir and Letters of Charles Sumner*, Vols. 3 & 4 (Boston: Roberts Brothers, 1893); and James Ford Rhodes, *History of the United States from the Compromise of 1850*, 2 vols. (New York: Harper & Brothers, 1893).

40. _____ . "The Art of Governing." In *PWW* 5 (ca. November 15, 1885): 50–54. An unpublished essay on administration.

41. _____ . "The Author Himself." In *PWW* 5 (ca. December 7, 1887): 635-45. [An unpublished redraft of **65**. Revised version published in *Atlantic Monthly* 68 (September 1891): 406–13. Reprinted in **26**, 28–49.] Argues that the rule for individuals is not to depend on the education which others organize or prepare for them, but to strive to see things as they are and to be themselves.

42. _____ . "Banker and the Nation." In *PWW* 18 (September 30, 1908): 424–34. [Originally published in *Moody's Magazine* 6 (October 1908): 250–53.] An address in Denver to the American Bankers Association, in which he discusses the social and political functions of modern business leaders.

43. _____ . "Before the English Came." In *PWW* 10 (ca. April 8, 1898): 503–17. An unpublished first chapter of a history of the United States for schools.

44. _____ . "The Bible." In *PWW* 1 (August 25, 1876): 184–85. [Originally published in the Wilmington *North Carolina Presbyterian*, August 30, 1876.] An essay about the richness of the Bible.

45. _____ . "Bryn Mawr College." In *PWW* 4 (ca. April 20, 1885): 505-8. [Originally published in the New York *Commercial Advertiser*, April 29, 1885.] An article commenting on the founding of Bryn Mawr College.

46. _____ . "Cabinet Government in the United States." In *PWW* 1 (August 1879): 493–510. [Originally published in the *International Review* 6 (August 1879): 146–63. Also published as *Cabinet Government in the United States* (Stamford, Conn.: Overbrook Press, 1947).] Wilson suggests that if the Cabinet were composed of House and Senate members, it would be more powerful and more responsible.

47. _____ . "A Calendar of Great Americans." In *PWW* 8 (ca. September 15, 1893): 368–80. [Originally published in New York *Forum* 16 (February 1894): 715-27. Also in **26**, 187–212.] An essay describing certain Americans whose greatness was distinctively national.

48. _____ . "Christ's Army." In *PWW* 1 (August 17, 1876): 180–81. [Originally published in the Wilmington *North Carolina Presbyterian*, August 23, 1876.] An essay about the fight against evil.

49. _____ . "Christian Progress." In *PWW* 1 (December 20, 1876): 234–35. [Originally published in the Wilmington *North Carolina Presbyterian*, December 20, 1876.] An essay on the difficulty of the Christian journey.

50. _____ . "A Christian Statesman." In *PWW* 1 (September 1, 1876): 188–89. [Originally published in the Wilmington *North Carolina Presbyterian*, September 6, 1876.] An essay focusing on Christian responsibility.

51. _____ . "Committee or Cabinet Government." In *PWW* 2 (ca. January 1, 1884): 614–40. [Originally published in *Overland Monthly*, 2nd ser., 3 (January 1884): 17–33.] An essay embracing cabinet government.

52. _____ . "Congress: Inside the House." In *PWW* 2 (ca. May 1, 1881): 55-60. An unpublished essay for a contest sponsored by the Philadelphia *American*, dealing with the committee system in the House of Representatives.

53. _____ . "Congressional Government." In *PWW* 1 (October 1, 1879): 548–74. An unpublished draft of an essay on the American system of government.

54. _____ . "Congressional Government in Practice." In *PWW* 4 (February 24, 1885): 288–93. [Originally published in *Bradstreet's* 11 (February 28, 1885): 133.] A letter to the editor discussing the closing session of the Forty-eighth Congress.

55. _____ . "Convict Labor in Georgia." In *PWW* 2 (ca. February 24, 1883): 306–11. [Originally published in the New York *Evening Post*, March 7, 1883.] A newspaper article criticizing the convict system in Georgia.

56. _____ . "The Country and the Colleges." In *PWW* 20 (ca. February 24, 1910): 157–72. An unpublished essay on the social reorganization of universities.

57. _____ . "The Course of American History." In *PWW* 9 (May 16, 1895): 257–74. [Also published as "The Proper Perspective of American History," in New York *Forum* 19 (July 1895): 544–59. Later published in **26**, 213–47.] Discusses the importance of local history and the evolution of writing the history of the United States.

58. _____ . "The Courtesy of the Senate." In *PWW* 5 (ca. November 15, 1885): 44–48. [Originally published in the Boston *Citizen* 1 (February 1886): 1–2.] An essay dealing with presidential nominations sent to the Senate.

59. _____ . "Culture and Education at the South." In *PWW* 2 (March 29, 1883): 326–32. An unpublished article submitted to Robert Bridges, discussing educational standards in the South.

60. _____ . "Daniel Webster and William Pitt." In *PWW* 1 (January 30, 1878): 396–97. Draft of an unfinished biographical essay.

61. _____ . "The December Lit." In *PWW* 1 (January 16, 1879): 446–47. [Originally published in *The Princetonian* 3 (January 16, 1879): 137–38.] A review of the December, 1878 issue of the Princeton literary magazine.

62. _____ . "Democracy and Efficiency." In *PWW* 12 (ca. October 1, 1900): 6–20. [Originally published in the *Atlantic Monthly* 87 (March 1901): 289–99.] An essay dealing with the effective application of democracy.

63. _____ . "The Democratic Opportunity." In *PWW* 19 (ca. November 1, 1909): 465-71. [Originally published in the Buffalo, N.Y. *National Monthly* 1 (January 1910): 249, 253.] An essay about the Democratic Party.

64. _____ . "Ecclesiastical Democracy." *Catholic Digest* 1 (February 1937): 38. Describes the Roman Catholic Church as democratic and the salvation of government in the Middle Ages.

65. _____ . "The Eclipse of Individuality: A One-sided Statement by Axson Mayte." In *PWW* 5 (ca. April 7, 1887): 476–83. An unpublished essay on individuality and reading.

66. _____ . "Editor's Study." In *PWW* 12 (January, 1901): 60–64. [Originally published in *Harper's Magazine* 102 (January 1901): 322–24.] An essay regarding the writing of history.

67. _____ . "Edmund Burke and the French Revolution." In *PWW* 10 (February 23, 1898): 408–23. [Originally published in *Century* 62 (September 1901): 784–92.] Donovan Lecture at Johns Hopkins University in 1898, in which Wilson argues that Edmund Burke gave the most striking proof of his character and genius during the last tumultuous days of his life.

68. _____ . "Education and Democracy." In *PWW* 17 (ca. May 4, 1907): 131–36. An unpublished essay dealing with the importance of popular education in a republic.

69. _____ . "The Education of the People." In *PWW* 1 (ca. August 20, 1880): 666–70. [Originally unsigned editorials in the Wilmington *Morning Star* on August 26, September 7, and September 30, 1880.] An essay on the importance of education for citizenship.

70. _____ . "The English Constitution." In *PWW* 7 (October 1890–January 1891):12–44. [Originally published in four installments in *Chautauquan* 12 (October 1890–January 1891): 5-9, 149–54, 293–98, 430–34.] An essay on the development and institutions of government in England.

71. _____ . "'English Lit. One Hour.'" In *PWW* 1 (January 30, 1879): 450–51. [Originally published in *The Princetonian* (January 30, 1879): 150.] An editorial concerning the study of English literature at Princeton.

72. _____ . "Exchanges." In *PWW* 1 (February 27, 1879): 463. [Originally published in *The Princetonian* 3 (February 27, 1879): 192.] An editorial concerning the Inter-Collegiate Literary Association.

73. _____ . "Football." In *PWW* 1 (September 26, 1878): 405-6. [Originally published in *The Princetonian* 3 (September 26, 1878): 70–71.] An essay about rugby.

74. _____ . "Government by Debate: Being a Short View of Our National Government as It Is and as It Might Be. An Essay in Five Parts." In *PWW* 2 (ca. December 4, 1882): 159–275. An unpublished essay on the American system of government.

75. _____ . "Government under the Constitution." In *PWW* 8 (ca. June 26, 1893): 254–70. [Originally published in **28**, 141–81.] An essay discussing American politics which asserts that the United States constitution is solid and preserved against precipitate change by the formidable difficulties of amending it.

76. _____ . "The Greville Memoirs." In *PWW* 5 (February 1886): 100–04. [Originally published in *Dial* 6 (February 1886): 269–71. A review of Charles C. F. Greville's *A Journal of the Reign of Queen Victoria from 1837-1852* (New York:

D. Appleton & Co., 1875).] Argues that the press has become a great revealer of private affairs and that the world has become an open laboratory in which one may quickly note the operation of social and political forces.

77. _____ . "Grover Cleveland, Man of Integrity." In *PWW* 17 (March 17, 1907): 73–78. [Originally published in the *New York Times* Magazine Section, March 17, 1907.] A tribute to Grover Cleveland on his seventieth birthday.

78. _____ . "Hide-and-Seek Politics." In *PWW* 20 (March 2, 1910): 192–207. [Originally published in the *North American Review* 191 (May 1910): 585-601.] An article on political reform that characterizes American electoral politics as unresponsive to the needs and desires of the people.

79. _____ . "Ideals of Public Life." In *PWW* 17 (November 16, 1907): 497–506. [Later published in *The Cleveland Chamber of Commerce Annual 1908*, 218–30.] Pleads for the recognition that there is a much bigger public life than is comprehended in party contests, and that government is created by public opinion.

80. _____ . "Intelligent Reading." In *PWW* 1 (June 7, 1877): 276–77. [Originally published in *The Princetonian* 2 (June 7, 1877): 44.] An editorial describing the best methods of reading.

81. _____ . "The Interpreter of English Liberty." In *PWW* 8 (ca. August 31, 1893): 318–43 under the title, "Edmund Burke: The Man and His Times." [Also in **26**, 104–160.] Chronicles the life and career of Edmund Burke and argues that Burke had the thoughts of a great statesman and uttered them with unmatched nobility.

82. _____ . "An Introduction to *The Autobiography of Benjamin Franklin*." In *PWW* 12 (July 18, 1901): 164–70. [Originally published in *The Autobiography of Benjamin Franklin*, ed. John Bigelow (New York: The Century Co., 1901): v-xix.] Praises the character of Franklin.

83. _____ . "An Introduction to *The Handbook of Princeton*." In *PWW* 15 (ca. August 1, 1904): 427–31. [Originally published in John Rogers Williams, *The Handbook of Princeton* (New York: 1905): xi-xvii.] Describes the distinctive charm and character of Princeton University.

84. _____ . "Is It Sufficient." In *PWW* 1 (March 21, 1878): 364–65. [Originally published in *The Princetonian* 2 (March 21, 1878): 209–10.] An editorial dealing with student discipline.

85. _____ . "John Bright." In *PWW* 1 (March 6, 1880): 608. [Originally published in *Virginia University Magazine* 19 (March 1880): 354–70.] Examines the character and career of Bright and says that Bright maintained the principles of his youth and that his name became synonymous with liberalism and reform.

86. _____ . *John Wesley's Place in History*. New York: Abingdon Press, 1915. [Also published in *1703-1903, Wesley Bicentennial, Wesleyan University*, 157–70. Middletown, Conn.: 1904, and *Together* (March 1964): 17+. Reprinted in *PWW* 14

(June 30, 1903): 502–14.] Calls Wesley a master evangelist who was poised in spirit, conversant with the nature of others, studious of the truth, sober to think, and prompt to act.

87. _____ . "Johns Hopkins University." In *PWW* 3 (April 11, 1884): 123–25. [Originally published in the New York *Evening Post*, April 15, 1884.] An article concerning lectures and papers at the Seminary of Historical and Political Science.

88. _____ . "Joseph R. Wilson." In *PWW* 30 (ca. May 25, 1914): 75. An unpublished, admiring description of Wilson's father.

89. _____ . "Joseph Ruggles Wilson." In *PWW* 30 (ca. May 25, 1914): 74. An unpublished epitaph for his father's tombstone.

90. _____ . "Last Will and Testament of Woodrow Wilson." In *PWW* 42 (May 31, 1917): 426. An unpublished manuscript, typed and signed.

91. _____ . "The Law and the Facts." *American Political Science Review* 5 (February 1911): 1–11. [Reprinted in *PWW* 22 (December 27, 1910): 263–72.] Presidential address at the Seventh Annual Meeting of the American Political Science Association on December 27, 1910. States that politics includes both the statesmanship of thinking and action, and that the law is subsequent to and based on facts.

92. _____ . "Lawyer with a Style." In *PWW* 10 (February 25, 1898): 443–61. [Originally published in *Atlantic Monthly* 82 (September 1898): 363–74.] Donovan Lecture at Johns Hopkins University on Henry Maine's life and accomplishments.

93. _____ . *Leaderless Government*. Richmond: James E. Goode Printing Co., 1897. [Reprinted in *PWW* 10 (December 27, 1910): 288–304. An address before the Virginia Bar Association, August 4, 1897.] Believes that the executive and legislative branches should be drawn together to give congressional leaders a better chance to determine who should be President, and in turn, the President should be more involved in the guidance of Congress.

94. _____ . "Letter to Representative A. Mitchell Palmer, February 3, 1913." *Congressional Digest* 17 (May 1938): 142–43. [Reprinted in *PWW* 27 (February 5, 1913): 98–101.] Discusses the constitutional amendment limiting the President to a single term.

95. _____ . "Life and Education." In *PWW* 21 (ca. August 1, 1910): 32–33. [Originally published in *Nassau Literary Magazine* 66 (October 1910): 167–69.] An essay on the interdependence of study and experience.

96. _____ . "A Literary Politician." In *PWW* 6 (July 20, 1889): 335-54. [Also in **26**, 69–103.] Outlines the life and career of Walter Bagehot calling Bagehot a talented writer who possessed an excellent understanding of politics and history.

97. _____ . "The Making of the Nation." In *PWW* 10 (April 15, 1897): 217–36. [Originally published in *Atlantic Monthly* 80 (July 1897): 1–14.] An essay concerning the development of the United States.

98. _____ . "The Man behind the Trust." In *PWW* 19 (August 3, 1909): 324–27. An unpublished essay on the modern corporation.

99. _____ . "Memorandum for 'The Modern Democratic State.'" In *PWW* 5 (ca. December 1 - December 20, 1885): 58–61. Unpublished samples written during the drafting of the essay.

100. _____ . "Mere Literature." In *PWW* 8 (ca. June 17, 1893): 240–52. [Originally published in *Atlantic Monthly* 72 (December 1893): 820–28. Also in **26**, 1–27.] An essay dealing with the benefits of literature.

101. _____ . "The Ministry and the Individual." In *McCormick Theological Seminary Historical Celebration*, 163–73. Chicago: R. R. Donnelley and Sons Co., 1910. [Reprinted in *PWW* 19 (November 2, 1909): 471–79.] Argues that the object of Christianity is the individual, and the individual is the vehicle for Christianity.

102. _____ . "The Modern Democratic State." In *PWW* 5 (ca. December 1 - December 20, 1885): 61–92. [Revised and published in *Atlantic Monthly*, November 1889 and **28**, 99–138, under the title "Character of Democracy in the United States."] An unpublished treatise on the nature and development of democratic government. Argues that democracy is the fullest form of state life.

103. _____ . "Monument and Site." In *PWW* 19 (ca. March 29, 1909): 126–28. An unpublished draft of a report to John Fairfield Dryden about a Cleveland memorial at Princeton.

104. _____ . "A More Excellent Way." *Princeton Alumni Weekly* (March 19, 1904): 391. Address to Brown University Teacher's Association, March 4, 1904.

105. _____ . "Mr. Cleveland's Cabinet." In *PWW* 8 (ca. March 17, 1893): 160–78. [Originally published in *Review of Reviews* 7 (April 1893): 286–97.] An article discussing the composition of Grover Cleveland's cabinet.

106. _____ . "Mr. Cleveland as President." In *PWW* 10 (January 15, 1897): 102–19. [Originally published in the *Atlantic Monthly* 79 (March 1897): 289–300.] An essay assessing the Cleveland presidency.

107. _____ . "Mr. Gladstone, A Character Sketch." In *PWW* 1 (April, 1880): 624–42. [Originally published in the *Virginia University Magazine* 19 (April 1880): 401–26.] Regards Gladstone as one of the great English orators, and asserts that no man was more consistently eloquent than Gladstone.

108. _____ . "My Ideal of the True University." In *PWW* 19 (July 6, 1909): 295-303. [Originally published in *Delineator* 74 (November 1909): 401, 437–38.] Believes that the ideal American university is a place combining genuine intellectual discovery and enlightenment, as well as moral and spiritual discipline.

109. _____ . "My Thought Is of America." *Register of the Kentucky Historical Society* 13, no. 37 (1915): 33–34. Discusses the effect of the war in Europe on the United States.

110. _____ . "The New Jersey Democratic Platform of 1911." In *PWW* 23 (October 3, 1911): 382–84. [Originally published in *Newark Evening News*, October 4, 1911.] Outlines thirteen of Wilson's platform principles designed to establish legislation free from private control.

111. _____ . "New Plans for Princeton." In *PWW* 16 (June 24, 1905): 146–49. [Originally published in *Harper's Weekly* 49 (June 24, 1905): 904.] An article on the new preceptorial system at Princeton.

112. _____ . "New Southern Industries." In *PWW* 2 (April 20, 1882): 119–25. [Originally published in the New York *Evening Post*, April 26, 1882.] Revision of the unpublished **170**, centering on industrial change in that region.

113. _____ . "Notes on Administration." In *PWW* 5 (ca. November 15, 1885): 49–50. An unpublished entry in a notebook concerning aspects of administration.

114. _____ . "Of the Study of Politics." In *PWW* 5 (ca. November 25, 1886): 395-406. [Originally published in *New Princeton Review* 3 (March 1887): 188–99, also published in **28**, 31–57.] Discusses politics and political economy, arguing that in order to understand and write about government the writer should paint the government to life.

115. _____ . "An Old Master." In *PWW* 5 (ca. February 1, 1887): 444–55. [Originally published in *New Princeton Review* 6 (September 1888): 210–20, also published in **28**, 3–28.] Examines the character and career of Adam Smith, calling him a major force in thought, an un-business-like professor, a man of books, and an eccentric, learned, and inspired individual.

116. _____ . "On an Author's Choice of Company." In *PWW* 9 (November 10, 1895): 338–47. [Originally published in *Century Magazine* 51 (March 1896): 775-79. Also in **26**, 49–68.] Covers the qualities of being a successful writer as well as the personality traits necessary to convey audibly one's message to others.

117. _____ . "On Being Human." *Atlantic Monthly* 80 (September 1897): 320–29. [Later published as **29**. Originally a commencement address at Miss Hersey's School, Boston, June 2, 1897. Reprinted in *PWW* 10 (June 2, 1897): 245-59.] Notes that "being human" was once simple, but now life has become more complex.

118. _____ . "On Board Steamship Anchoria: From Glasgow to New York, August 27 to September 7, 1896." In *PWW* 9 (September 5, 1896): 576. An unpublished poem.

119. _____ . "On the Writing of History with a Glance at the Methods of Macaulay, Gibbon, Carlyle, and Green." In *PWW* 9 (ca. June 17, 1895): 293–305.

[Originally published in *Century Magazine* 1 (September 1895): 787–93. Reprinted in **26**, 161–86, under the title "The Truth of the Matter." Also published as *On the Writing of History* (Albuquerque: American Classical College Press, 1978).] An essay dealing with the methods of various historians.

120. ———. "One Duty of a Son to His Parents." In *PWW* 1 (October 8, 1876): 205-7. [Originally published in the Wilmington *North Carolina Presbyterian*, December 27, 1896.] An essay on young people's conduct at home.

121. ———. "A Paper on the Actual Workings of the American Constitution." In *PWW* 38 (ca. Spring 1884): 680. A news report of a paper on the changing balance of constitutional government read by Wilson before the Historical and Political Science Association of Johns Hopkins University.

122. ———. "The Personal Factor in Education." In *PWW* 17 (ca. August 1, 1907): 325-33. [Originally published in *Youth's Companion* 81 (September 12, 1907): 423–24.] An essay on the importance of the teacher in education.

123. ———. "Platform Suggestions." In *PWW* 20 (ca. April 4, 1910): 315-17. An unpublished draft of a platform for the Democratic Party of Pennsylvania.

124. ———. "Political Sovereignty." In *PWW* 7 (ca. November 9, 1891): 325-341. [Also published in **28**, 61–96.] Asserts that law proceeds from the community as it develops out of the struggles against class, interest against interest, and from compromises and adjustments of public opinion.

125. ———. "Politics (1857–1907)." In *PWW* 17 (ca. July 31, 1907): 309–25. [Originally published in the *Atlantic Monthly* 100 (November 1907): 635-46.] An essay describing the political development of the United States during the last half-century.

126. ———. "The Politics and the Industries of the New South." In *PWW* 2 (April 30, 1881): 49–55. [An unpublished revision of **170**, submitted to *International Review*.] Believes that politically the South is "solid" and that industrial prospects for the region look bright.

127. ———. "The Positive in Religion." In *PWW* 1 (October 15, 1876): 211–12. [Originally published in the Wilmington *North Carolina Presbyterian*, October 25, 1876.] An essay about strict adherence to Christian principles.

128. ———. "The Preceptors." In *PWW* 16 (April 28, 1905): 84–85. [Originally published in the *Daily Princetonian*, April 28, 1905.] An article describing the new preceptorial system at Princeton.

129. ———. "A Preface to *The New Freedom*." In *PWW* 27 (ca. January 2, 1913): 6–7. [Originally published in **278**, vii-viii.] Explains that his book expresses the new spirit of politics; presents his New Freedom as only the old politics, clothed in the spirit of modern America.

130. _____ . "Preface to *The Proposed Graduate College of Princeton University*." In *PWW* 14 (February 17, 1903): 361. [Originally published in Andrew F. West, *The Proposed Graduate College of Princeton University* (Princeton: Trustees of Princeton University, 1903): 3.] Praises Dean West's plan to build and develop a graduate school at Princeton University.

131. _____ . "Preface to *Through Darkness to Dawn*." In *PWW* 43 (n.d.): 85. [Originally published in William North Rice, *Through Darkness to Dawn* (New York, 1917).] Brief preface in which Wilson describes Rice as an admirable friend and colleague.

132. _____ . "Preparatory Work in Roman History." In *PWW* 6 (October 15, 1889): 403–06. [Originally published in *Wesleyan University Bulletin* (October 15, 1889): 13–15.] Maintains that what is needed in the way of improvement in preparatory instruction in Roman history is a recognition of the fact that Roman history is the basis for much of the world's best literature.

133. _____ . "President Eliot's Views." In *PWW* 3 (February 22, 1884): 42–44. [Originally published in New York *Evening Post*, February 23, 1884.] An article describing a speech given at Johns Hopkins University by Harvard President Charles Eliot concerning educational reform.

134. _____ . "Prince Bismarck." In *PWW* 1 (November 1877): 307–13. [Originally published in *Nassau Literary Magazine* 33 (November 1877): 118–27.] Asserts that with the appearance of Bismarck upon the political stage a new rule of statesmen began and believes that Prussia will not soon find another Bismarck.

135. _____ . "Princeton and the Next I.C.L. Contest." In *PWW* 1 (May 10, 1877): 260–62. [Originally published in *The Princetonian* 2 (May 10, 1877): 19–20.] An editorial dealing with Princeton's membership in the Inter-Collegiate Literary Association.

136. _____ . "The Princeton Preceptorial System." In *PWW* 16 (ca. June 1, 1905): 107–09. [Originally published in *Independent* 59 (August 3, 1905): 239–40.] An article concerning the new system of preceptorial instruction at Princeton.

137. _____ . "Princeton's New Plan of Study." In *PWW* 15 (ca. August 29, 1904): 450–60. An unpublished draft of an article dealing with curricular reform at Princeton.

138. _____ . "Prolegomena." In *PWW* 2 (ca. January 1, 1881): 6. An unpublished memorandum in a journal describing its planned contents.

139. _____ . "Prospects for a New National Party." In *PWW* 5 (ca. September 1, 1886): 328–42. [Published in a briefer version as **228**.] An unpublished first draft of an essay about political parties.

140. _____ . "The Real Idea of Democracy." In *PWW* 12 (ca. August 31, 1901): 175-79. [Originally published in *Problems in Modern Democracy*, eds. Seymour

Eaton and Frederic W. Spiers, 59–67. Booklovers Reading Club Handbook, course 1. Philadelphia: Booklovers Library, 1901.] States that democracy as we know it is no older than the end of the eighteenth century and discusses the major problems of modern democracy.

141. _____ . "The Reconstruction of the Southern States." In *PWW* 11 (ca. March 2, 1900): 459–79. [Originally published in *Atlantic Monthly* 77 (January 1901): 1–15.] Discusses changes in the South thirty years after Reconstruction, and how the southern states were restored to their place in the Union.

142. _____ . "The Reorganization of the University." In *PWW* 19 (November 29, 1909): 536–37. An unpublished outline of an unpublished article for *Scribner's*.

143. _____ . "Responsible Government under the Constitution." In *PWW* 5 (ca. February 10, 1886): 107–24. [Originally published in the *Atlantic Monthly* 57 (April 1886): 542–53.] Explains that the governmental institutions of the United States rest upon the opinions of the people.

144. _____ . "Review of Adolphe de Chambrun's *Droit et Libertes aux Etats-Unis: Leurs Origines et Leurs Progres* (Paris: Ernest Thorin, 1891)." In *PWW* 7 (ca. April 1892): 534–36. [Originally published in the Philadelphia *Presbyterian and Reformed Review* 3 (April 1892): 396–98.] Review stating that Chambrun's work is more exhaustive than other English works written about rights and liberties in American history.

145. _____ . "Review of Edward Campbell Mason's *The Veto: Its Origin, Development, and Function in the Government of the United States (1789-1889)* (Boston: Ginn and Co., 1890)." In *PWW* 7 (April 1891): 185-86. [Originally published in *Annals of the American Academy of Political and Social Science* 1 (April 1891): 694–97.] Explains Mason's classification of vetoes and outlines the veto's development.

146. _____ . "Review of Emile Boutmy's *Studies in Constitutional Law: France-England-United States*" (New York: Macmillan and Co., 1891). In *PWW* 7 (ca. August 22, 1891): 275-76. [Originally published in the New York *Educational Review* 2 (November, 1891): 392–93.] Refers to the book as stimulating, suggestive, lively, and accurate. Further, Wilson asserts that in this translation the translator has preserved the true significance of the original.

147. _____ . "Review of Goldwin Smith's *The United States: An Outline of Political History, 1492-1871*" (New York: 1893). In *PWW* 8 (ca. September 5, 1893): 346–57. [Originally published under the title, "Mr. Goldwin Smith's 'Views' on Our Political History" in *Forum* 16 (December 1893): 489–99.] Calls Smith's work a strong pamphlet containing opinions rather than a real history containing dispassionate and well-considered truth.

148. _____ . "Review of H. von Holst's *The Constitutional Law of the United States of America*" (Chicago: Callahan and Co., 1887). In *PWW* 5 (April 17, 1887):

490–99. [Originally published in Philadelphia *Press*, April 17, 1887.] Describes von Holst's career and calls his book an important treatise on American constitutional law.

149. _____ . "Review of Hannis Taylor's *The Origin and Growth of the English Constitution*." In *PWW* 7 (January 1891): 87–91. [Originally published in the New York *Presbyterian and Reformed Review* 2 (January 1891): 179–81.] Calls Taylor's work a careful resume of the scholarly material, so various and so important, which has accumulated in recent years touching the history and development of the English constitution.

150. _____ . "Review of Henry Jephson's *The Platform: Its Rise and Progress* (New York: Macmillan and Co.)." In *PWW* 8 (October, 1892): 31–33. [Originally published in *Dial* 13 (October 1, 1892): 213–14.] Asserts that Jephson, like his book, has zeal and industry but no sense of humor. Further, Wilson believes that the real topic of this book is the history of political agitation between members of Parliament and their constitutients.

151. _____ . "Review of Henry Sidgwick's *The Elements of Politics*" (New York: Macmillan and Co.). In *PWW* 7 (ca. October 24, 1891): 318–20. [Originally published in *Dial* 12 (November 1891): 215-16.] Believes that Sidgwick accomplishes his main goal: to answer the question of what role the Constitution plays in the action of the government.

152. _____ . "Review of James Bryce's *American Commonwealth*." In *PWW* 6 (ca. January 31, 1889): 61–76. [Originally published in *Political Science Quarterly* 4 (March 1889): 153–69, under the title, "Bryce's American Commonwealth."] Believes that Bryce's excellent work will be invaluable to students of comparative politics.

153. _____ . "Review of John Richard Green's *A History of the English People*." In *PWW* 1 (May 2, 1878): 373–75. [Originally published in *The Princetonian* 3 (May 2, 1878): 7–8.] Upholds Green as an important English historian who adds vividness to history; also argues that this history of the English people is a history of the American people as well.

154. _____ . "Review of John W. Burgess's *Political Science and Comparative Constitutional Law*." In *PWW* 7 (May 1891): 195-203. [Originally published as "A System of Political Science and Constitutional Law," *Atlantic Monthly* 67 (May 1891): 694–99.] Praises Burgess's work as being excellent in both method and thought, but criticizes the work as being mechanically incorrect and dogmatic in spirit.

155. _____ . "The Revision of the Courses of Study." *Princeton Alumni Weekly* (June 18, 1904): 104. [Reprinted in *PWW* 15 (June 14, 1904): 379–83.] Introduces Wilson's proposed Bachelor of Letters degree program as well as new guidelines for undergraduate years.

156. ———. "A River's Course." In *PWW* 2 (December 1, 1881): 91–94. An unpublished poem in a private notebook.

157. ———. "Self-Government in France." In *PWW* 1 (September 4, 1879): 515-39. An unpublished essay about political development in France.

158. ———. "The Significance of American History." In *PWW* 12 (September 9, 1901): 179–84. [Originally published in *Harper's Encyclopedia of United States History* (10 vols., New York: 1902) 1:xxvii-xxxii.] This preface to a historical encyclopedia explains the importance of American history in the framework of world history.

159. ———. "Social Debating Clubs." In *PWW* 1 (February 6, 1879): 454–55. [Originally published in *The Princetonian* 3 (February 6, 1879): 164–65.] An editorial concerning literary and social clubs at Princeton.

160. ———. "Socialism and Democracy." In *PWW* 5 (ca. August 22, 1887): 559–62. An unpublished essay.

161. ———. "Some Legal Needs." In *PWW* 2 (ca. May 1, 1881): 60–63. An unpublished essay for a contest, sponsored by the Philadelphia *American*, regarding some limitations of federalism.

162. ———. "Some Thoughts on the Present State of Public Affairs." In *PWW* 1 (January 30, 1878): 347–54. An unpublished essay, probably submitted to *Nassau Literary Magazine*, dealing with the composition of Congress.

163. ———. "A Song." In *PWW* 2 (December 8, 1881): 94. An unpublished poem in a journal.

164. ———. "The Southern Colonist." In *PWW* 17 (ca. March 1, 1907): 51–56. [Originally published in *Youth's Companion* 81 (April 18, 1907): 184–85.] An essay for youth concerning the lives of Virginia colonists.

165. ———. "The State." In *PWW* 6 (ca. June 3, 1889): 253–311. Four chapters from **32**.

166. ———. *The State and Federal Governments of the United States*: *A Brief Manual for Schools and Colleges*. Boston: D. C. Heath, 1889. [A reprint of chapter eleven from **32**.]

167. ———. "State Rights (1850–1860)." In *PWW* 11 (ca. December 20, 1899): 303–48. [Originally published in A. W. Ward et al. (eds.) *The Cambridge Modern History* (13 vols., New York: 1903–1912) 7:405-42, 808–10.] Describes events leading up to the Civil War by focusing upon issues of slavery, states rights, and the 1860 presidential election.

168. ———. "The States and the Nation." *North American Review* 187, no. 3 (May 1908): 684–701. Essay describing the division of constitutional powers.

169. ———. "Stray Thoughts from the South." In *PWW* 2 (February 12, 1881): 19–25. [Originally published in the New York *Evening Post*, February 16, 1881.] An article discussing the condition and future of the South.

170. ———. "Stray Thoughts from the South." In *PWW* 2 (ca. February 22, 1881): 26–31. [Portions of it were published by the *Evening Post* on April 30, 1881, and April 26, 1882, under the titles "The Politics and the Industries of the New South" and "New Southern Industries" respectively.] Believes that the people of the South are determined to accomplish two goals: the unobstructed and peaceful development of its wealth and the conclusive establishment of its right of self-government within the provisions of the Constitution.

171. ———. *The Study of Public Administration*, Cadernos de Administracao Publica, 16. Rio de Janeiro: Escola Brasileira da Administracao Publica, Fundacao Getbulio Vargas, [1955?]. [Translation of **172.**]

172. ———. *The Study of Public Administration*. Washington, D.C.: Public Affairs Press, [1955]. [Reprint of Wilson's essay on public administration which originally appeared in the *Political Science Quarterly* in 1887.]

173. ———. "The Study of Administration." In *PWW* 5 (ca. November 1, 1886): 359–80. [Originally published in the *Political Science Quarterly* 2 (July 1887): 197–222.] Wilson's influential essay dealing with the science of administration in which he argues for the importance of politics in any analysis of administration.

174. ———. "The Study of Politics." In *PWW* 7 (September 1891): 278–84. [Originally published in the Philadelphia *Book News* 10 (September 1891): 36–39, and also in **28**, 31–57.] An essay including a reading list.

175. ———. "Suggestions for Platform Resolutions, September, 1910." In *PWW* 21 (August 9, 1910): 43–46. An unpublished proposal for the platform of the New Jersey Democratic Party.

176. ———. "The Tariff Make-Believe." In *PWW* 19 (September 5, 1909): 359–80. [Originally published in the *North American Review* (October 1909): 535-56.] An article concerning the Payne-Aldrich tariff bill.

177. ———. "Taxation and Appropriation." In *PWW* 5 (ca. January 12, 1888): 653–56. [Originally published in Albert Shaw, ed., *The National Revenues* (Chicago: A.C. McClurg and Co., 1888): 106–11.] An essay concerning tariff laws.

178. ———. "To E. L. A. on Her Birthday." In *PWW* 3 (May 15, 1884): 178–80. An unpublished poem to Ellen Louise Axson.

179. ———. "To the Women of the South." In *PWW* 27 (ca. January 1, 1910): 574. [Abridged version carved on a monument to women of the Confederacy in Rome, Ga., dedicated March 9, 1910.] An unpublished tribute.

180. _____ . "Translation of a Boudoir Scene." In *PWW* 7 (March 9, 1892): 462–66. Wilson's translation of a brief love scene taken from Theophile Gautier's *Mademoiselle de Maupin*. Nouv. ed. Paris: G. Charpentier, 1880.

181. _____ . "The True American Spirit." In *PWW* 8 (October 27, 1892): 37–40. [Originally published in the Boston *Congregationalist* 77 (October 27, 1892): 347.] An essay describing the essence of American democracy.

182. _____ . "True Scholarship." In *PWW* 1 (May 24, 1877): 268–69. [Originally published in *The Princetonian* 2 (May 24, 1877): 30–31.] An editorial describing the attributes of the scholar.

183. _____ . "The United States and the Armenian Mandate." *International Conciliation* 151 (June 1920): 271–74. [Reprinted from the *Congressional Record*, May 24, 1920.] Includes the Senate resolution and vote declining to grant power to the President to accept a mandate over Armenia.

184. _____ . "University Training and Citizenship." In *PWW* 8 (ca. June 20, 1894): 587–96. [Originally published in *Forum* 18 (September 1894): 107–14.] An essay on higher education.

185. _____ . "(Untitled)." In *PWW* 1 (May 24, 1877): 267–8. [Originally published untitled editorial in *The Princetonian* 2 (May 24, 1877): 28.] Concerns enthusiasm in study.

186. _____ . "(Untitled)." In *PWW* 1 (June 7, 1877): 274–5. [Originally published untitled editorial in *The Princetonian* 2 (June 7, 1877): 42–43.] Discusses oratory.

187. _____ . "(Untitled)." In *PWW* 1 (October 4, 1877): 294–5. [Originally published untitled editorial in *The Princetonian* 2 (October 4, 1877): 76.] Deals with the lack of oratory instruction at Princeton.

188. _____ . "(Untitled)." In *PWW* 1 (January 10, 1878): 333–37. [Originally published untitled editorial in *The Princetonian* 2 (January 10, 1878): 145-49.] Five editorials dealing with the Winter Term and the Lecture Association at Princeton, the Nassau and University Hotels, and laziness.

189. _____ . "(Untitled)." In *PWW* 1 (January 24, 1878): 342. [Originally published untitled editorial in *The Princetonian* 2 (January 24, 1878): 157.] A review of a Boston Philharmonic Club concert in Princeton.

190. _____ . "(Untitled)." In *PWW* 1 (January 24, 1878): 343–45. [Originally published untitled editorial in *The Princetonian* 2 (January 24, 1878): 157–59.] Three editorials concerning the Glee Club and Chapel Stage speakers at Princeton and the Inter-Collegiate Literary Association.

191. _____ . "(Untitled)." In *PWW* 1 (February 7, 1878): 356–58. [Originally published untitled editorial in *The Princetonian* 2 (February 7, 1878): 170.] Two editorials about two preachers and a lecture at Princeton.

192. _____. "(Untitled)." In *PWW* 1 (March 7, 1878): 362. [Originally published untitled editorial in *The Princetonian* 2 (March 7, 1878): 193.] Concerns a disturbance among freshmen and sophomores at Princeton.

193. _____. "(Untitled)." In *PWW* 1 (April 4, 1878): 367–68. [Originally published untitled editorial in *The Princetonian* 2 (April 4, 1878): 218–19.] Discusses the selection of successors to the boards of the campus newspaper and literary magazine.

194. _____. "(Untitled)." In *PWW* 1 (May 2, 1878): 369–73. [Originally published untitled editorial in *The Princetonian* 2 (May 2, 1878): 1–4.] Five editorials covering the introduction and election of new *The Princetonian* board members, college discipline, and sports.

195. _____. "(Untitled)." In *PWW* 1 (May 16, 1878): 376. [Originally published untitled editorial in *The Princetonian* 3 (May 16, 1878): 13–14.] Deals with the Inter-Collegiate Literary Association.

196. _____. "(Untitled)." In *PWW* 1 (May 30, 1878): 378–79. [Originally published untitled editorial in *The Princetonian* 3 (May 30, 1878): 25-26.] Three editorials concerning the resignation of the Princeton football captain and the Inter-Collegiate Athletic Association field meeting at Mott Haven, New York.

197. _____. "(Untitled)." In *PWW* 1 (June 27, 1878): 382–83. [Originally published untitled editorial in *The Princetonian* 3 (June 27, 1878): 50.] Discusses student disturbances at Princeton.

198. _____. "(Untitled)." In *PWW* 1 (September 26, 1878): 401–5. [Originally published untitled editorial in *The Princetonian* 3 (September 26, 1878): 64–66.] Three editorials covering football expenses, dormitory service, and baseball at Princeton.

199. _____. "(Untitled)." In *PWW* 1 (October 10, 1878): 413–17. [Originally published untitled editorial in *The Princetonian* 3 (October 10, 1878): 75-81.] Eight editorials dealing with aspects of campus life. The last two are titled "Dry" and "The I.C.L.A."; the six others are untitled.

200. _____. "(Untitled)." In *PWW* 1 (October 24, 1878): 422–23. [Originally published untitled editorial in *The Princetonian* 3 (October 24, 1878): 87–88.] Two editorials about college football.

201. _____. "(Untitled)." In *PWW* 1 (November 7, 1878): 429–32. [Originally published untitled editorial in *The Princetonian* 3 (November 7, 1878): 99–101.] Five editorials covering campus issues: the selection of editors at *The Princetonian*, attendance at chapel, stage oratory, and athletics.

202. _____. "(Untitled)." In *PWW* 1 (November 21, 1878): 436 [Originally published untitled editorial in *The Princetonian* 3 (November 21, 1878): 111.] Concerns Princeton football.

203. _____ . "(Untitled)." In *PWW* 1 (December 5, 1878): 437–39. [Originally published untitled editorial in *The Princetonian* 3 (December 5, 1878): 123–24.] Three editorials dealing with college athletics.

204. _____ . "(Untitled)." In *PWW* 1 (January 16, 1879): 444–45. [Originally published untitled editorial in *The Princetonian* 3 (January 16, 1879): 136.] Two editorials concerning the Inter-Collegiate Literary Association and a Princeton crew team.

205. _____ . "(Untitled)." In *PWW* 1 (January 30, 1879): 449–50. [Originally published untitled editorial in *The Princetonian* 3 (January 30, 1879): 147.] Discusses the organization of a cricket team at Princeton.

206. _____ . "(Untitled)." In *PWW* 1 (February 6, 1879): 453–54. [Originally published untitled editorial in *The Princetonian* 3 (February 6, 1879): 161–62.] Deals with commencement exercises at Princeton.

207. _____ . "(Untitled)." In *PWW* 1 (February 13, 1879): 457. [Originally published untitled editorial in *The Princetonian* 3 (February 13, 1879): 173.] Comments on the expected dramatic readings of Mary Frances Scott-Siddons.

208. _____ . "(Untitled)." In *PWW* 1 (February 27, 1879): 460–61. [Originally published in *The Princetonian* 3 (February 27, 1879): 183.] A review of Mary Frances Scott-Siddons' dramatic reading in Princeton.

209. _____ . "(Untitled)." In *PWW* 1 (February 27, 1879): 461–62. [Originally published untitled editorial in *The Princetonian* 3 (February 27, 1879): 183–84.] Two editorials dealing with college debating and commencement honors.

210. _____ . "(Untitled)." In *PWW* 1 (March 13, 1879): 464–65. [Originally published untitled editorial in *The Princetonian* 3 (March 13, 1879): 197.] Deals with classroom discipline.

211. _____ . "(Untitled)." In *PWW* 1 (March 27, 1879): 467–71. [Originally published untitled editorial in *The Princetonian* 3 (March 27, 1879): 207–9.] Five editorials covering aspects of campus life: gymnastic dress, the Lynde Debate, the Instrumental Club, the election of baseball captains, and the Boating Association.

212. _____ . "(Untitled)." In *PWW* 1 (April 10, 1879): 474–76. [Originally published untitled editorial in *The Princetonian* 3 (April 10, 1879): 220–21.] Two editorials dealing with college athletics and the Lynde Debate.

213. _____ . "(Untitled)." In *PWW* 1 (May 1, 1879): 478–79. [Originally published untitled editorial in *The Princetonian* 3 (May 1, 1879): 231–32.] Two editorials commenting on *The Princetonian* and boating at Princeton.

214. _____ . "(Untitled)." In *PWW* 3 (ca. August 24, 1884): 287. Fragment of an unpublished poem in a pocket notebook.

215. _____ . "(Untitled)." In *PWW* 5 (ca. September 1, 1886): 326–28. Unpublished outline for an essay having to do with leadership in government.

216. _____ . "(Untitled)." In *PWW* 17 (August 6, 1907): 335-38. An unpublished essay about constitutional government.

217. _____ . "(Untitled)." In *PWW* 17 (ca. February 1, 1908): 609–10. [Originally published in the Hamilton, Bermuda *Royal Gazette*, February 1, 1908.] A petition concerning the admission of automobiles onto the island of Bermuda.

218. _____ . "(Untitled)." In *PWW* 19 (October 8, 1909): 406. [Originally published in the *Daily Princetonian*, October 8, 1909.] A statement about the Bible.

219. _____ . "(Untitled)." In *PWW* 20 (June 6, 1910): 502–05. [Originally published in the Indianapolis *Jefferson Democracy* 1 (November 1910): 1–2.] An article about choosing a political party.

220. _____ . "(Untitled)." In *PWW* 21 (September 15, 1910): 94–96. [Originally published in the Trenton *True American*, September 16, 1910.] The platform of the New Jersey Democratic party.

221. _____ . "(Untitled)." In *PWW* 24 (June 11, 1912): 470. An unpublished draft of a plank on trusts for the Democratic platform.

222. _____ . "(Untitled)." In *PWW* 24 (ca. June 16, 1912): 476–77. An unpublished outline of a Democratic platform.

223. _____ . "(Untitled)." In *PWW* 24 (ca. June 16, 1912): 477–81. An unpublished draft of various planks for a Democratic platform.

224. _____ . "(Untitled)." In *PWW* 25 (October 1, 1912): 305-10. [Originally published in the *Trenton Evening Times*, October 2, 1912.] The New Jersey Democratic Party platform (attributed to Wilson as principal author).

225. _____ . "(Untitled)." In *PWW* 37 (ca. June 10, 1916): 190–200. An unpublished final draft of the National Democratic platform of 1916. The adopted platform incorporated most of Wilson's text verbatim.

226. _____ . "(Untitled)." In *PWW* 37 (August 1, 1916): 508–12. [Published as "The Mexican Question," *Ladies Home Journal* 33 (October 1916): 9.] An essay discussing United States' relations with Mexico.

227. _____ . "View of America's Future." *Journal of Education* 77 (February 6, 1913): 146–47. An exhortation on behalf of reform in business and banking, delivered by President-elect Wilson at Chicago on January 11, 1913.

228. _____ . "Wanted,—A Party." In *PWW* 5 (ca. September 1, 1886): 342–46. [Originally published in the *Boston Times*, September 26, 1886. See also **139**.] An essay concerning political parties.

229. _____ . "What Can Be Done for Constitutional Liberty: Letters from a Southern Young Man to Southern Young Men." In *PWW* 2 (ca. March 21, 1881): 33–40. Two unpublished letters to the editor calling for civil service reform.

230. _____ . "What Is a College For?" In *College Years: Essays of College Life*, ed. Joseph Bunn Heidler. New York: Ray Long and Richard R. Smith, 1933. Preceded by a sketch of Wilson by the editor.

231. _____ . "What Is a College For?" In *PWW* 19 (August 18, 1909): 334–47. [Originally published in *Scribner's Magazine* 46 (November 1909): 570–77.] An essay discussing the goals of higher education.

232. _____ . "When a Man Comes to Himself." In *PWW* 11 (ca. November 1, 1899): 263–73. [Originally published in *Century Magazine* 62 (June 1901): 268–73. Published as a book by Harper & Bros. in 1915.] An essay about self-understanding.

233. _____ . "William Earl Chatham." In *PWW* 1 (October 1878): 407–12. [Originally published in *Nassau Literary Magazine* 34 (October 1878): 99–105.] A prize biographical essay on the elder William Pitt.

234. _____ . "Wilson's Section for a History of Political Economy in the United States." In *PWW* 4 (ca. May 25, 1885): 631–63. An unpublished essay containing biographical sketches and commentaries on writings of political economists.

235. _____ . "Work-Day Religion." In *PWW* 1 (August 11, 1876): 176–78. [Originally published in the Wilmington *North Carolina Presbyterian*, August 16, 1876.] An essay concerning the need for more service in the church.

236. _____ . "The World and John Hart: A Sketch in Outline." In *PWW* 5 (ca. September 1, 1887): 567–84. An unpublished short story. This was an attempt to put **65** into fictional form. See *PWW* 5:645, footnote.

237. _____ . "Writing of Fiction in Princeton." In *PWW* 1 (June 7, 1877): 273–74. [Originally published in *The Princetonian* 2 (June 7, 1877): 40.] An editorial concerning the encouragement of fiction writing at Princeton.

C. Selections

238. American Association for International Conciliation. "The League of Nations." International Conciliation No. 131. New York: 1918. Contains speeches, documents, correspondence, letters, memos, and addresses by World War I leaders, including an address by Wilson at the Metropolitan Opera House, New York, September 27, 1918.

239. Birley, Robert, ed. *Speeches and Documents in American History*. World's Classics, vols. 3 and 4. London: Oxford University Press, 1942–1944. [Volumes cover 1865-1913, and 1914–1939.] Includes some of Wilson's more important addresses.

240. Braeman, John, ed. *Wilson*. Great Lives Observed Series. Englewood Cliffs, N.J.: Prentice-Hall, 1972. A collection of Wilson's writings and contemporary appraisals.

241. Brand, Katharine Edith. "The 'Inside Friends': Woodrow Wilson to Robert Bridges." *Library of Congress Quarterly Journal of Current Acquisitions* 10 (May 1953): 129–42. Selected letters, 1877–1923, and an editorial account of those not printed here.

242. Dickinson, Goldworthy Lowes. *Documents and Statements Relating to Peace Proposals and War Aims, (December 1916-November 1918)*, with an introduction by G. Lowes Dickinson. New York: Macmillan Co., 1919. Contains speeches and letters pertaining to World War I, including several by Wilson.

243. Fosdick, Dorothy, ed. "Woodrow Wilson in His Own Words." *New York Times Magazine* (June 10, 1956): 13, 58. Selected statements by Wilson on various topics.

244. Frost, Elizabeth, ed. *The Bully Pulpit: Quotations from America's Presidents*. New York: Facts on File Publications, 1988. Contains a short section on Wilson with various quotations by him.

245. Gailey, Robert R., ed. *Woodrow Wilson's Principles of Democracy*. Peking: Commercial Press, 1928. Wilson's wartime addresses and the Memorial Address delivered before the joint session of Congress.

246. Gauss, Christian Frederick, ed. *Democracy Today: An American Interpretation*. Lake English Classics. Chicago: Scott, Foresman, and Co., [ca. 1917]. Documents from American history designed to focus on the 1917 situation. Most of the entries are messages by Wilson.

247. Hurd, Charles, and Eleanor B. Hurd. *A Treasury of Great American Letters*, 252. New York: Hawthorn Books, 1961. Includes a short letter from Wilson to Senator William Borah, expressing his appreciation for a complimentary message.

248. Link, Arthur S., comp. *Woodrow Wilson: A Profile*. American Profile Series. New York: Hill and Wang, 1968. Selections from Wilson's writings, plus an essay on Wilson as a realist and an idealist.

249. Linthicum, Richard, ed. *Wit and Wisdom of Woodrow Wilson*. Garden City, N.Y.: Doubleday, Doran & Co., 1916. Excerpts from Wilson's public speeches covering a number of issues, arranged topically.

250. Padover, Saul Kussiel. "The American as Liberal: Woodrow Wilson." In *The Genius of America: Men Whose Ideas Shaped Our Civilization*, 304–20. New York: McGraw-Hill Book Co., 1960. Highlights of Wilson's speeches and writings, arranged topically.

251. Paine, Gregory Lansing, ed. *Southern Prose Writers*. American Writers Series, 365–76. New York: American Book Co., 1947. Brief biographical sketch which reviews and outlines **26** and **290**.

252. Pease, Otis, ed. *The Progressive Years: The Spirit and Achievement of American Reform.* New York: George Braziller, 1962. Includes writings by Wilson, using them to illuminate the goals of the progressive movement.

253. Rozwenc, Edwin Charles. *Roosevelt, Wilson and the Trusts.* Problems in American Civilization, no. 21. Boston: D. C. Heath and Co., 1950. [Includes an essay, "Woodrow Wilson: Monopoly or Opportunity?" reprinted from **278**, 54–63.] Believes that America was created in order that all persons should have an equal chance to exercise mastery over their own fortunes.

254. Van Doren, Carl Clinton, and Carl Lamson Carmer. "Crusade for Freedom." In *American Scriptures*, 244–47. New York: Boni and Gaer, 1946. Contains two short excerpts of Wilson speeches.

255. _____ . "Lincoln and Wilson." In *American Scriptures*, 43–50. New York: Boni and Gaer, 1946. A dramatic reading for radio which intermingles portions of Wilson's tribute to Lincoln in September, 1916, with portions of poems about Nancy Hanks (by Rosemary Benet), Ann Rutledge (by Edgar Lee Masters), and Lincoln himself (by Edwin Markham).

256. Warner, Charles Dudley, ed. *Library of the World's Best Literature.* 39:16047–60. New York: R. S. Peale and J. A. Hill, 1896. [Reprints Wilson's "The Truth of the Matter" and "The West in American History" from **26**.] Calls Wilson a brilliant scholar who makes the past and present vivid by his interpretations from the raw facts and figures.

257. Wilson, Woodrow. *Addresses Delivered by President Wilson on His Western Tour.* Washington, D.C.: Government Printing Office, 1919. [66th Cong., 1st sess., S. Doc. 120, September 4–25, 1919.] Speeches on the League of Nations, the peace treaty, and other topics.

258. _____ . *Addresses of President Wilson. Boston, Mass., February 24, 1919, New York, N.Y., March 4, 1919.* Washington, D.C.: Government Printing Office, 1919. Two speeches on the League of Nations, given between trips to Paris.

259. _____ . *Addresses of President Wilson on the First Trip to Europe.* Washington, D.C.: Government Printing Office, 1919. Speeches between December 3, 1918, and February 24, 1919, ending with "The Plan for the League of Nations."

260. _____ . *Addresses of President Wilson on National Defense.* Washington, D.C.: Government Printing Office, 1916. [Also in 64th Cong., 1st sess., H. Doc. 120. Addresses between January 27 and February 3, 1916.] Includes speeches in New York, Pittsburgh, Cleveland, Milwaukee, Chicago, Des Moines, Topeka, Kansas City, and St. Louis.

261. _____ . *America and Freedom: Being the Statements of President Wilson on the War.* London: G. Allen & Unwin, 1917. Selected addresses between December 20, 1916, and August 28, 1917.

262. _____ . *America Joins the World*. New York: Association Press, 1919. Selections from speeches and state papers, 1914–1918.

263. _____ . "American Universities." *New York Evening Post, or Evening Post for the Country* (June 27, 1884): 1. Describes the appeal of universities for two distinct groups of men: college graduates and those whose background is in the marketplace. Unsigned but attributed to Wilson.

264. _____ . *Americanism: Addresses by Woodrow Wilson, Franklin K. Lane, Theodore Roosevelt*. (n.p.): Veterans of Foreign Wars of the United States, 1926. Delivered in Philadelphia, May 10, 1915; New York, January 11, 1919; and New York, October 12, 1915, respectively.

265. _____ . *Americanism: Woodrow Wilson's Speeches on the War—Why He Made Them and What They Have Done*, comp. and annotated by Oliver Marble Gale. Chicago: Baldwin Syndicate, 1918. Wilson's most important remarks during the first year of World War I, with annotations.

266. _____ . *America's Greatness*. New York: W. H. Wise & Co., 1931. Selections from Wilson's works.

267. _____ . *The Bases of Durable Peace as Voiced by President Wilson*. Chicago: Union League Club, 1918. [Also issued by the Union League Club as *The Bases of Lasting Peace*.] Contains five addresses, January 8–September 27, 1918.

268. _____ . *A Crossroads of Freedom: The 1912 Campaign Speeches*, ed. John Wells Davidson. New Haven: Yale University Press, Woodrow Wilson Foundation, 1956. A compilation of Wilson's most important speeches. More complete texts are found in *PWW*.

269. _____ . *Day of Dedication: Essential Writings and Speeches*, ed. Albert Fried. New York: Macmillan Co., 1965. Wilson's political addresses, with a biographical introduction.

270. _____ . *The Frontier between Armenia and Turkey, as Decided by President Woodrow Wilson, November 22, 1920*. New York: Armenian National Committee, 1943. Contains Wilson's letter to the Supreme Council of the Allied Powers and his decision.

271. _____ . *Guarantees of Peace*. New York: Harper & Brothers, 1919. [This volume supplements two earlier collections: **305** and **274**.] Messages and addresses to the Congress and the people, January 31–December 2, 1918, together with the peace notes to Germany and Austria.

272. _____ . *Hope of the World: Messages and Addresses*. New York: Harper & Brothers, 1920. Addresses between July 10 and December 9, 1919, including some in behalf of the Versailles Treaty and the League of Nations.

273. _____ . *The Ideals of Education*, ed. August Heckscher. New York: Woodrow Wilson Foundation, 1958. [Reprinted from chapter five of **281**.]

274. _____ . *In Our First Year of the War.* Enl. ed. New York: Harper & Brothers, 1918. [First edition appeared earlier in 1918. This volume supplements **305** and precedes **271**.] Messages and addresses to Congress and the people, March 5, 1917 to April 6, 1918.

275. _____ . *International Ideals: Speeches and Addresses.* New York: Harper & Brothers, 1919. Addresses and speeches made during the President's European visit, December 14, 1918 to February 14, 1919.

276. _____ . "Make This League of Nations a Vital Thing." *International Organization* 10, no. 4 (1956): 525–28. In this address delivered before the second plenary session of the Peace Conference, January 25, 1919, Wilson urges that permanent justice be arranged and peace maintained.

277. _____ . "Message of President Wilson Transmitting to the Senate the Treaty with France of June 28, 1919." *American Journal of International Law* 13 (October 1919): 759–60. Treaty asserts that if Germany moved aggressively against France, the United States could immediately come to the aid of France.

278. _____ . *The New Freedom: A Call for the Emancipation of the Generous Energies of a People*, ed. William Bayard Hale. New York: Doubleday, Page and Co., 1913. [Originally published in *World's Work*, January to July, 1913.] Compiled from the stenographic reports of Wilson's campaign speeches in 1912. Several editions were published.

279. _____ . "Our Last Frontier." *Berea Quarterly* 4 (May 1899): 5–6. [Reprinted in *PWW* 11 (January 29, 1899): 97–100.] Address by Wilson at a meeting in New York about Berea College in January 1899. Wilson's "frontier" refers to the Appalachian area, allegedly skipped over during the march to the Pacific.

280. _____ . *The Political Thought of Woodrow Wilson*, ed. Edmund David Cronon. American Heritage Series. Indianapolis: Bobbs-Merrill Company [1965]. A collection of Wilson's writings with a biographical and analytical essay.

281. _____ . *The Politics of Woodrow Wilson: Selections from His Speeches and Writings*, ed. August Heckscher. New York: Harper & Brothers, 1956. One-volume selection of important writings and speeches.

282. _____ . *Pourquoi Nous Sommes en Guerre. Six Messages au Congres a au Peuple Americain, Suive du Message du President Wilson a la Russie*, trans. D. Roustan. Paris: Bossard, 1917. [No. 9 in: *World War, 1914-1918*. Pamphlets, 12.]

283. _____ . "President Extends to Women Subjects of Germany and Austria-Hungary Rules Governing Conduct of Alien Enemies." *Official Bulletin* 2 (April 22, 1918): 1–2.

284. _____ . *President Wilson's Addresses*, ed. George M. Harper. New York: Henry Holt and Co., 1918. Contains addresses from March 4, 1913 to April 6, 1918.

285. _____ . *President Wilson's Foreign Policy: Messages, Addresses, and Papers*, ed. James Brown Scott. New York: Oxford University Press, 1918. A collection of Wilson's works on foreign policy issues, focusing on Mexico and Europe.

286. _____ . *President Wilson's Great Speeches and Other History-Making Documents*. Chicago: Stanton and Van Vliet, [ca. 1917]. [A later edition was published in 1920.] Contains addresses from March 4, 1913, to April 6, 1918.

287. _____ . *President Wilson's Speeches on the World War*. Shanghai: Commercial Press, 1918. Translated into Chinese by Monlin Chiang.

288. _____ . *President Wilson's State Papers and Addresses*. New York: Review of Reviews Co., 1917. Major speeches and diplomatic notes through February, 1918.

289. _____ . "The Real Idea of Democracy: A Talk." In *Problems in Modern Democracy*, eds. Seymour Eaton and Frederic W. Spiers, 57–67. Booklovers Reading Club Handbook, course 1. Philadelphia: Booklovers Library, 1901. [Reprinted in *PWW* 12 (August 31, 1901): 175–79.] Believes that the real problem of modern democracy is how practical means are to be found for putting democratic ideals into actual use in the conduct of governments.

290. _____ . *Robert E. Lee: An Interpretation by Woodrow Wilson*. Chapel Hill: University of North Carolina Press, 1924. [Originally entitled "Robert E. Lee," an address at the University of North Carolina, January 19, 1909. Printed in the University of North Carolina *Record, Alumni Bulletin No. 2 Anniversary of Lee's Birth* (Chapel Hill, N.C., 1909), 6–21. Reprinted in *PWW* 18 (January 19, 1909): 631–45.] Describes Lee as a great soldier, leader, and gentleman.

291. _____ . *Selected Addresses and Public Papers of Woodrow Wilson*, ed. Albert Bushnell Hart. New York: Boni and Liveright, 1918. Contains letters and addresses, 1913–1918.

292. _____ . *A Selection from President Wilson's War Addresses, 1917-1918*. Historical Outlook, War Reprint, no. 6. Philadelphia: McKinley Publishing Co., 1918.

293. _____ . "Some Old Letters of Thomas Woodrow Wilson." *Pennsylvania Magazine of History and Biography* 67 (April 1943): 161–65. Two 1887 letters of Wilson to President James B. Angell of the University of Michigan expressing his ambition to become a leader of the nation.

294. _____ . "Statement Regarding the Disposition of Fiume." *American Journal of International Law* 13 (October 1919): 761–63. [Previously published in *Chicago Tribune*, Paris ed., Thursday, April 24, 1919, 1.] Calls Italy America's friend and charges that Fiume must be the outlet and inlet of commerce to the countries of Hungary, Bohemia, and Rumania.

295. _____ . "There Ought Never to Be Another Presidential Nominating Convention." *U.S. News and World Report* 72 (June 26, 1972): 92. [Letter reprinted in *PWW* 27 (February 5, 1913): 97–101.] Excerpts of a 1913 reply from Wilson to A. Mitchell Palmer, then Democratic leader of the House of Representatives, who had asked for his views on an amendment proposing a single, 6–year presidential term.

296. _____ . *The Triumph of Ideals.* New York: Harper & Brothers, 1919. Speeches, messages, and addresses between February 24, 1919, and July 8, 1919.

297. _____ . "Trust Crusading." *American Lawyer* 16 (May 1908): 267–68. [Also published as "Itch to Regulate" in *Nation's Business* 27 (May 1939): 78.] Wilson warns against too much regulative legislation, and compares it with government ownership of business.

298. _____ . *War Addresses of Woodrow Wilson*, ed. Arthur Roy Leonard. Boston: Ginn and Co., ca. 1918. Covers January 22, 1917 to February 11, 1918, and includes an introduction about Wilson, his writings, and World War I.

299. _____ . *War, Labor and Peace. Some Recent Addresses and Writings of President Wilson. Issued by the Committee on Public Information, Washington, D.C.* Red, White, and Blue Series, no. 9. March 1918. [Washington, D.C.: 1918]

300. _____ . *War Speeches and Messages of Woodrow Wilson.* Appeal Pocket Series, 125. Girard, Kans.: Appeal Publishing Co., [19—].

301. _____ . *War Speeches of Woodrow Wilson*, Little Blue Book, Vol. 5, no. 125. Girard, Kans.: Haldeman-Julius Co., ca. 1924.

302. _____ . *What Are We Fighting For?: A Question Answered from the Messages and Addresses of Woodrow Wilson, President of the United States of America.* Army and Navy Series. Boston: War Work Council of the Unitarian Churches, [1917].

303. _____ . *What President Wilson Says.* [New York: National Woman Suffrage Publishing Co., 1918]. Brief pamphlet explaining why and how Wilson supported woman suffrage.

304. _____ . *Why the U.S. President Must Not Wear a Uniform.* New York: Privately Printed, 1918. A letter from Wilson explaining that he will not wear a uniform because American military power is subordinate to civil authority.

305. _____ . *Why We Are at War.* New York: Harper & Brothers, 1917. [This volume was followed by two others: **274** and **271**.] Messages to Congress, January to April 1917.

306. _____ . *The Wilson Reader*, 4. Docket Series. ed. Frances Farmer. New York: Oceana Publications, 1956. Excerpts from Wilson's writings, arranged as a biography.

307. _____ . *Wilson's Ideals*, ed. Saul Kussiel Padover. Washington, D.C.: American Council on Public Affairs, 1942. Highlights of Wilson's speeches and writings, arranged topically.

308. _____ . *Winning the War: Nonpartisanship the Test*. St. Paul, Minn.: National Nonpartisan League, [1918]. From the letters, messages, and addresses of the President.

309. _____ . *The Wisdom of Woodrow Wilson*, ed. Charles J. Herold. New York: Brentano's, 1919. Selections from his thoughts and comments on political, social, and moral questions, with an introduction by the editor.

310. _____ . *Woodrow Wilson, 1856-1924: Chronology, Documents, Bibliographical Aids*. Presidential Chronologies Series. Vol. 11, ed. Robert I. Vexler. Dobbs Ferry, N.Y.: Oceana Publications, 1969. A selection of Wilson's significant speeches, supplemented by a fairly detailed chronology and a select bibliography.

311. _____ . *Woodrow Wilson at His Grandfather's Church at Carlisle. Address at the Lowther Street Congregational Church, Carlisle, England, December 29, 1918*. Stamford, Conn.: Overbrook Press, 1956.

312. _____ . *Woodrow Wilson: Selections for Today*, ed. Arthur Bernon Tourtellot. New York: Duell, Sloan and Pearce, 1945. A collection of Wilson's presidential speeches and writings.

313. _____ . *Woodrow Wilson's Case for the League of Nations*, comp. Hamilton Foley. Princeton: Princeton University Press, 1923. [Second edition, January 1924.] Combines Wilson's sentences from various occasions in order to provide a comprehensive explanation of the peace treaty and the League of Nations.

314. _____ . *Woodrow Wilson's Own Story*, ed. Donald Day. Boston: Little, Brown, and Co., 1952. Selections from Wilson arranged in an autobiographical form.

315. *The Woodrow Wilson Calendar, 1920*. New York: Hall, 1920. Contains selections from **278** and from addresses by Wilson.

3
General Biographies

316. Anderson, David D. *Woodrow Wilson*. Twayne's World Leaders Series, 76. Boston: Twayne Publishers, 1978. A brief biography focusing on Wilson's strengths and weaknesses as a man and a politician.

317. Archer, Jules. *World Citizen*: *Woodrow Wilson*. New York: J. Messner, 1967. A biography beginning with Wilson's childhood and ending with a discussion of the strong influence he had on the Presidents who followed him.

318. Archer, William Henry. *The Peace President*: *A Brief Appreciation*. New York: Henry Holt & Co., 1919. A short, laudatory biography taking Wilson through World War I and urging acceptance of the League of Nations.

319. Baker, Ray Stannard. *Life and Letters of Woodrow Wilson*. 8 vols. Garden City, N.Y.: Doubleday, Page and Co., 1927–1939. The authorized biography covering Wilson's life through the War. Filled with praise for Wilson, the study was the first to make use of his personal papers.

320. Bell, Herbert Clifford Francis. *Woodrow Wilson and the People*. Garden City, N.Y.: Doubleday, Doran, and Co., 1945. A laudatory biography, stressing Wilson's desire to stay in contact with the American public.

321. Blum, John Morton. *Woodrow Wilson and the Politics of Morality*. Library of American Biography Series. Boston: Little, Brown, and Co., 1956. An interpretation of Wilson's presidency, stressing his tendency to cast political issues in moral terms.

322. Bragdon, Henry Wilkinson. *Woodrow Wilson*: *The Academic Years*. Cambridge: Harvard University Press, 1967. Covers in detail Wilson's life prior to becoming governor of New Jersey.

323. Charles, Heinrich. *Der Wirkliche Woodrow Wilson*. [The Real Woodrow Wilson]. New York: Charles Publication Co., 1922.

324. Clements, Kendrick A. *The Presidency of Woodrow Wilson*. American Presidency Series. Lawrence: University Press of Kansas, 1992. A comprehensive, scholarly assessment of Wilson's presidency. Deals with the increase in presidential power under Wilson and with the impact of war on his administration and on the evolution of the presidency.

325. _____ . *Woodrow Wilson: World Statesman*, Twayne's Twentieth-Century American Biography Series. Boston: Twayne Publishers, 1987. A biography that probes into Wilson's personal life to answer questions surrounding his public life, accomplishments, and why his legacy has been subject to so much controversy.

326. Cooper, John Milton, Jr. *The Warrior and the Priest: Woodrow Wilson and Theodore Roosevelt*. Cambridge: Harvard University Press, 1983. A comparative biography, emphasizing how each contributed to the reshaping of American politics.

327. Cranston, Ruth. *The Story of Woodrow Wilson, Twenty-eighth President of the United States: Pioneer of World Democracy*. New York: Simon and Schuster, 1945. An admiring portrait by a family friend.

328. Daniels, Jonathan Worth. *The End of Innocence*. Philadelphia: J. B. Lippincott, 1954. Describes the activities of his father, Josephus Daniels, Wilson, and Franklin D. Roosevelt.

329. Daniels, Josephus P. *The Life of Woodrow Wilson, 1856–1924*. Philadelphia: John C. Winston Co., 1924. A portrayal of Wilson as tragic hero by his Secretary of the Navy.

330. _____ . *The Wilson Era*. 2 vols. Chapel Hill: University of North Carolina Press, 1944–1946. [Vol. 1: *Years of Peace, 1910–1917*; Vol. 2: *Years of War and After, 1917–1923*.] An insider traces Wilson's career and records how Wilson won the battles for the domestic reforms of the New Freedom and strengthened international friendships.

331. Dodd, William Edward. *Woodrow Wilson and His Work*. New York: Doubleday, Page and Co., 1920. [A revised edition was published in 1932.] A sympathetic biography, with notes, by the co-editor of the first series of Wilson's papers.

332. Eaton, William D., Harry C. Read, and Edmond McKenna. *Woodrow Wilson: His Life and Work*. Chicago: Peterson Co., 1919. An early, approving biography by journalists.

333. Elletson, D. H. *Roosevelt and Wilson: A Comparative Study*. London: J. Murray, 1965. Compares Wilson unfavorably with Theodore Roosevelt.

334. Ford, Henry Jones. *Woodrow Wilson, the Man and His Work: A Biographical Study*. New York: Appleton, Century, Crofts, 1916. Written by a Princeton colleague.

335. Garraty, John Arthur. *Woodrow Wilson: A Great Life in Brief.* New York: Alfred A. Knopf, 1956. A short study of Wilson as a principled leader and visionary politician with a flawed personality.

336. Gershov, Z. M. *Vudro Vilson.* [Woodrow Wilson]. Moscow: Mysl, 1983. Marxist interpretation of Wilson as a capitalist who repressed the lower classes and exported capitalism.

337. Hale, William Bayard. *Woodrow Wilson: The Story of His Life.* Garden City, N.Y.: Doubleday, Page, and Co., 1911. An early biography by a contemporary who later became disillusioned with Wilson.

338. Halevy, Daniel. *President Wilson,* trans. Hugh Stokes. New York: John Lane Co., 1919. [French version published in 1918.] Favorable biography by a French historical and literary critic who examines Wilson's career through late 1917, with special emphasis on the development of his political thought.

339. Harris, Henry Wilson. *President Wilson, His Problems and His Policy: An English View.* New York: Frederick A. Stokes Co., 1917. Political biography of Wilson which carries the story through the President's second inaugural address of March 5, 1917.

340. Heckscher, August. *Woodrow Wilson: A Biography.* New York: Charles Scribner's Sons, 1991. A full-scale, appreciative biography of Wilson making extensive use of *PWW*.

341. Hoover, Herbert Clark. *The Ordeal of Woodrow Wilson.* New York: McGraw-Hill Publishing Co., 1958. Argues that Wilson was a tragic hero, beset by character flaws.

342. Ions, Edmund S. *Woodrow Wilson: The Politics of Peace and War.* Library of the Twentieth Century. New York: American Heritage, 1972. Heavily illustrated, brief biography by a British scholar.

343. Jacobs, David. *An American Conscience: Woodrow Wilson's Search for World Peace.* New York: Harper and Row, 1973. A sympathetic account of Wilson's life, programs, and principles, written in popular style.

344. Jones, Charles Sheridan. *President Wilson: The Man and His Message.* London: W. Rider & Son, 1918. A brief, laudatory interpretation of Wilson's career through 1918.

345. Josephson, Matthew. *The President-Makers: The Culture of Politics and Leadership in an Age of Enlightenment, 1896–1919.* New York: Harcourt, Brace, and Co., 1940. Traces Wilson's extraordinary rise to the presidency and how he maintained his liberalism throughout World War I.

346. Kerney, James. *The Political Education of Woodrow Wilson.* New York: Century Co., 1926. An admiring account by a New Jersey newspaper editor, who argues that Wilson converted from a political conservative to a leader of liberal reform.

347. Knight, Lucian L. *Woodrow Wilson: The Dreamer and the Dream*. Atlanta: Johnson-Dallis, 1924. A contemporary biography of Wilson as tragic hero.

348. Kotzschke, Richard. *Thomas Woodrow Wilson, sein Leben und sein Wirken*. [Thomas Woodrow Wilson, His Life and His Work]. Dresden: W. Jess, 1931.

349. Latane, John Holladay. *From Isolation to Leadership*. Garden City, N.Y.: Doubleday, Page & Co., 1918. Chronicles the way in which Wilson was propelled into international affairs and the process by which he became a leader of world opinion.

350. Lawrence, David. *The True Story of Woodrow Wilson*. New York: George H. Doran Co., 1924. An analysis of Wilson's complex life and personality by a Washington journalist who covered the White House.

351. Leavell, J. Perry, Jr. *Woodrow Wilson*. New York: Chelsea House, 1987. Focuses on the war and the Paris Peace Conference.

352. Lehman, Lucien. *Wilson, Apotre et Martyr*. Paris: Maisonneuve, 1933.

353. Link, Arthur S. *Wilson: The Road to the White House*. Princeton: Princeton University Press, 1946. First volume analyzes Wilson's early career with a focus on the Princeton presidency, the New Jersey governorship, and the campaign of 1912.

354. _____ . *Wilson: The New Freedom*. Princeton: Princeton University Press, 1956. Volume two treats the initial years of Wilson's presidency, focusing primarily on his legislative triumphs, especially the tariff, the Federal Reserve Act, and antitrust issues.

355. _____ . *Wilson: The Struggle for Neutrality, 1914–1915*. Princeton: Princeton University Press, 1960. In this third volume Link analyzes the Wilson administration's response to European belligerence.

356. _____ . *Wilson: Confusions and Crises, 1915–1916*. Princeton: Princeton University Press, 1964. The fourth volume of Link's biography focuses on the debates over American preparedness for war and on foreign policy issues regarding the war in Europe and the intervention in Mexico.

357. _____ . *Wilson: Campaigns for Progressivism and Peace, 1916–1917*. Princeton: Princeton University Press, 1965. The fifth volume analyzes the 1916 campaign waged on progressivism at home and peace abroad through the declaration of war in 1917.

358. _____ . *Woodrow Wilson: A Brief Biography*. Cleveland: World Publishing Co., 1963. A short, popular biography for the general public.

359. _____ . *Woodrow Wilson: Pequena Biografia*. [Woodrow Wilson: A Brief Biography]. Sao Paulo: Livraria Martins, 1964.

360. _____ . *Woodrow Wilson and the Progressive Era, 1910–1917*. New American Nation Series. New York: Harper and Row, 1954. A study of Wilson as New Jersey governor and as President, ending with American entry into the war. Link's focus is domestic policy, highlighting Wilson's emergence as the leader of progressive reform.

361. Loth, David Goldsmith. *The Story of Woodrow Wilson*. New York: Woodrow Wilson Foundation, 1944. [A centennial edition was published in 1955 and a revised edition in 1957.] A brief, sympathetic biography.

362. McCombs, William F. *Making Woodrow Wilson President*. New York: Fairview Publishing Co., 1921. A political analysis of the events which gained the presidency for Wilson, beginning with his tenure as professor at Princeton, and proceeding up to 1920.

363. McKinley, Silas Bent. *Woodrow Wilson: A Biography*. New York: Praeger, 1957. Wilson as a tragic hero who could not compromise.

364. Mulder, John M. *Woodrow Wilson: The Years of Preparation*. A supplementary volume to *PWW*. Princeton: Princeton University Press, 1978. An intellectual biography of Wilson, tracing his religious, educational, and political thought up to 1910.

365. Rollins, Alfred Brooks. *Woodrow Wilson and the New America*. New York: Dell Publishing Co., 1965. Brief biography of Wilson which combines an original narrative with many extracts from Wilson's own writings and those of other historians.

366. Schulte Nordholt, Jan Willem. *Woodrow Wilson: A Life for World Peace*, trans. Herbert H. Rowen. Berkeley: University of California Press, 1991. Focus is on the failure of Wilson's emphasis on moral leadership in a volatile world.

367. Schwabe, Klaus. *Woodrow Wilson: Ein Staatsmann Zwischen Puritanertum und Liberalismus, Personlichkeit und Geschichte*. [Woodrow Wilson: A Statesman Between Puritanism and Liberalism, Personality and History]. Gottingen: Musterschmidt, 1971.

368. Smith, Gene. *When the Cheering Stopped: The Last Years of Woodrow Wilson*. New York: W. W. Morrow, 1964. A popular biography portraying Wilson as a tragic hero.

369. Steinberg, Alfred. *Woodrow Wilson*. Lives to Remember Series. New York: G. P. Putnam's Sons, 1961. A brief, favorable biography written in popular style.

370. Stevens, Alden. *Victory without Peace*. New York: Harcourt, Brace and Co., 1944. A popularly written survey of Wilson's presidency focusing on the impact of World War I.

371. Thorsen, Niels Aage. *The Political Thought of Woodrow Wilson, 1875–1910*. Princeton: Princeton University Press, 1988. Examines Wilson's pre-gubernatorial and pre-presidential political thought by analyzing key Wilsonian texts.

372. Walworth, Arthur Clarence. *Woodrow Wilson*. 2 vols. New York: Longmans, Green, & Co., 1958. [Vol. 1, *American Prophet*. Vol. 2, *World Prophet*. Revised editions were published in 1965 and 1978.] Comprehensive biography of Wilson as a wartime leader and a lifelong educator which identifies him as one of the foremost Presidents and statesmen of the twentieth century.

373. Weinstein, Edwin A. *Woodrow Wilson: A Medical and Psychological Biography*. Princeton: Princeton University Press, 1981. Contends that Wilson's occasional erratic behavior resulted from cerebrovascular illness rather than psychological difficulty.

374. White, William Allen. *Woodrow Wilson: The Man, His Times, and His Task*. Boston: Houghton, Mifflin Co., 1924. This important journalist argues that Wilson had noble strengths and fatal weaknesses.

375. Winkler, John Kennedy. *Woodrow Wilson: The Man Who Lives On*. New York: Vanguard Press, 1933. A Wilson biography explaining that his decision to enter war was necessary to make the world safe for democracy.

4

Biographical Essays and Sketches

See also entries under "Assessments of Wilson as President," "Presidential Power and Leadership," and "Contemporary Profiles and Assessments Following Wilson's Death"

376. Allen, Frederick Lewis. "Woodrow Wilson, 1856–1924." In *There Were Giants in the Land: Twenty-Eight Historic Americans as Seen by Twenty-Eight Contemporary Americans*, ed. U.S. Department of the Treasury, 114–22. New York: Farrar & Rinehart, 1942.

377. Ambruster, Maxim Ethan. *The Presidents of the United States and Their Administrations from Washington to Nixon*, 263–76. New York: Horizon Press, 1981. Short essays on each incumbent.

378. ———. *Presidents of the United States and Their Administrations from Washington to Reagan*. 3rd ed., 263–76. New York: Horizon Press, 1982.

379. Duplicate entry omitted.

380. Armour, Richard. *Our Presidents*, 64. New York: Norton, 1964.

381. ———. *Our Presidents*, 64–65. Santa Barbara: Woodbridge Press, 1983.

382. Ashley, Maurice Percy. *Mr. President: An Introduction to American History*, 369–431. London: J. Cape, 1948. Includes a biography of Wilson.

383. Baker, Ray Stannard. "A Thinker in the White House." *American Magazine* 77 (May 1914): 56–57+. Considers the advantages of having a great intellectual like Wilson in the White House.

384. Barclay, Barbara. *Lamps to Light the Way: Our Presidents*, 279–91. Glendale, Calif.: Bowmar, 1970.

385. Barmore, Irene M. "Facts Worth Knowing about Woodrow Wilson." *Popular Educator* 43 (December 1925): 202.

386. Beliavskaia, I. A. "Wilson, Thomas Woodrow." In **422**, 5:704–5. Brief entry stressing the interests of American business monopolies and Wilson's desire for American domination in international affairs.

387. Berger, Oscar, ed. *Presidents from George Washington to the Present*, 62. New York: Crown Publishers, 1968.

388. Blassingame, Wyatt. *Look-It-Up Book of Presidents*, 102–5. New York: Random House, 1968.

389. Blum, John Morton. *The Progressive Presidents: Roosevelt, Wilson, Roosevelt, Johnson*, 61–106. New York: W. W. Norton, 1980. Wilson as a champion of liberalism.

390. Bolton, Sarah K. *Famous American Statesmen*. New York: Thomas Y. Crowell Co., 1925.

391. Borie, Marcia. *Famous Presidents of the United States*, 88–98, 146–47. New York: Dodd Mead and Co., 1963.

392. Box, Pelham Horton. "Woodrow Wilson." In *Three Master Builders and Another: Studies in Modern Revolutionary and Liberal Statesmanship*, 297–392. Philadelphia: J. B. Lippincott Co., 1925.

393. Brown, Roscoe Conkling Ensign. "Woodrow Wilson [With Selections]." In *Columbia University Course in Literature Based on the World's Best Literature*. Warner Library, 18. New York: Columbia University Press, 1928–1929.

394. Canning, John, ed. *100 Great Modern Lives*, 215–20. New York: Hawthorn Books, 1965.

395. "Centennial Celebration of Woodrow Wilson." *Virginia Journal of Education* 49 (January 1956): 24–25.

396. Commager, Henry Steele and Allan Nevins, eds. *Heritage of America*. Rev. and enl. ed. Boston: Little, Brown and Co., 1949. Relevant articles listed by author.

397. *Contemporary American Biography*, eds. John A. Beckwith and Geoffrey G. Coope. New York: Harper, 1941. Relevant articles listed by author.

398. Cooke, Donald E. *Atlas of the Presidents*, 66–67. Maplewood, N.J.: Hammond, 1967.

399. Cottler, Joseph. *Champions of Democracy*, 285–310. Boston: Little, Brown, and Co., 1940. An inspirational work that tells the stories of twelve famous Americans, ending with Wilson.

400. Cunliffe, Marcus, et al. *A History of the Presidency*, 264–75. New York: American Heritage Publishing Co., 1965. Credits Wilson with adding a new sense of leadership and heightened stature to the presidency.

401. Curtin, Andrew. *Gallery of Great Americans*, 98. New York: Franklin Watts, 1965.

402. Daniels, Josephus P. "Woodrow Wilson." In *The Presidents of the United States*, ed. James Grant Wilson, 4:195–244. New York: Charles Scribner's Sons, 1914. Glowing biographical sketch of Wilson from childhood to the middle of his first term as President. Includes brief sketches of immediate family members.

403. DeGregorio, William A. *The Complete Book of U.S. Presidents*, 408–28. New York: Dembner Books, 1984.

404. Denniston, Elinore. *Famous Makers of America*, 137–46. New York: Dodd, Mead and Co., 1963.

405. DeWitt, William A. *Illustrated Minute Biographies*. Rev. ed., 156. New York: Grosset & Dunlap, 1953.

406. Dietz, August. *The Presidents of the United States of America*. 3rd ed., 59. Richmond: Dietz Press, 1953.

407. Donovan, Frank. *Famous Twentieth Century Leaders*, 37–48. New York: Dodd, Mead and Co., 1964.

408. Downs, Robert Bingham, John Theodore Flanagan, and Harold William Scott. *Memorable Americans, 1750–1950*, 354–57. Littleton, Colo.: Libraries Unlimited, 1983. A sketch describing Wilson as an educator and a United States President.

409. Durant, John, and Alice Durant. *The Presidents of the United States: With an Encyclopedic Supplement on the Office and Powers of the Presidency, Chronologies, and Records of Presidential Elections*. 2 vols. Miami: A. A. Gache, 1976.

410. *Encyclopedia of American Political History*, ed. Jack P. Greene. 3 vols. New York: Charles Scribner's Sons, 1984. Relevant articles listed by author.

411. "February Meeting." *Proceedings of the Massachusetts Historical Society* 57 (October 1923–June 1924): 241–77. Pages 243–44 contain a tribute to Wilson, who had been a member of the Massachusetts Historical Society.

412. Ferris, Robert G., ed. *The Presidents: Historic Places Commemorating the Chief Executives of the United States*, 233–39, 586–88. Washington, D.C.: Department of the Interior, National Park Service, 1976. Biographical sketch of Wilson and brief description of his birthplace.

413. Fitzhugh, Harriet Lloyd (LePorte), and Percy K. Fitzhugh. *Concise Biographical Dictionary of Famous Men and Women*. Rev. and enl. ed., 738–40. New York: Grosset and Dunlap, 1949.

414. Frank, Josef. *Amerikaners*. [Americans]. Leipzig: W. Goldman, 1936. Wilson is among the Americans profiled.

415. Freidel, Frank. *Our Country's Presidents*, 166–73. Washington: National Geographic Society, 1966. [Also published as "Woodrow Wilson: Twenty-Eighth President 1913–1921." *National Geographic Magazine*, 128 (October 1965): 554–61.]

416. Gibson, James B. *Great People—Great Americans*, 102–15. New York: Comet Press Books, 1959.

417. Gilmartin, John G., and Anne M. Skehan. *Great Names in American History*, 363–72. Chicago: Laidlaw Brothers, 1946.

418. Goebel, Edmund Joseph, Thomas J. Quigley, and John E. O'Loughlin. *Builders of Our Country*, 363–72. Chicago: Laidlaw Brothers, 1951.

419. Golson, K. K. *Presidents Are People*, 230–34. New York: Carlton Press, 1964.

420. Gounder, Howard M. *Woodrow Wilson: A Sketch; Together with a Short Review of the Career of Thomas R. Marshall, Vice-President*. Reading, Pa.: B. F. Owen and Co., 1916. Brief, highly laudatory sketch to 1916.

421. Graham, Alberta Powell. *Thirty-Three Roads to the White House*. Rev. ed., 202–8. New York: Thomas Nelson and Sons, 1953. Biographical sketch of Wilson, from his childhood to the end of his presidency.

422. *Great Soviet Encyclopedia*, ed. A. M. Prokhorov. Trans. of 3rd ed. 31 vols. New York: Macmillan Co., 1973–1983. Relevant articles listed by author.

423. Hagedorn, Hermann. *Americans: A Book of Lives*, 137–59. New York: John Day Co., 1946.

424. Hapgood, Norman. "James [sic] Woodrow Wilson, 1856–1924." In *Great Democrats*, ed. Alfred Barratt Brown, 665–76. London: I. Nicholson and Watson, 1934. Biographical sketch of Wilson, with emphasis on the development of his political thought throughout his life.

425. Harden, Maximilian. "Woodrow Wilson." In *I Meet My Contemporaries*, trans. William C. Lawton, 14–63. New York: Henry Holt and Co., 1925. A portrait of Wilson, concluding that America will one day revere the morality he tried to impart.

426. Hatch, Jane M., comp. and ed. *American Book of Days*. 3rd ed., 1163–65. New York: H. W. Wilson, 1978. Brief biographical sketch and a discussion of the activities of the Woodrow Wilson Foundation.

427. Hathaway, Esse Virginia. "Woodrow Wilson." In *The Book of American Presidents*, 287–303. New York: McGraw-Hill Book Co., 1933.

428. Hirst, David W. "Wilson, Woodrow." In *Academic American Encyclopedia*, 20:165–67. Danbury, Conn.: Grolier Publishers, 1988.

429. Hofstadter, Richard. *The American Political Tradition and the Men Who Made It*, 234–78. New York: Alfred A. Knopf, 1948. Includes a chapter on Wilson entitled, "Woodrow Wilson—the Conservative as Liberal." Chronicles Wilson's achievements and argues that his character and childhood were instrumental to his successes and failures.

430. Hollis, Christopher. *The American Heresy*, 213–89. London: Sheed and Ward, 1928. Detailed political sketch portraying Wilson as an important figure in the development of American political philosophy.

431. John Hancock Mutual Life Insurance Company. *Presidents of the United States*, 47–50. Boston: John Hancock Mutual Life Insurance Co., 1948.

432. Kane, Joseph Nathan. *Facts about the Presidents*, 185–94. New York: H. W. Wilson, 1959.

433. Kleine-Ahlbrandt, William Laird. "Woodrow Wilson." In *Great Lives from History: American Series*, ed. Frank N. Magill, 5: 2529–34. Pasadena, Calif.: Salem Press, 1987.

434. Kohlsaat, Herman Henry. *From McKinley to Harding: Personal Recollections of Our Presidents*, 212–25. New York: Charles Scribner's Sons, 1923. [Excerpted under same title in *Saturday Evening Post* 195 (January 13, 1923): 23.] Short chapters on Wilson cover the government's takeover of the cable lines following the armistice, his promotion of the League of Nations, and his break with Colonel House.

435. Lake, James. *Our Glorious Heritage: The Presidents from Washington to Eisenhower*, 78–80. New York: Vantage Press, 1961.

436. Lauzanne, Stephane. *Great Men and Great Days*. New York: Appleton, Century, 1921. Written by a member of the French mission to the United States and includes sketches of Wilson as college professor and President.

437. Law, Frederick Houk. "Woodrow Wilson: President of the United States." In *Modern Great Americans: Short Biographies of Twenty Great Americans of Modern Times Who Won Wide Recognition for Achievements in Various Types of Activity* 261–74. New York: Century Co., 1926. A portrait of Wilson as a spirited leader who held to his convictions despite declining popularity and eventual defeat.

438. Link, Arthur S. "Wilson, Thomas Woodrow." In *The Encyclopedia of American Biography*, ed. John A. Garraty, 1214–17. New York: 1974.

439. _____ . "Wilson, (Thomas) Woodrow." In *Princeton Companion*, ed. Alexander Leitch, 512–15. Princeton: Princeton University Press, 1978. Brief biographical sketch with a central focus on Wilson's years at Princeton.

440. _____ . "Wilson, (Thomas) Woodrow." In *Encyclopedia Americana*, 29:6–11. Danbury, Conn.: Grolier Society, 1989. Chronological sketch focusing on

Wilson's involvement with World War I and the Paris Peace Conference; includes a short bibliography.

441. _____. "Wilson, Woodrow." In *The World Book Encyclopedia*, 19:268–76. Chicago: World Book, Inc., 1962. Wilson's career outlined amidst changes in American culture.

442. _____. "Woodrow Wilson." In *The American Story*, ed. Earl Schenck Miers, 283–88. Great Neck, N.Y.: Channel Press, 1956. A brief account of Wilson's rise to political prominence and an overview of his presidency.

443. _____. "Woodrow Wilson." In *The Presidents: A Reference History*, ed. Henry F. Graff, 435–64. New York: Charles Scribner's Sons, 1984. Discusses his brand of leadership, his Cabinet, and the major challenges he confronted.

444. Lowry, Edward George. *Washington Close-ups: Intimate Views of Some Public Figures*. Boston: Houghton Mifflin Co., 1921. Profiles of prominent men in American politics, with occasional references to Wilson.

445. Madison, Charles Allan. "Woodrow Wilson: The New Freedom—A War Casualty." In *Leaders and Liberals in 20th Century America*, 65–134. New York: Frederick Ungar Publishing Co., 1961. A biographical sketch of Wilson, who is numbered among those who helped change the United States from an almost laissez-faire economy to a relatively well-regulated industrial society.

446. McConnell, Jane Tompkins, and Burt M. McConnell. *Presidents of the United States: The Story of Their Lives, Closely Interwoven with the Vast Political and Economic Changes of the Nation*, 247–58. New York: Thomas Y. Crowell, 1951.

447. Mendel, Roberta. "Woodrow Wilson: Living Martyr." *Daughters of the American Revolution Magazine* 110, no. 3 (1976): 332–35, 352.

448. Meyer, Edith Patterson. *Champions of Peace: Winners of the Nobel Prize*, 64–82. Boston: Little, Brown & Co., 1959.

449. Milhollen, Hirst Dillon, and Milton Kaplan. *Presidents on Parade*, 350–62. New York: Macmillan Co., 1948. Selected pictorial history covering Wilson's birth, his years at Princeton, and his final resting place at the Washington Cathedral.

450. Moran, Thomas Francis. "Wilson." In *American Presidents*, 231–37. New York: Thomas Y. Crowell, 1928. Emphasizes Wilson's contributions to American prosperity.

451. Morgan, James. *Our Presidents: Brief Biographies of Our Chief Magistrates from Washington to Truman, 1789–1949*. Enl. ed., 271–86. New York: Macmillan Co., 1949. A brief examination of Wilson's presidency, noting his keen intellect and the various events that shaped his presidency.

452. Morris, Richard Brandon, ed. *Encyclopedia of American History*, 732–33. New York: Harper & Brothers, 1953. Brief biography focusing on Wilson's involvement with World War I and the League of Nations.

453. Mothner, Ira. *Woodrow Wilson: Champion of Peace*. Immortals of History Series. New York: Franklin Watts, 1969. Short, sympathetic survey of Wilson's idealism in foreign policy.

454. Mowry, George Edwin. "Wilson, Thomas Woodrow." In *Chambers's Encyclopedia*, 14:576–77. Oxford: Pergamon Press, 1966.

455. ———. "Wilson, Woodrow." In *Collier's Encyclopedia*, 23: 507–10. New York: P. F. Collier, 1990.

456. New York University. *Hall of Fame for Great Americans at New York University: Official Handbook*, 131. New York: New York University Press, 1962.

457. Osgood, George Coleman. "Woodrow Wilson [1856–1924]." In *Lives of Eighteen from Princeton*, ed. Willard Thorpe, 282–301. Princeton: Princeton University Press, 1946.

458. Perkins, Dexter. "W. Wilson." In *The McGraw-Hill Encyclopedia of World Biography*, 11:403–6. New York: McGraw-Hill Book Co., 1973.

459. Petersham, Maud Fuller, and Miska Petersham. *Story of the Presidents of the United States of America*, 63–65. New York: Macmillan Co., 1953.

460. "President Wilson." *Living Age* 293 (June 30, 1917): 812–15. Short biography of Wilson taken from **339**.

461. Radek, Karl. "Woodrow Wilson." In *Portraits and Pamphlets*, 35–43. London: Wishart Books, 1935. A Marxist view of Woodrow Wilson's presidency, noting his unappreciative behavior toward the working class and portraying him as a slave of big business.

462. Rand, Clayton. *Sons of the South*, 188. New York: Holt, Rinehart & Co., 1961. Considers the American South as the preeminent "rookery" for men of statesmanship and independent thought. Includes a short biography on Woodrow Wilson.

463. Rose, Billy [pseud.]. "Brief Encounter." *Reader's Digest* 52 (April 1948): 99. [Reprinted from the author's column, "Pitching Horseshoes."] Recalls a short meeting with Wilson in 1918 when the author delivered a letter from Bernard Baruch.

464. Rowe, Jeanne A. *Album of the Presidents*, 62–65. New York: Franklin Watts, 1969.

465. Schnittkind, Henry Thomas. "Woodrow Wilson, the Professor in Politics." In *Story of the United States*, 367–74. New York: Doubleday, Doran & Co., 1938.

466. Schnittkind, Henry Thomas, and Dana Arnold Schnittkind. *Fifty Great Americans*, 312–20. Garden City, N.Y.: Doubleday and Co., 1948.

467. _____ . "Woodrow Wilson." In *Living Biographies of American Statesmen*, 295–307. Garden City, N.Y.: Garden City Publishing Co., 1943.

468. Schu, Pierre. *World of Great Men*, 110–13. North Easton, Mass.: Holy Cross Press, 1967.

469. Scott, Henry Edwards. "Hon. Woodrow Wilson." *New England Historical and Genealogical Register* 81 (April 1927): 115–19. A brief biographical sketch.

470. Sewell, W. Stuart, ed. *Brief Biographies of Famous Men and Women*, 210–11. New York: Permabooks, 1949. Brief sketch that mentions Wilson's "Fourteen Points."

471. Seymour, Charles. "Wilson, (Thomas) Woodrow." In *The New Encyclopaedia Britannica*. 15th ed., *Micropaedia* 12:690–92. Chicago: Encyclopaedia Britannica, 1986. Biographical sketch focusing on Wilson's foreign policy. Also lists significant biographies necessary to understand Wilson's accomplishments.

472. _____ . "Woodrow Wilson." In *American Plutarch*, ed. Edward T. James, 321–53. New York: Charles Scribner's Sons, 1936. Reprint of the article on Woodrow Wilson from the *DAB*, with a revised bibliography.

473. _____ . "Wilson, Woodrow." In *DAB* 20:352–68. New York: Charles Scribner's Sons, 1936. Biographical essay on Wilson's personal and political life.

474. Shapiro, Irwin. *Presidents of the United States*, 24. New York: Simon & Schuster, 1956.

475. Sobel, Robert, ed. *Biographical Directory of the United States Executive Branch, 1774–1971*. Westport, Conn.: Greenwood Press, 1971. Includes short biographies of Wilson and members of his cabinet.

476. Southworth, Gertrude Van Duyn, and John Van Duyn Southworth. *Heroes of Our America*, 353–65. Syracuse, N.Y.: Iroquois Publishing Co., 1952.

477. Stevens, Robley D. *Your Handbook of Presidents and the White House*, 55. Boston: Bruce Humphries, 1961.

478. Storer, Doug. *Amazing but True!: Stories about the Presidents*, 146–50. New York: Pocket Books, 1975. Lists Wilson's achievements as politician, President, and negotiator.

479. Synnott, Marcia Graham. "Woodrow Wilson." In 47:343–57. Detroit: Gale Research, 1986.

480. Taylor, Tim. *Book of Presidents*, 323–47. New York: Arno Press, 1972.

481. Thomas, Eleanor, and Mary G. Kelty. *Heroes, Heroines, and Holidays*, 179–83. Boston: Ginn & Co., 1947.

482. Thomas, Henry, and Dana Lee Thomas. *Fifty Great Americans: Their Inspiring Lives and Achievements*, 283–91. Garden City, N.Y: Hanover House, 1956.

483. "(Thomas) Woodrow Wilson, 28th President." In *Burke's Presidential Families of the United States of America*. 2d ed., 431–44. London: Burke's Peerage, 1981. Includes a biographical sketch, chronology, bibliography of Wilson's writings, and his genealogy.

484. Tugwell, Rexford Grey. *How They Became President: Thirty- Six Ways to the White House*, 339–55. New York: Simon & Schuster, 1968.

485. Vernon, Ambrose W. *Ten Pivotal Figures of History*, 35–36. Chicago: American Library Association, 1925.

486. Vinmont, Rolf Benjamin, comp. *Our Presidents at a Glance*, 33. Menlo Park, Calif.: Pacific Coast Publishers, 1961.

487. Warren, Louis Austin, comp. *From White House to Log Cabin: Roosevelt, Taft and Wilson, at the Birth Place of Abraham Lincoln*. Hodgenville, Ky.: Herald News Co., [ca. 1921.]

488. Wasson, Tyler, ed. *Nobel Prize Winners: An H. W. Wilson Biographical Dictionary*, 1140–43. New York: H. W. Wilson Co., 1987.

489. White, William Allen. *Masks in a Pageant*, 345–86. New York: Macmillan Co., 1928. Examines Wilson's rise to prominence and his importance in the resolution of World War I.

490. _____ . "White on Wilson: The Republican Sage of Emporia Gives His Version of the True Story of Democratic President Woodrow Wilson, 'The Man Who Would Be God.'" In *Treasury of Intimate Biographies*, ed. Louis Leo Snyder, 325–31. New York: Greenberg Press, 1951. [Reprinted from **489**.]

491. Whitney, David C. *The American Presidents: Biographies of the Chief Executive from Washington through Bush*, 224–38. Englewood Cliffs, N. J.: Prentice-Hall, 1990. [Originally published as **4211**. Revised and updated by Robert Vaughn Whitney.] Brief chronology and a biographical sketch. "Key Facts" at end of volume.

492. Williams, John Hargreaves Harley. "Woodrow Wilson." In *Men of Stress: Three Dynamic Interpretations, Woodrow Wilson, Andrew Carnegie, William Hesketh Lever*, 25–174. London: Jonathan Cape, 1948. Portrait of Wilson as both a moral crusader and a rancorous, very human politician.

493. "Wilson, (Thomas) Woodrow." In *The New Caxton Encyclopedia*. 18:5969–70. London: Thames Publishing Co., 1969.

494. "Wilson, (Thomas) Woodrow." In *The New International Year Book: 1924*, 792–93. New York: Dodd, Mead & Co., 1925.

495. "Wilson, (Thomas) Woodrow." In *The National Cyclopedia of American Biography*, 19:1–12. New York: James T. White & Co., 1926.

496. Wilson, Vincent. *Book of the Presidents*, 60–61. Silver Spring, Md.: American History Research Associates, 1963.

497. Wintterle, John, and R. S. Cramer. *Portraits of Nobel Laureates in Peace*, 74–78. London: Abelard-Schuman, 1971. Brief biographical sketch, focusing on Wilson's presidency and his fight for the League of Nations.

498. Wolfers, Arnold, and Laurence Woodward Martin. "Woodrow Wilson, 1856–1924." In *The Anglo-American Tradition in Foreign Affairs*: *Readings from Thomas More to Woodrow Wilson*, 263–279. New Haven: Yale University Press, 1956. Selections from **17**; includes a biographical sketch and analysis of Wilson's speeches.

499. *Woodrow Wilson: A Biography*. New York: New York Times Co., 1924. [Originally published as **3192**.] Short biography of Wilson written just after his death.

500. "Woodrow Wilson, 28th President of the United States, 1913– 1921." In *World Book of America's Presidents*: *Portraits of the Presidents*, ed. Robert O. Zeleny, 160–67. Chicago: World Book Co., 1988. A compact biographical article with illustrations and a full-page portrait.

5

Reference Works

A. Chronologies and Bibliographies

501. Bolling, John Randolph, et al. *Chronology of Woodrow Wilson*. New York: Frederick A. Stokes Co., 1927.

502. "Books on Woodrow Wilson." *Library Journal* 49 (February 15, 1924): 178.

503. Brand, Katharine Edith. "Books in the Woodrow Wilson Field." In **522**, 7–15.

504. Bremner, Robert H., comp. *American Social History Since 1860*. Goldentree Bibliographies in American History, 6–7. New York: Appleton-Century-Crofts, 1971.

505. British Museum. *Subject Index of the Books Relating to the European War, 1914-1918: Acquired by the British Museum, 1914-1920*. London: The Trustees, 1922.

506. Buckingham, Peter Henry. *Woodrow Wilson: A Bibliography of His Times and Presidency*. Twentieth-Century Presidential Bibliography Series. Wilmington, Del.: Scholarly Resources, 1990. Covers a wide array of topics in both domestic and foreign affairs and includes a chronology of Wilson.

507. Cassara, Ernest. *History of the United States of America: A Guide to Information Sources*. Detroit: Gale Publishers, 1977. Chapter eight contains an annotated bibliography covering the progressive era, the personalities of that period, and World War I.

508. Clemons, Harry. *An Essay Towards a Bibliography of the Published Writings and Addresses of Woodrow Wilson, 1875-1910*. Princeton: Library of Princeton University, 1913.

509. Coppa and Avery Consultants. *The Administration of Presidential Political Campaigns*. Monticello, Ill.: Vance Bibliographies, 1981.

510. Dargin, Marion. *Guide to American Biography. Part II: 1815-1933.* Albuquerque: University of New Mexico Press, 1952.

511. Davison, Kenneth E. *The American Presidency: A Guide to Information Sources,* 271–83. Detroit: Gale Publishing Co., 1983. A chapter on Wilson, listing sources to aid in research on his life and presidency.

512. *The Democratic and Republican Parties in America: A Historical Bibliography.* Santa Barbara, Calif.: ABC-Clio, 1983. Includes several references to Wilson and his contributions to the Democratic party.

513. Fitzgerald, Carol and Manfred F. Boemeke. "Toward a Bibliography of the Writings of Arthur S. Link." *American History: A Bibliographic Review* 5 (1989): 15–44. Provides a preliminary bibliography of the books, articles, and reviews by Link from 1941 to 1989, most of which deal with Wilson.

514. Leach, Howard S. *An Essay Towards a Bibliography of the Published Writings and Addresses of Woodrow Wilson, March 1917 to March 1921.* Princeton: Library of Princeton University, 1922. Primary documents from Wilson's second term.

515. Link, Arthur S. "Newspaper Reports of Woodrow Wilson's Speeches, Statements, and Papers, 1910–1912." In **522**, 137–43. Also published separately by Princeton University Press. An abridged bibliography of newspaper articles on Wilson's speeches and writings while he was Governor of New Jersey.

516. Link, Arthur S., and William M. Leary, Jr. *The Progressive Era and the Great War, 1896-1920.* New York: Appleton-Century-Crofts, 1969. Bibliography covering the presidencies of Theodore Roosevelt and Wilson.

517. Martin, Fenton S., and Robert V. Goehlert. *American Presidents: A Bibliography.* Washington, D.C.: Congressional Quarterly Books, 1987. Contains over 600 works on Wilson and his times.

518. Mauer, Donald J. *United States Politics and Elections: A Guide to Information Sources.* Detroit: Gale Publishing Co., 1971.

519. Noggle, Burt. "Woodrow Wilson, 1913–1921." In *The American Presidents,* ed. Frank N. Magill, 2:500–530. Pasadena, Calif.: Salem Press, 1986. Detailed Wilson chronology focusing on Wilson's foreign policies.

520. "The Published Writings of Wilson since 1895." *Annals of the American Academy of Political Science* 21 (March 1903): 294.

521. Schlacter, Gail. *The American Presidency: A Historical Bibliography,* 75–127. Santa Barbara, Calif.: ABC-Clio Information Services, 1984. Numerous references to Wilson's works, located mostly in section 3, "From Roosevelt through Roosevelt."

522. Turnbull, Laura Shearer. *Woodrow Wilson: A Selected Bibliography of His Published Writings, Addresses and Public Papers.* Princeton: Princeton University

Press, 1948. Includes reports of Wilson's remarks and writings between 1910 and 1912, compiled by Arthur S. Link, and books pertaining to Wilson, selected by Katharine E. Brand.

B. Historiographical Essays

523. Duplicate entry omitted.

524. Brand, Katharine Edith. "The Man in History." In **1038**, 183–205. Discusses the rich documentation of Wilson's presidency, including books and articles written by Wilson, his speeches, and his correspondence.

525. _____. "Woodrow Wilson in His Own Time." *Library of Congress Quarterly Journal of Current Acquisitions* 13 (February 1956): 61–105. "Catalogue of the Woodrow Wilson Centennial Exhibit," Library of Congress. The 219 items include manuscripts, imprints, and photographs, with a lengthy introduction to the Woodrow Wilson Collection.

526. Brown, William B. *The People's Choice: The Presidential Image in Campaign Biography*. Baton Rouge: Louisiana State University Press, 1960. Campaign biographers tend to idealize their subjects.

527. Burns, Richard Dean. *Guide to American Foreign Relations since 1700*. Santa Barbara, Calif.: ABC-Clio, 1983. Details United States-Latin America relations, relations with Africa and the Middle East, and World War I.

528. Cohen, Warren I. *The American Revisionists: The Lessons of Intervention in World War I*. Chicago: University of Chicago Press, 1967. Writings of revisionists who question the United States' motives in World War I.

529. Dodd, William Edward. *Wilsonism*. New York: Academy of Political Science, 1923. [Reprinted from *Political Science Quarterly* 38 (March 1923): 115–32.] Examines a range of books written on Wilson soon after he left office, in an attempt to gain a better understanding of the development of Wilson's political philosophy.

530. Dulles, Foster Rhea. "The New World Power: 1865–1917." In *Interpreting and Teaching American History*. National Council for the Social Studies Yearbook, ed. William H. Cartwright and Richard L. Watson, Jr., 215–30. New York: The Council, 1961. Appraises historians' views and contains a section on the Wilson era.

531. Leavell, J. Perry, Jr. "Woodrow Wilson: 1856–1924." In *Research Guide to American Historical Biography*, ed. Robert Muccigrosso, 2:1658–63. Washington, D.C.: Beacham Publishing Co., 1988. Brief overview of Wilson's historical significance, his literary works, and biographical sources.

532. Meaney, Neville K. "Arthur S. Link and Thomas Woodrow Wilson." *Journal of American Studies* 1, no. 1 (1967): 119–26. Critiques **353**, **354**, **355**, **356**, and **357**.

533. Moore, James R. "Woodrow Wilson and Post-Armistice Diplomacy: Some French Views." *Reviews in American History* 2, no. 2 (1974): 207–13. Studies three new perspectives on Wilsonian post-armistice diplomacy by French scholars.

534. Newell, William D. "The Problem of American Entry into Twentieth Century World War: A Study in Conflicting Historiography." Ph.D. diss., University of Idaho, 1982. Discusses whether Wilson was ever neutral or if he used German submarine attacks as an excuse to intervene. Also examines the argument that the United States entered the war because Wilson believed that a German victory would hurt American interests.

535. Porto, Victor John. "Woodrow Wilson, the War, and the Interpretations: 1917–1970." *Social Studies* 63 (January 1972): 22–31. Traces the changing opinions of historians on American entrance into World War I.

536. *Selected List of Biographies of the Presidents of the United States.* Washington, D.C.: U.S. Library of Congress, Bibliography Division, 1926.

537. Watson, Richard L., Jr. "Woodrow Wilson and His Interpreters, 1947–1957." *Mississippi Valley Historical Review* 44 (Spring 1957): 207–36. An enlargement of the author's original purpose to prepare a review of the following books on Wilson published in 1956: **268, 321, 335, 354, 4045**.

538. Wells, Samuel F., Jr. "New Perspectives on Wilsonian Diplomacy: The Secular Evangelism of American Political Economy." *Perspectives in American History* 6 (1972): 389–419. Discusses twelve recent publications on Wilson that deal with American political and economic expansionism.

6

Childhood, Education, and Early Career

A. Ancestry and Youth

539. Birkenhead, Frederick Edwin Smith, 1st Earl of. "Early Life of President Wilson." In *Last Essays*, 13–24. London: Cassell, 1930.

540. "Birthplace of a Scholar President: Woodrow Wilson's Birthplace." *Southern Living* 13 (October 1978): 90.

541. Bober, Robert Alexander. "Young Woodrow Wilson: The Search for Immortality." Ph.D. diss., Case Western University, 1980. A psychobiographical analysis of Wilson's personality, with emphasis on his relationship with his father.

542. Bridgman, William S. "Parentage of President Woodrow Wilson." *Munsey's Magazine* 48 (March 1913): 877–81. Brief essay on Wilson's immediate family and relatives. Includes several portraits of members of his family.

543. Cavanah, Frances. "Bending the Presidential Twig." *Publisher's Weekly* 138 (October 26, 1940): 1664–69. Books the Presidents read when they were young; Wilson's reading habits are included.

544. Davis, Elisabeth Logan. "Joseph Ruggles Wilson: Father of the Twenty-eighth President." In *Fathers of America: Our Heritage of Faith*, 13–24. Westwood, N.J.: Fleming H. Revell, 1958. A biographical sketch of Wilson's father, examining the ways in which he influenced Wilson's character.

545. Dowdey, Clifford. "The Birthplace." In **1038**, 1–14.

546. "The Early Life of President Wilson." *Empire Review* 47 (March 1928): 159–67. Biographical sketch based upon the first two volumes of **319**.

547. Eaton, Clement. "Professor James Woodrow and the Freedom of Teaching in the South." *Journal of Southern History* 28, no. 1 (1962): 3–17. Describes the 1880s controversy over the teaching of evolution by an uncle of Wilson at Columbia Theological Seminary in South Carolina.

548. Ezell, John S. "Woodrow Wilson as Southerner, 1856–1885: A Review Essay." *Civil War History* 15, no. 2 (1969): 160–67. Analyzes Wilson's early ideas as reflected in the first four volumes of *PWW*.

549. Faber, Doris. *The Mothers of American Presidents*. New York: New American Library, 1968. [Also published under title: *The Presidents' Mothers*. New York: St. Martin's Press, 1978.] Points to the indelible marks made by presidential mothers, hinting that Wilson harbored oedipal tendencies.

550. Gaines, William Harris. "From Staunton to the White House: Virginia, Virginians, and Woodrow Wilson." *Virginia Cavalcade: History in Picture and Story* 2, no. 3 (Winter 1952): 7–10. Summary of his childhood, study of law, and early ambition to be a senator from Virginia.

551. _____ . "A House on 'Gospel Hill': Homecoming to the Manse, 1912." *Virginia Cavalcade: History in Picture and Story* 6, no. 2 (Autumn 1956): 42–47. Discusses a visit by President-elect Wilson to his birthplace.

552. _____ . "A House on 'Gospel Hill': Woodrow Wilson's Birthplace Becomes a Shrine." *Virginia Calvacade: History in Picture and Story* 6, no. 3 (Winter 1956): 12–19. Describes the house in which Wilson was born in Staunton, Virginia, and the steps leading to its dedication as a national shrine by Franklin Delano Roosevelt on May 4, 1941.

553. Gatewood, Willard Badgette, Jr. "Woodrow Wilson: The Formative Years 1856–1880." *Georgia Review* 21, no. 1 (1967): 3–13. Emphasizes the significance of Wilson's home and college years at Princeton.

554. Handy, Edward Smith Craighill, and Elizabeth Handy. *President Woodrow Wilson's Irish and Scottish Heritage*. Staunton, Va.: Woodrow Wilson Birthplace Foundation, 1966. Genealogical study which maintains that Wilson's paternal grandfather, James Wilson, came from Strabane in County Tyrone, Northern Ireland; that all of the Wilsons were Irish; and all of the Woodrows were Scottish.

555. _____ . *Woodrow Wilson's Heritage and Environment: Ethnic and Cyclic Patterns in Time, Place, and Circumstance*. Philadelphia: Dorrance, 1969. Wilson as the product of his times.

556. Heller, Janet Seip. "Woodrow Wilson's Life Linked to Pennsylvania by Parentage, Teaching Career, and Politics." *Monthly Bulletin* 24, no. 12 (December 1956): 17–22, 28–29.

557. Henry, Reginald B. *Genealogies of the Families of the Presidents*. Rutland, Vt.: Tuttle, 1935.

558. "In Democracy's Darkest Hour the President Consecrates a National Shrine of Freedom." *Life* 10 (May 19, 1941): 29–33. Franklin Roosevelt's dedicatory address at the Wilson manse in Staunton, as he confronts the growing war in Europe.

559. Lescure, Dolores. "The Manse." *Commonwealth: The Magazine of Virginia* 26 (November 1959): 20–21. Discusses the Staunton house where Wilson was born.

560. Lewis, Frank Bell. "The Man of Faith." In **1038**, 35–48. Discusses Wilson's Scotch-Irish ancestry and its importance in shaping him as a man and a world leader.

561. Mulder, John M. "Joseph Ruggles Wilson: Southern Presbyterian Patriarch." *Journal of Presbyterian History* 52, no. 3 (1974): 245–71. An analysis of Wilson's father's personality, theology, and career in the southern Presbyterian church.

562. Noggle, Burt. "Predilections to Politics and the Lures of Love: The Further Education of Young Woodrow Wilson." *Louisiana History* 9, no. 4 (1968): 373–87. An essay review of volumes 2 and 3 of *PWW* covering the years 1881–1885.

563. Osborn, George Coleman. "The Influence of Joseph Ruggles Wilson on His Son Woodrow Wilson." *North Carolina Historical Review* 32 (October 1935): 519–43. Like other interpreters, Osborn points to the tremendous influence of Wilson's father on the future President.

564. _____ . *Woodrow Wilson: The Early Years*. Baton Rouge: Louisiana State University Press, 1968. Narrative biography of Wilson's life up to 1902.

565. Rosenberger, Francis Coleman. "The Young Woodrow Wilson." *Virginia Quarterly Review* 44, no. 2 (1968): 310–14. A review of Volumes 2, 3, and 4, covering 1881–1885, of *PWW* and **322**.

566. Smith, Bessie White. "The Seer: Woodrow Wilson (1856– 1924)." In *The Boyhoods of the Presidents*, 256–66. Boston: Lothrop, Lee, and Shepard Co., 1929. Portrays Wilson as a young dreamer who was largely educated by his father.

567. Virginia Education Association. "Homes of Virginia-born Presidents of the United States." *Virginia Journal of Education: Official Publication of the Virginia Education Association* 54 (September-November 1960): 1–3, (January-May 1961): 5–9. Contains photographs and brief histories, including Wilson's birthplace.

568. Weisenburger, Francis Phelps. "A Brief History of Immigrant Groups in Ohio." In *The Trek of the Immigrants: Essays Presented to Carl Wittke*, 81–93. Rock Island, Ill.: Augustana College Library, 1964. Chronicles the advent of immigrant groups into Ohio before 1825, including Wilson's grandparents.

569. _____ . "The Middle Western Antecedents of Woodrow Wilson." *Mississippi Valley Historical Review* 23 (1936): 375–90. Genealogical study of Wilson's family, noting its roots in Ohio before Wilson's father settled in the South.

570. "When He Was Just Tommy." *Ladies' Home Journal* 35 (November 1918): 138. A brief look at Wilson's childhood, focusing mainly on his poor health and unremarkable performance in school.

571. Wilson, John George. *The Wilsons: Their Origins and Past*, Scotland Alive Series, vol. 3. Paisley: Wilfion, 1984.

572. Wilson, Newton Allen. *Wilson-Rutherman-Woodburn-McElhattan: Genealogies and Working Papers*. Denver, Colo.: N. A. Wilson, 1980.

573. "Wilson Shrine." *Newsweek* 17 (May 12, 1941): 16. Describes the contents and the opening of the Wilson house located at his birthplace in Staunton, Virginia.

574. Wilson, Theodore Raymond. "The Birth of Greatness: A Psychological and Sociological Study of the Influences upon Woodrow Wilson during His Formative Years." Ph.D. diss., University of Pennsylvania, 1960. Social scientific study of Wilson up to age 26.

575. "You Are Invited to Virginia and Staunton for the Wilson Centennial." *Instructor* 65 (June 1956): 5. Pictures, captions, and a short introduction focusing on Wilson's birthplace.

576. Younger, Edward. "Woodrow Wilson: The Making of a Leader." *Virginia Magazine of History and Biography* 64, no. 4 (October 1956): 387–401. Focuses on the years before Wilson became President of Princeton and stresses his appeals to moral principles.

577. Zorn, Walter Lewis. *Descendants of the Presidents of the United States of America*, 118, 142. Monroe, Mich.: The Author, 1955. Wilson's family tree, beginning with Joseph Ruggles Wilson. Also includes pictures of Wilson's places of birth and burial.

B. College Years

578. Godwin, Harold. *A History of the Class of '79*. Trenton, N.J.: Princeton College, n.d. Wilson's undergraduate class at Princeton University.

579. Osborn, George Coleman. "Woodrow Wilson: The Evolution of a Name." *North Carolina Historical Review* 34 (October 1957): 507–16. Considers the changes from Tommy to Thomas W., to T. W., to T. Woodrow, and finally, in 1880, to Woodrow Wilson.

580. Princeton University. "Class Biographies." In *The Class of 1879: Princeton College, Quindecennial Record, 1879–1894*, 118. New York: Privately printed, 1894.

581. _____. Class of 1879. *Fifty Years of the Class of 'Seventy–nine, Princeton*. Princeton: Privately printed, 1931.

582. _____. "Who's Who in '79." In **581**, 237–304.

583. Wilhelm, Donald. "Candidates in College." *Independent* 88 (October 16, 1916): 99–101. Compares the college years of Wilson and Charles Evans Hughes.

584. Williams, Charles L. "Woodrow Wilson as an Undergraduate." *Current History* 31 (January 1930): 698–702. Explains that Wilson's undergraduate years at Princeton were crucial to forming his personality.

C. Law School, Legal Practice, and Doctoral Work

585. Gatewood, Willard Badgette, Jr. "Woodrow Wilson: Years of Trial and Decision, 1881–1885." *Georgia Review* 22, no. 3 (1968): 306–15. A review of volumes 2 and 3 of *PWW*.

586. Kent, Charles W. "Woodrow Wilson's Undergraduate Days at the Virginia Alpha." In *The Centennial History of Phi Kappa Psi Fraternity, 1852–1952*, ed. Harry Gorgas and James D. Campbell. Cleveland: Phi Kappa Psi Fraternity, 1952.

587. Latane, John Holladay. "Woodrow Wilson as Student and Lecturer." *Johns Hopkins Alumni Magazine* 12 (March 1924): 189–93. Wilson as graduate student and visiting professor.

588. Osborn, George Coleman. "Woodrow Wilson as a Young Lawyer, 1882–83." *Georgia Historical Quarterly* 41, no. 2 (June 1957): 126–42. Describes Wilson's brief and unhappy experience practicing law in Atlanta.

589. ———. "Woodrow Wilson's First Romance." *Ohio Historical Quarterly* 67 (January 1958): 1–20. Wilson's unsuccessful courtship of his cousin, Harriet Augusta Woodrow, between 1879 and 1881.

590. Patterson, Archibald W. *Personal Recollections of Woodrow Wilson and Some Reflections upon His Life and Character*. Richmond: Whittet and Shepperson, 1929. Memoir by a University of Virginia classmate.

591. Viar, Richard E. "Woodrow Wilson at the University of Virginia." *Magazine of Albermarle County History* 12 (1953): 11–23.

592. "When Woodrow Wilson Came to Hopkins." *Johns Hopkins Alumni Magazine* 28 (1940): 78–81. Contains three letters from Wilson to Heath Dabney, written between 1883 and 1885, while Wilson was a student at Johns Hopkins.

593. Williams, Charles L. "Woodrow Wilson's Student Days at the University of Virginia." *University of Virginia Magazine* 73 (1913): . Recollections of Wilson as a law student.

594. "Wilson at College." *Literary Digest* 45 (November 23, 1912): 970. Explains Wilson's attraction to public speaking and mentions selected Wilson experiences while he was attending the University of Virginia Law School.

7

Professor and Scholar

595. Alvarez, Eugene. "The Woodrow Wilsons in Gainesville, Georgia." *Georgia Historical Quarterly* 54 (1970): 563–70. Discusses the early years of Wilson's first marriage.

596. Archer, William Henry. "President Wilson as a Man of Letters." *Fortnightly Review* 109 (February 1918): 230–37. [Also published in *Living Age* 297 (May 4, 1918): 270–76.]

597. Athearn, Clarence Royalty. "Woodrow Wilson's Philosophy: Some Suggestions towards a Coherent Interpretation of Woodrow Wilson's Philosophy as Presented in His Published Works." Ph.D. diss., American University, 1931.

598. Bragdon, Henry Wilkinson. "Woodrow Wilson Addresses the Citizens of Baltimore, 1896." *Maryland Historical Magazine* 37 (June 1942): 150–70. Describes Wilson's first political battle and his first address to a partisan audience, at a meeting to support Mayor Hooper.

599. Bridges, Robert. "President Wilson and College Earnestness." *World's Work* 15 (January 1908): 9792–97. Wilson's career as an academic.

600. Carner, J. W. "Woodrow Wilson's Idea of the Presidency." *American Monthly Review of Reviews* 47 (January 1913): 47–51. Analysis of Wilson's scholarly writings on the role of the presidency.

601. Carpenter, Roland H. "On American History Textbooks and Integration in the South: Woodrow Wilson and the Rhetoric of Division and Reunion 1829–1889." *Southern Speech Communication Journal* 51, no. 1 (1985): 1–23. Discusses contemporary reactions to Wilson's 1893 history textbook.

602. Chitwood, John Carroll. "Selected Studies in the History of American Public Administration Thought from Wilson to Waldo: A Sociology of Knowledge Perspective (Volumes I and II)." Ph.D. diss., Ohio State University, 1980. Produces a survey of administrative theory during the first half-century of American public administration thought.

603. Couvreu, Emile. "Woodrow Wilson et son histoire du peuple americain." *Revue des Etudes Historiques* 85e (July 1919): 296–300. A review of **24**.

604. Daniel, Marjorie L. "Woodrow Wilson—Historian." *Mississippi Valley Historical Review* 21 (December 1934): 361–74.

605. Dennis, Alfred Pearce. "Princeton Schoolmaster." In *Great Teachers, Portrayed by Those Who Studied under Them*, ed. Houston Peterson, 131–52. New Brunswick, N.J.: Rutgers University Press, 1946. Written by a Wilson student who described him as an inspiring influence on Princeton students and Americans.

606. ———. "Woodrow Wilson, Princeton Schoolmaster." *Saturday Evening Post* 202 (February 15, 1930): 12–13+. [Reprinted in his *Gods and Little Fishes*, 84–117. Indianapolis: Bobbs-Merrill Co., 1931.] Reflections on Wilson by a former student.

607. Diamond, William. *The Economic Thought of Woodrow Wilson.* Johns Hopkins University Studies in Historical and Political Science, vol. 61, no. 4. Baltimore: Johns Hopkins Press, 1943. [Revision of "The Economic Thought of Woodrow Wilson." Ph.D. diss., Johns Hopkins University, 1942.] Examines Wilson's ideas concerning the nature of the American economy, how well it functioned, how its ills might be remedied, and its relation to the world at large.

608. Dilliard, Irving. "When Woodrow Wilson Was Invited to Head the University of Illinois." *Journal of the Illinois State Historical Society* 60, no. 4 (1967): 357–82. Recounts the 1892 offer of the presidency of the University of Illinois to Wilson, and his refusal.

609. Dimock, Marshall Edward. "The Study of Administration." *American Political Science Review* 31 (February 1937): 28–40. Argues that the acceptability of Wilson's theories of public administration is dependent upon their consistency and contribution to democratic values.

610. Dodd, Lawrence C. "Woodrow Wilson's *Congressional Government* and the Modern Congress: The 'Universal Principle' of Change." *Congress and the Presidency* 14, no. 1 (Spring 1987): 33–49. Evaluates Wilson's analysis of Congress in **19**.

611. Doig, Jameson W. "If I See a Murderous Fellow Sharpening a Knife Cleverly . . . : The Wilsonian Dichotomy and the Public Authority Tradition." *Public Administration Review* 43 (July-August 1983): 292–304. Cites Wilson's ideal of units of public administration exercising large powers with the efficiency of private business and evaluates the actual record.

612. Dudden, Arthur Power. "Woodrow Wilson at Bryn Mawr College." *Bryn Mawr Alumni Bulletin* 26 (1955): 6–7, 32–33. Wilson's brief service on the faculty.

613. Gallway, George B. "Congressional Reorganization: Unfinished Business." In **1149**, 214–27. Agrees with Wilson's argument in **19**.

614. Garfield, Harry A. "One of History's Great Souls: Some Personal Recollections of Woodrow Wilson '79." *Princeton Alumni Weekly* 30 (January 10, 1930): 355–57. [Delivered at the fiftieth anniversary of Wilson's 1879 graduation from Princeton.] Describes Wilson's Princeton days and his clarity in handling emergency administrations during World War I.

615. Gatewood, Willard Badgette, Jr. "Woodrow Wilson and the University of Arkansas." *Arkansas Historical Quarterly* 30, no. 2 (1971): 83–94. Discusses Wilson's consideration of a teaching position at Arkansas Industrial University.

616. Graham, George A. "How Professor Wilson Would Rate Public Administration Today." *Public Administration Review* 53 (September 1993): 486–502. A mock interview with Wilson to illustrate views on the current problems of public administration.

617. "A Great American Litterateur Praised by a British Critic." *Current Opinion* 64 (May 1918): 348–49. Examines Wilson's skills as a writer.

618. Grzybowski, Kazimierz. "Woodrow Wilson on Law, State and Society." *George Washington Law Review* 30 (1962): 808–52. Focuses on the prominence of law in Wilson's career before his election as Governor of New Jersey.

619. Henneman, John Bell. "The Work of a Southern Scholar." *Sewanee Review* 3, no. 2 (1895): 172–88. Brief biography of Wilson through the 1890s that focuses on his education and published works.

620. Howe, Frederic C. *The Confessions of a Reformer.* New York: Charles Scribner's Sons, 1925. Recounts his life and work, and remembers Wilson whom he first met at Johns Hopkins.

621. Hruska, Thomas Joseph, Jr. "Woodrow Wilson: The Organic State and His Political Theory." Ph.D. diss., Claremont Graduate School, 1978. Examines Wilson's philosophy of constitutional development and the role of liberally educated men in government.

622. Hunt, Rockwell Dennis. "These Were My Teachers." *Phi Delta Kappan* 28 (March 1947): 303–4.

623. Jacobs, Wilbur R. "Wilson's First Battle at Princeton: The Chair for Turner." *Harvard Library Bulletin* 8 (Winter 1954): 74–87. Wilson's unsuccessful attempt to attract Frederick Jackson Turner to a chair in Princeton's Department of History.

624. Jastrow, Joseph. "The Education of Woodrow Wilson." *Nation* 126 (February 8, 1928): 154–55. Discusses Wilson's academic pursuits and his political ambitions and their effects on his presidency.

625. Kirwan, Kent Aiken. "The Crisis of Identity in the Study of Public Administration: Woodrow Wilson." *Polity* 9 (Spring 1977): 321–433. The rejection of Wilson's theory by recent students and their lack of success in developing a more usable science leads the author to a new appreciation of Wilson's thought.

626. _____. "Historicism and Statesmanship in the Reform Argument of Woodrow Wilson." *Interpretation* 9 (September 1981): 339–51. Explores the principles which led Wilson to propose constitutional reform and evaluates his proposals.

627. _____. "Politics and Administration: An Analysis of Woodrow Wilson's 'The Study of Administration.' " Ph.D. diss., University of Chicago, 1971.

628. _____. "Woodrow Wilson and the Study of Public Administration: Response to Van Riper 'The American Administrative State: Wilson and the Founders,' " *Public Administration Review* 43 (November-December 1983): 477–490; and "The Politics-Administration Dichotomy: Concept and Reality?" In *Politics and Administration: Woodrow Wilson and American Public Administration*, ed. Jack Rabin and James S. Bowman. New York: Marcel Dekker, 1984; *Administration and Society* 18 (February 1987): 389–401. Assesses Wilson's contributions to the field of public administration in light of two Paul Van Riper essays.

629. Koch, F.-W. "Die Konzeption des Organischen Staates in der Politischen Philosophie Woodrow Wilsons: 1875–1912." [The Conception of the Organic State in the Political Philosophy of Woodrow Wilson, 1875–1912]. Ph.D. diss., University of Cologne, 1983.

630. Kraus, Michael. "Interpretive Writings." In *A History of American History*, 453–91. New York: Farrar & Rinehart, 1937. Wilson's career as a historian assessed.

631. _____. "Nationalist School." In *The Writing of American History*, 190–241. Norman: University of Oklahoma Press, 1953. Section describing the character and content of Wilson's historical writings.

632. Kurz, Alexander Thomson, Jr. "The Epistemology of Public Administration, Epistemic View." Ph.D. diss., University of Southern California, 1986. Study provides an analysis of selected public administration literature, from **173**, to Alberto G. Ramos's *The New Science of Administration* (1981).

633. Link, Arthur S. "Woodrow Wilson and the Study of Administration." *Proceedings of the American Philosophical Society* 112, no. 6 (1968): 431–33. [Also published in **1155**, 38–44.] Wilson's major contributions to the study of public administration.

634. _____. "Woodrow Wilson: The Making of a Writer." *Princeton History* 7 (1988): 11–29. Concise analysis of Wilson's development as a man of letters, with particular discussions of his writings on politics, history, and education.

635. Lippmann, Walter. "Woodrow Wilson's Approach to Politics." *New Republic* 133 (December 5, 1955): 15–18. A favorable reassessment of Wilson's writings on government.

636. "The Literary President." *Literary Digest* 46 (January 11, 1913): 76–77. Wilson's background as a scholar.

637. Martin, Daniel W. "The Fading Legacy of Woodrow Wilson." *Public Administration Review* 48 (March/April 1988): 631–66. Cites the waning enthusiasm for Wilson's writings and reassesses his position among scholars.

638. McKean, Dayton David. "Woodrow Wilson as a Debate Coach." *Quarterly Journal of Speech* 16 (November 1930): 458–63. Describes Wilson's efforts and methods while a debate coach at Princeton.

639. Meiklejohn, Alexander. "Woodrow Wilson, Teacher." *Saturday Review of Literature* 1 (May 30, 1925): 785–86. A review of Wilson's published papers which illustrate his attributes as a teacher and his philosophy of education.

640. Moran, W. A. "Woodrow Wilson's First Visit to Madison." *Wisconsin Magazine of History* 8 (June 1925): 459–60. Documents a 1892 textbook conference.

641. Mosher, O. W., Jr. "Woodrow Wilson's Methods in the Classroom." *Current History* 32, no. 3 (June 1930): 502–5. Focuses on Wilson's lectures, examinations, and attitude toward independent thinking.

642. Nevins, Allan. "The Sage and the Young Man." In *J. Franklin Jameson: A Tribute*, ed. Ruth Anna Fisher and William Lloyd Fox, 41–45. Washington, D.C.: Catholic University of America Press, 1965. Includes Jameson's recollections of Wilson.

643. Norris, Edwin M. "Some Writers of the Princeton Faculty." *Critic* 42 (June 1903): 509–16. A survey of the Princeton faculty notes that Wilson's best writing is "yet to come."

644. Osborn, George Coleman. "Woodrow Wilson and Frederick Jackson Turner." *Proceedings of the New Jersey Historical Society* 74 (July 1956): 208–29. Discusses their friendship and correspondence between 1889 and 1902.

645. Perry, Bliss. "Wilson." In *Commemorative Tributes*, ed. Robert Underwood Johnson, Academy Publications, no. 50. New York: American Academy of Arts and Letters, 1925. [Republished in a limited edition in 1942.] A tribute to the legacy of Woodrow Wilson, who was a member of the Academy of Arts and Letters from 1908.

646. ———. "Wilson as a Man of Letters." *Century Magazine* 85 (March 1913): 753–57. Promotes Wilson as the most able man of letters since Lincoln, both in style and content.

647. Pollin, Burton R. "Woodrow Wilson and Julian Hawthorne on Poe: Letters from an Overlooked Scholarly Resource." *Poe Studies* 12, no. 2 (1979): 35. Wilson's efforts with the Shakespearean Society of New York City to preserve a cottage Poe had lived in at Fordham University.

648. "President Wilson as a Man of Letters." *Current Opinion* 54 (May 1913): 410. Analyzes Wilson's attributes and successes as a writer.

649. Price, Carl F. "Woodrow Wilson at Wesleyan." *Wesleyan University Alumnus* 8 (March 1924): 3–7. Recounts stories about Wilson and the undergraduates at the university where he taught from 1888 until 1890.

650. Rabin, Jack, and James S. Bowman, eds. *Politics and Administration: Woodrow Wilson and Public Administration.* New York: Marcel Dekker, 1984. Describes Wilson's establishment of public administration; also covers the development of the theory and practice of public administration since Wilson's era.

651. Ranney, Joseph Austin. "Woodrow Wilson." In *The Doctrine of Responsible Party Government: Its Origins and Present State*, 25–47. Urbana: University of Illinois Press, 1962. [Originally published as Vol. 34, No. 3, in "Illinois Studies in the Social Sciences," 1954.] Describes Wilson as one of the first to consider seriously the function of political parties in the American democratic system, starting with **46**.

652. Rogal, Samuel J. "From Pedagogue to President: Thomas Woodrow Wilson as Teacher-Scholar." *Presidential Studies Quarterly* 24 (Winter 1994): 49–56. Examines how Wilson's political idealism developed from his academic experiences.

653. Rogers, Lindsay. "Professor with a Style." *Political Science Quarterly* 56 (December 1941): 507–14. Discusses some of Wilson's writings on government and public administration.

654. Rohde, David W., and Kenneth A. Shepsle. "Leaders and Followers in the House of Representatives: Reflections on Woodrow Wilson's *Congressional Government*." *Congress and the Presidency* 14 (Autumn 1987): 111–13. Analyzes the role of leadership in the House of Representatives in the context of both Wilson's book and the history of the House.

655. Sears, Louis M. "Woodrow Wilson." In *The Marcus W. Jernegan Essays in American Historiography*, ed. William T. Hutchinson, 102–21. Chicago: University of Chicago Press, 1937. An early historiographical essay on Wilson as a historian.

656. Sedgwick, Jeffrey Leigh. "Executive Leadership and Administration: Founding Versus Progressive Views." *Administration and Society* 17 (February 1986): 411–432. Compares the political attitudes of Wilson and the "Founding Fathers" on the proper nature of executive and administrative leadership.

657. Shannon, David A. "The Making of a Princeton President, 1896–1902: An Essay Review." *Pacific Northwest Quarterly* 65, no. 4 (1974): 184–86. An essay review of *PWW* volumes 10, 11, and 12.

658. Smith, John David. "James Ford Rhodes, Woodrow Wilson, and the Passing of the Amateur Historian of Slavery." *Mid-America* 64, no. 3 (October 1982): 17–24. Analyzes Wilson's anonymous review of Rhodes's *History of the United States from the Compromise of 1850*, 2 vols. (New York: Harper & Brothers, 1893) and compares the methods and attitudes of the two historians.

659. Stephenson, Wendell H. "The Influence of Woodrow Wilson on Frederick Jackson Turner." *Agricultural History* 19 (October 1945): 249–53. Includes a 1919 letter written by Turner, explaining Wilson's influence on him.

660. Stern, Bill. "No Place for Politics." *Coronet* 26 (October 1949): 73. [Also published, with minor alterations, in *Scholastic* 55 (October 12, 1945): 5, under the title "Scholars and Gentlemen: Sport and Politics Don't Mix."] Concerns an incident with the Princeton football team when Wilson was manager.

661. Stillman, Richard J., II. "Woodrow Wilson and the Study of Administration: A New Look at an Old Essay." *American Political Science Review* 67 (June 1973): 582–88. Argues that Wilson is best understood as a response to the issues raised in **19**.

662. Thorsen, Niels Aage. "Wilson and the Democratic State: A Historiographical Survey of Woodrow Wilson's View." *American History: A Bibliographic Review* 5 (1989): 1–14. Examines Wilson's thinking about democratic government before he entered politics in 1910.

663. ———. "Woodrow Wilson's Study of Administration." *American Studies in Scandinavia* (Norway) 21, no. 1 (1989): 16–29. Asserts that Wilson was the first American scholar to propose that public administration could not be divorced from political issues.

664. Tigert, John J. "Woodrow Wilson's *History of the American People*." *Methodist Quarterly Review* 52 (April 1903): 227–53. Assesses **24** as the greatest history from the pen of a southerner since the Civil War.

665. Tucker, Frank H. "East Meets West: Woodrow Wilson in 1894." *Colorado Magazine* 49, no. 2 (1972): 109–15. Describes Wilson's lectureship, "Value of Constitutional Government," at Colorado College Summer School of Science, Philosophy, and Languages in 1894.

666. Van Riper, Paul P. "The American Administrative State: Wilson and the Founders." *Public Administration Review* 43 (November-December 1983): 477–490. Examines **173**, and Wilson's role in the founding of the academic study of public administration.

667. ———. "The Politics-Administration Dichotomy: Concept and Reality?" In **650**, 203–218. Discusses Wilson's role in the development of public administration, as well as the nature and influence of his version of what later became known as the dichotomy between politics and administration.

668. ———. "On Woodrow Wilson: Van Riper Replies." *Administration and Society* 18, no. 4 (February 1987): 402–10. Responds to Kent Kirwan's critique of **666**.

669. Walker, Larry. "Woodrow Wilson, Progressive Reform, and Public Administration." *Political Science Quarterly* 104 (Fall 1989): 509–525. Reviews the contributions of Wilson to American public administration arguing he believed in a strong, active role for the federal government and as President succeeded in passing legislation that significantly enlarged its regulatory powers.

670. Wann, A. J. "The Development of Woodrow Wilson's Theory of the Presidency: Continuity and Change." In **1149**, 46–66. Explores Wilson's evolving ideas in **19**, **20**, and **32**.

671. Whyte, Frederic. "President Wilson as a Man of Letters." *Bookman* 55 (October 1918): 6–8. An appreciative evaluation.

672. "Wilson Twenty Years Ago." *Literary Digest* 60 (March 1, 1919): 31. Discusses Wilson's early career at Wesleyan University.

673. Wilson, Woodrow. *Bryn Mawr College Program, 1885–1886, 1886–1887, 1887–1888.* Philadelphia: 1886. Woodrow Wilson's own course descriptions.

674. Wolfe, Christopher. "Woodrow Wilson: Interpreting the Constitution." *Review of Politics* 41, no. 1 (January 1979): 121–42. Analyzes Supreme Court decisions in light of Wilson's interpretation of the Constitution.

675. "Woodrow Wilson, the Educator." *Journal of the National Education Association* 79 (April 16, 1914): 427–28. [Also published in *Journal of the National Education Association* 13 (March 1924): 109.]

676. Young, Roland. "Woodrow Wilson's *Congressional Government* Reconsidered." In **1149**, 201–13. Analyzes the book as a plea for congressional supremacy.

8

President of Princeton University

677. Bailey, Kenneth M. "Woodrow Wilson: The Educator Speaking." Ph.D. diss., University of Iowa, 1970. Wilson's educational philosophy and rhetoric.

678. Barzun, Jacques Martin. *The Tyranny of Idealism in Education*. Education in the Nation's Service, 6. New York: Woodrow Wilson Foundation, 1959. Covers the conflict between Wilson's ideas and those of John Dewey.

679. Beard, Charles Austin. "Woodrow Wilson and Science." *New Republic* 46 (April 14, 1926): 226–27. Argues that Wilson opposed advancing the teaching of sciences in the universities.

680. Bragdon, Henry Wilkinson. "Woodrow Wilson and Mr. Lowell." *Harvard Alumni Bulletin* 45 (May 22, 1943): 597. Compares the two university Presidents; tends to downplay the alleged influence of Wilson's educational ideas on Lowell.

681. Bridges, Robert. "President Woodrow Wilson." *American Monthly Review of Reviews* 26 (July 1902): 36–38. A biographical sketch.

682. Bundy, McGeorge. *An Atmosphere to Breathe: Woodrow Wilson and the Life of the American University College*. Education for the Nation's Service: A Series of Essays on American Education Today, 2. New York: Woodrow Wilson Foundation, 1960. Reviews Wilson's presidency of Princeton University, 1902–1910 and his statements on college education during those years.

683. *Cheer Up!* Printed for the family only, April 1, 1910. An anti-Wilson collection of quotations, with antique woodcut illustrations.

684. Clarke, Linda Lois. "Woodrow Wilson at Princeton: A Study in Leadership Ideals." Ph.D. diss., University of Iowa, 1991.

685. Clements, Edward W. "The Educational Contributions of Woodrow Wilson." Ph.D. diss., Stanford University, 1952.

686. _____ . *Educational Contributions of Woodrow Wilson: A Bibliography Submitted with a Dissertation in Partial Fulfillment of the Requirements for the Degree of Doctor of Philosophy, March, 1952 Together with Additions, As of December 1958.* New York: Woodrow Wilson Foundation, 1959.

687. Cooper, John Milton, Jr. "Woodrow Wilson: The Academic Man." *Virginia Quarterly Review* 58, no. 1 (Winter 1982): 38–53. Focuses on Wilson's tenure as President of Princeton.

688. Corwin, Edward Samuel. "Departmental Colleague." In **711**, 19–35. Admiring portrait by a member of Princeton's Department of History, Politics, and Economics.

689. Craig, Hardin. *Woodrow Wilson at Princeton.* Norman: University of Oklahoma Press, 1960. A memoir by one of the young preceptors hired by Wilson.

690. Daniels, Winthrop More. *Recollections of Woodrow Wilson.* New Haven, Conn.: Privately printed, 1944. A portrait of Wilson before he entered politics.

691. Demerly, John A. "Woodrow Wilson—Educator." Ph.D. diss., State University of New York at Buffalo, 1957.

692. Dodds, Harold Willis. "The Educator." In **1038**, 49–65.

693. Egbert, Donald Drew, and D. M. Lee. *Princeton Portraits*, 73–79. Princeton: Princeton University Press, 1947. Discusses Wilson's close and lifelong relationship with Princeton University and his major political achievements; includes nine portraits.

694. Eisenhart, Luther P. "The Far-Seeing Wilson." In **711**, 62–68. Portrait by a professor of mathematics.

695. Frankie, Richard John. "An Analysis of Selected Administrative Theories and Practices of Woodrow Wilson in the Field of Higher Education." Ed.D. diss., Wayne State University, 1966. Special attention is given to Wilson's years as President of Princeton University, in particular to his pioneering work in Princeton's development, reorganization, and expansion in the early twentieth century.

696. _____ . "Woodrow Wilson: Blueprint for Radical Change." *Journal of Education* 153, no. 2 (December 1970): 16–25. Examines Wilson's contributions as an innovative leader and reformer of higher education.

697. _____ . "Woodrow Wilson and Education." *School and Society* 96 (February 3, 1968): 80–82. Examines Wilson's philosophy of the purpose of higher education.

698. Frye, Roland Mushat. "Woodrow Wilson and the Nurture of Mind." *Emory University Quarterly* 11 (December 1955): 208–20. An analysis of Wilson's presidency of Princeton.

699. Garraty, John Arthur. "The Training of Woodrow Wilson: His Career at Princeton Prepared Him for a Larger Role, but also Showed His Strange Blend of Strength and Weakness." *American Heritage* 7, no. 5 (August 1956): 24–27.

700. Goheen, Robert F. *Essential Tasks: A Re-affirmation in the Present of Woodrow Wilson's Conviction That Liberal Education Is a Power, Not an Ornament.* Education in the Nation's Service, no. 3. New York: Woodrow Wilson Foundation, 1959. A defense of a broad, liberal education as essential for democracy by the then-President of Princeton University.

701. Gottlieb, Kevin Charles. "The Political Philosophy of Woodrow Wilson as President of Princeton, 1902 to 1910." Ph.D. diss., Syracuse University, 1970. Examines Wilson's speeches and writings while he was President of Princeton, tracing the development of his political philosophy before he ascended to elected office.

702. "Great Princetonian." *Newsweek* 47 (February 27, 1956): 86–87. Credits Wilson with rebuilding and remaking Princeton through the preceptorial system.

703. Hawley, Sherwin. "Wilson Garden at Princeton." *Country Life* 24 (September 1913): 44–45. Illustrated description of the extensive garden planned and developed by Mrs. Wilson.

704. "In Regard to Princeton University: Correspondence in *New York Evening Post* between an 'Alumnus' and a Trustee." *New York Evening Post*, March 4–18, 1910. An anonymous attack on Moses Taylor Pyne by David B. Jones, a Princeton trustee, answered by another trustee, the Rev. John DeWitt. Published by anti-Wilsonians.

705. Johnston, Charles. "Men of To-day." *Harper's Weekly* 50 (September 1, 1906): 1250–51. Portrait of Wilson as university President, including discussions of his philosophy of higher education and his scholarly writings.

706. "A Lasting Memorial to Woodrow Wilson." *Princeton Alumni Weekly* (May 9, 1947): Discusses plans for the enlargement of Princeton University's existing school for the training of public servants and its renaming as the Woodrow Wilson School of Public and International Affairs.

707. Lewis, McMillan. *Woodrow Wilson of Princeton.* Narberth, Pa.: Livingston Publishing Co., 1952. An informal sketch of Wilson's twenty-two years at Princeton which emphasizes Wilson as a human being and focuses primarily on his relations with Princeton University and its graduates, employing anecdotes as the chief means of illustrating Wilson's life.

708. MacLeish, Archibald. *Mr. Wilson and the Nation's Need, Education in the Nation's Service,* 1. New York: Woodrow Wilson Foundation, 1959. Considers the author's attendance at a speech delivered by Wilson at Harvard, July 1, 1909, on the purpose of American university education.

709. Medina, Harold R. "The Influence of Woodrow Wilson on the Princeton Undergraduate, 1902–1910." *Princeton Alumni Weekly* (June 2, 1956): 6. Describes Wilson as embodying Christian principles.

710. "Monument to Be Erected in Princeton." *School and Society* 39 (March 17, 1934): 343. An announcement concerning the plan for a Wilson monument.

711. Myers, William Starr, ed. *Woodrow Wilson: Some Princeton Memories.* Princeton: Princeton University Press, 1946. Fond reminiscences about Wilson by personal friends.

712. Nittoli, Michael J. "The Educational Ideals of Woodrow Wilson." Ph.D. diss., University of Ottawa (Canada), 1966.

713. O'Connor, Sister Brendan Marie. "Study of the Educational Ideas of Woodrow Wilson: Abridged." *Catholic Educational Review* 47 (November 1949): 617. Wilson's ideas from a Catholic perspective.

714. Princeton University. "The Inauguration of Woodrow Wilson as President of Princeton University." *Princeton University Bulletin* 14, no. 1 (December 1902): 1–36. Reprints the program of Wilson's inaugural ceremony on October 25, 1902, as well as Wilson's inaugural address.

715. *The Procter Gift: A History.* Printed at the request of many of the Alumni of Princeton, March 22, 1910. An anti-Wilson compilation of excerpts from trustees' minutes, correspondence, and other documents.

716. Spaeth, J. Duncan. "Wilson as I Knew Him and View Him Now." In **711**, 69–91. Admiring portrait of Wilson by a professor of Latin.

717. Synnott, Marcia Graham. *The Half-Opened Door: Discrimination and Admissions at Harvard, Yale, and Princeton, 1900–1970.* Contributions in American History, 80. Westport, Conn.: Greenwood Press, 1979. Examines racial quotas and admissions policies.

718. Taggart, Robert J. "Woodrow Wilson and Curriculum Reform." *New Jersey History* 93, no. 3–4 (1975): 99–114. Examines the conflict between Wilson's ideas for educational reform at Princeton and the goals of the university.

719. "That Pittsburgh Speech: and Some Comment." (April 17, 1910): Wilson's speech to Pittsburgh alumni, with hostile commentary from the *Princeton Alumni Weekly* and various newspapers.

720. Thwing, Charles Franklin. "Woodrow Wilson: College President." In *Friends of Men*, 413–35. New York: Macmillan Co., 1933. An admiring portrait.

721. Veysey, Laurence R. "The Academic Mind of Woodrow Wilson." *Mississippi Valley Historical Review* 49, no. 4 (March 1963): 613–34. Examines Wilson's reforms at Princeton.

722. Wall, Joseph Frazier. "What Princeton Really Needed: Excerpt from Andrew Carnegie." *American Heritage* 21 (June 1970): 91–92. Wilson's attempts to persuade Carnegie to endow Princeton. Excerpted from Wall's biography of Carnegie.

723. Watterson, John S., III. "The Football Crisis of 1909–1910: The Response of the Eastern 'Big Three.'" *Journal of Sport History* 8, no. 1 (1981): 33–49. Presidents' efforts to reform football in order to reduce injuries.

724. Wertenbaker, Thomas Jefferson. *Princeton, 1746–1896*, 344– 46. Princeton: Princeton University Press, 1946. Includes an account of the resignation of Princeton President Francis L. Patton and the sudden appointment of Wilson.

725. _____ . "Wilson's Educational Policies." In **1075**, 160–201. Wilson's years as President of Princeton University are covered.

726. Wilson, Edmund. "Woodrow Wilson at Princeton." In *The Shores of Light*, 298–324. New York: Farrar, Straus, 1952. A critical appraisal of Wilson by a literary critic who faults Wilson for his moralism.

727. "Woodrow Wilson: The First Lay President of Princeton." *Century Illustrated Monthly Magazine* 65 (November 1902): 161–62.

728. "Woodrow Wilson: The President as Professor." *Times* (London) *Literary Supplement* no. 3471 (September 5, 1968): 933–34. Examines the academic debate surrounding Wilson's career, with special attention paid to his years at Princeton.

9

Campaign for Governor of New Jersey

729. Bacon, Charles Reade. *A People Awakened: The Story of Woodrow Wilson's First Campaign.* Garden City, N.Y.: Doubleday, Page & Co., 1912. An account of Wilson's gubernatorial campaign, composed mostly of daily dispatches by a reporter from the Philadelphia *Record*.

730. "College President as Candidate." *Outlook* 96 (October 22, 1910): 396–97. Biographical sketch representing Wilson very favorably as a candidate but without naming a specific office.

731. Hosford, Hester Eloise. *The Forerunners of Woodrow Wilson.* East Orange, N.J.: Hosford Publications, 1914. A survey of previous leaders and legislation in New Jersey.

732. "How a Little Steel Ball Made Woodrow Wilson President." *Current Opinion* 61 (November 1916): 311–12. How a chauffeur's ingenuity in repairing a broken-down car got Wilson to the dinner where he decided to run for governor.

733. "An Inspiring Campaigner." *Nation* 91 (November 3, 1910): 408–9. Argues that Wilson's exciting gubernatorial campaign has pushed him to the forefront as one of the premier political leaders and reformers in the world.

734. Noble, Ransom Edward. "Four Wilson Campaign Speeches." *New Jersey History* 77 (1959): 71. Four speeches made by Wilson late in his gubernatorial campaign of 1910, with an introduction by Noble.

735. "Nomination of Woodrow Wilson." *Outlook* 96 (September 24, 1910): 140–41. A discussion of Wilson's nomination for governor and his political platform.

736. "Political Philosopher." *Outlook* 96 (November 5, 1910): 521. An endorsement.

737. "Real Scholar in Politics." *Nation* 91 (September 22, 1910): 256–57. Concerns the reaction to Wilson's Democratic nomination for the New Jersey governorship and believes that Wilson would attract many Republican voters along with national attention.

738. "States That Saw a New Light." *Literary Digest* 41 (November 19, 1910): 918–19. Two paragraphs describe Wilson as Judson Harmon's "most formidable rival" for the 1912 Democratic nomination.

739. Stickley, Gustav. "One of the Men Needed by the People." *Craftsman* 19 (November 1910): 116–23.

740. "Woodrow Wilson and the New Jersey Governorship." *American Monthly Review of Reviews* 42 (November 1910): 555–62. Describes Wilson's achievements while President of Princeton and his exceptional qualifications as he plans to run for the governorship of New Jersey.

741. "Woodrow Wilson's First Political Triumph." *Harper's Weekly* 54 (November 19, 1910): 8–9. Selections from newspapers' editorials across the nation, commenting on Wilson's election as governor of New Jersey.

10

Governor of New Jersey, 1911–1913

742. Alexander, Caroline Bayard (Stevens). "Wilson Legislation in New Jersey." *Survey* 30 (April 26, 1913): 140. Brief summary of some of Wilson's accomplishments as governor of New Jersey.

743. Buenker, John D. "Urban, New-Stock Liberalism and Progressive Reform in New Jersey." *New Jersey History* 87 (1969): 79–104. Examines Wilson's gubernatorial term within the context of progressive reform in New Jersey.

744. "Democracy's New Leader: A Few Sample Opinions from South, East, and West." *Harper's Weekly* 54 (November 26, 1910): 6. Brief excerpts from six newspapers rejoicing in Wilson's election as Governor of New Jersey and his apparent positioning as a candidate for President.

745. Franklin, Fabian. "New Democratic Governors." *Independent* 69 (November 17, 1910): 1067–69. Discusses the national excitement caused by Wilson's election as Governor of New Jersey.

746. "Governor Wilson's Vetoes." *Nation* 94 (April 18, 1912): 380–81. Defends Wilson's use of the veto to block a series of bills passed by the New Jersey legislature.

747. Hirst, David W. *Woodrow Wilson, A Reform Governor: A Documentary Narrative.* New Jersey History Series. Princeton, N.J.: Van Nostrand, 1965. A collection of primary sources describing Wilson's tenure as governor of New Jersey.

748. Hosford, Hester Eloise. *Woodrow Wilson: His Career, His Statesmanship, and His Public Policies.* 2nd ed., rev. and enl. New York: G. P. Putnam's Sons, 1912. Praises Wilson's record as a "conservative-progressive" Governor of New Jersey and promotes his election as President.

749. ———. *New Jersey Made Over.* New York: G. P. Putnam's Sons, 1912. An account of Wilson as a reforming Governor.

750. Johnston, Charles. "A Talk with Governor Wilson." *Harper's Weekly* 55 (August 19, 1911): 11–12. An interview focusing on his achievements as Governor.

751. Kerney, James. "Woodrow Wilson, Governor." *Independent* 70 (May 11, 1911): 986–89. A review of the rapid reforms Wilson brought to New Jersey after only three months as Governor.

752. Link, Arthur S. "Woodrow Wilson in New Jersey." In **1155**, 45–59. [Originally a public lecture at Princeton University on May 5, 1964.] An analysis of Wilson's impact on Princeton University as President and on the state as governor.

753. ———. "Woodrow Wilson and the Progressive Movement in New Jersey." *Princeton History* 1 (1971): 25–38. An evaluation of Wilson's contribution to the progressive movement in New Jersey.

754. Mahoney, Joseph F. "Backsliding Convert: Woodrow Wilson and the Seven Sisters." *American Quarterly* 18, no. 1 (Spring 1966): 71–80. A discussion of Wilson's policies regarding corporate monopolies during his tenure as New Jersey's governor.

755. ———. "New Jersey Politics after Wilson: Progressivism in Decline." Ph.D. diss., Columbia University, 1964. Concludes that New Jersey progressives lacked solid leadership after 1912 and soon merged with the Republicans.

756. Marcosson, Isaac Frederick. "Woodrow Wilson and Theodore Roosevelt." In *Adventures in Interviewing*, 79–93. New York: John Lane Co., 1919. An interview with Wilson while he was Governor of New Jersey, concerning his political philosophy and aspirations.

757. McCarter, Thomas Nesbitt. "Advanced Legislation of Governor Wilson." *Hampton's Magazine* 28 (May 1912): 258–62. A review of election, labor, and public utilities reform.

758. McLean, Joseph Erigina. "Early Modern Governor." *National Municipal Review* 46 (January 1957): 20–22. Explores Wilson's prophetic character that highlighted his tenure as Governor of New Jersey.

759. Noble, Ransom Edward. *New Jersey Progressivism before Wilson*. Princeton: Princeton University Press, 1946. A discussion of both Democratic and Republican reformers who preceded Wilson.

760. "The President in an Obdurate State." *Harper's Weekly* 57 (May 10, 1913): 3. Deplores Wilson's intervention in a New Jersey controversy over procedure for naming grand jurors and describes the criticism he received for it.

761. "President Wilson in New Jersey." *Outlook* 104 (May 17, 1913): 85–86. Examines President Wilson's trip to New Jersey to urge legislators there to pass legislation on jury selection reforms that Wilson had initiated while governor.

762. Rapport, George C. *The Statesman and the Boss: A Study of American Political Leadership Exemplified by Woodrow Wilson and Frank Hague.* New York: Vantage Press, 1961. Criticizes both men for cultivating exclusive groups and for failing to form a broader grassroots democracy.

763. Reynolds, John Francis. "Testing Democracy: Electoral Participation and Progressive Reform in New Jersey, 1888–1919." Ph.D. diss., Rutgers University, 1980. Despite high hopes, the reform of the electoral process in New Jersey was followed by declining voter participation.

764. _____. *Testing Democracy: Electoral Behavior and Progressive Reform in New Jersey, 1880–1920.* Chapel Hill: University of North Carolina Press, 1988. Discusses Wilson's relationship with New Jersey voters in gubernatorial elections of 1910 and 1913; in the Senate contest of 1911; and the presidential elections of 1912 and 1916.

765. "Speaking out about the Senatorship." *Nation* 91 (December 15, 1910): 571–72. Discusses Wilson's opposition to James Smith in the 1910 New Jersey senatorial contest.

766. Turner, Henry Andrew, Jr. "Woodrow Wilson and the New Jersey Legislature." *Proceedings of the New Jersey Historical Society* 74 (January 1956): 21–49. Praises Wilson's achievements as governor.

767. "Wilson in New Jersey." *Nation* 96 (May 8, 1913): 459–60. Describes President Wilson's activities regarding a proposed New Jersey jury reform bill.

768. "Wilson on Taft and Trusts." *Nation* 93 (October 19, 1911): 356. Criticizes a speech by Wilson on Taft's handling of trusts, arguing that Wilson offered no better solutions.

769. "Wilson on the Governorship." *Nation* 91 (December 8, 1910): 540–41. Recognizes Wilson as a man with a strong vision and excellent leadership.

770. "Wilson's Stormy Home-Coming." *Literary Digest* 46 (May 17, 1913): 1110–11. Praise from the national press regarding Wilson's first battle against New Jersey machine politics.

771. "Wilson's Work as Governor." *American Monthly Review of Reviews* 47, no. 2 (February 1913): 131–36. How Wilson used his national reputation to accomplish as much as possible in New Jersey before moving on to Washington, D.C.

772. "Woodrow Wilson's Promise and Performance: His Platform as a Candidate and His Work as Governor of New Jersey." *Democratic Campaign Documents* 2 (1912).

773. "Woodrow Wilson's Trust Treatment." *Literary Digest* 46 (February 1, 1913): 213–15. Discusses seven bills that Wilson believed would put an end to trusts and monopolies in New Jersey.

11
Presidential Campaigns

774. Boller, Paul F., Jr. *Presidential Campaigns*. New York: Oxford University Press, 1984.

775. Goldman, Ralph Morris. *The National Party Chairmen and Committees*: *Factionalism at the Top*, 220–21. Armonk, N.Y.: M.E. Sharpe, 1990. Includes a brief study of two party chairmen: William Frank McCombs and Vance Criswell McCormick.

776. Petersen, Svend. *A Statistical History of American Presidential Elections*, 77–82. Westport, Conn.: Greenwood Press, 1981. Contains a state-by-state breakdown.

777. Piccard, Paul J. "The Electoral Colleges of President Wilson." In **1112**, 29–64. An analysis of voting for Wilson in 1912 and 1916.

778. Robinson, Edgar Eugene. *The Presidential Vote, 1896–1932*. Stanford: Stanford University Press, 1934. Contains a compilation of election returns by counties for ten presidential elections, including those of 1912 and 1916.

779. Schlesinger, Arthur M., Jr., et al., eds. *History of American Presidential Elections, 1789–1968*. 4 vols. New York: Chelsea House Publishers, 1971. Relevant articles listed by author.

780. _____ . *Coming to Power: Critical Presidential Elections in American History*. New York: Chelsea House Publishers, 1972. Relevant articles listed by author.

12

Election of 1912

A. Early Presidential Campaign Activities and Pre-Convention Campaigns

781. Agranoff, Robert. *Political Campaigns: A Bibliography*. DeKalb: Center for Governmental Studies, Northern Illinois University, 1972.

782. Alderman, Edwin Anderson. "Virginia Democrat." *Harper's Weekly* 55 (May 6, 1911): 7. Transcript of a speech given by the President of the University of Virginia honoring Wilson.

783. "The Candidacy of Woodrow Wilson." *Harper's Weekly* 50 (April 21, May 19, 1906): 564, 716. Quotes from national newspapers assessing Wilson's prospects in 1908.

784. "Candidate from the East and South." *Harper's Weekly* 52 (January 25, 1908): 7. Argues for the nomination of Wilson for the presidency, citing his intellect as a sign of his being a natural statesman, and his citizenship in Virginia and New Jersey as a factor that can unify the country.

785. "A Consideration of Woodrow Wilson of Princeton." *Harper's Weekly* 51 (April 27, 1907): 601. Reports with approval an incipient movement to make Wilson the Democratic standard-bearer for President.

786. "Democracy Awaiting Its Leader." *Literary Digest* 44 (February 10, 1912): 252–53. Assesses damage by the Harvey-Watterson episode.

787. "Dr. Woodrow Wilson Defines Material Issues." *New York Times Magazine* November 24, 1907: 1. Interview with Wilson on pertinent issues of the day.

788. Ellis, Mary Louise. "Tilting on the Piazza: Emmet O'Neal's Encounter with Woodrow Wilson, September 1911." *Alabama Review* 39, no. 2 (1986): 83–95. Confrontation between Wilson and O'Neal, Governor of Alabama and an opponent of progressivism.

789. Fyfe, Harry Hamilton. "Some Possible American Presidents." *Fortnightly Review* 96 (November 1911): 899–906. [Also published in *Living Age* 272 (January 6, 1912): 3–8.] Examines Wilson's positions on various issues and his success as Governor of New Jersey, concluding that he would most likely win if he were to run for President.

790. "A Governor and Two Colonels." *Outlook* 100 (January 27, 1912): 149–50. Focuses on the break between Wilson and George Harvey.

791. "Governor Wilson and His Friends." *Independent* 72 (February 1, 1912): 219–20. Discusses Wilson's break with George Harvey and the possible ramifications it will have on his campaign.

792. "Governor Wilson's Candidacy." *Nation* 93 (August 17, 1911): 136–37. Discusses Wilson's increasing popularity among Democrats and considers his chances for the 1912 presidential nomination.

793. "Governor Wilson's Candidacy: A Poll of the Press." *Outlook* 100 (February 10, 1912): 307–9. Contains excerpts from American newspapers discussing Wilson's chances as a prospective presidential candidate.

794. "Governor Wilson's 'Cocked-Hat' Letter." *Literary Digest* 44 (January 20, 1912): 101–2. Reactions to a 1907 Wilson letter expressing his dislike for William Jennings Bryan.

795. Green, George N. "The Florida Press and the Democratic Presidential Primary of 1912." *Florida Historical Quarterly* 44, no. 3 (1966): 169–80. Argues that while most of the influential conservative papers did not endorse Wilson, he was not significantly damaged by their lack of support.

796. Griffin, Solomon Bulkley. "The Political Evolution of a College President." *Atlantic Monthly* 109 (January 1912): 43–51. A portrait of Wilson as an exceptionally promising presidential candidate.

797. Hale, William Bayard. "Woodrow Wilson: Possible President." *World's Work* 22 (May 1911): 14339–53. Examines Wilson's quick rise in politics, his talents as a scholar and orator, and his chances in the 1912 presidential election.

798. _____ . "Woodrow Wilson—a Biography." *World's Work* 22 (October 1911): 14940–53; 23 (November 1911): 64–77; 23 (March 1912): 229–35, 297–310, 466–72, 522–34. Covers Wilson's life from his youth to the possibility of his first presidential campaign.

799. Harrison, Marion Clifford. "Woodrow Wilson's Fairy Cross." *Virginia Cavalcade: History in Picture and Story* 8, no. 3 (Winter 1958): 4–6. Recounts his reception by faculty and students of Randolph-Macon College, February 2, 1912, and their gift to him of a cross-shaped fairy stone to wear on his watch chain.

800. Harvey, George Brinton McClellan. "Democratic Presidential Possibilities." *Independent* 71 (November 2, 1911): 449–54. [Also published in *Harper's Weekly*

55 (November 11, 1911): 4–5.] The author points to a variety of reasons as to why Wilson should be nominated, highlighting Wilson's intellect, effectiveness as a leader, and "radical" policy proposals.

801. _____. "The Political Predestination of Woodrow Wilson." *North American Review* 193 (March 1911): 321–30. [Also published in *North American Review* 196 (August 1912): 145–53.] Predicts that Wilson will be the Democrats' nominee.

802. Hazeltine, Mayo Williamson. "Claims as a Presidential Candidate." *North American Review* 187 (June 1908): 844–50. Considers Wilson's keen intellect, southern up-bringing, and northeastern education as factors that could lead to a powerful coalition of support.

803. Heard, Alexander. *The Cost of Democracy.* Chapel Hill: University of North Carolina Press, 1960. Mentions that Wilson's 1911–1912 publicity campaign created such strong irresistible public opinion in favor of his candidacy that the pressure could not be resisted by the party leaders.

804. Hendrick, Burton Jesse. "Woodrow Wilson: Political Leader. An Attempt to Introduce Genuine Party Responsibility into the Government of an American State." *McClure's Magazine* 38 (December 1911): 217–31. A complimentary, contemporary appraisal.

805. Hennings, Robert E. "James D. Phelan and the Woodrow Wilson Anti-Oriental Statement of May 3, 1912." *California Historical Quarterly* 42 (1963): 291–300. Discusses the anti-Asian statement issued by the Wilson campaign and written by Phelan, the mayor of San Francisco.

806. King, C. Richard. "Woodrow Wilson's Visit to Texas in 1911." *Southwestern Historical Quarterly* 65 (October 1961): 184–95. Describes a trip whose main purpose was to gain support for Wilson's presidential candidacy.

807. Lewis, Alfred Henry. "The Real Woodrow Wilson." *Hearst's Magazine* 21 (May 1912): 2265–74. Points out inconsistencies in his positions on a variety of issues.

808. Link, Arthur S. "The Democratic Pre-Convention Campaign of 1912 in Georgia." *Georgia Historical Quarterly* 29 (September 1945): 143–58. Discusses the efforts of Wilson, Champ Clark, and Oscar Underwood.

809. _____. "The Underwood Presidential Movement of 1912." *Journal of Southern History* 11 (May 1945): 230–45. [Also published in **1155**, 200–15.] How the Underwood delegates helped secure Wilson's nomination.

810. _____. "The Wilson Movement in Texas, 1910–1912." *Southwestern Historical Quarterly* 48 (October 1944): 169–85. [Also published in **1155**, 155–71.] Argues that an anticipated conservative backlash sent Wilson men to Texas in 1910, which probably saved Wilson's national candidacy.

811. Lissner, Edward. "Woodrow Wilson for President." *Harper's Weekly* 55 (July 29, 1911): 6. An endorsement of Wilson's candidacy.

812. Lyons, Maurice F. *William F. McCombs: President Maker*. Cincinnati: Bancroft, 1922. Explains McCombs's role in 1912.

813. "The March of Events." *World's Work* 22 (May 1911): 14292–93. Endorses Wilson's nomination.

814. Needham, Henry Beach. "Woodrow Wilson's Views." *Outlook* 98 (August 26, 1911): 939–51. A searching but friendly interview on regulation of big corporations, machine politics, federalism, and state reform.

815. "The Qualities of Wilson." *Harper's Weekly* 50 (May 26, 1906): 750. Analyzes the attributes and political ideology that make Wilson the consummate politician.

816. Ridgway, Erman Jesse. "Weighing the Candidates." *Everybody's Magazine* 26 (May 1912): 580–82. A brief summary of Wilson's political positions. Includes a photograph.

817. Russell, Francis. *Presidential Makers of the Twentieth Century: From Mark Hanna to Joseph P. Kennedy*. Boston: Little, Brown, and Co., 1976. Wilson's uneasy relationship with George Harvey.

818. Stevenson, Frederick Boyd. "The Presidential Skirmish Line: An Impartial Consideration of the Personalities and Tactical Strength of Those in the Vanguard of the Columns Advancing upon the National Conventions." *Harper's Weekly* 52 (May 16, 1908): 11–12. Wilson is among those considered.

819. Stockbridge, Frank Parker. "How Woodrow Wilson Won His Nomination." *Current History Magazine of the New York Times* 20 (July 1924): 561–72. Written by the 1911 director of publicity for Wilson's nomination for President.

820. ———. "With Governor Wilson in the West." *World's Work* 22 (August 1911): 14713–16. Describes several episodes in Governor Wilson's western train trip which illustrate aspects of his personality and outlook.

821. "Voice of the East, for President: Woodrow Wilson." *Harper's Weekly* 55 (December 2, 1911): 20. Editorials from four major eastern newspapers.

822. "The Voice of the People: Significant and Interesting Comment of the Southern and Western Press." *Harper's Weekly* 55 (April 8, 1911): 22–24. Editorial comment regarding George Harvey's endorsement of Wilson.

823. "Voice of the South, for President: Woodrow Wilson." *Harper's Weekly* 55 (November 18, 1911): 32. Excerpts from southern newspapers.

824. "Voice of the West, for President: Woodrow Wilson." *Harper's Weekly* 55 (November 25, 1911): 19. Excerpts from western newspapers.

825. "Wilson Winning—in England." *Literary Digest* 45 (August 3, 1912): 180. Excerpts from the London press praising Wilson and endorsing his candidacy.

826. "Wilson-Harvey Episode." *Outlook* 100 (February 10, 1912): 294–95. Explains that *Harper's Weekly* editor, Colonel George Harvey, abandoned publishing articles related to Wilson's presidential candidacy because the publicity was injurious to Wilson's campaign.

827. "Woodrow Wilson, a Presidential Possibility." *Current Literature* 49 (October 1910): 381–84. Reviews Wilson's background as professor and President of Princeton, and calls him a "safe and sane" candidate.

828. "Woodrow Wilson and the Two Colonels." *Independent* 72 (January 25, 1912): 207–8. Explains how and why Wilson lost support from once helpful political advisors Colonel Harvey and Colonel Watterson.

829. "Woodrow Wilson as a Candidate: Some Press Comments." *Harper's Weekly* 50 (March 10, 1906): 330. Wilson's prospects for 1908.

830. "Woodrow Wilson as a Possible Candidate." *Harper's Weekly* 50 (June 2, 1906): 782. Quotes from national newspapers assessing Wilson's prospects as a likely presidential candidate in 1908.

831. "Woodrow Wilson's Policies." *Outlook* 96 (October 8, 1910): 300–2. Gives Wilson's reasons for opposing Roosevelt's New Nationalism.

832. "Woodrow Wilson's Presidential Prospects." *Current Literature* 50 (June 1911): 575–78. Surveys numerous editorial pages around the country.

B. 1912 Convention

833. Brooks, Sydney. "Bryan, Wilson, and Democracy: An English View of the Democratic Party and Its Presidential Nominee." *Harper's Weekly* 56 (August 10, 1912): 22. The journal's London correspondent foresees improved relations between the Democratic Party and the rest of the world as a result of Wilson's nomination.

834. Bryan, William Jennings. *A Tale of Two Conventions: Being an Account of the Republican and Democratic National Conventions of June, 1912*, ed. Virgil V. McNitt. New York: Funk & Wagnalls Co., 1912. Bryan's reports as a correspondent at the conventions.

835. Chesnut, W. Calvin. "Mr. Baker Supports Mr. Wilson." *Johns Hopkins Alumni Magazine* 28 (1940): 81–82. First-hand impressions of the 1912 Democratic Convention, with a focus on Newton D. Baker's support of Wilson's candidacy.

836. Coletta, Paolo E. "Bryan at Baltimore, 1912: Wilson's Warwick." *Nebraska History* 57, no. 2 (1976): 200–225. Examines William Jennings Bryan's role at the convention.

837. Congressional Quarterly. *National Party Conventions, 1831–1988*, 72–81. Washington, D.C.: Congressional Quarterly, 1991. Describes the four candidates in the 1912 presidential election and lists Wilson's Democratic platform based on single-term presidencies, presidential primaries, judicial reform, and states' rights.

838. David, Paul T., Ralph Morris Goldman, and Richard C. Bain. *The Politics of National Party Conventions*. Washington, D.C.: Brookings Institution, 1960. Mentions Wilson, as well as his administrations, and believes that he fully developed the concept of the presidency.

839. *Democratic Campaign Text Book*. Washington, D.C.: Democratic National Committee.

840. Eaton, Herbert A. *Presidential Timber: A History of Nominating Conventions, 1868–1960*, 227–45. New York: Free Press, 1964. Describes the Convention of 1912, and the capture of the nomination by Wilson after months of political struggle.

841. "Effect of Woodrow Wilson's Nomination." *Literary Digest* 45 (July 13, 1912): 43–46. Reaction from national newspapers to Wilson's nomination and how it will affect the three-way presidential race.

842. "A Fine and Worthy Utterance." *American Review of Reviews* 46 (September 1912): 265–67. Quotes Wilson's speech accepting the Democratic nomination for the presidency and praises Wilson's intention to free political life from domination by private interests.

843. "Governor Wilson's Speech." *Independent* 73 (August 15, 1912): 393–94. Reviews Wilson's acceptance speech.

844. Hackett, Francis. "Tallulah's Grandfather and the Tammany Tigers: Francis Hackett Recalls the Crucial 1912 Democratic National Convention." *New Republic* 135 (August 20, 1956): 21–22. Describes the role of Alabama Senator Bankhead in breaking the convention stalemate.

845. Harriman, F. J. H. "Woodrow Wilson Is Nominated at Baltimore: Excerpt from 'From Pinafores to Politics.'" In **396**, 1053–58. An account of Wilson's 1912 nomination by one of the delegates.

846. Johnson, Evans C. "The Underwood Forces and the Democratic Nomination of 1912." *Historian* 31, no. 2 (1969): 173–93. Recounts efforts of Democratic Party regulars and conservative financial leaders to prevent the nomination of Wilson for the presidency.

847. Judah, Charles, and G. W. Smith. *The Unchosen*, 117–54. New York: Coward-McCann, 1962. Examines the selection of Wilson over Champ Clark at the Democrats' 1912 convention.

848. Link, Arthur S. "Baltimore Convention of 1912." *American Historical Review* 50 (July 1945): 691–713. [Also published in **1155**, 216–42.] Describes Wilson's triumph over party divisions and Clark's popularity.

849. ———— . "A Letter from One of Wilson's Managers." *American Historical Review* 50 (July 1945): 768–75. Contains a letter written by Thomas W. Gregory, a Texas progressive who supported Wilson, to Edward M. House.

850. Roseboom, Eugene H., and Alfred E. Eckes, Jr. *A History of Presidential Elections From George Washington to Richard M. Nixon.* 3d ed. New York: Macmillan Co., 1970. Describes Wilson's campaigns and their importance.

851. Sparlin, Estal E. "Bryan and the 1912 Democratic Convention." *Mississippi Valley Historic Review* 22 (1936): 537–47. Examines the reasons for the change of allegiance from Clark to Wilson.

852. Stoddard, Henry L. *Presidential Sweepstakes: The Story of Political Conventions and Campaigns*, ed. Francis W. Leary. New York: G. P. Putnam's Sons, 1948. Describes Wilson's struggles in the 1912 and 1916 Democratic conventions.

853. "What Wilson Would Do." *Literary Digest* 45 (August 17, 1912): 247–48. Outlines Wilson's campaign platform for the 1912 presidential election.

854. "Wilson's Speech of Acceptance." *Outlook* 101 (August 17, 1912): 864–67. Outlines Wilson campaign promises.

855. "Woodrow Wilson's Task." *Living Age* 274 (July 27, 1912): 252–53. Praises Wilson's Baltimore platform which dealt with the tariff issue and the trusts.

C. 1912 Campaign and Election

856. *100 Years of Presidential Elections, 1864–1964, Covered in the Evening Star and Sunday Star.* Washington, D.C.: Evening Star Newspaper Co., 1968. Reprints the *Evening Star* front page after the 1912 and 1916 elections.

857. Ander, O. Fritiof. "The Swedish-American Press in the Election of 1912." *Swedish Pioneer Historical Quarterly* 29 (1963): 175–92. Asserts that a significant number of Swedes left the Republican Party, mainly to support Roosevelt. Some favored Wilson over Taft.

858. "British Praise for Wilson." *Literary Digest* 45 (November 23, 1912): 952. Passages from the British press, including speculation about his foreign trade policies.

859. Broderick, Francis L. *Progressivism at Risk: Electing a President in 1912.* Westport, Conn.: Greenwood Press, 1989. A detailed narrative of the campaign and the four candidates.

860. Congressional Quarterly. *Historical Review of Presidential Candidates from 1788 to 1964. Including Third Parties, 1832 to 1968, with Popular and Electoral Vote.* 5th ed. Washington, D.C.: Congressional Quarterly, 1969. Includes information on the 1912 and 1916 presidential elections, such as Wilson's vital statistics, his opposition during the elections, and the state by state presidential election returns.

861. Crews, Kenneth D. "Woodrow Wilson, Wisconsin, and the Election of 1912." *Presidential Studies Quarterly* 12 (Summer 1982): 369–76. Wilson's efforts to build a more progressive Democratic Party.

862. Daniels, Josephus P. *Editor in Politics*. Chapel Hill: University of North Carolina Press, 1941. Several sections dealing with Wilson's 1912 campaign.

863. Davidson, John Wells. "Wilson in the Campaign of 1912." In **1149**, 85–99. [A portion of the paper appeared as "Woodrow Wilson and 1912: Intellectual on the Stump" in the *Saturday Review* 39 (December 22, 1956): 7–9, 39–40.] A re-examination of Wilson's campaign speeches as they illuminated his views on the powers of the federal government and social justice and as they provided clues to his personality.

864. "The Election." *World's Work* 25 (December 1912): 137–39. Welcomes Wilson's election as a victory of ideas rather than partisan politics.

865. Fischer, Roger A. *Tippecanoe and Trinkets Too: The Material Culture of American Presidential Campaigns, 1828–1984*. Urbana: University of Illinois Press, 1988. Describes buttons, slogans, and other campaign items that Wilson used in the 1912 and 1916 presidential elections.

866. Fishel, Jeff. *Presidents and Promises: From Campaign Pledge to Presidential Performance*. Washington, D.C.: Congressional Quarterly, 1985. Believes that Wilson's half-disguised preference for parliamentary government is no closer to adoption today than when he championed it.

867. "Governor Wilson on Law Enforcement." *Outlook* 102 (September 28, 1912): 148. Reports an incident to prove that Wilson is a champion of law enforcement in New Jersey.

868. Guiterman, Arthur. "Woodrow Wilson." *Collier's National Weekly* 50 (November 16, 1912): 11. A short poem celebrating Wilson's election.

869. Harvey, George Brinton McClellan. "Roosevelt or the Republic!" *North American Review* 196 (October 1912): 435–41. Endorses Wilson's candidacy for President.

870. Hill, Charles Peter. "American Radicalism: Jackson, Bryan, and Wilson." In *British Essays in American History*, ed. Harry Cranbrook Allen and Charles Peter Snow. London: E. Arnold, 1957. Covers the elections of 1828, 1896, and 1912.

871. "How Governor Wilson Feels." *Harper's Weekly* 56 (October 26, 1912): 7–8. An exclusive campaign statement written by Wilson.

872. "An Index to Presidential Election Campaign Biographies, 1824–1972." Ann Arbor: University Microfilms International, 1981. Includes several bibliographic references to Wilson in his campaigns for the governorship of New Jersey and for the presidency.

873. Inglis, William O. "Helping to Make a President." *Collier's National Weekly* October 7, 1916: 14–16, 37–41; October 14, 1916: 12–14, 40–41; October 21, 1916: 14–15, 20–24. Detailed account of a deliberate campaign begun in 1907 to elect Wilson President.

874. "Intimate Moments with the Leading Presidential Candidates." *Current Literature* 53 (October 1912): 397–99. Includes an account of an evening spent at Wilson's Sea Girt home.

875. Johnson, David E., and Johnny R. Johnson. "Three Hats in the Ring." *American History Illustrated* 19 (November 1984): 12–17. An analysis of the 1912 presidential campaign.

876. Johnson, Donald Bruce, and Kirk Harold Porter, comps. *National Party Platforms, 1840–1972*, 1:168–175, 194–200. 5th ed. Urbana: University of Illinois Press, 1940. Outlines the Democratic platform of the 1912 and 1916 presidential elections, and fully explains Wilson's foreign and domestic policies.

877. Kaufman, Burton Ira. "Virginia Politics and the Wilson Movement, 1910–1914." *Virginia Magazine of History and Biography* 77, no. 1 (1969): 3–21. Describes the power struggle in the state party.

878. Kelly, Frank K. *The Fight for the White House: The Story of 1912*. New York: Thomas Y. Crowell, 1961.

879. Kessel, John H. *Presidential Campaign Politics*. 2d ed. Homewood, Ill.: Dorsey Press, 1984. Believes that Wilson's intellectual heirs continue to champion stronger political parties.

880. Lawson, Hughie G. "Candidates and Issues in 1912: A Re-examination of the New Nationalism and the New Freedom." Ph.D. diss., Tulane University, 1970. Concludes that Wilson's and Roosevelt's platforms were not dissimilar.

881. Link, Arthur S. "Democratic Politics and the Presidential Campaign of 1912 in Tennessee." *East Tennessee Historical Society's Publications* 51 (1979): 114–37. [Also published in **1155**, 172–99.] Describes the campaign in a state where the party was divided over prohibition.

882. _____ . "The Negro as a Factor in the Campaign of 1912." *Journal of Negro History* 32 (January 1947): 81–99. [Also published in **1155**, 256–71.] Argues that Wilson's managers were worried enough about winning the election that Wilson courted the black vote, while making sure not to make any hard promises.

883. _____ . "The Progressive Movement in the South, 1870–1914." *North Carolina Historical Review* 23 (April 1946): 1–24. [Also published in **1155**, 272–97.] Examines the effort that culminated in Wilson's 1912 presidential campaign.

884. _____ . "The South and the Democratic Campaign of 1910–1912." Ph.D. diss., University of North Carolina, 1945. Analysis of Wilson's successful campaign to win southern Democratic support in the presidential election of 1912.

885. _____ . "Theodore Roosevelt and the South in 1912." _North Carolina Historical Review_ 23 (July 1946): 313–24. [Also published in **1155**, 243–55.] Concludes that southern liberals and conservatives alike viewed Wilson as more moderate than Roosevelt.

886. _____ . "The Wilson Movement in North Carolina." _North Carolina Historical Review_ 23 (October 1946): 483–94. Covers Wilson's 1912 state campaign and his support by Josephus Daniels and other progressives.

887. Linkuguel, Wil A., and Robert W. Sellen. "The Presidential Candidate in Behalf of Himself." _South Atlantic Quarterly_ 75, no. 3 (1976): 290–311. Deals with the transition from separation to involvement and from issues to personality in presidential candidates, and argues these are trends which began with Wilson.

888. Low, Alfred Maurice. "American Affairs." _Living Age_ 276 (January 4, 1913): 29–34. Considers Wilson's opportunity to restore people's faith in government.

889. Lubove, Roy. "The Election of Wilson: A Progressive Mandate?" _King's Crown Essays, The Columbia College of the Social Sciences_ 4, no. 1 (Winter 1956): 31–41, 53–55. Argues that the three-way 1912 presidential race was ambiguous as an index of progressive sentiment.

890. McInery, Thomas J. "The Election of 1912 in New York State." Ph.D. diss., University of Denver, 1977. Examines the 1912 election from the perspectives of Wilson, Taft, Theodore Roosevelt, and the state bosses from the two major parties.

891. McKeehan, Irene Pettit. "Virginia to Woodrow Wilson: Poem." _Independent_ 73 (November 21, 1912): 1181. From the state of Virginia to Wilson following his election.

892. McWilliams, Tennant S. _Harris Taylor: The New Southerner as an American._ Tuscaloosa: University of Alabama Press, 1978. Biography of a Republican attorney, diplomat, and writer who supported Wilson.

893. Morgenthau, Henry. "All in a Life-Time: Chapters from an Autobiography." _World's Work_ 42 (August 1921): 361–73. Morgenthau's account of his entrance into politics in 1912.

894. Mowry, George Edwin. "Election of 1912." In **779**, 3:2135–242. Party platforms, acceptance speeches, and electoral breakdown.

895. _____ . "Election of 1912, Wilson and T.R." In **780**, 264–95. Explains that because of shifting political alliances, Wilson was nominated and elected President in 1912.

896. "Mr. Bryan's Views of Governor Wilson and the Democratic Platform." *Outlook* 102 (September 7, 1912): 27–28. Takes issue with William Jennings Bryan's statement that the platform is the most progressive ever.

897. Mugleston, William F. "The 1912 Progressive Campaign in Georgia." *Georgia Historical Quarterly* 61 (1977): 233–45. Explains that because of the race issue and Wilson's southern background, Georgians accepted Wilson and mistrusted Roosevelt.

898. "The New President." *Register of the Kentucky Historical Society* 11, no. 31 (1913): 97–98. Comments on Wilson's election.

899. "The New President and His Party." *Living Age* 277 (April 19, 1913): 180–83. Speculation on the future direction of the party.

900. O'Gorman, James Aloysius. "Why I Am for Woodrow Wilson." *North American Review* 196 (October 1912): 460–67. Cites Senator O'Gorman's reasons for voting for Wilson in 1912.

901. Oster, Charles. "As a Foreigner Sees Them: Wilson, Taft, Roosevelt." *World's Work* 24 (September 1912): 575–78. A foreign journalist's view of the race.

902. "The Political Campaign." *Outlook* 102 (September 7, 1912): 5–6. Sympathetic report on a campaign week.

903. "The President-Elect." *Outlook* 102 (November 23, 1912): 613–14. A biographical sketch of Wilson, emphasizing his talent and education.

904. "President-Elect Wilson's Dilemma." *Literary Digest* 45 (November 16, 1912): 886–88. Affirms Wilson's public mandate and considers the difficulties he may have in keeping the nation's trust.

905. *Presidential Elections Since 1789.* 3d ed. Washington, D.C.: Congressional Quarterly, 1983. Detailed statistical analysis of presidential elections, including those in 1912 and 1916.

906. Quick, John Herbert. "Why I Prefer Wilson to Roosevelt." *American Magazine* 75 (November 1912): 14–17. Supports Wilson's brand of progressivism over that of Roosevelt's in the 1912 campaign.

907. Rorvig, Paul. "Clash of the Giants: The 1912 Presidential Election." *American History Illustrated* 14, no. 7 (November 1979): 12–15, 42–46. Examines the candidates for President in 1912 and the events surrounding the election.

908. Sarasohn, David. "The Democratic Surge, 1905–1912: Forging a Progressive Majority." Ph.D. diss., University of California, Los Angeles, 1976. Argues that the Democratically controlled House put together a progressive program foreshadowing the New Freedom, and that Wilson would have been elected in 1912 even without the Roosevelt-Taft split.

909. Scott, Robert Carl. "William McCombs and the 1912 Democratic Presidential Nomination of Woodrow Wilson." *Arkansas Historical Quarterly* 44, no. 3 (1985): 246–59. Focuses on the Arkansas native and New York City lawyer who initiated and managed Wilson's 1912 presidential strategy.

910. Stanwood, Edward. *A History of the Presidency.* 2 vols. New ed., revised by Charles Knaulen Bolton. Boston: Houghton Mifflin Co., 1928. Traces Wilson's nomination and election to the presidency in both the 1912 and 1916 elections.

911. Stoddard, Henry L. *It Costs to Be President*, 43–67. New York: Harper and Brothers, 1938. A New York editor describes the dynamics of political machinations.

912. "Three Hats in the Ring." *American History Illustrated* 19 (November 1984): 12. Concerns Wilson, Theodore Roosevelt, and William Howard Taft.

913. Tobin, Richard Lardner. "The Incredible Election of 1912." *Mankind* 1, no. 9 (1968): 28–31, 37–40. Analyzes the importance of the third-party candidate.

914. "The Torchlight Parade." *Yankee* 48 (December 1984): 150. Describes a 1912 Wilson parade in Hampton, New Hampshire.

915. "Trusts and the Candidates." *Literary Digest* 45 (November 2, 1912): 769–71. Explains Wilson's belief that American trusts were unjust and inhibited competition.

916. Warner, Robert M. "Chase S. Osborn and the Presidential Campaign of 1912." *Mississippi Valley Historical Review* 46, no. 1 (1959): 19–45. The role of the Republican Governor of Michigan.

917. Warren, Sidney. *Battle for the Presidency*, 176–215. Philadelphia: J.B. Lippincott, 1968. Describes Wilson's struggles with Taft and Roosevelt in the 1912 presidential election.

918. Watterson, Henry. "New Dispensation." *Collier's: The National Weekly* 50 (March 8, 1913): 10, 28. A Democrat's hopeful analysis of Wilson's potential.

919. Weisbord, Marvin R. *Campaigning for President*, 55–67. Washington, D.C.: Public Affairs Press, 1964. Examines the way Wilson broke tradition and re-shaped the role of the American President.

920. "What Europe Thinks of President-Elect Wilson." *American Monthly Review of Reviews* 47 (January 1913): 115. Includes comments from the German, British, and Russian press concerning Wilson's election to the presidency.

921. "Wilson and Bryan." *Independent* 73 (November 28, 1912): 1266. Describes Bryan's efforts to nominate and elect Wilson to the presidency, arguing that Bryan deserves a cabinet position.

922. "Wilson as a Campaigner." *Outlook* 102 (October 26, 1912): 370–71. Describes some of Wilson's campaign pledges, saying that some are unrealistic.

923. "Wilson as Viewed in the Roosevelt Camp." *Current Literature* 53 (August 1912): 127–28. States that many pro-Roosevelt newspapers support Wilson.

924. "Wilson in Connecticut." *Nation* 95 (October 3, 1912): 300. Attempts to distinguish Wilson's progressivism from Roosevelt's.

925. "Wilson versus Roosevelt." *Outlook* 102 (October 12, 1912): 297–300. Discusses Wilson's attacks upon two progressive planks, the proposal to regulate trusts by a Federal Industrial Commission, and the proposal to regulate the tariff by a scientific commission.

926. "Wilson-Taft-Roosevelt: The Candidates Compared." *World's Work* 24 (September 1912): 569–75. Concludes that all three candidates have considerable gifts but that Wilson will be elected because of his noble vision.

927. "Woodrow Wilson." *Outlook* 98 (August 26, 1911): 922–23. Favorable editorial recognizing Wilson as a candidate for the presidency and as the most popular leader in the Democratic Party.

13
Election of 1914

928. "Clinging to Wilson's Coat-tails." *Nation* 99 (October 22, 1914): 488–89. Describes Democrats' use of Wilson's popularity.

929. Harvey, George Brinton McClellan. "The Case Against Wilson." *North American Review* 200 (November 1914): 641–52. Republicans' campaign charges.

930. _____. "Uphold the President." *North American Review* 200 (October 1914): 481–94. Concludes that voters should return a Democratic Congress.

931. "The President and the Election." *Outlook* 108 (November 11, 1914): 575–76. Connects Wilson's decreasing popular opinion with his stand on big business.

932. "President Wilson's Popularity." *Literary Digest* 49 (August 1, 1914): 184–86. Remarks of a British writer.

933. Whelpley, James Davenport. "American Elections." *Fortnightly Review* 102, no. 6 (December 1914): 1033–40. [Also published in *Living Age* 284 (January 9, 1915): 67–72.]

934. "The Wilson Administration in Its First Trial at the Polls." *Current Opinion* 57 (November 1914): 305–8. Questions whether Wilson will get a Democratic Congress.

14

Election of 1916

935. "Allies Greet the President." *Literary Digest* 53 (December 16, 1916): 1589–90. The European press's favorable reaction to Wilson's re-election.

936. "As between Mr. Wilson and Mr. Hughes." *World's Work* 32 (October 1916): 600–1. Praises Wilson's renomination and expresses hope that he will address the European conflict.

937. Bohn, Frank. "The Reelection of Wilson." *Masses* 9 (January 1917): 15–16. Places Wilson in the historical context of labor reform and calls his reelection no socialist triumph but still a victory for progressives.

938. Brown, L. Ames. "President on the Independent Voter." *World's Work* 32 (September 1916): 494–98. Wilson's belief that ideas and character are more important to voters than party affiliation.

939. _____. "Wilson the Candidate." *American Monthly Review of Reviews* 54 (July 1916): 41–45. Portrait stressing his accomplishments and popularity.

940. Burnham, Walter Dean. *Critical Elections and the Mainspring of American Politics.* New York: W. W. Norton, 1966. How new technology in advertising boosted Wilson's 1916 campaign.

941. Claussen, E. Neal. "'He Kept Us out of War': Martin H. Glynn's Keynote." *Quarterly Journal of Speech* 52, no. 1 (1966): 23–32. Chronicles the 1916 presidential election and asserts that Wilson defeated Charles Evans Hughes because of Wilson's campaign slogan.

942. "A Comparison of the Chicago Platforms." *Literary Digest* 52 (June 17, 1916): 1762–63. Excerpts from American newspapers comparing the platforms of the Republican and Progressive parties.

943. Creel, George C. "Can Wilson Win?" *Century Magazine* 92 (June 1916): 266–72. Argues that the 1916 election is the most critical since the Civil War.

944. _____ . *Wilson and the Issues.* New York: Century Co., 1916. Looks at Wilson's positions on issues and argues that the 1916 election is the most critical one since 1860.

945. Croly, Herbert David. "The Two Parties in 1916." *New Republic* 8 (October 21, 1916): 286–91. An endorsement of the Democratic ticket.

946. Cuddy, Edward. "Irish-Americans and the 1916 Election." *American Quarterly* 21 (1969): 228–43. Explains the support Wilson received from most Irish-Americans in 1916.

947. Davenport, Frederick Morgan. "The Pre-Nomination Campaign: President of the United States." *Outlook* 112 (March 1, 1916): 511–15. Flattering portrait of Wilson as a man whose good character makes him deserving of the presidency.

948. _____ . "The Pre-Nomination Campaign: President Wilson's Foreign Policy." *Outlook* 113 (May 17, 1916): 142–47. Interviews of unnamed members of the Wilson administration.

949. _____ . "The Pre-Nomination Campaign: The Wilson Administration." *Outlook* 112 (March 8, 1916): 552+. Positive summary of Wilson's first term as President.

950. Deeg, D. M. "Supporting the President." *Nation* 103 (August 31, 1916): 200–1. Urges the *Nation* to support Wilson over Hughes in the 1916 election because of Wilson's excellent record in economics, foreign and domestic policy, and the numerous reforming measures passed during his first administration.

951. Eiselen, Malcolm R. "The Day That California Changed World History." *Pacific Historian* 10, no. 1 (1966): 49–57. Details California's role in the 1916 presidential election.

952. "The Election." *New Republic* 9 (November 11, 1916): 34–35. Examines the significance of Wilson's re-election and his coalition of western and southern states. Makes it clear that Wilson must still win over his critics if he is to succeed.

953. Eliot, Charles William. "The Achievements of the Democratic Party and Its Leader since March 4, 1913." *Atlantic Monthly* 118 (October 1916): 433–40. Concludes that Wilson accomplished just as much in one term as the four previous Republican administrations combined.

954. Fuller, Paul, Jr. "Case for Wilson." *World's Work* 32 (October 1916): 641–49. Gives reasons why independent voters should support Wilson.

955. Grant, Phillip A., Jr. "William Jennings Bryan and the Presidential Election of 1916." *Nebraska History* 63, no. 4 (1982): 531–42. Analyzes Bryan's role, particularly in his campaign in the Western states.

956. Hapgood, Norman. "Mr. Wilson's Leadership." *Independent* 88 (October 2, 1916): 15+. An endorsement of Wilson's bid for reelection.

957. _____ . "Wilson or Hughes." *Yale Review* n.s. 6 (October 1916): 26–43. Argues forcefully for Wilson's re-election.

958. _____ . "Wilson Tested, Hughes Dangerous." *Independent* 88 (November 6, 1916): 230–31. Blasts the policies proposed by Charles Evans Hughes during the campaign and argues that a vote for Wilson is a vote for the future of the nation.

959. Harvey, George Brinton McClellan. "The Paramount Issue: Character." *North American Review* 204 (November 1916): 641–57. An appraisal of Wilson.

960. _____ . "Wilson and a Second Term." *North American Review* 203 (February 1916): 161–70. Expresses dismay for the apparently hollow plank in the 1912 Democratic platform, which called for a one-term limit for the President.

961. "He Kept Us out of War." *Literary Digest* 53 (October 14, 1916): 933–34. Excerpts from American newspapers on the campaign slogan.

962. "How Woodrow Wilson Cultivated the Art of Expression." *Current Opinion* 61 (December 1916): 384–85. Discusses Wilson's power as writer and orator.

963. "Hughes or Wilson?" *New Republic* 8 (October 28, 1916): 311– 13. Explains the publication's difficulty in deciding which presidential candidate to endorse. Comes out unenthusiastically for Wilson.

964. Lawrence, David. "Man to Man: Comparison of Wilson and Hughes." *Independent* 87 (July 24, 1916): 121–22. Compares presidential candidates Wilson and Charles Evans Hughes.

965. _____ . "One Term for Wilson?" *Collier's National Weekly* 56 (November 6, 1915): 7–8. Considers whether Wilson will abide by a presidential one-term limit in the 1912 platform.

966. Leary, William M., Jr. "Woodrow Wilson, Irish-Americans, and the Election of 1916." *Journal of American History* 54, no. 1 (June 1967): 57–72. Analyzes the voting patterns of Irish-Americans in urban counties and wards, given their stated positions about Wilson.

967. Link, Arthur S. "President Wilson's Plan to Resign in 1916." *Princeton University Library Chronicle* 23 (Summer 1962): 167–72. Reports Wilson's idea to resign immediately after the 1916 election if Hughes won. In this way there would be no lame duck executive from November to March during a time of crisis.

968. Link, Arthur S., and William M. Leary, Jr. "Election of 1916." In 779, 3:2245–345. Contains an historical overview of the election, the major party platforms, acceptance speeches by Wilson and Charles Evans Hughes, several contemporary journal articles, and a state-by-state breakdown of the popular and electoral vote.

969. _____ . "Election of 1916: 'He Kept Us out of War.'" In **780**, 296–321. Believes that in 1916 the United States elected a man destined to influence the course of human events in an more profound way than any of his predecessors.

970. Lippmann, Walter. "The Case for Wilson." *New Republic* 8 (October 14, 1916): 263–64. An endorsement of Wilson's candidacy.

971. _____ . "A Progressive's View of the Election." *Yale Review* n.s. 6 (January 1917): 225–32. Sees Wilson's reelection as a victory for progressivism.

972. Lovell, S. D. *The Presidential Election of 1916.* Carbondale: Southern Illinois University Press, 1980. Argues that Wilson's 1916 election was a personal victory since he was the one who mapped out the strategies for appealing to progressives and independent voters.

973. Martin, Edward Sandford. "Root, Roosevelt, and Wilson." *World's Work* 31 (April 1916): 603–4. A character analysis of the three statesmen, noting in particular Wilson's emphasis on morality.

974. Meyer, Jonah N. "The Presidential Election of 1916 in the Middle West." Ph.D. diss., Princeton University, 1966. Considers Wilson's progressive reforms, opposition to involvement in the European conflict, and Hughes's negative campaign.

975. "Mr. Root's Assault on the Wilson Administration." *Literary Digest* 52 (February 26, 1916): 485–88. A collection of opinions on the viability of Elihu Root as an opponent of Wilson during his second campaign for office.

976. "Mr. Wilson's Acceptance." *Nation* 103 (September 7, 1916): 213–14. A discussion of both Wilson's acceptance speech and his first term.

977. "Mr. Wilson's Hat in the Ring." *Literary Digest* 52 (January 22, 1916): 159–60. Cites various opinions concerning Wilson's decision to accept the nomination for the presidency in 1916.

978. Olin, Spencer C., Jr. "Hiram Johnson, the California Progressives, and the Hughes Campaign of 1916." *Pacific Historical Review* 31 (1962): 403–12. Argues that Johnson and his progressive followers ran a weak campaign for Hughes.

979. Pinchot, Amos. "What the Election Means." *Masses* 9 (January 1917): 18–19. Asserts that Wilson advanced the cause of internationalism by maintaining that narrow nationalism is out of date.

980. "The Pomp and the Glory, the Drama and the Deals." *Life* 49 (July 4, 1960): 54–55. Wilson at a Chicago auditorium, outside of which suffragists demonstrated.

981. "Possible Democratic Candidates in 1916." *Everybody's Magazine* 32 (June 1915): 761–64. A rating of Wilson as "the Party Man," "the Book Man," "the Business Man," and "the Peace Man."

982. Prasad, Y. D. "The German-Americans and the Election of 1916." *Indian Journal of American Studies* (India) 11, no. 1 (1981): 49–57. Describes Wilson's inability to secure the majority of the 1916 German-American vote.

983. "The President and the Crowd." *Nation* 102 (February 10, 1916): 153. Differentiates between audiences at speaking tours and Wilson's actual popular support.

984. "President Wilson and Prosperity." *Outlook* 114 (September 13, 1916): 64–65. Analyzes the economic achievements of the Wilson administration and believes that American prosperity is due to Wilson's encouragement of business.

985. "President Wilson Stands on His Record and Appeals to the Country for Reelection." *Current Opinion* 61 (October 1916): 225–26. A sampling of newspaper opinion.

986. "President Wilson's Challenge to His Political Foes." *Current Opinion* 58 (February 1915): 69–71. Examines Wilson's campaign for the presidency in 1916, and the efforts of his opponents.

987. "The President's Defense of His Record." *Literary Digest* 53 (September 16, 1916): 654–56. Assesses first-term legislation.

988. "The President—Why He Should and Should Not Be Reelected." *World's Work* 32 (August 1916): 367–69. Considers the prospects of Wilson's domestic and foreign agenda if reelected in 1916.

989. Ratcliffe, Samuel Kerkham. "President Wilson's Victory and Its Significance." *Contemporary Review* 110 (December 1916): 705–14. [Also published in *Living Age* 292 (January 13, 1917): 67–74.] Analyzes the significance of Wilson succeeding himself as President in 1916.

990. "Reelection of Mr. Wilson." *New Republic* 9 (November 11, 1916): 31–32. Calls Wilson's reelection "remarkable."

991. Roberts, George C. "Woodrow Wilson, John W. Kern, and the 1916 Indiana Election: Defeat of a Senate Majority Leader." *Presidential Studies Quarterly* 10, no. 1 (1980): 63–73. Explores the relationship between Wilson and his first Senate Majority Leader.

992. Sarasohn, David. "The Election of 1916: Realigning the Rockies." *Western Historical Quarterly* 11 (July 1980): 285–305. Explains the importance of Rocky Mountain states.

993. Schurman, Jacob Gould. "Weakness of Mr. Wilson." *Independent* 87 (August 21, 1916): 273. Outlines Hughes' criticisms of Wilson as an executive.

994. "Shall We Vote for Wilson?" *Outlook* 113 (August 23, 1916): 941–42. Opposes Wilson's reelection on the basis of his weaknesses in economic policies and his failure to protest against the invasion of Belgium.

995. Singh, Cathleyne. "Presidential Election in the U.S.A." *London Quarterly Review* 127 (January 1917): 116–19. Explains that Wilson's failure to pursue a stronger line of action against Germany was not due to his own weakness.

996. Storey, Moorfield. "President Wilson's Administration." *Yale Review* n.s. 5 (April 1916): 449–73. Argues that Wilson's accomplishments strengthen his candidacy.

997. Taft, William Howard. "Democratic Record." *Yale Review* n.s. 6 (October 1916): 1–25. Attacks Wilson's foreign policy and domestic programs.

998. Thomas, Phyllis H. "The Role of Mississippi in the Presidential Election of 1916." *Southern Quarterly* 4 (1966): 207–26. Discusses Wilson's strong victory in Mississippi.

999. "Three Candidates." *Nation* 103 (October 26, 1916): 394–96. Examines the three platforms while favoring Wilson.

1000. "The Two Parties after the Election." *New Republic* 9 (November 18, 1916): 63–64. Argues that the election endorsed Wilson, not the Democrats, and that both parties should beware of any return to partisanship.

1001. Walling, William English. "Socialists for Wilson." *Masses* 9 (January 1917): 24. Describes the Socialists' temporary transfer of support to Wilson in the 1916 election.

1002. Whelpley, James Davenport. "American Presidential Campaign." *Fortnightly Review* 106, no. 1 (July 1916): 157–66. [Also published in *Living Age* 290 (August 5, 1916): 323–29.] A British perspective.

1003. "Why Wilson Won." *Literary Digest* 53 (November 18, 1916): 1312–15. The American press reacts to the 1916 presidential election.

1004. "Wilson and Roosevelt." *New Republic* 9 (November 4, 1916): 3–5. Suggests that few Presidents have been more profoundly distrusted and misinterpreted.

1005. "Wilson on the Second Term." *Nation* 102 (January 13, 1916): 35. Supports Wilson's opposition to a proposed constitutional amendment that would limit a President to one term.

1006. Wister, Owen. "If We Elect Mr. Wilson." *Collier's National Weekly* 58 (November 4, 1916): 5–6+. Opposes Wilson's reelection because of his bungling of foreign and domestic policies.

1007. "Working up the Case against President Wilson." *Current Opinion* 60 (February 1916): 78–82. Believes Wilson is entitled to seek renomination.

15

Election of 1918

1008. Abbott, Lawrence Fraser. "Making America Safe for Autocracy: An Open Letter on the President's Congressional Appeal." *Outlook* 120 (November 6, 1918): 349–50. Argues that it would be fatal to elect a Congress controlled by Wilson.

1009. Adler, Selig. "The Congressional Election of 1918." *South Atlantic Quarterly* 36 (October 1937): 447–65. Notes the rare importance of the election of a Republican Congress in the face of Wilson's appeal for support at the Paris Peace Conference.

1010. "Choose Ye This Day." *Nation* 107 (November 16, 1918): 573. Blames Wilson for losing the congressional elections.

1011. Davison, C. S. "President Wilson's Position." *Spectator* 122 (June 21, 1919): 791. States that the elections were a solid rejection of Wilson.

1012. Eastman, Max. "The Campaign Issue." *Liberator* 1 (October 1918): 23–25. Expresses disillusionment over Wilson's support of freedom from autocracy for the Russian people and his failure to endorse the Bolsheviks.

1013. "An Election in a Fog." *New Republic* 16 (October 26, 1918): 363–65. Criticizes the lack of discussion on specific issues.

1014. Hoopes, Roy. "'Politics Is Adjourned!'" *American History Illustrated* 21, no. 7 (November 1986): 18–23. Focuses on Wilson's involvement in the Michigan senatorial campaign.

1015. Livermore, Seward W. "The Sectional Issue in the 1918 Congressional Elections." *Mississippi Valley Historical Review* 35, no. 1 (June 1948): 29–60. Argues that blaming Wilson oversimplifies the facts leading up to the election.

1016. Parsons, Edward B. "Some International Implications of the 1918 Roosevelt-Lodge Campaign against Wilson and a Democratic Congress." *Presidential Studies Quarterly* 19 (Winter 1989): 141–57. Studies Theodore Roosevelt's and Henry Cabot Lodge's fears that Germany would remain strong after the war, and Great Britain would be weakened.

1017. "President Wilson to Face a Republican Congress." *Literary Digest* 59 (November 16, 1918): 14–15. Excerpts from the American press.

1018. "The War and the New Congress." *Literary Digest* 59 (October 26, 1918): 17–18. The American press debates the effect of World War I on the 1918 congressional elections.

1019. "Woodrow Wilson, Politician." *Nation* 107 (November 2, 1918): 503. Criticizes Wilson's appeal to partisan voting.

16

Election of 1920

1020. Bagby, Wesley Marvin. *The Road to Normalcy: The Presidential Campaign and Election of 1920.* Johns Hopkins University Studies in Historical and Political Science. Baltimore: Johns Hopkins University Press, 1962. The first study to demonstrate that Wilson wanted a third term.

1021. ———. "William Gibbs McAdoo and the 1920 Presidential Nomination." *East Tennessee Historical Society's Publications* 31 (1959): 43–58. Presents evidence that McAdoo feared Wilson would run for a third term.

1022. ———. "Woodrow Wilson, a Third Term, and the Solemn Referendum." *American Historical Review* 60 (April 1955): 567–75. Describes the 1920 Democratic Convention.

1023. Burchell, R. A. "Did the Irish and German Voters Desert the Democrats in 1920?" *Journal of American Studies* 6 (1972): 153–64. Blames their desertion on the postwar downturn in the economy.

1024. Burner, David. "The Breakup of the Wilson Coalition of 1916." *Mid-America* 45 (January 1963): 18–35. [Also published in **1544**, 3:1047–65.] Argues that Wilson's coalition failed in 1920 because Wilson was unable to focus on crucial domestic issues following the war.

1025. "Defeat of Wilsonism." *Nation* 111 (November 10, 1920): 520. Welcomes the rejection of Wilson by the people.

1026. Eliot, Charles William. "The Voter's Choice in the Coming Election." *Atlantic Monthly* 126 (October 1920): 527–40. A defense of Wilson's presidency.

1027. "The Fight for Control of the Democratic Party." *Literary Digest* 65 (June 12, 1920): 17–19. Leadership fight between Wilson and Bryan.

1028. Hapgood, Norman. "Wilsonism as an Issue." *Independent* 102 (June 5, 1920): 319. Lists Wilson's mistakes but praises his achievements.

1029. Laskine, Edmond. "La Crise de la Democratie Presidentielle aux Etats-Unis." *Revue Politique et Litteraire Reveu Bleu* 58 (July 3, 1920): 392–96.

1030. Merritt, Richard L. "Woodrow Wilson and the Great and Solemn Referendum, 1920." *Review of Politics* 27, no. 1 (January 1965): 78–104. Demonstrates the effect of Wilsonian idealism on his appeal for a referendum on the peace treaty and League of Nations and on the 1920 campaign.

1031. Taft, William Howard. "Mr. Wilson and the Campaign." *Yale Review* n.s. 10 (October 1920): 1–25. An attack on Wilson's policies.

1032. "Why Wait until March 4th?" *New Republic* 24 (November 10, 1920): 255–56. Gives suggestions for Wilson's future, considering his illness and his recent loss to Harding in the 1920 election.

1033. "Wilson in Defeat." *Review* 3 (November 10, 1920): 435. Concedes that Wilson made serious mistakes.

1034. Wimer, Kurt. "Woodrow Wilson and a Third Nomination." *Pennsylvania History: Quarterly Journal of the Pennsylvania Historical Association* 29 (April 1962): 193–211. Disputes the notion that Wilson was not mapping out future plans during his illness in 1920 and argues that he planned to seek a third term with the League as the central issue.

17

President of the United States

A. Assessments of Wilson as President

See also entries under "Biographical Essays and Sketches," "Presidential Power and Leadership," and "Contemporary Profiles and Assessments Following Wilson's Death"

1035. Abrams, Richard M. "American Visions of the Good Society." *Reviews in American History* 12, no. 4 (1984): 533–40. Essay review of **326**. Argues that the contrast between Woodrow Wilson and Theodore Roosevelt helps to illuminate two traditions in American politics.

1036. Agar, Herbert. "Roosevelt, Taft, Wilson and Harding." In *People's Choice*: *From Washington to Harding. A Study in Democracy*, 288–305. Boston: Houghton-Mifflin Co., 1933. Biographical sketch followed by a summary of Wilson's presidency. The success of his domestic policy is contrasted with his anemic handling of foreign affairs.

1037. Allen, Gary. "Deadly Lies." *American Opinion* 19 (May 1976): 29–46, 87–94. Article on liberal Presidents' tendencies to make promises of peace, only to enter into war. The first part focuses on Wilson's 1916 campaign.

1038. Alsop, Em Bowles, ed. *The Greatness of Woodrow Wilson, 1856–1956*. New York: Holt, Rinehart & Co., 1956. Collection of essays written by historians and friends of Wilson commemorating the centennial anniversary of his birth. Each essay is listed separately by author.

1039. Ambrosius, Lloyd E. "The Orthodoxy of Revisionism: Woodrow Wilson and the New Left." *Diplomatic History* 1, no. 3 (1977): 199–214. Wilson's internationalism and the Cold War.

1040. Anderson, Isabel (Perkins). *Presidents and Pies*: *Life in Washington, 1897–1919*. Boston: Houghton Mifflin and Co., 1920. Traces Wilson's political accomplishments and the unusual fluctuations in his popularity.

1041. Bailey, Thomas Andrew. *Presidential Greatness: The Image and the Man from George Washington to the Present*, 310–12. New York: Appleton-Century-Crofts, 1966. Balances the judgment that Wilson's early domestic achievements make him one of the great Presidents against the verdict that he failed with foreign policies.

1042. ———. *Presidential Saints and Sinners*, 168–85. New York: Free Press, 1981. Believes that Wilson was a man with Christian principles and that the force of circumstances led him to abandon, reverse, or apply these principles inconsistently.

1043. ———. *The Pugnacious Presidents: White House Warriors on Parade*. New York: Free Press, 1980. Agrees that Wilson hated war but presents the paradox that Wilson, an idealist who was dedicated to peace, led the United States into World War I.

1044. Baillie, Hugh. "Wilson." In *High Tension*, 43–65. New York: Harper and Brothers, 1959. Wilson during his second term, written by a reporter for United Press International.

1045. Baker, Ray Stannard. "Woodrow Wilson—Prophet." In **1255**, 18–22. Regards Wilson as a gifted leader and visionary.

1046. Barkley, Alben W., et al. "Woodrow Wilson: His Ambitions and Achievements." *Town Meeting* 22 (January 22, 1956): 1–12. ABC radio broadcast from Wilson's birthplace to observe the 100th anniversary of his birth.

1047. Baruch, Bernard Mannes. "The Wilsonian Legacy for Us." *New York Times Magazine* December 23, 1956: 12, 18. Wilson's devotion to the ideals of individual liberty and democracy.

1048. ———. "Wilson's Words—Words for Today." *New York Times Magazine* January 2, 1955: 8, 26. Deals with Wilsonian idealism and its legacy.

1049. ———. "Woodrow Wilson's Claims to Greatness." *Vital Speeches of the Day* 14 (December 15, 1947): 158–60. Admiring portrait of Wilson.

1050. Bassett, Margaret. *Profiles and Portraits of American Presidents*, 267–73. Freeport, Maine: Bond Wheelwright, 1964. Overview of Wilson's presidency.

1051. Beard, Charles Austin. *Presidents in American History*, 127–30. New York: J. Messner, 1953. Brief summary of Wilson's career as an independent President.

1052. ———. *Presidents in American History*. Rev. ed., 126–30, 202–3. New York: J. Messner, 1985.

1053. Bellot, Hugh Hale. *Woodrow Wilson*. Creighton Lecture in History, 1954. London: Athlone Press for the University of London, 1955. Discussion of Wilson as a visionary thinker and powerful public speaker who was impatient with the means necessary to achieve his goals.

1054. Block, Harold B. *The True Woodrow Wilson: Crusader for Democracy*. New York: Fleming H. Revell, 1946. An analysis of why Wilson ranks as one of the greatest American Presidents.

1055. Blum, John Morton. "Woodrow Wilson: A Study in Intellect." *Confluence: An International Forum* 5, no. 4 (Winter 1957): 367–75. A critical assessment of Wilson's ideas of politics and society as outmoded and inadequate for the realities of the twentieth century.

1056. Bolitho, William. *Twelve Against the Gods: The Story of Adventure*, 331–51. New York: Simon & Schuster, 1929. The sociological and psychological struggles of individuals throughout history, with a final chapter on Wilson.

1057. _____. "Woodrow Wilson." *Saturday Review of Literature* 6 (October 12, 1929): 238–39. Portrays Wilson as a humanitarian, a champion of democracy, and a tragic hero.

1058. Bourquin, Maurice. "L'Oeuvre du President Wilson." In **1073**, 5–16.

1059. Bowers, Claude Gernade. "The Statesman." In **1038**, 151–66. Argues that Wilson's reputation as a brilliant statesman and diplomat is justified not only by his wartime leadership, but also by his handling of affairs in South America before the war.

1060. _____. "Woodrow Wilson: A Reappraisal." *Current History* 34, no. 1 (April 1931): 1–6. Emphasizes Wilson's consistency.

1061. Bradford, Gamaliel. "Brains Win and Lose: Woodrow Wilson." *Atlantic Monthly* 147 (February 1931): 152–64. [Reprinted in **397**, 13–34.] Portrays Wilson as a great intellectual, devoted to his causes.

1062. _____. *The Quick and the Dead*, 43–78. Boston: Houghton, Mifflin Co., 1931. Studies by a Wilson contemporary.

1063. Broesamle, John J. "The Democrats from Bryan to Wilson." In *The Progressive Era*, ed. Lewis L. Gould, 83–113. Syracuse: Syracuse University Press, 1974. Argues that Wilson's presidency, which formed a bridge between the urban and the agrarian Democrats, was an aberration in the history of the Democratic Party. The party became increasingly urbanized, though still divided.

1064. Bundy, McGeorge. "Woodrow Wilson and a World He Never Made." *Confluence: An International Forum* 5, no. 4 (Winter 1957): 281–90. An analysis of Wilson's failure to rally political support for his foreign policy.

1065. Burch, Philip H., Jr. *Elites in American History, Vol. II: The Civil War to the New Deal*, 201–44. New York: Holmes and Meier, 1981. Overview of the Wilson Administration, including Cabinet and Supreme Court appointments, major issues confronted, and World War I.

1066. Burns, James MacGregor. "Wilson, Roosevelt, and Eisenhower: Three Approaches to Leadership." In **1251**, 43–56. An address describing the changes in Wilson's leadership from representative to uncompromising, and comparing Wilson's style to that of two other Presidents.

1067. Burt, Nathaniel. *First Families: The Making of an American Aristocracy.* Boston: Little, Brown and Co., 1970. Mentions Wilson's contributions to the presidency but believes that he is overshadowed by the Roosevelts.

1068. Burton, David Henry. "Woodrow Wilson, Righteous Scholar." In *The Learned Presidency: Theodore Roosevelt, William Howard Taft, Woodrow Wilson,* 136–92. Cranbury, N.J.: Fairleigh Dickinson University Press, 1988. Describes Wilson as a Protestant intellectual untutored in international power politics.

1069. Butler, Nicholas Murray. *Across the Busy Years: Recollections and Reflections.* New York: Charles Scribner's Sons, 1939–1940. 2 vols. Contains scattered impressions of Wilson as candidate and President by the President of Columbia University.

1070. _____ . *Things Seen and Heard in Politics.* New York: Charles Scribner's Sons, 1936. Comments on American public figures, including Wilson.

1071. Canfield, Leon Hardy. *Presidency of Woodrow Wilson: Prelude to a World in Crisis.* Rutherford, N.J.: Fairleigh Dickinson University Press, 1966. Partisan biography of Wilson, defending him as a hero defeated by opponents.

1072. Carleton, William Graves. "A New Look at Woodrow Wilson." *Virginia Quarterly Review* 38, no. 4 (Autumn 1962): 545–66. [Reprinted in his *Technology and Humanism,* 114–31. Nashville: Vanderbilt University Press, 1970.] Regards Wilson as a great leader and superb politician.

1073. Carnegie Endowment for International Peace. European Center. *Centenaire Woodrow Wilson, 1856–1956.* Geneva: Atar Arts Graphiques, 1956. A tribute to Wilson by professors at the Institut Universitaire de Hautes Etudes Internationales in Geneva.

1074. Chiang Kai-Shek, Madame. "Wilson to Asia." In **1038**, 209–13. Argues that Wilson's moral idealism draws a striking contrast to the dealings of other Presidents with Southeast Asia.

1075. Chicago, University of. *Lectures and Seminar at the University of Chicago, January 30–February 3, 1956, in Celebration of the Centennial of Woodrow Wilson, 1856–1956. Centennial Theme: Freedom for Man: A World Safe for Mankind.* Chicago: University of Chicago Press, 1956. Ten lectures by Wilson scholars, half of them followed by discussion. The lectures are listed by author.

1076. Clor, H. M. "Woodrow Wilson." In *American Political Thought,* ed. Morton J. Frisch and Richard G. Stevens, 191–218. New York: Charles Scribner's Sons,

1971. Examines Wilson's writings and speeches, both as academician and politician, to give a broad overview of the term "Wilsonian."

1077. Colby, Bainbridge. "Roosevelt: Story of an Animosity: His Hostility to Woodrow Wilson." *Current History* 32 (August 1930): 857–63. Discusses Owen Wister's comparison of Theodore Roosevelt and Wilson in Wister's *Roosevelt: The Story of a Friendship, 1880–1919*. New York: Macmillan Company, 1930.

1078. Conn, Nathan A. *Modern Prophets True and False*, 27–40, 65–67. New York: Exposition Press, 1967. Biographical sketch that focuses on Wilson's keen intellect, foreign policy, and especially the Fourteen Points.

1079. Connally, Thomas Terry. "Wilson to the United Nations." In **1038**, 232–37. Argues that the creation of the United Nations was a direct, if not delayed, result of Wilson's idealism and efforts to bring about world order.

1080. Cook, Sherwin Lawrence. *Torchlight Parade*, 160–214. New York: Minton, Balch & Co., 1929. Three chapters summarizing Wilson's presidency.

1081. Coon, Horace Campbell. *Triumph of the Eggheads*, 47–171. New York: Random House, 1955. Includes Wilson among the leading intellectuals in American politics between 1800 and 1952.

1082. Cooper, John Milton, Jr. "'The Warrior and the Priest': Toward a Comparative Perspective on Theodore Roosevelt and Woodrow Wilson." *South Atlantic Quarterly* 80 (Autumn 1981): 419–28. Based on **326**.

1083. Cooper, John Milton, Jr., and Charles E. Neu, eds. *The Wilson Era: Essays in Honor of Arthur S. Link*. Arlington Heights, Ill.: Harlan Davidson, Inc., 1991. Essays pertaining to Wilson will be found under individual authors.

1084. Coyle, David Cushman. "Crucified Peacemaker." In *Ordeal of the Presidency*, 292–336. Washington, D.C.: Public Affairs Press, 1960. Biographical sketches of the most disparaged Presidents.

1085. Craven, Avery, et al. "Woodrow Wilson: Prophet or Visionary?" *University of Chicago Round Table* 249 (December 27, 1942): 1–26. NBC Radio broadcast panel evaluates Wilson's life and work on the 86th anniversary of his birth.

1086. Croly, Herbert David. "Paradox of Woodrow Wilson." In *New Republic Anthology, 1915–1935*, ed. Groff Conklin, 197–200. New York: Dodge Publishing Co., 1936. Wilson as a man of many paradoxes, including his focus on domestic issues during his first term, tempered by his international concerns during the second.

1087. Cronon, Edmund David. "Woodrow Wilson." In *America's Ten Greatest Presidents*, ed. Morton Bordon. Chicago: Rand McNally, 1971. Argues that Wilson was tragically heroic.

1088. Curry, Roy Watson. "Duty and Woodrow Wilson." *Carnegie Magazine* 30 (December 1956): 335–38. Contends that devotion to duty, based on his Christian convictions, was Wilson's strongest character trait.

1089. Cusack, Michael. "To End All Wars." *Senior Scholastic* 112 (March 6, 1980): 12–14. Says Wilson was the first President to take personal responsibility for foreign policy in time of crisis and the President who suffered the most drastic fluctuation in public approval.

1090. Dallek, Robert. "Woodrow Wilson, Politician." *Wilson Quarterly* 15 (Autumn 1991): 106–114. Reviews the life and political career of Wilson who is remembered most for the failings of his administration, rather than for his political victories and achievements.

1091. Daniels, Jonathan Worth. "The Long Shadow of Woodrow Wilson." *Virginia Quarterly Review* 32 (Autumn 1956): 481–93. An analysis of Wilson's political skills, particularly in conveying the ideals of American foreign policy.

1092. _____. "Woodrow Wilson: Politician and Statesman." In **1075**, 45–58. [Address delivered February 1, 1956, by the son of Wilson's Secretary of the Navy.] Remembers Wilson as the man who carried the American democratic dream into world diplomacy.

1093. Daniels, Josephus P. "Wilson: Idealist and Statesman." *Saturday Review of Literature* 8 (December 19, 1931): 389–90+. Focuses on the first two volumes of **319**, with an emphasis on Wilson's emergence into politics.

1094. _____. *Virginia Quarterly Review* 20 (October 1944): 584–90. Describes two different writers' interpretations of Wilson as an individual and as a President.

1095. Davidson, John Wells. "Wilson as Presidential Leader." *Current History* 39 (October 1960): 198–202. Surveys Wilson's life and presidential achievements.

1096. De Casseres, Benjamin. "Complete American." *American Mercury* 10 (February 1927): 146–67. Wilson as the personification of American idealism.

1097. De Jouvenal, Bertrand. "Woodrow Wilson." *Confluence: An International Forum* 5, no. 4 (Winter 1957): 320–31. A personal appraisal of Wilson by a European.

1098. Dickson, Thomas H. "Bernard Shaw and Woodrow Wilson." *Virginia Quarterly Review* 7, no. 1 (1931): 1–17. Assesses Shaw's influence on Wilson.

1099. Dodd, William Edward. *Woodrow Wilson and His Work*. New York: Doubleday, Page and Co., 1920. An admiring portrait of Wilson as President.

1100. Dudden, Arthur Power. "Grover Cleveland and Woodrow Wilson." *New Republic* 133 (December 26, 1955): 23. Reprints a quote by Wilson which asserts that Cleveland provided a vivid example of the kind of leadership which Wilson himself asserted.

1101. Dudden, Arthur Power, ed. *Woodrow Wilson and the World of Today: Essays by Arthur S. Link, William L. Langer, and Eric F. Goldman.* Philadelphia: University of Pennsylvania Press, 1957. A compilation of lectures delivered at Bryn Mawr College on January 5–6, 1956, in honor of the Wilson Centennial.

1102. Dulles, Allen Welsh. "Woodrow Wilson: Prophecy and Perspective for the Present." *Vital Speeches of the Day* 23 (January 1, 1957): 176–80. Lamont Lecture at Yale, November 27, 1956, offering recollections of Wilson and his policies by the Director of the Central Intelligence Agency, who began his foreign service under Wilson in 1916.

1103. Dulles, Foster Rhea. "Woodrow Wilson—A Contemporary Evaluation." *United Asia* (India) 9, no. 2 (1957): 115–22. Compares the humanitarian idealism of Wilson and Jawaharlal Nehru of India.

1104. Dulles, John Foster. "Woodrow Wilson's Three Prescriptions for Peace." *Freedom and Union* 4 (February 1949): 5–6. States the relevance of Wilsonian principles for the success of the United Nations.

1105. Dumond, Dwight L. *Roosevelt to Roosevelt.* New York: Henry Holt and Co., 1937. A survey of Presidents from Theodore Roosevelt to Franklin Roosevelt which describes Wilson as a preacher in the sense that he believed the essence of national life to be moral power, drawn from the whole of the people.

1106. _____. "Woodrow Wilson: A Century View [1856–1956]." *Michigan Alumnus Quarterly Review* 63 (December 1956): 67–74. Historical assessment of Wilson and his contribution to American politics.

1107. Egger, Rowland Andrews. *The President of the United States.* 2d ed. New York: McGraw-Hill and Co., 1972. Sums up Wilson's belief that leadership in government naturally belongs to its executive officers.

1108. Eisenhower, Dwight David. "Woodrow Wilson Centennial Year: Proclamation." *United States Department of State Bulletin* 34 (May 14, 1956): 806.

1109. Fehr, Joseph Conrad. "The Vision of Woodrow Wilson." *South Atlantic Quarterly* 40 (January 1941): 22–29. Argues that in light of recent events in Europe, even Wilson's strongest critics must recognize that his basic vision of the interdependence of nations was correct.

1110. Ferrell, Robert H. "Woodrow Wilson: Man and Statesman." *Review of Politics* 18, no. 2 (April 1956): 131–45. Argues that Wilson was a forceful and successful leader, except when he refused to compromise in the battle over the League of Nations.

1111. Filler, Louis, ed. *The Presidents in the 20th Century. Vol. I: The Ascendant President: From William McKinley to Lyndon B. Johnson,* 93–138. Englewood, N.J.: J. S. Ozer, 1983. Considers Wilson a significant progressive and discusses his importance in World War I.

1112. Florida State Research Council. *Woodrow Wilson Centennial Issue*. Florida State University Studies, 23. Tallahassee: Florida State University, 1956. Essays are listed separately by author.

1113. Fosdick, Dorothy. "The Living Heritage of Woodrow Wilson." *New York Times Magazine* January 1, 1956: 9, 30. Describes the United Nations as a Wilsonian legacy.

1114. Frankfurter, Felix. "Woodrow Wilson." In *Of Law and Life & Other Things that Matter: Papers and Addresses of Felix Frankfurter, 1956–1963*, ed. Philip B. Kurland, 63–69. Cambridge: Harvard University Press, 1965. Ranks the influence of Wilson alongside that of Jefferson, Jackson, and Lincoln.

1115. Garraty, John Arthur. "Link's Wilson." *Virginia Quarterly Review* 42 (1966): 149–54. Criticizes Link's loss of objectivity in his writings on Wilson.

1116. Gillis, James Martin. "Wilson to Chamberlain to Hitler." *Catholic World* 148 (November 1938): 129–35. Accuses Wilson of being unfaithful to his principles.

1117. "Give Wilson back to the South." *Christian Century* 81 (January 1, 1964): 5. Wilson, not Lyndon B. Johnson, was the first southerner in the White House since Andrew Johnson.

1118. Glass, Carter. *Woodrow Wilson: Remarks of Hon. Carter Glass of Virginia in the Senate of the United States, January 27, 1931. Remarks of James Brown Scott and John H. Clarke . . . at a Meeting of the Woodrow Wilson Foundation, Washington, D.C., on January 4, 1931*. Washington, D.C.: Government Printing Office, 1931.

1119. Gottfried, Paul. "Wilsonianism: The Legacy that Won't Die." *Journal of Libertarian Studies* 9 (Fall 1990): 117–126. Believes that liberals, who admire Wilson for his creation of a federal administrative bureaucracy and his activist foreign policy, ignore his punishment of Germany and its allies during and after World War I.

1120. Gould, Lewis L. "The President in the Age of the Politico." In **4200**. Believes the weak presidency of the late nineteenth century ended when Roosevelt and Wilson revived the heritage of Lincoln and Jackson.

1121. ———. *Reform and Regulation: American Politics from Roosevelt to Wilson*. 2d ed. New York: Alfred A. Knopf, 1986. Analyzes the political process leading to Wilson's election as President and the effect of his administration.

1122. Graham, Otis L., Jr. *The Great Campaign: Reform and War in America, 1900–1928*. Englewood Cliffs, N.J.: Prentice-Hall, 1971. Argues that Wilson should have kept the United States out of the war and concentrated instead on domestic reforms.

1123. Grattan, Clinton Hartley. "The 'Failure' of Woodrow Wilson." *North American Review* 237 (March 1934): 263–69. Analyzes the conflict of Wilson's principle of self-determination with his ideal of internationalism.

1124. ———. "Wartime President." *New Republic* 100 (September 27, 1939): 219–20. Stresses the importance of **319** in illuminating Wilson's presidency and his times.

1125. Guerard, Albert Leon. "Confessions of an Unrepentant Wilsonian." *American Scholar* 9, no. 4 (October 1940): 461–72. Defends many of Wilson's beliefs about the importance of the League of Nations, arguing that his legacy can still serve the world well in shaping a new international order.

1126. Hammarskjold, Dag Hjalmar Agne Carl. "A Salute." In **1038**, 243–50. Tribute to Wilson originally made during ceremonies in the Hall of Fame in New York University on the occasion of the unveiling of the Woodrow Wilson bust and tablet.

1127. Harley, John Eugene. "Heritage of Woodrow Wilson." In *Problems of the Peace. Interim Proceedings of the Institute.* Institute of World Affairs, 21, ed. Charles E. Martin and Rufus B. Kleinsmid, 103–18. Los Angeles: University of Southern California, 1945. Comments on Wilson's contributions to world peace and world order, praising him highly.

1128. Harley, John Eugene, ed. *Woodrow Wilson Still Lives—His World Ideals Triumphant.* Los Angeles: Center for International Understanding, 1944. A collection of tributes to Wilson written by his daughter, Herbert Hoover, Cordell Hull, Ray Stannard Baker, and others.

1129. Harvey, A. R. "Woodrow Wilson." *Queen's Quarterly* 34 (January 1927): 241–62. Biographical sketch of Wilson, with a critical estimate of his intellect and character.

1130. Heckscher, August. "Woodrow Wilson: An Appraisal and Recapitulation." In **1149**, 244–59. Wilson as an inspirational moral leader.

1131. ———. "Woodrow Wilson in Perspective." In **1251**, 29–42. Highlights Wilson's abilities as stylist, moralist, and liberal, and describes his immense scale as a man and the dimensions of his stage.

1132. Hohner, Robert A. "Woodrow Wilson and the Presidency." *Canadian Review of American Studies* 13, no. 2 (1982): 213–21. Discusses Wilson's quickness of mind, his oratorical talent, and his literary skills.

1133. Holmes, John Haynes. "Ein Urteil nach zehn Jahren: Woodrow Wilson, Amerika und der Weltkrieg." [Ten Years Later: A Judgment on Woodrow Wilson, America and the World War]. *Kriegsschuldfrage* 6 (June 1928): 552–69.

1134. Hugh-Jones, Edward Maurice. *Woodrow Wilson and American Liberalism.* Teach Yourself History Library. London: English Universities Press, 1947. Regards Wilson's presidency as the culmination of an epoch of American liberalism.

1135. Hyman, Sidney. *The American President.* New York: Harper and Brothers, 1954. A popular survey of presidential power and personalities, citing Wilson as an effective leader.

1136. "In Wilson's Town." *Time* 37 (May 12, 1941): 13. Franklin Roosevelt's dedicatory address at Staunton, Virginia, where he declared that Wilson's character symbolized faith in the freedom of democracy.

1137. Jenkins, Starr. "Woodrow Wilson: Writer, Leader, Prophet." In *Profiles of Creative Political Leaders*, 193–221. Ardmore, Pa.: Whitmore Publishing Co., 1975. A portrait of Wilson as a great scholar, thinker, and orator.

1138. Johnson, Gerald White. "Cream of the Jest." In *American Heroes and Hero-Worship*, 251–77. New York: Harper and Brothers, 1943. Discusses the irony of the repudiation of Wilson by the American people just before and after his death, in light of the events that culminated in World War II.

1139. _____ . "Ghost of Woodrow Wilson." *Harper's Magazine* 183 (June 1941): 1–9. [Also published in *Reader's Digest* 39 (August 1941): 81–84.] Argues that the ghost of Wilson, who initially believed that the war could be contained in Europe, now hangs ominously over the United States as Hitler gains power.

1140. _____ . "Since Wilson." *Virginia Quarterly Review* 8 (July 1932): 321–36. A portrait of Wilson as the last man in American politics who could arouse intense hatred and anger.

1141. Kaiser, Philip. "Woodrow Wilson." In *History Makers*, ed. Lord Frank Pakenham Longford and Sir John Wheeler-Bennett, 34–53. New York: St. Martins Press, 1973. A critical evaluation of Wilson's life and influence.

1142. Kaltenborn, Hans von. *It Seems Like Yesterday*, 39–42. New York: G. P. Putnam's Sons, 1956. Views Wilson as more a prophet than a politician, a man who could inspire the world to accept the League of Nations but could not lead his own nation into it.

1143. Kennedy, John F., and Julian P. Boyd. "A White House Luncheon, June 17, 1963." *New York History* 45, no. 2 (1964): 151–60. Statements by President Kennedy and Professor Boyd at a luncheon promoting publication of the papers of leading Americans, including those of Wilson.

1144. Kirk, Russell. "Wilson: Abstraction, Principle, and the Antagonist World." *Confluence: An International Forum* 5, no. 3 (Autumn 1956): 204–15. Comments on Wilson as a natural conservative, the conflict with liberal abstraction, and his consequent failure to establish a lasting peace.

1145. Kozenko, B. D. "Vudro Vil'son: Burzhuaznyi Reformator." [Woodrow Wilson: Bourgeois Reformer]. *Voprosy Istorii* (USSR) 4 (1979): 133–47. Questions the progressive content of Wilsonian policies.

1146. Langbaum, Robert. "Woodrow Wilson: Tragic Hero." *Commentary* 27, no. 2 (February 1959): 159–65. Interprets Wilson's ideals and failures.

1147. Langer, William Leonard. "The Faith of Woodrow Wilson." *New York Times Magazine* May 4, 1941: 5. Discusses Wilson's faith in democracy and his belief that the League of Nations was the best way to avert another world war.

1148. Laski, Harold Joseph. "Woodrow Wilson after Ten Years." *Forum* 85 (March 1931): 129–33. A brief review of Wilson's presidency, praising the great effort he put into leading the nation even when he failed to meet a certain goal.

1149. Latham, Earl, ed. *The Philosophy and Policies of Woodrow Wilson.* Chicago: University of Chicago Press, 1958. Essays are listed separately.

1150. Lawrence, David. "Woodrow Wilson, Man of Half Century." *U.S. News & World Report* 28 (January 6, 1950): 41. Argues that Wilson, through his love of freedom and democracy, put America back on the right track after a century of upheaval.

1151. Lerner, Max. "Woodrow Wilson and FDR." In *Public Journal,* 339–42. New York: Viking Press, 1945. [Appeared in the New York newspaper *PM,* between February 4, 1943 and November 15, 1944.] Argues that FDR had a better sense of his strengths and weaknesses than did Wilson, making him more adept at fulfilling his agenda.

1152. _____. "Woodrow Wilson: The New Freedom and the New Deal." In *Ideas Are Weapons,* 113–16. New York: Viking Press, 1939. Examines the historical continuity and differences between the two eras.

1153. Lewis, Wyndham. "Presbyterian Priest." In *America and Cosmic Man,* 92–100. Garden City, N.Y.: Doubleday and Co., 1949. Describes the novel appeal of Wilson's political persona, focusing on his early years running for office.

1154. Link, Arthur S. "The Contributions of Woodrow Wilson." In **1251**, 12–19. Wilson's contributions as scholar, historian, governor, statesman, and President.

1155. _____. *The Higher Realism of Woodrow Wilson and Other Essays.* Nashville: Vanderbilt University Press, 1971. Interprets and analyzes in detail specific aspects of Wilson's career. Essays are listed separately.

1156. _____. "Portrait of the President." In **1149**, 3–27. A description of Wilson's character, intellect, ideas, religion, and relationships with others.

1157. _____. "The President as Progressive." In **4200**, 153–63. Emphasizes Wilson's achievements in domestic policy. Gives Wilson a prominent place in a sequence of "progressive" Presidents extending from Theodore Roosevelt to Truman.

1158. _____ . "The Progressive." In **1038**, 137–50. Argues that Wilson, as a progressive leader, was a product of his times and changed his mind on issues as his own understanding of them increased.

1159. _____ . "Wilson the President." In **1075**, 112–59. [Address delivered January 30, 1956.] The personal side of Wilson, with emphasis on his contradictions.

1160. _____ . "Woodrow Wilson: The American as Southerner." *Journal of Southern History* 36, no. 1 (February 1970): 3–17. [Also published in **1155**, 21–37.] An analysis of Wilson's perception of himself as a southerner and his ability to appeal to southern voters.

1161. _____ . "Woodrow Wilson: The Philosophy, Methods, and Impact of Leadership." In **1101**, 1–21. Argues that historians will judge Wilson as one who expanded and added significance to presidential powers. Demonstrates Wilson's conviction that presidential leadership includes being both spokesman for the people and also architect of effective legislation.

1162. Lippmann, Walter. *Public Persons*, 147–49. New York: Liveright, 1976. Argues that history's judgment of Wilson depends upon whether that generation learns from Wilson's experiences.

1163. Long, John Cuthbert. *The Liberal Presidents*, 124–38. New York: Thomas Y. Crowell, 1948. Two sections, one focusing on the New Freedom, the other on World War I.

1164. Longaker, Richard P. "Woodrow Wilson and the Presidency." In **1149**, 67–81. Wilson as a positive and negative model for later Presidents.

1165. Longworth, Alice Roosevelt. *Crowded Hours: Reminiscences of Alice Roosevelt Longworth*. New York: Charles Scribner's Sons, 1933. The daughter of Theodore Roosevelt and wife of a Republican congressional leader recalls political struggles.

1166. Lord, Walter. *The Good Years: From 1900 to the First World War*, 272–342. New York: Harper & Brothers, 1960. Discusses Wilson as an academic President and focuses on his involvement with woman suffrage and child labor issues.

1167. Low, Alfred Maurice. *Woodrow Wilson: An Interpretation*. Boston: Little, Brown, and Co., 1918. An admiring appraisal of Wilson by an Englishman.

1168. Lukacs, John Adalbert. "Wilson Is Overtaking Lenin." *National Review* 26 (February 15, 1974): 199–203. Compares the legacies and influences of Wilson and Lenin on global politics.

1169. Madariaga, Salvador de. "Wilson and the Dream of Reason." *Virginia Quarterly Review* 32 (Autumn 1956): 594–97. A portrait of Wilson as high-minded, yet reasonable, in times of turmoil and dissent.

1170. Madison, Charles Allen. "Woodrow Wilson: Crusader for Democracy." *Chicago Jewish Forum* 14 (Spring 1956): 167–73. Recognizes the centenary of Wilson's birth and calls him one of the very few men who has helped the nation to achieve greatness.

1171. Maranell, Gary M. "The Evaluation of Presidents: An Extension of the Schlesinger Polls." *Journal of American History* 57 (1970): 104–13.

1172. Maranell, Gary M., and Richard A. Doddler. "Political Orientation and the Evaluation of Presidential Prestige: A Study of American Historians." *Social Science Quarterly* 51 (1970): 415–21. Another Schlesinger poll evaluating Presidents.

1173. McGill, Ralph Emerson. "The President." In **1038**, 79–128.

1174. Mencken, Henry Louis. "Archangel Woodrow: Excerpt from 'Prejudices: Sixth Series.'" In *Mencken Chrestomathy*, 248–51. New York: Alfred A. Knopf, 1949. A collection of excerpts from Mencken's writings, including several allusions to Wilson.

1175. Merriam, Charles Edward. "Woodrow Wilson." In *Four American Party Leaders*. Henry Ward Beecher Foundation Lectures, Delivered at Amherst College. Political Parties and Practical Politics Series. New York: Macmillan Co., 1926. A study of the qualities of leadership exhibited by Lincoln, Theodore Roosevelt, Bryan, and Wilson.

1176. "Message du President Roosevelt pour l'anniversaire de Woodrow Wilson, 29 decembre 1933; texte." *L'Europe Nouvelle* 17 (January 27, 1934): 101–2.

1177. Miller, Karl Palmer. "Woodrow Wilson and World Brotherhood." In *How in the World Do Americans? A Biographical Inquiry*, 181–202. New York: Pageant Press, 1957. A biographical speech in praise of Wilson and his ideals.

1178. Mosca, Rudolfo. "Woodrow Wilson e F. D. Roosevelt." In *Questioni di Storia Contemporanea*, ed. Ettore Rota, 3:831–70. Milan: C. Marzorati, 1952.

1179. Mowry, George Edwin. "The Uses of History by Recent Presidents." *Journal of American History* 53 (June 1966): 5–18. A study of Presidents from Harding to Kennedy, with references to Wilson.

1180. Moynihan, Daniel Patrick. "The Legacy of Woodrow Wilson." In *Counting Our Blessings*, 6–22. Boston: Little, Brown & Co., 1980. Depicts Wilsonianism as the keystone to twentieth century political thought, dissecting both its good and bad elements.

1181. ———— . "Morality and American Foreign Policy: Was Woodrow Wilson Right?" *Foreign Service Journal* 51, no. 9 (1974): 8–12, 24–25. Appraises Wilson's definition of American citizenship.

1182. Murray, Robert K., and Tim H. Blessing. *Greatness in the White House: Rating the Presidents, Washington through Carter: Final Report, the Presidential Performance Study*. University Park: Pennsylvania State University Press, 1988. Rates Wilson's success as President and considers Wilson one of the top five United States Presidents.

1183. ———— . "The Presidential Performance Study: A Progress Report." *Journal of American History* 70 (1983): 535–55. A quantitative analysis of past Presidents which places Wilson in several of the top categories.

1184. Muzzey, David Saville. "President Wilson's Purgatory." *Political Science Quarterly* 53 (June 1938): 272–78. A critique of volumes V and VI of **319** covering the period between 1914 and 1917.

1185. *The National Memorial to Woodrow Wilson*, Pamphlets on Education, 90. New York: Woodrow Wilson Foundation, 1968. Presented by Whitfield J. Bell, July 1968.

1186. Naveh, Eyal Jehoshua. "The Martyr Image in American Political Culture (Lincoln, Sermons, Obituaries)." Ph.D. diss., University of California, Berkeley, 1986. Argues that Wilson was a political martyr, second only to Lincoln.

1187. Nicholas, Herbert George. "Wilsonianism at Mid-Century." In **1073**, 95–110.

1188. Nixon, Richard Milhous. "The Wilsonian Principle after Half a Century." *United States Department of State Bulletin* 64 (March 15, 1971): 312–14. Remarks at the Smithsonian at the dedication of the Woodrow Wilson International Center for Scholars on February 18, 1971, calling Wilson "one of America's greatest men."

1189. Noble, Ransom Edward. "Woodrow Wilson: Centennial Interpretations." *Proceedings of the New Jersey Historical Society* 75 (April 1957): 79–95. Commentary on seven books published in 1956.

1190. Duplicate entry omitted.

1191. "One Hundred Years of Woodrow Wilson." *Saturday Review* 39 (December 29, 1956): 19. Marks the centennial anniversary of Wilson's birth, with a brief biography and a review of six books.

1192. Opie, Evarts Walton. "The Immortal." In **1038**, 239–42. Reprinted eulogy delivered in a memorial service at Wilson's tomb on the centennial anniversary of his birth.

1193. Payne, John Barton. *An Address at the Unveiling of the Bust of Woodrow Wilson.* Richmond: 1931. At the Hall of the House of Delegates, Richmond, November 17, 1931.

1194. _____ . "Woodrow Wilson." In *Virginia Born Presidents: Addresses Delivered on the Occasions of Unveiling the Busts of Virginia Born Presidents at Old Hall of the House of Delegates, Richmond, Virginia,* comp. John Garland Pollard, 213–32. New York: American Book Co., 1932. Asserts that Wilson was a brave and fearless man who upheld humanity, peace, and freedom, and fought that these principles might be realized.

1195. Perkins, Dexter. "Woodrow Wilson: An Interpretation." In *Transactions of the Royal Historical Society,* 4th ser., 29 (1947): 115–34. Admiring appraisal by a British scholar.

1196. Pisney, Raymond F., ed. *Woodrow Wilson: Idealism and Reality.* Verona, Va.: McClure Press, 1977. Brief addresses honoring Woodrow Wilson and Edith Bolling Wilson by nineteen prominent persons at Staunton, Virginia, for the Woodrow Wilson Birthplace Foundation.

1197. _____ . *Woodrow Wilson in Retrospect.* Verona, Va.: McClure Press, 1978. Addresses given at Wilson's birthplace.

1198. Plischke, Elmer. "Rating Presidents and Diplomats in Chief." *Presidential Studies Quarterly* 15, no. 4 (1985): 725–42. Numbers Wilson among twentieth century Presidents who were most involved in foreign affairs.

1199. Pomeroy, Earl Spencer. "Woodrow Wilson: The End of His First Century." *Oregon Historical Quarterly* 57, no. 4 (December 1956): 315–32. Wilson as lonely idealist, more at home with crowds than with individuals.

1200. Porter, Henry Alford. *Woodrow Wilson the Dreamer.* Charlottesville, Va.: Surber Publishing Co., 1929. An address following the unveiling of a memorial tablet on Jefferson Day, April 13, 1929, at the University of Virginia.

1201. "Prophet and His Time of Trial: 100th Birthday Recalls Wilson and the League." *Life* 41 (December 17, 1956): 103–7. Believes that the defeat of the League of Nations broke Wilson physically, but it did not destroy his prophetic vision or end the debate on his ideas.

1202. Pruessen, Ronald W. "Woodrow Wilson to John Foster Dulles: A Legacy." *Princeton University Library Chronicle* 34, no. 2 (1973): 109–29. Analyzes Wilson's influence on Dulles.

1203. Ramsey, Darley Hiden. "Nineteen Years Ago—and Today." *South Atlantic Quarterly* 42 (April 1943): 154–61. Notes that Wilson's ideals survived his death.

1204. Randall, James Garfield. "Lincoln's Task and Wilson's." *South Atlantic Quarterly* 29, no. 4 (October 1930): 349–68. Contrasts the two Presidents.

1205. Redfield, William Cox. "Woodrow Wilson: An Appreciation." *American Monthly Review of Reviews* 75 (April 1927): 371–75. Reprints Wilson's war address to Congress, April 2, 1917, ten years after the event, and comments that it was a strange fate that led Wilson, the peace-seeker, into the paths of war.

1206. Robertson, Walter S. "Ideals of Woodrow Wilson: Address, April 25, 1956." *United States Department of State Bulletin* 34 (May 14, 1956): 805–10. Address in praise of Wilson at the centennial celebration at Staunton, Virginia, on April 28, 1956.

1207. Robinson, Edgar Eugene. "The Internationalist." In **1038**, 167–82. Argues that Wilson evolved into being a great internationalist through hard work and study and that his principles were applied around the world.

1208. Roosevelt, Franklin Delano. *Dinner in Connection with the Birthday of Woodrow Wilson, Thursday, December Twenty-eight, 1933, The Mayflower. Address by Franklin Delano Roosevelt.* New York: Woodrow Wilson Foundation, 1934. Praises Wilson's contributions.

1209. ———. "Power of Spiritual Force: Address at the Birthplace of Woodrow Wilson." *Vital Speeches of the Day* 7 (May 15, 1941): 457. Sees Wilson as the proponent of a faith in democracy.

1210. Rosenman, Samuel, and Dorothy Rosenman. *Presidential Style: Some Giants and a Pygmy in the White House*, 124–263. New York: Harper and Row, 1976. Sympathetic treatment of Wilson.

1211. Rossiter, Clinton Lawrence. *The American Presidency*. New York: Harcourt, Brace and World, 1956. Evaluates Wilson as one of the great Presidents.

1212. ———. "The Presidents and the Presidency." *American Heritage* 7, no. 3 (1956): 28–33, 94–95. Describes Wilson as one of the great Presidents.

1213. Ryerson, Edward. "The Leadership of Woodrow Wilson." *American Scholar* 21 (July 1952): 301–8. Analyzes five Wilson traits: his Presbyterianism, his isolation, his response to public attack, his demands on himself and others, and his destructive impulse.

1214. Salter, Sir James Arthur. "Woodrow Wilson: The Inflexible Will." In *Personality in Politics: Studies of Contemporary Statesmen*, 149–59. London: Faber and Faber, 1947. Discusses Wilson's unbending personality and its consequences.

1215. Sayre, Francis Bowes. "The World Vision of Woodrow Wilson." In **1075**, 27–44b. Address delivered January 31, 1956. Describes Wilson as the prophet of a changed world whose vision derived from a profound religious faith.

1216. Schlesinger, Arthur Meyer, Sr. "Our Presidents: A Rating by Seventy-Five Historians." *New York Times Magazine* July 29, 1962: 12ff. An update of the first poll; Wilson's standing remains unchanged.

1217. ———— . "The United States Presidents." *Life Magazine* 25 (November 1, 1948): 65+. Wilson emerges as the fourth greatest President.

1217a. Schulte Nordholt, Jan Willem. "Woodrow Wilson en de Droom van de Wereldvrede." [Woodrow Wilson and the Dream of World Peace]. *Spiegel Historiael* (Netherlands) 18, no. 7/8 (1983): 370–72. Analyzes Wilson the peacemaker in the light of his personality.

1218. Sellen, Robert W. "Theodore Roosevelt and Woodrow Wilson as 'World Politicians.'" Ph.D. diss., University of Chicago, 1959.

1219. Seymour, Charles. "Woodrow Wilson in Perspective." *Foreign Affairs* 34 (January 1956): 175–86. [Also printed under the same title as a book (Stamford, Conn.: Overlook Press, 1956) and as chapter 11 in **1149**.] A centennial reevaluation of Wilson's position in history, which the author says has been primarily determined by his role on the international stage.

1220. ———— . "Woodrow Wilson: A Political Balance Sheet." *Proceedings of the American Philosophical Society* 101, no. 2 (April 1957): 135–41. Concludes that Wilson had notable domestic policy successes and a fine record as a war leader, despite failure to secure approval of the League of Nations.

1221. Shotwell, James Thomson. "Leadership of Wilson." *Current History* 21 (November 1951): 263–68. Evaluates the statesmanship of Woodrow Wilson by focusing upon Wilsonian economics, the Treaty of Versailles, open covenants, and the League of Nations.

1222. Skau, George Henry. "Woodrow Wilson's Impact on the American Presidency." In *Power and the Presidency*, ed. Philip C. Dolce and George H. Skau, 75–87. New York: Charles Scribner's Sons, 1976. An analysis of Wilson as one who transformed the presidency.

1223. Smith, Bradford. *Men of Peace*, 239–82. Philadelphia: J. B. Lippincott & Co., 1964. Brief biographical sketch of Wilson's life, focusing on peace efforts.

1224. Smuts, Jan Christiaan, et al. *Woodrow Wilson: Addresses to Commemorate the 87th Anniversary of Woodrow Wilson's Birth.* New York: Woodrow Wilson Foundation, 1944. Authors discuss Wilson's political principles, leadership abilities, international diplomacy, and domestic policies.

1225. Sokolsky, Eric. *Our Seven Great Presidents*, 75–84. New York: Exposition Press, 1964. States that Woodrow Wilson continues unparalleled in history as a supreme patriot, a magnificent legislator, an excellent peacetime President, a great commander-in-chief, a pioneer in the formation of the League of Nations, and an incorruptible public servant.

1226. St. John, Jacqueline D., and Jane Keller. "Student Perceptions of Post Civil War Presidents: A Survey Conducted at the University of Nebraska at Omaha,

1979–1981." A Research Report, 1984. Reports on a study to discover what college freshmen knew about post-Civil War Presidents.

1227. Stanton, Theodore. "Le nouveau president des Etats-Unis: son caractere, ses opinions, ses methodes." [The New President of the United States: His Character, His Opinions, His Methods]. *Revue des Deux Mondes* 14 (March 15, 1913): 358–80.

1228. Steigerwald, David. "The Synthetic Politics of Woodrow Wilson." *Journal of the History of Ideas* 50 (July-September 1989): 465–84. Wilson is portrayed as a political centrist who sought to bring together an individualistic past and a collective future.

1229. Steinberg, Samuel. "Woodrow Wilson." In *Great American Liberals*, ed. Gabriel Richard Mason, 129–40. Boston: Starr King Press, 1956. A survey of Wilson's political achievements as a liberal in both domestic and foreign policy.

1230. Stevenson, Adlai E. "Die Politische Philosophie Woodrow Wilsons in Heutiger Sicht. Gedanken Zum 100. Geburtstag." [Wilson's Political Philosophy Seen Today. Reflections on His 100th Birthday]. *Europa Archiv* 11, no. 3 (1956): 8573–76.

1231. Swing, Raymond. "The Contribution of Woodrow Wilson to the World Today." In **1255**, 13–17. Sees Wilson not as a leader who failed to achieve lasting peace but as a prophet who applied democratic principles to the conduct of international affairs.

1232. "Top Ten Presidents." *Scholastic Update* 115 (May 13, 1983): 16–17. Places Wilson as the sixth most important President in American history because of his vision of the League of Nations, the forerunner of the United Nations.

1233. Tucker, Robert W. "Brave New World Orders: Woodrow Wilson, George Bush, and the 'Higher Realism.'" *New Republic* 206, no. 8 (February 24, 1992): 24–34. Describes the outcome of the Wilsonian vision as seen in three works: **340**; **366**; and vols. 62–64 of *PWW*.

1234. Tugwell, Rexford Guy, and Thomas E. Cronin, eds. *The Presidency Reappraised.* New York: Fredrick A. Praeger, 1974. Believes that the revival of presidential initiative under Theodore Roosevelt and Wilson resulted in congressional opposition to the Versailles Treaty and future foreign entanglements.

1235. Duplicate entry omitted.

1236. Villard, Oswald Garrison. "Retrospect: Objects of American Entry into World War." *Nation* 146 (April 2, 1938): 388. Concludes that Wilson failed to achieve his war aims.

1237. Wallace, Henry Agard. *America's Part in World Reconstruction: An Address Given on December 28, 1942, the Eighty-Sixth Anniversary of the Birth of Woodrow Wilson.* New York: Woodrow Wilson Foundation, 1943.

1238. Wecter, Dixon. *The Hero in America: A Chronicle of Hero-Worship*, 392–414. New York: Charles Scribner's Sons, 1941. Analyzes Wilson's failure to join Washington and Lincoln as one of the nation's great wartime leaders.

1239. Wells, Wells [pseud.]. *Wilson the Unknown: An Explanation of an Enigma of History*. New York: Charles Scribner's Sons, 1931. A vigorous attack on Wilson and his policies.

1240. White, William Allen. *The Autobiography of William Allen White*. New York: Macmillan Co., 1946. Discusses Wilson and his administration, World War I, and the battle over the Treaty of Versailles.

1241. _____ . "End of an Epoch: Passing of the Apostles of Liberalism in the United States." *Scribner's Magazine* 79, no. 6 (June 1926): 561–70. Points to Wilson as the last major prophet of American liberalism in the populist cycle.

1242. Williams, William Appleman. *Some Presidents: Wilson to Nixon*. New York: New York Review, 1972. The first chapter contains an essay on a number of recent works about Wilson.

1243. Wills, Gary. "The Presbyterian Nietzsche." *New York Review of Books* 39 (January 16, 1992): 3–4, 6–7. Discusses Wilson's devotion to the cult of the individual. Books reviewed are **340**; **366**; **1746**; and Carl Pletsch, *Young Nietzsche: Becoming a Genius* (New York: Free Press, 1991).

1244. "Wilson and Bessemer Celebrate Together." *Christian Century* 73 (December 26, 1956): 1499. Celebrates Wilson's achievements and the 100th anniversary of his birth.

1245. Wilson, Francis Graham. "New Freedom, American." *America* 96 (March 16, 1957): 679–81. Review of **268**; **354**; and **4045**.

1246. _____ . "Woodrow Wilson, 1856–1956." *America* 96 (December 15, 1956): 321–23. A philosophical evaluation of Wilson from a Catholic perspective.

1247. "Wilson and His Faults." *Newsweek* 24 (July 17, 1944): 82. Concludes that Wilson was arrogant, puritanical, and self-righteous, but also scrupulously honest, learned, and impatient with ignorance.

1248. "Wilson's 21 Blunders." *Time* 43 (January 10, 1944): 23. Lists the peacemaking mistakes made by Wilson, according to Thomas A. Bailey. Notes that Franklin Roosevelt has vowed not to repeat them.

1249. "Wilson's Birthday." *Outlook* 142 (January 6, 1926): 9. Describes a gathering in New York to celebrate what would have been Wilson's sixty-ninth birthday.

1250. Wittmer, Felix. "As Woodrow Wilson Said." *Freeman* 5 (September 1954): 94–96. Examines the erosion of Wilson's liberalism and government restraint.

1251. *Woodrow Wilson Centennial Addresses*. Oxford, Ohio: Miami University Press, 1957. A program commemorating the one hundredth anniversary of Wilson's birth. Delivered at Miami University, Oxford, Ohio, November-December 1956. Essays are listed by author.

1252. Woodrow Wilson Centennial Celebration Commission. *Handbook on Information and Suggestions for the Woodrow Wilson Centennial, 1856–1956.* Washington, D.C.: United States Government Printing Office, 1956.

1253. ———. *Woodrow Wilson Centennial: Final Report.* Washington, D.C.: United States Government Printing Office, 1958. Includes "Woodrow Wilson Reappraised—The Literature of the Centennial Year" by August Heckscher, and "Preliminary Survey of Woodrow Wilson Manuscripts" by David W. Hirst.

1254. "Woodrow Wilson Centennial Number." *Virginia Quarterly Review* 32 (Autumn 1956): 481–540, 546–610. A collection of articles on Wilson as political leader, man of letters, and political theorist, published on occasion of the centennial of his birth.

1255. Woodrow Wilson Foundation. *Woodrow Wilson: Addresses by Field Marshall Jan Christiaan Smuts, Raymond Swing, [and] Ray Stannard Baker, to Commemorate the Eighty-Seventh Anniversary of Woodrow Wilson's Birth, December 28, 1943.* New York: Woodrow Wilson Foundation, [1944]. Articles are found under each author.

1256. ———. *Woodrow Wilson: Addresses upon the Occasion of His Ninety-Second Birthday Anniversary, December 28, 1948.* Stamford, Conn.: Overbrook Press, 1949. Addresses by John Foster Dulles, Allen Welsh Dulles, and Adlai Stevenson, and an undelivered address by Sumner Welles. Also a commemorative broadcast to France by the Voice of America.

1257. ———. *Woodrow Wilson. Radio Addresses in Commemoration of Woodrow Wilson's Ninetieth Birthday Anniversary, December 28, 1946.* New York: The Woodrow Wilson Foundation, 1946. Contains addresses by Raymond Swing, Adlai E. Stevenson, William C. Benton, Francis B. Sayre, William W. Waymack, and Josephus P. Daniels.

1258. Woodrow Wilson International Center for Scholars. *Woodrow Wilson: A Commemorative Celebration.* Washington, D.C.: Wilson Center, 1982. Essays listed by author.

1259. *Woodrow Wilson Memorial: Hearings March 9, 1967–May 14, 1968 on S. 277, A Bill to Authorize the Preparation of Plans for a Memorial to Woodrow Wilson, and S. 3174, A Bill to Establish a National Memorial to Woodrow Wilson in the Smithsonian Institution.* Washington, D.C.: Government Printing Office, 1968. [Committee on Rules and Administration. Subcommittee on the Smithsonian Institution. (90th Congress, 1st and 2d sessions).]

1260. "Woodrow Wilson and the Problems of Liberalism [symposium]." *Confluence: An International Forum* 5, no. 6 (Fall 1956 and Winter 1957): 183–276, 281–375. Essays are listed by author.

1261. "Woodrow Wilson's Hide-and-Seek Politics." *North American Review* 261 (Summer 1976): 62–68. Describes governmental decline and many new governmental changes since Wilson's presidency.

B. Presidential Power and Leadership

See also entries under "Biographical Essays and Sketches," "Assessments of Wilson as President," and "Contemporary Profiles and Assessments Following Wilson's Death"

1262. Balch, Stephen H. "Do Presidents Really Want Strong Legislative Parties?" *Presidential Studies Quarterly* 7, no. 4 (1977): 231–38. Argues that Wilson's strong presidential leadership meant that he disparaged strong legislative parties.

1263. Bennett, Ira E. "The Vacancy in the White House." *Christian Science Monitor Weekly Magazine* (September 6, 1941): 6+. Describes roles and significance of Cabinet members, Supreme Court justices, and the Vice President during Wilson's illness.

1264. Binkley, Wilfred Ellsworth. *The Powers of the President: Problems of American Democracy.* Garden City, N.Y.: Doubleday, Doran and Co., 1937. Contains a section on Wilson's theory and practice of the presidency.

1265. Brent, Robert A. "The Myth of Separation of Powers." *Southern Quarterly* 7, no. 4 (1969): 433–42. Discusses Wilson's failure to appoint a member of the Senate to the Peace Commission in 1918 and concludes that such an appointment would have violated the Constitution.

1266. Burns, James MacGregor. *Presidential Government: The Crucible of Leadership.* Boston: Houghton, Mifflin Co., 1965. Discusses Wilson's administration as being a model for future leaders.

1267. Cooper, John Milton, Jr. "Another 'Irony of Fate': Woodrow Wilson's Domestic Politics." In **1258**, 13–19. Explains the irony that Wilson's administration dealt primarily with foreign problems while Wilson's preparation had actually been in domestic matters.

1268. Corwin, Edward Samuel. "The Literary Sources of Presidential Leadership—Woodrow Wilson." In *The President, Office and Powers: History and Analysis of Practice and Opinion.* 4th ed., 256–64. New York: New York University Press, 1957. Legal history, containing Wilson's ideas on congressional relations, foreign affairs, and war.

1269. _____. "Woodrow Wilson and the Presidency." *Virginia Law Review* 42 (October 1956): 761–83. [Also published in *Presidential Power and the Constitution*, 32–53. Ithaca: Cornell University Press, 1976.] An examination of the depth and added dimensions Wilson brought to the presidency, from his early academic writings to his strong leadership of the Congress and the United States.

1270. Cunliffe, Marcus. "Changing Factors." In *American Presidents and the Presidency*, 243–72. 2d rev. ed. New York: McGraw-Hill Publishing Co., 1976. [Also published in *The American Heritage History of the Presidency*. New York: American Heritage Publishing Co., 1968.] Refers to Wilson's theories of the presidency and describes the increasing executive energy since Taft.

1271. Daniels, Jonathan Worth. *Washington Quadrille: The Dance Beside the Documents*. Garden City, N.Y.: Doubleday and Co., 1968. Chronicles Washington political and social events including the Wilson era.

1272. Dowie, James Iverne. "Wilson and Gladstone: Perils and Parallels in Leadership." In *The Immigration of Ideas*. James Iverne Dowie and J. Thomas Tredway, eds. Augustana Historical Society, no. 21, 127–42. Rock Island, Ill.: The Augustana Historical Society, 1968. Portrays the two as probably the last great statesmen who approached politics and diplomacy assuming that God is active in history.

1273. Edwards, George C. III, and Stephen J. Wayne. *Presidential Leadership: Politics and Policy Making*. New York: St. Martin's Press, 1985. Wilson's legislative achievements are attributed to his leadership and his rhetorical power.

1274. Fersh, Seymour H. *The View from the White House: A Study of the Presidential State of the Union Messages*. Washington, D.C.: Public Affairs Press, 1961. Describes the consolidation of the presidency and the development of a closer cooperation between the President and Congress during the Wilson administration.

1275. Fosdick, Raymond Blaine. "Personal Recollections of Woodrow Wilson." In **1075**, 1–26. [Also published in **1149**, 28–45.] Warm memoir by a close friend. Identifies Wilson's religion and moral principles as keys to understanding his life.

1276. Gabriel, Ralph Henry. *The Course of American Democratic Thought: An Intellectual History Since 1815*. 2nd ed., 352–404. New York: Ronald Press, 1956. Describes Wilson's leadership in the progressive era and in the "Great Crusade" of World War I.

1277. Gahl, Leslie L. "Moral Courage: The Essence of Leadership." *Presidential Studies Quarterly* 14, no. 1 (1984): 43–52. Seeks a redefinition of presidential leadership in the wake of Watergate, with discussion of Wilson's presidency.

1278. Gillman, Howard. "The Constitution Besieged: T.R., Taft, and Wilson on the Virtue and Efficacy of a Faction-Free Republic." *Presidential Studies Quarterly* 19, no. 1 (Winter 1989): 179–201. Examines the politics and policies of the twentieth century's first three Presidents during the transition to a post-industrial economy.

1279. Goldsmith, William M. *The Growth of Presidential Power: A Documentary History*. 3 vols. New York: Chelsea House, 1974. The third volume covers the impact of the progressive movement on Wilson's domestic agenda and leadership. Also discussed is Wilson's role as a world leader.

1280. Gould, Lewis L. "Theodore Roosevelt, Woodrow Wilson and the Emergence of the Modern Presidency: An Introductory Essay." *Presidential Studies Quarterly* 19, no. 1 (Winter 1989): 41–50. Looks at Wilson's importance in adding power and influence to the role of the President.

1281. Hargrove, Erwin C. *Presidential Leadership: Personality and Political Style*, 32–53. New York: Macmillan Co., 1966. Concludes that Wilson was most effective as President when public opinion was on his side and he could confront one issue at a time.

1282. Hart, James. *The Ordinance-Making Powers of the President of the United States*. Baltimore: Johns Hopkins University Press, 1925. Examines several emergency proclamations relating to exports and imports made by Wilson.

1283. Hollingsworth, William Wiley. "Woodrow Wilson's Political Ideals as Interpreted from His Works." Ph.D. diss., University of Pennsylvania, 1918.

1284. _____ . *Woodrow Wilson's Political Ideals as Interpreted from His Works*. Princeton: Princeton University Press, 1918. Describes Wilson's political principles and comments on their application in the executive office.

1285. Jackson, Carlton. *Presidential Vetoes, 1792–1945*. Athens: University of Georgia Press, 1967. Brief treatment of Wilson's exercise of this aspect of presidential power.

1286. Johnson, Gerald White. "The Superficial Aspect." *New Republic* 130 (June 21, 1954): 17. A description of Wilson's political savvy.

1287. _____ . "Woodrow Wilson: A Challenge to the Fighting South." In *Southern Pioneers in Social Interpretation*, ed. Howard W. Odum, 29–49. Chapel Hill: University of North Carolina Press, 1925. [Also published in *Journal of Social Forces* 3 (January 1925): 231–36.] A southern perspective on Wilson's presidency, challenging people in the region to live up to his legacy.

1288. Kallenbach, Joseph E. *The American Chief Executive: The Presidency and the Governorship*. New York: Harper and Row, 1966. Analyzes "the psychological, political, and personality factors" that shaped decisions by Presidents and governors. Wilson's tenure discussed as governor of New Jersey and President are discussed.

1289. Kessler, Frank. *The Dilemmas of Presidential Leadership: Of Caretakers and Kings*. Englewood Cliffs, N.J.: Prentice-Hall, 1982. Notes that Wilson was the first President to visit foreign capitals officially and to participate personally in an international conference outside the United States.

1290. Koenig, Louis W. *The Chief Executive*. 6th ed. New York: Harcourt, Brace, Jovanovich, 1986. Discusses the variety of presidential powers and the role of the President in American politics. Wilson's influence on the shaping of a number of aspects of the presidency is treated.

1291. Kundanis, George. "Ardent Advocates of Action: The Idea of Strong Presidential Leadership in the United States 1885–1965." Ph.D. diss., University of Wisconsin—Madison, 1982. One chapter on Wilson as strong, moral leader.

1292. Laski, Harold Joseph. *The American Presidency: An Interpretation.* New York: Harper & Brothers, 1940. Wilson is a frequent example used in discussions of Congress and foreign affairs.

1293. Laudi, Regina M. "Woodrow Wilson: A Case Study of Ideological Change." Ph.D. diss., Bowling Green State University, 1975.

1294. Link, Arthur S. "Woodrow Wilson and the Democratic Party." *Review of Politics* 18, no. 2 (April 1956): 146–56. [Also published in **1155**, 60–71, and in **1544**, 3:1035–45.] An assessment of Wilson's skill at building coalitions of progressives and conservatives. Argues that Wilson alone rebuilt the Democratic party in 1912, enabling him to press for his domestic agenda and control foreign affairs during the period of American neutrality.

1295. Lippmann, Walter. "The Political Philosopher." In **1038**, 67–78. Describes Wilson's evolution as a political philosopher, from his belief in the central power of the Congress to his emphasis on the importance of strong executive leadership.

1296. Longaker, Richard P. *The Presidency and Individual Liberties.* Cornell Studies in Civil Liberties. Ithaca: Cornell University Press, 1961. Discusses the issues of executive power and legal authority under Wilson and other Presidents.

1297. Loomis, Richard T. "The White House Telephone and Crisis Management." *United States Naval Institute Proceedings* 95, no. 12 (1969): 63–73. Describes Wilson as the exception to presidential dependence on the telephone since its inception at the White House in 1877.

1298. Loss, Richard. "Alexander Hamilton and the Modern Presidency: Continuity or Discontinuity?" *Presidential Studies Quarterly* 12, no. 1 (1982): 6–25. Treats Wilson as inheriting but also distorting Hamilton's conception of the presidency as the locus of strong executive power.

1299. Marion, David E. "Alexander Hamilton and Woodrow Wilson on the Spirit and Form of a Responsible Republican Government." *Review of Politics* 42, no. 3 (July 1980): 309–28. Noting their similarities, Marion argues that Wilson's view of executive leadership surpassed that of Hamilton because of his commitment to equality and democracy.

1300. McConnell, Grant. *The Modern Presidency.* 2d ed. New York: St. Martin's Press, 1976. Uses the presidency as a way to illuminate the interplay of all branches of government. Refers to Wilson, his personality as a leader, and his relationship with Congress.

1301. McCormick, Richard L. *The Party Period and Public Policy: American Politics from the Age of Jackson to the Progressive Era.* New York: Oxford

University Press, 1986. Analyzes Wilson's criticism of political parties and maintains that Wilson was a perceptive student of American politics.

1302. McQueen, Danny. "The Evolving Prophecy of Woodrow Wilson." *E.C. Barksdale Student Lectures* 11 (1989–1990): 3–31. Traces Wilson's switch from an affinity for the cabinet system of government during his early career as a political scientist in the 1880's to his later support of the presidential/congressional system.

1303. Mervin, David. "Woodrow Wilson and Presidential Myths." *Presidential Studies Quarterly* 11, no. 4 (Fall 1981): 559–64. An examination of Wilson's work habits during the initial months of his presidency.

1304. Milton, George Fort. "Spokesman of the People." In *Use of Presidential Power, 1789–1943*, 197–223. Boston: Little, Brown and Co., 1944. Examines Wilson "the scholar" in comparison to Wilson "the practical politician."

1305. Moos, Malcolm Charles. *Politics, Presidents, and Coattails.* Baltimore: Johns Hopkins University Press, 1952. Argues that Wilson was an excellent example of a vigorous presidential leader.

1306. Mullen, William F. *Presidential Power and Politics.* New York: St. Martin's Press, 1976. Argues for the necessity of a strong and assertive executive branch of government, frequently using Wilson as an example.

1307. Munro, William Bennett. "Woodrow Wilson and the Accentuation of Presidential Leadership." In *The Makers of the Unwritten Constitution*, 117–47. New York: Macmillan Co., 1930. Four lectures explaining how Hamilton, Marshall, Jackson, and Wilson interpreted the Constitution to achieve their goals.

1308. Noble, Charles Ira. "Wilson's Choice: The Political Origins of the Modern American State." *Comparative Politics* 17 (April 1985): 313–36. An analysis of Wilson as the leader of progressivism.

1309. Ong, Bruce Nelson. "Constitutionalism and Political Change: James Madison, Thomas Jefferson, and Progressive Reinterpretations." Ph.D. diss., University of Virginia, 1985. Deals with the issue of managing change while preserving the rule of law and Wilson's attempts to loosen constitutional restrictions in order to expand governmental power.

1310. "The Palmer Letter." *New Republic* 5 (January 15, 1916): 268. [Published by Louis Seibold, Washington correspondent of the New York *World*.] Concerns a letter written by Wilson to A. Mitchell Palmer, explaining Wilson's objection to presidential term limitations.

1311. Paolucci, Henry. *War, Peace, and the Presidency.* New York: McGraw-Hill, 1968. Argues that because of Wilson's leadership, the United States emerged from World War I more dominant than any nation in modern times.

1312. Patterson, Caleb Perry. *Presidential Government in the United States: The Unwritten Constitution.* Chapel Hill: University of North Carolina Press, 1947.

Examines the changing role of the President, arguing that the position has taken on powers that stretch beyond the Constitution. Wilson is discussed throughout.

1313. Pyne, John Michael. "Woodrow Wilson's Abdication of Domestic and Party Leadership: Autumn 1918 to Autumn 1919." Ph.D. diss., University of Notre Dame, 1979.

1314. Ringelstein, Albert C. "Presidential Vetoes: Motivation and Classification." *Congress and the Presidency* 12 (Spring 1985): 43–55. Briefly describes Wilson's theory of the presidential veto and how his ideas have been adapted over the years.

1315. Rogin, Michael Paul. "The King's Two Bodies: Abraham Lincoln, Richard Nixon, and Presidential Self-Sacrifice." *Massachusetts Review* 20, no. 3 (1979): 553–73. [Also published in *Public Values and Private Power in American Politics*, ed. J. David Greenstone, 71–108. Chicago: University of Chicago Press, 1982.] Deals with the doctrine that subordinates the officeholder to the law and contains a brief passage on Richard Nixon's feelings about Wilson.

1316. Rossiter, Clinton Lawrence. *Constitutional Dictatorship: Crisis Government in the Modern Democracies*, 207–314. Princeton: Princeton University Press, 1948. Deals with the use of emergency powers under Lincoln, Wilson, and Franklin Roosevelt.

1317. Rovere, Richard H. "The Loneliest Place in the World." *American Heritage* 15 (August 1964): 29–32. Discusses Wilson's isolation in the White House.

1318. Ruiz, George W. "The Ideological Convergence of Theodore Roosevelt and Woodrow Wilson." *Presidential Studies Quarterly* 19, no. 1 (Winter 1989): 159–77. Focuses on the evolution of Wilson's thought, while comparing the development and outcome of his philosophy to that of Theodore Roosevelt.

1319. Schlesinger, Arthur Meyer, Jr. *The Imperial Presidency*. Boston: Houghton, Mifflin Co., 1973. Wilson is included in this survey of the rise of presidential power.

1320. "Should Presidents Control Their Own Renomination?" *U.S. News and World Report* 25 (July 19, 1948): 30–31. Reprint of a letter from Wilson to A. Mitchell Palmer, saying that a President should not be deprived of the right to run for a second term.

1321. Skau, George Henry. "Woodrow Wilson and the American Presidency: Theory and Practice." Ph.D. diss., St. John's University, 1969. An evaluation of Wilson's changing political views from his advocacy of a form of cabinet government to his espousal of strong presidential leadership.

1322. Small, Norman J. *Some Presidential Interpretations of the Presidency*. Johns Hopkins Study Series 50, no. 2. Baltimore: Johns Hopkins University Press, 1932. Explores views and actions of Wilson and several earlier Presidents.

1323. Sobota, E. "Diktatura Lincolnova a Wilsonova." [The Dictatorship of Lincoln and Wilson]. *Nase Doba* 38 (October 1930): 11–16; (November 1930):76–80.

Discusses the way in which the Constitution enabled the two Presidents to increase their power.

1324. Stid, Daniel Diehl. "Woodrow Wilson, Responsible Government, and the Founders' Regime." Ph.D. diss. Harvard University, 1994. Studies Wilson's efforts, both as a political scientist and as a politician, to replace the political independence of and competition between the President and Congress in the Founders' era with interdependence and cooperation.

1325. Stoddard, Henry L. *As I Knew Them: Presidents and Politics from Grant to Coolidge*, 426–37, 480–519. New York: Harper and Brothers, 1927. The two chapters on Wilson concern his nomination for the presidency and his friendship with Colonel House.

1326. Stout, Wesley Winans. "White House Newsreel." *Saturday Evening Post* 207 (January 12, 1935): 12–13+. Points out White House "firsts" during several presidential administrations, including Wilson's.

1327. Thompson, Charles Willis. *Presidents I've Known and Two Near Presidents*, 253–321. Indianapolis: Bobbs-Merill Co., 1929. Believes that Wilson was unable to separate his own personality from criticism of himself, favorable or unfavorable.

1328. Tourtellot, Arthur Bernon. *The Presidents on the Presidency*. Garden City, N.Y.: Doubleday & Co., 1964. Examines the way in which the different Presidents carved their roles in governing and shaping society. Wilson is featured prominently throughout.

1329. Tugwell, Rexford Guy. *The Enlargement of the Presidency*. Garden City, N.Y.: Doubleday & Co., 1960. Contends that Wilson's presidency finally brought the office to a size and complexity no one person could direct.

1330. Turner, Henry Andrew, Jr. "Woodrow Wilson: Exponent of Executive Leadership [1913–21]." *Western Political Quarterly* 4 (March 1951): 97–115. An analysis of Wilson as a strong party leader, whose effectiveness diminished after 1918.

1331. Van Alstyne, Richard Warner. "Woodrow Wilson and the Idea of the Nation State." *International Affairs* 37, no. 3 (July 1961): 293–308. Deals with the views and actions of Wilson the nationalist leader at the end of the era of the liberal nation state.

1332. Vinyard, Dale. *The Presidency*. New York: Charles Scribner's Sons, 1971. States that both Wilson and Franklin Roosevelt lobbied relentlessly for passage of their recommendations and that both also sensed the great potential of their office to mobilize public opinion behind their legislative programs.

1333. "Wilson in Iowa." *Palimpsest* 29 (October 1948): 310–16. Describes Wilson's visits to Iowa in 1916 and 1919.

1334. *Woodrow Wilson Still Lives—His World Ideals Triumphant*. Los Angeles: Auspices of the Center for International Understanding, 1944. A lengthy treatise arguing in favor of an improved and revitalized League of Nations or United Nations. Includes excerpts from Wilson's speeches and tributes to him by leaders of the movement for international organization.

1335. "Would Change to Single Six-Year Term for President Be Advisable?" *Congressional Digest* 7 (April 1928): 121–23. Takes the form of a short debate, with Wilson and Henry Cabot Lodge making the case against a single term, and Senators John D. Works and Albert B. Cummins taking the affirmative. Wilson's remarks are reprinted from his February 3, 1913, letter to A. Mitchell Palmer. Part of an issue entitled "The Third Term Controversy."

1336. Zentner, Scot James. "Leadership and Partisanship in the Thought of Woodrow Wilson and the American Founders." Ph.D. diss., Michigan State University, 1994. Discusses Wilson's view of liberalism and the administrative state, political leadership, Wilson's historicism, and modern parties and party theory.

C. Inaugurations

1337. "American Philosophical Society and President Wilson." *Science* n.s. 37 (March 28, 1913): 476. Letter of congratulations from the American Philosophical Society to Wilson upon his accession to the presidency.

1338. Baldwin, Elbert Francis. "Exit Wilson; Enter Harding." *Outlook* 127 (March 16, 1921): 414–15. Wilson on the day of Warren G. Harding's inauguration.

1339. *The Chief Executive*, Conceived by Chelsea House Publishers, 220–30. New York: Crown Publishers, 1965. Presidential inaugural addresses, including both of Wilson's.

1340. Christensen, Bonniejean. "Style Is the Man: A Sampling of Prose from Presidential Inaugural Addresses." *North Dakota Quarterly* 48, no. 1 (1980): 5–27. Includes Wilson's March 4, 1913 Inaugural Address.

1341. Durbin, Louise. *Inaugural Cavalcade*, 140–44. New York: Dodd, Mead and Co., 1971. A survey of presidential inaugurations.

1342. Freitag, Ruth S. *Presidential Inaugurations: A Selected List of References*. 3d ed., 140–46. Washington, D.C.: Library of Congress, 1969. Brief bibliography of sources pertaining to Wilson's two inaugurations.

1343. Henry, Laurin L. *Presidential Transitions*, 13–194. Washington, D.C.: Brookings Institute, 1960. Compares the differences between the Taft-Wilson and Wilson-Harding presidencies.

1344. "High Conceptions of Public Duty." *American Monthly Review of Reviews* 47 (April 1913): 388–90. Discusses Wilson's first inaugural address.

1345. Housman, Laurence. "The Instrument." In *Dethronements*: *Imaginary Portraits of Political Characters, Done in Dialogue*: *Charles Stewart Parnell, Joseph Chamberlain, Woodrow Wilson*, 71–95. New York: Macmillan Co., 1923. A dialogue between Wilson and Joseph Tumulty on the day of Harding's inauguration, looking back at Wilson's handling of World War I and the peace.

1346. Hurja, Emil E. *History of Presidential Inaugurations*. New York: New York Democratic Publishing Co., 1933. Describes Wilson's 1912 and 1916 presidential inaugurations as well as American involvement in World War I.

1347. "Inaugural and Its Policy." *Nation* 96 (March 6, 1913): 222–23. An enthusiastic and supportive reaction.

1348. Kittler, Glenn D. *Hail to the Chief!*: *Inaugural Days of Our Presidents*, 154–61. Philadelphia: Chilton Books, 1965.

1349. La Fontaine, Charles V. "God and Nation in Selected U.S. Presidential Inaugural Addresses, 1789–1945." *Journal of Church and State* 18 (1976): 39–60, 503–21. Wilson's inaugural addresses are included in the discussion and found similar to those of Lincoln.

1350. Lott, David Newton, comp. *The Presidents Speak*, 198–205. New York: Holt Rinehart Wilson, 1963. Reprints Wilson's two inaugural addresses.

1351. Low, Alfred Maurice. "The New Era: Wilson's Inauguration Marks the Passing of the Old Days and Methods and the Beginning of Another Phase." *Harper's Weekly* 57 (March 1, 1913): 8–13. Provides pictures of the 1913 inauguration, with one page of text.

1352. "The President and His Problems." *Outlook* 103 (March 15, 1913): 573–75. An analysis of Wilson's inaugural and the obstacles that stand in the way of his success.

1353. "The President and the People." *Bellman* 22 (March 10, 1917): 258–59. Editorial which quotes extensively from Wilson's second inaugural address (March 5, 1917) and declares that Wilson has the full support of the American people.

1354. President, United States. *Inaugural Address of the Presidents of the United States from George Washington to Richard Milhous Nixon*, 198–205. Washington, D.C.: Government Printing Office, 1973–1974. [Reprints of Wilson's two inaugural addresses.] Includes a biographical sketch, a summary of issues facing the nation at the time, and explanatory editorial notes.

1355. Stathis, Stephen W. "Our Sunday Inaugurations." *Presidential Studies Quarterly* 15, no. 1 (1985): 12–24. Deals with the inaugural precedent established by Wilson in 1917.

1356. Storer, James Wilson. *These Historic Scriptures*: *Meditations upon the Bible Texts Used by Our Presidents, from Lincoln to Truman, at Their Inaugurations*,

89–96. Nashville: Broadman Press, 1952. Brief devotional essays based on the biblical passages. Wilson selected Psalm 119: 43–46.

1357. "To Woodrow Wilson." *Register of the Kentucky Historical Society* 11, no. 32 (1913): 81. A short greeting to the President.

1358. "The Triumph of an Idea: Beginning and Conclusion of Seven Years of Public Service." *Harper's Weekly* 57 (March 8, 1913): 35–74. Selections from a number of editorial and special articles on Wilson, published in *Harper's Weekly* and *North American Review* between March 10, 1906 and March 8, 1913.

D. Vice President, Cabinet, and Advisors

See also the section, Wilson's Associates

1359. Auchincloss, Louis. *Love without Wings: Some Friendships in Literature and Politics*, 3–19. Boston: Houghton Mifflin Co., 1991. Describes the Wilson-House friendship, calling it the most important in American political history.

1360. Birkenhead, Frederick Edwin Smith, 1st Earl of. "New Light on President Wilson." In *Last Essays*, 348–74. London: Cassell, 1930. Examines House's recently published personal documents and what they reveal about his relationship with Wilson.

1361. Brands, Henry William, Jr. "Unpremeditated Lansing: His 'Scraps.'" *Diplomatic History* 9, no. 1 (1985): 25–33. Examines Robert Lansing's private writings and insights.

1362. Brown, John Eugene. "Woodrow Wilson's Vice President: Thomas R. Marshall and the Wilson Administration, 1913–1921." Ph.D. diss., Ball State University, 1970.

1363. "Bryan and Wilson." *Nation* 98 (January 22, 1914): 74. Portrays Bryan as a great asset to the Wilson administration.

1364. Chalmers, David. "Ray Stannard Baker's Search for Reform." *Journal of the History of Ideas* 19, no. 3 (1958): 422–34. Describes Baker's shifting allegiance from Theodore Roosevelt to Wilson.

1365. Clymer, Ernest Fletcher. *Cabinets of the Presidents and the Speakers of the House of Representatives, Presidential Electoral Votes by States, 1900–1916. Special Notes on the Presidents*, 33–34. New York: Chandler and Co. Inc., 1920.

1366. "A Costly Resignation." *New Republic* 6 (February 19, 1916): 56–57. Argues that Secretary Garrison's resignation is symbolic of the inconsistencies and lack of strong leadership in the Wilson administration.

1367. Creel, George C. "Break between Wilson and Colonel House." *Collier's National Weekly* 77 (May 22, 1926): 7–8. Describes their eventual split over the peace treaty.

1368. Curtis, Richard, and Maggie Wells. *Not Exactly a Crime: Our Vice Presidents from Adams to Agnew*, 138–44. New York: Dial Press, 1972.

1369. Daniels, Adelaide W. *Recollections of a Cabinet Minister's Wife*. Raleigh, N.C.: Mitchell, 1945. Reflections on social life in Washington during Wilson's presidency, written by the wife of Josephus Daniels.

1370. Daniels, Josephus P. "Wilson and Bryan: What Brought Them Together in 1912 and What Separated Them in 1915." *Saturday Evening Post* 198 (September 5, 1925): 6–7. An in-depth look at the political alliance forced between Wilson and William Jennings Bryan; concludes that the war brought about Bryan's resignation.

1371. Dell, Christopher, comp. *Vice Presidents of the United States, 1789–1961*. Washington, D.C.: Library of Congress Legislative Reference Service, 1962.

1372. Elms, A. C. "From House to Haig: Private Life and Public Style in American Foreign Policy Advisors." *Journal of Social Issues* no. 42 (Summer 1986): 33–53. Includes a study of House as Wilson's friend and advisor.

1373. Fenno, Richard F. *The President's Cabinet: An Analysis in the Period from Wilson to Eisenhower*. Harvard Political Studies. Cambridge: Harvard University Press, 1959. Emphasizes the degree to which Wilson depended on his cabinet to run the government on a day-to-day basis.

1374. Fester, Richard. "Wilson and House." *Deutsche Rundschau* 208 (September 1926): 211–28.

1375. Floto, Inga. "Colonel House in Paris: The Fate of a Presidential Adviser." *American Studies in Scandinavia* (Norway) 6, no. 1–2 (1973–74): 21–45. Discusses House's skills as a negotiator and his breach with Wilson.

1376. Gaines, Anne-Rosewell J. "Political Reward and Recognition: Woodrow Wilson Appoints Thomas Nelson Page Ambassador to Italy." *Virginia Magazine of History and Biography* 89, no. 3 (1981): 328–40. Recounts the circumstances surrounding the 1913 appointment of the wealthy Potomac literary figure.

1377. Gooch, George Peabody. "The Final Revelations of Colonel House." *Contemporary Review* 135 (January 1929): 11–18. Cites the recently published volumes three and four of **3695** as evidence that House was the able and faithful colleague of Wilson.

1378. Grattan, Clinton Hartley. "Colonel House's Self-Defense." *Nation* 135 (December 14, 1932): 588–89. Points out Wilson's inconsistencies.

1379. Grayson, Cary Travers. "The Colonel's Folly and the President's Distress." *American Heritage* 15 (October 1964): 4–7. An account in 1926 by Wilson's personal physician.

1380. Hammer, S. C. "Colonel House og praesident Wilson." *Samtiden* ([Oslo] 1926): 396–406.

1381. Holt, William Stull. "What Wilson Sent and What House Received: Or, Scholars Need to Check Carefully." *American Historical Review* 65 (April 1960): 569–71. Compares the message that Wilson wrote with the decoded cable received by House on October 29, 1918.

1382. Hoover, Irwin Hood (Ike). "The Case of Colonel House." *Saturday Evening Post* 207 (July 14, 1934): 16–17+. Discusses House's role in the administration and his eventual break with Wilson.

1383. Julhiard-Pellisson, Th. "Wilson Raconte par Tumulty." *Revue de Paris* 29, pt. 1 (February 1, 1922): 647–62.

1384. Kerney, James. "Warwicks of the Wilson Cabinets." *Saturday Evening Post* 196 (May 3, 1924): 7+. Discusses Wilson's choices for cabinet positions.

1385. Koenig, Louis W. *The Invisible Presidency*. New York: Rinehart and Co., 1960. A book about the influence of advisors and friends on different presidents. Sections on Wilson focus mainly on Edward M. House.

1386. Le Verrier, Charles. "Silences of President Wilson." *Living Age* 311 (October 29, 1921): 269–71. Describes the disagreements between Wilson and Secretary of State Lansing.

1387. Lippmann, Walter. "Wilson and House." In *Men of Destiny*, 120–39. New York: Macmillan Co., 1927. Argues that despite failures, they set a positive precedent for future statesmen.

1388. Livermore, Seward W. "'Deserving Democrats': The Foreign Service under Woodrow Wilson." *South Atlantic Quarterly* 69, no. 1 (1970): 144–60. Discusses the neglect of the career diplomatic service under Wilson.

1389. MacDonald, William. "Colonel House's Latest Disclosures." *Current History* 29 (December 1928): 430–33. A review of the third and fourth volumes of **3695** in which Wilson plays a major role.

1390. Marshall, Thomas Riley. "Constructive Work of the Wilson Administration." *Forum* 56 (July 1916): 46–62. A defense by the Vice-President.

1391. McWilliams, Tennant S. "John W. Davis and Southern Wilsonianism." *Virginia Quarterly Review* 64 (Summer 1988): 398–416. Wilson's Ambassador to the Court of St. James who was devoted to the cause of the League.

1392. Neu, Charles E. "Woodrow Wilson and Colonel House: The Early Years, 1911–1915." In **1083**, 248–78. Describes the beginnings of the House-Wilson friendship, with special emphasis on their declining dependency.

1393. "The New Administration." *Nation* 96 (March 13, 1913): 248. Examines the individuals in Wilson's first cabinet.

1394. "The New Page Letters, from the Files of President Wilson: Edited by Burton Jesse Hendrick." *World's Work* 50 (June-November 1925): 23–36, 139–47, 251–59,

361–75, 475–85, 585–602. Letters from the Ambassador to England, Walter A. Page, to Wilson, 1913–1917.

1395. Olson, Keith W. "Woodrow Wilson, Franklin K. Lane, and the Wilson Cabinet Meetings." *Historian* 32, no. 2 (February 1970): 270–75. Disagrees with Lane's contention that Wilson did not make good use of his cabinet.

1396. "The President and the Dismissal of Lansing." *Review* 2 (February 21, 1920): 168–69. A denunciation of Wilson's firing of Lansing as Secretary of State.

1397. "President-Elect Wilson's Cabinet-Making." *Outlook* 103 (January 11, 1913): 65–68. Examines Wilson's cabinet appointees in the new administration of 1916.

1398. "President Wilson as Secretary Lane Knows Him." *Literary Digest* 54 (June 30, 1917): 2016. A thumbnail sketch by Secretary of the Interior Franklin K. Lane.

1399. "The President's Appointments." *Outlook* 103 (March 22, 1913): 606–7. Reports that Wilson will delegate authority to cabinet members to place office-seekers in the new administration.

1400. Reinertson, John. "Colonel House, Woodrow Wilson and European Socialism, 1917–1919." Ph.D. diss., University of Wisconsin-Madison, 1971.

1401. Rifkind, Robert S. "The Colonel's Dream of Power." *American Heritage* 10, no. 2 (February 1959): 62–64, 111. Assesses the influence on Wilson and Franklin D. Roosevelt of Edward M. House's novel *Philip Dru: Administrator, a Story of Tomorrow* (New York: B.W. Huebsch, 1919).

1402. Seymour, Charles. "End of a Friendship." *American Heritage* 14 (August 1963): 4–9, 78–80. An account of the break with Wilson, containing a statement by House.

1403. ———. "The Role of Colonel House in Wilson's Diplomacy." In **1870**, 11–33. Maintains that House was a crucial influence in formulating but not implementing policy.

1404. Straus, Oscar S. *Under Four Administrations*, 307–430. Boston: Houghton, Mifflin Co., 1922. Autobiography of a career diplomat.

1405. Tompkins, Dorothy L. C. *The Office of Vice President: A Selected Bibliography*. Berkeley: Bureau of Public Administration, University of California, 1957.

1406. Tumulty, Joseph Patrick. "Close-up View of Woodrow Wilson." *Current Opinion* 69 (December 1920): 789–94. Wilson's personal secretary describes his ten-year tenure with Wilson.

1407. ———. *Woodrow Wilson as I Know Him*. New York: Doubleday, Page, and Co., 1921. An admiring account and strong defense of Wilson and his policies.

1408. Viereck, George Sylvester. "Behind the House-Wilson Break." In *The Inside Story, by Members of the Overseas Press Club of America*, ed. Robert Spiers Benjamin, 139–56. New York: Prentice-Hall, 1940. Believes that the jealousy of Mrs. Wilson, the connivance of Dr. Cary Grayson, and the ambition of a daring Wall Street operator upset the friendship between House and Wilson.

1409. ———. *The Strangest Friendship in History: Woodrow Wilson and Colonel House*. New York: Horace Liveright, 1932. Examines the Wilson Administration and the complex story of the friendship between Woodrow Wilson and Edward Mandell House.

1410. White, William Lindsay. *Bernard Baruch: Portrait of a Citizen*. New York: Harcourt, Brace & Co., 1950. Contains a chapter on Baruch and Woodrow Wilson.

1411. Williams, Joyce G. *Colonel House and Sir Edward Grey: A Study in Anglo-American Diplomacy*. Lanham, Md.: University Press, 1984. Discusses how they used their friendship to avoid a confrontation over violations of American neutrality rights.

1412. ———. "The Resignation of Secretary of State Robert Lansing." *Diplomatic History* 3, no. 3 (1979): 337–43. Reproduces a memorandum by Edith Bolling Galt Wilson's secretary concerning Lansing's resignation in 1920.

1413. Willsie, Honore McCue. "How the Cabinet Was Selected." *Harper's Weekly* 58 (September 27, 1913): 26–27. Upholds Wilson's cabinet selections as brave, efficient, and imaginative.

1414. "Wilson's Administration." *Current Opinion* 54 (April 1913): 265–70. Describes members of the Wilson administration and summarizes some of Wilson's campaign promises.

1415. Wish, Harvey. "Toward the New Freedom: The Wilson-House Regime." In *Contemporary America: The National Scene Since 1900*, 167–92. New York: Harper & Brothers, 1945. Discusses the importance of Wilson's relationship with Col. Edward M. House in setting his domestic agenda.

1416. Woolsey, Lester H. "The Personal Diplomacy of Colonel House." *American Journal of International Law* 21 (October 1927): 706–15. Describes the involvement of Colonel House with prewar international events.

E. Wilson as Administrator

1417. Arnold, Peri E. *Making the Managerial Presidency: Comprehensive Reorganization Planning, 1905–1980*. Princeton: Princeton University Press, 1986. Credits Wilson for pioneering the study of administration but argues that he did not make administrative reorganization a priority.

1418. Bain, E. "Woodrow Wilson (1856–1924): 'Herwaardering.' [Woodrow Wilson (1856–1924): Reevaluation"]. *Politeia* (UNISA) 6, no. 1 (1987): 72–80.

Reappraises Wilson's contribution to public administration, particularly as it relates to contemporary South Africa.

1419. Brownlow, Louis. "Woodrow Wilson and Public Administration." *Public Administration Review* 16 (Spring 1956): 77–81. Tribute to Wilson as one of the architects of modern public administration in the United States.

1420. Cohen, Michael. "Religious Revivalism and the Administrative Centralization Movement." *Administration and Society* 9, no. 2 (1977): 219–32. Discusses a movement, promoted by Wilson and others, which emphasized the centralization of departments in the executive branch.

1421. Cuff, Robert D. "Wilson and Weber: Bourgeois Critics in an Organized Age." *Public Administration Review* 38 (May 1978): 240–44. The similarities and differences between the Wilson administration and the model of public administration created by Max Weber.

1422. Devine, Donald. "American Culture and Public Administration." *Policy Studies Journal* 11, no. 2 (December 1982): 255–60. Wilson's influence in shaping modern administrations.

1423. Gawthrop, Louis C. "Administrative Responsibility: Public Policy and the Wilsonian Legacy." *Policy Studies Journal* 5 (Autumn 1976): 108–13. Discusses Wilson's emphasis on operating techniques in administrative responsibility and the modern need for individual morality in that field.

1424. MacMahon, Arthur Whittier. "Woodrow Wilson: Political Leader and Administrator." In **1075**, 202–93. [Also published in **1149**, 100–22.] An analysis of Wilson's theories on the presidency, his legislative leadership, and his administrative organization.

1425. Turner, Henry Andrew, Jr. "The Administrative Theory and Practice of Woodrow Wilson." Ph.D. diss., University of Chicago, 1950.

1426. _____ . "Woodrow Wilson as an Administrator." *Public Administration Review* 16 (Fall 1956): 249–57. Commends Wilson's administrative theory and practice for being as important as his social reform, wartime leadership, and his advocacy of the League of Nations.

F. Wilson as Commander in Chief

1427. Daniels, Josephus P. *Our Navy at War*. New York: George H. Doran, 1922. A detailed account of the Navy's wartime role by Wilson's Secretary of the Navy.

1428. Davidson, Eugene. "Presidential Wars." *Modern Age* 12, no. 3 (1968): 226–31. Deals with the presidency and Congress, right to declare war, beginning with the Wilson era.

1429. Esposito, David M. "Woodrow Wilson and the Origins of the AEF." *Presidential Studies Quarterly* 19, no. 1 (Winter 1989): 127–40. [Taken from his Ph.D. diss., Pennsylvania State University, 1988.] Explores Wilson's decision to send the American Expeditionary Force to France in 1917.

1430. Ferrell, Robert H. "Woodrow Wilson: A Misfit in Office?" In *Commanders in Chief: Presidential Leadership in Modern Times*, ed. Joseph G. Dawson III. 65–86. Lawrence: University Press of Kansas, 1993. Believes that Wilson's role as commander-in-chief during World War I was minimal and unusual because of his background—his confidence in the Victorian era, his success as a university professor, and his dogmatic hatred of war itself.

1431. Link, Arthur S., and John Whiteclay Chambers, II. "Woodrow Wilson as Commander in Chief." In *The United States Military under the Constitution of the United States, 1789–1989*, ed. Richard H. Kohn, 317–75. New York: New York University Press, 1991. Wilson's use of the constitution to direct the nation's military and civilian resources in time of crisis.

1432. May, Ernest R. "Wilson (1917–1918)." In *The Ultimate Decision: The President as Commander-in-Chief*, 109–31. New York: George Braziller, 1960. Argues that Wilson's wish to avoid the role of Commander in Chief was based on his desire for American neutrality. Wilson also made it clear that should the United States enter the war, his goals would be different than those of his predecessors.

1433. Palmer, John McAuley. *Washington, Lincoln, Wilson: Three War Statesmen.* New York: Doubleday, Doran & Co., 1930. Focuses on Wilson's military decisions and examines his role as a wartime President.

1434. Ray, Christopher. "Woodrow Wilson as Commander-In-Chief." *History Today* (Great Britain) 43 (April 1993): 24–30. Focuses on Wilson's performance as head of the United States armed forces during World War I, as well as his relationship with the generals.

1435. Reilly, Henry Joseph. "Wilson, the Greatest War Leader of Them All." *American Magazine* 106 (December 1928): 18–21+. An admiring portrait by a brigadier general who at first bitterly opposed Wilson's policy of neutrality but then came to admire him.

G. Wilson and Congress

1436. Abrams, Richard M. "Woodrow Wilson and the Southern Congressmen, 1913–1916." *Journal of Southern History* 22 (November 1956): 417–37. The influence of southern Congressmen on New Freedom legislation.

1437. Acheson, Dean Gooderham. "Legislative-Executive Relations." *Yale Review* 45 (June 1956): 481–95. Discusses the relationship between the legislative and executive branches of government, using **19** as its basis.

1438. Barkley, Alben W. "Woodrow Wilson and the Congress." In **1075**, 59–79. Reviews Wilson's legislative accomplishments and his international diplomacy, judging him to be the world's great benefactor despite his mistakes.

1439. Billington, Monroe L. "Thomas P. Gore and the Election of Woodrow Wilson." *Mid-America* 39, no. 3 (July 1957): 180–91. Examines the Senator's overlooked role in Wilson's first election.

1440. _____ . "Thomas P. Gore and Oklahoma Public Opinion, 1917–1918." *Journal of Southern History* 27, no. 3 (August 1961): 344–53. Discusses Gore's opposition to many of Wilson's war measures and the reaction against him in Oklahoma.

1441. Carter, Jean. "Woodrow Wilson and His Congress." *Vassar Journal of Undergraduate Studies* 9 (May 1935): 112–34. A mixed review of Wilson's character and presidency, blaming his inability to work well with Congress for his failure to achieve total success.

1442. Curran, George A. "Woodrow Wilson's Theory and Practice Regarding Relations of President and Congress." Ph.D. diss., Fordham University, 1949.

1443. Dimock, Marshall Edward. "Woodrow Wilson as Legislative Leader." *Journal of Politics* 19, no. 1 (February 1957): 3–19. Positively appraises Wilson's leadership of Congress through his personality and persuasion.

1444. "The End of Congress." *Nation* 100 (March 11, 1915): 266. Criticizes the performance of the Sixty-third Congress, but praises Wilson's efforts in trying to lead it.

1445. Fleming, Denna Frank. *The Treaty Veto of the American Senate*. New York: G. P. Putnam's Sons, 1930. Discusses the power of the United States Senate over treaties, including the rejection of the Treaty of Versailles.

1446. Hendrix, J. A. "Presidential Addresses to Congress: Woodrow Wilson and the Jeffersonian Tradition." *Southern Speech Journal* 31, no. 4 (1966): 285–94. Wilson's success in appealing to Congress in person to support his legislative program in 1913.

1447. Herring, Pendleton. *Presidential Leadership: The Political Relations of Congress and the Chief Executive*. New York: Farrar and Rinehart, 1940. Discusses the relations between the branches of the federal government, focusing on the role of the President. Wilson discussed throughout.

1448. Holt, Laurence James. *Congressional Insurgents and the Party System, 1909–1916*. Cambridge: Harvard University Press, 1967. A book on the insurgents within the Republican party during the Taft and Wilson years. Discusses their increased political isolation due to the hostility they aimed at old guard Republicans, the Progressive Party, and the Wilson administration.

1449. Livermore, Seward W. *Politics Is Adjourned: Woodrow Wilson and the War Congress, 1916–1918.* Middletown: Wesleyan University Press, 1966. Examines Wilson's wartime relationship with Congress and the gradual development of partisanship and ill feelings.

1450. MacMahon, Arthur Whittier. "Woodrow Wilson as a Legislative Leader and Administrator." *American Political Science Review* 50, no. 3 (Spring 1956): 641–75. An analysis of Wilson's relationships with Congress.

1451. McGregor [pseud.]. "The President and the Congress." *Harper's Weekly* 58 (April 18, 1914): 15. Attributes Wilson's power with Congress to his clearly formulated goals and his reputation as a friend of the people.

1452. Mansfield, Harvey V., Sr., ed. *Congress Against the President.* New York: Academy of Political Science, 1975. Describes the 1913 revolt of the progressive Democrats in the Senate, the removal of majority leader Thomas Martin, and his replacement by John Worth.

1453. "Mr. Wilson's Congress." *Nation* 103 (September 14, 1916): 251–52. Describes the legislative accomplishments of Congress in 1916 and Wilson's ability to control that branch of government.

1454. Osborn, George Coleman. "The Friendship of John Sharp Williams and Woodrow Wilson." *Journal of Mississippi History* 1 (1939): 3–13. Recounts the experiences shared with the Mississippi Senator.

1455. ———. "John Sharp Williams Among the Wilson Reformers." *Journal of Mississippi History* 5 (January 1943): 3–13. Deals with the interaction between Williams and Wilson during the tariff, currency, and anti-trust battles in 1913 and 1914.

1456. Overman, Lee Slater. "President Wilson as a World Leader." *Forum* 60 (December 1918): 641–47. Analysis by the North Carolina Senator.

1457. Pious, Richard M. *The American Presidency.* New York: Basic Books, 1979. An analysis of the office of the presidency; Wilson and his relations with Congress are frequently discussed.

1458. Polsby, Nelson W. *Congress and the Presidency.* Englewood Cliffs, N.J.: Prentice-Hall, 1986. Wilson is discussed as both a student of American politics and as President.

1459. "The President and Congress." *Outlook* 107 (August 8, 1914): 834–35. An endorsement of Bryan's views during the Wilson administration on increasing executive power.

1460. "The President and Congress." *Outlook* 109 (March 17, 1915): 612–14. Wilson's success in getting his legislative agenda passed.

1461. "The President and Legislation." *Nation* 96 (April 10, 1913): 350. Discusses Wilson's desire to work with Congress in the lawmaking process.

1462. "The President and the Recalcitrant Democrats." *Independent* 85 (March 13, 1916): 368. An examination of Wilson's struggle to keep unity in the Democratic party so as to ensure passage of his legislation.

1463. "The President and the Senate." *Nation* 99 (July 16, 1914): 61. Wilson's difficulties in getting confirmation for his nominees to the Federal Reserve Board.

1464. "President Wilson on Capitol Hill." *Harper's Weekly* 57 (April 19, 1913): 3–4. Applauds Wilson's renewal of the practice of going personally to address the opening session of Congress.

1465. "President Wilson and Presidential Primaries: A Poll of Congress and of the Press." *Outlook* 105 (December 13, 1913): 792–95. Quotes the responses of two Congressmen and several American newspapers to Wilson's message convening the 63rd Congress.

1466. "President Wilson's Indianapolis Speech." *Outlook* 109 (January 20, 1915): 121–27. Wilson's January 8, 1915 speech, in which politics dominated.

1467. "President Wilson's Message, 1913." *Current Opinion* 56 (January 1914): 1–2. Reviews Wilson's annual message to Congress on foreign and domestic issues.

1468. "President Wilson's Message, December 7, 1915." *Independent* 84 (December 20, 1915): 461–62. Analyzes Wilson's annual message to Congress on foreign and domestic issues.

1469. "Presidential Peace-Message in War-Time." *Literary Digest* 51 (December 18, 1915): 1411–14. A compilation of reviews of Wilson's message to Congress, in which Pan-Americanism, disloyal citizens, preparedness, taxation, and problems with the railroad were discussed.

1470. "The President's Absence." *Outlook* 120 (December 11, 1918): 576. Analyzes Congress' responsibilities in the absence of Wilson during the Paris Peace Conference.

1471. "The President's Address to Congress, December, 1913." *Independent* 76 (December 11, 1913): 480–81. Addresses Wilsonian foreign policy in relation to Mexico and the Philippines. Also deals with domestic issues, specifically farm credits, trust problems, and election reform.

1472. "The President's Message." *Outlook* 108 (December 16, 1914): 853–54. Addresses conservation of natural resources, the extension of Philippine self-government, the shipping bill, rural credits, and the general state of the economy.

1473. "The President's Message." *Outlook* 111 (December 15, 1915): 890–93. Divides Wilson's annual message to Congress into four categories: national defense, internal treason, foreign relations, and domestic industry and taxation.

1474. "The President's Message." *Outlook* 114 (December 13, 1916): 782–83. Discusses Wilson's annual message before Congress, delivered during the preceding week.

1475. "The President's Program." *Independent* 100 (December 13, 1919): 176–77. Analyzes Wilson's December 2 message to Congress.

1476. Rayburn, Sam. "Speaker Speaks of Presidents." *New York Times Magazine* June 4, 1961: 32. Democratic representative Sam Rayburn of Texas reflects on the Presidents with whom he served, beginning with Wilson.

1477. Reed, Thomas H. "The Presidency of Woodrow Wilson—A Symposium: Wilson's Theory of the Relation of President and Congress." *Pacific Review* 1 (March 1921): 581–87. Examines Wilson's belief that the President must lead Congress and Wilson's ultimate inability to overcome party partisanship in trying to fulfill that role.

1478. Roady, Elston Edward. "Party Regularity in the Sixty-third Congress, 1913–1921." Ph.D. diss., University of Illinois, 1951.

1479. Ryley, Thomas W. *A Little Group of Willful Men: A Study of Congressional-Presidential Authority*. Port Washington, N.Y.: Kennikat Press, 1975. A study of the group of Senators opposing the United States' entry into World War I.

1480. "The Senate against Mr. Wilson: Concerning Several Appointments to Office." *Independent* 81 (January 4, 1915): 10–11. Describes sharp disagreements between the Senate and Wilson because of appointments to state offices.

1481. Stratton, David Hodges. "President Wilson's Smelling Committee." *Colorado Quarterly* 5 (Summer 1956): 164–84. Concerns a subcommittee of the Senate Foreign Relations Committee, appointed to confer with Wilson in December 1919 during his illness.

1482. U.S. Congress. House. *Biographical Directory of the American Congress, 1774–1961*, (85th Cong., 2nd session, 1961). H. Doc. 442. Washington, D.C.: Government Printing Office, 1961. Sketches of Congressmen during the Wilson administration.

1483. Watson, James E. *As I Knew Them: Memoirs of James E. Watson, Former United States Senator from Indiana*. Indianapolis: Bobbs-Merrill Co., 1936. Includes discussion of Wilson's presidency.

1484. Westwood, Howard C. "The Joint Committee on the Conduct of the War: A Look at the Record." *Lincoln Herald* 80, no. 1 (1978): 3–15. Examines the Civil War committee in light of its later condemnation by Wilson and others.

1485. "Wilson and Congress." *Nation* 98 (February 12, 1914): 150. Discusses the differing opinions between Wilson and Congress on the topic of the proposed Panama Act.

1486. "Wilson and Legislation." *Nation* 97 (August 14, 1913): 136. Discusses Wilson's skillful politics and the methods he used to achieve his goals.

1487. "Wilson's Use of Defeat." *Nation* 99 (July 30, 1914): 121–22. Explains how Wilson used defeat to gain an advantage.

1488. "Wilson Touch." *Nation* 98 (March 5, 1914): 228. Praises Wilson's efficiency and his ability to get Congressional cooperation.

H. Wilson, Progressivism, and Domestic Affairs

1. General Works

1489. Aaron, Daniel. *Men of Good Hope: A Story of American Progressives*, 281–86. New York: Oxford University Press, 1951. Includes a short section on Wilson.

1490. Allen, Frederick Lewis. *Only Yesterday*, 1–62. New York: Blue Ribbon Books, 1931. Social history of the 1920s, with the first three chapters covering postwar America under Wilson.

1491. Barth, Hans. "The Decline of Liberal Values since 1914." *Confluence: An International Forum* 5, no. 4 (Winter 1957): 355–66. Defines liberalism and finds its demise foreshadowed by nineteenth-century currents and hastened by the restriction of freedoms in Europe during World War I.

1492. Bassett, John Spencer. "Wilson and Domestic Issues." In *Makers of a New Nation*, 268–92. New Haven: Yale University Press, 1928. Argues that Wilson was a strong proponent of progressive reform.

1493. Binkley, Wilfred Ellsworth. *The Man in the White House: His Powers and Duties*, *1958*. Rev. ed. New York: Harper and Row, 1968. Wilson's skillful manipulation of social forces during his first administration in the creation of his "New Freedom."

1494. ———. "Present-Day Democracy." In *American Political Parties*. 2d ed., 359–402. New York: Alfred A. Knopf, 1945. Argues that Wilson's New Freedom marked a turning-point for political parties and set a precedent for activism.

1495. Burner, David. *The Politics of Provincialism: The Democratic Party in Transition, 1918–1932*. New York: Alfred A. Knopf, 1968. Describes the role of the Democratic party following Wilson's second term and argues that any Democratic presidential candidate would have had the burden of Wilson's League of Nations.

1496. Chamberlain, John. *Farewell to Reform: The Rise, Life and Decay of the Progressive Mind in America*. New York: John Day, 1932. Concludes that the progressive movement was often too cautious and reactionary and argues that Wilson mistakenly equated liberalism with morality.

1497. Chambers, Clarke. *Seedtime of Reform: American Social Service and Social Action, 1918–1933*. Minneapolis: University of Minnesota Press, 1963. Argues that many voluntary welfare agencies had their origins in the progressive era.

1498. Chambers, John Whiteclay, II. *The Tyranny of Change: America in the Progressive Era, 1900–1917*. New York: St. Martin's Press, 1980. A book on the concerted effort in American history to deal with the vast problems emerging in industrial America.

1499. *Change and Continuity in Twentieth-Century America*, ed. John Braeman, et al. Columbus: Ohio State University Press, 1964. Relevant articles listed by author.

1500. Childs, Richard Spencer. "Woodrow Wilson's Legacy: Recalling the Educator-President's Role in Early Development of the League's Program." *National Municipal Review* 46 (January 1957): 14–19. Wilson's contributions to municipal reform during the progressive era.

1501. Cooper, John Milton, Jr. "New Freedom." In **410**, 2:890–95. Discusses the conflict between Woodrow Wilson's New Freedom and Theodore Roosevelt's New Nationalism.

1502. Crunden, Robert. *Ministers of Reform: The Progressives' Achievement in American Civilization, 1889–1920*. New York: Basic Books, 1982. Argues that a shared sense of moral values shaped the progressive vision for the United States.

1503. Davidson, John Wells. "The Response of the South to Woodrow Wilson's New Freedom, 1912–1914." Ph.D. diss., Yale University, 1954. Demonstrates the southern congressional support for the Underwood Tariff, Federal Reserve, trade commission, and Clayton antitrust bills.

1504. DeSantis, Vincent P. *The Shaping of Modern America: 1877–1916*, 207–26. Boston: Allyn and Bacon, 1973. Includes a chapter on Wilson's domestic policies.

1505. Dewitt, Benjamin Parke. "The Progressive Movement in the Democratic Party." In *The Progressive Movement*, 26–45. New York: Macmillan Co., 1915. Discusses the progressive movement not in terms of the formation of one Progressive Party but as a force affecting all of American politics. Wilson is mentioned throughout.

1506. Diggins, John Patrick. "Republicanism and Progressivism." *American Quarterly* 37, no. 4 (1985): 572–98. Discusses eleven political leaders and thinkers, including Wilson, in order to answer the question why the ideals of classical republicanism are no longer a part of political life.

1507. Downs, Robert Bingham. "Conquest of Freedom: Woodrow Wilson's *The New Freedom*." In *Molders of the Modern Mind: 111 Books that Shaped Western Civilization*, 350–53. New York: Barnes and Noble, 1961. Brief analysis of Wilson's domestic agenda.

1508. Dulles, Foster Rhea. "New Freedom." In *Twentieth Century America*, 128–45. Boston: Houghton-Mifflin Co., 1945. Focuses on Wilson's domestic policies during his first term, placing them in the context of the progressive era.

1509. Ekirch, Arthur Alphonse, Jr. *Progressivism in America: A Study of the Era from Theodore Roosevelt to Woodrow Wilson*, 214–75. New York: Viewpoints, 1974. The final chapters cover the New Freedom and World War I, arguing that progressives borrowed ideas liberally from European counterparts.

1510. Faulkner, Harold Underwood. *American Political and Social History*. 4th ed., 586–627. New York: F. S. Crofts, 1945. Two chapters on the Wilson years, entitled "The New Democracy," and "The World War."

1511. ———. *The Decline of Laissez-Faire, 1897–1917*. New York: Holt Rinehart & Co., 1951. Comments on Wilson's desire for a new democratic freedom from extremes of business monopoly and power.

1512. ———. *The Quest for Social Justice, 1898–1914*. New York: Macmillan Co., 1931. Describes Wilson as a social reformer while governor and President.

1513. Forcey, Charles Budd. *The Crossroads of Liberalism: Croly, Weyl, Lippmann, and the Progressive Era, 1900–1925*. New York: Oxford University Press, 1961. Deals with "the men of ideas" who were associated with the *New Republic* after 1914 and their relations with Wilson and Theodore Roosevelt.

1514. Frisch, Michael H. "Urban Theorists, Urban Reform, and American Political Culture in the Progressive Period." *Political Science Quarterly* 97, no. 2 (1982): 295–315. Wilson's view of the positive role of government is seen as his contribution to progressive reform.

1515. Goldman, Eric Frederick. *Rendezvous with Destiny: A History of Modern American Reform*, 208–84. New York: Alfred A. Knopf, 1952. A popular history of twentieth-century reform, with Wilson portrayed as a leader of the reformers who was then rejected by them after the war.

1516. Grantham, Dewey W. "The Contours of Southern Progressivism." *American Historical Review* 86, no. 5 (1981): 1035–59. Examines the forces shaping progressivism in the South during the early twentieth century. The author argues that the end of Wilson's presidency marked the collapse of southern progressivism.

1517. ———. "Southern Congressional Leaders and the New Freedom, 1913–1917." *Journal of Southern History* 13 (November 1947): 439–59. Argues that southern congressional leaders like Oscar Underwood were crucial to the passage of New Freedom legislation.

1518. Graves, John Temple. "The Magnificent American Proposition: The New Freedom of Woodrow Wilson." *Virginia Quarterly Review* 20 (July 1944): 404–12. Concludes that the ideals and principles of the New Freedom were more timeless and more American than those expressed in the New Deal.

1519. _____ . "Wilson and the South Today." *Virginia Quarterly Review* 6 (July 1930): 382–88. Examines the contemporary South in the context of Wilson's philosophy of competitive individualism.

1520. Haber, Samuel. *Efficiency and Uplift: Scientific Management in the Progressive Era, 1890–1920*. Chicago: University of Chicago Press, 1964. Shows Wilson balancing the drive for efficient wartime production with concern for the rights of labor.

1521. Hawley, Ellis W. *The Great War and the Search for a Modern Order: A History of the American People and Their Institutions, 1917–1933*. New York: St. Martin's Press, 1979. An assessment of Wilson's presidency as the prelude to government intervention in economic problems.

1522. Hofstadter, Richard. *The Age of Reform: From Bryan to F.D.R.* New York: Alfred A. Knopf, 1955. Discusses Wilson's role in helping to restore a sense of political and economic power to all Americans.

1523. Hofstadter, Richard, ed. *The Progressive Movement: 1900–1915*, 153–57, 169–77. Englewood Cliffs, N.J.: Prentice-Hall, 1963. Includes 1912–1913 speeches by Wilson on the New Freedom and tariff revision.

1524. Kennedy, David M. *Progressivism: The Critical Issues*. Boston: Little, Brown & Co., 1971. Includes reprints and excerpts of scholarly writings by Wilson, among other progressives.

1525. Kolko, Gabriel. *The Triumph of Conservatism: A Reinterpretation of American History, 1900–1916*, 190–305. New York: Free Press, 1963. Argues that big business succeeded by supporting progressive leaders like Wilson, because federal regulations under him preserved existing economic structures.

1526. Leuchtenburg, William E. "The New Deal and the Analogue of War." In **1499**, 81–144. Includes a discussion of the New Freedom as a precursor to the New Deal.

1527. _____ . *The Perils of Prosperity, 1914–1932*, 1–84. Chicago: University of Chicago Press, 1958. Sees the Wilson years as the beginning of growing American power. Covers Wilson, World War I, the peace, and the Red Scare.

1528. Lewis, Edward Rieman. *A History of American Political Thought from the Civil War to the World War*. New York: Macmillan Co., 1937. Discusses progressivism, the New Freedom, woman suffrage, and executive leadership. Wilson discussed throughout.

1529. Link, Arthur S. *American Epoch: A History of the United States since the 1890's*, 118–250. New York: Alfred A. Knopf, 1955. [Later editions include the 2d ed. in 1963 with the collaboration of William B. Catton; the 3d ed. in 1967 with the collaboration of William B. Catton and the assistance of William M. Leary; the 4th ed. in 1973 entitled *American Epoch: A History of the United States since 1900* in

3 vols. with William B. Catton; two 5th eds., each in 2 vols., in 1980, also with William B. Catton, and one with maps and charts by Theodore R. Miller; and the 6th ed. in 1987 in 2 vols. with William B. Catton and William A. Link. A 3 vol. Borzoi paperback was also published in 1967.] Covers Wilson's early agenda, both of Wilson's campaigns, his domestic and foreign policies between 1913–1921, World War I, and the peace talks.

1530. ――――. "The South and the 'New Freedom': An Interpretation." *American Scholar* 20 (July 1951): 314–24. [Also published in **1155**, 298–308.] Discusses the influence of southern agrarians in persuading Wilson to move away from the policy of laissez-faire towards one of more government action.

1531. ――――. "What Happened to the Progressive Movement in the 1920s?" *American Historical Review* 64 (July 1959): 833–51. [Also published in **1155**, 349–69.] Questions the view that progressivism died during the twenties and argues that it persisted throughout the decade.

1532. Link, Arthur S., and Richard L. McCormick. *Progressivism*. Arlington Heights, Ill.: Harlan Davidson, 1983. Discusses Wilson as a leader of progressive reform.

1533. Link, William A. "The Social Context of Southern Progressivism: 1880–1930." In **1083**, 55–82. Believes that the real significance of progressive era social reform is to be found in the society which reformers confronted: a dispersed, rural population with strong traditions of individualism and localism.

1534. Mann, Arthur, ed. *The Progressive Era: Liberal Renaissance or Liberal Failure?* New York: Holt, Rinehart and Winston, 1963. A political analysis of the nature and effect of the progressive era. Wilson is cited throughout.

1535. May, Henry F. *End of American Innocence: A Study of the First Years of Our Own Time, 1912–1917*. New York: Alfred A. Knopf, 1959. Notes significant changes in American society especially in literature, politics, and American self-expression, prior to the United States' entry into World War I.

1536. McCormick, Richard L. "Progressivism: A Modern Reassessment." In **1258**, 3–12. Describes the changing historical interpretation of the progressive era and asserts that progressive reforms were distinguished by an optimism about the ability to improve conditions and environment through human endeavor.

1537. McKown, Paul. "Certain Important Domestic Policies of Woodrow Wilson." Ph.D. diss., University of Pennsylvania, 1932. An analysis of Wilson's growing belief in the positive role of the federal government in social reform.

1538. Mowry, George Edwin. *The Era of Theodore Roosevelt*. New York: Harper & Brothers, 1958. Contains scattered discussions of Wilson's brand of progressivism, mainly in the context of being a new challenge to Roosevelt.

1539. _____ . *The Progressive Era, 1900–1920.* Washington, D.C.: American Historical Association, 1972. Pamphlet no. 212. Explores recent literature on the progressive era, emphasizing its origins and ideas.

1540. Newman, Simon P. "The Hegelian Roots of Woodrow Wilson's Progressivism." *American Presbyterians: Journal of Presbyterian History* 64, no. 3 (Fall 1986): 191–201. Examines Wilson's reconciliation of conservatism and progressivism through his introduction to the thought of Hegel.

1541. Norris, John M. "The Influence of British Nineteenth- Century Liberalism on Woodrow Wilson." *World Affairs Quarterly* 28, no. 3 (1957): 219–28. Explores the similarities and differences between nineteenth-century British liberalism and twentieth-century American progressivism and identifies Wilson's place in the spectrum.

1542. Nye, Russel Blaine. "Betrayal and Survival, 1908–1920." In *Midwestern Progressive Politics*, 263–309. East Lansing: Michigan State College Press, 1951. Discusses the disillusionment of midwestern progressives with the Taft administration and the rebound of their hopes under Wilson.

1543. Osborn, George Coleman. "Woodrow Wilson Visits Mobile, October 27, 1913." *Alabama Historical Quarterly* 19 (Spring 1957): 157–69. Describes Wilson's journey and attendance at the fifth annual convention of the Southern Commercial Congress in Mobile, where Wilson met with Deep South governors.

1544. *Political Parties in American History: 1890-Present*, comp. Winfred E. A. Bernhard, et. al. 3 vols. New York: G.P. Putnam's Sons, 1974. Relevant articles listed by author.

1545. Roberts, Derrel. "Mobile and the Visit by Woodrow Wilson." *Alabama Historical Quarterly* 27, no. 1–2 (1966): 81–90. Describes the presidential visit to Mobile in 1913 to meet with southern governors.

1546. Ross, Edward A. *Seventy Years of It.* New York: D. Appleton-Century, 1936. A former student of Wilson and an advocate of the Wisconsin progressives describes the progressive movement.

1547. Sarasohn, David. *The Party of Reform: Democrats in the Progressive Era.* Jackson: University of Mississippi Press, 1989. Focuses on Wilson's affiliation with the Democratic party and gives several different historical interpretations.

1548. Seltzer, Alan L. "Woodrow Wilson as 'Corporate Liberal': Toward a Reconsideration of Left Revisionist Historiography." *Western Political Quarterly* 30, no. 2 (June 1977): 183–212. A critique of New Left interpretations of Wilson as a corporate liberal.

1549. Strum, Phillippa. "Louis D. Brandeis, The New Freedom and The State." *Mid-America* 69 (October 1987): 105–24. Contends that the New Freedom would not have been possible without Brandeis's vision.

1550. Sullivan, Mark. *Our Times: The United States, 1900–1925.* 6 vols. New York: Charles Scribner's Sons, 1926–1935. Written by a journalist. Volume 5, *Over Here*, covers World War I; and volume 6, *The Twenties*, includes the latter part of the Wilson administration.

1551. Swisher, Carl Brent. "Woodrow Wilson and the New Freedom." In *American Constitutional Development*, 567–95. Boston: Houghton, Mifflin Co., 1943. Devotes a chapter to a discussion of several changes in American government brought about by the New Freedom.

1552. Tindall, George Brown. *The Emergence of the New South, 1913–1945*, 1–69. Baton Rouge: Louisiana State University Press, 1967. The first two chapters discuss Wilson's special relationship with the South and the effects that his war policies had on the region.

1553. Wiebe, Robert H. *Businessmen and Reform: A Study of the Progressive Movement.* Cambridge: Harvard University Press, 1962. Includes a description of the impact of Wilson's policies on American business.

1554. ———. *The Search for Order, 1877–1920.* New York: Hill and Wang, 1967. Argues that during this period a fundamental shift in American values occurred, from small town mores to those of a rising, bureaucratic middle class. Wilson featured throughout.

1555. Williams, Jack Kenny. "Roosevelt, Wilson, and the Progressive Movement." *South Atlantic Quarterly* 54 (April 1955): 207–11. Argues that progressivism began under Theodore Roosevelt, came to maturity with Wilson, and was cut short by a "world gone mad with war."

2. Agriculture, Business, and Economic Policy

1556. "Are We a Democracy?" *Public* 21 (February 8, 1918): 164–66. Deals with Wilson's economic views.

1557. Benson, Allan L. "Our New President." *Masses* 4 (May 1913): 3. A socialist's critique and appreciation of Wilson's economic theory and attempts at reform.

1558. Brownlee, W. Elliot. "Wilson and Financing the Modern State: The Revenue Act of 1916." *Proceedings of the American Philosophical Society* 129 (June 1985): 173–210. Discusses the role of the Wilson administration in enacting the Revenue Act of 1916 and explains the implications of the act.

1559. Bullock, Charles T., et al. "The Balance of Trade of the United States." *Review of Economic Statistics* 1 (July 1919): 215–66. Includes a description of the United States' expanding international trade under Wilson, 1914–1919.

1560. Burdick, Frank. "Woodrow Wilson and the Underwood Tariff." *Mid-America* 50, no. 4 (October 1968): 272–90. Reinterprets the Underwood Tariff Act and Wilson's role in its passage.

1561. Chandler, Lester V. "Wilson's Monetary Reform." In **1149**, 123–31. Discusses the passage of the Federal Reserve Act of 1913.

1562. Connolly, Christopher P. "Business Men against Wilson." *Everybody's Magazine* 35 (October 1916): 412–21. Records the discontent of businessmen from around the country with the Wilson administration.

1563. Cuff, Robert D. "Woodrow Wilson's Missionary to American Business, 1914–1915: A Note." *Business History Review* 43 (Winter 1969): 545–51. Assesses the role of Charles Ferguson in winning the support of big business.

1564. Cuff, Robert D., and Melvin I. Urofsky. "The Steel Industry and Price-Fixing during World War I." *Business History Review* 44 (1970): 291–306. Discusses the bargaining between the Wilson administration and the steel industry and Wilson's desire to coordinate production without interfering in the private sector.

1565. Davis, George C., Jr. "The Federal Trade Commission: Promise and Practice in Regulating Business, 1900–1929." Ph.D. diss., University of Illinois, 1969. Traces the early history of the F.T.C., from its success as a major part of the New Freedom to its decline after 1920.

1566. Dimock, Marshall Edward. "Wilson the Domestic Reformer." In **1075**, 294–333. [Also published in *Virginia Quarterly Review* 32 (Autumn 1956): 546–65; and **1149**, 228–43.] Argues that Wilson's greatest achievement was his reform of the American economic system.

1567. Fetner, Gerald Lawrence. "Counsel to the Situation: The Lawyer as Social Engineer, 1900–1945." Ph.D. diss., Brown University, 1973. Includes a discussion of a critique made by Wilson and others of the lawyer as an adjunct to the corporation.

1568. Fisher, Louis. *Presidential Spending Power*, 31–35. Princeton: Princeton University Press, 1975. Examines presidential influence on federal spending with some attention to Wilson.

1569. Garrison, Elisha E. *Roosevelt, Wilson, and the Federal Reserve Law: A Story of the Author's Relations with Theodore Roosevelt, Woodrow Wilson, and Other Public Men, Principally as Related to the Development and Writing of the Federal Reserve Law*. Boston: Christopher Publishing House, 1931. Discusses his involvement in writing the Federal Reserve Act.

1570. Giddings, Franklin Henry. "Mr. Wilson on the Cost of Living." *Independent* 99 (August 23, 1919): 249–50. Reviews Wilson's plan for restoring the peacetime economy.

1571. Grosscup, Peter Stenger. "Can Republicans and Progressives Unite?" *North American Review* 199 (March 1914): 353–65. Expresses distrust of Wilson's economic philosophy and considers forming a new opposition to it that does not rely on traditional, old-guard Republican thinking.

1572. Hall, Tom G. "Wilson and the Food Crisis: Agricultural Price Control during World War I." *Agricultural History* 47 (1973): 25–46. Focuses on Wilson's imposition of controls on wheat prices in 1917.

1573. Hansen, Alvin Harvey. "Woodrow Wilson as an Economic Reformer." *Virginia Quarterly Review* 32 (Autumn 1956): 566–77. Argues that Wilson was a conservative in the reform movement but saw the positive role of government in addressing social problems.

1574. Harvey, George Brinton McClellan. "Politics and Business: The President's Change of Mind." *North American Review* 200 (August 1914): 161–74. Examines the politics of Wilson's new-found desire to court business leaders.

1575. Henderson, Gerald C. *The Federal Trade Commission: A Study in Administrative Law and Procedure.* New Haven: Yale University Press, 1924. The first part covers the Wilson administration's attempts to regulate business through the F.T.C.

1576. Hill, John Wylie. "The Progressive Movement and the Graduated Income Tax, 1913–1919." Ph.D. diss. University of Texas, 1966. Traces Wilson's support of the graduated income tax.

1577. Hovenstine, E. Jay, Jr. "Lessons of World War I." *Annals of the American Academy of Political and Social Science* 238 (1945): 180–87. Criticizes the post-World War I demobilization program that led to another world conflict, warning that the same mistakes should not be made again in 1945.

1578. Howard, Vincent W. "Woodrow Wilson, the Press, and Presidential Leadership: Another Look at the Passage of the Underwood Tariff, 1913." *Centennial Review* 24 (Spring 1980): 167–84. A case study of Wilson's personal leadership in securing passage of the landmark tariff legislation.

1579. Ingle, Harry L. "The Dangers of Reaction: The Repeal of the Revenue Act of 1918." *North Carolina Historical Review* 44, no. 1 (1967): 72–88. Refers to Wilson and William G. McAdoo as progressives of the 1920s who presented a united front opposing excess profit taxes.

1580. Kaufman, Burton Ira. *Efficiency and Expansion: Foreign Trade Organization in the Wilson Administration, 1913–1921.* Contributions in American History, 34. Westport, Conn.: Greenwood Press, 1974. Contends that the Wilson administration fundamentally altered American foreign commercial policy by integrating foreign trade activity and by defining new business-government relationships aimed at trade promotion.

1581. ———. "The Organizational Dimension of United States Economic Foreign Policy, 1900–1920." *Business History Review* 46 (1972): 17–44. Discusses the means by which American businesses became more competitive and expanded abroad and Wilson's doubts about some of those measures.

1582. _____ . "Wilson's 'War Bureaucracy' and Foreign Trade Expansion." *Prologue* 6, no. 1 (1974): 19–31. Examines wartime coordination and centralization of economic activity, including trade.

1583. Kenkel, Joseph C. "The Tariff Commission Movement: The Search for a Nonpartisan Solution of the Tariff Question." Ph.D. diss., University of Maryland, 1962. Argues that business interests and difficulties arising from World War I forced Wilson to change his position and support the creation of a tariff commission in 1916.

1584. Klebaner, Benjamin J. "Potential Competition and the American Anti-Trust Legislation of 1914." *Business History Review* 38 (1964): 163–85. Argues that progressives hoped to use the Clayton Antitrust Act and the Federal Trade Commission Act to restore competition as a way of regulating trusts.

1585. Laughlin, J. Laurence. *The Federal Reserve Act: Its Origins and Problems.* New York: Macmillan Co., 1933. Concludes that Wilson led the campaign for responsible banking reform.

1586. Link, Arthur S. "The Federal Reserve Policy and the Agricultural Depression of 1920–1921." *Agricultural History* 20 (July 1946): 166–75. [Also published in **1155**, 330–48.] Describes the backlash against the Federal Reserve as farm prices plummeted in late 1920.

1587. Low, Alfred Maurice. "American Affairs." *Living Age* 278 (July 5, 1913): 15–22. Discusses Wilson's early call to Congress to pass new tariff legislation.

1588. McCauley, Daniel J., Jr. "Trade Regulation—The Wilsonian Concepts in a Regulatory Climate." *Food Drug Cosmetic Law Journal* 15 (February 1960): 93–98. Includes Wilson's recommendations regarding government proceedings against business misconduct.

1589. Miller, John Perry. "Woodrow Wilson's Contribution to Antitrust Policy." In **1149**, 132–43. Comments on the way in which Wilson built consensus for a policy of competition—avoiding the alternatives of laissez-faire on the one hand and a regulated economy on the other.

1590. "Modern Jeffersonianism." *Outlook* 103 (January 11, 1913): 59–60. Compares Wilson's views on the correct relationship between business and community interests with those of Jefferson.

1591. Moore, Thomas Lane, III. "The Establishment of a 'New Freedom' Policy: The Federal Trade Commission, 1912–1918." Ph.D. diss., University of Alabama, 1980. Finds that the agency in 1917–1918 adopted a policy consistent with the basic economic program that Wilson had advocated during the 1912 presidential campaign.

1592. "Mr. Wilson's Business Policy." *Moody's Magazine* 17 (July 1914): 344. A speech given by Wilson to the press, calling for a more conservative national policy regarding business.

1593. Noyes, Alexander Dana. *The War Period of American Finance, 1908–1925.* New York: G. P. Putnam's Sons, 1926. Comments on Wilson's financial policies and their effects.

1594. O'Brien, Dennis J. "The Oil Crisis and the Foreign Policy of the Wilson Administration." Ph.D. diss., University of Missouri, Columbia, 1974. Argues that the cooperation between oil companies and the State Department during the crisis with Mexico set a precedent for the era of international petroleum diplomacy.

1595. Poole, Robert, Jr. "Fly the Frenzied Skies." *Freeman* 20, no. 5 (1970): 273–86. Includes a section on Wilson's formation in 1915 of the National Advisory Committee on Aeronautics (NACA), which emerged after the war as an advocate for government control of aviation.

1596. "President Wilson Subjects All Foreign Trade of the United States to License Requirements." *Economics World* n.s. 15 (February 23, 1918): 265. Full text of presidential proclamation of February 14, 1918.

1597. "President Wilson and the Trade Commission." *Outlook* 106 (January 31, 1914): 233–35. Presents some recommendations of Wilson designed to control trusts, the most important of which was the establishment of the F.T.C.

1598. "President Wilson's Trust Program." *Literary Digest* 48 (January 31, 1914): 187–89. Examines the response of "big business" and the general public to Wilson's antitrust legislation.

1599. "Presidential Complacency." *New Republic* 1 (November 21, 1914): 7. Considers the benefits of Wilson's progressive views on the banking system, tariffs, and antitrust laws.

1600. "The President's Anti-Trust Message." *Outlook* 106 (January 31, 1914): 223–24. A list of Wilson's proposed legislation on commerce and its chances of success.

1601. "The President's Trust Address." *Independent* 77 (February 2, 1914): 146. Analyzes public support for Wilson's trust measures.

1602. Ratner, Sidney. *Taxation and Democracy in America.* New York: Samuel Wiley, 1967. Covers the Wilson administration's fiscal policies.

1603. Roady, Elston Edward. "Woodrow Wilson's Role as Party Leader: Trust Legislation." In **1112**, 1–27. Examines Wilson's abilities in achieving passage of the Clayton Antitrust Act and in creating the F.T.C.

1604. Seager, Henry R., and Charles A. Bulick. *Trust and Corporation Problems.* New York: Harper and Brothers, 1929. Describes the passage of the Clayton Act and the establishment of the F.T.C. as part of a longer fight for antitrust legislation.

1605. "Tariff Ideas of Roosevelt and Wilson." *Literary Digest* 45 (September 14, 1912): 408–9. Excerpts from speeches, editorials, and political cartoons about Wilson and Theodore Roosevelt on the tariff issue.

1606. Torodash, Martin. "Woodrow Wilson and the Tariff Question: The Importance of the Underwood Act in His Reform Program." Ph.D. diss., New York University, 1966.

1607. ———. "Woodrow Wilson's Views on the Tariff." *New Jersey History* 88, no. 3 (1970): 133–52. Chronicles Wilson's views from their first articulation in 1882 to his action on the tariff during his final day in office.

1608. "Trust Remedies of Roosevelt and Wilson." *Literary Digest* 45 (September 28, 1912): 499–501. Excerpts of speeches by Wilson and Theodore Roosevelt on corporate trusts and related issues. Includes editorial comments and cartoons from several newspapers.

1609. Urofsky, Melvin I. *Big Steel and the Wilson Administration: A Study in Business-Government Relations.* Columbus: Ohio State University Press, 1969. Examines Wilson's failure to acknowledge important issues in the steel industry.

1610. ———. "Wilson, Brandeis and the Trust Issue, 1912–1914." *Mid-America* 49 (January 1967): 3–28. Details the development of the relationship between Wilson and Louis Brandeis during the formation of a federal policy and agency for control of trusts.

1611. Vivian, James F. "The Last Tax-Exempt President." *Presidential Studies Quarterly* 19, no. 1 (Winter 1989): 107–16. Reviews the developments leading to the exemption of both Taft and Wilson under legislation enforcing the 16th Amendment and the aftermath.

1612. Walling, William English. "Woodrow Wilson and Business." *New Review* 1 (March 22, 1913): 364–69. Judges Wilson as an opponent of legalized monopoly but not as an opponent of the business class or a friend of the workers.

1613. West, Robert C. *Banking Reform and the Federal Reserve, 1863–1923.* Ithaca: Cornell University Press, 1977. Describes the progressives' attempts to regulate the monetary system.

1614. Willis, Henry P., and William H. Steiner. *The Federal Reserve System.* New York: Ronald Press, 1923. A mixed review of the progressives in this history of the Federal Reserve system.

1615. Wood, Richardson. "Morgan, Wilson, and Ford: Their Ideas about Money." *American Monthly Review of Reviews* 94 (July 1936): 31–34. Compares the opinions of John Morgan, Woodrow Wilson, and Henry Ford in relation to high-finance, the gold-standard, centralized banking, and big business.

1616. Woodward, Carl R. "Woodrow Wilson's Agricultural Philosophy." *Agricultural History* 14 (1940): 129–42. Traces the development of Wilson's ideas on agriculture.

3. Labor

1617. Adamic, Louis. "The Assassin of Wilson." *American Mercury* 21 (October 1930): 138–46. Deals with the International Workers of the World's alleged role in Wilson's collapse in Seattle in 1919 and his eventual death.

1618. Andrews, Gregory Alan. "American Labor and the Mexican Revolution, 1910–1924." Ph.D. diss., Northern Illinois University, 1988. Asserts that the AFL's response to the Mexican Revolution was the product of an interplay between progressive forces and the tendencies toward cooperation which became more pronounced during Wilson's presidency.

1619. Best, Gary Dean. "President Wilson's Second Industrial Conference, 1919–20." *Labor History* 16, no. 4 (1975): 505–20. Discusses the proposal for representation of employees through shop committees at the Second Industrial Conference and its transformation into company unions in the 1920s.

1620. Boemeke, Manfred F. "The Wilson Administration, Organized Labor, and the Colorado Coal Strike." Ph.D. diss., Princeton University, 1983. Argues that Wilson's intervention in the Colorado coal strike was part of his plan to establish a progressive partnership between business and labor.

1621. Brown, Jerold E., and Patrick D. Reagan. *Voluntarism, Planning, and the State: The American Planning Experience, 1914–1916*. Westport, Conn.: Greenwood Press, 1988. Describes Wilson's attempts to ease tensions between striking labor and uncooperative employers.

1622. "Hughes and Wilson on the Eight-Hour Law." *Literary Digest* 53 (October 7, 1916): 875–77. Contains lengthy excerpts from speeches made by both presidential candidates on the law in question.

1623. Hurvitz, Haggai. "Ideology and Industrial Conflict: President Wilson's First Industrial Conference of October 1919." *Labor History* 18, no. 4 (Fall 1977): 509–24. Focuses on the ideological conflict between labor and management.

1624. Jensen, Billie Barnes. "Woodrow Wilson's Intervention in the Coal Strike of 1914." *Labor History* 15, no. 1 (Winter 1974): 63–77. Assesses the pressures on Wilson to intervene in the Colorado coalfields strikes.

1625. Johnson, Michael R. "The I.W.W. and Wilsonian Democracy." *Science and Society* 28, no. 3 (1964): 257–74. Surveys the history of the IWW and focuses on its postwar growth.

1626. Jones, Dallas Lee. "The Enigma of the Clayton Act." *Industrial and Labor Relations Review* 10 (January 1957): 201–21. Considers Wilson's contribution to the 1914 law's ambiguity about labor organizations.

1627. ———. "The Wilson Administration and Organized Labor, 1912–1919." Ph.D. diss., Cornell University, 1954. Cites Wilson as a strong supporter of the rights of labor, with the exception of the 1919 steel workers' strike.

1628. Kirkpatrick, Ivy E. "The Struggle for Industrial Democracy: Croly, Lippmann, and Weyl—1912–1917." Ph.D. diss., Texas Christian University, 1974. Describes the support of these men for Wilson and Wilson's pro-labor legislation in 1916.

1629. Larson, Simeon. "The American Federation of Labor and the Preparedness Controversy." *Historian* 37, no. 1 (1974): 67–81. Discusses the anti-military sentiments arising largely from labor interests and the shift in Wilson's thinking from relative unconcern to a policy of military preparedness.

1630. McGovern, George S. "The Colorado Coal Strike, 1913–1914." Ph.D. diss., Northwestern University, 1953. Describes the coal strike as an industrial struggle that had been gathering since the 1880s and maintains that a final proposal by Wilson convinced miners to end the strike.

1631. "Mr. Wilson Justifies the Eight-Hour Law." *Independent* 88 (October 2, 1916): 5–6. Debates the merits of Wilson's stance against Charles Hughes's opposition to the eight-hour law.

1632. "Mr. Wilson's Defense." *Nation* 103 (September 28, 1916): 293. Criticizes Wilson's recent defense of new railway labor legislation as rash and without the popular support he claims.

1633. Murray, Robert K. "Communism and the Great Steel Strike of 1919." *Mississippi Valley Historical Review* 38 (1951): 445–66. An analysis of the strike and Wilson's attempts at conciliation.

1634. ———. "Public Opinion, Labor, and the Clayton Act." *Historian* 21 (1959): 255–70. Examines Wilson's attempts to pass the Clayton Act in the face of organized labor's claims that the legislation simply maintained the status quo.

1635. "President Wilson and Union Labor." *Public* 21 (September 21, 1918): 1201–2. Contends that Wilson had no choice but to discipline the Bridgeport strikers who agreed to arbitration but rejected the arbitrator's decision.

1636. "The President's Anti-Strike Message." *Literary Digest* 53 (December 16, 1916): 1581–83. Disparate opinions concerning the right of the President to intervene in labor disputes.

1637. Smith, John S. "Organized Labor and Government in the Wilson Era, 1913–1921: Some Conclusions." *Labor History* 3, no. 3 (1962): 265–86. Deals with the new and changing relationship between the federal government and organized labor under Wilson.

1638. Watkins, Gordon S. *Labor Problems and Labor Administration in the United States during the World War*. Urbana: University of Illinois Press, 1919. Describes the steps by which Wilson formulated a labor policy and created labor administrative agencies.

1639. "Woodrow Wilson." *American Federationist* 31 (March 1924): 222–40. A tribute to Wilson's progressive leadership in labor issues.

4. Women and Woman Suffrage

1640. Buechler, Steven M. *Women's Movements in the United States*: *Woman Suffrage, Equal Rights, and Beyond*. New Brunswick: Rutgers University Press, 1990. Asserts that the suffrage movement won the vote because it built a broadly based coalition of supportive groups, gained support from Wilson and the Democratic party, and neutralized antisuffragist forces by offering multiple rationales for why women needed the vote.

1641. Caplan, Judith. "Woodrow Wilson and Women: The Formative Influences on Wilson's Attitudes toward Women." *New Jersey History* 104, no. 1–2 (1986): 22–35. Discusses the influence of Wilson's mother and wives.

1642. Flexner, Eleanor. *Century of Struggle*: *The Woman's Rights Movement in the United States*. Cambridge: Harvard University Press, 1959. How the woman suffrage movement finally convinced men that women deserved the vote.

1643. Graham, Sally Hunter. "Woodrow Wilson, Alice Paul, and the Woman Suffrage Movement." *Political Science Quarterly* 98 (Winter 1983–1984): 665–79. Discusses Wilson's attempts to silence the criticism of American suffragists.

1644. Grimes, Alan Pendleton. *The Puritan Ethic and Woman Suffrage*. New York: Oxford University Press, 1967. Describes Wilson's important role in reforming education, lifting immigration restrictions, and becoming involved in suffrage efforts.

1645. Hendrickson, Rick. "Mother's Day and the Mother's Day Shrine: A History." *Upper Ohio Valley Historical Review* 13, no. 2 (1984): 2–4. Recounts events leading to Wilson's proclamation of Mother's Day in 1914.

1646. Kraditor, Aileen S. *The Ideas of the Woman Suffrage Movement, 1890–1920*. New York: Columbia University Press, 1965. Discusses the political pressures employed by suffragists to get Wilson to support them.

1647. Lunardini, Christine Anne. *From Equal Suffrage to Equal Rights*: *The National Woman's Party, 1913–1923*. Ph.D. diss., Princeton University, 1981.

1648. ———. *From Equal Suffrage to Equal Rights*: *Alice Paul and the National Woman's Party, 1910–1928*. New York: New York University Press, 1986. The reinvigoration of the suffrage movement through mass demonstrations, lobbying, and picketing.

1649. Lunardini, Christine Anne, and Thomas J. Knock. "Woodrow Wilson and Woman Suffrage: A New Look." *Political Science Quarterly* 95, no. 4 (Winter 1980–1981): 655–71. Discusses Wilson's conversion to support the 19th Amendment.

1650. McFarland, Charles K., and Nevin E. Neal. "The Reluctant Reformer: Woodrow Wilson and Woman Suffrage, 1913–1920." *Rocky Mountain Social Science Journal* 11, no. 2 (1974): 33–43. Wilson's support came gradually and only under pressure.

1651. "The President and the Suffragists." *Literary Digest* 47 (December 20, 1913): 1209–11. Discusses the opinions of several suffragists after Wilson's brief statements to Congress about suffrage.

1652. Scott, Anne Firor, and Andrew Mackay Scott. *One Half the People*: *The Fight for Woman Suffrage*. Philadelphia: J. B. Lippincott & Co., 1975. Includes a chapter on Wilson's education about women's issues.

1653. Snapp, Meredith A. "Defeat the Democrats: The Congressional Union for Woman Suffrage in Arizona, 1914 and 1916." *Journal of the West* 14 (October 1975): 131–39. Details two woman suffrage campaigns against the incumbent party, with the one in 1916 particularly directed against Wilson.

1654. Trecker, Janice L. "The Suffrage Prisoners." *American Scholar* 41 (1972): 409–23. Describes the intense protesting at the White House by suffragists during 1917.

1655. "Woodrow Wilson for Suffrage." *Literary Digest* 51 (October 16, 1915): 827–28. Outlines Wilson's conversion to the movement.

5. Prohibition

1656. Asbury, Herbert. *The Great Illusion*: *an Informal History of Prohibition*. New York: Greenwood Press, 1968. Explains that Wilson's approval of national prohibition was caused by entry into World War I and not from pressures executed by the "drys" such as the Anti-Saloon League.

1657. Blocker, Jack S. *Retreat from Reform*: *the Prohibition Movement in the United States, 1890–1913*. Westport, Conn.: Greenwood Press, 1976. By 1917 even Wilson had to negotiate with the Anti-Saloon League for the postponement of wartime prohibition.

1658. Cashman, Sean Dennis. *Prohibition*: *the Lie of the Land*. New York: The Free Press, 1981. Argues that because of his background, Wilson might have been sympathetic to prohibition, but his political instincts opposed it until the end of his career.

1659. Kerr, K. Austin. *Organized for Prohibition: A New History of the Anti-Saloon League*. New Haven: Yale University Press, 1985. Before 1912 the Anti-Saloon League applauded Wilson for his progressive reforms in New Jersey, but after Wilson became President he equivocated and lost support from the "drys."

1660. Kobler, John. *Ardent Spirits: The Rise and Fall of Prohibition*. New York: Putnam, 1973. Explains that Wilson vetoed the Volstead Act because he objected that the Congress had combined wartime prohibition and constitutional prohibition.

1661. Kyvig, David E. *Repealing National Prohibition*. Chicago: University of Chicago Press, 1979. Asserts that Wilson, a temperance advocate but an opponent of prohibition, maintained an absolute neutrality toward the Eighteenth Amendment as it progressed through Congress.

1662. Merz, Charles. *The Dry Decade*. Seattle: University of Washington Press, 1931. Argues that Wilson vetoed the Volstead Act primarily because Congress had confused wartime prohibition with constitutional prohibition.

1663. Sinclair, Andrew. *Prohibition, the Era of Excess*. Boston: Little, Brown, 1962. Believes that after America rejected his League proposal, Wilson turned toward supporting national prohibition.

1664. Timberlake, James H. *Prohibition and the Progressive Movement, 1900–1920*. Cambridge: Harvard University Press, 1963. Explains that Wilson never used prohibition as a political issue and in 1919 vetoed the Volstead Act because he believed that there was no reason for war prohibition or its enforcement.

6. Children

1665. Abbott, Grace. *The Child and the State*. 2 vols. Chicago: University of Chicago Press, 1938. Explains that in 1912 Wilson demanded the passage of a child labor bill which later resulted in the passage of the Keating-Owen bill, the first federal child labor law.

1666. Bradbury, Dorothy E. *Five Decades of Action for Children: A History of the Children's Bureau*. Washington, D.C.: Government Printing Office, 1962. Describes the growth of the Children's Bureau during the Wilson administration.

1667. Bremner, Robert H., ed. *Children and Youth in America: A Documentary History. Vol. II: 1866–1932*. Cambridge, Mass.: Harvard University Press, 1971. Mentions special conferences called by Theodore Roosevelt, Wilson, and Hoover which considered the welfare of children and pointed to the importance of preventing the break-up of the home on the grounds of poverty alone.

1668. _____. *From the Depths: The Discovery of Poverty in the United States*. New York: New York University Press, 1967. Describes child labor reform legislation passed during the Wilson administration as well as the activities of the National Child Labor Committee.

1669. Cox, J. Robert. "The Rhetoric of Child Labor Reform: An Efficacy—Utility Analysis." *Quarterly Journal of Speech* 60 (October 1974): 359–70. Explains the Congressional battle for the passage of the Keating-Owen child labor bill which Wilson signed into law on September 1, 1916.

1670. Davidson, Elizabeth H. *Child Labor Legislation in the Southern Textile States*. Chapel Hill: University of North Carolina Press, 1939. Describes Wilson's efforts to encourage Congress to pass a child labor bill.

1671. "The President and the Mill-Child." *Literary Digest* 53 (August 5, 1916): 290. American newspapers react to Wilson's call for a child labor law.

1672. Tiffin, Susan. *In Whose Best Interest? Child Welfare Reform in the Progressive Era*. Westport, Conn.: Greenwood Press, 1982. Refers to Wilson as an important leader in bringing together opinions concerning the welfare of children in the United States.

1673. Tobey, James A. *The Children's Bureau: Its History, Activities and Organization*. Baltimore: Johns Hopkins University Press, 1925. Explains that a Children's Year campaign was formally launched on April 6, 1918 with the approval and support of Wilson, who allotted $150,000 from the National Security and Defense appropriation for carrying on this work.

1674. Trattner, Walter I. *Crusade for the Children: A History of the National Child Labor Committee and Child Labor Reform in America*. Chicago: Quadrangle Books, 1970. Describes Wilson's support for child labor reform and his signing of the Keating-Owen bill.

1675. ———. "The First Federal Child Labor Law (1916)." *Social Science Quarterly* 50, no. 3 (1969): 507–24. Recounts Wilson's changing views on child labor laws and his support of the Keating-Owen bill, which he signed into law September 1, 1916.

1676. Wood, Stephen B. *Constitutional Politics in the Progressive Era: Child Labor and the Law*. Chicago: University of Chicago Press, 1968. Contends that as Wilson's first administration began, progressives enthusiastically heralded the efficacy of national legislation for fulfilling the reform programs.

7. Judicial System

1677. Abraham, Henry Julian. *Justices and Presidents: A Political History of Appointments to the Supreme Court*, 173–82. New York: Oxford University Press, 1985. Discusses Wilson's criteria for selecting his Supreme Court justices: Louis D. Brandeis, John H. Clarke, and James C. McReynolds.

1678. Bickel, Alexander M. and Benno C. Schmidt, Jr. *History of the Supreme Court of the United States. Vol 9: The Judiciary and Responsible Government*. New York: Publishing Co., 1984. Records Wilson's three appointments to the Court: James C. McReynolds, Louis Brandeis, and John H. Clarke.

1679. Romine, Ronald Hale. "The 'Politics' of Supreme Court Nominations from Theodore Roosevelt to Ronald Reagan: The Construction of a 'Politicization Index.'" Ph.D. diss., University of South Carolina, 1984. Analyzes Supreme Court nominations.

1680. Ross, William G. *A Muted Fury: Populists, Progressives, and Labor Unions Confront the Court, 1890–1937.* Princeton: Princeton University Press, 1994. Asserts that Wilson's 1912 election was cheered by progressives and trade unionists, who hoped that the appointment of liberal judges would reduce their conflict with the federal judiciary.

1681. White, G. Edward. *The American Judicial Tradition: Profiles of Leading American Judges.* New York: Oxford University Press, 1976. Examines Wilson's decision to appoint his Attorney General, James C. McReynolds, to the Supreme Court.

8. Immigration

1682. Boyer, Paul. *Urban Masses and Moral Order in America, 1820–1920.* Cambridge, Mass: Harvard University Press, 1978. Restates Wilson's promise that if civic loyalty were to become an effective instrument of urban social control, it had to be compelling through sustained appeals to people's feeling and emotions.

1683. Jones, Maldwyn Allen. *American Immigration.* Chicago: University of Chicago Press, 1960. Explains that upon his return to the United States from Europe in 1919 Wilson discovered that practically every immigrant group in the United States found some fault with the treaty signed at Versailles.

1684. Kraut, Alan M. *The Huddled Masses: The Immigrant in American Society, 1880–1921.* The American History Series. Arlington Heights, Il.: Harlan Davidson Inc., 1982. Maintains that despite Wilson's vetoes during the war, proponents of the literacy test, such as the Immigration Restriction League, took advantage of fears that the United States would be inundated by unfit immigrants after the war.

1685. McBride, Paul. *Culture Clash-Immigrants and Reformers, 1880–1920.* San Francisco: R and E Research Associates, 1975. Suggests that Wilson vetoed the literacy test in 1915 not because of the profound principles which he publicized but for political reasons.

1686. Parmet, Robert D. *Labor and Immigration in Industrial America.* Boston: Twayne Publishers, 1981. Describes Wilson's consistent practice of vetoing immigration restrictions.

1687. Saveth, Edward Norman. *American Historians and European Immigrants, 1875–1925,* 137–49. New York: Columbia University Press, 1948. Explains Wilson's positive views on the large influx of immigrant populations into American cities and his belief in the "melting pot" ideology.

1688. Stephenson, George M. *A History of American Immigration, 1820–1924.* Boston: Ginn and Company, 1926. Describes Wilson's objections to the literacy test bill of 1915 and how despite Wilson's veto the bill passed Congress.

1689. Vought, Hans. "Division and Reunion: Woodrow Wilson, Immigration, and the Myth of American Unity." *Journal of American Ethnic History* 13 (Spring 1994): 24–50. Asserts that Wilson sought to achieve American strength by blending together the best characteristics of every nationality and opposed Lodge's nativist view that American civilization must be based on an Anglo-Saxon foundation.

1690. Zeidel, Robert F. "The Literacy Test for Immigrants: A Question of Progress." Ph.D. diss., Marquette University, 1986. Discusses the tightening of immigration rules during the progressive era and the passage of the literacy test bill, despite Wilson's veto.

9. African Americans

1691. Blumenthal, Henry. "Woodrow Wilson and the Race Question." *Journal of Negro History* 48, no. 1 (January 1963): 1–21. Analyzes the decreasing importance of African-Americans during Wilson's administration.

1692. Crosby, Earl W. "Progressive Segregation in the Wilson Administration." *Potomac Review* 6, no. 2 (1973): 41–57. Discusses the support for racial segregation by the southern progressive movement and by the federal government.

1693. Franklin, John Hope. "'Birth of a Nation': Propaganda as History." *Massachusetts Review* 20, no. 3 (1979): 417–34. Describes Thomas Dixon's attempts to overcome opposition to the movie and Wilson's part in its promotion.

1694. Friedman, Lawrence. "In Search of Uncle Tom: Racial Attitudes of the Southern Leadership, 1865–1920." Ph.D. diss., University of California, Los Angeles, 1967. Examines the racial attitudes of six leaders, including Wilson.

1695. Glazier, Kenneth M. "Document: W. E. B. Du Bois' Impressions of Woodrow Wilson." *Journal of Negro History* 58, no. 4 (1973): 452–59. An evaluation of Wilson and racial policy by a prominent African-American contemporary of Wilson.

1696. Green, Cleveland M. "Prejudices and Empty Promises: Woodrow Wilson's Betrayal of the Negro, 1910–1919." *Crisis* 87 (November 1980): 380–88. Traces Wilson's abandonment of African-Americans after campaigning actively for their support in 1912.

1697. Hellwig, David J. "The Afro-American Press and Woodrow Wilson's Mexican Policy, 1913–1917." *Phylon* 48 (Winter 1987): 261–270. Examines twenty journals indicating African-American reactions to United States policy in Mexico from 1913 to 1917, emphasizes the discrepancy between Wilson's eagerness to help the poor and establish democratic institutions in Mexico and his silence on the treatment of African-Americans, especially those living in the South.

1698. Kellogg, Charles Flint. *NAACP: A History of the National Association for the Advancement of Colored People, 1909–1920.* Baltimore: Johns Hopkins University Press, 1967. Includes a discussion of the NAACP's clash with the Wilson administration over its increasingly segregationist policies.

1699. Kluger, Pearl. "Progressive Presidents and Black Americans." Ph.D. diss., Columbia University, 1974. Discusses Wilson's segregationist policies and his token gestures to African-Americans.

1700. Lunardini, Christine Anne. "Standing Firm: William Monroe Trotter's Meetings with Woodrow Wilson, 1913–1914." *Journal of Negro History* 64, no. 3 (Summer 1979): 244–64. Concerns two meetings about segregation in the federal government.

1701. Meier, August. "The Negro and the Democratic Party, 1875–1915." *Phylon* 17 (1956): 173–91. Discusses attempts by black leaders to join the Democratic party, their support of Wilson, and their subsequent disillusionment.

1702. Miller, M. Sammy. "Woodrow Wilson and the Black Judge." *Crisis* 84, no. 2 (February 1977): 81–86. Deals with the reappointment of Robert H. Terrell to the municipal bench of the District of Columbia.

1703. Osborn, George Coleman. "The Problem of the Negro in Government, 1913." *Historian* 23 (May 1961): 330–47. Discusses Wilson's decision to segregate civil service employees and to exclude blacks from high office.

1704. ———. "Woodrow Wilson Appoints a Negro Judge." *Journal of Southern History* 24 (November 1958): 481–93. Documents Wilson's selection of Robert Terrell.

1705. ———. "Woodrow Wilson Appoints Robert H. Terrell Judge of Municipal Court, District of Columbia." *Negro History Bulletin* 22, no. 5 (February 1959): 111–15. Discusses Wilson's reappointment of the African-American Republican judge and his confirmation by the Senate.

1706. Paolucci, Henry. *The South and the Presidency: From Reconstruction to Carter, A Long Day's Task.* Whitestone, N.Y.: Published for the Bagehot Council by Griffin House Publishers, 1978. Describes Wilson's 1912 pledge to reverse past racial policies in the United States.

1707. "The President and the Negro." *Nation* 97 (August 7, 1913): 114. Considers the plight of African-Americans and Wilson's intentions to promote them in his administration.

1708. "President Wilson and the Color Line." *Literary Digest* 47 (August 23, 1913): 270. Excerpts from American newspapers detailing Wilson's difficulty in gaining support from African-Americans.

1709. Rogin, Michael Paul. "'The Sword Became a Flashing Vision:' D.W. Griffith's the Birth of a Nation." *Representations* 9 (1985): 150–195. Provides a psychohistory of Griffith and his films by examining the origins of the filmmaker's racism, his attitudes toward women, and his relationship to his father. Notes the influence of his friends, Thomas Dixon and Woodrow Wilson.

1710. Rudwick, Elliott M. *Race Riot at East St. Louis, July 2, 1917.* Carbondale: Southern Illinois University Press, 1964. Includes a chapter on Wilson's refusal to authorize federal intervention.

1711. Scheiber, Jane Lang, and Harry Noel Scheiber. "The Wilson Administration and the Wartime Mobilization of Black Americans, 1917–1918." *Labor History* 10 (Summer 1969): 433–58. Analyzes the lack of civil rights legislation during Wilson's administration.

1712. Sosna, Morton. "The South in the Saddle: Racial Politics during the Wilson Years." *Wisconsin Magazine of History* 54 (1970): 30–49. Discusses Wilson's racial policies and their influences on other issues, notably woman suffrage.

1713. Steinfiel, Melvin. *Our Racist Presidents: From Washington to Nixon.* San Ramon, Calif.: Consensus, 1972. Chapter seven examines Wilson's segregationist and racial attitudes towards African-Americans.

1714. Toppin, Edgar A. "A Half-Century of Struggle for Equal Rights, 1916–1965." *Negro History Bulletin* 28, no. 8 (1965): 176–77, 188–89, 197. A survey which includes Wilson's role in segregation policies.

1715. Villard, Oswald Garrison. "The President and the Segregation at Washington." *North American Review* 198 (December 1913): 800–7. Calls Wilson a noble and inspired leader but believes that his 1912 African-American policy of full equality will be extremely difficult to implement especially in government positions.

1716. Weiss, Nancy J. "The Negro and the New Freedom: Fighting Wilsonian Segregation." *Political Science Quarterly* 84, no. 1 (1969): 61–79. Discusses African-American support of Wilson in 1912 and subsequent disillusionment with him as his administration moved toward racial segregation.

1717. Wolgemuth, Kathleen Long. "Woodrow Wilson and Federal Segregation." *Journal of Negro History* 44 (April 1959): 158–73. [Also published in *Understanding Negro History*, ed. Dwight W. Hoover, 369–82. Chicago: Quadrangle Books, 1969.] Explains Wilson's establishment of federal segregation in several governmental departments.

1718. _____ . "Woodrow Wilson's Appointment Policy and the Negro." *Journal of Southern History* 24 (November 1958): 457–71. Evaluates Wilson's policy on appointing African-Americans to high governmental positions.

10. Other Ethnic and Religious Groups

1719. Bailey, Thomas Andrew. "California, Japan, and the Alien Land Legislation of 1913." *Pacific Historical Review* 1 (1932): 36–59. Discusses Wilson's embarrassment over the anti-Japanese actions taken by the California legislature in 1906 and 1913.

1720. Bernstein, Herman. "Jewish Favor for Mr. Wilson." *Literary Digest* 54 (January 6, 1917): 24. Describes Wilson's strong support among American Jews.

1721. Buell, Raymond L. "The Development of Anti-Japanese Agitation in the United States." *Political Science Quarterly* 37 (1922): 605–38; 38 (1923): 57–81. Includes a discussion of the Wilson administration's attempts to persuade the California legislature to write a land law that did not discriminate against Japanese-Americans.

1722. Coletta, Paolo E. "'The Most Thankless Task': Bryan and the California Alien Land Legislation." *Pacific Historical Review* 36 (1967): 163–87. Analyzes the influence of Wilson's numerous distractions on Bryan's attempts to intervene on behalf of the Japanese in California.

1723. Cuddy, Joseph E. *Irish-America and National Isolationism, 1914–1920.* New York: Arno Press, 1976. Discusses the abandonment of the Democratic party by Irish-Americans over their opposition to the United States' role in World War I.

1724. Daniels, Roger. *The Politics of Prejudice: The Anti-Japanese Movement in California and the Struggle for Japanese Exclusion*, 54–60. Berkeley: University of California Press, 1962. Discusses racist writings by Wilson about Asian immigrants and how his support of exclusionary immigration laws affected his 1912 presidential campaign in California.

1725. LePore, Herbert P. "Prelude to Prejudice: Hiram Johnson, Woodrow Wilson, and the California Alien Land Law Controversy of 1913." *Southern California Quarterly* 61, no. 1 (1979): 99–110. Describes the circumstances and motives surrounding the passage of the Webb-Heney Act of 1913, which forbade land ownership by Japanese aliens.

1726. Penrose, Eldon. "Grape Juice Diplomacy and a Bit of Political Buncombe." *Pacific Historical Review* 37, no. 2 (1968): 159–62. Takes issue with Paolo E. Coletta's explication in **1722** of Bryan's involvement with the California Alien Land issue of 1913 and the motives of Wilson.

1727. "The President and the Hyphen." *Literary Digest* 59 (October 14, 1916): 935. Discusses Wilson, ethnic groups, and loyalty.

1728. Quinlan, Patrick L. "Mr. Baker's Wilson." *Commonweal* 16 (June 1, 1932): 131–32. Attempts to discredit Ray Stannard Baker's notion that there was an inherent conflict between Wilson and Irish-Americans.

1729. "Woodrow Wilson and American Catholics." *America* 96 (December 15, 1956): 319. Focuses on Wilson's conflicts with American Catholics, especially in regard to Mexico and Ireland.

I. Wilson and World War I — Domestic

1. General Works

1730. Addams, Jane. *Peace and Bread in Time of War*. New York: Macmillan Co., 1922. Reviews the war years from the viewpoint of a pacifist and social activist, with an introduction by John Dewey.

1731. Brandon, Betty Jane. "A Wilsonian Progressive: Alexander Jeffrey McKelway." *Journal of Presbyterian History* 48 (Spring 1970): 2–17. McKelway's relationship with and influence on Wilson.

1732. Chambers, Frank P. *The War behind the War, 1914–1918. A History of the Political and Civilian Fronts*. New York: Harcourt, Brace and Co., 1939. Explores the political, economic, and social forces that guided the course of World War I.

1733. Churchill, Allen. *Over Here! An Informal Re-creation of the Home Front in World War I*. New York: Dodd, Mead, and Co., 1968. An account of life on the American home front during the war, concluding that the conflict led to domestic disillusionment.

1734. Davis, Allen F. "Welfare, Reform, and World War I." *American Quarterly* 19 (Fall 1967): 516–553. [Also published as his "The Flowering of Progressivism," in **1741**, 44–56.] Argues against the view that World War I ended progressivism in the United States.

1735. Dos Passos, John R. *Mr. Wilson's War*. Garden City, N.Y.: Doubleday and Co., 1962. A narrative portraying the turbulent twenty years between McKinley's assassination and the defeat of the League of Nations.

1736. Ellis, Edward R. *Echoes of Distant Thunder: Life in the United States, 1914–1918*. New York: Coward, McCann and Geoghegan, 1975. Begins with Wilson's first inauguration and ends with the outbreak of the Red Scare, arguing that Americans were not emotionally prepared for war.

1737. Ferrell, Robert H. *Woodrow Wilson and World War I, 1917–1921*. New York: Harper & Row, 1985. Examines the second Wilson administration, paying special attention to Wilson's role as a war leader.

1738. Hirschfeld, Charles. "National Progressivism and World War I." *Mid-America* 45 (1963): 139–56. Argues that nationalist progressives viewed the war as an opportunity to push for more reforms. Wilson's policies seen as furthering their cause.

1739. Kennedy, David M. *Over Here: The First World War and American Society*. New York: Oxford University Press, 1980. Examines the war's impact on the politics, economics, culture, and society as a whole in the United States.

1740. Leuchtenburg, William E. "The Impact of the War on the American Political Economy." In **1741**, 57–70. [Also published as "The New Deal and the Analogue of War," in **1499**, 81–144.] Discusses wartime governmental controls and argues that they were a precedent for other reform movements.

1741. Link, Arthur S., ed. *The Impact of World War I.* New York: Harper & Row, 1969. A collection of essays analyzing the war's repercussions for the American people.

1742. Millis, Walter. *Road to War: America, 1914–1917.* Boston: Houghton, Mifflin Co., 1935. Deals with social, economic, political, and racial developments during American neutrality.

1743. Olssen, Erik N. "Dissent from Normalcy: Progressives in Congress, 1918–1925." Ph.D. diss., Duke University, 1970. Argues that Wilson's failings and the Red Scare created a new, more radical breed of progressive.

1744. Paxson, Frederic Logan. *American Democracy and the World War,* 3 vols. Boston: Houghton Mifflin Co., 1936–48. Shows how American democracy responded to the outbreak of a war of such magnitude.

1745. Pearlman, Michael. *To Make Democracy Safe for America: Patricians and Preparedness in the Progressive Era,* 35–186. Urbana: University of Illinois Press, 1984. Examines Wilson's policy of preparedness, World War I, and postwar America.

1746. Schaffer, Ronald. *America in the Great War: The Rise of the War Welfare State.* New York: Oxford University Press, 1991. Depicts war as welfare for large corporations in war production.

1747. Slosson, Preston William. *The Great Crusade and After, 1914–1928,* 1–129. New York: Macmillan Co., 1930. The first three chapters discuss the war years and the beginning of prohibition.

1748. Wehle, Louis Brandeis. *Hidden Threads of History: Wilson through Roosevelt.* New York: Macmillan Co., 1953. Describes Wilson's domestic policies emphasizing war production, labor, and foreign trade.

2. Preparedness, Mobilization, and War Policy

1749. Abrams, Ray H. *Preachers Present Arms: A Study of Wartime Attitudes and Activities of the Churches and the Clergy in the United States, 1914–1918.* Philadelphia: Round Table Press, 1933. Discusses the split in the American clergy during the war and finds that most were caught up in the wartime hysteria, while a vocal minority stood up against the government's repression of dissenters.

1750. "Are We Militarists?" *New Republic* 2 (March 20, 1915): 166–67. Defends the publication's support of Wilson's policy of national preparedness and criticizes the pacifists who claimed such support made the *New Republic* a militarist journal.

1751. Bean, Rodney. "President among the People." *World's Work* 31 (April 1916): 610–20. Discusses Wilson's development as a public orator and includes his 1916 tour through the Midwest, where he spoke on the importance of national preparedness.

1752. Beaver, Daniel R. "Newton D. Baker and the Genesis of the War Industries Board." *Journal of American History* 52 (1965): 43–58. Discusses Baker's difficulties in heading the mobilization for war but does not blame him for the Board's failures.

1753. Chambers, John Whiteclay, II. "Conscriptive for Colossus: The Adoption of the Draft in the United States in World War I." Ph.D. diss., Columbia University, 1973. Factors that contributed to the adoption of the draft.

1754. _____. *To Raise an Army: The Draft Comes to Modern America.* New York: Free Press, 1987. The importance of a conscripted army in major conflicts beginning with World War I. Also discusses resistance to the draft during and after World War I.

1755. Child, Clifton J. "German-American Attempts to Prevent the Exportation of Munitions of War, 1914–1915." *Mississippi Valley Historical Review* 25 (December 1938): 351–68. Failed attempts to keep the United States from supplying weapons to nations fighting against Germany.

1756. Clarkson, Grosvenor B. *Industrial America in the World War: The Strategy behind the Main Line, 1917–1918.* Boston: Houghton Mifflin Co., 1923. Examines the transition of American industry from peacetime to wartime with specific attention given to the role of the War Industries Board.

1757. Conner, Valerie Jean. *The National War Labor Board: Stability, Social Justice, and the Voluntary State in World War I.* Papers of Woodrow Wilson. Supplementary Volume. Chapel Hill: University of North Carolina Press, 1983. Explains how Wilson's NWLB worked both to centralize federal war-labor policies and to secure voluntary acceptance of its rulings.

1758. Crowell, Benedict, and Robert F. Wilson. *How America Went to War; The Giant Hand: Our Mobilization and Control of Industry and Natural Resources, 1917–1918.* New Haven: Yale University Press, 1921. Gives special attention to the machinery and resources employed.

1759. Cuff, Robert D. "We Band of Brothers—Woodrow Wilson's War Managers." *Canadian Review of American Studies* 5, no. 2 (1974): 135–48. Explores management practices and policy-making by Wilson's War Council in 1918.

1760. _____. "Woodrow Wilson and Business-Government Relations during World War I." *Review of Politics* 31 (July 1969): 385–407. Details government-business cooperation in Wilson's Advisory Commission of the Council of National Defense.

1761. "A Disentangling Alliance." *Nation* 19 (June 3, 1916): 277–78. Questions whether Wilson's recent speech favoring international guarantees of peace will convince an isolationist American electorate and Congress.

1762. "Effect of the President's Appeals to the People for National Defense." *Current Opinion* 60 (March 1916): 149–52. A review of a speech-making tour through the Midwest by Wilson on the issue of national preparedness, praising his inspirational appeals but noting a lack of detail in his plans.

1763. "Effect of the President's Pleas for Preparedness." *Literary Digest* 52 (February 12, 1916): 359–61. Praise for Wilson from the national press for his call for national preparedness.

1764. "Evasions by Mr. Wilson." *New Republic* 5 (November 13, 1915): 29–30. Criticizes the vagueness of Wilson's first national speech on preparedness.

1765. Finnegan, John Patrick. *Against the Spector of the Dragon: The Campaign for American Military Preparedness, 1914–1917.* Westport, Conn.: Greenwood Press, 1974. Concludes that Wilson provided little leadership either for or against preparedness, partly because of the political sensitivity of the issue and partly because of his own aversion to military matters.

1766. Genders, William L. "Woodrow Wilson and the 'Preparedness Tour' of the Midwest, January-February, 1916." *Australasian Journal of American Studies* (Australia) 9, no. 1 (1990): 75–81. Analyzes contemporary newspaper reports and evaluates the effectiveness of Wilson's tour in raising regional support for the idea of preparedness as national defense.

1767. Gilbert, Charles. *American Financing of World War I.* Westport, Conn.: Greenwood Publishing Corporation, 1970. Examines economic panic and prosperity during the years 1914–1916; the actual financing of the war 1916–1920; and the lasting effects of wartime finance.

1768. Glass, Carter. "The Integrity of a United States President." *Vital Speeches of the Day* 2 (January 27, 1936): 275–77. Stout defense in the Senate on January 17, 1936, against a charge made there two days earlier that Wilson yielded to pressure from banking's House of Morgan to drag the nation into war.

1769. Harvey, George Brinton McClellan. "President at Sea." *North American Review* 203 (March 1916): 321–31. A blistering criticism of Wilson's national defense policies.

1770. Hessen, Robert. "Charles Schwab and the Shipbuilding Crisis of 1918." *Pennsylvania History* 38, no. 4 (1971): 389–99. Discusses Wilson's appointment of Schwab as head of the Emergency Fleet Corporation, which was designed to speed up ship production.

1771. Hoover, Herbert Clark. *The Hoover-Wilson Wartime Correspondence, September 24, 1914, to November 11, 1918,* ed. Francis William O'Brien. Ames: Iowa State University Press, 1974. Presents correspondence between Wilson and Food Administrator Herbert Hoover explaining the food situation during World War I.

1772. Hurley, Edward Nash. *The Bridge to France*. Philadelphia: J. B. Lippincott Co., 1927. Details the development of the United States Shipping Board and the Emergency Fleet Corporation.

1773. "If the United States Should Go to War." *Scientific American* 116 (February 17, 1917): 168. Argues that if America is drawn into the world war, America would be the decisive factor; however, supplying and supporting American soldiers in Europe may prove to be difficult.

1774. Johnson, James P. "The Wilsonians as War Managers: Coal and the 1917–18 Winter Crisis." *Prologue* 9, no. 4 (1977): 193–208. Describes government regulation of the coal industry, administrators' attitudes toward coal producers, and the effects on war production.

1775. Kerr, K. Austin. "Decision for Federal Control: Wilson, McAdoo, and the Railroads, 1917." *Journal of American History* 54, no. 3 (1967): 550–60. Discusses Wilson's and McAdoo's decision to have the government take over the railroads during the war.

1776. Koistinen, Paul A. C. "The 'Industrial-Military Complex' in Historical Perspective: World War I." *Business History Review* 41 (1967): 378–403. Examines the legacy of government-business relations formed during the mobilization for World War I.

1777. Lael, Richard L., and Linda R. Killen. "The Pressure of Shortage: Platinum Policy and the Wilson Administration during World War I." *Business History Review* 56 (1982): 545–58. Explains why the Wilson administration placed few controls on the platinum market, even though it was a vital source for the war effort.

1778. Littell, Philip. "Books and Things." *New Republic* 6 (February 19, 1916): 77. Deals with the controversy between Wilson and Garrison over preparedness.

1779. Mooney, Chase C., and Martha E. Layman. "Some Phases of the Compulsory Military Training Movement, 1914–1920." *Mississippi Valley Historical Review* 38 (March 1952): 633–56. Discusses the attempts by Wilson to require a permanent military draft and his ultimate failure after the war.

1780. Mullendore, William Clinton. *History of the United States Food Administration, 1917–1919*. Stanford: Stanford University Press, 1941. Summarizes the work and purposes of the United States Food Administration.

1781. "Multitude of Counsels: Mr. Wilson's Preparedness Speeches." *Nation* 102 (February 3, 1916): 123. A discussion of Wilson's attempts to sell his ideas on the urgency of rearming for war.

1782. Nash, Gerald D. "Experiments in Industrial Mobilization: WIB and NRA." *Mid-America* 45 (1963): 157–74. Describes how Franklin Roosevelt used Wilson's War Industries Board as a model for his own National Recovery Administration.

1783. ————. "Franklin D. Roosevelt and Labor: The World War I Origins of the Early New Deal Policy." *Labor History* 1 (1960): 39–52. Traces the origins of Roosevelt's labor policy to his earlier work in Wilson's war administration.

1784. "Our State of Preparedness for War." *Literary Digest* 54 (February 17, 1917): 385–87. Argues that America's navy and army are unprepared for European action.

1785. Paxson, Frederick Logan. "The American War Government, 1917–1918." *American Historical Review* 26 (1920): 54–76. Focuses on the organization of the American government for war and the restructuring of military and civil services.

1786. Piper, John F., Jr. *The American Churches in World War I.* Athens: Ohio University Press, 1985. Argues that most churches did support the war effort without celebrating the war itself.

1787. "President Eliot's Support of President Wilson." *Outlook* 114 (October 4, 1916): 254–55. Believes that **953** which gave support to Wilson failed to address Wilson's many mistakes.

1788. "The President and Preparedness." *Nation* 101 (October 21, 1915): 485. An analysis of Wilson's support for rearmament and the subsequent effect it will have on other world powers.

1789. "President Wilson and National Defense." *Outlook* 111 (November 17, 1915): 641–42. Describes a speech made by Wilson, recommending a moderate increase in the regular army and the training of 400,000 citizen soldiers.

1790. "The President's Preparedness Tour." *Independent* 85 (February 14, 1916): 216–17. Suggests that Wilson's emphasis on preparedness is born of his desire to maintain both the honor of the United States and the Monroe Doctrine, and to be ready in case America is forced to go to war.

1791. "The President's Program of Preparedness." *Independent* 84 (December 20, 1915): 455–56. Analyzes Wilson's call for a military buildup and the economic requisites associated with it.

1792. "The President's Speech at Indianapolis." *Nation* 100 (January 14, 1915): 41. A description of Wilson's speech on Andrew Jackson, presented in Indianapolis.

1793. "The President's Speech before the Manhattan Club of New York." *Nation* 101 (November 11, 1915): 561–62. Outlines Wilson's speech, in which national defense was discussed.

1794. "The President's Speeches on Preparedness." *Outlook* 112 (February 9, 1916): 291–92. Analyzes Wilson's call for preparedness by examining the text of various speeches.

1795. Pringle, Henry Fowles. "T.R.'s Feud with Wilson." *Outlook* 159 (December 30, 1931): 560–62+. A segment from the book *Roosevelt: A Biography*, describing

Roosevelt's disagreement with Wilson over American pacifism in the face of German militarism.

1796. ———. "Shifting Administration: Mr. Wilson's Changes on Preparedness, the Tariff Commission, and Other Policies." *Nation* 102 (February 17, 1916): 189–91. Examines Wilson's positions on preparedness, the tariff commission, and other policies.

1797. Ward, Robert D. "The Origins and Activities of the National Security League, 1914–1919." *Mississippi Valley Historical Review* 47 (1960): 51–65. Traces the development of the National Security League and its advocacy of such ideas as compulsory military training.

1798. Ward, Robert D., and Fredrick W. Brogdan. "The Revolt against Wilson: Southern Leadership and the Democratic Caucus of 1920." *Alabama Historical Quarterly* 38, no. 2 (1976): 144–57. Describes Wilson's struggle for military training.

1799. Willoughby, William Franklin. *Government Organization in War Time and After: A Survey of Federal Civil Agencies Created for the Prosecution of the War.* New York: D. Appleton and Co., 1919. Outlines the duties of a wartime President.

3. Peace Movements

1800. Addams, Jane. "President Wilson's Policies." *Survey* 47 (January 28, 1922): 659–63. Excerpts from **1730**. Expresses a critical, pacifist view of Wilson's handling of the war.

1801. Chambers, John Whiteclay, II, ed. *The Eagle and the Dove: The American Peace Movement and United States Foreign Policy, 1900–1922.* 2nd ed. Syracuse: Syracuse University Press, 1991. Includes numerous Wilson documents relating to the development of early pacifist organizations into a broader social movement to restructure international relations.

1802. Chatfield, Charles. *For Peace and Justice: Pacifism in America, 1914–1941.* Knoxville: University of Tennessee Press, 1971. Analyzes interaction between Wilson and organized pacifists.

1803. ———. "World War I and the Liberal Pacifists in the United States." *American Historical Review* 75 (December 1970): 1920–37. Explains the negative connotation of the word "pacifist" during World War I.

1804. Cook, Blanche Wiesen. "Woodrow Wilson and the Antimilitarists, 1914–1917." Ph.D. diss., Johns Hopkins University, 1970. Wilson and the peace movement in the years leading up to American entry into World War I.

1805. DeBenedetti, Charles. *Origins of the Modern American Peace Movement, 1915–1929.* Millwood, N.Y.: KTO Press, 1978. Describes the dynamic relationship between Wilson and organized groups that advocated international peace programs.

1806. Edwards, John Carver. "The Price of Political Innocence: The Role of the National Security League in the 1918 Congressional Election." *Military Affairs* 42, no. 4 (1978): 190–95. Chronicles the development and views of the organization that opposed American military preparedness before World War I.

1807. Filene, Peter. "The World Peace Foundation and Progressivism, 1910–1918." *New England Quarterly* 36 (1963): 478–501. Compares the challenges to pacifism and to Wilson's "New Freedom" by the world conflict.

1808. "Mr. President, We Demand Peace and Democracy at Home as Well as Abroad." *Appeal to Reason* (March 1, 1919): 2. Appeals for amnesty to radicals prosecuted under the Espionage Act.

1809. Patterson, David S. "Woodrow Wilson and the Mediation Movement, 1914–17." *Historian* 33 (August 1971): 535–56. Examines pacifist pressures on Wilson to end the war by bringing the belligerents to the conference table.

1810. Peterson, Horace C., and Gilbert C. Fite. *Opponents of War, 1917–1918.* Seattle: University of Washington Press, 1957. Examines the conflict between prowar and antiwar groups. Also covers the persecution of immigrants, African-Americans, teachers, conscientious objectors, and others.

1811. "Swinging around the Circle." *Survey* 36 (April 22, 1916): 95–96. Reports on mass protest meetings organized in New York and ten other major American cities in opposition to Wilson's campaign for naval and military preparedness.

1812. Taylor, Alan John Percivale. *The Troublemakers: Dissent over Foreign Policy, 1792–1939,* 132–66. London: Hamish Hamilton, 1957. Originally the Ford Lectures delivered at the University of Oxford in 1956 dealing with the English radical tradition. Briefly portrays Wilson as the radicals saw him.

1813. Weinstein, James. "Anti-War Sentiment and the Socialist Party, 1917–1918." *Political Science Quarterly* 74 (1959): 215–39. Traces Socialist party opposition to the war and advocacy of a peaceful resolution.

1814. "Will the Peace League Prevent War?" *Literary Digest* 60 (March 1, 1919): 11–13. The American press on how to make the League more effective.

4. Propaganda and Civil Liberties

1815. Beck, James Montgomery. *The War and Humanity.* New York: G. P. Putnam's Sons, 1916. A collection of essays criticizing the handling of World War I and calling for a greater sense of moral awareness to replace the indifference Americans felt towards violations of human rights in times of war.

1816. Buchanan, Russell. "European Propaganda and American Public Opinion 1914–1917." Ph.D. diss., Stanford University, 1935.

1817. Coben, Stanley. "A Study in Nativism: The American Red Scare of 1919–1920." *Political Science Quarterly* 79 (March 1964): 52–75. [Also published as his

"Postwar Upheaval: The Red Scare," in **1741**, 100–11.] A study of American xenophobia and political discrimination in the years immediately following World War I.

1818. Commager, Henry Steele. "Woodrow Wilson as Propagandist." *Scholastic* 41 (November 9, 1942): 9. Calls Wilson the "greatest propagandist of the Twentieth Century."

1819. Cornwell, Elmer Eckert, Jr. "Wilson, Creel, and the Presidency." *Public Opinion Quarterly* 23 (Summer 1959): 189–202. Public relations and communication during Wilson's presidency.

1820. Creel, George C. *How We Advertised America: The First Telling of the Amazing Story of the Committee on Public Information that Carried the Gospel of Americanism to Every Corner of the Globe.* New York: Harper and Brothers, 1920. An account of American publicity and propaganda campaigns at home and abroad during World War I.

1821. Johnson, Donald Oscar. "Wilson, Burleson, and Censorship in the First World War." *Journal of Southern History* 28, no. 1 (Fall 1962): 46–58. Focuses on the Postmaster General's rigorous enforcement of the Espionage Act of 1917.

1822. Lasswell, Harold D. *Propaganda Technique in the World War.* New York: Alfred A. Knopf, 1927. A general discussion of the role of propaganda in controlling public opinion and specifically in directing American public opinion during the First World War.

1823. Mock, James R., and Cedric Larson. *Words That Won the War: The Story of the Committee on Public Information, 1917–1919.* Princeton: Princeton University Press, 1939. A study of America's initial propaganda efforts and its energetic leader, George Creel.

1824. Murray, Robert K. *Red Scare: A Study in National Hysteria, 1919–1920.* Minneapolis: University of Minnesota Press, 1955. Includes material on the raids by Wilson's Attorney General.

1825. Nicholas, Wayne Alfred. "Crossroads Oratory: A Study of the Four Minute Men of World War I." Ph.D. diss., Columbia University, 1953. Deals with the more than 70,000 volunteer speakers, conceived by a group of young businessmen in Chicago and mobilized by the Committee on Public Information, to build national morale.

1826. "The President's Indignant Arraignment of Disloyal Americans." *Current Opinion* 60 (January 1916): 1–1b. Newspaper opinions concerning Wilson's denunciation in an address to Congress of unpatriotic American activity.

1827. Preston, William, Jr. *Aliens and Dissenters: Federal Suppression of Radicals, 1903–1933.* Cambridge: Harvard University Press, 1963. Surveys the evolution of thought on the immigration question in America from 1905 to 1921, noting Wilson's approval of the IWW's repression of other immigrant radicals.

1828. Scheiber, Harry Noel. *The Wilson Administration and Civil Liberties, 1917–1921.* Cornell Studies in American History, Literature and Folklore, 6. Ithaca, N.Y.: Cornell University Press, 1960.

1829. Swisher, Carl Brent. "Civil Liberties in War Time." *Political Science Quarterly* 55 (September 1940): 321–47. Argues that certain wartime policies had a grossly negative impact on the protection of civil liberties.

1830. Vaughn, Stephen L. *Holding Fast the Inner Lines: Democracy, Nationalism, and the Committee on Public Information.* Papers of Woodrow Wilson. Supplementary Volume. Chapel Hill: University of North Carolina Press, 1980. Details the creation and purposes of Wilson's Committee on Public Information.

1831. Viereck, George Sylvester. *Spreading Germs of Hate.* New York: Horace Liveright, 1930. A book about World War I propaganda, by the editor of the pro-German weekly, *The Fatherland.* With a foreword by Colonel Edward M. House.

1832. Ward, Larry W. "'Official' European War Films in Neutral America, 1914–1917." *Indiana Social Studies Quarterly* 34 (1981): 57–68. Explains how Wilson adopted many of the ideas from early European films for his own propaganda campaign in 1917.

1833. Warth, Robert D. "The Palmer Raids." *South Atlantic Quarterly* 48, no. 1 (1949): 1–23. Describes the 1920s raids of Attorney General Mitchell A. Palmer.

5. Politics

1834. Dayer, Roberta Allbert. "Strange Bedfellows: J. P. Morgan & Co., Whitehall and the Wilson Administration during World War I." *Business History* (Great Britain) 18, no. 2 (1976): 127–51. Deals with the suspicions of Wilson administration personnel regarding J. P. Morgan & Co.'s role as British agent for purchasing and banking during World War I.

1835. Draper, Theodore. "Intellectuals in Politics." *Encounter* (Great Britain) 49, no. 6 (1977): 47–60. Discusses the increased political engagement of intellectuals during and after World War I.

1836. ———. "The Versailles Treaty and the Irish-Americans." *Journal of American History* 55, no. 3 (December 1968): 582–98. Traces growing Irish-American sentiment against the Treaty of Versailles.

1837. Gerson, Louis L. *The Hyphenate in Recent American Politics and Diplomacy.* Lawrence: University of Kansas Press, 1964. The influence of immigrant groups on Wilson's consideration of a variety of issues related to World War I.

1838. Holman, H. L. A. *How!: How to Organize Society: An Open Letter to President Wilson.* Dayton: Miami Valley Socialist, [1917?].

1839. "In the Next Four Years." *New Republic* 10 (March 3, 1917): 123–24. Calls on Wilson to reform the federal government so that it does not rely directly on his leadership to function and to pass legislation.

1840. Keen, Jean B. "Wilson in Iowa." *Palimpsest* 29 (October 1948): 310–16. Discusses two trips to Iowa by Wilson: in 1916 during the American turn to preparedness, and in 1919 during the fight over the League of Nations.

1841. Lawrence, David. "A Crisis in the Leadership of President Wilson." *Outlook* 120 (December 4, 1918): 528–29. Discusses dissatisfaction within the Democratic party over Wilson's handling of preparations for the peace conference.

1842. Link, Arthur S. "The Cotton Crisis, the South, and Anglo-American Diplomacy, 1914–1915." In *Studies in Southern History in Memory of Albert Ray Newsome, 1894–1951*, ed. J. Carlyle Sitterson, 122–38. Chapel Hill: University of North Carolina Press, 1957. [Also published in **1155**, 309–29.] Explores a phase of the struggle between Wilson and the southern agrarian radicals.

1843. ———. "The Middle West and the Coming of the First World War." *Ohio State Archaelogical and Historical Quarterly* 62 (April 1953): 109–21. Describes midwestern opposition to intervention.

1844. Newby, I. A. "States' Rights and Southern Congressmen during World War I." *Phylon* 24 (1963): 34–50. Maintains that the Wilson administration undermined states' rights and that the southern congressmen knowingly supported these measures.

1845. O'Grady, Joseph P. "Irish-Americans, Woodrow Wilson, and Self-Determination." *Records of the American Catholic Historical Society of Philadelphia* 74, no. 3 (1963): 159–73. Discusses Wilson's views on Irish freedom and their resolution at Versailles.

1846. O'Grady, Joseph P., ed. *The Immigrants' Influence on Wilson's Peace Policies.* Lexington: University of Kentucky Press, 1967. An analysis of the roles played by ethnic groups in Wilson's decision-making process.

1847. "The President to Congress and the People." *Nation* 104 (March 1, 1917): 228. A report of Wilson's speech to Congress, asking for greater executive power because of the ever-widening war in Europe.

1848. "A Presidential Homily." *Literary Digest* 52 (January 1, 1916): 23. A report on Wilson's message to the Federal Council of Churches, in which he contrasted cooperation with organization.

1849. Price, Theodore Hazeltine. "President Wilson and Prosperity." *Outlook* 113 (August 23, 1916): 998–1002. Insists that the economic prosperity in the United States is due to the Wilson administration and is not coincidental to the war in Europe.

1850. Shapiro, Stanley. "The Great War and Reform: Liberals and Labor, 1917–1919." *Labor History* 12 (1971): 323–44. Concludes that the fight over Wilson's peace proposals, and not the war itself, ended the period of liberal reform.

1851. Trattner, Walter I. "Progressivism and World War I: A Re-appraisal." *Mid-America* 44 (1962): 131–45. Disagrees with the prevalent notion that progressives were uniformly in favor of American participation.

1852. "A War Program for Liberals." *New Republic* 10 (March 31, 1917): 249–50. Provides a set of eight principles for liberals to follow during wartime.

1853. "Why Is Roosevelt Unjailed?" *Nation* 107 (November 2, 1918): 546. A blistering criticism of Theodore Roosevelt for his verbal assaults on Wilson. Suggests, somewhat mockingly, that Roosevelt be arrested for violation of the Espionage Act.

J. Wilson and Foreign Affairs

1. General Works

1854. Adams, P. L. "Woodrow Wilson and the Idealism of American Foreign Policy." *Gordon Review* 4 (Summer 1958): 51–61. Praises Wilson's commitment to morality in his foreign policy but recognizes that he made mistakes, particularly in dealing with the Mexican conflict. Concludes that while many of his contemporaries maligned him, history judges him well.

1855. Anderson, George La Verne, ed. *Issues and Conflicts: Studies in Twentieth Century Diplomacy.* Lawrence: University of Kansas Press, 1959. Relevant articles listed by author.

1856. Asinof, Eliot. *1919: America's Loss of Innocence.* New York: D. I. Fine, 1990. Detailed examination of American society and politics following World War I.

1857. Bailey, Thomas Andrew. "America's Emergence as a World Power: The Myth and the Verity." *Pacific Historical Review* 30 (1961): 1–16. Reveals historical incongruities present in American history texts.

1858. Banks, William. "President Wilson in World Politics." *Canadian Magazine* 55 (July 1920): 241–46. Gives credit to Wilson for forcing the United States to become an active participant in world politics, permanently altering the American public's perception of foreign affairs.

1859. Barclay, Sir Thomas. *Le President Wilson et l'Evolution de la Politique Etrangere des Etats-Unis.* Paris: Colin, 1918.

1860. Bell, Herbert Clifford Francis. "Genesis of Wilson's Foreign Policy." *Thought* 23 (December 1948): 657–64. The influence of Christian teachings on Wilson's foreign policy.

1861. Bell, Sidney. *Righteous Conquest: Woodrow Wilson and the Evolution of the New Diplomacy.* Port Washington, N.Y.: Kennikat Press, 1972. Reviews the democracy, peace, and stability of Wilson's "New Diplomacy" policy.

1862. Bellve, Mariano. "Wilson and Monroe." *Living Age* 305 (May 22, 1920): 457–59. Praises Wilson's efforts in trying to create a lasting world peace which is not focused exclusively on the United States' interests.

1863. Beloff, Max. "Self Determination Reconsidered." *Confluence: An International Forum* 5, no. 3 (Autumn 1956): 195–203. Addresses the implications of self-determination and Wilson's role in unifying the concepts of nation and state.

1864. Bennett, Ira E. "Two Architects of Peace." *Christian Science Monitor Weekly Magazine* (March 17, 1945): 3, 16. Compares the methods of Wilson and Franklin D. Roosevelt for promoting world peace systems.

1865. ――――. "Two War Presidents: Mistakes Avoided, Mistakes Repeated." *Christian Science Monitor Weekly Magazine* (October 3, 1942): 7+. Discusses Wilson and Franklin D. Roosevelt.

1866. Bishirjian, Richard J. "Croly, Wilson, and the American Civil Religion." *Modern Age* 23, no. 1 (1979): 33–38. An analysis of Herbert Croly's and Wilson's views on morality in world affairs.

1867. Block, Robert Hoyt. "Southern Opinion of Woodrow Wilson's Foreign Policies, 1913–1917." Ph.D. diss., Duke University, 1968. Concludes that the majority of southern elected officials supported Wilson's foreign policies, giving him a valuable bloc of support.

1868. Buehrig, Edward Henry. "Idealism and Statecraft." *Confluence: An International Forum* 5, no. 3 (Autumn 1956): 252–63. Wilson as a case study in the tension between realism and idealism in American foreign policy.

1869. ――――. *Woodrow Wilson and the Balance of Power.* Bloomington: Indiana University Press, 1955. Discusses American trade policies before World War I, the emergence of Wilson's League of Nations, and his efforts for peace.

1870. Buehrig, Edward Henry, ed. *Wilson's Foreign Policy in Perspective.* Bloomington: Indiana University Press, 1957. A collection of lectures by scholars on several aspects of Wilson's foreign policy. Essays are listed separately by author.

1871. Burns, Richard Dean, and Donald Urquidi. "Woodrow Wilson and Disarmament: Ideas vs. Realities." *Aerospace Historian* 18, no. 4 (1971): 186–94. Describes the maneuvering over disarmament after 1917 and Wilson's shaping of an international commitment to disarm.

1872. Calhoun, Frederick Sill. *Power and Principle: Armed Intervention in Wilsonian Foreign Policy.* Kent: Kent State University Press, 1986. Argues that Wilson's instinct to reform the world was limited by a realistic understanding of the problems of using armed force.

1873. ———. *Uses of Force and Wilsonian Foreign Policy*. Kent: Kent State University Press, 1994. Analyzes Wilson's military interventions, and concludes that Wilson turned to force to promote American ideology, enforce international law, encourage international cooperation, and effect collective security.

1874. ———. "The Wilsonian Way of War: American Armed Power from Veracruz to Vladivostok." Ph.D. diss., University of Chicago, 1983. Examines the role of force in American foreign policy and analyzes each of the seven interventions undertaken by Wilson.

1875. Carroll, John M. "The Making of the Dawes Plan, 1919–1924." Ph.D. diss., University of Kentucky, 1972. Focuses on the Republicans' efforts in settling the issue of reparations, with some discussion of Wilson's economic foreign policy and his desire to create a world order based on the Open Door.

1876. Commager, Henry Steele. "Woodrow Wilson Charts the New Path." *Scholastic* 52 (May 3, 1948): 10. Discusses the rational and moral aspects of Wilson's foreign policy.

1877. Cooper, John Milton, Jr. "Progressivism and American Foreign Policy: A Reconsideration." *Mid-America* 51 (October 1969): 260–77. Examines the three different views on foreign policy held by progressives: imperialist, anti-imperialist, and liberal internationalist.

1878. Crossman, Richard Howard Stafford. "Did F.D.R. Escape Wilson's Failure? Idealism vs. Power Politics in American Foreign Policy." *Commentary* 8 (November 1949): 418–23. Argues that Franklin Roosevelt's foreign policy failures were due to his departure from the idealistic precedent set by Wilson.

1879. Dallek, Robert. *The American Style of Foreign Policy: Cultural Politics and Foreign Affairs*. New York: Mentor, 1983. Includes a chapter on Wilson's foreign policy, arguing that it was increasingly designed to save foreign peoples from themselves.

1880. Davis, Norman H. *Woodrow Wilson's Foreign Policy and Its Effect on World Peace*. Philadelphia: [s.n. 1930?]. Address before the Democratic Women's Luncheon Club of Philadelphia, March 17, 1930.

1881. Duplicate entry omitted.

1882. DeWitt, Howard A. "Hiram W. Johnson and Economic Opposition to Wilsonian Diplomacy: A Note." *Pacific Historian* 19, no. 1 (1975): 15–23. Johnson's opposition to Wilson's foreign policy, especially the League of Nations.

1883. Dexter, Byron. "Wilsonian Idealism [1913–52]." *Confluence: An International Forum* 2 (June 1953): 88–99. Believes that of the American statesmen of the last hundred years, only Wilson took the pains to establish guiding principles for future American foreign policy.

1884. Dobson, John M. *America's Ascent: The United States Becomes a Great Power, 1880–1914.* DeKalb: Northern Illinois University Press, 1978. Wilson's early foreign policies and his difficulties in reconciling altruism and national self-interest.

1885. Dodd, William Edward. "The Presidency of Woodrow Wilson—A Symposium: Wilson and the American Tradition." *Pacific Review* 1 (March 1921): 576–81. Argues that the United States has never been able to maintain an isolationist position and that Wilson's intervention was based on traditional American idealism.

1886. ———. "Woodrow Wilson, Ten Years After." *Contemporary Review* 135 (January 1929): 26–38. An admiring tribute, praising his boldness in international affairs.

1887. Dodds, Harold Willis. "Woodrow Wilson: A True Liberal." *Vital Speeches of the Day* 12 (May 15, 1946): 477–78. Argues that, in retrospect, Wilson's belief in the League of Nations and world order was not misguided.

1888. Dostert, Leon. "The Wilsonian Ideal and World Reconstruction." *World Affairs Interpreter* 13 (1942): 135–43. A plea for the reaffirmation of the Wilsonian ideal, with flexibility and sanctions, after World War II.

1889. Dougherty, Patrick T. "Catholic Opinion and United States Recognition Policy." Ph.D. diss., University of Missouri, 1963. Discusses the support of American Catholics for Wilson's policy of nonrecognition towards Latin America and the Soviet Union.

1890. Dulles, Foster Rhea. *America's Rise to World Power, 1898–1954*, 87–128. New American Nation Series. New York: Harper and Brothers, 1955. How the war and treaty negotiations affected the United States' role in international affairs.

1891. Dulles, John Foster. *Peaceful Change within the Society of Nations, Delivered at Princeton University on March 19, 1936, As One of the Stafford Little Foundation Series.* n.p., 1936. A defense of Wilson's vision of collective security by the future secretary of state.

1892. Duroselle, Jean-Baptiste. *From Wilson to Roosevelt: Foreign Policy of the United States, 1913–1945*, trans. Nancy Lyman Roelker, 3–129. Cambridge: Harvard University Press, 1963. [A translation of his *De Wilson a Roosevelt, politique exterieure des Etats-Unis, 1913–1945*. Paris: A. Colin, 1960.] Describes the "failure" and "defeat" of Wilsonian internationalism.

1893. Easum, Chester Verne. "Woodrow Wilson: Zu Seinem Hundertjahrigen Geburtstag am 28. Dezember 1956." [Woodrow Wilson: In Commemoration of the 100th Anniversary of His Birth on 28 December 1956]. *Jahrbuch fur Amerikastudien* (West Germany) 2 (1957): 8–18. Argues that Wilson's realism in foreign policy was as important as his idealism.

1894. Eddy, George Sherwood, and Kirby Page. "Freedom from International Anarchy: Woodrow Wilson." In *Makers of Freedom*, 200–30. New York: George H. Doran Co., 1926. Discusses Wilson's words and actions in the realm of foreign affairs.

1895. Eiland, Murray Lee. *Woodrow Wilson: Architect of World War II*. American University Studies. Series 9, History, vol. 113. New York: P. Lang, 1992. Argues that Wilson's untempered idealism may have posed a threat to peace.

1896. Eliot, Charles William. "Wilson's Foreign Policies." *Harper's Weekly* 59 (August 22, 1914): 177–78. Calls Wilson's actions in international affairs a great service to the republic.

1897. *Encyclopedia of American Foreign Policy: Studies of the Principal Movements and Ideas*, ed. Alexander DeConde. 3 vols. New York: Charles Scribner's Sons, 1978. Relevant articles listed by author.

1898. Ferrell, Robert H. "Woodrow Wilson and Open Diplomacy." In **1855**, 193–209. Argues that Wilson's open diplomacy was timely because the public wanted a change, because he needed a counteroffensive against the spread of Bolshevism, and because it advocated democracy around the world.

1899. Ford, Harold P. "Centennial Thoughts about Wilsonian Diplomacy." *Christianity and Crisis* 16, no. 22 (December 24, 1956): 176–78. Critiques Wilsonian diplomacy and its consequences.

1900. Fowler, Wilton B. *American Diplomatic History since 1890*. Northbrook, Ill.: A.H.M. Publishing Corp., 1975. Numerous references to Wilson, World War I, and the peace treaty.

1901. Franklin, Fabian. "Woodrow Wilson Again." *Independent* 110 (March 3, 1923): 150–52. Examines three books: **2733**; **3611**; and **3563**, to establish a framework for evaluating Woodrow Wilson's handling of foreign affairs.

1902. Gandi, Vera. "I Limiti Dell'Internazionalismo Wilsoniano." [The Limits of Wilsonian Internationalism]. *Comunita* (Italy) 35, no. 183 (1981): 96–152. Traces the evolution of Wilson's ideas on international order from a British-type liberalism to the "New Freedom."

1903. Gardner, Lloyd C. "American Foreign Policy, 1900–1921: A Second Look at the Realist Critique of American Diplomacy." In *Towards a New Past: Dissenting Essays in American History*, ed. Barton J. Bernstein, 202–31. New York: Pantheon Books, 1968. A critique of the realists, regarding Wilson as the most imperialistic of the progressive Presidents.

1904. _____. *A Covenant with Power: America and World Order from Wilson to Reagan*, 3–28. New York: Oxford University Press, 1984. Discusses Wilson's use of liberal capitalism against the threat of war.

1905. ———. "A Progressive Foreign Policy, 1900–1921." In *From Colony to Empire*: *Essays in the History of American Foreign Relations*, ed. William A. Williams, 203–51. New York: John Wiley, 1972. Argues that Wilson used the United States' assumed role of world savior to seek American economic interests overseas.

1906. ———. *Safe for Democracy*: *Anglo-American Response to Revolution, 1913–1923*. New York: Oxford University Press, 1984. Views World War I as a means by which Wilson hoped to curb revolutions around the world and establish an international order made necessary by the industrial age.

1907. ———. *Wilson and Revolutions*: *1913–1921*. Philadelphia: J. B. Lippincott Co., 1976. Interventions in Mexico and Russia, including primary documents.

1908. Gelfand, Lawrence Emerson. "The Mystique of Wilsonian Statecraft." *Diplomatic History* 7 (Spring 1983): 87–101. Examines Wilson's management of foreign policy.

1909. Glen, Johnson M. "Human Rights and United States Foreign Policy." *India Quarterly* 35 (1978): 471–90. Contends that Wilson was the first President to use human rights as a principle in the formation of foreign policy.

1910. Graebner, Norman A. *America as a World Power*: *A Realist Appraisal from Wilson to Reagan*, 1–30. Wilmington, Del.: Scholarly Resources, 1984. Argues that the United States' rejection of the League of Nations resulted from an unrealistic vision of its new role.

1911. Graham, Malbone Watson. "The Reconstruction of the International Order, 1914–1919." In *American Diplomacy in the International Community*. Albert Shaw Lectures on Diplomatic History, 1946, 122–225. Baltimore: Johns Hopkins University Press, 1948. Describes American diplomacy during Wilson's presidency.

1912. Gregory, Ross. "To Do Good in the World: Woodrow Wilson and America's Mission." In *Makers of American Diplomacy*, ed. Frank J. Merli and T. A. Wilson, 359–83. New York: Charles Scribner's Sons, 1974. Examines Wilson's foreign policy and its legacy through the 1960s.

1913. Grenville, John Ashley Soames, and George Berkeley Young. "The Quest for Social Security: Admiral Dewey and the General Board, 1900–1917." In *Politics, Strategy, and American Diplomacy*: *Studies in Foreign Policy, 1873–1917*, 297–336. New Haven: Yale University Press, 1966. Includes discussion of the Wilson presidency and policies.

1914. Harley, John Eugene. *The Heritage of Woodrow Wilson*. Los Angeles: Auspices of the Center for International Understanding, 1945. Lists Wilson's twenty-nine direct and indirect contributions to world peace and world order.

1915. Herman, Sondra R. "Woodrow Wilson: The Polity as an Instrument of National Policy." In *Eleven against War*. Hoover Institution Publications, 82,

179–216. Stanford, Calif.: Hoover Institution Press, Stanford University, 1969. Discusses Wilson's brand of internationalism and the League of Nations.

1916. Hilderbrand, Robert C. *Power and the People*: *Executive Management of Public Opinion in Foreign Affairs, 1897–1921*, 93–197. Chapel Hill: University of North Carolina Press, 1981. Analyzes the influence of public opinion on the progressive era Presidents, including Wilson.

1917. Hill, David Jayne. "President Wilson's Administration of Foreign Affairs." *North American Review* 204 (September-October 1916): 345–61, 550–74. Takes issue with Wilson's claim that his foreign policy has been a success, arguing that he has, in fact, involved American soldiers in at least two warlike incursions.

1918. Howe, Frederic C. "Dollar Diplomacy and Financial Imperialism under the Wilson Administration." *Annals of the American Academy of Political and Social Science* 68 (November 1916): 312–20. Criticizes dollar diplomacy as a form of imperialism benefitting only a small group of financiers.

1919. Huthmacher, J. Joseph, and Warren I. Susman, eds. *Wilson's Diplomacy*: *An International Symposium*. American Forum Series. Cambridge: Schenkman Publishing Co., 1973. Essays on Wilsonian foreign policy as seen from several different national perspectives. Written by Arthur S. Link, Jean-Baptiste Duroselle, Ernst Fraenkel, and Herbert G. Nicholas.

1920. Johansson, Karl Magnus. "The Inherent Dialectic of International Politics." *Statsvetenskaplig Tidskrift* (Sweden) 93, no. 3 (1990): 269–92. Examines tensions between liberal idealism and realism in North American international political thought from 1775–1990, as exemplified particularly in Wilson's approach.

1921. Johnson, Gerald White. "Wilson: Character as Statecraft." In **1251**, 20–28. Credits Wilson with the restoration of the "politics of morality" to diplomacy.

1922. Johnston, Whittle. "Reflections on Wilson and the Problems of World Peace." In **1941**, 190–231. Argues that the real meaning and merit of Wilson's foreign policies was his definition of their goals as the organization of the common interest.

1923. "Kant and Wilson on Peace without Victory." *American Monthly Review of Reviews* 55 (April 1917): 426–27. Discusses Kant's influence on Wilson's foreign policy.

1924. Katz, Milton. "Woodrow Wilson and the Twentieth Century." *Confluence*: *An International Forum* 5, no. 3 (Autumn 1956): 229–38. Portrays Wilson as a President who saw the emerging character of world politics and prepared America to assume its role of leadership.

1925. Kennan, George Frost. "Comments on the Paper Entitled 'Kennan Versus Wilson' by Professor Thomas J. Knock." In **1083**, 327–330. Expresses a willingness to modify his former views on Wilson.

1925a. _____ . "The Legacy of Woodrow Wilson." *Princeton Alumni Weekly* 75 (October 1, 1974): 11–13. An assessment by the influential historian and diplomat.

1926. _____ . "World War I." In *American Diplomacy, 1900–1950*, 55–73. Chicago: University of Chicago Press, 1951. Argues that the outbreak of World War I and the failure to come up with an adequate plan for peace is much to blame for the decline of the security of the West during and after World War II.

1927. Kesler, Charles R. "Woodrow Wilson and the Statesmanship of Progress." In *Natural Right and Political Right: Essays in Honor of Harry V. Jaffa*, ed. Thomas B. Silver and Peter W. Schramm, 103–27. Durham: Carolina Academic Press, 1984. Says Wilson claimed statesmanship based on historical vision and leadership shared with the people, rather than that based on natural law or right.

1928. Knock, Thomas J. "Kennan Versus Wilson." In **1083**, 302–26. Detects a Kennan-Wilson "convergence," finding elements of realism and idealism in both men.

1929. Langer, William Leonard. "Woodrow Wilson: His Education in World Affairs." *Confluence: An International Forum* 5, no. 3 (Autumn 1956): 183–94. [Also published in **1149**, 165–74.] Discusses Wilson's growing understanding of the complexities of foreign relations.

1930. "The Larger Effects." *Nation* 100 (May 20, 1915): 553. Discusses the new moral tone being struck in Wilson's foreign policy.

1931. Leopold, Richard William. "The Emergence of America as a World Power: Some Second Thoughts." In **1499**, 3–34. Examines the modifications of American foreign policy, caused by the Spanish-American War, using World War I as the prime example.

1932. _____ . "The Mississippi Valley and American Foreign Policy, 1890–1941: An Assessment and an Appeal." *Mississippi Valley Historical Review* 37 (1951): 625–42. Examines the historiography of sectional attitudes toward American foreign policy, including discussions of World War I and the Treaty of Versailles.

1933. Leuchtenburg, William E. "Progressivism and Imperialism: The Progressive Movement and American Foreign Policy, 1898–1916." *Mississippi Valley Historical Review* 39 (1952): 483–504. Includes discussions of Wilson's domestic agenda and his Mexico policy.

1934. Link, Arthur S. "The Higher Realism of Woodrow Wilson." *Journal of Presbyterian History* 41, no. 1 (March 1963): 1–13. [Also published in **1155**, 127–39.] Contends that Wilson's politics demonstrated a realism that went beyond short-term political considerations.

1935. _____ . "Wilson the Diplomatist." In **1149**, 147–64. [Includes portions of **1936**, 4–28.] Discusses Wilson's early career and the formulation of his philosophy on foreign policy. Argues that his temperament and acute concern for ideals added to his troubles in executing his policies.

1936. _____ . *Wilson the Diplomatist: A Look at His Major Foreign Policies.* Albert Shaw Lectures on Diplomatic History. Baltimore: Johns Hopkins University Press, 1957. Five essays discussing Wilson's diplomatic skills, his handling of American neutrality, the decision to enter the war, and his ideas of collective security.

1937. _____ . "'Wilson the Diplomatist' in Retrospect." In **1155**, 72–87. [Originally an address at Harvard University under the auspices of the Charles Warren Center for the Study of American History on December 3, 1969. Adapted from **1936**.] Focuses on Wilson's foreign policy successes, which left a foundation for establishing peace through cooperation.

1938. _____ . "Woodrow Wilson and American Traditions." In *Outstanding American Statesmen*, ed. Russell H. Lucas, 17–33. Cambridge: Schenkman Publishing Co., 1970. Wilson's contribution as teacher to other American statesmen.

1939. _____ . "Woodrow Wilson: Hinge of the 20th Century." In **1258**, 20–26. Emphasizes Wilson's achievements as an international statesman, a legacy based on a firmly held body of political principles and Christian beliefs.

1940. _____ . *Woodrow Wilson: Revolution, War, and Peace.* Arlington Heights, Ill: Harlan Davidson, 1979. A substantial revision of **1936**.

1941. Link, Arthur S., ed. *Woodrow Wilson and a Revolutionary World, 1913–1921.* Papers of Woodrow Wilson. Supplementary Volume. Chapel Hill: University of North Carolina Press, 1982. Papers given at a 1979 symposium on Wilsonian foreign policy. Essays listed separately by author.

1942. Link, Arthur S., and William M. Leary Jr., eds. *The Diplomacy of World Power: The United States, 1889–1920*, 82–178. Documents of American History Series. New York: St. Martin's Press, 1970. International relations during the Wilson years; covers Latin America, the Far East, and World War I.

1942a. Madariaga, Salvador de. "Wilson and the Dream of Reason." *Virginia Quarterly Review* 32, no. 4 (1956): 594–98. Argues that Wilson's vision of world politics was destroyed by the realities of the early twentieth century.

1943. Martel, Gordon. "America's First Bid for Empire." *Canadian Review of American Studies* (Canada) 17, no. 1 (1986): 81–92. Discusses several books on American imperialism during the progressive era and World War I.

1944. Martin, Laurence Woodward. "Necessity and Principle: Woodrow Wilson's Views." *Review of Politics* 22, no. 1 (January 1960): 96–114. Analyzes Wilson's attempt to balance international cooperation with national interests.

1945. Martin, William. *Statesmen of the War in Retrospect, 1918–1928*, 217–33. New York: Minton, Balch and Co., 1928. Considers the motives of the various statesmen.

1946. McMahon, John L. "Recent Changes in the Recognition Policy of the United States." Ph.D diss., Catholic University of America, 1933. Wilson's actions in Central America, Mexico, and Russia.

1947. Mitchell, Paul. *The Rape of America*. New York: Comet Press Books, 1960. Describes the author's civilian and naval service from 1918 until after World War II and includes a critique of Wilson and his foreign policy.

1948. Moynihan, Daniel Patrick. "Was Woodrow Wilson Right? Morality and American Foreign Policy." *Commentary* 57 (May 1974): 25–31. Believes that Wilson, like Lenin, inspired and mobilized public opinion unlike any modern leader since, and contends that Wilsonian ideas were and are still carried over into other presidential administrations.

1949. Nicholas, Herbert George. "Woodrow Wilson and Collective Security." In **1941**, 174–89. Describes some of the factors that encouraged Wilson to lead the United States and others away from an earlier emphasis on the nation-state and toward a commitment to national security. Discusses Wilson's expectations for the League of Nations.

1950. Niermeijer, J. F. "Ideaal en werkelijkheid in de buitenlandsche politiek van Woodrow Wilson. 1914–1917." [Ideals and Reality in Woodrow Wilson's Foreign Policy, 1914–1917]. *De Gids* 102, no. 3 (1938): 188–207, 314–30; no. 4 (1938): 84–99, 163–84.

1951. Notter, Harley A. *The Origins of the Foreign Policy of Woodrow Wilson*. Baltimore: Johns Hopkins University Press, 1937. Examines the influence of Wilson's life as a scholar and intellectual on the formulation of his foreign policy. Concludes that he had already developed many of his policies before assuming the presidency.

1952. _____ . "The Origins of the Foreign Policy of Woodrow Wilson." Ph.D. diss., Stanford University, 1937.

1953. Osgood, Robert Endicott. *Ideals and Self-Interest in America's Foreign Relations: The Great Transformations of the Twentieth Century*. Chicago: University of Chicago Press, 1953. Devotes several chapters to the foreign policy of Wilson before and during World War I, using the framework of "realism" and "idealism."

1954. _____ . "Woodrow Wilson, Collective Security, and the Lessons of History." *Confluence: An International Forum* 5, no. 4 (Winter 1957): 341–54. [Also published as chapter 12 in **1149**, 187–98.] Compares modern collective security to the Wilsonian ideal.

1955. Parrine, Carl P. *Heir to Empire: United States Economic Diplomacy, 1916–1923*. Pittsburgh: University of Pittsburgh Press, 1969. Assesses the economic interests of the Wilson and Harding administrations, which vigorously attempted to open foreign markets.

1956. Patterson, Richard S. "Woodrow Wilson in Foreign Affairs." *United States Department of State Bulletin* 35 (December 17, 1956): 954–56. Summarizes Wilson's transition from a President without diplomatic experience to a skilled negotiator, only to be thwarted by partisan resistance and ill health.

1957. Phillips, William. *Ventures in Diplomacy*, 59–99. Boston: Beacon Press, 1953. Autobiography of a State Department officer, which includes numerous personal encounters with Wilson.

1958. Pierce, Anne Rice. "Mission and Power in Twentieth Century American Foreign Policy: Woodrow Wilson and Harry Truman." Ph.D. diss., University of Chicago, 1990.

1959. Pomerance, Michla. "The United States and Self-Determination: Perspectives on the Wilsonian Conception." *American Journal of International Law* 70, no. 1 (1976): 1–27. Assesses the idealist, realist, and radical perspectives on self-determination.

1960. Pratt, Julius William. *Challenge and Rejection: The United States and World Leadership, 1900–1921*. New York: Macmillan Co., 1967. Describes Wilson's role in American neutrality, World War I diplomacy, the Paris Peace Conference, and the return of world peace.

1961. "President Eliot on Wilson." *Weekly Review* 3 (November 3, 1920): 406–7. Criticizes Wilson's foreign policy as idealistic and moralistic.

1962. "President Wilson." *Public* 22 (March 8, 1919): 232. Portrays Wilson as an unparalleled advocate of democracy within nations and open friendship among them.

1963. Robinson, Edgar Eugene, and Victor J. West. *The Foreign Policy of Woodrow Wilson, 1913–1917*. New York: Macmillan Co., 1917. Presents the foreign policy developments of Wilson during 1913–1917 and provides the important statements announcing these policies.

1964. Root, Elihu. "Bankrupt Diplomacy: A Review of the Foreign Policies of the Wilson Administration." *American Monthly Review of Reviews* 53 (March 1916): 298–303. Criticizes Wilson's foreign policy, especially toward Mexico, Germany, and Belgium, and explains the ultimate consequences of those mistakes.

1965. Safford, Jeffrey Jaeger. "The American Merchant Marine as an Expression of Foreign Policy: Woodrow Wilson and the Genesis of Modern Maritime Diplomacy, 1914–1920." In *The Atlantic World of Robert G. Albion*, ed. Benjamin W. Labaree, 144–68. Middletown: Wesleyan University Press, 1975. Explains how

Wilson raised the American merchant marine to a level to compete with other nations.

1966. _____ . "Edward Hurley and American Shipping Policy: An Elaboration on Wilsonian Diplomacy, 1918–1919." *Historian* 35, no. 4 (August 1973): 568–86. Explores the objectives of the chairman of the United States Shipping Board and member of Wilson's war council.

1967. _____ . *Wilsonian Maritime Diplomacy: 1913–1921.* New Brunswick: Rutgers University Press, 1978. Focuses on the numerous maritime accomplishments of the Wilson administration.

1968. Sayre, Francis Bowes. *Woodrow Wilson and Economic Disarmament.* U.S. Dept. of State Publication no. 823. Washington, D.C.: U.S. Government Printing Office, 1936. Address by the Assistant Secretary of State and Wilson's son-in-law before the Democratic Women's Luncheon Club, Philadelphia, December 28, 1935.

1969. Schaefer, Dietrich. "Wilson as a Statesman." *Living Age* 305 (April 10, 1920): 75–80. Summarizes Wilson's leadership in foreign policy.

1970. Sellen, Robert W. "Why Presidents Fail in Foreign Policy: The Case of Woodrow Wilson." *Social Studies* 64, no. 2 (February 1973): 64–70, 75–77. Discusses Wilson's foreign policy and recounts significant events in his life.

1971. Sidey, Hugh. "Hazardous Course for Carter." *Time* 109 (June 27, 1977): 9. Compares Presidents Carter and Wilson in their missionary approach to the world.

1972. Sklar, Martin J. "Woodrow Wilson and the Political Economy of United States Liberalism." *Studies on the Left* 1, no. 3 (1960): 17–47. [Also published in *For a New America*, ed. James Weinstein and David W. Eakins, 46–100. New York: Random House, 1970.] Calvinism and the economics of Adam Smith decisively shaped Wilson's understanding of the liberal state.

1973. Soward, Frederic Hubert. "Woodrow Wilson and the Struggle for a New World Order." In *Moulders of National Destinies.* 2d ed., 1–9. London: Oxford University Press, 1940. Short, favorable account of Wilson's life and diplomacy.

1974. Tobin, Richard Lardner. *Decisions of Destiny*, 180–214. Cleveland: World Publishing Co., 1961. Explores political, diplomatic, and military decisions made by Wilson and other Presidents between 1782 and 1950.

1975. Trask, David F. "The American Presidency, National Security, and Intervention from McKinley to Wilson." *Revue Internationale d'Histoire Militaire* (France) 69 (1990): 290–316. Asserts that under Wilson the United States changed its foreign policy from isolationism to interventionism, and from a passive to an active policy.

1976. _____ . *Victory without Peace: American Foreign Relations in the Twentieth Century*, 51–82. New York: John Wiley & Sons, 1968. Analyzes Wilson's attempts to remain out of war.

1977. U.S. Department of State. *Papers Relating to the Foreign Relations of the United States, 1913–1921.* 21 vols. Washington, D.C.: Government Printing Office, 1920–1936.

1978. ———. *Papers Relating to the Foreign Relations of the United States: General Index, 1900–1918.* Washington, D.C.: Government Printing Office, 1941. [Including the regular annual volumes and the appendices for 1901 and 1902.]

1979. U.S. Department of the Army. *United States Army in the World War, 1917–1919.* 17 vols. Washington, D.C.: Government Printing Office, 1948.

1980. Van Alstyne, Richard Warner. *American Diplomacy in Action.* Stanford: Stanford University Press, 1944. Includes scattered sections on Wilson's role in policies directed towards Latin America, Asia, and Europe during World War I.

1981. Williams, Wayne C. "Wilson's Foreign Policies: A Defense." *Outlook* 126 (October 6, 1920): 234–35. Gives several reasons why Wilson is one of the great Presidents.

1982. Williams, William Appleman. *The Tragedy of American Diplomacy.* Cleveland: World Publishing Co., 1959. [Rev. and enl. ed., New York: Dell Publishing Co., 1962.] Critically examines Wilson's actions as President and the reasons for American entry into World War I.

1983. "The Wilson Administration Reviewed." *American Monthly Review of Reviews* 54, no. 5 (November 1916): 545–46. Surveys President Wilson's handling of foreign affairs, especially the President's reaction to European events, by using contributions from David J. Hill's articles for the *North American Review.*

1984. "Wilson's Legacy to Harding." *Nation* 112 (February 23, 1921): 282–83. Argues that a foreign policy in shambles cannot be easily fixed.

1985. Woodward, Sir Llewellyn. "A British View of Mr. Wilson's Foreign Policy." In **1870**, 141–76. Discusses how Wilson is regarded by British historians.

2. Mexico, Central America, and the Caribbean

1986. Adler, Selig. "Bryan and Wilsonian Caribbean Penetration." *Hispanic-American Historical Review* 20 (May 1940): 198–226. Examines William Jennings Bryan's role in the increasing American activity in the Caribbean under Wilson.

1987. Anderson, William W. "The Nature of the Mexican Revolution as Viewed from the United States, 1910–1917." Ph.D. diss., University of Texas, 1967. Argues that the United States' incompatible ideas of idealistic reform and selfish economic expansion split Americans' attitudes toward the Mexican Revolution.

1988. Duplicate entry omitted.

1989. Archer, Jules. "Woodrow Wilson's Dirty Little War." *Mankind* 1, no. 5 (1968): 44–55. Analyzes Wilson's involvement in Mexico.

1990. Astorino, Samuel J. "Senator Albert B. Fall and Wilson's Last Crisis with Mexico." *Duquesne Review* 13 (1968): 3–17. The disagreement between Wilson and New Mexico Senator Albert B. Fall over the response to Carranza's threats to American oil companies.

1991. Baker, George Walter, Jr. "The Caribbean Policy of Woodrow Wilson, 1913–1917." Ph.D. diss., University of Colorado, 1961. Argues that Wilson's policies, while paternalistic, were a direct predecessor of the goodwill policies of later administrations.

1992. ———. "Ideals and Realities in the Wilson Administration's Relations with Honduras." *Americas* 21 (July 1964): 3–19. Describes Wilson's policies toward Honduras as starting out as new and idealistic promises of goodwill, then regressing into policies similar to those of previous administrations.

1993. ———. "Robert Lansing and the Purchase of the Danish West Indies." *Social Studies* 57, no. 2 (1966): 64–71. Describes the purchase of the Virgin Islands, as a guarantee against German influence.

1994. ———. "The Wilson Administration and Cuba, 1913–1921." *Mid-America* 46, no. 1 (1964): 48–63. Describes the policies toward Cuba as well-meaning but inconsistent.

1995. ———. "The Wilson Administration and Nicaragua, 1913–1921." *Americas* 22 (April 1966): 339–76. Observes the ways in which the early Wilsonian idealism was altered by the pragmatism of his Secretaries of State.

1996. ———. "The Wilson Administration and Panama, 1913–1921." *Journal of Inter-American Studies* 8 (April 1966): 279–93. Describes the mixed legacy in Panamanian relations left by Wilson's Secretaries of State.

1997. ———. "The Woodrow Wilson Administration and El Salvadoran Relations, 1913–1921." *Social Studies* 56, no. 3 (1965): 97–103. The failure of Wilson's Pan-American Pact, and the deterioration of relations with El Salvador.

1998. ———. "The Woodrow Wilson Administration and Guatemalan Relations." *Historian* 27 (February 1965): 155–69. Examines Wilson's indirect role in Guatemalan affairs.

1999. ———. "Woodrow Wilson's Use of the Non-Recognition Policy in Costa Rica." *Americas* 22 (July 1965): 3–21. Wilson's policy was an example of his naive and idealistic foreign policies at their worst.

2000. Baker, James F. "Invasion Flashback." *Newsweek* 102 (November 21, 1983): 32–33. Compares the 1983 United States invasion of Grenada to Wilson's misguided policy of sending troops to Veracruz in 1914.

2001. Baldridge, Donald C. "Mexican Petroleum and United States- Mexican Relations, 1919–1923." Ph.D. diss., University of Arizona, 1971. Discusses Wilson's refusal to mount a new offensive against Mexico to protect American oil companies, the near break-out of war, and his refusal to recognize the new government until it guaranteed protection for American interests.

2002. Balmaseda-Napoles, Francisco A. "Mexico and the United States, 1912–1917: A Study of Selected Writings of Isidro Fabela." Ph.D. diss., Case Western Reserve University, 1974. Analyzes Mexican-American relations during the Wilson years.

2003. Block, Robert Hoyt. "Southern Congressmen and Wilson's Call for Repeal of the Panama Canal Toll Exemption." *Southern Studies* 17, no. 1 (1978): 91–100. Wilson's changing views on the American exemption from payment of Panama Canal tolls and his support from southern congressmen.

2004. Blythe, Samuel George. "Mexico: The Record of a Conversation with President Wilson." *Saturday Evening Post* 186 (May 23, 1914): 3. A conversation with Wilson about establishing a democratic government in Mexico.

2005. Brown, L. Ames. "President Wilson's Mexican Policy." *Atlantic Monthly* 117 (June 1916): 732–44. Positive assessment of Wilson's policies towards Mexico, arguing that they were part of his attempt to promote peace and freedom in the Americas.

2006. Calder, Bruce J. "Some Aspects of the United States Occupation of the Dominican Republic, 1916–1924." Ph.D. diss., University of Texas, Austin, 1974.

2007. _____ . *The Impact of Intervention: The Dominican Republic during the U.S. Occupation of 1916–1924.* Austin: University of Texas Press, 1984. Argues that there were several unofficial reasons for the intervention in the Dominican Republic, and that the military occupation received little help from Washington in formulating a policy there.

2008. Callcott, Wilfrid H. *The Caribbean Policy of the United States, 1890–1920.* Baltimore: Johns Hopkins University Press, 1942. A dated survey of the period.

2009. Calvert, Peter. *The Mexican Revolution, 1910–1914: The Diplomacy of Anglo-American Conflict.* Cambridge, Eng.: Cambridge University Press, 1968. Argues that Wilson's policy was a form of dollar diplomacy.

2010. Carter, Purvis M. *Congressional and Public Reaction to Wilson's Caribbean Policy, 1913–1917.* New York: Vantage Press, 1977. Explains the support for Wilson's decisions to intervene in Haiti, the Dominican Republic, and Nicaragua.

2011. Clements, Kendrick A. "Emissary from a Revolution: Luis Cabrera and Woodrow Wilson." *Americas* 35, no. 3 (January 1979): 353–71. An appraisal of the Mexican envoy to the United States from 1914–1917.

2012. _____ . "Woodrow Wilson's Mexican Policy, 1913–15." *Diplomatic History* 4, no. 2 (1980): 113–36. Re-evaluates Wilson's policies in Mexico.

2013. Clendenen, Clarence Clemens. *The United States and Pancho Villa: A Study in Unconventional Diplomacy.* Ithaca: Cornell University Press, 1961. Analyzes problems with Mexico, which confronted Wilson from the day of his inauguration.

2014. Coker, William S. "Dollar Diplomacy versus Constitutional Legitimacy." *Southern Quarterly* 6, no. 4 (1968): 428–37. Compares the responses of Presidents Grant, Hayes, and Taft to conditions in Mexico with that of Wilson and notes the extent of American interference.

2015. ———. "Mediacion Britanica en el Conflicto Wilson-Huerta." [British Mediation in the Wilson-Huerta Conflict]. *Historia Mexicana* 18, no. 70 (1968): 244–57.

2016. ———. "The Panama Canal Tolls Controversy: A Different Perspective." *Journal of American History* 55, no. 3 (1968): 555–64. Considers Wilson's changing attitudes toward arbitration treaties with England and repeal of the tolls clause.

2017. ———. "United States-British Diplomacy over Mexico, 1913." Ph.D. diss., University of Oklahoma, 1965. Discusses Wilson's refusal to recognize the Huerta government in Mexico, the more pragmatic response by the British, and resulting tensions.

2018. Cumberland, Charles C. "Huerta, Carranza, and the Occupation of Veracruz." *Historia Mexicana* 6 (1957): 534–47. Discusses the strengthening of Huerta's regime following the American landing at Veracruz and Carranza's eventual success in toppling the Mexican government.

2019. "A Defense of the President's Mexican Policy." *American Monthly Review of Reviews* 54 (November 1916): 546–47. Argues that Wilson achieved more success in dealing with South American countries than either Theodore Roosevelt or William Howard Taft.

2020. Dinwoodle, David H. "Expedient Diplomacy: The United States and Guatemala, 1898–1929." Ph.D. diss., University of Colorado, 1966. Argues that United States-Guatemalan relations revealed the nature of Wilson's policies in Latin America.

2021. Edwards, Warrick R., III. "United States-Mexican Relations, 1913–1916: Revolution, Oil, and Intervention." Ph.D. diss., Louisiana State University, 1971. Traces the unprecedented pattern of interference in Mexico.

2022. "Exit Huerta." *Nation* 99 (July 23, 1914): 91. Praises Wilson's Mexican policy.

2023. Fabela, Isidro. *Historia Diplomatica de la Revolucion Mexicana.* 2 vols. Mexico City: Fondo de Cultura Economica, 1958–1959.

2024. Facio, Gonzalo J. "Los Golpes de Estado, la Solidaridad Democratica y la No Intervencion." [Coups d'etat, Democratic Solidarity, and Nonintervention]. *Panoramas* 1, no. 1 (1963): 5–66.

2025. "The First Act of President Wilson." *Harper's Weekly* 57 (March 22, 1913): 3. Applauds Wilson's early statement of policy concerning Mexico, Cuba, Central America, and South America.

2026. Fitzgibbon, Russell Humke. *Cuba and the United States, 1900–1935*, 145–70. Menasha, Wis.: Banta Publishing Co., 1935. Argues that Wilson's policies showed little difference from those of his predecessors.

2027. Gardner, Lloyd C. "Woodrow Wilson and the Mexican Revolution." In **1941**, 3–48. Discusses Wilson's changed understanding of the Mexican revolution and his unwillingness to intervene.

2028. Gilderhus, Mark Theodore. *Diplomacy and Revolution: U.S.-Mexican Relations under Wilson and Carranza.* Tucson: University of Arizona Press, 1977. Discusses the misunderstandings and disagreements between Wilson and Carranza.

2029. ———. "Wilson, Carranza, and the Monroe Doctrine: A Question in Regional Organization." *Diplomatic History* 7, no. 2 (1983): 103–15. Investigates Wilson's attempts to expand the Monroe Doctrine to provide for regional integration and Latin America's fears of United States domination.

2030. Glaser, David. "1919: William Jenkins, Robert Lansing, and the Mexican Interlude." *Southwestern Historical Quarterly* 74 (1971): 337–56. Discusses the kidnapping of the American consular agent, the near decision by Lansing and Albert Fall to invade, and Wilson's intervention to stop the plan.

2031. Grieb, Kenneth J. "The Lind Mission to Mexico." *Caribbean Studies* 7 (1968): 24–43. Argues that Wilson's decision to send John Lind on a diplomatic mission to Mexico was a mistake.

2032. ———. *The United States and Huerta.* Lincoln: University of Nebraska Press, 1969. Examines the ramifications of Wilson's refusal to recognize Huerta.

2033. Haley, P. Edward. *Revolution and Intervention: The Diplomacy of Taft and Wilson with Mexico, 1910–1917.* Cambridge: M.I.T. Press, 1970. Discusses how the instability in Mexico affected Wilson's promise not to intervene there.

2034. Hall, Linda B. "The Mexican Revolution and the Crisis in Naco, 1914–1915." *Journal of the West* 16 (1977): 27–35. Discusses Wilson's decision not to intervene in Mexico after a battle between two Mexican factions resulted in the killing of several Americans across the border.

2035. Harrison, Benjamin T. "Chandler Anderson and American Foreign Relations (1896–1928)." Ph.D. diss., University of California, Los Angeles, 1969. Includes a discussion of Anderson's political involvement while representing businesses in Mexico during the Wilson years.

2036. Harrison, John P. "Henry Lane Wilson, el Tragico de la Decena." [Henry Lane Wilson, The Tragedian of the Ten Days]. *Historia Mexicana* 6, no. 3 (1956/57): 374–405.

2037. Harvey, George Brinton McClellan. "The President and Mexico." *North American Review* 198 (December 1913): 737–44. A mixed review of Wilson's early policies toward Mexico.

2038. ———. "We Appeal to the President to Save Mexico, to Save His Party, to Save Himself." *North American Review* 199 (April 1914): 481–504. Excerpts from editorials calling for changes in Wilson's Mexico policy.

2039. ———. "Why the President Is Right." *North American Review* 199 (May 1914): 641–64. Supports Wilson's position on the Panama Canal treaty.

2040. Healy, David. *Drive to Hegemony: The United States in the Caribbean, 1898–1917.* Madison: University of Wisconsin Press, 1988. Examines Wilson's foreign policy in regard to Latin America and the Caribbean.

2041. ———. *Gunboat Diplomacy in the Wilson Era: The U.S. Navy in Haiti, 1915–1916.* Madison: University of Wisconsin Press, 1976. Argues that American gunboat diplomacy in Haiti was influenced by racism and the strategic importance of having a foothold in the Caribbean.

2042. Henderson, Paul V. N. "Woodrow Wilson, Victoriano Huerta, and the Recognition Issue in Mexico." *Americas* 41, no. 2 (October 1984): 151–76. Examines Wilson's new requirements for United States recognition of Mexico upon taking office in 1913.

2043. Hill, Larry D. *Emissaries to a Revolution: Woodrow Wilson's Executive Agents in Mexico.* Baton Rouge: Louisiana State University Press, 1973. An examination of the work done by the numerous agents Wilson sent to negotiate with the Mexican government.

2044. Hinckley, Ted C. "Wilson, Huerta, and the Twenty-One Gun Salute." *Historian* 22, no. 2 (1960): 197–206. Deals with the "Tampico Incident" of 1914, in which American Marines were arrested in Mexico. United States troops subsequently occupied the area.

2045. Hoernel, David. "Large Corporations and the Big Stick Policy in Cuba and Mexico." *Historia Mexicana* 30 (1980): 209–46. Argues that Wilson refused to cater to the American businesses with interests in Mexico and Cuba.

2046. Holcombe, Harold E. "United States Arms Control and the Mexican Revolution, 1910–1924." Ph.D. diss., University of Alabama, 1968. Maintains that the United States was able to affect the revolution by limiting the export of arms.

2047. Hopper, James Marle. "Wilson and the Border." *Collier's National Weekly* 57 (July 8, 1916): 7–8. Criticizes Wilson's Mexico policy.

2048. "Idealism of President Wilson and Its Effects upon Our Foreign Policy." *Current Opinion* 57 (August 1914): 81–84. Wilson's foreign policy on Latin America and the Panama Canal.

2049. Katz, Friedrich. "Pancho Villa and the Attack on Columbus, New Mexico." *American Historical Review* 83 (1978): 101–30. Discusses Villa's attack across the border as an attempt to spread fear about a possible Wilson-Carranza conspiracy.

2050. ———. *The Secret War in Mexico: Europe, the United States, and the Mexican Revolution.* Chicago: University of Chicago Press, 1972. Discusses the United States' policy of giving top priority to the protection of American businesses in Mexico, and how by 1920 that policy had enabled the United States to gain a firm economic grasp on that country.

2051. Kelley, Francis Clement. "History Points Finger at U.S.A. for Mexican Troubles: Personal Experiences during the Wilson Administration." *America* 60 (March 11, 1939): 537–39. Wilson shares some of the blame for the United States' meddling in Mexico.

2052. Kestenbaum, Justin L. "The Question of Intervention in Mexico, 1913–1917." Ph.D. diss., Northwestern University, 1963. Maintains that most Americans supported Wilson's use of economic and diplomatic pressure.

2053. "The Key to President Wilson's Mexican Policy." *Literary Digest* 48 (May 30, 1914): 1297–99. Excerpts from American newspapers, expressing a variety of opinions on Wilson's policy toward Mexico.

2054. Knight, Alan. *The Mexican Revolution,* 2 vols. Cambridge: Harvard University Press, 1986. Takes into account local and regional differences, as well as politics and diplomacy.

2055. Lael, Richard L. "Struggle for Ratification: Wilson, Lodge, and the Thomson-Urrutia Treaty." *Diplomatic History* 2, no. 1 (1978): 81–102. Discusses Wilson's success in negotiating the treaty stabilizing United States-Colombian relations and his neglect of the Senate.

2056. Langley, Lester D. *The Banana Wars: An Inner History of American Empire, 1900–1934.* Lexington: University Press of Kentucky, 1983. Asserts that Wilson opposed the interventionist policies of his Republican predecessors and looked upon the regular naval patrols of the Mexican coasts as signs of gunboat diplomacy.

2057. Lansing, Robert. "Drama of the Virgin Islands Purchase." *New York Times Magazine* July 19, 1931: 4–5. Describes efforts to obtain the Virgin Islands from Denmark, partly in an attempt to keep Germany from gaining a foothold in the hemisphere.

2058. Lind, John. "Un analisis norteamericano de la Revolucion Mexicana en 1913." [A North American Analysis of the Mexican Revolution in 1913]. *Historia Mexicana* 5 (April-June 1956): 598–18. Report to William Jennings Bryan by a special agent of Wilson, from Veracruz on September 19, 1913.

2059. Lopes de Roux, Maria Eugenia. "Relaciones Mexicano-Norteamericanas (1917–1918)." [Mexican-North-American Relations (1917–1918)]. *Historia Mexicana* 14, no. 55 (1965): 445–68.

2060. Lowry, Edward George. "What the President Is Trying to Do for Mexico." *World's Work* 27 (January 1914): 261–66. Delineates how Wilson is forming his Mexico policy so that it can be applied to all of Latin America and be the basis for improved relations.

2061. Lowry, Philip H. "The Mexican Policy of Woodrow Wilson." Ph.D. diss., Yale University, 1949. Contrasts Wilson's idealism and the exigencies of diplomacy with Mexico.

2062. Lutzker, Michael A. "Can the Peace Movement Prevent War? The U.S.-Mexican Crisis of April 1914." In *Doves and Diplomats: Foreign Offices and Peace Movements in Europe and America in the 20th Century*, ed. Solomon Weeks, 127–53. Westport, Conn.: Greenwood Press, 1978. Argues that Wilson's bold leadership did more than the peace movement in dealing peacefully with the Mexican crisis.

2063. Lyon, Jessie C. "Diplomatic Relations between the United States, Mexico, and Japan: 1913–1917." Ph.D. diss., Claremont Graduate School, 1975. Discusses the disagreement between the United States and Japan over American policy toward Mexico.

2064. "Machiavelli in a Mortarboard." *Spectator* 112 (February 7, 1914): 215–16. Describes Wilson's Mexican policies and his opinions regarding General Huerta's government.

2065. Mason, Gregory. "Wilson, Hughes, Taft, and Mexico; Interviews with Carranza, Obregon, Gonzales, and Aguilar." *Outlook* 114 (November 1, 1916): 505–12. The Mexican perspective on Wilson.

2066. ———. "President Wilson's Mexican Policy: An Interpretation." *Outlook* 113 (May 3, 1916): 36–39. An analysis of the advancing stages of Wilson's policy toward Mexico and a clarification of the American interests there.

2067. McMillen, Fred E. "San Juan de Ulua under the American Flag." *United States Naval Institute Proceedings* 62 (1936): 1155–66. An account of the two occasions, in 1847 and 1914, when the United States captured and controlled the fortress in the harbor of Veraco Mexico.

2068. Meier, Matt S., and Feliciano Rivera, eds. *Readings on La Raza: The Twentieth Century*. New York: Hill and Wang, 1974. Survey includes material on Wilson's presidency, during which thousands of Mexicans fled to America to escape revolution and to seek economic opportunity.

2069. Meyer, Leo J. "The United States and the Cuban Revolution of 1917." *Hispanic American Historical Review* 10 (1930): 138–66. Discusses United States support for the Cuban government in the face of the threat created by Alberto Zaya's liberal revolutionaries.

2070. Meyer, Michael C. "The Arms of the *Ypiranga*." *Hispanic American Historical Review* 50 (1970): 543–56. Discusses the purchase of American arms by German agents who then resold them in Mexico.

2071. Mitchell, Nancy. "The Danger of Dreams: Weltpolitik Versus Protective Imperialism." Ph.D. diss., Johns Hopkins University, 1993. Maintains that when Wilson sent the Marines into Haiti and the Dominican Republic, he justified his policy by referring to the Germany threat to Latin America.

2072. "Mr. Wilson's Catholic Critics." *Literary Digest* 51 (December 25, 1915): 1481–82. Details several sources that condemned Wilson for supporting the Carranza government in Mexico in the wake of atrocities against Catholics.

2073. Munro, Dana Gardner. *Intervention and Dollar Diplomacy in the Caribbean, 1900–1921*. Princeton: Princeton University Press, 1964. Examines the political circumstances which colored United States perceptions of the Caribbean and Central America.

2074. Murillo-Jimenez, Hugo. "Wilson and Tinoco: The United States and the Policy of Non-Recognition in Costa Rica, 1917–1919." Ph.D. diss., University of California, San Diego, 1978. Discusses Wilson's refusal to recognize the Tinoco government after it overthrew the legitimate regime, and the ramifications of that policy for Costa Rica.

2075. Plummer, Brenda G. "Black and White in the Caribbean: Haitian-American Relations, 1902–1934." Ph.D. diss., Cornell University, 1981. Argues that the United States kept Haiti unstable by undermining local leadership and preserving the status quo.

2076. Posner, Walter H. "American Marines in Haiti, 1915–1922." *Americas* 20 (1963): 231–66. Describes the seven years of United States intervention in Haiti.

2077. "The President on the Canal Tolls." *Outlook* 106 (March 14, 1914): 561. Reprints one of Wilson's speeches to Congress urging the repeal of the Panama Canal tolls exemption on American coastwide trade.

2078. "President Wilson." *Living Age* 285 (April 3, 1915): 56–58. Upholds Wilson as a successful President despite an unpopular Mexican policy.

2079. "President Wilson and the Panama Tolls." *Spectator* 112 (June 20, 1914): 1021–22. English praise for Wilson's restructuring.

2080. "President Wilson's Best Way in Mexico." *Spectator* 112 (March 7, 1914): 378–79. British advice on the Mexican crisis.

2081. "President Wilson's Difficulties." *Spectator* 112 (April 18, 1914): 635–36. Discusses the problems of the formation of Wilson's Mexican policy.

2082. "President Wilson's Good Fortune." *Spectator* 113 (July 18, 1914): 81–82. Questions the future of American involvement in Mexico, given General Huerta's elimination from the political scene.

2083. Prisco, Salvatore, III. "John Barrett's Plan to Mediate the Mexican Revolution." *Americas* 27 (1971): 413–25. Discusses Wilson's refusal of a multilateral commission to mediate between Huerta and himself.

2084. Pyron, Darden A. "Mexico as an Issue in American Politics, 1911–1916." Ph.D. diss., University of Virginia, 1975. Describes how American leaders and political parties attempted to exploit the situation with Mexico.

2085. Quirk, Robert E. *An Affair of Honor: Woodrow Wilson and the Occupation of Veracruz.* Lexington: Published for the Mississippi Valley Historical Association by the University Press of Kentucky, 1962. Employs the Veracruz example to demonstrate that Wilson's ideal of ethical government was irreconcilable with the reality of the Mexican situation.

2086. ———. *The Mexican Revolution, 1914–1915: The Convention of Aguascalientes.* Bloomington: Indiana University Press, 1960. Detailed look at Wilson's role in the negotiations between the contending parties.

2087. Rausch, George J., Jr. "Poison-Pen Diplomacy: Mexico, 1913." *Americas* 24, no. 3 (1968): 272–80. Describes William Bayard Hale's role as Wilson's confidential agent in Mexico.

2088. Romer, Hans G. *Amerikanischen Interessen-und Prinzipienpolitik in Mexiko, 1910–1914; ein Beitrag zur Kritik des Wilsonismus.* [American Interests and Political Principles in Mexico, 1910–1914: An Introduction to a Critique of Wilsonism]. Hamburg: Friederichsen, de Gruyter und Co., ca. 1929.

2089. "Roosevelt and Wilson." *Nation* 99 (July 9, 1914): 35. Describes Theodore Roosevelt's outrage at Wilson's foreign policy and his proposed treaty with Colombia.

2090. Rosenberg, Emily S. "Economic Pressures in Anglo-American Diplomacy in Mexico, 1917–1918." *Journal of Inter-American Studies and World Affairs* 17 (1975): 123–52. Describes the failure of Americans to sway the course of the Mexican Revolution with money and food and how the Mexicans turned to Great Britain and Latin America for help.

2091. ———. "La Politicia del Presidente Wilson en America Central: La Lucha Contra la Inestabilidad Economica." [The Politics of President Wilson in Central America: The Struggle Against Economic Instability]. *Revista de Historia* (Costa Rica) 5, no. 9–10 (1980): 33–58. Argues that to insure stability and continued United States domination in Central America, Wilson relied on "dollar diplomacy" as well as direct military intervention.

2092. Sandos, James Anthony. "The Mexican Revolution and the United States, 1915–1917: The Impact of Conflict in the Tamaulipas-Texas Frontier Upon the Emergence of the Revolutionary Government in Mexico." Ph.D. diss., University of California, Berkeley, 1978. Believes that the United States' importance to the Mexican Revolution resulted from Mexico's great dependence upon both American business interests and the Wilson administration.

2093. _____. "Pancho Villa and American Security: Woodrow Wilson's Mexican Diplomacy Reconsidered." *Journal of Latin American Studies* (Great Britain) 13, no. 2 (1981): 293–311. Focuses on the 1916 Mexican border disturbances, Wilson's dispatch of troops to the area, and Carranza's securing of the border.

2094. Schmidt, Hans. *The United States Occupation of Haiti, 1915–1934.* New Brunswick: Rutgers University Press, 1971. Examines the occupation of Haiti in terms of economics, racism, the long-term need for expansion, and short-term concerns over German influence in the region.

2095. Scholes, Walter Vinton, and Marie V. Scholes. "Wilson, Grey, and Huerta." *Pacific Historical Review* 37 (May 1968): 151–58. Discusses the reaction of Sir Edward Grey to Wilson's Mexican policy.

2096. Schurman, Jacob Gould. "Wilson's Mexican Failure." *Independent* 88 (October 16, 1916): 103. Argues that Wilson abandoned a primary duty as President by interfering in the domestic politics of Mexico.

2097. Selfridge, G. S. "Is the Country Safe with Wilson?" *North American Review* 204 (August 1916): 316–17. Criticizes Wilson's Mexican policy but believes that Mexico needs a dictator like Huerta.

2098. Sessions, Tommie Gene. "American Reformers and the Mexican Revolution: Progressives and Woodrow Wilson's Policy in Mexico, 1913–1917." Ph.D. diss., American University, 1974.

2099. Shoemaker, Raymond L. "Henry Lane Wilson and Republican Policy Toward Mexico, 1913–1920." *Indiana Magazine of History* 76, no. 2 (1980): 103–22. Describes Wilson's Mexican policy and his adversarial relationship with Republican diplomat Henry Lane Wilson.

2100. Simpson, H. "Woodrow Wilson and Mexico." *New Review* 1 (October 1913): 805–9. Praises Wilson's determination to refuse recognition to Huerta but says no enduring peace can prevail until the land is redistributed.

2101. Smith, Robert Freeman. *The United States and Revolutionary Nationalism in Mexico, 1916–1932*, 1–150. Chicago: University of Chicago Press, 1972. Discusses the early challenges that the Revolution posed to the industrial, capitalistic world order.

2102. Sutton, Walter A. "The Wilson Administration and a Scandal in Santo Domingo." *Presidential Studies Quarterly* 12, no. 4 (1982): 552–60. Describes the

1914 scandal surrounding James M. Sullivan, American Minister to Santo Domingo.

2103. Tate, Michael L. "Pershing's Punitive Expedition: Pursuer of Bandits or Presidential Panacea?" *Americas* 32, no. 1 (July 1975): 46–71. Discusses Wilson's 1916 decision to intervene in Mexico, given his attitudes toward Latin America generally.

2104. Teitelbaum, Louis M. *Woodrow Wilson and the Mexican Revolution (1913–1916): A History of United States-Mexican Relations from the Murder of Madero until Villa's Provocation across the Border.* New York: Exposition Press, 1967. Concludes that without Wilson's cool leadership, the United States could very well have gone to war against Mexico.

2105. Trow, Clifford W. "'Tired of Waiting': Senator Albert B. Fall's Alternative to Woodrow Wilson's Mexican Policies, 1920–1921." *New Mexico Historical Review* 57, no. 2 (1982): 159–82. Explores the attempts by various interests to influence the recognition of Mexico by the United States during the Wilson administration and focuses on the New Mexico senator's opposition.

2106. _____. "Woodrow Wilson and the Mexican Interventionist Movement of 1919." *Journal of American History* 58, no. 1 (June 1971): 46–72. Centers on the resolution introduced into the Senate by Albert B. Fall to withdraw recognition from the government of Carranza.

2107. Turchen, Lesta V. "The Oil Expropriation Controversy, 1917–1942." Ph.D. diss., Purdue University, 1972. Discusses the threat Carranza's Mexican government posed to American oil interests.

2108. Ulloa Ortiz, Berta. "Carranza y el Armamento Norte- Americano." [Carranza and United States Armament]. *Historia Mexicana* 17, no. 66 (1967): 253–62.

2109. _____. *La Revolucion Intervenida: Relaciones Diplomaticas entre Mexico y Estados Unidos, 1910–1914.* [The Revolutionary Intervention: Diplomatic Relations Between Mexico and the United States, 1910–1914]. Mexico City: El Colegio de Mexico, 1971. Argues that the Tampico incident was minor and used as an excuse by Wilson to intervene.

2110. Venzon, Anne C. "The Papers of General Smedley Darlington Butler, USMC, 1915–1918." Ph.D. diss., Princeton University, 1982. An account of the American intervention in Haiti.

2111. Villard, Oswald Garrison. "Tried Administration: Its Versatility in Handling International Problems." *Nation* 101 (August 12, 1915): 197–98. Praises Wilson's character but criticizes his Mexican and Haitian policies.

2112. Webster, Arthur. "Woodrow Wilson's Mexican Policy: March 3, 1913 to April 21, 1914." Ph.D. diss., University of Chicago, 1963.

2113. Whelpley, James Davenport. "President Wilson and His Problems." *Fortnightly Review* 101, no. 1 (January 1914): 107–14. [Also published in *Living Age* 280 (February 7, 1914): 323–29.] Discusses Wilson's Mexican policy and his popular American support.

2114. ―――. "President Wilson's Waning Political Power." *Fortnightly Review* 102, no. 1 (July 1914): 135–41. [Also published in *Living Age* 282 (August 29, 1914): 515–20.] Explains how Wilson's Congressional support declined after the Panama Canal tolls controversy.

2115. "Wilson and Mexico." *Collier's National Weekly* 53 (June 13, 1914): 17. Charges Wilson with unwitting support of Pancho Villa by refusing to recognize the government of Huerta and with masking that error in deceptive rhetoric.

2116. "Wilson's Populist Views about Mexico." *New Review* 2 (July 1914): 420–22. Part of the section, "A Socialist Digest," that deals with Wilson's resolution to prevent capitalists from exploiting the situation in Mexico.

2117. Woodbury, Ronald G. "Wilson y la Intervencion de Veracruz (Analisis Historiografico)." [Wilson and the Intervention of Veracruz (A Historical Analysis)]. *Historia Mexicana* 17, no. 66 (1967): 263–92.

2118. Wright, Theodore P., Jr. "Honduras: A Case Study of United States Support of Free Elections in Central America." *Hispanic American Historical Review* 40 (1960): 212–23. Discusses the American interventions in Honduras in 1919 and 1923.

3. Latin America

2119. Bemis, Samuel Flagg. "Woodrow Wilson and Latin America." In **1870**, 105–40. [Also published in Bemis's *American Foreign Policy and the Blessings of Liberty, and Other Essays*, 379–95. New Haven: Yale University Press, 1962.] Discusses Wilson's policies towards nations in the western hemisphere before and during World War I.

2120. "Can President Wilson Inaugurate a Moral Pan-American Empire?" *Current Opinion* 56 (June 1914): 450–51. Examines the morality of United States' influence on revolutions in Central and South America.

2121. Carlisle, Charles H. "Woodrow Wilson's Pan-American Pact." *Proceedings of the South Carolina Historical Association* (1949): 3–15. Argues that Wilson's Pan-American Pact failed because it could not shake the perception by Latin American countries that United States' policies would remain interventionist and imperialistic.

2122. Garcbia Calderbon, Francisco. *El Wilsonismo: Con una Semblanza del Autor por Gonzalo Zaldumbide*. Biblioteca Latino-Americana. Paris: Agencia General De Librerbia, [1920].

2123. Gil, Enrique. *Evolucion del panamericanismo: el credo de Wilson y el panamericanismo*. Buenos Aires: Menedez, 1933.

2124. Gilderhus, Mark Theodore. "Pan-American Initiatives: The Wilson Presidency and Regional Integration, 1914–1917." *Diplomatic History* 4, no. 4 (1980): 409–23. Discusses efforts by Wilson to coordinate trade and investment in the western hemisphere and to resist potential European intervention.

2125. ———. *Pan-American Visions: Woodrow Wilson and the Western Hemisphere*. Tucson: University of Arizona Press, 1986. Argues that the United States used the war to gain economic control over Latin America.

2126. Goodell, Stephen. "Woodrow Wilson in Latin America: Interpretations." *Historian* 28, no. 1 (November 1965): 96–127. Reviews the historiography of Wilson's Latin American policy.

2127. Guastavino, J. E. "Argentine Estimate of Wilson." *Bellman* 26 (March 8, 1919): 274. Wilson described as the transcendent political figure of the historical moment.

2128. Healy, David. *Pan American Visions: Woodrow Wilson in the Western Hemisphere, 1913–1921*. Tucson: University of Arizona Press, 1986. Explores Wilson's policies and relations with Latin America.

2129. Kaufman, Burton Ira. "United States Trade and Latin America: The Wilson Years." *Journal of American History* 58, no. 2 (1971): 342–63. Describes how the Wilson administration sought to increase exports and how the withdrawal of Germany and Britain from some markets after 1914 helped them to meet that goal.

2130. Knott, Alexander Waller. "The Pan-American Policy of Woodrow Wilson, 1913–1921." Ph.D. diss., University of Colorado, 1968. Argues that Wilson was committed to the ideals of Pan-Americanism, citing his efforts to promote hemispheric solidarity and security during the period of American neutrality.

2131. Krenn, Michael L. *U.S. Policy Toward Economic Nationalism in Latin America, 1917–1929*. Wilmington, Del.: Scholarly Resources, 1990. Discusses United States' relations with Colombia, Brazil, and Venezuela and how they illustrate the nature of economic nationalism in Latin America.

2132. Livermore, Seward W. "Battleship Diplomacy in South America: 1905–1925." *Journal of Modern History* 16 (1944): 31–48. Traces United States' reliance upon the Navy to maintain order during the administrations of Theodore Roosevelt, Taft, and Wilson.

2133. Low, Alfred Maurice. "President Wilson's Latin-American Policy." *Contemporary Review* 105 (January 1914): 21–29. [Also published in *Living Age* 280 (February 21, 1914): 451–57.] Examines the idealism and morality in Wilson's Latin American policies.

2134. McGann, Thomas F. *Argentina, the United States, and the Inter-American System, 1880–1914*, 305–6. Cambridge: Harvard University Press, 1957. Brief discussion of Wilson's non-recognition policy toward undemocratic Latin American governments.

2135. "Monroe and Wilson." *Independent* 85 (January 17, 1916): 73. Weighs the merits of the Monroe Doctrine against the Wilsonian view of a new world civilization.

2136. Murphy, Donald J. "Professors, Publicists, and Pan-Americanism, 1905–1917: A Study in the Origins of the Use of 'Experts' in Shaping American Foreign Policy." Ph.D. diss., University of Wisconsin, 1970. Discusses the role of academics, including Wilson, in forming a policy of mediation in South America.

2137. "President Wilson Expands the Idea of National Defense to Cover the Hemisphere." *Current Opinion* 60 (January 1916): 1b-d. Examines Wilson's ideas on Pan-American defense, and the new thinking on the Monroe Doctrine.

2138. "President Wilson and Latin America." *American Journal of International Law* 7 (April 1913): 329–33. Applauds Wilson's statement of policy toward Latin America, issued on March 12, 1913.

2139. "President Wilson and Latin America: A Poll of the Press." *Outlook* 105 (November 8, 1913): 523–25. Reports journalistic reactions to Wilson's stand against local tyranny and against European intervention in Latin America, emphasizing favorable response.

2140. "President Wilson's Visit to the Moreno." *Bulletin of the Pan American Union* 40 (April 1915): 434–37. Describes Wilson's visit aboard the Argentine battleship Moreno on March 29, 1915 at Annapolis. The text of his remarks stating his affection for Latin America is included.

2141. Quintanilla, Luis. "Wilson to South America." In **1038**, 214–26. Praises Wilson's attempts to encourage the spread of democracy throughout the western hemisphere.

2142. "Re-creating Mr. Wilson." *New Republic* 1 (January 16, 1915): 9–10. Argues that American independence is undermined by strict compliance with the Monroe Doctrine and its insistence on isolationism.

2143. Rogers, Lindsay. "President Wilson's Pan-American Policy." *Contemporary Review* 111 (April 1917): 437–47. Upholds Wilson's desire to have the United States cooperate with the Latin American countries and enter into a friendly and peaceful endeavor for a possible united front toward Europe.

2144. Rosenberg, Emily S. "Dollar Diplomacy under Wilson: An Ecuadorean Case." *Inter-American Economic Affairs* 25, no. 2 (1971): 47–53. Wilson's relations with Ecuador as an example of his use of war powers in economic diplomacy.

2145. ———. "World War I and 'Continental Solidarity.'" *Americas* 31 (1975): 313–34. Examines the formation of two rival political blocs in the Western Hemisphere after the war: United States-Brazil and Mexico-Argentina.

2146. Seidel, Robert N. "Progressive Pan Americanism: Development and United States Policy toward South America, 1906–1931." Ph.D. diss., Cornell University, 1973. Explains the reasons why progressive internationalists supported American involvement in the economic affairs of the Southern Hemisphere.

2147. Smith, Daniel Malloy. "Bainbridge Colby and the Good Neighbor Policy, 1920–1921." *Mississippi Valley Historical Review* 50, no. 1 (June 1963): 56–78. Reexamines Latin-American relations during Wilson's last year as President.

2148. Trask, Roger R. "Missionary Diplomacy." In **1896**, 2:575–83. A criticism of Wilson's foreign policies as moralistic particularly as they related to Latin America.

2149. Tulchin, Joseph S. *The Aftermath of War: World War I and U.S. Policy toward Latin America.* New York: New York University Press, 1971. Argues that the American experience in World War I altered United States policy toward Latin America for years to come, creating a good deal of antipathy toward the idea of protectorates but maintaining the right to intervene.

2150. Vivian, James F. "Wilson, Bryan, and the American Delegation to the Abortive Fifth Pan American Conference 1914." *Nebraska History* 59, no. 1 (1978): 56–69. Deals with the cancellation of the conference, the makeup of the American delegation, and the effect on it of World War I.

2151. Woods, Randall B. "Hull and Argentina: Wilsonian Diplomacy in the Age of Roosevelt." *Journal of Inter-American Studies* 16, no. 3 (1974): 350–71. Describes Cordell Hull as a product of the Wilsonian tradition in American foreign policy.

2152. Yepes, J. M. "Bolivar et Wilson—le traite de Panama de 1826 et le pacte de la Societe des nations de 1919." *Friedens-Warte* 40 (1940): 1–2, 37–46.

4. Asia and the Far East

2153. Braisted, William R. *The United States Navy in the Pacific, 1909–1922.* Austin: University of Texas Press, 1971. Discusses Wilson's "New Freedom," the Japanese crisis of 1913, and the role of the Pacific in World War I.

2154. Curry, Roy Watson. "Woodrow Wilson and the Far East." Ph.D. diss., Duke University, 1952.

2155. ———. "Woodrow Wilson and Philippine Policy." *Mississippi Valley Historical Review* 41 (December 1954): 435–52. Chronicles the halting movement toward Philippine independence between 1912 and 1916 and the extent of Wilson's support for it.

2156. _____ . *Woodrow Wilson and Far Eastern Policy, 1913–1921.* New York: Bookman Associates, 1957. Focuses on United States' attempt to maintain interests in China and the Philippines, while confronting Japanese expansion and the war in Europe.

2157. Evans, Benjamin Ifor. "Disease of Wilsonism." *Saturday Review* 140 (October 31, 1925): 498–99. [Also published in *Living Age* 327 (December 5, 1925): 489–91.] A sharp criticism of Wilson's policies in East Asia, particularly his belief in self-determination.

2158. Griswold, A. Whitney. *The Far Eastern Policy of the United States.* New York: Harcourt, Brace and World, 1938. Wilson's Asian policies, including his "war-inspired gospel," and relations with China and Britain.

2159. Gundappa, D. V. "Liberalism in India." *Confluence*: *An International Forum* 5, no. 3 (Autumn 1956): 216–28. Matches key dates in Wilson's life with the record of Indian nationalism and alludes to the deeper psychological harmony between them.

2160. Hiroshi, Yoshii. "Der Americanische Eintritt in den Ersten Weltkrieg Und Wilsons Fernost-Politik." [The American Entry into World War I and Wilson's Far East Policy]. *Revue Internationale d'Histoire Militaire* (France) 63 (1985): 21–25. Believes that traditional concepts of the origins of America's entry into World War I fail to recognize the global range of Wilson's foreign policy.

2161. Soberano, Rawlein G. "Proposals for the American Annexation of the Philippines: A Study of Dissenting Views (1900–1935)." Ph.D. diss., St. John's University, 1974. Discusses Wilson's position favoring independence for the Philippines but argues that he bowed to Congressional pressure in keeping them.

2162. Van Alstyne, Richard Warner. "The Pacific Becomes a Crisis Area (1918–1941)." In *American Crisis Diplomacy*: *The Quest for Collective Security, 1918–1952,* 1–29. Stanford: Stanford University Press, 1952. Wilson's build-up of the United States Navy, and his concerns about British and Japanese inroads in the Pacific and Far East.

2163. Verma, Dina N. *India and the League of Nations.* Patra, India: Bharati Bhawan, 1968. Examines Wilson's wish to keep India out of the League, mainly because he feared its admittance would spur the Philippines to demand participation.

2164. Vinacke, Harold M. "Woodrow Wilson's Far Eastern Policy." In **1870**, 61–104. Argues that Wilson's policies in Asia, specifically China and Japan, were aimed at bringing them into the world community and set a precedent for other administrations in dealing with that part of the world.

a. China

2165. Bose, Nemai Sadhan. *American Attitudes and Policy to the Nationalist Movement in China, 1911–1921.* Bombay: Orient Longmans, 1970. Blames the growth of Chinese animosity toward the United States following the 1911 revolution on American misconceptions and failed foreign policies.

2166. Cameron, Meribeth E. "American Recognition Policy toward the Republic of China, 1912–1913." *Pacific Historical Review* 2 (June 1933): 214–30. Argues that Wilson's recognition of the Chinese government was meant to free United States foreign policy from big business and the interests of other nations. Concludes that the resulting benefits were only slight.

2167. Chi, Madeleine. *China Diplomacy, 1914–1918.* Cambridge: Harvard University Press, 1970. Includes a discussion of the United States' role in trying to contain Japanese expansion into China during World War I, concluding that American policy-makers lacked a good deal of information and understanding about China.

2168. _____ . "China and Unequal Treaties at the Paris Peace Conference of 1919." *Asian Profile* (Hong Kong) 1, no. 1 (1973): 49–61. Argues that Wilson traded his support on the question of Chinese territorial integrity for Allied support of the League of Nations, leading China to refuse to sign the peace treaty.

2169. Chih Yu-ju. "Goodnow's Mission to China." *Tsing Hua Journal of Chinese Studies* 13 (1981): 197–220. Discusses Frank J. Goodnow's advice to the Chinese on writing their constitution, concluding that he was too ignorant about China and too conservative to be of much help.

2170. Cohen, Warren I. "America and the May Fourth Movement: Response to Chinese Nationalism, 1917–1921." *Pacific Historical Review* 35 (1966): 83–100. Explains American failure to win over China, and the appeal of communism to the Chinese.

2171. Crane, Daniel M., and Thomas A. Breslin. *An Ordinary Relationship: American Opposition to Republican Revolution in China.* Miami: Florida International University Press, 1986. Taft's dollar diplomacy and Wilson's missionary diplomacy.

2172. Dayer, Roberta Allbert. "Struggle for China: The Anglo-American Relationship, 1917–1925." Ph.D. diss., State University of New York, Buffalo, 1972. Discusses the influence of corporations on Wilson's China policy, which was designed to prevent Britain from regaining its prewar influence on Chinese markets.

2173. Ellison, Duane C. "The United States and China, 1913–1921: A Study of the Strategy and Tactics of the Open Door Policy." Ph.D. diss., George Washington University, 1974. Discusses Wilson's dollar diplomacy and believes that control over China clearly remained a means, not an end, in American foreign policy during Wilson's administration.

2174. Fifield, Russell Hunt. *Woodrow Wilson and the Far East: The Diplomacy of the Shantung Question.* New York: Thomas Y. Crowell, 1952. Believes Wilson's Shantung settlement at the Paris Peace Conference, which was interpreted as a sacrifice of China's fundamental interests in favor of Japan's expansionist aims, was a significant factor in the Senate's rejection of the Treaty of Versailles.

2175. Israel, Jerry. *Progressivism and the Open Door: America and China, 1905–1921.* Pittsburgh: University of Pittsburgh Press, 1971. Devotes a chapter to Wilson's China policy.

2176. King, Wunsz. *Woodrow Wilson, Wellington Koo, and the China Question at the Paris Peace Conference.* Leyden: A. W. Sythoff, 1959. A brief account of the roles of Wilson and Wellington Koo in the decision of the conference to deny unconditional return of Shantung to China.

2177. Li, Tien-yi. *Woodrow Wilson and Far Eastern Policy, 1913–1917.* Kansas City, Mo.: University of Kansas City Press, 1952. [Also published under the title *Woodrow Wilson's China Policy*, Kansas City, Mo.: University of Kansas City Press, 1952, and New York: Twayne Publishers, 1952.] Based on a Yale dissertation reporting the mixed results of Wilson's attitudes and actions toward China during his first term.

2178. ———. "Woodrow Wilson's China Policy, 1913–1917." Ph.D. diss., Yale University, 1950. Examines Wilsonian dollar diplomacy and Wilson's anger over inroads made by Japan during World War I.

2179. Matsuda, Takeshi. "Woodrow Wilson's Dollar Diplomacy in the Far East: The New Chinese Consortium, 1917–1921." Ph.D. diss., University of Wisconsin-Madison, 1979. Maintains the Wilson administration adopted a new Consortium policy because it feared that a glut of capital and manufactured goods would threaten the United States economy.

2180. Metallo, Michael V. "The United States and Sun Yat-sen, 1911–1925." Ph.D. diss., New York University, 1974. Discusses the United States preference that Yuan Shih-k'ai lead the new China, not Sun Yat-sen, even though the latter was Christian and pro-American.

2181. Nuernberger, Richard. "Die Chinesische Frague auf der Pariser Frien-denskonferenz 1919." [The Chinese Question at the Paris Peace Conference of 1919]. *Festschrift fur Hermann Heimpel* 1 (1971): 238–56.

2182. Posey, John P. "David Hunter Miller and the Far Eastern Question at the Paris Peace Conference, 1919." *Southern Quarterly* 7 (1969): 373–92. Discusses Miller's influence on both Wilson and the Chinese delegation.

2183. "President Wilson's Message to China." *American Monthly Review of Reviews* 59 (January 1919): 88. A letter from Wilson to Hsu-Shih-Chang on the Chinese national holiday, October 10, 1919, with various opinions about the letter from Chinese newspapers.

2184. Pugach, Noel. "Embarrassed Monarchist: Frank J. Goodnow and Constitu-tional Development in China, 1913–1915." *Pacific Historical Review* 42 (1973):

499–517. Claims that Goodnow's outspoken support of China's monarchy was an embarrassment to the Wilson administration.

2185. _____. "Making the Open Door Work: Paul S. Reinsch in China, 1913–1919." *Pacific Historical Review* 38 (1969): 157–75. Discusses the limitations that hindered the United States' ability to develop improved Sino-American relations.

2186. _____. "Standard Oil and Petroleum Development in Early Republican China." *Business History Review* 45 (1971): 452–73. Discusses the failure of Standard Oil's plan to cooperate with the Chinese government in exploring for oil.

2187. Trani, Eugene Paul. "Woodrow Wilson, China, and the Missionaries, 1913–1921." *Journal of Presbyterian History* 49, no. 4 (Winter 1971): 328–51. Examines the missionary influence on Wilson's foreign policies in China.

b. Japan

2188. Asada, Sadao. "Japan and the United States, 1915–1925." Ph.D. diss., Yale University, 1963. Opening chapters concentrate on Wilson's growing concerns about Japan.

2189. Beers, Burton F. "Robert Lansing's Proposed Bargain with Japan." *Pacific Historical Review* 26, no. 4 (1957): 391–400. Robert Lansing's differences with Wilson on how to deal with Japanese economic expansion abroad.

2190. _____. *Vain Endeavor: Robert Lansing's Attempts to End the American-Japanese Rivalry.* Durham: Duke University Press, 1962. Examines Lansing's role in formulating a foreign policy for the Far East.

2191. Clinard, Outten Jones. *Japan's Influence on American Naval Power, 1897–1917,* 101–71. Berkeley: University of California Press, 1947. Includes numerous references to Wilson's Asian policies.

2192. Fulton, Lloyd G. "Japanese-American Relations, 1918–1922." Ph.D. diss., Michigan State University, 1975. United States' attempts to block Japanese imperialism.

2193. Hosoya, Chihiro. "The United States and Japan's Twenty-One Demands in 1915." *Hitotsu-bashi* (Japan) 43 (1960): 28–50. Discusses increasing tensions between the United States and Japan, beginning with Wilson's threat to refuse to recognize Japan's special interest in China.

2194. "Japanese Student on Wilson." *Asia Journal of the American Asiatic Association* 19 (July 1919): 693. Japanese student, who had never met Wilson, gives his favorable impressions of the President as world leader.

2195. Kimitada, Miwa. "Japanese Opinions on Woodrow Wilson in War and Peace." *Monumenta Nipponica* 22, no. 3/4 (1967): 368–89. Examines the way in which Japanese feelings about their own country reflected on their opinions about Wilson.

2196. Lauren, Paul Gordon. "Human Rights in History: Diplomacy and Racial Equality at the Paris Peace Conference." *Diplomatic History* 2, no. 3 (1978): 257–78. Describes the efforts of Japanese to have a statement on racial equality.

2197. Lyman, Donald R. "The United States and Japan, 1913–1921." Ph.D. diss., University of North Carolina, Chapel Hill, 1976. Argues that Wilson's shift from passive to active policies in the Far East confused Japan and ensured American failure there.

2198. Lyon, Jessie C. "Diplomatic Relations between the United States, Mexico, and Japan: 1913–1917." Ph.D. diss., Claremont Graduate School, 1975. Discusses the disagreement between the United States and Japan over American policy toward Mexico.

2199. Maga, Timothy P. "Prelude To War? The United States, Japan, and the Yap Crisis, 1918–22." *Diplomatic History* 9, no. 3 (1985): 215–31. Examines the international conflict over the island of Yap in the Carolines, following the Japanese takeover in 1914.

2200. Matsuda, Takeshi. "Wilson Seiken to Wall Street: Taika Rokkakoku Shakkandan Dattai Mondai o Chushin to Shite." [The Wilson Administration and Wall Street]. *Seiyo Shigaku* (Japan) 112, 113 (1979): 1–17; 33–44. Analyzes Wilson's 1913 statement withdrawing from the Sextuple Consortium to China.

2201. Prescott, Francis C. "The Lansing-Ishii Agreement." Ph.D. diss., Yale University, 1949.

2202. Tsurumi, Yusuke. "Woodrow Wilson: A Japanese Appreciation of the Scholar-Statesman." *Trans-Pacific* 16 (February 25, 1928): 6.

5. Middle East

2203. Brecher, Frank W. "Woodrow Wilson and the Origins of the Arab-Israeli Conflict." *American Jewish Archives* 39 (April 1987): 23–47. Inconsistencies in Wilson's pro-Zionist stance.

2204. DeNovo, John A. *American Interests and Policies in the Middle East, 1900–1939.* Minneapolis: University of Minnesota Press, 1963. Examines Wilson's dramatic departure from Middle East foreign policy.

2205. Evans, Laurence. *United States Policy and the Partition of Turkey, 1914–1924.* Baltimore: Johns Hopkins University Press, 1965. Argues that the only influence the United States could have had on the Middle East at this time would have come from coercing governments in the region.

2206. Grabill, Joseph L. "Cleveland H. Dodge, Woodrow Wilson, and the Near East." *Journal of Presbyterian History* 48, no. 4 (Winter 1970): 249–64. Describes efforts by Wilson's friend and advisor to gain protection for Armenians during and after World War I.

2207. Howard, Henry N. *Turkey, the Straits, and U.S. Policy.* Baltimore: Johns Hopkins University Press, 1974. Includes a discussion of the strategic importance of the Turkish waterways and of Wilson's interest in becoming a more prominent player in the Near East.

2208. Kislov, A. K. "Belyi Dom I Sionistskoe Lobbi." [The White House and the Zionist Lobby]. *Voprosy Istorii* (USSR) 1 (1973): 48–61. Begins with Zionist ties to the White House under Wilson.

2209. Laffey, Robert M. "United States Policy toward and Relations with Syria, 1914 to 1949." Ph.D. diss., University of Notre Dame, 1981. Wilson's policies and attitudes toward the Middle East are covered.

2210. Lebow, Richard Ned. "Woodrow Wilson and the Balfour Declaration." *Journal of Modern History* 40, no. 4 (December 1968): 501–23. Explores the motivation behind Wilson's approval of the declaration favoring the establishment of a Jewish state.

2211. Levitas, Irving. "Reform Jews and Zionism." *American Jewish Archives* 14 (1962): 3–19. Discusses the presentation of an anti-Zionist petition to Wilson in 1919 and the opposition it received from many Reform Jews.

2212. Raphalides, Samuel J. "The United States and the Question of the Greco-Turkish War, 1919–1922." *Byzantine and Modern Greek Studies* 8 (1982): 171–89. Discusses the humanitarian concerns expressed by Wilson and Harding during the Greco-Turkish War, even though both avoided getting involved in the conflict.

2213. Sabki, Hisham. "Woodrow Wilson and Self-Determination in the Arab Middle-East." *Journal of Social and Political Studies* 4, no. 4 (1979): 381–99. Examines the impact of Wilsonian self-determination on the Arabs of the Ottoman Empire between 1915 and 1920.

2214. Stivers, William. "Woodrow Wilson and the Arab World: The Liberal Dilemma." *Colorado College Studies* no. 20 (1984): 106–23. Assesses Wilson's endorsement of the mandate system and limited self-determination in the Middle East.

2215. Urofsky, Melvin I. *American Zionism from Herzl to the Holocaust.* Garden City, N.Y.: Anchor Books, 1976. The Americanization of Zionism during World War I.

6. World War I and the Period of Neutrality

2216. Abbott, Lawrence Fraser. "President Wilson, Mr. Roosevelt, and Belgium." *Outlook* 112 (March 29, 1916): 732–35. Examines the positions taken by Wilson and Theodore Roosevelt regarding the violation of Belgian neutrality in 1914.

2217. Adler, Selig. *The Isolationist Impulse: Its Twentieth-Century Reaction*, 35–200. New York: Abelard-Schuman, 1957. Six chapters discussing the American impulse to remain isolationist in foreign affairs, including Wilson's failure to convince the public to depart from that inclination.

2218. "An Ally or a Hindrance." *North American Review* 10 (February 10, 1917): 321–26. Argues that when Wilson broke off diplomatic relations with Germany, he advanced the cause of peace and increased the potential of United States influence in world affairs.

2219. "America Speaks: President Wilson's Address to the Senate." *New Republic* 9 (January 27, 1917): 340–42. Praises Wilson's attempts to offer aid in negotiating the peace.

2220. Angell, Norman. "Mr. Wilson's Contribution." *War and Peace* 3 (June 1916): 136–38.

2221. Auerbach, Jerold S. "Woodrow Wilson's 'Prediction' to Frank Cobb: Words Historians Should Doubt Ever Got Spoken." *Journal of American History* 54 (December 1967): 608–17. Questions the date and authenticity of the conversation between Wilson and the editor of the *New York World*, in which Wilson allegedly predicted dire consequences of the war.

2222. "Autocrat of American Policy." *North American Review* 205 (February 1917): 161–66. Criticizes the undemocratic fashion in which Wilson conducted foreign policy, attacking his notion that the opposition should remain silent.

2223. Avery, Laurence G. "Maxwell Anderson's Report on Frank Cobb's Interview with Woodrow Wilson: The Documentary Source." *North Dakota Quarterly* 45, no. 3 (1977): 5–14. Manuscript version of the interview on the day Wilson delivered his war message to Congress, plus an introductory note.

2224. Bailey, Thomas Andrew. *The Policy of the United States Toward the Neutrals, 1917–1918*. Baltimore: Johns Hopkins University Press, 1942. Concludes that the United States did not violate international law.

2225. ———. "The United States and the Blacklist during the Great War." *Journal of Modern History* 6 (March 1934): 14–35. Describes Allied blacklisting focusing briefly on Britain's blacklisting of the still-neutral United States and Wilson's response.

2226. Bailey, Thomas Andrew, and Paul B. Ryan. *The "Lusitania" Disaster: An Episode in Modern Warfare and Diplomacy*. New York: Free Press, 1975. Argues that, while the sinking of the Lusitania was legally justified by the Germans and was not a part of any British conspiracy, it had serious repercussions for American neutrality.

2227. Barie, Ottavio. *L'opinione interventistica negli Stati Uniti, 1914–1917*. Milan: Istituto Editoriale Cisalpino, 1960.

2228. Bartlett, Ruhl J. *The League to Enforce Peace*. Chapel Hill: University of North Carolina Press, 1944. Discusses the activities of the League to Enforce Peace, its excitement over the League of Nations, and the organization's eventual decline.

2229. "Belligerent Raps at the President." *Literary Digest* 54 (January 27, 1917): 184. Excerpts from the European press, expressing doubt and mistrust over Wilson's claims of neutrality in the European war.

2230. "Bill of Rights for the World: President Wilson's Address before the League to Enforce Peace." *Survey* 36 (June 10, 1916): 281–82. In the address Wilson argued that the great nations should reach agreement on common interests, as well as decide upon a method of acting when any nation or group of nations disturbs the agreed-upon fundamentals.

2231. Billington, Monroe L. "The Gore Resolution of 1916." *Mid-America* 47 (1965): 89–98. Discusses Senator Thomas Pryor Gore's failed attempt to form a policy that would declare war on Germany if any ship carrying an American was sunk.

2232. ———. "The Sunrise Conference: Myth or Fact?" *Southwestern Social Science Quarterly* 37 (March 1957): 330–40. Deals with an alleged announcement by Wilson at a secret conference in April 1916 that the United States would enter the war.

2233. Birdsall, Paul M. "Neutrality and Economic Pressures, 1914–1917." *Science and Society* 3 (1939): 217–28. Using the initial neutrality position as an example, this author argues that it is nearly impossible for a nation to remain neutral if it maintains economic ties with belligerents.

2234. Buehrig, Edward Henry. "Wilson's Neutrality Re-Examined." *World Politics* 3 (October 1950): 1–19. Argues that inconsistencies and lack of clarity regarding neutrality complicated the eventual entry into the conflict.

2235. Coletta, Paolo E. "William Jennings Bryan's Plans for World Peace." *Nebraska History* 58 (Summer 1977): 193–217. Bryan's strenuous efforts, as Secretary of State, to provide settlement of disputes without war.

2236. Coogan, John W. *The End of Neutrality: The United States, Britain, and Maritime Rights, 1899–1915*. Ithaca: Cornell University Press, 1981. Origins of the British blockade and Wilson's neutrality policies.

2237. Cooper, John Milton, Jr. "'An Irony of Fate': Woodrow Wilson's Pre-World War I Diplomacy." *Diplomatic History* 3 (Fall 1979): 425–37. Reviews vols. 27–30 of *PWW* which cover 1913–1914.

2238. ———. *The Vanity of Power: American Isolationism and the First World War, 1914–1917*. Westport, Conn.: Greenwood Press, 1969. Shows how Wilson finally felt compelled to lead the nation away from isolationism, justifying overseas involvement on idealistic grounds.

2239. Croly, Herbert David. "The Structure of Peace." *New Republic* 9 (January 13, 1917): 287–91. Looks favorably upon the formation of the League to Enforce Peace.

2240. Dalton, Brian J. "Wilson's Prediction to Cobb: Notes on the Auerbach-Link Debate." *Historian* 32 (August 1970): 545–63. An examination of the circumstances under which Wilson decided to declare war, with attention to a purported conversation with Frank Cobb.

2241. "A Declaration of Interdependence." *Independent* 86 (June 5, 1916): 357. Stresses Wilson's belief in the League to Enforce Peace.

2242. Devlin, Patrick Baron. *Too Proud to Fight: Woodrow Wilson's Neutrality*. New York: Oxford University Press, 1974. A comprehensive examination of Wilson's foreign policy prior to World War I, emphasizing the complexity of the issues with which he dealt.

2243. Dickinson, Goldsworthy Lowes. "The War and the Way Out." *Atlantic Monthly* 114 (December 1914): 820–37. Concludes that the only way to prevent more wars from occurring is to create a League of Europe.

2244. "The End of Isolationism." *New Republic* 1 (November 7, 1914): 9–10. Declares that the European conflict has called into question the United States' ability to remain completely independent of the affairs of other nations.

2245. "Europe's Disapproval of the President." *Literary Digest* 51 (December 25, 1915): 1467–68. Excerpts from European newspapers expressing universal dissatisfaction with Wilson's behavior as a neutral leader.

2246. Fay, Sidney Bradshaw. "Wilson and Neutrality." *Nation* 142 (January 22, 1936): 109–10. Examines Wilson's decision to intervene in World War I.

2247. "Feasibility of the President's Peace-Program." *Literary Digest* 54 (February 3, 1917): 229–32. Excerpts from European newspapers expressing support for Wilson's peace program.

2248. Fenton, Charles A. "A Literary Fracture of World War I." *American Quarterly* 12 (1960): 119–32. Examines the criticisms by members of the American Academy of Arts and Letters of Wilson's policy of neutrality.

2249. Fitz-Gerald, William George [Ignatius Phayre, pseud.]. "Dr. Wilson's Household Foes." *Living Age* 289 (April 29, 1916): 308–12. Discusses Wilson's political opposition in light of his stand on German submarine warfare.

2250. Folliard, Edward Thomas. "Roosevelt's Neutrality Views Compared to Those of Wilson." *Congressional Digest* 18 (October 1939): 238–39. Argues that events following Wilson's speech taught the Congress to proceed cautiously in times of war, even as a neutral.

2251. Gardiner, Alfred G. "Footnote to History." *Nation and the Athenaeum* 28 (March 12, 1921): 815. Reports an interview in which Wilson explained his request in December of 1916 that all belligerent governments state plainly what they were fighting for.

2252. Grenville, John Ashley Soames. "The United States Decision for War, 1917: Excerpts From the Manuscript Diary of Robert Lansing." *Renaissance and Modern Studies* 4 (1960): 59–81. Examines the diary for an understanding of Wilson's decision to enter World War I and of Lansing's relations with Wilson.

2253. Handlin, Oscar. "A Liner, a U-boat . . . and History." *American Heritage* 6 (1955): 40–45, 105. Argues that the sinking of the *Lusitania* forced Wilson to view U-boat warfare as an act of war by Germany.

2254. Harbaugh, William Henry. "Woodrow Wilson, Roosevelt, and Interventionism, 1914–1917: A Study of Domestic Influences on the Formulation of American Foreign Policy." Ph.D. diss., Northwestern University, 1954. A survey of the debate over American entry into World War I. Concludes that both Wilson and Theodore Roosevelt failed to articulate their positions on the war, leaving the American people partially unprepared for what was required of them in time of crisis.

2255. Heaton, John Langdon, ed. *Cobb of "The World": A Leader in Liberalism.* New York: E. P. Dutton and Co., 1924. Recounts Cobb's famous, if controversial, interview with Wilson soon before the declaration of war, revealing Wilson's anguish over making the decision about entering the war.

2256. ———. " 'To Fight You Must Be Brutal and Ruthless': Excerpt from Cobb of 'The World.' " In **396**, 1058–87. Describes Wilson's struggle over asking Congress to declare war on Germany without destroying the Constitution.

2257. Herrick, Robert. "Le President Wilson et le Pacifisme Americain." [President Wilson and American Pacifism]. *Revue de Paris* 24, pt. 2 (April 15, 1917): 711–32.

2258. "How the President Met the Crisis." *Literary Digest* 50 (June 5, 1915): 1340–46. Positive reactions by the press to Wilson's handling of the *Lusitania* crisis.

2259. "Is the President's Note Pro-German? One Reason Why the Allies Think It Is." *Outlook* 115 (January 3, 1917): 17. Describes United States and European reactions to Wilson's December 18, 1916 peace note.

2260. Jensen, Billie Barnes. "House, Wilson and American Neutrality, 1914–1917." Ph.D. diss., University of Colorado, 1962. Describes House's three peace missions to Europe as an educational experience for both him and Wilson, helping them to understand the importance of the European war to America's future.

2261. Johnson, William Hannibal. "The President's Idealism." *Nation* 104 (February 1, 1917): 129. Criticizes Wilson's complacency in dealing with the European war.

2262. Kaplan, Phillip S. "The Crisis in Anglo-American Relations of 1913–1914." Ph.D. diss., Johns Hopkins University, 1966. Discusses disagreements over South American oil, the Panama Canal tolls, and the handling of the Mexican Revolution.

2263. Keller, Albert Galloway. "The Conceivable Virtue of Patience." *Nation* 104 (February 22, 1917): 209–11. Sees the United States decision not to enter the war rashly as a desirable precedent in American statesmanship.

2264. Kernek, Sterling J. "The British Government's Reactions to President Wilson's 'Peace' Note of December 1916." *History Journal* 13, no. 4 (1970): 721–66. Assesses the attitude of the British government toward American peace negotiations during World War I.

2265. Langer, William Leonard. "From Isolation to Mediation." In **1101**, 22–46. Focuses on Wilson's desire to play mediator during World War I and its effect on his policy during the period of American neutrality.

2266. Lansing, Robert. "The Difficulties of Neutrality." *Saturday Evening Post* 203 (April 18, 1931): 6–7+. Excerpts of notes written by Lansing describing the tenuous United States position as a neutral power.

2267. "A League of Peace." *New Republic* 2 (March 20, 1914): 167–69. Supports the idea for the League to Enforce Peace, but gives credence to the German complaint that such a league would be unfair to them.

2268. "The League to Enforce Peace." *Independent* 86 (June 5, 1916): 358. A brief account of *Independent*'s early advocacy of a League to Enforce Peace.

2269. Link, Arthur S. "That Cobb Interview." *Journal of American History* 72, no. 1 (June 1985): 7–17. Discusses Cobb's interview with Wilson on March 19, 1917, which was published as a memorandum in 1924.

2270. ———. "Wilson and the Ordeal of Neutrality." In *History of the Twentieth Century*, 652–56. London: B.P.C. Publishing, 1968. [Also published in **1155**, 88–98.] Discusses the limiting effects of public opinion on Wilson's policy of neutrality.

2271. ———. "Wilson and the Struggle for Neutrality." In **1741**, 8–28. [Also published in **1936**, 31–60.] Argues that Wilson succeeded in making the case for American neutrality before 1917, based upon moral principle and tactical pragmatism.

2272. Littell, Philip. "Books and Things." *New Republic* 3 (June 26, 1915): 208. Concerns Wilson's speech on Flag Day.

2273. ———. "Books and Things." *New Republic* 4 (September 18, 1915): 186. Describes Wilsonian quietness in the face of German aggression as cool strength.

2274. ———. "Books and Things." *New Republic* 9 (January 13, 1917): 300. Discusses Wilson's involvement in World War I.

2275. _____ . "Books and Things." *New Republic* 10 (April 14, 1917): 324. Examines the change in Wilson's attitude toward the inevitability of war.

2276. "The Logothete at Large." *Spectator* 116 (February 12, 1916): 213. Wilson's diplomacy regarding the sinking of the *Lusitania*.

2277. Mason, Gregory. "The President's Mind Made Up." *Outlook* 111 (September 1, 1915): 20–21. Suggests that Wilson was preparing for war following the sinking of the *Lusitania* and the *Arabic*.

2278. May, Ernest R., ed. *The Coming of War, 1917*. Chicago: Rand McNally, 1963. A collection of primary sources to document the end of American neutrality.

2279. _____ . *The World War and American Isolation, 1914–1917*. Cambridge: Harvard University Press, 1959. A comprehensive analysis of Wilson's dilemmas and decision to enter World War I.

2280. McDonald, Timothy G. "The Gore-McLemore Resolutions: Democratic Revolt against Wilson's Submarine Policy." *Historian* 26, no. 1 (1963): 50–74. Examines Wilson's Democratic congressional supporters and detractors on the issues of Allied shipping and the possibility of German submarine attacks upon United States vessels.

2281. Meine, Arnold. *Wilsons Diplomatie in der Friedensfrage 1914–1917*. Stuttgart: Kohlhammer, 1938. Originally a Ph.D. dissertation, University of Bonn.

2282. Mooney, Christopher. "Moral Consensus and Law: *The Lusitania Case*, after May 7, 1915." *Thought* 51, no. 202 (September 1976): 231–54. Wilson's attempts to generate a moral consensus.

2283. Morrissey, Alice M. *The American Defense of Neutral Rights, 1914–1917*. Cambridge: Harvard University Press, 1939. Stresses the relationship of foreign policy to economic interests and public opinion.

2284. "Mr. Wilson's Great Utterance: Speech on May 22 before the League to Enforce Peace." *New Republic* 7 (June 3, 1916): 102–4. Extols Wilson's role as peacemaker just as war has broken out across Europe.

2285. "Mr. Wilson's Interpretation of American Public Opinion on the War." *New Republic* 5 (January 15, 1916): 278–79. Explores the degree to which Wilson acted either in response to "the will of the people" or to public opinion.

2286. "Nemesis of Neutrality." *Spectator* 115 (December 11, 1915): 817. [Reprinted in *Living Age* 288 (January 15, 1916): 177–79.] Discusses Wilson's plea for an adequate defense in light of his neutrality on the moral issues of the war.

2287. "Peace without Victory." *New Republic* 9 (December 23, 1916): 201–2. Criticizes the European Allies for fighting for nothing more than territory and prestige.

2288. Peterson, Horace C. *Propaganda for War: The Campaign against American Neutrality, 1914–1917*. Norman: University of Oklahoma Press, 1939. A study of the effect of British propaganda on the United States in the years of neutrality and its role in changing Wilson's view on neutrality.

2289. "The President and Congress: A Poll of the Press." *Outlook* 112 (March 8, 1916): 549–52. Diversity of opinions about Wilson's anti-German stance.

2290. "The President as Peace-Pilot." *Literary Digest* 53 (December 30, 1916): 1694–95. Describes Wilson's efforts and suggestions about bringing peace to Europe.

2291. "The President on Militarism." *Survey* 36 (May 20, 1916): 198–99. Describes Wilson's attempt to avoid capitulating to the militarists or to the opponents of preparedness.

2292. "The President on the Enforcement of Peace." *Independent* 86 (June 5, 1916): 357. Impressions of a speech given by Wilson at a banquet honoring the League to Enforce Peace.

2293. "The President on the Job." *Literary Digest* 49 (September 19, 1914): 496–97. Praises Wilson for his domestic policies and efforts to establish peace in Europe.

2294. "President Wilson Calls on Congress to Define Its Views of American Rights." *Current Opinion* 60 (April 1916): 235–38. Opinions from various newspapers regarding freedom of the seas and Wilson's appeals to Congress to follow his lead.

2295. "President Wilson and the German Memorandum." *Living Age* 289 (April 8, 1916): 111–13. Criticizes Wilson for being too idealistic in his responses to German war atrocities, arguing that it is not always possible to maintain a peaceful stance in foreign affairs.

2296. "President Wilson as a Leader." *Outlook* 113 (June 7, 1916): 303–4. Examines Wilson's call for mediation to end the war.

2297. "President Wilson's Message." *Spectator* 113 (December 12, 1914): 834–35. Urges American involvement on the side of the Allies.

2298. "President Wilson's Mistake." *Spectator* 114 (March 27, 1915): 428–29. A critical analysis of Wilson's understanding of the term "neutrality" and its practical uses.

2299. "President Wilson's Note." *Living Age* 292 (January 27, 1917): 248–51. An analysis of Wilson's "Note to the Central Powers and the Allies," expressing a hope of limiting the war.

2300. "President Wilson's Peace-Plan." *Literary Digest* 52 (June 10, 1916): 1683–85. Newspaper opinions on the practicality of Wilson's peace plan and the League to Enforce Peace.

2301. "The President's Latest Note to Germany: A Poll of the International Press." *Outlook* 110 (June 23, 1915): 413–17. Contains excerpts from newspapers in the United States, Germany, France, and England.

2302. "The President's Note to the Powers: A Poll of the Press." *Outlook* 115 (January 3, 1917): 15–16. Includes selections from American and European newspapers regarding Wilson's peace message to the belligerents.

2303. "The President's Proclamation Asks Prayers for Peace." *Journal of Education* 80 (September 17, 1914): 231. Proclaims October 4, 1914, a day of prayer.

2304. "The President's Speeches Relating to Plans for National Defense." *Independent* 85 (February 7, 1916): 179. Reports on several speeches on defense.

2305. "The President's Unasked Advice." *Outlook* 115 (January 3, 1917): 13–14. Remarks on Wilson's haste in forwarding the German note to the European Allies.

2306. "Recent Talk with President Wilson." *American Monthly Review of Reviews* 51 (February 1915): 238–39. Describes an extensive interview by Samuel G. Blythe, which appeared in the *Saturday Evening Post*, January 9, 1915. Blythe maintains that Wilson is the most conscientiously neutral man of all neutral men.

2307. "Responses to the President." *Nation* 103 (December 28, 1916): 599. Describes European reactions to Wilson's call for an end to war and his efforts to begin peace negotiations.

2308. Rogers, Lindsay. "President Wilson's Neutrality: An American View." *Contemporary Review* 107 (May 1915): 602–9. [Also published in *Living Age* 285 (June 26, 1915): 771–76.] Describes mixed reactions to Wilson's neutrality policy.

2309. Scheiber, Harry Noel. "What Woodrow Wilson Said to Cobb in 1917: Another View of Plausibility." *Wisconsin Magazine of History* 52, no. 4 (1969): 344–47. Examines the possibility that a much-discussed interview of Wilson by journalist Frank I. Cobb never took place.

2310. Seymour, Charles. *American Neutrality, 1914–1917: Essays on the Causes of American Intervention in the World War.* New Haven: Yale University Press, 1935. Essays centering on Wilson, notably his role in the submarine campaign and Lansing's portrayal of him in **3568**.

2311. Simpson, Colin. *The "Lusitania."* Boston: Little, Brown and Co., 1973. Provides the German point of view that the sinking was part of a British conspiracy to outrage the world and bring the United States into the war on the side of the Allies.

2312. Small, Melvin. "Woodrow Wilson and U.S. Intervention in World War I." In *Modern American Diplomacy*, ed. John M. Carroll and George C. Herring. Wilmington, Del.: Scholarly Resources, 1986. Discusses the gradual loosening of Wilson's policy of neutrality by making concessions to benefit the Allies and allowing arms trade to belligerents.

2313. Smith, Daniel Malloy. "Robert Lansing and the Formulation of American Neutrality Policies, 1914–1915." *Mississippi Valley Historical Review* 43, no. 1 (June 1956): 59–81. Argues that Lansing had more influence with the President than previous scholars have noted.

2314. Spector, Ronald. " 'You're Not Going to Send Soldiers over There Are You!': The American Search for an Alternative to the Western Front 1916–1917." *Military Affairs* 36, no. 1 (1972): 1–4. Wilson's consideration of an alternative front.

2315. Swain, Joseph Ward. "Woodrow Wilson's Fight for Peace." *Current History* 35, no. 6 (March 1932): 805–12. Wilson's attempt to keep the United States out of war, in light of the 1931 publication of the Government Printing Office's *Foreign Relations of the United States, 1917.*

2316. Syrett, Harold C. "The Business Press and American Neutrality, 1914–1917." *Mississippi Valley Historical Review* 32 (1945): 215–230. Evaluates the theory that America entered World War I because of large-scale business interests.

2317. Tarbox, James Jeffrey. "The Constitutive Function of Woodrow Wilson's Rhetoric, 1914 to 1917." Ph.D. diss. Pennsylvania State University, 1992. Analyzes twenty-eight Wilson speeches in terms of context, the argument, and the characteristics that Wilson attributes to Americans and America in discussing war.

2318. Thornton, Willis. "The Sunrise Conference." In *Fable, Fact, and History*, 188–93. New York: Greenberg Publishers, 1957. Examines whether Wilson planned all along to enter the war, concluding that there is no definite proof to support the theory.

2319. Turlington, Edgar W. "The World War Period." In *Neutrality, Its History, Economics, and Law*, ed. Philip C. Jessup, et al. New York: Columbia University Press, 1935–1936. Volume 3 includes a discussion of Wilson's rationale for taking over neutral ships in Allied or American ports for use in the war effort.

2320. U.S. Department of State. *Diplomatic Correspondence between the United States and Belligerent Governments Relating to Neutral Rights and Duties.* Washington, D.C.: Government Printing Office, 1916. Covers correspondence from June 3, 1915 to June 19, 1916.

2321. Whelpley, James Davenport. "President Wilson and His Message." *Fortnightly Review* 105, no. 1 (January 1916): 141–52. [Also published in *Living Age* 288 (February 12, 1916): 387–96.] Summary of Wilson's opening Congressional message delivered on December 1915, which focused on the European war and neutrality.

2322. _____ . "President Wilson in the Toils." *Fortnightly Review* 105, no. 3 (March 1916): 516–25. [Also published in *Living Age* 289 (April 8, 1916): 67–74.] Addresses the issue of armed American merchant ships after the Lusitania incident.

2323. _____ . "President Wilson's Pro-Ally Propaganda." *Fortnightly Review* 107, no. 2 (February 1917): 348–56. [Also published in *Living Age* 292 (March 3, 1917): 515–21.] Shows how Wilson used propaganda to uphold the British Allies and expose the Germans.

2324. Williams, William J. *The Wilson Administration and the Shipbuilding Crisis of 1917: Steel Ships and Wooden Steamers.* Lewiston, N.Y.: Mellen, 1992. Discusses the confusion and disputes that hampered the initial efforts of the Wilson administration to meet the merchant shipping crisis caused by U-boat attacks.

2325. "Wilson, the Country, and War." *Nation* 103 (October 26, 1916): 389. Characterizes different American opinions of Wilson's anti-war sentiments.

2326. "Wilson's War Policy." *Moody's Magazine* 19, no. 12 (December 1916): 610–11. Praises Wilson's foreign policy in light of the war in Europe.

7. Europe and World War I

a. General Works

2327. Adkins, Francis James. *Historical Background of the Great War.* New York: R. M. McBride & Co., 1918. Focuses almost exclusively on Europe's prewar history and the involvement of England, France, and Germany.

2328. "Allied Admiration for Wilson." *Literary Digest* 52 (May 27, 1916): 1526–27. Quotations from the European press praising Wilson.

2329. "The Allies Ask Restitution, Reparation, Security." *Literary Digest* 53 (December 30, 1916): 1691–93. Allies' conditions for peace, with lengthy quotations.

2330. Ambrosius, Lloyd E. *Wilsonian Statecraft: Theory and Practice of Liberal Internationalism during World War I.* Wilmington, Del.: Scholarly Resources, 1991. Wilson's emerging conception of collective security.

2331. "America's Part in the War." *New Republic* 10 (February 10, 1917): 33–34. Maintains that because of the hard facts presented, Wilson acted appropriately in entering World War I.

2332. Baker, Newton Diehl. *Why We Went to War.* New York: Harper and Brothers, 1936. [Published for the Council on Foreign Relations. Also published in *Foreign Affairs* 15 (October 1936): 1–86.] A defense of Wilson's decision to declare war, written by his Secretary of War.

2333. Bolt, Robert. "American Involvement in World War I." In *The Wars of America: Christian Views*, ed. Ronald Wells, 127–46. Grand Rapids, Mich.: Eerdmans Publishing Co., 1981. Interprets Wilson's contributions and applauds him for his postwar accomplishments.

2334. Buckingham, Peter Henry. "Diplomatic and Economic Normalcy: America's Open Door Peace with the Former Central Powers, 1921–1929." Ph.D. diss., Washington State University, 1980.

2335. ———. *International Normalcy: The Open Door Peace with the Former Central Powers, 1921–1929.* Wilmington, Del.: Scholarly Resources, 1983. Includes a comparison of Wilson's views on American expansion and those of his Republican successors.

2336. Buehrig, Edward Henry. "Wilson and Europe." In **1075**, 334–76. Describes the evolution of Wilson's European policy.

2337. Bullard, Arthur. *The Diplomacy of the Great War.* New York: Macmillan Co., 1916. An attempt to explain the historical events that caused the war.

2338. Cantor, Milton. "The Radical Confrontation with Foreign Policy: War and Revolution, 1914–1920." In *Dissent: Exploration in the History of American Radicalism,* ed. Alfred F. Young, 217–49. DeKalb: Northern Illinois University Press, 1968. Social radicals, at first supportive of Wilson's ideals and crusade, came to denounce the Versailles settlement and even the League in favor of Russian Bolshevism.

2339. Chaplin, W. W. "Gloria Mundi." In *Deadline Delayed,* Members of the Overseas Press Club of America, 282–84. New York: E. P. Dutton and Co., 1947. Veteran's recollection that Wilson raised the justification of American involvement to a plane of idealism and morality.

2340. Churchill, Sir Winston Spencer. *The World Crisis: European War, 1911–1918,* 1:690–704. New York: Charles Scribner's Sons, 1923. Commentary on Wilson's role.

2341. Civitello, Maryann. "The State Department and Peacemaking, 1917–1920: Attitudes of State Department Officials toward Wilson's Peacemaking Efforts." Ph.D. diss., Fordham University, 1981. Analyzes the reactions of six officials.

2342. Coffman, Edward M. "The American Military and Strategic Policy in World War I." In *War Aims and Strategic Policy in the Great War, 1914–1918,* ed. Barry Hunat and Adrian Preston, 67–84. London: Croom Helm, 1977. Argues that John Pershing cooperated with the Allies only on his terms.

2343. ———. *The War to End All Wars: The American Military Experience in World War I.* New York: Oxford University Press, 1968. Discusses the military history of World War I and shows Wilson's compassion and support for the American soldiers.

2344. Coletta, Paolo E. "A Question of Alternatives: Wilson, Bryan, Lansing, and America's Intervention in World War I." *Nebraska History* 63, no. 1 (1982): 33–57. Analyzes Wilson's diplomacy from the perspective of William Jennings Bryan.

2345. Cooper, John Milton, Jr. "World War I: European Origins and American Intervention." *Virginia Quarterly Review* 56 (Winter 1980): 1–18. Observes the breakdowns in Europe leading to World War I and the reasons for American involvement in the war.

2346. Davenport, Frederick Morgan. "War, Congress, and the President." *Outlook* 115 (April 11, 1917): 646–47. Congressional response to Wilson's declaration of war.

2347. DeWeerd, Harvey A. *President Wilson Fights His War: World War I and American Intervention.* New York: Macmillan Co., 1968. Argues that American success in achieving its goals in the conflict was limited.

2348. Esposito, David M. "Force Without Stint or Limit: Woodrow Wilson and the Origins of the American Expeditionary Force." Ph.D. diss., Pennsylvania State University, 1988. Maintains that the Russian Revolution was the catalyst that brought Wilson to accept American participation in the war.

2349. "Europe's Ideas of Wilson the Man." *Current Opinion* 66 (January 1919): 18–19. Wilson's personal popularity.

2350. "Europe's New Estimates of Woodrow Wilson." *Current Opinion* 62 (April 1917): 243–44. Discusses the admiration for Wilson expressed by the European press.

2351. "Europe's Revised Idea of Wilson the Man." *Current Opinion* 67 (October 1919): 226–27. European press' disappointment with Wilson during his tour of the continent.

2352. "Europe's Suspicion Regarding President Wilson's Designs on the Old World." *Current Opinion* 62 (April 1917): 238–41. Discusses the general feeling within the European press that Wilson is ignorant of many issues and concerns confronting Europe, resulting in ill effects on the postwar world.

2353. "European Comment on President Wilson's Visit." *Living Age* 300 (January 25, 1919): 208–19. Reports from European newspapers and journals on the receptions Wilson received in different countries during his postwar tour of the continent.

2354. "European Views of Autocratic America." *Literary Digest* 64 (February 28, 1920): 24. The European press' sharp criticisms of Wilson for imposing his ideas on Europe without consideration for other countries.

2355. Fay, Sidney Bradshaw. *The Origins of the World War.* 2 vols. New York: Macmillan Co., 1928. An attempt to explain the war. Criticizes the propaganda campaigns that placed the blame solely on Germany.

2356. Fleming, Denna Frank. "Woodrow Wilson and Collective Security Today." *Journal of Politics* 18, no. 4 (November 1956): 611–24. Emphasizes Wilson's wartime activities, the League of Nations, and the effects of these actions on World War II.

2357. Fleming, Thomas James. "Woodrow Wilson's Fight for Peace." *Reader's Digest* 99 (September 1971): 87–91. Argues that Wilson's desire to use United States involvement in the conflict as a means toward establishing a lasting world order transformed the nature of the war.

2358. Floto, Inga. "Woodrow Wilson: War Aims, Peace Strategy, and the European Left." In **1941**, 127–45. Explicates Arno Mayer's thesis that Wilson's foreign policy proclamations were propaganda designed to undermine Germany and to bolster liberal and socialistic forces among the Allies.

2359. "Follow Your Leader." *North American Review* 206 (November 1917): 661–63. Praises Wilson's call for "no peace without victory."

2360. "Force to the Utmost." *Outlook* 118 (April 17, 1918): 614–15. Speech given by Wilson on the anniversary of the declaration of war, restating United States resolve to stop aggression.

2361. Fraser, Sir John Foster. "What Europe Thinks of Woodrow Wilson." *Current Opinion* 67 (July 1919): 16–18. Portrays Wilson as personally cold and unpopular but a valued world leader.

2362. Frothingham, Thomas Goddard. *The Naval History of the World War*. 3 vols. Cambridge: Harvard University Press, 1924–1926. Describes offensive operations and developing naval power, and analyzes the United States significance for American and Allied policies.

2363. Gannett, Lewis Stiles. "President Wilson's Achievement." *Survey* 41 (March 8, 1919): 826–30. Praises Wilson's steadfastness for a new order of world peace instead of a relapse into the old imperialism.

2364. Gelfand, Lawrence Emerson. *The Inquiry: American Preparations for Peace, 1917–1919*. New Haven: Yale University Press, 1963. Deals with the organization commissioned by Wilson, before the cessation of military hostilities, to prepare for America's program for peace.

2365. Goldman, Eric Frederick. "Woodrow Wilson: The Test of War." In **1101**, 47–66. Describes Wilson's wartime leadership and the public hysteria that undercut it.

2366. Grattan, Clinton Hartley. *Why We Fought*. Indianapolis: Bobbs-Merrill Co., 1969. A revisionist work blaming British propaganda campaigns and economic factors for forcing Wilson into the war.

2367. ———. "Wilson Was for War in March, 1916." *Nation* 135 (July 27, 1932): 76–78. Argues that the President's powers in war should be severely limited.

2368. Gray, Tony. "The World at War." In *Champions of Peace: The Story of Alfred Nobel, the Peace Prize, and the Laureates*, 102–22. New York: Paddington Press, 1976. Describes Wilson's leadership during the war years and his acceptance of the Nobel Peace Prize in 1919.

2369. "The Great Decision." *New Republic* 10 (April 7, 1917): 279–80. Expresses confidence in Wilson's leadership and diplomacy.

2370. Greene, Fred. "The Military View of American National Policy, 1904–1940." *American Historical Review* 66 (January 1961): 354–77. How the war shaped the military's view of the formation of American foreign policy.

2371. Gregory, Ross. *The Origins of American Intervention in the First World War*. New York: W. W. Norton, 1971. Argues that Wilson's neutrality benefited the Allies and concludes that he led the United States into war to protect American honor and interests.

2372. Gullberg, Tom. "Woodrow Wilsons Utrikes-politik Och Den Nya Europa." [Woodrow Wilson's Foreign Policy and the New Europe]. *Historisk Tidskrift fr Finland* (Finland) 79, no. 2 (1994): 277–299. Examines changing scholarly assessments of Wilson's European foreign policy with particular attention to studies published in the United States from 1920 to 1994.

2373. Hard, William. "The Keystone of Our Coordination." *New Republic* 13 (January 12, 1918): 302–4. Criticizes Wilson for not coordinating the many aspects of foreign policy.

2374. Harvey, George Brinton McClellan. "The President Must Win the War." *North American Review* 206 (September 1917): 337–50. Argues that the time has come to defeat Germany and ensure the safety of America and democracy around the world.

2375. ――――. "Thank God for Wilson: The President at His Best." *North American Review* 207 (January 1918): 2–17. Focuses on Wilson's performance as a wartime President.

2376. Herron, George Davis. *Woodrow Wilson and the World's Peace*. New York: Mitchell Kennerley, 1917. Five papers in support of Wilson first published for European readers.

2377. Hogan, Michael J. "The United States and the Problem of International Economic Control: American Attitudes toward European Reconstruction." *Pacific Historical Review* 44 (1975): 84–103. Wilson's opposition to any postwar economic controls in Europe.

2378. Hornbeck, Stanley Kuhl. "Cause and Occasion of Our Entry into the World War, 1917." *Annals of the American Academy of Political and Social Science* 192 (July 1937): 56–66. Argues that Wilson struggled to champion the rights and interests of his own country, as well as to punish Germany.

2379. "How President Wilson Is Waging the War." *Literary Digest* 56 (February 9, 1918): 15–16. American newspaper articles on Wilson's performance managing the war.

2380. "How Washington Heard the President's Message of April 19." *Independent* 86 (May 1, 1916): 169. An account of Wilson's request for a declaration of war before a joint session of Congress.

2381. "Inquisitors Call Wilson a Falsifier." *News-Week* 7 (January 25, 1936): 12–14. Discusses accusations by Champ Clark that Wilson gave dishonest reasons for entering the war and that he was influenced by business leaders in making the decision to intervene. Details the Senate hearings that took place twelve years after Wilson's death.

2382. Ivie, Robert L. "Presidential Motives for War." *Quarterly Journal of Speech* 60 (1974): 337–45. Examines Wilson's choice of words used to justify war.

2383. Jacks, Lawrence Pearsall. "President Wilson's War Mind." *Living Age* 298 (July 13, 1918): 99–104. Uses Wilson's speeches on the war in Europe in an attempt to trace the evolution of his thought on the matter, and to see what the future course might be.

2384. James, Edith. "Wilsonian Wartime Diplomacy: The Sense of the Seventies." In *American Foreign Relations: A Historiographical Review*, ed. Gerald K. Haines and J. Samuel Walker, 115–31. Westport, Conn.: Greenwood Press, 1981. Reviews World War I historiography of the 1970s, with a focus on Wilson's diplomacy.

2385. Karp, Walter. "How to Think about Politicians." *Horizon* 19 (January 1977): 14–15. Explores the possibility that Wilson deliberately entered the war in order to preside over the peace.

2386. Kellogg, Paul Underwood. "The 'Wilson Policies.'" *Survey* 41 (October 19, 1918): 59–61. Calls on all Americans to support Wilson as America's and the world's moral leader in ending the war.

2387. Kosberg, Roberta Louise. "Executive-Legislative Rhetoric Regarding American Participation in an Association of Nations, 1916–1920 and 1935–1945." Ph.D. diss., Pennsylvania State University, 1982. Compares efforts by Wilson and Franklin Roosevelt to insure American membership in a community of nations.

2388. Kuhn, Johannes. "Die Friedensvermittlung des Prasidenten Wilson im Weltkrieg." [President Wilson's Mediation During the World War]. *Zeitschrift fur Politik* 18, no. 4 (1928): 209–30. Examines Wilson's mediation policy from the standpoint of his ultimate aim, which was to control the peace settlement.

2389. "Leader of Civilization." *Bellman* 25 (August 3, 1918): 117–18. Argues that Wilson had become the preeminent political leader of the world because of his "unshakable faith in peace founded on mutual understanding and good will."

2390. Leopold, Richard William. "The Problem of American Intervention, 1917: An Historical Retrospect." *World Politics* 2, no. 3 (April 1950): 404–25. Surveys literature covering United States intervention.

2391. Levin, Norman Gordon, Jr. *Woodrow Wilson and World Politics: America's Response to War and Revolution.* New York: Oxford University Press, 1968. Interprets Wilson's wartime policy as an effort to create a liberal-capitalist world order.

2392. Link, Arthur S. "Wilson Moves to the Center of the Stage of World Affairs." In **1741**, 37–43. [Also published as his "Woodrow Wilson and Peace Moves." *Listener* 75 (June 16, 1966): 869–71, and in **1155**, 99–109.] Traces Wilson's early offers of mediation, entry into the war, and the "uncharted waters" of trying to establish a new world order.

2393. ———. "World War I." In *Interpreting American History: Conversations with Historians*, ed. John A. Garraty, 121–44. New York: Macmillan Co., 1970. An interview with Link about World War I, its causes, and the ramifications of American participation.

2394. Lukacs, John. "1918." *American Heritage* 44 (November 1993): 46–51. Argues that America's involvement in World War I was perhaps the major event of the century, but due to Wilson's inability to deal with his allies at the Versailles Peace Conference, the resulting treaty contributed to World War II.

2395. Manning, Clarence A. "Woodrow Wilson and American Foreign Policy." *Ukrainian Quarterly* 12, no. 4 (1956): 332–39. Deals with Wilson's prewar stance, his plan for world reorganization, and his opponents on both topics.

2396. March, Peyton C. *The Nations at War.* Garden City, N.Y.: Doubleday, Doran & Co., 1918. Examines Wilson's decisions as Commander-in-Chief and his often difficult interactions with the War Department.

2397. Massie, Robert K. *Dreadnought: Britain, Germany, and the Coming of the Great War.* New York: Random House, 1991. Describes the European naval battles, technological developments, and strategic positioning prior to the outbreak of World War I.

2398. May, Ernest R. *American Intervention: 1917 and 1941.* Washington, D.C.: Service Center for Teachers of History, 1960. Compares Wilson's intervention with that of Franklin Roosevelt.

2399. Mayer, Arno J. *Political Origins of the New Diplomacy, 1917–1918.* New Haven: Yale University Press, 1959. [Also published under the title *Wilson vs. Lenin: Political Origins of the New Diplomacy.* Cleveland: World Publishing Co., 1964.] Maintains that American peace policy was intended to compete for world leadership with the ideas of the Bolsheviks.

2400. McMaster, John Bach. *The United States in the World War*. New York: D. Appleton and Co., 1927. An overview of the United States' role in World War I.

2401. Milton, George Fort. "But There Was No Peace." In *Use of Presidential Power, 1789–1943*, 224–50. Boston: Little, Brown and Co., 1944. Explores the incongruities of Wilson's diplomacy, his efforts for a lasting peace, and his troubles with political opposition.

2402. Morris, Richard Brandon. "The Decision to Go to War with Germany." In **2912**, 344–55. Details Wilson's decision to go to war, to issue his Fourteen Points, and to promote the League of Nations.

2403. Mowat, Robert Balmain. *A History of European Diplomacy, 1914–1925*, 44, 54, 179–88. New York: Longmans, Green & Co., 1927. United States' aloofness toward Europe in 1915 and 1916 and the failure of Wilson to bring about ratification of the League.

2404. "The Need for Wilson Diplomacy." *New Republic* 14 (March 9, 1918): 156–59. Champions the virtues of Wilson's "Peace Offensive."

2405. Noring, Nina J. "American Coalition Diplomacy and the Armistice, 1918–1919." Ph.D. diss., University of Iowa, 1972. Argues that American national interests soon triumphed over coalition politics.

2406. Odell, Joseph Henry. "Interpreting the People to the President." *Outlook* 118 (March 6, 1918): 368+. A consideration of America's war aspirations.

2407. Owen-Cruise, Sian Elizabeth. "'Out into Pastures of Quietness and Peace Such as the World Never Dreamed of Before:' An Examination of Woodrow Wilson's Peace Rhetoric as Covenant Creation." Ph.D. diss., University of Minnesota, 1993. Examines Wilson's use of covenant rhetoric to create an international peace.

2408. Parsons, Edward B. *Wilsonian Diplomacy: Allied-American Rivalries in War and Peace*. St. Louis: Forum Press, 1978. Wilson's abandonment of early peace proposals and the formation of new ones in 1918.

2409. Potter, Pitman Benjamin. "The United States and the War." *Harper's Monthly Magazine* 136 (March 1918): 521–31. An analysis of America's history, motives, and capabilities as a fighting nation.

2410. "The President Abroad." *Bellman* 23 (August 18, 1917): 174. Editorial which declares that the people of both the United States and the rest of the world now recognize Wilson's wisdom and leadership and the many obstacles he overcame to successfully lead his nation during wartime.

2411. "The President at Mount Vernon." *Nation* 107 (July 13, 1918): 30–31. Comments on Wilson's Fourth of July address dealing with the war.

2412. "The President on the Peace." *Nation* 108 (May 24, 1919): 846–47. Extracts from Wilson's 1917 addresses to Congress, pledging a peace without victory and making the world safe for democracy.

2413. "The President Voices the World's Desire." *Independent* 96 (October 12, 1918): 39–40. Wilson's speech at the Metropolitan Opera House, New York City, opening the Fourth Liberty Loan campaign in which he addressed goals for peace.

2414. "President Wilson and the Lessons of History." *Spectator* 116 (June 3, 1916): 678. Compares Wilson's and Abraham Lincoln's wartime policies.

2415. "President Wilson Calls upon Congress to Act." *Outlook* 115 (April 11, 1917): 637. Analyzes Wilson's April 2, 1917 call to war, with excerpts from his address to Congress.

2416. "President Wilson in Europe." *Current History Magazine of the New York Times* 9 (January-February 1919): 1–7, 198–215. A description of Wilson's journey to Europe and the subsequent reception upon his arrival.

2417. "President Wilson Tells Us When and How the War Will End." *Current Opinion* 64 (January 1918): 1–4. Tabloid opinions on Wilson's proposed conditions for ending World War I. Cites Wilson as a visionary and world architect.

2418. "President Wilson's Address to the Senate." *Spectator* 118 (January 27, 1917): 93. Argues that the only sure way to maintain world peace is by preserving the letter and spirit of the treaties.

2419. "President Wilson's Idealism." *Living Age* 298 (August 10, 1918): 348–50. Wilson as preeminent spokesman for the Allies.

2420. "The President's Attitude as Seen Abroad." *Literary Digest* 54 (April 7, 1917): 973–74. European opinion about Wilson's commitment to the war.

2421. "The President's Responsibility." *New Republic* 16 (October 26, 1918): 360–61. Calls for Americans to rally behind Wilson.

2422. "The President's Speech to the World." *Survey* 41 (October 5, 1918): 19–21. Wilson's New York City address on September 27, 1918.

2423. "The President's World Leadership." *Nation* 106 (January 17, 1918): 54. Wilson's terms for ending the war and the ways of ensuring lasting peace.

2424. Redfield, William Cox. "Glimpses of Our Government: The Storm Center." *Saturday Evening Post* 197 (September 13, 1924): 42, 200–2. Wilson's Secretary of Commerce uses the enactment of the Webb-Pomerene Act and United States entry into war to demonstrate Wilson's readiness to take advice.

2425. Rozwenc, Edwin Charles, and Thomas Lyons. *Realism and Idealism in Wilson's Peace Program.* Boston: D.C. Heath and Co., 1965. Analyzes Wilson's diplomacy despite his conflicts with other political leaders at home and abroad.

2426. "Rubicon Crossed." *Bellman* 22 (April 7, 1917): 369–70. Calls the war message one of the "most masterly and superb public utterances in the history of America."

2427. Schmickle, William Edgar. "For the Proper Use of Victory: Diplomacy and the Imperatives of Vision in the Foreign Policy of Woodrow Wilson, 1916–1919." Ph.D. diss., Duke University, 1979.

2428. Schmidtchen, Paul W. "The Man Who Won the War, but Lost the Peace." *Hobbies* May 1979: 102–4; June 1979: 102–4; July 1979: 102–3. Summarizes the changes in Wilson's views on foreign policy, culminating in the entrance into World War I and its consequences.

2429. Schnetzler, Hedwig. *Das Problem Wilson untersucht as der amerikanischen Aussenpolitik im besonderen wahrend des Weltkrieges.* [The Wilson Problem Explored in Relation to American Foreign Policy in Particular During the World War]. Jena: Universitatsbuchdruckerei G. Neuenhahn, 1932. A study of Wilson's personality and policy toward Europe, before and during World War I.

2430. "Scorn of Yesteryear." *Bellman* 23 (October 20, 1917): 425–26. Editorial contrasting the widespread vilification of Wilson both at home and abroad in late 1916 with the nearly universal approbation of him in late 1917.

2431. Seymour, Charles. *American Diplomacy During the World War.* Baltimore: Johns Hopkins University Press, 1934. [The Albert Shaw Lectures on Diplomatic History, 1933.] A study of the developments that "forced" Wilson to bring the United States into World War I and to promote a plan for an international organization.

2432. _____ . *Woodrow Wilson and the World War.* Chronicles of America Series. New Haven: Yale University Press, 1921. Believes that Wilson lacked the capacity for implementing the ideals that he preached, but his ideals greatly contributed to the development of modern international relations.

2433. Sheikholislam, Ali. "Open Diplomacy and Registration of Treaties." Ph.D. diss., New York University, 1959. Wilson's proposal that only open treaties be valid.

2434. Shriver, Philip R., ed. "A Wilsonian Paradox." *Ohio State Archaeological and Historical Quarterly* 63 (April 1954): 147–50. Three letters by Wilson in 1913, declining to travel to Europe while President. Article speculates how events might have gone if Wilson had declined to attend the peace conference.

2435. Smith, Daniel Malloy. *The Great Departure: The United States and World War I, 1914–1917.* New York: John Wiley Co., 1965. Describes Wilson as a moral leader and the relationship of his policies and principles to his goal of peace.

2436. _____ . "National Interest and American Intervention, 1917: An Historical Appraisal." *Journal of American History* 52, no. 1 (June 1965): 5–24. Focuses on the theme of national interest and its influence on American foreign policy makers.

2437. Smuts, Jan Christiaan. "Address by Field Marshall Smuts Accepting the Woodrow Wilson Award for Distinguished Service." In **1255**, 3–12. Rejects the criticism that the League of Nations Covenant demanded too much.

2438. Spencer, Samuel R., Jr. *Decision for War, 1917*. Ridge, N.H.: R. R. Smith, 1953. Analyzes the significance of the Zimmerman telegram and Wilson's decision that war could not be avoided.

2439. Tansill, Charles C. *America Goes to War*. Boston: Little, Brown and Co., 1938. Surveys the events which lead to the United States' entry into World War I. Much attention is given Wilson's administration, policies, and views on neutrality.

2440. Thompson, John A. "Woodrow Wilson and World War I: A Reappraisal." *Journal of American Studies* 19, no. 3 (December 1985): 325–48. Reassesses Wilson's foreign policies during and after World War I and their relationship to fundamental American interests.

2441. Trask, David F. "Remarks for the Bicentennial Lecture Series, U. S. Department of State, May 1, 1981: Woodrow Wilson and the Coordination of Force and Diplomacy." *Society for the History of American Foreign Relations* 12, no. 3 (1981): 12–19. Argues that Wilson was successful in striking this balance during the war but not after.

2442. _____ . "Woodrow Wilson and International Statecraft: A Modern Assessment." *Naval War College Review* 36, no. 2 (1983): 57–68. An appraisal of Wilson's struggle to keep the United States out of the war and his decision to enter the conflict in order to shape the peace.

2443. _____ . "Woodrow Wilson and the Reconciliation of Force and Diplomacy: 1917–1918." *Naval War College Review* 27, no. 4 (1975): 23–31. A favorable assessment of Wilson as a war leader.

2444. "An 'Unconditional Surrender.'" *Literary Digest* 59 (November 23, 1918): 12–13. Reaction from the American press on what it sees as a crushing defeat for Germany.

2445. U.S. Department of State. *Papers Relating to the Foreign Relations of the United States, 1914–1918. Supplement: The World War.* 9 vols. Washington, D.C.: Government Printing Office, 1928–1933.

2446. Van Meter, Robert H., Jr. "The United States and European Recovery, 1918–1923: A Study of Public Policy and Private Finance." Ph.D. diss., University of Wisconsin, 1971. Discusses Wilson's hope that United States private enterprise, not the government, would aid in Europe's recovery.

2447. Villard, Oswald Garrison. "Wilson and the World." *Nation* 108 (February 15, 1919): 252. Describes Wilson's crusade to fight for the interests of the United States as well as the Allies.

2448. Vosnjak, Bogumil. "Wilson to Europe." In **1038**, 227–31. Praises Wilson as a great prophet of democracy and a promoter of world order.

2449. Warren, Sidney. *The President as World Leader*, 62–138. Philadelphia: J. P. Lippincott, 1964. An examination of Wilson's attempt to use the presidency to change the isolationism of the American public.

2450. "Who Willed American Participation: Leadership of Mr. Wilson." *New Republic* 10 (April 14, 1917): 308–10. Regards Wilson's decision to enter World War I as intelligent and well-considered.

2451. Wimer, Kurt. "Woodrow Wilson and World Order." In **1941**, 146–173. Concentrates on Wilson's vision at the time when he formed the elements of his policy, shortly after the outbreak of World War I.

2452. Wister, Owen. "Roosevelt and the War." *Harper's Magazine* 161, no. 6 (June 1930): 34–49. Contains a number of comparisons of Wilson and Theodore Roosevelt, focusing on the years 1914–1918.

2453. Woodbridge, Homer E. "Criticism of the Nation." *Nation* 111 (November 17, 1920): 564–65. Criticizes the *Nation* for bitterly opposing Wilson's decision to enter World War I.

2454. Wright, Esmond. "Foreign Policy of Woodrow Wilson: A Re-Assessment." *History Today* (Great Britain) 10, no. 3–4 (March, April 1960): 149–57, 223–31. Pt. 1: Woodrow Wilson and the First World War. Pt. 2: Wilson and the Dream of Reason. Explores Wilson's passage from neutrality to intervention and his European policy in 1919.

b. France

2455. Ambrosius, Lloyd E. "Wilson, Clemenceau, and the German Problem at the Paris Peace Conference of 1919." *Rocky Mountain Social Science Journal* 12, no. 2 (1975): 69–80. Argues that Wilson's disagreement with Clemenceau was over means, not ends. Concludes that Wilson's faith in moral suasion and his failure to understand the German threat provided neither security for France nor a lasting peace.

2456. ———. "Wilson, the Republicans, and French Security after World War I." *Journal of American History* 59, no. 2 (1972): 341–52. Explores Republicans' attention to French security and Wilson's refusal to separate that question from the League Covenant.

2457. Barbusse, Henri. "Barbusse's View of President Wilson." *Dial* 66 (January 25, 1919): 92. Flattering view of Wilson by the leader of the French Socialist Party.

2458. Blumenthal, Henry. *Illusion and Reality in Franco-American Diplomacy, 1914–1945*. Baton Rouge: Louisiana State University Press, 1986. Discusses the negative effects of the disagreement between Wilson and Clemenceau on the peace treaty.

2459. "Clash of French and American Peace Plans." *Literary Digest* 60 (January 11, 1919): 9–11. Examination by the national press of the disagreement between Wilson and Clemenceau over the nature of the peace plan.

2460. Clemenceau, Georges Eugene Benjamin. "Grandeur and Misery of Victory." *Collier's National Weekly* 85 (April 19, 1930): 19–21+. Adapted from Clemenceau's book of the same title. He praises Wilson for his efforts to create a new world order but strongly condemns the United States Congress, and by implication the American people, for their rejection of the Versailles Treaty, the League of Nations, and the mutual security treaty.

2461. Dewey, Stoddard. "Opposition in France—Senator Clemenceau and President Wilson." *Nation* 102 (March 2, 1916): 246. Clemenceau's views of Wilson and the role of the United States in the European conflict.

2462. Duroselle, Jean-Baptiste. "Wilson et Clemenceau." In **1073**, 75–94. In a detailed comparison of the lives, personalities, and policies of the two statesmen, the author concludes that Wilson was more realistic and Clemenceau more idealistic than is usually assumed.

2463. Farrar, Marjorie M. "Toward a Complete Blockade: The American Adherence to France's Objectives of Economic War, April-August, 1917." *Revue d'Histoire Diplomatique* 89 (1975): 127–43. Examines the Wilson Administration's decision to begin an embargo on exports to European neutrals in 1917.

2464. "French Exegesis of American Politics." *Living Age* 304 (March 6, 1920): 565–69. Blames Wilson for the failure of the League of Nations, characterizing his leadership as reckless and dictatorial.

2465. Gannett, Lewis Stiles. "Temper of the French Workers: Their Attitude toward President Wilson, the Peace Conference and Reconstruction." *Survey* 41 (January 11, 1919): 488–89. Says Wilson is very popular with French laborers who want a new world order and believe he is their best representative at the Peace Conference.

2466. ———. "Vive Vill-son!" [Long Live Wilson!]. *Nation* 108 (January 18, 1919): 86–87. Examines French editorials written about Wilson.

2467. Gauvain, Auguste. "Les Initiatives du President Wilson." *Revue de Paris* 24, pt. 2 (March 1, 1917): 198–224.

2468. Ginsburg, Shaul. "Du Wilsonisme au Communisme: L'Itineraire du Pacifiste Raymond Lefebvre en 1919." [From Wilsonism to Communism: The Itinerary of the Pacifist Raymond Lefebrve in 1919]. *Revue d'Histoire Moderne et Contemporaine* 23, no. 4 (1976): 581–605.

2469. Goutel, Hennet de. *Vergennes and the American Independence: Vergennes and Wilson*, trans. L. Ensor. Paris: Editions de la Nouvelle Revue Nationale, 1918. Compares Wilson with Louis XVI's minister of foreign affairs.

2470. ———. *Vergennes et l'independence americaine*: *Vergennes et Wilson*. Paris: Editions de La Nouvelle Revue Nationale, 1918.

2471. "How President Wilson Impresses the French Mind." *American Monthly Review of Reviews* 59 (January 1919): 85–86. Contains excerpts from articles written by Emile Boutroux of the French Academy about his impressions of Wilson.

2472. Lavedan, Henri. "France Salutes President Wilson." *Living Age* 300 (January 18, 1919): 151–53. Praise for Wilson's idealism and hard work.

2473. Leffler, Melvyn P. *The Elusive Quest*: *America's Pursuit of European Stability and French Security, 1919–1933*. Chapel Hill: University of North Carolina Press, 1979. Although Wilson and his Republican successors sank back into isolationism, they continued to understand the importance of Europe's economic security for American prosperity.

2474. Louis, Paul. "L'evolution de la Politique Wilsonnienne." *Revue Politique et Litteraire* (Revue Bleu) 55 (February 24, 1917): 145–50.

2475. ———. "Les Idees Wilsoniennes." *Revue Politique et Litteraire* (Revue Bleu) 56 (February 2, 1918): 88–91.

2476. ———. "Wilson en Europe." *Revue Politique et Litteraire* (Revue Bleu) 56 (December 21, 1918): 741–3.

2477. Maurras, Charles Marie Photius. *Les trois aspects du president Wilson*; *la neutralite, l'intervention, l'armistice*. [Three Aspects of President Wilson: Neutrality, Intervention, Armistice]. 2 vols. Paris: Nouvelle Librairie Nationale, 1920.

2478. Merriman, Howard Maxwell. "The French and Woodrow Wilson, 1912–1918: A Study in Public Opinion." Ph.D. diss., Harvard University, 1937. Variations of French public opinion leading up to the Paris Peace Conference.

2479. Noble, George Bernard. *Policies and Opinions at Paris, 1919*: *Wilsonian Diplomacy, the Versailles Peace, and French Public Opinion*. New York: Macmillan Co., 1935. An attache to the American peace commission on French public opinion.

2480. Nouailhat, Yves-Henri. "A French Loan in the United States in July 1916: The Loan of the 'American Foreign Securities Company.'" *Revue d'Histoire Moderne et Contemporaine* 14 (1967): 356–74. Discusses the negotiations of a loan from the United States to France in 1916.

2481. Poincare, Raymond. *Victoire et Armistice*. [Victory and Armistice]. Paris: Plon et Nourrit, 1933. Memoirs of the President of France, including American participation in the war and Wilson's arrival in Paris.

2482. "President Wilson's Charge and French Replies." *Literary Digest* 64 (March 27, 1920): 27–29. Describes reaction to Wilson's charge that French imperialism was hindering a proper peace settlement.

2483. Renouvin, Pierre. "Le Destin du Pacte d'Assistance Americain a la France en 1919." [The Fate of the American Assistance Pact with France in 1919]. *Annals d'Etudes Internationales* (Switzerland) 1 (1970): 9–22.

2484. Roz, Firmin. "Le cas Wilson." [The Wilson Case]. *Revue des Deux Mondes* 60, no. 7 (December 1, 1930): 519–49.

2485. Stevenson, David. "French War Aims and the American Challenge, 1914–1918." *Historical Journal* (Great Britain) 22, no. 4 (1979): 887–94. Maintains that Wilson's entry into the war was a chance not only to eliminate an immediate threat to American interests but also to transform international relations.

2486. Trask, David F. *The United States in the Supreme War Council: American War Aims and Inter-Allied Strategy, 1917–1918.* Middletown: Wesleyan University Press, 1961. An analysis of military strategy in the French theater, arguing that decisions by field commanders were critical.

c. Germany

2487. Bergmann, Carl. *The History of Reparations.* London: Ernest Benn, 1927. A German moderate's views on reparations, with the opening chapters focusing on Wilson's peace efforts.

2488. "Bernstorff on the Witness Stand: German Ex-Ambassador's Testimony on Why President Wilson's Peace Efforts Failed." *Current History* 11 (March 1920): 513–19. Testimony by the former German Ambassador to the United States on his peace negotiations with Wilson during the war.

2489. Brooks, Sydney. *America and Germany, 1918–1925.* New York: Macmillan Co., 1925. Deals with the need for Americans to overcome wartime prejudices and the German dependence on American aid.

2490. Fitzgerald, Oscar P., IV. "The Supreme Economic Council and Germany: A Study of Inter-Allied Cooperation after World War I." Ph.D. diss., Georgetown University, 1971. Examines the role of the Supreme Economic Council in providing relief to Germany after the war.

2491. Fraenkel, Ernst. "Das deutsche Wilsonbild." [The German Image of Wilson]. *Jahrbuch fur Amerikastudien* 5 (1960): 66–120. Discusses the blame placed on Wilson by Germans for the harshness of the peace treaty and the rise of Fascism.

2492. "German Attitudes to President Wilson." *Living Age* 300 (February 8, 1919): 380. Excerpts from the *Frankfurter Zeitung* expressing a sense of betrayal over the armistice, while still holding out hope that Wilson can create an equitable peace.

2493. "German Ideas of the President's Aims." *Literary Digest* 56 (February 16, 1918): 15. Wilson's "infamous designs" on the world. The introduction is highly critical of the Germans.

2494. "Germany and the League of Peace." *New Republic* 9 (November 18, 1916): 60–62. Looks approvingly upon the German Chancellor's willingness to participate in a league to enforce peace and criticizes those who argue that the offer is insincere.

2495. "Germany's Peace Plot: Mr. Wilson's Warning." *Living Age* 294 (July 28, 1917): 253–54. Excerpts from a speech given by Wilson in response to an early, unacceptable peace proposal made by Germany.

2496. Kautsky, Karl. *Die Wursein der Politik Wilsons.* Berlin: Verlag Neues Vaterland, 1919.

2497. Kimmich, Christoph M. *Germany and the League of Nations.* Chicago: University of Chicago Press, 1976. Focuses on Wilson's role in the decision to exclude Germany from the League of Nations.

2498. Kober, August Heinrich. *Wilson und der Weltkrieg; Ratsel einer Freudschaft.* [Wilson and the World War; the Riddle of a Friendship]. Frankfurt: Societatsverlag, 1938.

2499. Kromer, Claudia. "Diplomatie und Volksabstimmung [Diplomacy and Plebiscite]." *Osterreich in Geschichte und Literatur* 14, no. 8 (1970): 401–13.

2500. Kruger, Peter. *Versailles: Deutsche Aussenpolitik Swischen Revisionismus und Friedensicherung.* Munich: Deutscher Taschenbuch Verlag, 1986.

2501. Ludendorff, Erich von. "The American Effort." *Atlantic Monthly* 129 (May 1922): 676–87. Examines the way in which American involvement influenced the development and outcome of World War I from the German viewpoint.

2502. Lutz, Ralph Haswell, ed. *Fall of the German Empire, 1914–1918.* 2 vols. Stanford: Stanford University Press, 1932. An extensive collection of primary documents.

2503. Martin, William S., Jr. "The Colonial Mandate Question at the Paris Peace Conference of 1919: The United States and the Disposition of the German Colonies in Africa and the Pacific." Ph.D. diss., University of Southern Mississippi, 1982. Examines attempts to prevent the annexation of African colonies by other European nations and the expansion by the Japanese in the Pacific islands.

2504. Nelson, Keith L. *Victors Divided: America and the Allies in Germany, 1918–1923.* Berkeley: University of California Press, 1975. Argues that United States forces remained in Germany to preserve unity, ensure obedience to the peace, and prevent the Allies from beginning any form of aggression.

2505. "Opening a Way to Peace." *Literary Digest* 53 (November 25, 1916): 1398. The German press's reaction to the German Chancellor's expressed willingness to seek a peaceful settlement.

2506. "Our President's Fantastic Ideas Unmasked by the Kolnische Zeitung." *Literary Digest* 57 (April 6, 1918): 30. Surveys the German tabloid view of Wilson.

2507. "President Wilson: The Perfect Ally." *Spectator* 118 (June 23, 1917): 694–95. Examines Wilson's relationship with Germany from a British perspective.

2508. "President Wilson's Vindication." *Living Age* 299 (November 23, 1918): 506–8. Defense of Wilson's overtures to the German leadership.

2509. "The President's Reply and the People's Reply." *Literary Digest* 59 (October 19, 1918): 7–9. Examines the demand of the American public that Germany surrender unconditionally.

2510. Reventlow, Ernst Christian Einar Ludwig Detlev, graf zu. "Germany's Opinion of Wilson as a Mediator." *Current History Magazine of the New York Times* 5 (October 1916): 148–51. Attacks Wilson by revealing the state of mind underlying the German opposition to American mediation.

2511. Schwabe, Klaus. *Deutsche Revolution und Wilson-Frieden. Die amerikanische und deutsche Friedensstrategie zwischen Ideologie und Machtpolitik 1918/19.* Dusseldorf: Droste, 1971.

2512. _____ . "Die Amerikanische und die Deutsche Geheimidiplomatie und das Problem eines Verstandigungsfriendens im Jahre 1918." [American and German Secret Diplomacy and the Problem of Peace by Consultation in 1918]. *Vierteljahrshefte fur Zeitgeschichte* (West Germany) 19, no. 1 (1971): 1–32.

2513. _____ . "U.S. Secret War Diplomacy, Intelligence, and the Coming of the German Revolution in 1918: The Role of Vice Consul James McNally." *Diplomatic History* 16 (Spring 1992): 175–200. Discusses Wilson's contradictory position in dealing with Germany about the armistice negotiations and the crucial source who claimed to speak for him.

2514. _____ . "Woodrow Wilson and Germany's Membership in the League of Nations, 1918–19." *Central European History* 8, no. 1 (March 1975): 3–22. Deals with Wilson's changing attitude in 1918 and 1919 about Germany's membership in the League of Nations.

2515. _____ . *Woodrow Wilson, Revolutionary Germany, and Peacemaking, 1918–1919: Missionary Diplomacy and the Realities of Power,* trans. Rita Kimber and Robert Kimber. Chapel Hill: University of North Carolina Press, 1985. Studies the relations between the United States and the first German Republic at the end of the World War and during the Paris Peace Conference.

2516. "Shall the Peace League Include Germany." *Literary Digest* 59 (October 12, 1918): 11–12. The world press on the importance of having Wilson's endorsement in order for the League of Nations to remain a viable idea.

2517. Small, Melvin. "The United States and the German 'Threat' to the Hemisphere, 1905–1914." *Americas* 28 (1972): 252–70. Argues that Germany never posed a serious threat to Latin America, but that a growing German presence in the region was a further justification for American entry into World War I.

2518. Smith, Daniel Malloy. "President Wilson and the German 'Overt Act' of 1917—a Reappraisal." *University of Colorado Studies Series in History* 2 (1961): 129–39.

2519. Smith, Dean. "The Zimmermann Telegram, 1917." *American History Illustrated* 13, no. 3 (1978): 28–37. Chronicles the events surrounding British interception of the note from the German foreign secretary which offered to help Mexico recover territories lost to the United States if Mexico joined an alliance with Germany.

2520. ———. "German Socialist Reaction to Wilsonian Diplomacy: From Neutrality to Belligerency." *Journal of Central European Affairs* 9 (April 1949): 61–79. Describes the variety of opinions concerning Wilson which generally moved toward disapproval.

2521. ———. "Wilson's Peace Program and German Socialism, January-March 1918." *Mississippi Valley Historical Review* 38 (September 1951): 187–214. Examines Wilson's ability to keep the German Socialists from supporting the Bolsheviks.

2522. ———. "Wilsonian Rhetoric Goes to War." *Historian: A Journal of History* 14 (Spring 1952): 191–208. Examines the ideological confrontation between Germany and the United States before and after World War I.

2523. Sondermann, Fred A. "The Wilson Administration's Image of Germany." Ph.D. diss., Yale University, 1953.

2524. ———. "The Wilson Administration's Attitude toward the German Emperor." *Colorado College Studies* 1 (Spring 1958): 3–16. [Based on the author's dissertation for Yale University.]

2525. "Teutonic Ire Stirred by the President." *Literary Digest* 55 (September 15, 1917): 19–20. Describes German and Austrian rage due to Wilson's peace efforts.

2526. "Teutonic Tact at Washington." *Literary Digest* 80 (February 23, 1924): 15. Discusses the German embassy's refusal to fly its flag at half-staff at the death of Wilson.

2527. Tuchman, Barbara Wertheim. *The Zimmermann Telegram.* New York: Viking Press, 1958. Explains how the discovery of the Zimmerman telegram helped push America into World War I.

2528. "Two German Tributes to Woodrow Wilson." *American Monthly Review of Reviews* 69, no. 5 (May 1924): 545.

2529. "An Unpublished Wilson Conversation." *Living Age* 333 (July 1, 1927): 9–10. Summarizes a conversation with Wilson concerning peace with Germany, relations with Allied Europe, and other post-Armistice questions.

2530. Vagts, Alfred. "Hopes and Fears of an American-German War, 1870–1915." *Political Science Quarterly* 54 (1939–1940): 514–35; 55 (1940): 53–76. Argues that the growth of navies and expansion of natural spheres of influence vastly altered international diplomacy, created new competitors and enemies for nations, and raised the possibility of a tragic world conflict.

2531. Wolfe, James H. "Woodrow Wilson und das Selbstbestimmungsrecht. Das Problem der Bohmischer Grenze." [Woodrow Wilson and the Right of Self-Determination. The Problem of the Bohemian Border]. *Bohemia. Jahrbuch des Collegium Carolinum* (West Germany) 8 (1967): 217–26. Deals with self-determination and the relocation of the Sudeten Germans after World War I.

2532. Wolff-Metternich, Paul Graf. "Eine Kriegskabinetts-Sitzung. [vom 29. Okt. 1918 uber die Antwort, die dem Prasidenten Wilson wegen der geforderten Aufgabe des U-Bootkrieges zu erteilen war]." [A War Cabinet Meeting (on October 29, 1918) in Which the Answer That Was to be Given President Wilson in Response to His Demand That the Submarine War Cease Was Discussed]. *Europaische Gesprache* 5 (1927): 39–46.

d. Great Britain and Its Dominions

2533. Boothe, Leon Estel. "A Fettered Envoy: Lord Grey's Mission to the United States, 1919–1920." *Review of Politics* 33, no. 1 (1971): 78–94. Describes some of Wilson's domestic difficulties concerning the League of Nations.

2534. Brand, Carl Fremont. "The Attitude of British Labor toward President Wilson during the Peace Conference." *American Historical Review* 42 (1937): 244–55. Believes that the appearance of Wilson in England at the close of 1918 called forth a welcome which proclaimed how fully and completely the British Labor party had accepted him as its spokesman.

2535. ———. "Reaction of British Labor to the Policies of President Wilson during the World War." *American Historical Review* 38 (January 1933): 263–85. British labor was generally united in support of Wilson's ideal of a just peace and a new international order.

2536. Brindley, Ronan. "Woodrow Wilson, Self-Determination and Ireland 1918–1919: A View from the Irish Newspapers." *Eire-Ireland* 23 (Winter 1988): 62–80. Asserts that although Wilson was not interested in Irish self-determination, Irish nationalists in 1918–1919 fully expected his support for a self-governing Ireland.

2537. Burk, Kathleen. *Britain, America, and the Sinews of War, 1914–1918.* Boston: George Allen & Unwin, 1985. Describes a complex economic structure, built up over four years of war, which deeply connected the British economy with American industry and finance.

2538. Carroll, Francis M. "The American Commission on Irish Independence and the Paris Peace Conference of 1919." *Irish Studies in International Affairs* (Ireland) 2, no. 1 (1985): 103–118. Examines the role of Irish-Americans and Irish leaders to bring the issue of self-rule for Ireland before the Paris Peace Conference and how they were unable to win the support of Wilson.

2539. Cooper, John Milton, Jr. "The British Response to the House-Grey Memorandum: New Evidence and New Questions." *Journal of American History* 59 (March 1973): 958–71. Includes documents from Sir Edward Grey and Arthur Balfour and minutes from a War Committee meeting.

2540. Egerton, George William. "Britain and 'The Great Betrayal': Anglo-American Relations and the Struggle for United States Ratification of the Treaty of Versailles, 1919–1920." *Historical Journal* 21 (1978): 885–911. Examines Edward Grey's inability to mediate between Wilson and the United States Senate over the treaty's ratification and his publication of a letter in *The Times* that further strained Anglo-American relations.

2541. _____. *Great Britain and the Creation of the League of Nations: Strategy, Politics, and International Organization, 1914–1919*. Papers of Woodrow Wilson. Supplementary Volume. Chapel Hill: University of North Carolina Press, 1978. Argues that British leaders wanted a League of Nations that would help establish them as a world power along with the United States.

2542. _____. "The Lloyd George Government and the Creation of the League of Nations." *American Historical Review* 79 (April 1974): 419–44. Focuses on the British involvement in the Paris Peace Conference but includes a discussion of Wilson's participation.

2543. "Ex-President Wilson and Ireland." *Spectator* 127 (December 10, 1921): 779. Believes that because of his Virginia background, Wilson was a believer in "states-rights" and secession.

2544. Fowler, Wilton B. *British-American Relations, 1917–1918: The Role of Sir William Wiseman*. Papers of Woodrow Wilson. Supplementary Volume. Princeton: Princeton University Press, 1969. An account written by a British Army captain who earned Wilson's trust and served as a liaison between the American and British governments.

2545. Girard, Jolyon P. "Congress and Presidential Military Policy: The Occupation of Germany, 1919–1923." *Mid-America* 56, no. 4 (1974): 211–20. Congressional pressure on Wilson and Harding to withdraw American troops from Germany after the war.

2546. "Great Scot, by the Gentleman at the Keyhole." *Collier's National Weekly* 84 (November 30, 1929): 36. Describes Lloyd George and Wilson as religious missionaries for world peace.

2547. Gregory, Ross. "The Superfluous Ambassador: Walter Hines Page's Return to Washington, 1916." *Historian* 28, no. 3 (May 1966): 389–404. Describes the failure of the American Ambassador to England to win his superiors to the British cause during his 1916 recall to the United States.

2548. "Grey on Wilson." *Nation* 105 (October 25, 1917): 444. Discusses a brief piece written by Sir Edward Grey on Wilson and the peace negotiations.

2549. Harris, Henry Wilson. "Has President Wilson Failed?" *Contemporary Review* 116 (August 1919): 154–61. [Also published in *American Monthly Review of Reviews* 60 (October 1919): 421–22.] Examines the irony of Wilson's new-found support among the British press, who once vilified him, just as his popularity at home is on the decline.

2550. Hopkinson, Michael. "President Woodrow Wilson and the Irish Question." *Studia Hibernica* (Ireland) 27 (1993): 89–111. Argues that although Wilson had no notable sympathy for Irish self-rule, he realized the need to influence the British on the question to improve his position within his own party.

2551. Kernek, Sterling J. "Distractions of Peace during War: The Lloyd George Government's Reactions to Woodrow Wilson, December, 1916–November, 1918." *Transactions of the American Philosophical Society* n.s. 65, pt. 2 (1975): 1–117. While still occupied in waging war, the British government was under constant pressure to react to Wilson's ambitious plans for peace and world order.

2552. Kihl, May R. "A Failure of Ambassadorial Diplomacy." *Journal of American History* 57 (December 1970): 636–53. Discusses the breakdown of communication between the American and British governments in late 1916.

2553. Link, Arthur S. *President Wilson and His English Critics: An Inaugural Lecture Delivered before the University of Oxford on 13 May 1959.* Oxford University Inaugural Lectures. Oxford: Oxford University Press, 1959. [Also published under the title, "President Wilson and His English Critics: Survey and Interpretation," in **1155**, 110–26.] Discusses the disregard British leaders showed toward Wilson during the period of American neutrality and at the Peace Conference.

2554. Machray, Robert. "President Wilson's Greatest Achievement." *Nineteenth Century and After* 82 (November 1917): 1088–1100. [Also published in *Living Age* 295 (December 29, 1917): 771–80.] A British analysis of Wilson's superb political leadership in mobilizing popular support for entering the war.

2555. Martin, Laurence Woodward. *Peace Without Victory: Woodrow Wilson and the British Liberals.* New Haven: Yale University Press, 1958. Compares the philosophies of Wilson and the British radicals.

2556. ———. "Woodrow Wilson's Appeals to the People of Europe: British Radical Influence on the President's Strategy." *Political Science Quarterly* 74 (December 1959): 498–516. Analyzes the effect of British radical influence on Wilson's strategy during World War I.

2557. Martin, Lawrence. *Presidents and the Prime Ministers*, 86–89. New York: Doubleday and Co., 1982. Describes Wilson's political relationship with Canadian Prime Minister Robert Borden during the Paris Peace Conference.

2558. McCarthy, Dennis J. "The British-Americans and Wilson's Peacemaking." *Duquesne Review* 9 (Spring-Fall 1964): 115–36. Examines a pressure group the author feels has been previously ignored.

2559. Meaney, Neville K. "The American Attitude towards the British Empire from 1919 to 1922: A Study in the Diplomatic Relations of the English-Speaking Nations." Ph.D. diss., Duke University, 1959. Discusses the effect of the changing attitudes of the British Empire on the League of Nations negotiations.

2560. _____ . "The British Empire in the American Rejection of the Treaty of Versailles." *Australian Journal of Politics and History* 9, no. 2 (1963): 213–34. Examines the debate over British domination of the League of Nations and its treaty, Wilson's role in the talks, and his American tour in support of the treaty.

2561. Murray, Arthur Cecil (3rd Viscount Elibank). *At Close Quarters: A Sidelight on Anglo-American Diplomatic Relations*. London: John Murray, 1946. Primarily a discussion of the role of Sir William Wiseman in confidential wartime communications between Wilson, Colonel House, and the British government.

2562. "Premier and President." *Living Age* 296 (February 23, 1918): 489–90. Advises Lloyd George to convince Wilson to cut off all raw materials to Entente nations as long as they remain occupied territories.

2563. "President Wilson as a German Catspaw in the Eyes of the British." *Current Opinion* 61 (July 1916): 7–10. A British tabloid opinion on Wilson's policies.

2564. "President Wilson's Visit and Its Sequels." *Spectator* 121 (December 14, 1918): 684–85. Expresses British support of Wilson's peace mission, analyzes the idea of freedom of the seas, and demands strong terms for Germany.

2565. Rappaport, Armin. *The British Press and Wilsonian Neutrality*. Stanford: Stanford University Press, 1951. Analyzes British attitudes toward Wilsonian neutrality by using the views and opinions expressed by dailies, weeklies, monthlies, and quarterlies.

2566. Ratcliffe, Samuel Kerkham. "Re-election of President Wilson." *Nineteenth Century and After* 80 (December 1916): 1186–97. Argues that Wilson's reelection is a favorable sign for British interests in the war.

2567. Schwartz, Donald R. "From Rapprochement to Appeasement: Domestic Determinants of Anglo-American Relations under Lloyd George and Wilson." Ph.D. diss., New York University, 1977. Discusses the clash between Britain and the United States during and after World War I due to Britain's loss of strength and America's resurgence.

2568. Swanwick, Helen Maria. *Builders of Peace*, 112–26. London: Swarthmore Press, 1924. Includes a letter from the British Union of Democratic Control to Wilson, supporting the Fourteen Points and the League of Nations.

2569. Trask, David F. *Captains and Cabinets*: *Anglo-American Naval Relations, 1917–1918*. Columbia: University of Missouri Press, 1972. Examines the somewhat uneasy relationship between the British and American navies during World War I, exploring American fears that Great Britain might still have used its naval power for imperial gain.

2570. Wallace, Robert. *Letters to President Woodrow Wilson*. London: A. H. Stockwell, 1931. Letters written by an Edinburgh professor, encouraging Wilson to intervene.

2571. Willert, Arthur. *The Road to Safety*: *A Study in Anglo-American Relations*. New York: Frederick A. Praeger, 1953. Describes Wilson's place in the diplomatic process.

2572. Woodruff, Douglas. "America's Crucial Years: Woodrow Wilson and Anglo-American Relations." *Tablet* 229 (March 22, 1975): 279–80.

2573. Woodward, David R. "Great Britain and President Wilson's Efforts to End World War I in 1916." *Maryland Historian* 1 (1970): 45–55. Shows British suspicions of Wilson's motives.

2574. Zimmern, Alfred E. "A European View of President Wilson." *Pacific Review* 1 (March 1921): 443–51. An account of the British people's disapproval of Wilson's foreign policy, beginning in 1916.

e. Italy

2575. Andriulli, G. A. "How We Alienated Wilson." *Living Age* 308 (January 29, 1921): 266–70. Wilson's relationship with the Italian government.

2576. Arbib-Costa, Alfonso. "Wilson and Italy." *Living Age* 305 (May 29, 1920): 520–23. [Also published in *Pan American Magazine* 31 (June 1920): 82–83.] Wilson's opposition to Italy's postwar claims.

2576a. Bobnio, Norberto. "Liberalism Old and New." *Confluence*: *An International Forum* 5, no. 3 (Autumn 1956): 239–51. Focuses on three proponents of liberalism who contributed to its decline in Italy: Benedetto Croce, Gaetano Mosca, and Vilfredo Pareto.

2577. Cimbali, Edoardo. *La Guerra degli Stati dell'Intesa. I 14 punti di Wilson e la revisione dei mandati e dei trattati internazionali*. Catania: Giannotta, 1931.

2578. Collins, Joseph. "American Eagle Changes His Perch." In *Idling in Italy*, 293–316. New York: Charles Scribner's Sons, 1920. Discusses Italians' reactions to Wilson and his peace efforts when he visited Italy soon after the war.

2579. De Capariis, Vittorio. "The Crisis of Contemporary Philosophy." *Confluence*: *An International Forum* 5, no. 4 (Winter 1957): 307–19. Introduces his remarks with a brief discussion of a prewar "golden age" of liberalism in the United States and Italy.

2580. De Santo, Vincenzo. "Italian View of the President." *New York Times* Sect. 4 (January 5, 1919): 1. Positive assessment of Wilson published just before his visit to Italy and written by an Italian soldier and former faculty member at the University of Pennsylvania.

2581. Fusco, Jeremiah N. "Diplomatic Relations between Italy and the United States, 1913–1917." Ph.D. diss., George Washington University, 1969. Discusses the increasingly strained relations between Italy and the United States over the issue of immigration and Italian opposition to Wilson's peace plan.

2582. Gannett, Lewis Stiles. "Mr. Wilson and the Italians." *Nation* 108 (May 3, 1919): 682. Discusses Wilson's handling of the conflict between the Italians and Yugoslavs.

2583. Gould, John W. "Italy and the United States, 1914–1918: Background to Confrontation." Ph.D. diss., Yale University, 1969. Argues that the Italian government made a serious mistake by failing to recognize the importance of American involvement in World War I, and that the blunder haunted Italy at the Peace Conference.

2584. Kernek, Sterling J. "Woodrow Wilson and National Self-Determination along Italy's Frontier: A Study of the Manipulation of Principles in the Pursuit of Political Interests." *Proceedings of the American Philosophical Society* 126, no. 4 (1982): 243–300. Analyzes Wilson's conduct over Italian boundary questions at the Paris Peace Conference.

2585. Nigro, Louis J., Jr. "Propaganda, Politics, and the New Diplomacy: The Impact of Wilsonian Propaganda on Politics and Public Opinion in Italy, 1917–1919." Ph.D. diss., Vanderbilt University, 1979. Examines Wilson's popularity among Italians.

2586. "Preference of Justice over Interest: President Wilson's Appeal to the Italian People." *Independent* 98 (May 3, 1919): 168. Wilson's appeal from Paris to Italians to support his program of partitioning in Yugoslavia, Austria, and Hungary.

2587. "The President and the Italians." *Nation* 108 (May 3, 1919): 676. Praises Wilson's behavior at the conference and forecasts the role that Italy will play in the process.

2588. "President Wilson Honored with Citizenship of Rome." *Official Bulletin* 3 (January 6, 1919): 1, 6–7. Provides full texts of speeches by the King of Italy and Wilson on a state occasion.

2589. Richardson, Norval. "A President in an Embassy." *Saturday Evening Post* 195 (May 12, 1923): 23+. Wilson's visit to Rome by the United States Ambassador to Italy.

2590. Ruffini, Francesco. *Il Presidente Wilson*. [President Wilson]. Milan: Fratelli Treves, 1919. Ranks Wilson as the equal of Washington and Lincoln in statesmanship and their superior in ideals.

2591. Schmitz, David F. "Woodrow Wilson and the Liberal Peace: The Problem of Italy and Imperialism." *Peace and Change* 12, no. 1/2 (1987): 29–44. Seeks to bridge a gap in the historical appraisal of Wilson's diplomacy, specifically his policy toward Italy and its territorial demands. Also undertakes to serve as a reminder that Wilson's original goal, the defeat of militarism in Europe, was not abandoned.

2592. Tobia, Bruno. "Il Partito Socialista Italiano e la Politica di W. Wilson (1916–1919)." [The Italian Socialist Party and the Policy of Woodrow Wilson, 1916–1919]. *Storia Contemporanea* 5, no. 2 (1974): 275–303. Reaction of the Italian Socialist Party to Wilson's peace proposals and the Paris Peace settlements.

2593. ———. "Vilson, Italija i Cetrnaest Tacaka." [Wilson, Italy and the Fourteen Points]. *Istoriski Casopis* 16/17 (1966–1967): 55–78.

2594. Zivojinovic, Dragan R. "The Emergence of American Policy in the Adriatic: December 1917–April 1919." *East European Quarterly* 1, no. 3 (1967): 173–215. Argues that Wilson's insistence upon the League and its role in the prevention of future wars brought Italy to despair; further, Italian trust in the force of arms could not have been more contrary to Wilson's idealism and optimism.

f. Poland

2595. Albee, Parker B., Jr. "American and Allied Policies at the Paris Peace Conference: The Drawing of the Polish-German Frontier." Ph.D. diss., Duke University, 1968. Argues that the resolution of the dispute over securing access to the sea for Poland revealed the personalities and diplomatic styles of many of the negotiators in Paris, especially Wilson and Colonel House.

2596. Biskupski, M. B. "The Poles, the Root Mission, and the Russian Provisional Government, 1917." *Slavonic and East European Review* (Great Britain) 63, no. 1 (1985): 56–68. Appraises the failure of the Root delegation, Wilson's interest in Polish independence, and his "Peace without Victory" speech.

2597. Duplicate entry omitted.

2598. Gerson, Louis L. *Woodrow Wilson and the Rebirth of Poland, 1914–1920: A Study in the Influence on American Policy of Minority Groups of Foreign Origin.* [Originally a Ph.D. diss., Yale University, 1952.] New Haven: Yale University Press, 1953. Describes the pressures brought to bear on Wilson by Polish groups seeking the reformation of Poland.

2599. Jezierske, Bronislas A. "The Wilson Monument in Poland." *Polish American Studies: Official Organ of the Polish American Historical Commission* 12 (January-June 1955): 19–34. Reminiscences of events at the unveiling of a monument to Woodrow Wilson at Poznan, 1931, involving several Polish political personalities.

2600. Kusielewicz, Eugene. "Paderewski and Wilson's Speech to the Senate, January 22, 1917." *Polish American Studies* 13 (July- December 1956): 65–71. Discusses the influence of the future Prime Minister of Poland on Wilson's decision to include Poland in the "Peace without Victory" speech.

2601. ———. "Wilson and the Polish Cause at Paris." *Polish Review* 1, no. 1 (Winter 1956): 64–79. Argues that the Thirteenth Point makes it clear that Wilson favored an independent Poland but that his positions on other issues relating to Poland are more difficult to understand.

2602. ———. "Woodrow Wilson and the Rebirth of Poland." *Polish American Studies* 12 (January-June 1955): 1–10.

2603. Lundgreen-Nielsen, Kay. "Woodrow Wilson and the Rebirth of Poland." In **1941**, 105–26. Discusses Wilson's Polish policy, 1917–1919.

2604. Manijak, William. "Polish American Pressure Groups, Woodrow Wilson and the Thirteenth Point: The Significance of Polish Food Relief, the Polish Vote in the 1916 Presidential Election, and European Events in the Eventual Self-Determination for Poland." Ph.D. diss., Ball State University, 1975.

2605. Sukiennicki, Wiktor. "Amerykanski Memorial Paderewskiego." [Paderewski's American Memo]. *Zeszyty Historyczne* (France) no. 26 (1973): 166–85. Considers the Polish leader's January, 1917 memo to Wilson urging the restoration of an independent Poland.

2606. "Un monument polonais au president Wilson." [A Polish Monument to President Wilson]. *L'Illustration* 179 (July 11, 1931): 380. Deals with the erection of a monument in Poznan in appreciation of Wilson.

g. Russia and the Soviet Union

2607. Bolger, Daniel P. "Cruel Russian Winter." *Military Review* 67 (June 1987): 63–77. Believes that Wilson's A.E.F. politically influenced the Allied presence in Russia.

2608. Bullitt, William C. *The Bullitt Mission to Russia*: *Testimony before the Committee on Foreign Relations, U.S. Senate*. New York: B. W. Huebsch, 1919. Records of the committee proceedings concerning William C. Bullitt's role during the American intervention in the Russian civil war.

2609. Creel, George C. "The Presidency of Woodrow Wilson—A Symposium: Wilson's Russian Policy." *Pacific Review* 1 (March 1921): 562–69. Explains why Wilson's Russian policy changed from supporting the revolution to refusing to recognize the Bolshevik state.

2610. Eastman, Max. "Lenin and Wilson." *Liberator* 2, no. 3 (March 1919): 8–11. Uses a fictional dialogue to contrast Lenin's clear language of concrete purpose with Wilson's unctuous moral language and opportunistic conduct.

2611. Farnsworth, Beatrice. *William C. Bullitt and the Soviet Union.* Bloomington: Indiana University Press, 1967. An assessment of the Soviet diplomat.

2612. Fike, Claude E. "Aspects of the New American Recognition Policy toward Russia following World War I." *Southern Quarterly* 4 (1965): 1–16. Wilson's refusal to recognize the new Soviet government.

2613. ――――. "The United States and Russian Territorial Problems, 1917–1920." *Historian* 24 (1962): 331–46. Argues that the Bolshevik Revolution made it difficult for Wilson to maintain his commitment to national self-determination.

2614. Filene, Peter G. *Americans and the Soviet Experiment, 1917–1933,* 9–63. Cambridge: Harvard University Press, 1967. Wilson's failed Russian policies are analyzed.

2615. Fithian, Floyd J. "Soviet-American Economic Relations, 1918–1933: American Business in Russia during the Period of Nonrecognition." Ph.D. diss., University of Nebraska, 1964. The loss of American business holdings in Russia, when Wilson offered no protection.

2616. Geyer, Dietrich. "Wilson und Lenin: Ideologie und Friedenssicherung in OstEuropa 1917–1919." [Wilson and Lenin: Ideology and the Security of Peace in Eastern Europe, 1917–1919]. *Jahrbucher fur Geschichte Osteuropas* 3, no. 4 (1955): 430–41.

2617. Goodman, Melvin A. "The Diplomacy of Nonrecognition: Soviet-American Relations, 1917–1933." Ph.D. diss., Indiana University, 1972. Includes a discussion of the origins of Wilson's policy of nonrecognition of the Soviet Union.

2618. Graves, William S. *America's Siberian Adventure.* New York: J. Cape and H. Smith, 1931. An account of the ultimately disasterous invasion of Siberia by the United States.

2619. Grayson, Benson L. *Russian-American Relations in World War I.* New York: Frederick Ungar, 1979. Russian-American relations from the outbreak of the European conflict through 1917.

2620. Hanna, William. "American Intervention into Siberia." *American History Illustrated* 19 (April 1984): 8–11, 44–47. Explains Wilson's decision to participate in the Allied Expeditionary Force sent to Russia in 1918.

2621. Hofer, W. "Lenin and Wilson in 1917. The 'Dominant Tendency' of Our Century." *Modern World* 6 (1968): 67–74. Analyzes the twentieth-century conflict between democracy and totalitarianism, especially in 1917.

2622. Hopkins, C. Howard, and John W. Long. "American Jews and the Root Mission to Russia in 1917: Some New Evidence." *American Jewish History* 69 (1980): 342–54. Discusses Elihu Root's trip to Russia in an effort to bolster the provisional government and to keep it in the war.

2623. Kennan, George Frost. "Russia and the Versailles Conference." *American Scholar* 30 (Winter 1960–61): 13–42. Wilson's hopes for support by the Russian people, a keystone in his plan for the postwar era.

2624. _____ . *Russia and the West under Lenin and Stalin*, 3–150. Boston: Little, Brown & Co., 1961. Notes Wilson's reactions to the Russian Revolution and states that Wilson believed Russia's absence at the Paris Peace Conference was little short of tragic.

2625. _____ . *Soviet Foreign Policy, 1917–1941*, 10–37. Princeton: Princeton University Press, 1960. Outlines Wilson's hopes for Russian involvement in the war following the Allied announcement of a more liberal and inspiring concept of war aims.

2626. _____ . "Soviet Historiography and America's Role in the Intervention." *American Historical Review* 65 (1960): 302–22. [Also published in *Contemporary History of the Soviet Mirror*, ed. John Keep, 286–305. New York: Praeger, 1964.] A rebuttal to Soviet military historian S. F. Naida's narrative on the United States intervention.

2627. _____ . *Soviet-American Relations, 1917–1920*. 2 vols. Princeton: Princeton University Press, 1958. [The first volume, entitled *Russia Leaves the War*, covers the 1917 Revolution through March 1918. Volume two, *The Decision to Intervene*, ends with United States intervention in Siberia.] Asserts that Wilson had no particular interest or knowledge of Russian affairs and that he used the network of America's foreign diplomatic missions as a vital and intimate agency of policy.

2628. _____ . "Wilsons Vierzehn Punkte und die Sowjets." [Wilson's Fourteen Points and the Soviets]. *Monat* 12, no. 133 (1959): 3–14.

2629. Killen, Linda R. *Russian Bureau: A Case Study in Wilsonian Diplomacy*. Lexington: University Press of Kentucky, 1983. Wilson's failed attempt to withhold recognition of the Bolshevik government.

2630. _____ . "The Search for a Democratic Russia: Bakhmetev and the United States." *Diplomatic History* 2 (1978): 237–56. Examines the recognition of Bakhmetev by Wilson long after his Russian government had lost power.

2631. _____ . "Self-Determination vs. Territorial Integrity: Conflict within the American Delegation at Paris over Wilsonian Policy toward the Russian Borderlands." *Nationalities Papers* 10, no. 1 (1982): 65–78. Emphasizes Wilson's contradictory policies.

2632. Kitsikis, Dimitri. "Religion and Politics: Tsar Alexander I and Woodrow Wilson: A Comparative Essay." *Patristic and Byzantine Review* 3, no. 3 (1984): 233–48. Compares the personalities and pacifist programs of two religious statesmen who lived a century apart.

2633. Kornfield, Louis D. "President Wilson on Siberia." *Nation* 109 (August 23, 1919): 258–61. Criticizes the American intervention in Siberia.

2634. Lasch, Christopher. "American Intervention in Siberia: A Reinterpretation." *Political Science Quarterly* 77 (1962): 205–23. Argues that concerns about Germany, not the spread of Bolshevism, brought about the intervention.

2635. Levine, Isaac Don. "President Wilson Has Saved Russia." *Independent* 93 (January 19, 1918): 102. Argues that Wilson's diplomatic overtures toward the Russian government saved Russia from German conquest.

2636. Long, John W. "American Intervention in Russia: The North Russian Expedition, 1918–19." *Diplomatic History* 6 (1982): 45–67. Claims that the Allies pressured Wilson into taking part in the intervention.

2637. Maddox, Robert James. "President Wilson and the Russians." *American History Illustrated* 2, no. 1 (1967): 40–47. Describes Wilson's futile one-year attempt to send American troops to Siberia.

2638. _____ . *The Unknown War with Russia*: *Wilson's Siberian Adventure*. San Rafael, Calif.: Presidio, 1977. Argues that the American intervention in Russia makes sense only in the greater context of Wilson's peace proposals and the threat posed to them by the Bolsheviks.

2639. _____ . "Woodrow Wilson the Russian Embassy and Siberian Intervention." *Pacific Historical Review* 36 (November 1967): 435–48. Wilson's motives for sending United States troops to Siberia.

2640. McFadden, David W. *Alternative Paths*: *Soviets and Americans, 1917–1920*. New York: Oxford University Press, 1993. Believes that Wilson's decision to commit American troops to defeat Germany in World War I was an important milestone in the complex and multifaceted relationship between the Soviet Union and the United States.

2641. Melton, Carol Kingsland. "Between War and Peace: Woodrow Wilson and the American Expeditionary Force in Siberia, 1918–1920." Ph.D. diss., Duke University, 1991. Explains that because of the uneasy political situation in Siberia, in 1920 the Wilson administration ordered the A.E.F.'s withdrawal from Russia.

2642. "Mr. Wilson on Russia: The Eleventh Hour." *New Republic* 25 (February 2, 1921): 273–74. An analysis of Wilson's official and unofficial policies.

2643. "Mr. Wilson Speaks Out: Note to Russia." *Living Age* 294 (July 14, 1917): 123–25. Discusses Wilson's communication with the Russian government and a British delegation concerning the steadfastness of American resolve.

2644. Radosh, Ronald. "John Spargo and Wilson's Russian Policy, 1920." *Journal of American History* 52 (December 1965): 548–65. Wilson requested official relations because the Russians were determined to conspire against American institutions.

2645. Richard, Carl J. "'The Shadow of a Plan': The Rationale behind Wilson's 1918 Siberian Intervention." *Historian* 49 (November 1986): 64–84. Concludes that had there not been a war in Europe already, Wilson would never have pursued the new Bolskevik regime.

2646. Schulman, Ephraim. "Of Betty Unterberger and Woodrow Wilson." *Society for Historians of American Foreign Relations. Newsletter* 18, no. 3 (1987): 35–38. Refutes Unterberger's portrayal of Wilson as consistent in his rhetoric and action, particularly in regard to noninterference in Russian affairs.

2647. Seal, Enoch, Jr. "The Attitude of the United States toward the Russian Provisional Government, March 15 to November 7, 1917." *Southern Quarterly* 4 (1966): 331–47. Claims that American aid was too little too late, demonstrating a lack of understanding of the Bolshevik movement.

2648. Shapiro, Sumner. "Intervention in Russia (1918–1919)." *United States Naval Institute Proceedings* 99, no. 4 (1973): 52–61. Wilson's purpose was to safeguard Allied military equipment and to secure the eastern terminus of the Trans-Siberian Railroad.

2649. Shelton, Brenda Kurtz. *President Wilson and the Russian Revolution.* University of Buffalo Studies 23:111–55. Buffalo: University of Buffalo, 1957. Explores Wilson's changing attitudes toward the revolution.

2650. Stamatopulos, Stephen. "Woodrow Wilson's Russian Policy: A Case Study of American-Russian Relations, 1913–1921." Ph.D. diss., Harvard University, 1957.

2651. Thompson, John M. "Allied and American Intervention in Russia, 1918–1921." In *Rewriting Russian History: Soviet Interpretations of Russia's Past*, ed. Cyril Edwin Black, 334–400. New York: Frederick A. Praeger, 1956. Soviet accounts of Allied-American intervention.

2652. ———. *Russia, Bolshevism, and the Versailles Peace.* Princeton: Princeton University Press, 1966. The uneasy stalemate in Eastern Europe and the inability of the Western powers to destroy the Bolsheviks or establish peaceful relations with them.

2653. Trani, Eugene Paul. "Woodrow Wilson and the Decision to Intervene in Russia: A Reconsideration." *Journal of Modern History* 48, no. 3 (September 1976): 440–61. Reexamines the question of why Wilson decided to send American troops to Siberia.

2654. Unterberger, Betty Miller. *America's Siberian Expedition: 1918–1920*. Durham: Duke University Press, 1956. Maintains that American intervention was motivated primarily by a desire to halt Japanese expansion.

2655. ———. "President Wilson and the Decision to Send American Troops to Siberia." *Pacific Historical Review* 24 (February 1955): 63–74. Wilson's decision to send forces, after long resisting Allied pressure to intervene.

2656. ———. "The Russian Revolution and Wilson's Far Eastern Policy." *Russian Review* 16, no. 2 (1957): 35–46. Motivations behind United States foreign policy.

2657. ———. *The United States, Revolutionary Russia, and the Rise of Czechoslovakia*. Chapel Hill: University of North Carolina Press, 1989. Explains Wilson's efforts to implement principles for which the United States had entered the war, and which he sought to apply universally.

2658. ———. "Woodrow Wilson and the Russian Revolution." In **1941**, 49–104. Contends that Wilson's policy of neutrality and non-interference can be understood within the context of his moral principles.

2659. ———. "Woodrow Wilson and the Bolsheviks: The 'Acid Test' of Soviet-American Relationships." *Diplomatic History* 11, no. 2 (1987): 71–90. Discusses the influence of Wilson's commitment to self-determination on his decision first to intervene in Russia in 1918 and later to withdraw.

2660. Unterberger, Betty Miller, ed. *American Intervention in the Russian Civil War*. Lexington, Mass.: D.C. Heath & Co., 1969. Essays and official documents illustrating Wilson's response to the Russian Revolution.

2661. U.S. Department of State. *Papers Relating to the Foreign Relations of the United States. Russia. 1918–1919*. 3 vols. Washington, D.C.: Government Printing Office, 1931–1937.

2662. Vinogradov, K. B., and V. V. Sergeev. "Vudro Vil'son v dni Voiny i Mira." [Woodrow Wilson in Days of War and Peace]. *Novaia i Noveishaia Istoriia* (USSR) 5, 6 (1975): 122–34, 100–13. A Marxist analysis of Wilson's presidency.

2663. Walsh, William James. "Secretary of State Robert Lansing and the Russian Revolutions of 1917 (Liberalism, Bolshevism, Nonrecognition, Resistance, Woodrow Wilson)." Ph.D. diss., Georgetown University, 1986. Chronicles Lansing's formulation of diplomatic responses to the two 1917 revolutions, his advice to Wilson, and Wilson's ultimate decision regarding Bolshevism.

2664. White, John A. *The Siberian Intervention*. Princeton: Princeton University Press, 1950. Wilson's concern over Japanese expansion was the motivating factor in his decision to send troops.

2665. Williams, William Appleman. *American-Russian Relations, 1781–1947*, 49–175. New York: Rinehart and Co., 1952. Examines the collapse of American relations with Russia during the Wilson years.

2666. ———. "The American Intervention in Russia, 1917–1920 (Part I)." *Studies on the Left* 3 (Fall 1963): 24–48. Argues that Wilson intervened because of concern over overseas economic expansion and Lenin's challenge to American ideals.

2667. ———. "The American Intervention in Russia, 1917–1920 (Part II)." *Studies on the Left* 4 (Spring 1964): 39–57. Discusses Wilson's rejection of a French proposal to aid the Bolsheviks.

2668. "Wilson on Russia." *New Republic* 20 (September 17, 1919): 189–90. Criticizes Wilson's new Russian policy as irrational.

2669. Wise, Jennings Cropper. *Woodrow Wilson: Disciple of Revolution.* New York: Paisley Press, 1938. An acerbic view of Wilson who is seen as prompting the Russian Revolution.

h. Other Nations

2670. Adam, Magda. "Woodrow Wilson and the Successor States." *Danubian Historical Studies* (Hungary) 1, no. 4 (1987): 19–32. Asserts that Wilson was committed to a policy of maintaining the economic and political integrity of the Hapsburg Empire and wanted to create a federation of states within its established borders.

2671. Ambrosius, Lloyd E. "Wilsonian Self-Determination." *Diplomatic History* 16 (Winter 1992): 141–48. This essay review of **2657** focuses on Wilson's efforts to implement his principles, especially national self-determination in Czechoslovakia.

2672. Barany, George. "Wilsonian Central Europe: Lansing's Contribution." *Historian* 28, no. 2 (1966): 224–51. Analyzes Lansing's influence on Wilson's policies.

2673. Biskupski, M.B. "Poland in American Foreign Policy, 1918–1945: 'Sentimental' or 'Strategic' Friendship? A Review Article." *Polish American Studies* 38, no. 2 (1981): 5–15. Believes that long-established friends of Poland such as Wilson, Hoover, and Franklin Roosevelt were sympathetic but seldom offered support just to benefit Poland.

2674. Bonn, Moritz J. "President Wilson: An Austrian View." *Living Age* 300 (March 1, 1919): 522–26. Portrays Wilson as passionate in his belief in American ideals but as overly cautious in the peace negotiations.

2675. Bousa, Joseph. "Wilson and T. G. Masaryk." *Slovakia* 10, no. 6 (1960): 29–36. Wilson's difficulties in dealing with Masaryk.

2676. Bryson, Thomas Archer. "Woodrow Wilson, the Senate, Public Opinion, and the Armenian Mandate, 1919–1929." Ph.D. diss., University of Georgia, 1965. Wilson could not accept a mandate for Armenia because of Senate opposition to Article 10 of the League of Nations Covenant.

2677. ———— . "Woodrow Wilson and the Armenian Mandate: A Reassessment." *Armenian Review* 21 (Autumn 1968): 10–29. Background and events regarding the Senate rejection of the Armenian mandate.

2678. Burian von Rajecz, Baron Stephan. "Austro-Hungarian Foreign Minister Discusses the President's Mount Vernon Address." *Current History Magazine of the New York Times* 8 (August 1918): 194–96. Shows a willingness to accept many of Wilson's peace proposals but refers to other Allies as being obstinate.

2679. Caldwell, R. J. *The Economic Situation in Czechoslovakia in 1920.* Washington, D.C.: Government Printing Office, 1920.

2680. Cardashian, Vahan. "A 1921 Memorandum to the President on Armenia." *Armenian Review* 26, no. 2 (1973): 46–63. A reprint of the document prepared at Wilson's request and Cardashian's letter, with an editorial note.

2681. Cizmic, Ivan. "Americka Politika Prema Bivsoj Jugoslaviji." [American Policies Toward Yugoslavia from Wilson to Roosevelt]. *Casopis za Suvremenu Povijest* (Crotia) 26, no. 1 (1994): 7–25. Argues that even though the principal of national self- determination encouraged the South Slavs to seek the breakup of the Austro-Hungarian monarchy, Wilson persisted in advocating the preservation of the monarchy, only offering Slavs autonomy in the Fourteen Points.

2682. Cramon, August von. "Kaiser Karl und Prasident Wilson; zu den neuen amerikanischen Dokumenten." [Kaiser Karl and President Wilson: Regarding Recent American Documents]. *Berliner Monatshefte fur International Aufklarung* 11 (1933): 1148–56. [Drawn from the "Papers Relating to the Foreign Relations of the United States, 1918 . . . World War," issued by the Department of State (Washington, 1933).] Deals with the Austrian peace overtures of 1918.

2683. Devasia, A. Thomas. "The United States and the Formation of Greater Romania, 1914–1918: A Study in Diplomacy and Propaganda." Ph.D. diss., Boston College, 1970. Argues that Wilson hoped to deal leniently with Austria-Hungary, but that public opinion persuaded him to create a Greater Romania.

2684. "General Smuts's Estimate of Wilson." *Current Opinion* 70 (April 1921): 449–50. Admiring tribute paid to Wilson on the eve of his retirement into private life.

2685. Gibson, Hugh. *A Journal from Our Legation in Belgium.* Garden City, N.Y.: Doubleday, Page & Co., 1917. A record of life and events in Belgium.

2686. Hajek, Jiri S. *Wilsonovska legenda v dejinach Ceskoslovenske Republiky.* [The Wilsonian Legend in the History of the Czechoslovak Republic]. Praha: Statni nakl. Politicke Literatury, 1953.

2687. Harbored, Maj. Gen. James G. "American Military Mission to Armenia." *International Conciliation* 151 (June 1920): 275–312. Report from the Chief of the Mission to the Secretary of State.

2688. Hitchins, Keith. "Woodrow Wilson and the Union of Transylvania with Rumania, 1917–1918." *Revue Roumaine d'Histoire* (Romania) 18, no. 4 (1979): 803–10. Evolution of Wilson's attitudes toward Austria-Hungary, particularly the Romanians of Transylvania.

2689. Kelly, David. "Woodrow Wilson and the Creation of Czechoslovakia." *East European Quarterly* 26 (Summer 1992): 185–207. Recounts the events that created Czechoslovakia in 1918 and concludes that Wilson was not primarily responsible for the emergence of the new state.

2690. Kisch, Guido. "Woodrow Wilson and the Independence of Small Nations in Central Europe." *Journal of Modern History* 19 (Summer 1947): 235–38. Discusses new documents that illuminate more fully Wilson's role in the breakup of Austria-Hungary and the creation of Czechoslovakia.

2691. Lederer, Ivo J. *Yugoslavia at the Paris Peace Conference: A Study in Frontier Making.* New Haven: Yale University Press, 1963. A study of Yugoslavia's formative period between 1918 and 1920, during which its frontiers were secured. Notes Wilson's contributions to the process.

2692. Mamatey, Victor S. "United States and the Dissolution of Austria-Hungary." *Journal of Central European Affairs* 10 (October 1950): 256–70. Examines American policy toward Austria, focusing on the declaration of May 29, 1917, the events leading up to it, and Wilson's motives and actions.

2693. _____ . *The United States and East Central Europe, 1915–1918: A Study in Wilsonian Diplomacy and Propaganda.* Princeton: Princeton University Press, 1957. A comprehensive study of Wilsonian self-determination in the Austro-Hungarian Empire.

2694. Masaryk, Thomas G. *The Making of a State.* London: George Allen & Unwin, 1927. [Also published under the title, *Memories and Observations, 1914–1918*.] The founding of the state of Czechoslovakia, written by its first President.

2695. Mrazek, Jaroslav. "Woodrow Wilson a americke uznani Ceskoslovenske Narodni rady za vladu de facto." [Woodrow Wilson and the Recognition of the National Czechoslovakian Council as the *De Facto* Government by the United States of America]. *Nase Revoluce* 9 (1933): 129–55, 379–427.

2696. Netea, Vasile. "Romanians in America up to 1918." In *Nouvelle Etudes d'Histoire*, 259–67. Bucharest: Editura Academiei, 1975. Efforts by the Romanian government to persuade Romanian immigrants in the United States to influence the Wilson Administration on such matters as Romanian claims to Transylvania.

2697. Oprea, Ion M. "Contributia Romaniei la Intemeierea Societatii Natiunilor." [Romania's Contribution to the Formation of the League of Nations]. *Revista de Istorie* (Romania) 33, no. 10 (1980): 1891–1903. Maintains that Wilson's League exerted a positive influence on the victorious nations after World War I.

2698. Pastor, Peter. "The Hungarian Revolution's Road from Wilsonianism to Leninism, 1918–19." *East Central Europe* 3, no. 2 (1976): 210–19. Although Hungarian revolutionary leader Mihaly Karoliy embraced Wilsonism, Wilson favored a hands-off policy toward Eastern Europe because he considered conditions there too volatile.

2699. Petko, Petko M. "Sasht I Bulgaria 1917–1918." [The United States and Bulgaria, 1917–1918]. *Godishnik na Sofiiskiia U. "Kliment Okhridski." Istoricheski Fakultet* (Bulgaria) 73 (1979): 61–107. Concerns United States-Bulgarian relations before World War I and at the 1918 peace conference.

2700. "President Wilson and the Adriatic." *New Statesman* 14 (February 21, 1920): 574–75. Describes Wilson's frustrated involvement in the division of territory between Italians and Yugoslavs.

2701. "President Wilson on Austria-Hungary." *Nation* 107 (October 5, 19, 1918): 392–94, 467. Includes a compendium of Wilson's pronouncements on the role he envisioned for Austria-Hungary.

2702. Rhue, Algot. *Woodrow Wilson, Mhanniskan och Statsmannen.* Stockholm: Svenska Andelsfhorlaget, [n.d.].

2703. Seymour, Charles. "Woodrow Wilson and Self-Determination in the Tyrol." *Virginia Quarterly Review* 38, no. 4 (Autumn 1962): 567–87. Examines traditional explanations for Wilson's attitudes toward the German-speaking Tyrolese.

2704. "Sick-Bed Politics." *Spectator* 124 (February 21, 1920): 232–33. Analyzes Wilson's intervention in the Adriatic conflict following the peace settlement.

2705. Smallwood, James. "Banquo's Ghost at the Paris Peace Conference: The United States and the Hungarian Question." *East European Quarterly* 12 (1978): 289–307. Wilson's staff and the Allies in Paris made it nearly impossible to accept the Communist government in Hungary.

2706. Snell, John Leslie. "Benedict XV, Wilson, Michaelis, and German Socialism." *Catholic Historical Review* 37 (July 1951): 151–78. Believes that Wilson's 1917 peace efforts have been over-emphasized while the Pope's peace efforts have been ignored.

2707. Tarulis, Albert N. *American-Baltic Relations, 1918–1922: The Struggle over Recognition.* Washington, D.C.: Catholic University of America Press, 1965. Discusses the United States' "do-nothing" policy toward the Baltic states who wished independence from Russia.

2708. Vesa, Vasile. "Wilsonian Principles in Transylvania, 1918." *Southeastern Europe* 6, no. 1 (1979): 81–86. Notes Wilson's great influence as an advocate and symbol of self-determination.

2709. Wojstomski, Stefan. "Pojecie samostanowienia w polityce sowieckiej w okresie rokowan brzeskich 1917–1918 r. [Przyczynek do badan nad sprawa narodowosciowa w Z. S. R. R.] (L'idee wilsonienne dans la politique de U.R.S.S. au temps des negociations de Brzesc 1917–1918. [Contribution a l'etude sur la question nationale de U.R.S.S.])." *Sprawy narodowosciowe* 9 (1935): 38–44.

2710. "Woodrow Wilson and the Liberation of Nations." *Ukrainian Quarterly* 12, no. 4 (1956): 293–98. Assesses the application of the theory of self-determination by Wilson and his assistants.

2711. Ybarra, Thomas Russell. "Prague! Wilson Station!" *Outlook* 151 (March 20, 1929): 447. Describes Wilson's continuing popularity in Czechoslovakia.

2712. Zivojinovic, Dragan R. *America, Italy, and the Birth of Yugoslavia (1917–1919)*. New York: Columbia University Press, 1972. Argues that Wilson was much more flexible than has been thought.

2713. ———. "The Vatican, Woodrow Wilson, and the Dissolution of the Hapsburg Monarchy, 1914–1918." *East European Quarterly* 3, no. 1 (1969): 31–70. The Vatican's efforts to safeguard the survival of Austria-Hungary.

8. Paris Peace Conference and the League of Nations

2714. "Agitation for a League of Nations without Criticism." *New Republic* 18 (March 15, 1919): 200–2. Advocates uncritical support.

2715. Almond, Nina, and Ralph Haswell Lutz. *An Introduction to a Bibliography of the Paris Peace Conference: Collections of Sources, Archive Publications, and Source Books*. Hoover War Library Bibliographical Series 2. Stanford: Stanford University Press, 1935. Sources, archival publications, and source books.

2716. Aman, John A. "Views of Three Iowa Newspapers on the League of Nations." *Iowa Journal of History and Politics* 34 (July 1941): 227–85. Uses the debate among Iowa's three major newspapers to survey the variety of arguments, offered by the press about the proposed League.

2717. Ambrosius, Lloyd E. *Woodrow Wilson and The American Diplomatic Tradition: The Treaty Fight in Perspective*. Cambridge: Harvard University Press, 1987. World War I as the first test of the United States' role in an interdependent global community.

2718. ———. "Woodrow Wilson's League of Nations." *Maryland Historical Magazine* 65, no. 4 (1970): 369–93. Wilson's actions at the Paris Peace Conference were only the "first, cautious steps" away from traditional American isolationism.

2719. "America and the League of Nations." *New Republic* 17 (November 30, 1918): 116–18. Expresses support for a League of Nations.

2720. Angell, Norman. *After All*. London: H. Hamilton, 1951. Outlines Wilson's peace plans following World War I.

2721. Armstrong, Gary Thomas. "The Domestic Politics of War Termination: The Political Struggle in the United States Over the Armistice, 1918 (World War I)." Ph.D. diss., Georgetown University, 1994. Asserts that the Wilson administration upheld a moderate policy for ending the war in order to solidify its peace proposals.

2722. Armstrong, Hamilton Fish. "American Misgivings." *New Europe* 14 (March 18, 1920): 232–34. Discusses Wilson's hopes and compromises during the peace negotiations.

2723. _____. "The Chain of Coincidences." In *Peace and Counterpeace: From Wilson to Hitler: Memoirs*, 9–178. New York: Harper and Row, 1971. Memoir by an army officer present at the Paris peace negotiations in 1919. The first section covers the war and the peace talks.

2724. Artaud, Denise. "Sur L'Entre-Deux-Guerres: Wilson a la Conference de la Paix (1919)." [On the Interwar Period: Wilson at the Peace Conference, 1919]. *Revue d'Histoire de la Deuxieme Guerre Mondiale* (France) 31, no. 124 (1981): 97–107. Failure of European financial reconstruction.

2725. Asquith, Herbert Henry. "President Wilson and the League of Nations." *Current History Magazine of the New York Times* 8 (September 1918): 511–13. Praises Wilson's efforts to create a League of Nations, ranking him alongside Washington and Lincoln.

2726. Bailey, Thomas Andrew. *Wilson and the Peacemakers.* Combining *Woodrow Wilson and the Lost Peace* and *Woodrow Wilson and the Great Betrayal.* 2 vols. in 1. New York: Macmillan Co., 1947.

2727. _____. *Woodrow Wilson and the Great Betrayal.* New York: Macmillan Co., 1945. Believes that the unwillingness or inability of the United States to accept Wilson's League of Nations plan resulted in the betrayal of the Allies, the Treaty of Versailles, worldwide liberal opinion, and the American people themselves.

2728. _____. *Woodrow Wilson and the Lost Peace.* New York: Macmillan Co., 1944. Interprets Wilson's role at the Peace Conference as the struggle of American idealism against European realism.

2729. _____. "The Woodrow Wilson Worshippers." *Society for the History of American Foreign Relations* 12, no. 4 (1981): 13–15. A revisionist account of the negotiations at the Paris Peace Conference.

2730. _____. "Woodrow Wilson Wouldn't Yield." *American Heritage* 8, no. 4 (June 1957): 20–25, 105–6. [Also published in *Essays Diplomatic and Undiplomatic of Thomas A. Bailey*, ed. Alexander Deconde and Armin Rappaport, 221–35. New York: Appleton-Century-Crofts, 1969.] Discusses the clash between Wilson and Henry Cabot Lodge in the struggle over the Treaty of Versailles.

2731. Baker, Ray Stannard. *The Versailles Treaty and After: An Interpretation of Woodrow Wilson's Work at Paris.* Christianity and World Problems, 5. New York: George H. Doran, 1924. Wilson's efforts to secure a just peace.

2732. _____ . *What Wilson Did at Paris.* Garden City, N.Y.: Doubleday, Page & Co., 1919. Interpretative glimpses of Wilson's battles and the kind of foes he confronted.

2733. _____ . *Woodrow Wilson and World Settlement.* 3 vols. Garden City, N.Y.: Doubleday, Page and Co., 1922. Taken from the author's unpublished material. Vols. 1 and 2 concern the Paris Peace Conference, and vol. 3 contains documents cited in the previous volumes.

2734. Barany, George. "A Note on the Genesis of Wilson's Point Ten. The Meinl Mission and the Department of State, 1917–18." *Journal of Central European Affairs* 23, no. 2 (July 1963): 219–22. Calls into question some of the diplomatic jockeying that led to the formulation of the Tenth Point.

2735. Barth, Frank, comp. *The Lost Peace: A Chronology: The League of Nations and the United States Senate, 1918–1921.* New York: Woodrow Wilson Foundation, 1945. Describes important dates and events during the Paris Peace Conference.

2736. Baruch, Bernard Mannes. *The Making of the Reparation and Economic Sections of the Treaty*, 298–315. New York: Harper and Brothers, 1920. States that Wilson's Fourteen Points proceeded from the basis of existing international law and specified the further and special acts of justice necessary for a proper settlement of the war.

2737. Berle, Adolf A., Jr. "Betrayal at Paris." *Nation* 109 (August 9, 1919): 170–71. Contends that Wilson betrayed the world.

2738. Best, Gary Dean. *Politics of American Individualism: Herbert Hoover in Transition, 1918–1921.* Westport, Conn.: Greenwood Press, 1975. Material on the battle for the League of Nations is contained here, as is information on the Second Industrial Conference.

2739. Binkley, Robert Cedric. "Ten Years of Peace Conference History." *Journal of Modern History* 1 (1929): 607–29. Argues that some documentation of the Paris Peace Conference is incomplete.

2740. Birdsall, Paul M. "Second Decade of Peace Conference History." *Journal of Modern History* 11 (1939): 362–78. An addendum to the Binkley article of 1929 containing further documentation of the Paris Peace Conference.

2741. _____ . *Versailles Twenty Years After.* New York: Reynal and Hitchcock, 1941. The struggle between Wilsonian principles and the tenets of nationalism, including a section on Wilson as "American Prophet" and a chapter on Wilson and Colonel House.

2742. Bonsal, Stephen. "Conference Runs into Heavy Weather: The Little Nations at Versailles." In *Suitors and Suppliants*, 245–81. New York: Prentice-Hall, 1946. Diary entries recounting events at the Paris peace talks, including Wilson's failings.

2743. ———. *Unfinished Business*. Garden City, N.Y.: Doubleday, Doran and Co., 1944. Account of the peace negotiations, taken from private notes and diaries.

2744. Boothe, Leon Estel. "Anglo-American Pro-League Groups Lead Wilson, 1915–1918." *Mid-America* 51, no. 2 (1969): 92–107. Investigates pro-League movements in England and America and Wilson's early reluctance to support them.

2745. ———. "Woodrow Wilson's Cold War: The President, the Public, and the League Fight, 1919–1920." Ph.D. diss., University of Illinois at Urbana-Champaign, 1966. Blames Wilson's obstinacy and his alienation of the Republican party and the American public for the failure of the League of Nations Treaty.

2746. Bowie, Robert R. "Progress toward Collective Security." In **1251**, 2–11. Traces the development of collective security from Wilson's early actions, through the lifetime of the League of Nations, and up to and including the United Nations' response to the 1956 Suez and Hungarian crises.

2747. Brinkley, Robert Cedric. "New Light on the Paris Peace Conference: From the Armistice to the Organization of the Peace Conference." *Political Science Quarterly* 46, no. 3 (September 1931): 335–61. Examines the contradictory agreements that came out of the Paris Peace Conference.

2748. Brooks, Sydney. "Mr. Wilson and the Treaty." *Nineteenth Century and After* 86 (December 1919): 1180–88. Blames Wilson for the failure of the treaty, claiming that he formed his foreign policy as a one-man crusade, alienating many.

2749. Brown, Daniel Patrick. *Woodrow Wilson and the Treaty of Versailles: The German Leftist Press' Response*. Ventura, Calif.: Golden West Historical Publications, 1977. Examines Wilson's peacemaking efforts during the Weimar era.

2750. Bruggeman, Felix. *Woodrow Wilson und die Vereinigten Staaten von Amerika. Betrachtungen zum Weltkrieg und Versailler Vertrag*. [Woodrow Wilson and the United States of America. Deliberations on the World War and the Versailles Treaty]. Giessen: Giessen University, 1933.

2751. Buehrig, Edward Henry. "Woodrow Wilson and Collective Security." In **1870**, 34–60. [Also published in **1741**, 29–36.] Argues that it is impossible to say with any certainty that the failure to adopt Wilson's postwar policies led directly to World War II and the events leading up to it.

2752. Bullitt, William C. "Tragedy of Versailles." *Life* 16 (March 27, 1944): 98–102. Examines the diplomatic errors at Versailles which precluded a lasting peace.

2753. Burlingame, Roger, and Alden Stevens. *Victory without Peace*. New York: Harcourt, Brace and Co., 1944. A fictional treatment of Wilson's fight for the peace treaty.

2754. Burnett, Phillip M. *Reparations at the Paris Peace Conference from the Standpoint of the American Delegation*. 2 vols. New York: Columbia University Press, 1940. Contains a synopsis and most of the pertinent documents dealing with reparations, chiefly from American sources.

2755. Bush, Irving T. "When Dreams Come True." *Independent* 97 (February 22, 1919): 254–55. Wilson's decision to attend the Peace Conference.

2756. Chalmers, Thomas. "Wilson et l'entree de l'Amerique dans la Societe des Nations." [Wilson and the Entry of America into the League of Nations]. *Nouvelle Revue* 87 (February 1, 1927): 175–82.

2757. Chan, Loren B. "Fighting for the League: President Wilson in Nevada, 1919." *Nevada Historical Society Quarterly* 22, no. 2 (1979): 115–27. Explores Wilson's appeal in Nevada for support of the League and the opposition to it in that state and by its senators.

2758. Churchill, Sir Winston Spencer. *The World Crisis: The Aftermath*, 4:104–202. New York: Charles Scribner's Sons, 1929. Concerns the period 1918–1928. Chapters on the Fourteen Points, the Paris Peace Conference, and the League of Nations contain numerous references to Wilson.

2759. Ciechanowski, Jan. "Woodrow Wilson in the Spotlight of Versailles." *Polish Review* 1, no. 2/3 (1956): 12–21. A reprint of an address delivered at the celebration of the 100th anniversary of Wilson's birth, which discusses Wilson's role in the Versailles settlement.

2760. Colcord, Lincoln (Ross). "Why Wilson Was Defeated at Paris." *Nation* 108 (May 17, 1919): 782–84. Blames Wilson and the State Department for the failure to negotiate a peace treaty, citing their early knowledge of secret imperialistic treaties between Entente nations and Wilson's willingness to join them in the war despite his anti-imperialism rhetoric.

2761. Cole, Beverly A. "A Critical Battle of Modern Times." *Social Studies* 39 (December 1948): 355–59. Discusses the parts played by Wilson and the Senate in the debate over ratification of the League of Nations. Blames, in part, the failure of the United States to join the League for the aggressive actions of Germany in the 1930s.

2762. Cooper, John Milton, Jr. "Fool's Errand or Finest Hour? Woodrow Wilson's Speaking Tour in September 1919." In **1083**, 198–220. Wilson's whirlwind tour on behalf of American membership in the League of Nations.

2763. Corwin, Edward Samuel. "Wilson and the Senate." *Review* 1 (July 26, 1919): 228–29. [Also published in *Presidential Power and the Constitution*, 28–31. Ithaca,

N.Y.: Cornell University Press, 1976.] Analyzes the deteriorating relationship between Wilson and the Senate over the League of Nations.

2764. Cousins, Norman. "Woodrow Wilson and His Clients." *Saturday Review of Literature* 33 (September 23, 1950): 24–25. Describes Wilson's efforts for the League on behalf of the "clients" who were all the members of the next generation.

2765. Cranston, Ruth. "Fact vs. Fiction: On-the-Record Story of Wilson and the Peacemaking of 1919." *Christian Science Monitor Weekly Magazine* (July 29, 1944): 7, 14. Correction of a popular perception that Wilson was obstinate and that he failed to consult adequately with members of the Senate.

2766. ———. "Myths of the League Battle." *New York Times Magazine* August 20, 1944: 14+. Among the "myths" are popular support, support by business and most churches, and defeat by a small group of powerful men.

2767. Creel, George C. "Mr. Wilson among the Lions at the Paris Peace Conference." *Literary Digest* 66 (August 14, 1920): 50–55. A defense of Wilson's performance and correctness.

2768. ———. *The War, the World and Wilson.* New York: Harper & Brothers, 1920. Views Wilson's performance at Versailles as one of the great diplomatic moments in history, marred only by the response of the Senate Republicans.

2769. Curry, George. "Woodrow Wilson, Jan Smuts, and the Versailles Settlement." *American Historical Review* 66 (July 1961): 968–86. Interplay of compromise and principle on the settlement.

2770. Curtis, George H. "The Wilson Administration, Elihu Root, and the Founding of the World Court." Ph.D. diss., Georgetown University, 1972. Examines Wilson's gradual conversion to the idea of a World Court and Root's promise to help.

2771. Czernin, Ferdinand. *Versailles, 1919: The Forces, Events and Personalities that Shaped the Treaty.* New York: Capricorn Press, 1965. Divides the peace negotiations into six phases: the first five weeks; the period of Wilson's absence; the two weeks immediately following Wilson's return; the dark period; the period during which compromises were made; and the final face-to-face meetings of the belligerents.

2772. Darien, George. "How President Wilson Did Not Fail." *Public* 22 (September 20, 1919): 1017–19. Denies that Wilson was naive or stubborn as a negotiator but was instead a committed advocate of a new order for the world's people.

2773. ———. "How President Wilson Has Succeeded." *Public* 22 (September 27, 1919): 1045–47. Says Wilson has made plain to the world's governments that the people are sovereign and can lead through the League of Nations.

2774. Darling, H. Maurice. "Who Kept the United States out of the League of Nations?" *Canadian Historical Review* 10 (September 1929): 196–211. Lays much of the blame on Henry Cabot Lodge.

2775. "Defeat Article Ten." *New Republic* 18 (March 29, 1919): 263–65. An editorial opposing Article Ten of the League Covenant, which would require members to insure the preservation of the national integrity of all other members.

2776. "Defeat the Treaty!" *Nation* 108 (June 21, 1919): 972. An editorial attempt to overcome the praise being heaped upon the peace treaty by the national press, pointing out the treaty's many flaws.

2777. "Democratic Ways of the Wilsons with Foreign Kings and Things." *Literary Digest* 61 (May 3, 1919): 64–66. Describes Wilson's informality and lack of deference during his meetings with European royalty.

2778. Dexter, Byron. "The Liberal Values and Collective Security." *Confluence: An International Forum* 5, no. 4 (Winter 1957): 307–19. Compares the systems of collective security under the League of Nations, whose rationale was supplied by Western liberal values.

2779. Dickinson, Goldsworthy Lowes. *The Choice Before Us*. New York: Dodd, Mead and Co., 1917. Deals with the problems of World War I and the League of Nations.

2780. Dickman, Fritz. "Die Kriegsschuld Frage auf der Friedenskonferenz von Paris, 1919." [The Question of Reparations at the Peace Conference in Paris, 1919]. *Historiche Zeitschrift* (1963): 1–101.

2781. Dillion, Emile Joseph. *Inside Story of the Peace Conference*. New York: Harper and Brothers, 1920. Argues that ignoring the problems with Russia and worldwide labor and linking the peace treaty with the League were the largest of many blunders.

2782. Dodd, William Edward. "President Wilson, His Treaty, and His Reward." *World's Work* 39 (March 1920): 440–47. Praises Wilson's tireless effort for the peace treaty.

2783. Duff, John Bernard. "The Politics of Revenge: The Ethnic Opposition to the Peace Policies of Woodrow Wilson." Ph.D. diss., Columbia University, 1964. Presents the difficulties and eventual opposition Wilson faced from a number of immigrant groups while negotiating the peace treaty.

2784. Dulles, Foster Rhea. "Return to Peace." In *Twentieth Century America*, 235–56. Boston: Houghton-Mifflin Co., 1945. Discusses Wilson's failure at Paris and his repudiation by the public.

2785. East, Dennis, II. "Irreconcilable Differences: Wilson's Whistlestop Campaign for the League." *Timeline* 3, no. 6 (1986–87): 12–17. Recounts Wilson's 1919 national tour.

2786. Eastman, Max. "A World's Peace." *Liberator* 1 (March 1918): 10. Eastman's interpretation of and comments upon each of Wilson's Fourteen Points of January 8, 1918.

2787. Erlenwein, Gustav. "Die Gegensatze zwischen dem amerikanischen Prasidenten Woodrow Wilson und seinem Staatssekretar Robert Lansing in Fragen des Volkerbundsstatus unter Berucks. D. Volkerbundsentwurfe." [The Conflict Between the American President Woodrow Wilson and His Secretary of State Robert Lansing on Questions of the Status of the League of Nations Taking into Account the Articles of the League of Nations Charter]. Wurzburg: Rechts-u. Staatswiss. Diss., 1929.

2788. "Europe's Idea about Mr. Wilson's Position." *Current Opinion* 67 (December 1919): 277–80. British and French press reactions.

2789. "Europe's Joyous Agony over Mr. Wilson's Visit." *Current Opinion* 66 (February 1919): 76–79. European disagreements with the Fourteen Points.

2790. "European Bewilderment at President Wilson's Diplomacy." *Current Opinion* 65 (September 1918): 148–49. Discusses Wilson's unorthodox diplomacy regarding the Versailles Council and the slowly growing opposition in the European press to his peace plan.

2791. Fels, Mary. "President Wilson and the Treaty." *Public* 22 (June 21, 1919): 658–59. Answers liberals who charge Wilson with failure because they are displeased with the peace treaty.

2792. Finch, George Augustus. "The Treaty of Peace with Germany in the United States Senate: An Exposition and a Review." *American Journal of International Law* 14 (1920): 155–206.[Also published in *International Conciliation* 153 (August 1920): 359–420.] Includes the final form, with the fifteen reservations, of the resolution of ratification and an analysis of votes on each part.

2793. Finger, Charles J. "If You Were Wilson in Paris." *Public* 22 (July 5, 1919): 712–13. Exonerates Wilson for the failure to achieve real peace and names several others as the culprits.

2794. Firth, John Benjamin. "President Wilson and the League of Nations." *Fortnightly Review* 111 (April 1919): 553–65. Considers the League inevitable but questions its usefulness and Wilson's reputation.

2795. Fitz-Gerald, William George [Ignatius Phayre, pseud.]. "President Wilson's Dream—and His Dilemma." *Nineteenth Century and After* 81 (January 1917): 18–30. Examines Wilson's desire to establish a world order and the complications of rebuilding Europe.

2796. ———. "Wilson and Housetop Diplomacy." *Living Age* 299 (December 21, 1918): 749–52. Describes Wilson's role as an "absolute Dictator" in conducting foreign affairs.

2797. Fleming, Denna Frank. *The United States and the League of Nations, 1918–1920.* New York: G.P. Putnam's Sons, 1932. An early account of the League of Nations controversy between Wilson and the Senate, supporting Wilson's position on the issue.

2798. ———. *The United States and World Organization, 1920–1933.* New York: Columbia University Press, 1938. Details the creation by Wilson of a model for the League and its rejection by the Senate.

2799. Floto, Inga. *Colonel House in Paris: A Study of American Policy at the Paris Peace Conference, 1919.* Papers of Woodrow Wilson. Supplementary Volume. Princeton: Princeton University Press, 1981. [A corrected edition of a limited edition published by the Aarhus University Press in 1973.] A history of the Paris Peace Conference with emphasis on the interaction between Wilson and House.

2800. Forster, Kent. *The Failures of Peace: The Search for a Negotiated Peace during the First World War.* Washington, D.C.: American Council on Public Affairs, 1941. Describes Wilson's attempts to establish peace as early as 1916 and until 1919.

2801. Fosdick, Raymond Blaine. "Before Wilson Died." *Survey* 51 (February 15, 1924): 495. The author recounts a conversation about the League of Nations that he had with Wilson two weeks before his death.

2802. ———. *Letters on the League of Nations. From the Files of Raymond B. Fosdick.* Papers of Woodrow Wilson. Supplementary Volume. Princeton: Princeton University Press, 1966. Letters written to and from Wilson's Under Secretary-General of the League of Nations who helped in the planning of the new international body.

2803. "Fourteen Points." In **422**, 29:388. Summary listing of the aims, stressing American imperialism.

2804. "Fourteen Questions to Mr. Wilson." *Nation* 109 (July 19, 1919): 70. Criticizes Wilson's inability to compromise or heed the advice of others at the Paris Peace Conference.

2805. Frank, Glenn. "Has Wilson Failed? An Examination of the Liberal Outlook." *Century Magazine* 98 (August 1919): 506–20. Examines flaws in the current League of Nations covenant and proposes measures to correct them.

2806. Franklin, Fabian. "Our 'Ignoble Isolation.'" *Independent* 11 (November 24, 1923): 245–46. Assigns responsibility for the failure of the Senate to ratify the League Covenant.

2807. Frear, Mary Reno. "Did President Wilson Contradict Himself on the Secret Treaties?" *Current History* 30 (June 1929): 435–43. Addresses Wilson's alleged knowledge of secret treaties and his denial of that knowledge.

2808. "A Friend Writes to Mr. Wilson." *New Republic* 19 (July 9, 1919): 301–2. An imaginary letter urging Wilson to keep fighting until the spirit of the peace is reached.

2809. Fuller, Howard de Wolf. "Anti-Wilson." *Review* 1 (November 1, 1919): 424–25. Argues that party politics should be put aside.

2810. Fullerton, William Morton. "Bewilderment of America." *World's Work* 39 (March 1920): 448–55. Discusses Wilson's poor handling of the peace process and his rejection by the American people.

2811. Grantham, Dewey W., Jr. "The Southern Senators and the League of Nations, 1918–1920." *North Carolina Historical Review* 26 (April 1949): 187–205. Contends that southern senators wanted to support Wilson and the League but that partisanship prevented the necessary compromises.

2812. Graves, John Temple. "Return of a Lonely Warrior." *Virginia Quarterly Review* 21, no. 4 (October 1945): 614–18. Compares the 1945 compromises for the United Nations charter to Wilson's inflexibility about the League.

2813. "Great Failure." *Review* 3 (October 20, 1920): 332–33. Quotes a recent speech by Herbert Hoover characterizing Wilson's refusal to compromise as "the greatest failure of American statesmanship since the Civil War."

2814. Greene, Theodore P., ed. *Wilson at Versailles*. Problems in American Civilization, no. 23. Boston: D. C. Heath and Co., 1957. Readings in primary and secondary sources to illustrate the debate over the League.

2815. Haeften, V. "President Wilson und der Vorfriede vom 5. November 1918." [President Wilson and the Preliminary Armistice Agreement of November 5, 1918]. *Wissen und Wehr* (1935): 838–42.

2816. Halperin, S. William. "Anatomy of an Armistice." *Journal of Modern History* 43, no. 1 (1971): 107–12. Agrees that Wilson was very concerned with the spread of Bolshevism.

2817. Hansen, Harry. *The Adventures of the Fourteen Points*. New York: Century Co., 1919. A first-hand account of the Paris Peace Conference.

2818. ———. "Forgotten Men of Versailles." In *The Aspirin Age, 1919–1941*, ed. Isabel Leighton, 1–33. New York: Simon and Schuster, 1949. Correspondent's retrospective account.

2819. Hard, William. "Article Ten of the League." *New Republic* 18 (March 22, 1919): 237–40. Letter to the editor opposing the League based upon its linkage to the peace treaty as a whole.

2820. Harris, Henry Wilson. *The Peace in the Making*. New York: E. P. Dutton & Co., 1920. Laments the delayed peace conference and its treaties. Also sees the League of Nations as the sole bulwark against chaos.

2821. "Has President Wilson Failed in Europe?" *Current Opinion* 66 (June 1919): 348–49. Records opinions expressed in European newspapers on the issue of Wilson's peace-making efforts.

2822. "Has President Wilson Made Good at the Peace Conference?" *Current Opinion* 66 (March 1919): 137–39. Excerpts from American newspapers, expressing a variety of opinions on Wilson's performance at the Peace Conference.

2823. Haskins, Charles Homer, and Robert Howard Lord. *Some Problems of the Peace Conference.* Cambridge: Harvard University Press, 1920. Focuses on the territorial settlements in Europe that came out of the Paris Peace Conference but omits a discussion of Russia.

2824. Helbich, Wolfgang J. "American Liberals in the League of Nations Controversy." *Public Opinion Quarterly* 31 (1967–1968): 568–96. Liberals' lack of support for the League.

2825. Hewes, James E., Jr. "Henry Cabot Lodge and the League of Nations." *Proceedings of the American Philosophical Society* 114, no. 4 (1970): 245–55. Argues that the debate surrounding the League grew out of moral and ideological conflict, not partisanship.

2826. Hill, David Jayne. "Betrayal of the Monroe Doctrine." *North American Review* 212 (November 1920): 577–93. Argues that Article Ten was the final step taken to wipe out the principles of the Monroe Doctrine.

2827. ———. "President's Attack on the Senate." *North American Review* 210 (November 1919): 587–603. Criticizes Wilson's assumption that he can dictate the terms of the peace settlement and keep the Senate from performing its constitutional role in the process.

2828. Hofstadter, Richard. "Wilson, the Intransigent." *New Republic* 113 (August 6, 1945): 164. Considers what might have happened had Wilson been more flexible and had the United States joined the League of Nations.

2829. Holt, Hamilton. "The People and the President." *Independent* 98 (June 28, 1919): 476–77. Defends Wilson against the barrage of criticism.

2830. Holt, William Stull. *Treaties Defeated by the Senate: A Study of the Struggle between President and Senate over the Conduct of Foreign Relations*, 249–307. Baltimore: Johns Hopkins University Press, 1933. Treaty of Versailles as part of an ongoing fight between branches of the federal government.

2831. "Homecoming of President Wilson." *Current History Magazine of the New York Times* 10 (August 1919): 206–8. An account of Wilson's departure from France and his arrival in the United States.

2832. Hoover, Herbert Clark. *America's First Crusade.* New York: Charles Scribner's Sons, 1942. [Originally published as **2833**.] Memoirs of the Paris Peace Conference, slightly rearranged and enlarged.

2833. ———. "First American Crusade." *Saturday Evening Post* 214 (November 1, 1941): 9–11+; (November 8, 1941): 14–15+; (November 15, 1941): 31+. A description of the Paris Peace Conference by Hoover when he was a member of the advisory economic committee of the United States delegation.

2834. Hoover, Irwin Hood (Ike). "Germany Signs." *Saturday Evening Post* 207 (July 7, 1934): 16–17+. A journal of the conclusion of the peace conference.

2835. ———. "With Wilson in France." *Saturday Evening Post* 206 (June 30, 1934): 16–17+. A chronicle of the beginning of the Paris Peace Conference.

2836. House, Edward Mandell, and Charles Seymour, eds. *What Really Happened at Paris: The Story of the Peace Conference, 1918–1919, by American Delegates.* New York: Charles Scribner's Sons, 1921. Attempts to deal honestly with the facts of the Paris Peace Conference and praises Wilson.

2837. "How Canada Views the President's Trip." *Literary Digest* 59 (December 14, 1918): 19. Excerpts from Canadian newspapers praising Wilson.

2838. "How Lansing and Wilson Fell Out." *Current Opinion* 70 (April 1921): 438–40. Discusses Lansing's account of his break with Wilson at the Paris Peace Conference.

2839. "How the Press Answer the President's Plea for the League of Nations." *Literary Digest* 62 (July 19, 1919): 9–11. American newspapers respond, mostly negatively.

2840. Howe, Mark Antony de Wolfe. "Swords, Ploughshares, and Woodrow Wilson." In *Causes and Their Champions*, 267–306. Boston: Little, Brown and Co., 1926. Views the League as the most promising agent against war.

2841. Huddleston, Sisley. *Peace-Making at Paris.* London: T. F. Unwin, 1919. Traces the conference's major developments and describes the interactions among the chief statesmen. A chapter on the differences over the League of Nations is included.

2842. Hudson, Manley O. *Woodrow Wilson's Fourteen Points after Eight Years. An Address at a Dinner in Commemoration of the Birthday of Woodrow Wilson, Minneapolis, Minn., December Twenty- Eighth, 1925.* New York: Woodrow Wilson Foundation, [1926?]. Discussion of the extent to which Wilson's Fourteen Points had been realized by the end of 1925.

2843. Hughes, H. Stuart. "Thirty-Five Years after Versailles." *New Leader* 37 (1954): 16–19. [Also published as "Am Einer Diskussion. Versailles Nach 35 Jahren." *Monat* 6, no. 71 (1954): 446–51.] Argues that the United States has an obligation to maintain world order.

2844. "Idealism at Its Worst: Mr. Wilson's Letter to Senator Hitchcock." *Review* 2 (March 13, 1920): 241. Criticizes Wilson's rhetorical arguments in favor of Article Ten as not being grounded in reality or fact.

2845. "Idealism in Vacuo: Mr. Wilson and the League of Nations Controversy." *Review* 2 (May 15, 1920): 505–6. Argues that Wilson could have secured ratification had he been willing to make minor concessions.

2846. "The Innocent Abroad." *Nation* 109 (August 30, 1919): 272–74. Expresses disbelief that Wilson knew nothing about the secret treaties.

2847. James, Edwin Leland. "If We Had Joined the League There Might Not Have Been a Hitler." *New York Times Magazine* July 13, 1941: 3, 23. Believes that Wilson's rejected League of Nations was intended to halt tyrants and aggressors such as Adolf Hitler.

2848. Jennings, David H. "President Wilson's Tour in September, 1919: A Study of Forces Operating during the League of Nations Fight." Ph.D. diss., Ohio State University, 1958. Concludes that Wilson's tour would have been more effective had he played up American self-interest.

2849. Johnson, Robert David. "Article XI in the Debate on the United States' Rejection of the League of Nations." *International History Review* (Canada) 15 (August 1993): 502–524. Explains why Wilson lost the battle in the League of Nations fight.

2850. Johnson, Walter. "Senatorial Strategy, 1919–1920." *Antioch Review* 3 (Winter 1943): 512–29. [Also published in *Recent America: Conflicting Interpretations of the Great Issues*, ed. Sidney Fine, 154–67. New York: Macmillan Co., 1962.] Argues that the partisanship of the Senate debate clouded public perception of what was at stake.

2851. Jouvenel, B. de. "Woodrow Wilson." *Confluence: An International Forum* 5, no. 4 (Winter 1957): 320–31. Focuses on the place of information and goodwill in Wilson's actions in Europe.

2852. "Justice for All: President Wilson's Speech in New York, September 27, 1918." *Bellman* 25 (October 5, 1918): 371–72. The coming peace settlement must be based upon the desires of the world's peoples, not on the bargaining of diplomats.

2853. Keynes, John Maynard. "Council of Four, Paris, 1919." In *Essays in Biography*, 11–31. New York: Harcourt, Brace and Co., 1933. [Also published in *Modern Short Biographies and Autobiographies*, ed. Marston Balch, 389–410. New York: Harcourt, Brace and Co., 1940.] Includes a discussion of a variety of European opinions about Wilson at the peace conference.

2854. ———. *The Economic Consequences of the Peace*. New York: Harcourt, Brace and Howe, 1920. Predicts the failure of the peace treaty and blames it on Wilson's impracticality.

2855. ———. "When the Big Four Met." In **3075**, 51–54. Written December 24, 1919, about Wilson's inadequate diplomacy at the Paris Peace Conference.

2856. "The Kind of League the Republicans Want." *Literary Digest* 60 (March 15, 1919): 13–16. Republican newspapers on the issue of the League of Nations.

2857. Knock, Thomas J. *To End All Wars: Woodrow Wilson and the Quest for a New World Order.* New York: Oxford University Press, 1992. Places new emphasis on the evolution of the League of Nations that took place before Wilson went to the Paris Peace Conference.

2858. ———. "Woodrow Wilson and the Origins of the League of Nations." Ph.D. diss., Princeton University, 1982. Intellectual, political, and diplomatic origins of Wilson's League proposal and the Pan-American Pact.

2859. Kuehl, Warren F. *Seeking World Order: The United States and World Organizations to 1920.* Nashville: Vanderbilt University Press, 1969. A study of America's effort between 1890 and 1920 to create an international organization for global cooperation.

2860. Lancaster, James L. "The Protestant Churches and the Fight for Ratification of the Versailles Treaty." *Public Opinion Quarterly* 31 (1967–1968): 597–619. Believes that American Protestant involvement in the struggle for ratification of the Versailles Treaty was the culmination of a vigorous campaign waged during the Great War by many prominent church leaders who saw Wilson's vision for a new world order as a moral issue.

2861. Langer, William Leonard. "Peace and the New World Order." In **1101**, 67–96. Discusses Wilson's role in the postwar period when he could no longer serve as a detached mediator.

2862. "Lansing's Disagreements with Wilson." *Literary Digest* 68 (March 26, 1921): 40–42. Discusses the Secretary of State's disagreements with Wilson about the Peace Conference and the League of Nations. Contains numerous excerpts from **2865**.

2863. Lansing, Robert. *The Big Four and Others of the Peace Conference*, 37–76. Boston: Houghton Mifflin Co., 1921. Lansing focuses on the changes in Wilson's character as the negotiations progressed.

2864. ———. "Big Four of the Peace Conference—Wilson." *Saturday Evening Post* 193 (March 19, 1921): 3–4+. How aspects of Wilson's character that enabled him to lead so well before were somehow "suppressed or submerged" during the negotiations.

2865. ———. *The Peace Negotiations, A Personal Narrative.* Boston: Houghton Mifflin Co., 1921.

2866. ———. "When Wilson Failed as Peacemaker." *Saturday Evening Post* 203 (June 20, 1931): 10–11+. Concludes that Wilson did not give enough attention to rival nations, American government, and public opinion.

2867. Lawrence, David. "The Crusade That Failed but Lives On." *New York Times Magazine* November 14, 1943: 3+. Relevance of Wilson's 1919 speech-making tour to developments in 1943.

2868. Lazo, Dimitri D. "A Question of Loyalty: Robert Lansing and the Treaty of Versailles." *Diplomatic History* 9 (1985): 35–53. The Peace Conference from Lansing's perspective, borrowing extensively from his memoirs and diaries.

2869. "The League of Nations." *Liberator* 1 (December 1918): 5–6. Contends that the League of Nations will be only a commercial league for capitalists.

2870. *The League of Nations: Text of the Covenant and Addresses by Woodrow Wilson, William Howard Taft, Henry Cabot Lodge, Philander C. Knox.* Cleveland: Otis & Co., 1920.

2871. "A League of Which Nations?" *The Liberator* (February 1919): 7–8. Argues that the only way that the proposed League of Nations can be a true federation of the peoples of the world is for the Soviet Republic to be invited to participate on equal terms with all other nations.

2872. Lentin, Anthony. *Lloyd George, Woodrow Wilson and the Guilt of Germany: An Essay in the Prehistory of Appeasement.* Baton Rouge: Louisiana State University Press, 1985. Asserts that Wilson, for all his faults and detractors, was the tragic hero of the Conference, but his defeat was the world's loss.

2873. Levering, Ralph B. "Public Culture and Public Opinion: The League of Nations Controversy in New Jersey and North Carolina." In **1083**, 159–97. Focuses on two states with very different cultures, economies, and politics.

2874. Levin, Norman Gordon, Jr. "Wilsonian Liberalism, the German Problem, and the League of Nations." In **1741**, 112–28. [Also published in **2391**, 161–182.] Argues that Wilson believed he could create a family of nations, which included Germany.

2875. Link, Arthur S. "Inga Flotto's Colonel House in Paris: A Study in American Foreign Policy at the Paris Peace Conference 1919." *Historisk Tidsskrift* (Denmark) 78, no. 1 (1978): 335–37.

2876. ———. "Wilson and the Great Debate over Collective Security." In **1741**, 129–47. [Also published in **1936**, 127–156.] Discusses Wilson's failure to sell the peace treaty to the American public.

2877. "The Living Ideas of Woodrow Wilson." *New Republic* 22 (March 17, 1920): 73–74. Wilson as a visionary but inept negotiator.

2878. Lloyd George, David. "Wilson at the Peace Conference." *Saturday Review of Literature* 19 (February 25, 1939): 13–14. An excerpt from **3899**, describing Wilson as idealistic, keenly intelligent, and a man who did not wish to be distracted from his preconceived notions.

2879. Logan, Rayford Whittingham. *The Senate and the Versailles Mandate System.* Washington, D.C.: Minorities Publishers, 1945. The defeat by imperialist nations and the United States Senate of Wilson's efforts to place colonial territories under international authority.

2880. "The Lone Hand." *New Republic* 17 (January 4, 1919): 264–67. Examines Wilson's isolated position among world leaders.

2881. Loth, David Goldsmith. *Woodrow Wilson: The Fifteenth Point.* Philadelphia: J. B. Lippincott Co., 1941. Disputes a once-common theory that all postwar international tragedies stemmed from the Versailles settlement.

2882. Lovett, Robert Morse. "The Covenant—and After." *Dial* 66 (March 8, 1919): 219–20. Calls upon liberals to support the League as a first step toward creating a world order based upon cooperation and the equality of nations.

2883. Ludwig, Emil. "Wilson." In *Genius and Character,* trans. Kenneth Burke, 91–118. New York: Harcourt, Brace and Co., 1927. A fictitious dialogue between Wilson and George Washington, dramatizing Wilson's coming to terms with his failure at the Peace Conference.

2884. "The Madness at Versailles." *Nation* 108 (May 17, 1919): 778–80. Criticizes participants for ignoring Wilson's rhetoric about making the world safe for democracy and freeing Germany from tyranny.

2885. "Making War on Our Chief Peacemaker." *Literary Digest* 59 (December 14, 1918): 9–12. A survey of newspaper opinions weighing American support for Wilson's actions at Versailles.

2886. Mantoux, Etienne. *The Carthaginian Peace, or The Economic Consequences of Mr. Keynes.* London: Oxford University Press, 1946. Disputes Keynes's interpretation of the failure of the peace treaty.

2887. Mantoux, Paul Joseph. "Le president Wilson et le droit des peuples a disposer d'eux-memes." [President Wilson and the Right of People to Self-Determination]. *L'Europe Nouvelle* 21 (October 8, 1938): 1085–86.

2888. ———. "Le President Wilson au Conseil des Quatre." In **1073**, 17–28.

2889. ———. *Les deliberations du Conseil des quatre, 24 mars-28 juin 1919: Notes de l'officier interprete Paul Mantoux,* trans. John Boardman Whitton. 2 vols. Paris: Editions du Centre national de la recherche scientifique, 1955. Minutes from the Council of Four's meetings, provided by a French secretary, including some otherwise unpublished material.

2890. ———. *Paris Peace Conference, 1919: Proceedings of the Council of Four, (March 24-April 18),* trans. John Boardman Whitton. Geneva: Librairie Droz, 1964. The first English translation, without annotation of any kind, of Mantoux's notes of the first thirty-eight sessions of the Council of Four.

2891. Marburg, Theodore. *Development of the League of Nations Idea: Documents and Correspondence of Theodore Marburg*, ed. John H. Latane. 2 vols. New York: Macmillan Co., 1932. Documentary collection by one of the key leaders of the League to Enforce Peace.

2892. ———. *The League of Nations.* 2 vols. New York: Macmillan Co., 1917–1918. Examines the importance of security in a peacetime world; argues that after Germany has been defeated, an intelligent and practical plan to discourage future war should be immediately implemented.

2893. Margulies, Herbert F. *The Mild Revisionists and the League of Nations Controversy in the Senate.* Columbia: University of Missouri Press, 1989. The ten Republican senators who wished to form a League and complete the peace but who could not support the treaty.

2894. Marsh, Arthur Richmond. "President Wilson's Proposed Sojourn in Europe." *Economic World* n.s. 16 (November 23, 1918): 723–24. Criticizes Wilson's decision to go personally to France for the peace talks.

2895. Marston, Frank Swain. *The Peace Conference of 1919: Organization and Procedure.* London: Oxford University Press, 1944. An attempt to recount the Conference objectively.

2896. Mason, Augustus Lynch. "The Psychology of Woodrow Wilson." *Review* 1, no. 3 (May 31, 1919): 58. Letter to the editors, arguing that the Wilsonian principles of self-determinism and internationalism are destructive.

2897. Maxwell, Kenneth R. "Irish-Americans and the Fight for Treaty Ratification." *Public Opinion Quarterly* 31 (1967–1968): 620–41. Irish-Americans' opposition to Wilson's peace efforts.

2898. Mayer, Arno J. *Politics and Diplomacy of Peacemaking: Containment and Counterrevolution at Versailles, 1918–1919.* New York: Alfred A. Knopf, 1967. Believes that Wilson was on the "left" of other world leaders at the Paris Peace Conference and that his political leverage was nullified by the strong "moderate" pressure.

2899. McCallum, R. B. *Public Opinion and the Lost Peace.* London: Oxford University Press, 1944. Looks at the negative effects of the United States' withdrawal from the League of Nations.

2900. McClure, Wallace. "Wilson's Fourteen Points as Followed in the Post-War Commercial Treaties of the United States." *Tennessee Law Review* 6 (February 1928): 86–94. Speculates on possibilities of success of the equality of trade conditions submitted in the Fourteen Points.

2901. McDermott, Louis M. "Three Who Made an Evolution." *Mid-America* 52 (January 1970): 31–54. Efforts by Wilson, Jan Smuts, and David Lloyd George to end imperialism after the war.

2902. McGinty, Brian. "'Remember, No Compromise': The Debate over the League of Nations." *American History Illustrated* 15, no. 9 (1971): 8–17. Examines the Senate's refusal to ratify the treaty.

2903. Mee, Charles L. *End of Order: Versailles, 1919.* New York: E.P. Dutton and Co., 1980. Detailed description of the events leading up to the signing of the Treaty of Versailles, with particular emphasis upon Wilson's decisive role at the Conference.

2904. Miller, David Hunter. "Some Legal Aspects of the Visit of President Wilson to Paris." *Harvard Law Review* 36 (November 1922): 51–78. A study, written by a participant in the peace negotiations, of the constitutionality of Wilson's trip to Paris and his authority as executive to make treaties.

2905. Miquel, Pierre. "Le 'Journal des Debats' et la Paix de Versailles." [The 'Journal des Dabats' and the Peace of Versailles]. *Revue Historique* 232, no. 2 (1964): 379–414. Describes the opposition of the director and political editor of the *Journal des Debats* to positions taken by Lloyd George and Wilson on the Treaty of Versailles.

2906. "Misrepresentation of Mr. Wilson to Europeans." *Current Opinion* 66 (May 1919): 278–81. Outlines the conservative European view against Wilson's plans for peace and order in Europe and the methods employed to contravene enactment of his plans.

2907. Mitchell, David. "Woodrow Wilson as World Saviour: Peace-Making in 1919." *History Today* 26, no. 1 (January 1976): 3–14. Examines Wilson's role in establishing the League of Nations at the Paris Peace Conference.

2908. Molin, Alma L. "Die Pariser Friedenskonferenz, Wilson und das Deutche Problem." [The Paris Peace Conference, Wilson, and the German Problem]. *Internationales Jahrbuch fur Geschichts-und-Geographie-Unterricht* 11 (1967): 54–66.

2909. Moll, Kenneth L. "Writing on Water with a Fork: 1919 Disarmament Efforts at Versailles." *Military Review* 44, no. 8 (August 1964): 29–37. Says Wilson's plan for peace failed because of public resistance.

2910. Moors, John Farwell. "The President at the Peace Conference." *Public* 22 (July 26, 1919): 794–97. Answers charges leveled against Wilson.

2911. ———. "President Wilson and Senator Lodge." *Public* 22 (September 6, 1919): 952–55. Evaluates Wilson and chronicles Lodge's development as his bitter and unrelenting critic.

2912. Morris, Richard Brandon. *Great Presidential Decisions*, 356–72. Philadelphia: J. B. Lippincott, 1960. Examines the idealistic and self-righteous elements inherent in the Fourteen Points.

2913. "Mr. Wilson and His Promises." *New Republic* 19 (May 24, 1919): 104–6. Sets out to destroy the belief that the treaty fulfilled the promises made in Wilson's Fourteen Points.

2914. "Mr. Wilson Forgets: Speech to Congress, July 10, 1919." *New Republic* 19 (July 23, 1919): 370–72. Admonishes Wilson for not laying down a timetable for the planned League.

2915. "Mr. Wilson on the Stump." *New Republic* 6 (February 12, 1916): 30. Editorial criticizing Wilson's speechmaking tour, arguing that he was short on specifics, did little to educate the people, and made no attempt to seek a compromise.

2916. "Mr. Wilson on the Stump." *Review* 1 (September 13, 1919): 376–77. A commentary of Wilson's oratorical ability and his prospects of selling the idea of the League of Nations.

2917. "Mr. Wilson Rants." *Nation* 109 (October 4, 1919): 453. Criticizes Wilson's argument that Americans either support the League of Nations or else prepare to adjust to a German military-type government.

2918. "Mr. Wilson Testifies: The White House Conference." *New Republic* 20 (September 3, 1919): 134–35. Criticizes Wilson's concealment of possible secret treaties following the meeting of the Council of Four.

2919. "Mr. Wilson's Critics." *New Republic* 7 (May 6, 1916): 4–5. Reproaches Lodge, Roosevelt, and Root for denouncing Wilson's policies without offering alternatives.

2920. "Mr. Wilson's Idealism at the Peace Table." *Literary Digest* 59 (November 23, 1918): 19. Four foreign viewpoints on Wilson's role.

2921. Munson, Gorham Bert. "Propaganda of Peace Aims: Wilson's Fourteen Points." In *12 Decisive Battles of the Mind*, 239–46. New York: Greystone Press, 1942. A study of the use of propaganda in shaping world opinion, including Wilson's Fourteen Points.

2922. Muret, Maurice. "M. Lansing contre M. Wilson." [Mr. Lansing Versus Mr. Wilson]. *Revue de Paris* 28, pt. 6 (November 15, 1921): 364–75.

2923. "Nation-wide Press Poll on the League of Nations." *Literary Digest* 61 (April 5, 1919): 13–16, 120–28. The poll shows a wide variety of opinion among newspaper editorial boards on the issue of the League.

2924. Nelson, Keith L. "What Colonel House Overlooked in the Armistice." *Mid-America* 51 (April 1969): 75–91. Concludes that House failed to understand how Britain and France were manipulating the Peace Conference.

2925. "The Net Result." *Nation* 108 (February 22, 1919): 268. Concludes that the League of Nations is the only new idea to come out of the Paris Peace Conference, an idea destined to fail.

2926. Nicholson, Harold. *Peacemaking, 1919: Being Reminiscences of the Paris Peace Conference.* Boston: Houghton, Mifflin Co., 1933. Stresses the element of confusion at the conference, the impossibility of Wilson's ideals, and the consequent need for compromise.

2927. Northedge, F. S. *The League of Nations: Its Life and Times, 1920–1946.* New York: Holmes and Meier, 1986. Discusses Wilson's role in the formation of the League and the disavowal of it by the United States.

2928. "Notes Exchanged on the Russian-Polish Situation by the United States, France and Poland." *International Conciliation* 155 (October 1920): 461–77. Consists of August 1–August 28, 1920 communications.

2929. Nowak, Karl Friedrich. *Versailles.* New York: Payson and Clarke, 1929. Details the Versailles Peace Conference and Treaty, as well as Wilson's efforts to establish the League of Nations.

2930. Orlando, Vittorio Emanuele. "Wilson and Lansing." *Saturday Evening Post* 201 (March 23, 1929): 6–7. Examines the roles played by Wilson and his Secretary of State at the Paris Peace Conference.

2931. Pange, Jean de. "Les preliminaires de l'armistice et les quatorze articles du President Wilson; d'apres des documents allemands." [The Armistice Preliminaries and Fourteen Points of President Wilson According to German Documents]. *Correspondant* 242 (March 25, 1920): 1113–22.

2932. Paris Peace Conference. *The Deliberations of the Council of Four (March 24–June 28, 1919): Notes of the Official Interpreter, Paul Montoux,* ed. Arthur S. Link. 2 vols. Papers of Woodrow Wilson. Supplementary Volume. Princeton: Princeton University Press, 1992. An annotated text of the meetings in a modern edition.

2933. Parmoor, Charles Alfred Cripps, 1st baron. "President Wilson and the Peace Settlement." *Contemporary Review* 115 (January 1919): 10–14. Considers the prospects of the League.

2934. Partridge, Edward Bellamy. "On the King's Carpet." *Sunset: The Pacific Monthly* 42 (June 1919): 30–33, 78+. An article describing some ceremonial aspects of Wilson's 1919 visit to England—the first by an American President.

2935. Perkins, Dexter. "Woodrow Wilson's Tour [in Support of the League of Nations, 1919]." In *America in Crisis,* ed. Daniel Aaron, 245–65. New York: Alfred A. Knopf, 1952. An account of Wilson's last speaking tour.

2936. Phifer, Gregg. "Woodrow Wilson's Swing around the Circle in Defense of His League, September 3–28, 1919." In **1112,** 65–102. Describes Wilson's September 3–28, 1919, speaking tour to advocate his League proposal and believes that he clearly gained a significant amount of popular opinion.

2937. Phillips, Walter Alison. "President's Peace Programme and the British Empire." *Edinburgh Review* 225 (April 1917): 227–48. Argues that Wilson's vision of collective security was a noble but illusory dream that was at odds with British imperial interests.

2938. Pierre, A. "Wilson et Clemenceau vus par Lloyd George." [Wilson and Clemenceau as Seen by Lloyd George]. *Les Annales Politiques et Litteraires* 112 (September 25, 1938): 306–8.

2939. Post, Louis Freeland. "The President's Fourteen Points." *Public* 22 (August 23, 1919): 898–99. Pleads for the Fourteenth Point, which would establish the League.

2940. "The President and Peace." *Bellman* 25 (November 30, 1918): 593–94. An analysis of the outrage and bias displayed by Europeans following Wilson's announcement that he would attend the Paris Peace Conference.

2941. "The President as Conquering Hero." *Independent* 99 (July 19, 1919): 71. Describes the warm welcome Wilson received by Americans upon returning from the Peace Conference.

2942. "The President at His Worst in His Western Tour." *North American Review* 210 (October 1919): 433–36. Believes that Wilson's absence from the White House during the Paris Peace Conference and during his Western United States campaign for the League of Nations was inappropriate and an amazing exhibition of Wilson at his worst.

2943. "The President at the Peace Table." *Literary Digest* 59 (November 30, 1918): 14–15. Expresses several opinions regarding Wilson's decision to attend the Versailles Peace Conference.

2944. "The President, the Senate and the Treaty: A Poll of the Press." *Outlook* 122 (July 23, 1919): 464–66. Includes selections from press opinion about the Versailles treaty and the League of Nations.

2945. "President Wilson and the World." *New Statesman* 14 (December 6, 1919): 266–67. Chides Wilson for failure to deliver American leadership.

2946. "President Wilson as Evangelist." *Nation* 109 (September 13, 1919): 360. Employs crusading imagery to depict Wilson's Western tour, noting his missionary zeal.

2947. "President Wilson at Versailles." *World's Work* 37 (January 1919): 249–51. Explores the precedent set by Wilson's personal attendance.

2948. "President Wilson at the Guildhall." *Public* 22 (January 4, 1919): 7–8. Says Wilson's speaking tour was intended to commit European leaders and citizens to a program for permanent peace.

2949. "President Wilson Carries the Treaty to the People." *Current Opinion* 67 (October 1919): 205–9. Various tabloid opinions concerning the content of the Covenant of the League of Nations and its chances of success in passing Congress.

2950. "President Wilson in Belgium: Address to the Deputies." *Current History* 10 (July 1919): 50–52. Describes Wilson's June 18–19, 1919, visit to Belgium highlighted by his meeting with King Albert, his receiving of a Doctor of Laws degree from the University of Louvain, and a motorcade tour through the war ravaged countryside.

2951. "President Wilson Smashes Another Precedent and Goes to France." *Current Opinion* 66 (January 1919): 1–5. Analyzes Wilson's reasons for going to Paris and the expected result of his trip.

2952. "President Wilson Stops an Inquiry." *New Republic* 85 (January 29, 1936): 326–27. Questions how much Wilson knew about the secret treaties.

2953. "President Wilson's Address to Congress before Leaving the United States for the Peace Conference." *Economics World* n.s. 16 (December 7, 1918): 796–800. Full text of Wilson's 1918 State of the Union Message.

2954. "President Wilson's Opponents." *New Statesman* 12 (February 22, 1919): 438–39. British reporter describes the increasing hostility toward Wilson at home while he was concentrating on peace negotiations in Europe.

2955. "Presidents Abroad." *Department of State Bulletin* 81 (September 1981): 1–9. Describes the domestic furor created by Wilson's trips to Europe in 1918 and 1919.

2956. "The President's Conditions of Peace." *Outlook* 120 (October 9, 1918): 208–9. Refers to Wilson's speech at the Metropolitan Opera House in New York City on September 27, 1918.

2957. "The President's Departure." *Bellman* 25 (December 7, 1918): 621–22. Stresses the importance of Wilson's role in the Conference.

2958. "The President's European Visit." *Outlook* 120 (November 27, 1918): 487–88. Examines the reasons for Wilson's personal appearance at the Peace Conference.

2959. "Psychology of Woodrow Wilson." *Review* 1, no. 2 (May 24, 1919): 30–31. A critique of Wilson's idealism and limitations, and of public expectations concerning the peace talks in Paris.

2960. "Quoting the President." *Public* 22 (May 31, 1919): 566–67. Wilson's need for support in the face of his earlier loss of a "peace without victory."

2961. Rabl, Kurt O. "Woodrow Wilson und das Selbstbestimmungsrecht der Volker." [Woodrow Wilson and the Right of Self-Determination for Nations]. *Zeitschrift fur d. ges. Staatswiss* 98 (1938): 585–624; 99 (1939): 116–47.

2962. Raffo, Peter. "Anglo-American Preliminary Negotiations for a League of Nations." *Journal of Contemporary History* 9 (October 1974): 153–76. Describes the emergence of an Anglo-American front at the League of Nations negotiations, and Lord Robert Cecil's courtship of a disinterested and unresponsive Wilson.

2963. Randall, James Garfield. *Lincoln's Peace and Wilson's*. New York: Dodd, Mead & Co., 1947. [Reprinted from *South Atlantic Quarterly* 42, no. 3 (July 1943): 225–42, and in his *Lincoln the Liberal Statesman*, New York: Dodd, Mead & Co., 1947.] Compares the peace efforts made by Lincoln and Wilson, calling both superior statesmen who valiantly battled against an unfriendly Congress during a time of extreme bloodshed.

2964. Rappard, William E. "Woodrow Wilson, la Suisse et Geneve." [Woodrow Wilson, the Swiss and Geneva]. In **1073**, 29–74. Author draws extensively on his notes of conversations with Wilson in Washington and Paris to reveal Wilson's attitudes towards the Swiss and the location of the permanent headquarters of the League of Nations in Geneva.

2965. Rastignac. "Wilson's Defeat." *Living Age* 305 (May 8, 1920): 334–36. Attributes Wilson's failure to self-righteous authoritarianism and deference to big business.

2966. Ratcliffe, Samuel Kerkham. "President Wilson, in Europe and America." *Contemporary Review* 115 (April 1919): 404–10. Measures the degree to which Wilson's actions reflect the will of the American people.

2967. Reinfeld, Fred. *Biggest Job in the World*, 155–70. New York: Thomas Y. Crowell, 1964. Argues that because of a number of fatal blunders, the League of Nations failed to gain support in America.

2968. Reisiger, Hans, and Harold Nicolson. "Friedensmacher 1919/Wilsonismus; auszug, ubers." [Peacemaking 1919/Wilsonism: Excerpts and Summary]. *Neue Rundschau* 44, no. 2 (October 1933): 433–44.

2969. "Results of the President's Tour." *Review* 1 (October 4, 1919): 442. Argues that after Wilson recovers, a compromise on the League is possible.

2970. "Return." *Nation* 109 (July 12, 1919): 30. Discusses Wilson's return to America after the Paris Peace Conference and his lack of accomplishment.

2971. Riddell, George Allardice. *Lord Riddell's Intimate Diary of the Paris Peace Conference and After, 1918–1923*. New York: Reynal & Hitchcock, 1934. A British reporter on Wilson as a member of the stellar cast he observed during sixteen conference sessions.

2972. Riddell, George Allardice, et al. *The Treaty of Versailles and After*. London: Oxford University Press, 1935. Includes analysis of Wilson as a prominent participant in treaty negotiations.

2973. Rifkind, Robert S. "The Wasted Mission." *American Heritage* 12, no. 3 (1961): 40–45, 72–74. Describes William Bullitt's first trip to Russia and Wilson's refusal to release Bullitt's report at the Paris Peace Conference.

2974. Rochester, Stuart I. *American Liberal Disillusionment in the Wake of World War I*. University Park: Pennsylvania State University Press, 1975. Dynamics of disillusionment in the American liberal community, largely due to the war.

2975. Rosenberger, Homer T. "The American Peace Society's Reaction to the Covenant of the League of Nations." *World Affairs* 141 (1978): 139–52. The mixed reaction to Wilson's many compromises.

2976. Rudin, Harry Rudolph. *Armistice, 1918*. New Haven: Yale University Press, 1944. Argues that Wilson saved the Germans from being forced to surrender unconditionally.

2977. Sainte-Aulaire, Auguste Felix Charles de Beaupoil, comte de. "Forbidden Knowledge." *American Mercury* 89 (September 1959): 30–32. Contends that foreign agents were responsible for Wilson's plans for the peace settlement and the League of Nations.

2978. Sandberger, Dietrich. "Die Freiheit der Meere, der zweite Punkt des Präsidenten Wilson." [Freedom of the Seas, President Wilson's Second Point]. *Welt als Gesch* 4 (1938): 473–501.

2979. Sarolea, Charles. "America and the League of Nations." In *Europe and the League of Nations*, 240–93. London: G. Bell and Sons, 1919. Contemporary work on the importance of the League, including a chapter on the importance of United States membership.

2980. Schmid, Karl. "Some Observations on Certain Principles of Woodrow Wilson." *Confluence* 5, no. 3 (Autumn 1956): 264–76. Discusses Wilson's goals and methods in his quest for an enduring peace.

2981. Schmitt, Bernadotte E. "The Peace Conference of 1919." *Journal of Modern History* 16 (March 1944): 49–59. Concerns the then-impending publication of official United States documents on the Peace Conference.

2982. Schulte Nordholt, Jan Willem. "Wilson in Versailles." *Tijdschrift voor Geschiedenis* 80, no. 2 (1967): 177–99.

2983. Scott, Arthur Pearson. *An Introduction to the Peace Treaties*. Chicago: University of Chicago Press, 1920. Describes Wilson's efforts to establish the League of Nations.

2984. Sears, Joseph Hamblen. "Robert Lansing and Woodrow Wilson." *Forum* 65 (April 1921): 466–68. Discusses **2865**, which treats Wilson as a heroic figure of the Paris Peace Conference.

2985. Seeberg, Joachim. *Wilson's Botschaft der 14 Punkte vom 8 Januar 1918 in Urteil der Grossen Deutschen Tagespresse vom Januar bis zum Oktober 1918.* Berlin: Triltsch & Huther, 1936.

2986. Seymour, Charles. *Geography, Justice, and Politics at the Peace Conference of 1919.* New York: American Geographical Society, 1951. How politics and geography shaped the treaty and why Wilson failed.

2987. _____. *Le Politique de Wilson et le Senat.* [The Politics of Wilson and the Senate]. Brussels: Imprimie Scientifique Litteraire, 1925. [Reprinted from *Revue de l'Institut de Sociologie* 5 (January 1925).]

2988. _____. *Letters from the Paris Peace Conference*, ed. Harold B. Whiteman, Jr. New Haven: Yale University Press, 1965. Maintains that Wilson was a powerful influence at the Conference, despite the 1918 elections.

2989. _____. "The Paris Education of Woodrow Wilson." *Virginia Quarterly Review* 32, no. 4 (Autumn 1956): 578–93. Discusses Wilson's conduct and decisions at the Peace Conference.

2990. _____. "The Presidency of Woodrow Wilson—A Symposium: President Wilson at Paris." *Pacific Review* 1 (March 1921): 569–75. Wilson's inability to convince the Senate of the advantages of the League.

2991. Shaw, George Bernard. *Peace Conference Hints.* London: Constable and Co., 1919. Emphasizes security, disarmament, neutrality, and freedom of the seas, and questions the effectiveness of Wilson's League of Nations.

2992. Shepardson, Donald E. "Versailles Plus Sixty." *Worldview* 22 (January–February 1979): 10–15. A recounting of Wilson's crusade for peace.

2993. Shotwell, James Thomson. *At the Paris Peace Conference.* New York: Macmillan Co., 1937. A topical treatment of the events at the Paris Peace Conference, noting the central role played by Wilson.

2994. Silbert, Frederic. "Les Habits Neufs du President Wilson." [President Wilson's New Clothes]. *Historie* (France), no. 56 (1983): 94–97. Explores Wilson's attempts to fashion a peace treaty.

2995. Sinha, Sushil Chandra. "The Role of President Woodrow Wilson in the Evolution of the Mandates System." *Indian Journal of Political Science* 3 (April-June 1942): 424–36. Analysis of the origins of the mandates system which concludes that Wilson was the driving force in pushing it through the Paris Peace Conference.

2996. Slocombe, George Edward. *A Mirror to Geneva*, 15–36. New York: Henry Holt and Co., 1938. A brief account of the work of Wilson and foreign leaders at the Conference.

2997. Smith, Daniel Malloy. "The Fourteen Points." In **1896**, 2:380–86. Brief sketch outlining Wilson's Fourteen Points.

2998. ———. "Robert M. Lansing and the Wilson Interregnum, 1919–1920." *Historian* 21, no. 2 (February 1959): 135–61. Appraises the increasingly strained relationship between Wilson and his Secretary of State at the Paris Peace Conference and during Wilson's illness.

2999. Smith, Marion Couthouy. "Syllogisms and Presidents." *Review* 1 (December 6, 1919): 641–42. Describes Wilson's League of Nations as a question of nationalism versus internationalism.

3000. Snell, John Leslie. "Wilson on Germany and the Fourteen Points." *Journal of Modern History* 26 (December 1954): 364–69. Contains notes by Sir William Wiseman, Chief of British Intelligence in the United States, from an interview with Wilson on October 16, 1918, which were subsequently relayed to the British government.

3001. Spector, Sherman D. *Rumania at the Paris Peace Conference.* New York: Bookman Associates, 1962. Wilson's addresses, attitudes, policies, and knowledge of secret treaties are discussed.

3002. ———. "Early Press Reaction to Wilson's League Proposal." *Journalism Quarterly* 39 (Summer 1962): 301–8. Describes press reaction to Wilson's League of Nations proposal.

3003. ———. "The Uneasy Partnership: Wilson and the Press at Paris." *Mid-America* 52 (January 1970): 55–69. Wilson's high regard for public opinion and his inability to develop better press relations during the Conference.

3004. ———. "Wilson's Mission to Paris: The Making of a Decision." *Historian* 30 (August 1968): 599–616. Considers the negative impact of Wilson's personal diplomacy.

3005. ———. "Wilson's Trip to Paris: Profile of Press Response." *Journalism Quarterly* 46, no. 4 (1969): 737–42. Discusses press response to the announcement of Wilson's trip to the Paris Peace Conference.

3006. Spencer, Frank. "The United States and Germany in the Aftermath of the War: 'I. 1918 to 1929.'" *International Affairs* 43, no. 4 (1967): 693–703. Argues that the repudiation of Wilson by the Senate, rightly or wrongly, represented the popular will of the people.

3007. Stone, Ralph A. "The Irreconcilables' Alternatives to the League." *Mid-America* 49 (1967): 163–73. Divides the irreconcilables into three distinct groups: supernationalists, realists, and idealists.

3008. _____. *The Irreconcilables: The Fight against the League of Nations.* Lexington: University Press of Kentucky, 1970. Examines how the "irreconcilables" interacted with the two protagonists, Wilson and Lodge.

3009. _____. "Two Illinois Senators among the Irreconcilables." *Mississippi Valley Historical Review* 50 (December 1963): 443–65. Discusses the roles of Medill McCormick and Lawrence Yardell Sherman.

3010. Stone, Ralph A., ed. *Wilson and the League of Nations: Why America's Rejection?* New York: Holt, Rinehart & Winston, 1967. A collection of documents and historical interpretations of the League's defeat.

3011. Stromberg, Roland N. *Collective Security and American Foreign Policy: From the League of Nations to NATO,* 3–45. New York: Frederick A. Praeger, 1963. Covers the inception of the idea for an international body, the League of Nations Treaty, and its defeat.

3012. _____. "The Riddle of Collective Security, 1916–1920." In **1855**, 147–70. Wilson's "collective security" policies as embodied in the League of Nations and the United Nations.

3013. Strunsky, Simeon. "Peace-Makers." *Atlantic Monthly* 123 (April 1919): 528–36. [Reprinted in *Literary Digest* 61 (May 3, 1919): 102–4.]

3014. _____. "The President's Homecoming." *Atlantic Monthly* 124 (August 1919): 267–75. Argues that it is not so easy to draw conclusions about Wilson's "victories" and "failures."

3015. Tardieu, Andre. *La Paix.* [The Peace]. Paris: Payot & Cie, 1921.

3016. _____. *The Truth about the Treaty.* Indianapolis: Bobbs-Merrill Co., 1921. A vehement defense of the treaty from a French perspective.

3017. Temperley, H. W. *A History of the Peace Conference at Paris.* 5th ed., 6 vols. London: H. Frowde and Hodder and Stoughton, 1920–24. Wilson's addresses, memoranda, principles, and attitudes.

3018. Thompson, Charles T. *The Peace Conference Day by Day.* New York: Brentano's, 1920. The record of the conference by an Associated Press reporter based in Paris.

3019. Tillman, Seth P. *Anglo-American Relations at the Paris Peace Conference of 1919.* Princeton: Princeton University Press, 1961. From the Pre-Armistice agreement through the Peace Conference.

3020. Trachtenberg, Marc. "Versailles after Sixty Years." *Journal of Contemporary History* 17 (July 1982): 487–506. Evaluates the historiography of the Paris Peace Conference as political, simplistic, and overschematized.

3021. Trow, Clifford W. "'Something Desperate in His Face': Woodrow Wilson in Portland at the 'Very Crisis of His Career.'" *Oregon Historical Quarterly* 82, no. 1

(1981): 40–64. Recounts the events of Wilson's visit to Portland on September 15, 1919 to raise support for the League of Nations; includes a discussion of senatorial opposition to the League.

3022. Turner, John Kenneth. "Pledge to the World." *Nation* 109 (July 5, 1919): 14–16. Describes Wilson's address immediately following the war concerning justice for the German people and the Allies.

3023. ———. "Standing behind the President: An Impossibility." *Nation* 111 (October 6, 1920): 370–72. Description of Wilson's lack of support from American and Allied leaders during his negotiations at the Paris Peace Conference.

3024. Uhler, John Earle. "Do Not Make the Atlantic Charter Official." *South Atlantic Quarterly* 42 (April 1943): 162–71. Compares the Atlantic Charter and the circumstances surrounding it with Wilson's Fourteen Points.

3025. Unger, Debi, and Irwin Unger. *The Vulnerable Years: The United States, 1896–1917.* Hinsdale, Ill.: Dryden Press, 1977. Argues that the Fourteen Points and the League of Nations were the finest expression of progressivism.

3026. U.S. Department of State. *General Records of the American Commission to Negotiate Peace, 1918–1931.* Washington, D.C.: National Archives and Records Administration, n.d. Microfilm. A complete compilation of the papers of the Commission at the Paris Peace Conference.

3027. ———. *Papers Relating to the Foreign Relations of the United States. The Paris Peace Conference, 1919.* 13 vols. Washington, D.C.: Government Printing Office, 1942–1948. Includes most of the important documents from the Paris Peace talks.

3028. U.S. Library of Congress. Division of Bibliography. *Check List of Documents Relating to the Paris Peace Conference, 1919.* Washington, D.C.: 1922.

3029. ———. *List of References on the Treaty of Versailles.* Washington, D.C.: 1922.

3030. Veblen, Thorstein. "Peace." *Dial* 66 (May 17, 1919): 485–87. Views the peace treaty as the best, if imperfect, solution.

3031. "A Victory of Justice vs. a Victory of Power." *New Republic* 16 (October 5, 1918): 271–73. Praises Wilson for his role in ending the war and for advocating the acceptance of democratic principles.

3032. Villard, Oswald Garrison. "Issues and Men: Lesson of the Failure of 1919." *Nation* 149 (October 14, 1939): 414. Mentions Wilson's activities during the Paris Peace Conference and compares the European situation in 1919 to the unstable situation there in 1939.

3033. ———. "Measure of America's Betrayal: With Editorial Comment." *Nation* 142 (January 29, 1936): 116, 119. Describes Wilson's changing reputation after the

Nye Committee hearings on the war and criticizes Wilson's decision to enter the war.

3034. ———. "Open Letter to Colonel House." *Nation* 136 (April 5, 1933): 364–65. Criticizes Colonel House and Wilson for creating an unstable peace.

3035. ———. "President Wilson's Task." *Nation* 108 (January 4, 1919): 15. Wilson's correspondence from London discussing efforts toward organizing a peace conference.

3036. ———. "The Truth about the Peace Conference." *Nation* 108 (April 19, 1919): 646–47. Calls the Paris Peace Conference a "palpable fraud upon the world" being overseen by four heads of state bent on "parceling out the globe."

3037. Villiers, Brougham. "President Wilson's Opportunity." *Contemporary Review* 114 (September 1918): 279–85. [Also published in *Living Age* 299 (November 9, 1918): 321–27.] Describes Wilson's unique opportunity to establish peace and structure after the disorganization caused by the war.

3038. Vinson, John Chalmers. *Referendum for Isolation: Defeat of Article Ten of the League of Nations Covenant.* Athens: University of Georgia Press, 1961. Argues that basic differences of opinion about the wisest course for American foreign policy were most sharply drawn in the debates on Article Ten of the Covenant.

3039. "Visit of President Wilson." *Nature* 102 (January 2, 1919): 349–50. Emphasizes the importance of Wilson's diplomatic journey to England in order to negotiate a European peace.

3040. Walters, Francis P. *A History of the League of Nations.* 2 vols. New York: Oxford University Press, 1952. Summarizes the creation, growth, conflict, and defeat of Wilson's League of Nations.

3041. Walworth, Arthur Clarence. *America's Moment, 1918: American Diplomacy at the End of World War I.* New York: W. W. Norton, 1977. Examines Wilson's decisions made after World War I and his efforts to establish world peace.

3042. ———. *Wilson and His Peacemakers: American Diplomacy at the Paris Peace Conference, 1919.* New York: W. W. Norton, 1986. Concerns the performance of Wilson and of other Americans assigned to negotiate peace treaties to end World War I.

3043. Wetjen, Hermann. "Die grossen Vier auf der Pariser Friedenskonferenz von 1919. Clemenceau, Wilson, Lloyd George u. Orlando." [The Big Four at the Paris Peace Conference of 1919. Clemenceau, Wilson, Lloyd George, and Orlando]. *Archiv fur Polit und Geschichte* 6 (1926): 401–23.

3044. Weyl, Walter Edward. "Prophet and Politician." *New Republic* 19 (June 7, 1919): 173–78. [Also published in **3075**, 45–49.] Believes that Wilson's failure at the Paris Peace Conference was due to his overconfidence, stubbornness, and a lack of preparation.

3045. "What Wilson Said." *Newsweek* 25 (May 21, 1945): 40. Includes a story by Eleanor Wilson McAdoo that on his deathbed, Wilson said that the United States should have stayed out of the League because Americans did not support it.

3046. "Whither Bound?" *Nation* 107 (December 14, 1918): 718. Commentary at the eve of the Paris Peace Conference.

3047. "Wilson vs. Clemenceau." *Literary Digest* 61 (April 5, 1919): 25. Includes excerpts from an essay written by a Spanish journalist.

3048. Wilson, Woodrow. "Presenting the Treaty of Versailles for Ratification, 1919." In *12 Americans Speak: Facsimiles of Original Editions Selected and Annotated*, ed. John Edwin Pomfret. San Marino, Calif.: Huntington Library, 1954. A facsimile of Wilson's address to the Senate on July 10, 1919.

3049. Wimer, Kurt. "Executive-Legislative Tensions in the Making of the League of Nations." Ph.D. diss., New York University, 1957. Discusses the political and ideological struggle between Wilson and the Senate over the League of Nations.

3050. _____. "The League of Nations: A Victim of Executive-Legislative Rivalry." *Lock Haven Bulletin* 2 (February 1960): 1–12. Argues that the League was defeated because of long-standing tensions between the President and Congress.

3051. _____. "Woodrow Wilson Tries Conciliation: An Effort That Failed." *Historian* 25, no. 4 (1963): 419–38. Reappraises Wilson's efforts at persuading the Senate to support the Versailles Treaty.

3052. _____. "Woodrow Wilson's Plan for a Vote of Confidence." *Pennsylvania History: Quarterly Journal of the Pennsylvania Historical Association* 28 (July 1961): 279–93. Examines Wilson's desire to settle the League question with a public referendum.

3053. _____. "Woodrow Wilson's Plans to Enter the League of Nations through an Executive Agreement." *Western Political Quarterly* 11, no. 4 (December 1958): 800–12. Compares Wilson's and Theodore Roosevelt's use of the executive agreement.

3054. Wittkovsky, Isidore Maximilian Harden, Prince of Baden [pseud.]. "The Eclipse of the Fourteen Points." *Living Age* 302 (August 23, 1919): 449–53. Declares that the promises contained in the Fourteen Points have been broken.

3055. *Woodrow Wilson's Fourteen Points. The Atlantic Charter's Eight Points.* New York: Woodrow Wilson Foundation, 1942.

3056. Wright, Quincy. "Woodrow Wilson and the League of Nations." *Social Research* 24 (Spring 1957): 65–86. Portrait of Wilson as a political pragmatist.

3057. Wyatt, Harold Frazer. "After the Signature." *Nineteenth Century and After* 86 (July 1919): 24–33. A British critique of the peace treaty for failing to punish Germany sufficiently.

3058. Zacharewicz, Mary M. "The Attitude of the Catholic Press toward the League of Nations." *Records of the American Catholic Historical Society of Philadelphia* 67 (1956): 3–30, 88–104; 68 (1957): 46–60. Examines the variety of opinions on the League of Nations expressed by different Catholic publications.

3059. Zilliacus, Konni. "How the War Ended." In *Mirror of the Past: A History of Secret Diplomacy*, 150–218. New York: Current Books; A. A. Wyn, 1946. Argues that the Allies made agreements to prolong the fighting so they could control the Peace Conference.

3060. Zweig, Stefan. "Wilson's Failure." In *Tide of Fortune: Twelve Historical Miniatures*, trans. E. Paul and C. Paul, 263–85. New York: Viking Press, 1940. Wilson's tragic failure at the Paris peace talks.

K. Wilson and the Press

3061. Boaz, John K. "The Presidential Press Conference." Ph.D. diss., Wayne State University, 1969. Includes coverage of Wilson.

3062. Brown, L. Ames. "President Wilson and Publicity." *Harper's Weekly* 58 (November 1, 1913): 19–21. Describes Wilson's open and informative relationship with the press, stating that he was more willing to meet with reporters than any President before him.

3063. Cobb, Frank Irving. *Cobb of "The World": A Leader in Liberalism*, ed. John Langdon Heaton, 178–230, 250–87. New York: E.P. Dutton & Co., 1924. Compiled from Cobb's articles and addresses.

3064. Cornwell, Elmer Eckert, Jr. "The Press Conferences of Woodrow Wilson." *Journalism Quarterly* 39, no. 3 (1962): 292–300. Wilson's innovative use of the press conference.

3065. ———. *Presidential Leadership of Public Opinion*. Bloomington: Indiana University Press, 1965. Wilson introduced formal press conferences and used them skillfully.

3066. "The Disaffection of Mr. Hearst." *Harper's Weekly* 57 (April 26, 1913): 3–4. Reasons for William Randolph Hearst's break with Wilson.

3067. Douglas, Susan J. "Media." In **410**, 2:815–30. Wilson's contribution to information management.

3068. "First Time." *New Yorker* 32 (March 17, 1956): 34–35. Discusses Wilson's first presidential press conference, held on March 15, 1913.

3069. Gatewood, Willard Badgette, Jr. "James Calvin Hemphill: Southern Critic of Woodrow Wilson, 1911–1912." *Georgia Review* 13 (Winter 1959): 378–92. Hemphill's views in the Charlotte *Daily Observer*.

3070. Glasner, Philip D. "Pacific Northwest Press Reaction to Wilson's Mexican Diplomacy, 1913–1916." Ph.D. diss., University of Idaho, 1965. Various journalists believed that people in the Northwest supported Wilson's initial Mexico policy but later became disenchanted with it.

3071. "Governor Wilson and Business: A Poll of the Press." *Outlook* 103 (January 25, 1913): 155–57. Excerpts from American newspapers reacting to a speech by Wilson on business in America.

3072. Hard, William. "Is This Adulation?" *New Republic* 14 (April 13, 1918): 323–24. The author defends columns he has written criticizing and praising both Wilson and Theodore Roosevelt.

3073. Juergens, George. *News from the White House: The Presidential-Press Relationship in the Progressive Era*, 126–272. Chicago: University of Chicago Press, 1981. Discusses the way in which the power of the modern presidency and the professionalization of the press affected political history under the progressive Presidents.

3074. Krock, Arthur. *Memoirs: Sixty Years on the Firing Line*. New York: Funk and Wagnalls, 1968. A journalist recalls covering Wilson as governor and President.

3075. Luce, Robert B., ed. *The Faces of Five Decades: Selections from Fifty Years of The New Republic 1914–1964*. New York: Simon & Schuster, 1964. Relevant articles listed by author.

3076. Moon, Gordon A., II. "George F. Parker: A 'Near Miss' as First White House Press Chief." *Journalism Quarterly* 41, no. 2 (1964): 183–90. Includes the institution of the position of press secretary under Wilson.

3077. Nevins, Allan. *American Press Opinion: Washington to Coolidge. A Documentary Record of Editorial Leadership and Criticism, 1785–1927*. 2 vols. Boston: D.C. Heath and Co., 1928. Uses selected newspaper and journal articles to chronicle Wilson's ascendancy to the White House, his stormy battles during the Peace Conference, and the League fight.

3078. Paul, Edward. "Newspapers versus President Wilson." *Public* 21 (April 27, 1918): 532–56. Defends Wilson against a pro-Japanese press in America.

3079. Pollard, James Edward. *Presidents and the Press*, 630–96. New York: Macmillan Co., 1947. Wilson realized the power of the press and was effective in using it.

3080. "President Wilson at the Peace Conference." *Outlook* 120 (December 4, 1918): 529–30. A poll of American newspapers over the propriety of Wilson's personal representation of America at the Paris Peace Conference.

3081. Seideman, David. *The New Republic: A Voice of Modern Liberalism*. New York: Praeger Books, 1986. Includes discussion of the *New Republic*'s support of Wilson and most of his policies.

3082. Startt, James Dill. "American Editorial Opinion of Woodrow Wilson and the Main Problems of Peacemaking in 1919." Ph.D. diss., University of Maryland, 1965.

3083. Steel, Ronald. *Walter Lippmann and the American Century.* Boston: Little, Brown & Co., 1980. Includes the Wilson years.

3084. Stein, Meyer L. *When Presidents Meet the Press*, 54–67. New York: Julian Messner, 1969. Concise discussion of Joseph P. Tumulty's role in the Wilson administration, especially as an unofficial press secretary.

3085. Stockstill, Michael A. "Walter Lippmann: His Rise to Fame, 1899–1945." Ph.D. diss., Mississippi State University, 1970. Discusses Lippmann's interests in socialism, his associations with Wilson, and his disillusionment with the Treaty of Versailles.

3086. Tebbel, John, and Sarah Miles Watts. "Wilson: A 'Modern President.'" In *The Press and the Presidency: From George Washington to Ronald Reagan*, 363–90. New York: Oxford University Press, 1985. Examines Wilson's relationship with and use of the press during his presidency and his influence on the relationships between journalists and the Presidents who followed.

3087. Thompson, John A. "American Progressive Publicists and the First World War, 1914–1917." *Journal of American History* 58 (September 1971): 364–83. Examines opinions expressed by progressive editors and writers, mainly on preparedness and intervention.

3088. ———. *Reformers and War: American Progressive Publicists and the First World War.* Cambridge: Harvard University Press, 1987. Wilson as a major player in a wartime era which publicists have seen as a time of decline for progressivism.

3089. Thompson, Kenneth W., ed. *The Presidents and the Press.* Washington, D.C.: University Press of America, 1988. Credits the two Roosevelts and Wilson for building the modern presidency.

3090. Villard, Oswald Garrison. *Fighting Years: Memoirs of a Liberal Editor.* New York: Harcourt, Brace, & Co., 1939. Memoir of a personal friend of Wilson, focusing on Wilson's personal life during his campaigns for Governor and President.

3091. Walker, Don D. "Woodrow Wilson and Walter Lippmann: A Narrative of Historical Imagery." *Western Political Quarterly* 12 (December 1959): 939–47. Lippmann's evaluation of Wilson.

3092. Watterson, Henry. *Marse Henry: An Autobiography.* 2 vols. New York: Doubleday, Doran & Co., 1919. Argues that the League was only a fad that would eventually become obsolete.

3093. Wilson, Woodrow. *The Papers of Woodrow Wilson: The Complete Press Conference, 1913–1919*, vol. 50, ed. by Robert C. Hilderbrand. Princeton: Princeton University Press, 1985. Contains the transcripts of all of Wilson's press conferences.

3093a. ———. *Press Conferences, March 22, 1913–July 10, 1919*. Wilton, Conn.: National Micropublishing Corporation, 1971. 1 reel. Contains all of the transcripts and other records of Wilson's press conferences known to exist covering the years 1913 to 1919.

3094. Wreszin, Michael. *Oswald Garrison Villard: Pacifist at War*. Bloomington: Indiana University Press, 1965. Examines Villard's differences with Wilson, especially on America's entry into World War I.

18
Contemporary Profiles and Assessments Following Wilson's Death

See also entries under "Biographical Essays and Sketches," "Assessments of Wilson as President," and "Presidential Power and Leadership"

3095. Abbott, Lawrence Fraser. "Reformers and Pioneers." *Outlook* 137 (June 18, 1924): 261–62. Praises Wilson's idealism but criticizes his approach to foreign affairs as impractical and unrealistic.

3096. Alderman, Edwin Anderson. "Woodrow Wilson." Washington, D.C.: Government Printing Office, 1924. [Also published: Garden City, N.Y.: Doubleday, Page and Co., 1925.] Memorial address delivered before a joint session of Congress, December 15, 1924. 68th Cong., 2d sess. S. Doc. 174.

3097. ———. "Woodrow Wilson." *Outlook* 136 (February 13, 1924): 254–59. Admiring portrait of Wilson, written soon after Wilson's death, by the President of the University of Virginia.

3098. Andrews, Sandford. "Woodrow Wilson." *Cosmopolitan* 33 (October 1902): 651–54. [Reprinted in *Century Magazine* 65 (November 1902): 161–62.] A biographical sketch.

3099. "Animated Conservatism of Woodrow Wilson." *Independent* 81 (January 18, 1915): 75–76. Praises Wilson's progressivism and criticizes his partisanship.

3100. "An Appreciation." *Independent* 82 (April 12, 1915): 58. Contends that the problems Wilson had to confront as President were more difficult and complex than those faced by any since Lincoln.

3101. Araquistain, Louis. "As the Actors Leave the Stage." *Living Age* 320 (March 22, 1924): 541–42. Praises the greatness of Wilson and Lenin and the historical importance of their convictions. Written soon after their deaths.

3102. Baker, Ray Stannard. "Wilson—After Twenty Months." *American Magazine* 78 (December 1914): 43+. Praises Wilson's calm, steady, serious leadership.

3103. ———. "Wilson." *Collier's National Weekly* 58 (October 7, 1916): 5–6. Portrait of Wilson as a great thinker.

3104. Barnes, Harry Elmer. "More about Wilson." *New Republic* 40 (October 1, 1924): 3–5. Reviews of **350** and **4025**.

3105. ———. "Woodrow Wilson." *American Mercury* 1 (April 1924): 479–90. Portrait of Wilson written soon after he died, examining the many complexities of his character and times.

3106. ———. "Woodrow Wilson: An Estimate; Woodrow Wilson: Contemporary Appraisal." In *History and Social Intelligence*, 505–61. New York: Alfred A. Knopf, 1926. Examines the many conflicting views of Wilson. Includes excerpts from works by Robert Edwards Annin and William Allen White.

3107. Barron, C. W. *They Told Barron: The Notes of Clarence W. Barron*, ed. Arthur Pound and Samuel T. Moore. New York: Harper & Brothers, 1930. A record of the 1918–1928 conversations between the publisher of the *Wall Street Journal* and important people, including Wilson.

3108. Barton, George. "Woodrow Wilson: His Human Side." *Current History Magazine of the New York Times* 22 (April 1925): 1–9. Wilson's complex and often contradictory personality.

3109. Beck, James Montgomery. *The Passing of the New Freedom*. New York: George H. Doran Co., 1920. A critical, partly satirical, review of Wilson's policies, foreign and domestic. Much of the book is written in the form of imaginary conversations among world leaders, including Wilson.

3110. Bender, Robert J. *"W. W.": Scattered Impressions of a Reporter Who for Eight Years "Covered" the Activities of Woodrow Wilson*. New York: United Press Associations, 1924. Insider's personal view of Wilson by an international reporter who was with him, at home and abroad, through both his presidential terms.

3111. Bernstein, Herman. "Woodrow Wilson." In *Celebrities of Our Time*, 335–47. New York: J. Lawren, 1924.

3112. Blythe, Samuel George. "Lonely Man in the White House: Why a President of These United States Can Have No Intimates." *Ladies' Home Journal* 31 (April 1914): 11. Argues that the President can have no close relationships because everyone wants something from him.

3113. Bok, Edward William. "President." *Scribner's Magazine* 77 (January 1925): 93–95. Compares Wilson to Abraham Lincoln.

3114. Bridges, Robert. *Woodrow Wilson: A Personal Tribute*. [n.p., n.d.] Profile by Wilson's college classmate.

3115. "Britisher's Glimpse of the President." *Literary Digest* 47 (November 22, 1913): 1036–39. Portrait of Wilson at a press reception.

3116. Brooks, Eugene Clyde. *Woodrow Wilson as President.* New York: Row, Peterson and Co., 1916. Summary of Wilson's first term, including excerpts from some of his speeches in an appendix.

3117. Brooks, Sydney. "President Wilson." *English Review* 17 (June 1914): 372– 84. [Reprinted in *Living Age* 282 (July 4, 1914): 3–10.] Analysis of Wilson's evolution from strong executive leader to what his critics see as a presidential dictator.

3118. Catt, Carrie Lane Chapman. "Woodrow Wilson." *Woman Citizen* n.s. 8 (February 9, 1924): 14. Insists the insight of time will rank him with Washington and Lincoln as the nation's three mightiest leaders.

3119. Chapman, John Jay. "President's Dictatorship." *North American Review* 208 (October 1918): 518–23. Praises Wilson's thoughtfulness and ability to speak for the American public.

3120. "Common Sense in the White House: Non-Partisan Questions on which President Wilson Begins Well." *Century Magazine* 86 (May 1913): 149. Praises Wilson's willingness to avoid partisan politics and to depart from the traditional way of doing things in Washington.

3121. "The Complete Statesman." *Collier's National Weekly* 58 (October 28, 1916): 18. Takes issue with Ida Tarbell's positive report on an interview with Wilson published in the same issue, and attacks Wilson as a pompous moralist.

3122. Condon, Randall Judson. "A Tribute to Woodrow Wilson." *National Education Association of the United States, Addresses and Proceedings* 62 (1924): 838–39.

3123. Corbin, John. "From Jefferson to Wilson." *North American Review* 210 (August 1919): 172–85. Compares the political ideals and theories of Thomas Jefferson with those of Wilson.

3124. Crane, Frank. "Who Killed Wilson?" *Current Opinion* 70 (May 1921): 595. Blames Wilson's belief in partisan political parties for his downfall.

3125. Creel, George C. "The Next Four Years: An Interview with the President." *Everybody's Magazine* 36 (February 1917): 129–39. Enthusiastically supports Wilson and his progressive policies.

3126. ———. "Our Visionary President: An Interpretation." *Century Magazine* 89 (December 1914): 192–201. Praises Wilson for restoring the public's faith in American ideals and dreams.

3127. "Crisis. Not Victory." *Nation* 107 (December 7, 1918): 690. Focuses on Wilson's neglect of the great issues of the day: railways, reconstruction, and the peace.

3128. Croly, Herbert David. "Unregenerate Democracy: President Wilson's Administration." *New Republic* 6 (February 5, 1916): 17–19. Criticizes Wilson's failure to resurrect and unify the Democratic party.

3129. *Czechoslovakia's Tribute to the Memory of Woodrow Wilson.* New York: Czechoslovak Consulate General, 1924.

3130. Daniels, Winthrop More. "Woodrow Wilson: An Appraisal." *Independent* 73 (November 14, 1912): 1111–14. Portrait of Wilson as a man of high convictions.

3131. Dennis, Alfred Lewis Pinneo. "Career of Wilson." *Contemporary Review* 102 (December 1912): 790–800. [Reprinted in *Living Age* 276 (January 4, 1913): 3–11.] A portrait of Wilson and his background, in anticipation of his assuming the presidency.

3132. Dodd, William Edward. "The Social and Economic Background of Woodrow Wilson." *Journal of Political Economy* 25 (March 1917): 261–85. Describes the dynamic of the Wilson years in terms of regional and political interests rather than in terms of the personal principles of the President.

3133. Dos Passos, John R. "Meester Veelson." *New Republic* 69 (January 13, 1932): 240–41. [Also published in *Essays for Better Reading*, ed. Jacob Hooper Wise, 107–13. New York: Harcourt, Brace, 1940; in **397**, 35–42; and in *Heritage of American Literature*, ed. Lyon Norman Richardson, 789–93. Boston: Ginn, 1951.] Satirical poem criticizing Wilson's handling of World War I.

3134. "Dr. Woodrow Wilson and Political Courage." *Spectator* 110 (March 8, 1913): 392–94. Names Wilson a man of political courage and suggests several reforms for which he and the Democrats should be commended.

3135. Dunn, Arthur Wallace. *From Harrison to Harding: A Personal Narrative, Covering a Third of a Century, 1888–1921*, 2:181–415. New York: G.P. Putnam's Sons, 1922. Includes a political history of the 1912 and 1916 presidential elections and summarizes Wilson's two administrations.

3136. Durant, Will. "American Liberals and the War." *Dial* 64 (April 11, 1918): 366. Praises Wilson's leadership and his vision of the postwar world.

3137. Duplicate entry omitted.

3138. Eastman, Max. "Wilson and the World's Future." *Liberator* 1 (May 1918): 19–24. Praises Wilson for wisdom, restraint, and openness to liberal ideas, and hopes he will prove hospitable to socialist goals as well.

3139. _____ . "Wilson's Style." *Liberator* 4 (March 1921): 24–27. Uses Wilson's language in **4055** to attack him as a trickster who substitutes verbiage for fact or action.

3140. Eliot, Charles William. "Woodrow Wilson." *Atlantic Monthly* 133 (June 1924): 815–23. An admiring and emotional tribute to Wilson.

3141. "Exhortation and Government." *Nation* 96 (January 23, 1913): 72. Discusses the power of a President's speeches and exhortations, cautioning Wilson that if he raises hopes, he will be expected to see them realized.

3142. "Fair Play for the President." *Unpopular Review* 5 (April– June 1916): 427–49. Calls Wilson a religious sentimentalist who has made serious mistakes but urges all critics to play fair.

3143. "First Year of the Wilson Administration: A Review." *Outlook* 106 (March 7, 1914): 523–29. Views the first year of Wilson's presidency as a time during which he was able to win respect.

3144. Fisher, Irving. *Woodrow Wilson*. New Haven: Yale University Press, 1924. Address before the Woodrow Wilson Birthday Club, St. Joseph, Mo., April 29, 1924.

3145. Ford, Henry Jones. "The Record of the Administration." *Atlantic Monthly* 117 (May 1916): 577–90. In reviewing Wilson's first term as President, the author concludes that Wilson has set a new standard for the role of the executive branch of government.

3146. _____ . "Woodrow Wilson,—A Character Sketch." *American Review of Reviews* 46 (August 1912): 177–84. Indicates that the candidate has great vitality and a love of fun and of dramatic narrative.

3147. "Foreign Appraisals of Woodrow Wilson." *Literary Digest* 80 (February 16, 1924): 20–22. Excerpts of tributes to Wilson by European newspapers.

3148. "Foreign Raps at the President." *Literary Digest* 50 (June 12, 1915): 1391–92. European newspapers' criticisms of Wilson.

3149. "Foreign Views of Wilson." *Nation* 95 (November 28, 1912): 500. Discusses different impressions of Wilson put forth in European newspapers.

3150. Fort, John Franklin. "Wilson the Man." *Harpers Weekly* 58 (March 7, 1914): 7. Argues that Wilson is neither an enigma nor a mystery but a man with a deep sense of official responsibility.

3151. Frank, Glenn. *An American Looks at His World: Variations on a Point of View*, 277–94. Newark: University of Delaware Press, 1923. Asserts that the army of Wilson's liberal supporters has been put on guard but not defeated.

3152. Franklin, Fabian. "President and Public Opinion." *North American Review* 207 (April 1918): 533–40. An article discussing the complexity of issues and the opposition Wilson faced.

3153. "French Historian on Wilson." *Literary Digest* 65 (June 12, 1920): 41. Contains a brief essay by Joseph Reinach, praising Wilson's efforts to establish a world order.

3154. "A Fresh and Striking Composite Picture of President Wilson." *Current Opinion* 68 (March 1920): 328–33. Portrays Wilson as a man who is difficult to understand.

3155. Fuller, Harold de Wolf. "Anti-Wilson." *Review* 1 (September 27, 1919): 424–25. Examines Wilson's sharply declining popularity.

3156. Gardiner, Alfred G. "My Interview with Mr. Wilson." *Nation and the Athenaeum* 29 (April 2, 1921): 11–12. Reports a 1919 interview in which Wilson acknowledged the depth of American isolationism but was convinced he could overcome it.

3157. ———. "President Wilson." *Collier's National Weekly* 65 (March 20, 1920): 5–6, 55–56. [Also published in *Contemporary Review* 117 (May 1920): 626–34.] Portrays Wilson as a heroic figure continually subverted in a vast international drama.

3158. Gerard, James Watson. "The Statesmanship of Woodrow Wilson." *Current History Magazine of the New York Times* 19 (March 1924): 895–98. A tribute to Wilson and a brief review of his presidency, written shortly after his death.

3159. "Getting a Line on Mr. Wilson." *Literary Digest* 48 (April 25, 1914): 1005+. Excerpts from American newspapers attempting to write accurate portraits of Wilson.

3160. Gilbert, Clinton Wallace. *The Mirrors of Washington*, 25–45. New York: G. P. Putnam's Sons, 1921. Acerbic treatment of Wilson's Washington.

3161. Grasty, Charles Henry. "The Personality behind the President." *Atlantic Monthly* 125 (January 1920): 1–11. Ranks Wilson with Washington and Lincoln.

3162. "The Growing Isolation of President Wilson." *Current Opinion* 68 (April 1920): 446–50. Discusses Wilson's souring relations with European leaders and his declining popularity at home.

3163. Guehenno, Jean. "Whitman, Wilson et L'esprit Moderne." *Revue de Paris* 26, pt. 1 (January 1, 1919): 109–30.

3164. Hale, William Bayard. "Professor in the White House." *Collier's National Weekly* 50 (November 16, 1912): 11. Praises Wilson's openness, his scholarly writings, and his talents as an orator.

3165. ———. "Watching President Wilson at Work." *World's Work* 26 (May 1913): 69–77. Compares Wilson's White House to that of Roosevelt and Taft.

3166. Halevy, Daniel. "In Regard to President Wilson." *Living Age* 304 (January 24, 1920): 191–94. The author defends his positive portrayals of Wilson.

3167. Hamilton, Joseph Gregoire de Roulhac. "Woodrow Wilson: A Memorial Note." *Journal of Social Forces* 2 (March 1924): 425–29. A retrospective of Wilson's presidency, arguing that he was a prophet for his times.

3168. Hamlett, Earl G. "Immortality of Woodrow Wilson." *Methodist Quarterly Review* 74 (July 1925): 575–76. An assessment in which Wilson's reputation is found in his idealism.

3169. Hapgood, Norman. "Roosevelt, Perkins and Wilson." *Harper's Weekly* 58 (June 20, 1914): 11–12. Considers the role of Theodore Roosevelt and the Progressive Party, given the success and popularity of Wilson's own brand of progressivism.

3170. ———. "Spirit of the Administration." *Independent* 86 (May 22, 1916): 277–78. An enthusiastic description of Wilson's statesmanship, intellect, and leadership.

3171. Harris, Frank. "Gargoyles: Roosevelt, Wilson, and Harding." In *Contemporary Portraits*, 4th ser., 262–80. New York: Berntano's, 1923. Includes a bitter, angry portrait of Wilson as one who betrayed both his country and those who supported him.

3172. Harris, Henry Wilson. "Woodrow Wilson." *Contemporary Review* 125 (March 1924): 282–89. Refers to his conversations with Wilson and others in a critical analysis of Wilson's public service.

3173. Hart, James. "Classical Statesmanship as Exemplified in Woodrow Wilson." *Sewanee Review* 33 (October 1925): 396–403. Wilson as the first classical statesman to provide strong leadership for both the United States and the world.

3174. Harvey, George Brinton McClellan. "The President's Message." *North American Review* 199 (February 1914): 174–76. Criticizes the style of Wilson's State of the Union address, but praises the substance, particularly on the role of business.

3175. ———. "The President's Vision: Is It True or Is It Illusive?" *North American Review* 199 (January 1914): 1–13. Considers the many problems Wilson may have to face in the coming year, expressing confidence in him but also an unwillingness to share his seemingly unbridled optimism.

3176. ———. "Six Months of Wilson." *North American Review* 198 (November 1913): 577–87. A mostly positive assessment of the domestic and economic legislation passed during Wilson's first months in office.

3177. Hay, James, Jr. "The Working Habits of the President of the United States." *American Magazine* 81 (January 1916): 55–57. Admires Wilson's daily work routine and schedule.

3178. Holt, Hamilton. "Woodrow Wilson and the Service He Has Rendered His Country and Humanity." *Independent* 105 (March 5, 1921): 231–33. Positive summation.

3179. Hosford, Hester Eloise. "Woodrow Wilson." *Independent* 73 (July 11, 1912): 68–79. A portrait of Wilson by a family friend.

3180. Houston, Herbert Sherman. "Woodrow Wilson and World Peace." *Our World* 4 (March 1924): 1. Obituary tribute.

3181. "How the President's Message Is Received." *Literary Digest* 47 (December 13, 1913): 1155–58. Generally favorable reactions by American newspapers to Wilson's first year in office.

3182. Hyman, Sidney. "When He Enters the Oval Room." *New York Times Magazine* January 22, 1961: 5+. Wilson's accomplishments during his first days in the White House.

3183. "Idealism of Woodrow Wilson." *Christian Century* 41 (February 21, 1924): 230–32. A eulogy for Wilson, stating that his greatness came from his eloquence and moral leadership, and that his downfall came about only when he lost sight of those gifts.

3184. "In Memory of Woodrow Wilson." *Outlook* 138 (December 24, 1924): 662–64. Brief description of an event paying tribute to Wilson.

3185. Irwin, William Henry. "The World's Leading Democrat: And His Influence in Spreading the Spirit of World Democracy." *World Outlook* 4 (November 1918): 3. Calls Wilson the greatest diplomat in the world and explains his philosophy that true democracy rests on the foundation of Christianity.

3186. "Is President Wilson Great or Only Near-Great?" *Journal of Education* 79 (May 28, 1914): 602. Editorial asserting that Wilson's reputation will depend on his Mexican policy.

3187. "Judging an Administration." *Nation* 102 (March 23, 1916): 328. Discusses a number of nonpartisan responses to the Republicans' attempts to label Wilson as the worst President since James Buchanan.

3188. Keller, Albert Galloway. "Case for Wilson, At Its Worst." *Nation* 103 (November 2, 1916): 420. Defends Wilson's first term.

3189. Kirk, Harris E. "In Memoriam: Woodrow Wilson." *Johns Hopkins Alumni Magazine* 12 (March 1924): 202–8. [Delivered at the memorial service held under the auspices of the Baltimore Federation of Churches at the Mt. Vernon Place Methodist Episcopal Church, 6 February 1924.] Believes that the pathway for future leadership was opened by the political idealism, humanitarian passion, and religious faith of Woodrow Wilson.

3190. Klein, Felix. "Le President Wilson." [President Wilson]. *Revue Hebdomadaire* 33 (March 1, 1924): 73–93.

3191. Latane, John Holladay. "Woodrow Wilson: Memorial Address." *Johns Hopkins Alumni Magazine* 12 (March 1924): 194–200. Dispels the belief that Wilson's life was a tragedy by calling him a great President in times of peace, a greater leader of a mighty nation in war, a spokesman for the liberal forces of humanity, and the creator and founder of the League of Nations idea.

3192. "The Late President's Record of Achievement." *Current History* 19 (March 1924): 899–941. Reviews Wilson's career as academician, Governor, and President. Examines the major events of his presidency.

3193. Lawrence, David. "How Does He Stand It?" *Ladies' Home Journal* 34 (November 1917): 8, 87. Lawrence asserts that Wilson is in much better physical condition than he was before he became President.

3194. ———. "The President and His Day's Work." *Century Magazine* 93 (March 1917): 641–52. [Also published as "White House Burdens, They Are Older than Kennedy." *U.S. News & World Report* 51 (November 13, 1961): 58–60.] Discusses the effects of the presidency on Wilson's recreational activities and describes a regular day at the White House.

3195. Leach, Henry. "Woodrow Wilson: Man and Statesman." *Living Age* 295 (October 13, 1917): 67–72. An admiring portrait of Wilson as a great leader who delivers his message in a simple yet eloquent fashion.

3196. "Leaders in a Democracy." *Nation* 95 (December 26, 1912): 604. Discusses Wilson's great talent of alternately leading the people forcefully and then going to them for support.

3197. Lechartier, Georges. "Le President Wilson." [President Wilson]. *Le Correspondant* 294 (February 25, 1924): 577–99.

3198. "The Legend of Woodrow Wilson." *Independent* 112 (February 16, 1924): 90–91. Argues that Wilson's legacy will be the great irony of his presidency: his dictatorial efforts to be the world's moral leader.

3199. Leupp, Francis Ellington. "The President—and Mr. Wilson." *Independent* 76 (November 27, 1913): 390–95. Wilson as an independent reformer, comparing him to Theodore Roosevelt and Taft.

3200. Levi, Alessandro. "Il Pensiero Politico di Woodrow Wilson." *Nuova Antologia* 234 (March 16–April 1, 1924): 162–75, 193–206.

3201. Lloyd, J. William. "Woodrow Wilson in the White House." *New Review* 1 (1913): 24–25. Article written by a Socialist at the outset of Wilson's presidency, expressing little hope for change as the result of electing a Democrat to office.

3202. Lord, Frank B., and James William Bryan. *Woodrow Wilson's Administration and Achievements: Being a Compilation from the Newspaper Press of Eight Years of the World's Greatest History, Particularly as Concerns America, Its People and Their Affairs.* Washington, D.C.: J.W. Bryan, 1921.

3203. Low, Alfred Maurice. "An Englishman's Review of President Wilson's First Year." *Century Magazine* 88 (May 1914): 26–32. Credits Wilson with quickly restoring prestige to the executive office.

3204. _____ . "The Burden." *Good Housekeeping* 66 (April 1918): 31–32+. A fictional piece on how the war affected Wilson.

3205. _____ . "New Bossism." *Harper's Weekly* 57 (April 19, 1913): 8. Washington correspondent comments on the speed with which Wilson asserted his leadership of both the executive and legislative branches.

3206. _____ . "President Wilson's Leadership." *Harper's Weekly* 57 (March 29, 1913): 7. Washington correspondent advises Wilson on the kind of leadership needed to achieve stability.

3207. _____ . "President Wilson's Service to the World." *American Monthly Review of Reviews* 59 (January 1919): 66– 68. Praises Wilson's sense of morality.

3208. Lowry, Edward George. "The Wilson Personality." *Collier's National Weekly* 53 (July 25, 1914): 5–6+. The difficulties in gaining a firm grasp of Wilson's character.

3209. Macfarlane, Peter Clark. "President in Practice." *Collier's National Weekly* 53 (April 18, 1914): 5–7. A blistering critique of Wilson's first two years.

3210. MacRae, D. A. "An Appreciation of Woodrow Wilson." *Dalhousie Review* 4 (April 1924): 86–97. Describes Wilson's ability to establish traditions as President of Princeton and President of the United States.

3211. "Man of Letters." *Literary Review* 4 (February 16, 1924): 517.

3212. McAdoo, William Gibbs. "The Kind of Man Woodrow Wilson Is." *Century Magazine* 85 (March 1913): 744–53.

3213. McClintock, R. M. "What Does President Wilson Mean?" *Collier's National Weekly* 52 (November 22, 1913): 23. Prefers the progressivism of Theodore Roosevelt to Wilson's "New Freedom."

3214. McDonald, P. B. "Woodrow Wilson: Teacher of the American People." *Texas Review* 6 (January 1921): 138–42. Depicts Wilson as an idealistic teacher and compares him to Theodore Roosevelt.

3215. Michaelis, Karin. "On President Wilson's Trail." *Living Age* 326 (July 18, 1925): 131–39. A reporter's recollections about an interview with the President-elect.

3216. Miller, David Hunter. *Woodrow Wilson. Memorial Address Delivered at the Madison Avenue Presbyterian Church, February 10, 1924.* New York: Appeal Printing Co., 1924. Describes Wilson as the noblest statesman known in history and praises his peaceful ideals.

3217. Mims, Edwin. "Woodrow Wilson: The Happy Warrior." *Methodist Quarterly Review* 73 (April 1924): 195–214.

3218. Morley, Christopher Darlington. "Christmas Card." In *Power of Sympathy*, 213–17. Garden City, N.Y.: Doubleday, Page & Co., 1923. Short Christmas piece, praising Wilson's efforts for world peace.

3219. _____. "The Man." *Ladies' Home Journal* 34 (June 1917): 14. A fanciful account of Wilson's decision to go to war.

3220. _____. "The Man." In *Shandygaff*, 72–81. Garden City, N.Y.: Doubleday, Page & Co., 1918. Sympathetic portrait that describes how the pressures of Wilson's public life chipped away at his idealism.

3221. "The Most Useful Americans." *Independent* 74 (May 1, 1913): 960–61. A poll of *Independent* readers voting Wilson one of the "Most Useful Americans" and their reasons.

3222. "Mr. Wilson, Psychologically." *North American Review* 211 (May 1920): 577–89. [Also published in *Literary Digest* 66 (September 11, 1920): 56–58.] A review of Joseph Collins' article concerning the psychology of Wilson, depicting him as a non-emotional, practical idealist.

3223. "Mr. Wilson as a War-President." *Literary Digest* 56 (February 2, 1918): 5–7. A collection of editorial opinions.

3224. "Mr. Wilson's Mind." *Collier's National Weekly* 58 (November 11, 1916): 10–11. Criticizes Wilson as willing to dress in artful words any power or action he favors.

3225. "Mr. Wilson's Theory of the Presidential Office." *World's Work* 37 (December 1918): 134. An examination of Wilson's political theories on the necessity for strong executive leadership.

3226. "National State of Mind." *Nation* 96 (January 16, 1913): 48. Discusses Governor Wilson's views on the right relationship among business, labor, and government.

3227. "The New Administration." *Literary Digest* 46 (March 15, 1913): 556–58. Speculation concerning the course of the new Wilson administration.

3228. "The New Administration." *Survey* 29 (March 15, 1913): 840–41. Examines the cabinet of the first Wilson administration and the new offices that were created.

3229. "The New National Administration." *Chautauquan* 70 (May 1913): 249–51. Describes Wilson's new administration as "hardheaded, practical, earnest, and progressive."

3230. "The New Start in America." *Living Age* 275 (November 30, 1912): 569–71. Discusses foreign and domestic problems facing the newly-elected Wilson.

3231. "Obituary." *Current Opinion* 76 (March 1924): 265–67. Describes Wilson as an idealist, doomed to failure.

3232. "Obituary." *American Antiquarian Society. Proceedings* n.s. 34 (April 1924): 25–26. Tribute to Wilson as a member in the Society.

3233. Odell, Joseph Henry. "Who Is the United States?" *Outlook* 118 (February 20, 1918): 281–83. The author's answer is Wilson.

3234. O'Malley, Frank Ward. "War-Whirl in the White House." *Century Magazine* 96 (May 1918): 62–72. Describes the austere, businesslike atmosphere of the Wilson White House during wartime.

3235. "One Month of Wilson." *Hearst's Magazine* 23 (May 1913): 827–30. A favorable analysis.

3236. "One Year of Wilson." *Harper's Weekly* 58 (March 7, 1914): 6–13. Seven prominent American politicians recite Wilson's achievements.

3237. "The Other-Worldliness of Wilson." *New Republic* 2 (March 27, 1915): 194–95. An assessment praising Wilson's idealistic literary style.

3238. "Our Literary President." *Literary Digest* 55 (December 29, 1917): 34–35. Reconciles the seeming contradiction between Wilson as "man of letters" and Wilson as "man of politics" by a professor who knew Wilson at Princeton.

3239. Packh, Cecilia Hoerr de. "If Woodrow Wilson Were a Woman: A Woman's View." *Public* 22 (June 7, 1919): 598–99. Argues that if Wilson were a woman, the League of Nations treaty would have been ratified because only women can bring about revolutionary change.

3240. "Paradox of Woodrow Wilson." *New Republic* 37 (February 13, 1924): 299–300. Examines discrepancy between his views on international cooperation and national isolation.

3241. Parkman, Mary Rosetta. "Champion of Peace: President Wilson." In *Fighters for Peace*, 285–311. New York: Century Co., 1919. Calls Wilson a champion of peace who thought deeply about the vital concerns of his nation suddenly thrust into World War I.

3242. "The Passing of Mr. Wilson." *Nation* 112 (March 2, 1921): 328. A memorial to Wilson, noting his idealistic, yet tragic, legacy.

3243. "The Passing of Woodrow Wilson." *Round Table* 11 (December 1920): 14–31. A tribute to Woodrow Wilson as he passed from national political life after his party lost the 1920 presidential election.

3244. Pearson, Edmund Lester. "Books about Mr. Wilson." *Review* 2 (March 6, 1920): 237. A review of laudatory Wilson books.

3245. Pepper, George Wharton. "What Is an Anarchist?" *North American Review* 210 (October 1919): 470–74. Poses the question about Wilson, while accusing him of actions that discredit government.

3246. Perkins, L. M. "Schoolma'am and Schoolmaster." *North American Review* 199 (January 1914): 156–59. Criticizes Wilson's "intellectual arrogance."

3247. "Personal Leadership of Woodrow Wilson." *Current Opinion* 54 (May 1913): 353–55. An early assessment of Wilson's leadership as President, including his relations with Congress and his stand on tariffs.

3248. "The Political Transformation of Woodrow Wilson." *Current Literature* 52 (February 1912): 153–57. Wilson's political evolution as a progressive.

3249. "Premier-President." *Living Age* 277 (June 28, 1913): 821– 23. Compares the powers enjoyed by the President of the United States and the Prime Minister of Great Britain, and describes Wilson's attempt to strengthen the executive office.

3250. "The President and Foreign Affairs." *Nation* 103 (July 6, 1916): 5–6. An evaluation of Wilson's lack of personal knowledge and experience in foreign policy.

3251. "The President at Work." *Literary Digest* 46 (May 24, 1913): 1191–92. Reprint of an article from the New York *Evening World*, describing Wilson as the hardest working President in recent memory.

3252. "The President of the United States." *Forum* 53 (June 1915): 792. Believes that Wilson's contributions have not been fully recognized and that Wilson should be regarded as one of the most important and influential Presidents.

3253. "President or Prime Minister?" *Nation* 102 (March 9, 1916): 271–72. Compares the United States Congress to England's House of Commons and the President to a Prime Minister.

3254. "President Wilson." *Independent* 74 (March 6, 1913): 487–88. Describes Wilson's character prior to taking the presidency and urges his administration to focus on issues such as foreign relations and the growth of the Socialist party.

3255. "President Wilson." *Living Age* 320 (March 15, 1924): 483– 86. Gives several journalistic responses, written as obituaries, concerning the contributions of Wilson.

3256. "President Wilson Alone." *New Republic* 20 (October 8, 1919): 277–79. Examines the cause of Wilson's breakdown in 1919.

3257. "President Wilson Comes Back." *Literary Digest* 64 (February 28, 1920): 13–15. Cites opinions of civic leaders and physicians about Wilson's ability to govern during and following his illness.

3258. "President Wilson, a Political and Personal Interpretation." *Outlook* 121 (April 23, 1919): 693–96. A first-hand study of Wilson as an academician, a politician, a diplomatist, and a national leader.

3259. "President Wilson and the Trusts: A Poll of the Press." *Outlook* 106 (January 31, 1914): 240–42. Reviews Wilson's message to Congress, dealing with trust legislation, as well as press reaction to it.

3260. "President Wilson Will Put Progressives Only on Guard." *Current Opinion* 54 (February 1913): 92–93. Suggests that Wilson will remain firmly behind the progressives in the Democratic party at the expense of the conservative wing.

3261. "President Wilson's Baffling Methods of Handling Men." *Current Opinion* 56 (January 1914): 18–20. Characterizes Wilson's technique for dealing with reporters, congressmen, and other visitors as adroit, clever, and secretive.

3262. "President Wilson's Illness: Abrupt End of His Tour." *Current History Magazine of the New York Times* 11 (November 1919): 236–37. A discussion of the nature of Wilson's illness, and the many rumors about the degree of its severity.

3263. "Presidential Promptness." *Literary Digest* 52 (January 15, 1916): 142. Examines Wilson's emphasis on punctuality.

3264. "The President's Address." *Public* 21 (December 7, 1918): 1470–71. Contends that Wilson has been a leader in war but has failed to shape domestic programs.

3265. "The President's Illness." *Spectator* 123 (October 11, 1919): 462–63. Analyzes the causes of Wilson's illness, citing the unnecessarily heavy load that burdened Wilson.

3266. "The President's Opportunity." *Outlook* 114 (December 13, 1916): 792–93. Studies the criticisms of the Wilson administration as it enters a second term.

3267. "Professor as President." *Living Age* 275 (December 7, 1912): 624–26. Argues that the same attributes which elevated Wilson to eminence as a professor also elevated him to the presidency.

3268. Risque, Bert. *Seven Wonders of Woodrow Wilson, Father of the Family of Nations.* Lancaster, Pa.: H. E. Winters, 1924. Laudatory poetry and brief justifications of Wilson's major diplomatic policies.

3269. Robinson, Edgar Eugene. "The Presidency of Woodrow Wilson— A Symposium: Woodrow Wilson and the Democratic Party, 1913–1921." *Pacific Review* 1 (March 1921): 588–95. Brief look at how Wilson's leadership changed the Democratic Party.

3270. ———. "The President or His Party." *New Republic* 7 (May 13, 1916): 40–42. Describes the importance of the Democratic Party in determining United States Presidents and how Wilson's first administration changed that structure.

3271. Robinson, Luther Emerson. "President Wilson in Contemporary Critique." *Bookman* 46 (October 1917): 201–4. Interpretations of Wilson's character and accomplishments by both foreign and American authors.

3272. Rogers, Lindsay. "President Wilson's Theory of His Office." *Forum* 51 (February 1914): 174–86. Examines Wilson's ability to pass legislation and carry out his policies with little friction from opposition.

3273. ———. "Presidential Dictatorship in the United States." *Quarterly Review* 231 (January 1919): 127–48. Deals with presidential power in time of war. Written during Wilson's second administration.

3274. S., E. "The President." *Atlantic Monthly* 111, no. 13 (March 1913): 289–95. Characterizes Wilson as a visionary who will take important values into the White House.

3275. Shadwell, Bertrand. "Portrait of a President: Poem." *Spectator* 121 (October 12, 1918): 390. Short poem written after viewing a portrait of Wilson at a Chicago art museum.

3276. Shannon, Frederick Franklin. "Woodrow Wilson: Martyr." *Methodist Quarterly Review* 74 (April 1925): 295–308. Believes that in the post-Armistice period, the one bright light shining through the darkness is the memory of Wilson.

3277. Shaw, Albert. "Woodrow Wilson's Leadership." *American Monthly Review of Reviews* 69, no. 3 (March 1924): 260–67. Sketch of Wilson that focuses upon the unexpected successes and superb leadership of his presidency.

3278. Shorey, Paul. "Wilson—the Man and the Statesman." *Weekly Review* 4 (April 30, 1921): 414–15. Argues that Wilson's legacy will be measured by the unpredictable outcome of his policies and the incalculable reverberations of his rhetoric.

3279. Showerman, Grant. "Woodrow Wilson: An Appreciation." *Sewanee Review* 32 (April 1924): 139–45. An acquaintance of Wilson recalls specific encounters and summarizes Wilson's achievements.

3280. "Simplicity at Washington." *Nation* 96 (January 30, 1913): 96–97. Explains how Wilson transformed the presidency from a glamorous office into a position heavily burdened with responsibility.

3281. Smith, J. W. Rixey. "My Neighbor Woodrow Wilson." *Collier's National Weekly* 70 (October 21, 1922): 5–6. [Also published in *Literary Digest* 75 (December 9, 1922): 38–40.] Written by a Washington neighbor, giving accounts of some incidents of the ex-President's daily life in the Capital.

3282. Smuts, Jan Christiaan. "Woodrow Wilson's Place in History." *Current History Magazine of the New York Times* 14 (April 1921): 45–48. [Also published in *American Monthly Review of Reviews* 63 (April 1921): 426–27; and in *Essays on Current Themes*, ed. Charles Alphonso Smith, 90–96. Boston: Ginn & Co., 1923.]

3283. Strunsky, Simeon. "Wilsoniana." *Foreign Affairs* 2 (September 1923): 147–60. A review of four books.

3284. Tarbell, Ida Minerva. "A Talk with the President of the United States." *Collier's National Weekly* 58 (October 28, 1916): 5–6, 37, 40–41. An admiring interview with Wilson that supports his bid for reelection.

3285. Tattler [pseud.]. "Notes from the Capital: 'When a Man Comes to Himself.'" *Nation* 102 (March 16, 1916): 310. Wilson's failed experiments with availability to the press and open discussions with Congress.

3286. "That Old Presbyterian, Woodrow Wilson, in War and Peace." *Literary Digest* 66 (August 7, 1920): 60–66. Explains Wilson's confrontations with Congress before entering World War I, his criticisms as a war leader, and his triumph over diplomats at the Paris Peace Conference.

3287. Thayer, William Roscoe. "Close of an Epoch." *North American Review* 213 (March 1921): 289–307. Regards Wilson as an egoist and the 1920 presidential election as an important event ending a democratic crisis.

3288. "To Woodrow Wilson: Greetings!" *Harper's Weekly* 57 (March 8, 1913): 7. [Also published in *North American Review* 221 (March 1925): 387–89.] Friendly editorial encouraging the newly elected Wilson to lead democracy against economic monopoly.

3289. Turner, George Kibbe. "What Wilson Is up Against." *McClure's Magazine* 40 (February 1913): 148+. Delineates the political, economic, and social forces which will impact Wilson as President and questions whether he can possibly resist the weight of the conservatives.

3290. "Two Mr. Wilsons." *New Republic* 8 (September 9, 1916): 128– 29. Describes Wilson's second administration and considers Wilson to be a progressive Democrat.

3291. "Two Personalities in Politics." *World's Work* 28 (August 1914): 369–70. Compares Theodore Roosevelt with Wilson.

3292. "Two-Year Record." *World's Work* 29 (March 1915): 489–91. Explains presidential power and the restoration of the Democratic Party during Wilson's first administration.

3293. Van Dyke, Henry. "Single Star Mind." *Forum* 71 (March 1924): 388–89. A tribute to Wilson by his former colleague at Princeton.

3294. Villard, Oswald Garrison. "Isolation of the President." *Independent* 84 (December 6, 1915): 384–85. Describes Wilson's presidential personality as being isolated and his administration as being ineffective due to lack of communication and little cooperation.

3295. _____. "Mystery of Woodrow Wilson." *North American Review* 204 (September 1916): 362–72. Traces the drastic change of Wilson from an open New Jersey Governor to a secluded President.

3296. _____. "Woodrow Wilson: A Supreme Tragedy." In *Prophets, True and False*, 158–68. New York: Alfred A. Knopf, 1928. [Also published in *Nation* 118 (February 13, 1924): 156–58.] Holds Wilson culpable for entering the war and for failing to shape the peace. One of a series of portraits of contemporary public figures by the editor of *Nation*.

3297. Virginia General Assembly. *Exercises in Respect to the Memory of Woodrow Wilson, Former President of the United States, Held in the Hall of the House of Delegates by the General Assembly of Virginia, Wednesday, February 6, 1924.* Richmond: William Byrd Press, 1924.

3298. Walling, William English. "Woodrow Wilson and the Class Struggle." *New Review* 1 (1913): 399–405. Discusses Wilson's ability to understand and use socialist language in articulating the need for certain reforms.

3299. ———. "Woodrow Wilson and State Socialism." *New Review* 1 (1913): 329–35. Argues that many of Wilson's proposals for the roles of government and business come close to a form of socialism.

3300. "War-Time Day with the President." *Literary Digest* 55 (September 8, 1917): 38. Examines Wilson's personal seclusion and intense study before American entry into World War I.

3301. "We Can't Seem to Get Away from Mr. Wilson." *Current Opinion* 71 (December 1921): 711–16. States that the responsibility given to Wilson can only be compared to the responsibility placed upon Lincoln and questions whether Wilson will ever return to public affairs.

3302. "What We May Anticipate." *Independent* 74 (March 6, 1913): 496–97. Anticipates from Wilson a prudently progressive and safely conservative administration.

3303. Whittlesey, Walter Lincoln. "The Woodrow We Knew." *Collier's National Weekly* 73 (March 1, 1924): 7. A Princeton professor's admiring description of Wilson written as the lowered campus flag marked Wilson's death.

3304. "Why President Wilson Collapsed." *Current Opinion* 67 (December 1919): supp. 4.

3305. "Why Woodrow Wilson Belongs to the Ages." *Literary Digest* 80 (February 16, 1924): 7–10. Chronology of Wilson, which also explains that his principles are deeply embedded in American political thinking.

3306. Whyte, Frederic. "Two Presidents: Woodrow Wilson and Raymond Poincare." *Cornhill Magazine* 117 (February 1918): 181–92. [Also published in *Living Age* 297 (May 11, 1918): 331–39.] Compares Wilson with Raymond Poincare, who is described as the first "adequate" President of the French Republic.

3307. Wilhelm, Donald. "When You Drop in on Mr. Wilson." *Independent* 98 (June 21, 1919): 442. Describes the interior of Wilson's White House as being simplistic but holding within its walls extensive worldwide powers.

3308. "The Wilson Administration." *Outlook* 127 (March 9, 1921): 367–71. Sums up the numerous achievements of Wilson's administrations.

3309. "The Wilson Administration Closes Its First Year." *Current Opinion* 56 (April 1914): 253–55. Reports various opinions, focusing on his economic, Mexican, and partisan policies.

3310. "The Wilson Administration to Date." *New England Magazine* n.s. 51 (August 1914): 257–62.

3311. "Wilson after Four Years." *Nation* 104 (March 8, 1917): 259– 60. Argues that Wilson's first term has been a success.

3312. "Wilson after Two Years." *Independent* 81 (March 1, 1915): 303–4. Describes Wilson's first two years by commending him as a party leader and an international President.

3313. Wilson, Albert Frederick. "Woodrow Wilson: After Seeing Drinkwater's Lincoln." *Poetry* 16, no. 6 (September 1920): 314–23. Poem.

3314. "Wilson and Lenin." *Christian Century* 41 (February 14, 1924): 197–99. Compares the lives and careers of the two leaders.

3315. "Wilson and Political Courage." *Living Age* 277 (April 12, 1913): 116–19. Points out that since the Democrats have not been in power for over twenty years, Wilson will need to see how the old Democratic principles are to be applied to new conditions.

3316. "Wilson and the Presidency." *Nation* 102 (June 22, 1916): 661. Reviews the first administration and suggests ways to correct its mistakes.

3317. "Wilson the Idealist—and Scapegoat." *Literary Digest* 68 (March 19, 1921): 40–42. Examines Wilson's decline in public opinion.

3318. Wilson, Samuel Mackay. *Woodrow Wilson. Memorial Address on the Death of the Twenty-Eighth President of the United States of America, Delivered at the Memorial Service Held at the New Lexington Opera House in Lexington, Kentucky, on Sunday, February 10, 1924.* Lexington, 1924.

3319. "Wilson's Second Year." *Nation* 100 (January 7, 1915): 7. Praises him as strong and intelligent.

3320. "Wilson's Superior Prestige." *American Monthly Review of Reviews* 57, no. 1 (January 1918): 10–12. Argues that Wilson has more worldwide prestige than either Clemenceau or Lloyd George.

3321. "Wisdom of Woodrow Wilson." *Living Age* 295 (December 8, 1917): 614–18. Considers Wilson to be more interested in his own rather than his party's success.

3322. Wittkovsky, Isidore Maximilian Harden, Prince of Baden, [pseud.]. "Woodrow Wilson." *Living Age* 320 (March 22, 1924): 537–40. Short biographical article written by a German pacifist.

3323. Woodhouse, Edward S. "The Place of Woodrow Wilson in American Politics—An Estimate." *South Atlantic Quarterly* 21 (January 1922): 1–13. Compares Wilson to a soldier who was politically disabled by World War I.

3324. "Woodrow Wilson." *Independent* 93 (January 19, 1918): 89. Upholds Wilson as a democratic leader engaged in the overthrow of absolutism and also as a great champion of liberalism.

3325. "Woodrow Wilson." *New Republic* 24 (November 17, 1920): 284–85. Outlines the differing interpretations by Wilson's biographers of his motives, career, and character.

3326. "Woodrow Wilson." *Weekly Review* 4 (March 9, 1921): 214–16. An appraisal of Wilson's presidency at its conclusion, granting that Wilson achieved much but failed to get the League approved because of "radical defects of mind and spirit."

3327. "Woodrow Wilson." *Saturday Review* 137 (February 9, 1924): 124–25. Describes the reaction to Wilson's death and discusses his importance in American as well as world history.

3328. "Woodrow Wilson." *Deutsche Rundschau* 198 (March 1924): 225– 33. [Signed by "Diplomaticus."]

3329. "Woodrow Wilson, 28 December, 1856–3 February, 1924." *Outlook* 136 (February 13, 1924): 245–47. Assesses Wilson's greatest achievements, primarily focusing on his last ten years of life.

3330. "Woodrow Wilson, a Biography." *Current History Magazine of the New York Times* 19 (March 1924): 887–942. Series of four lengthy articles by James Watson Gerard: **3158**; **3932**; **3192**; and "Phrases that Woodrow Wilson Made Famous," all of which evaluate Wilson's life and achievements.

3331. "Woodrow Wilson the Man." *Harper's Weekly* 58 (January 10, 1914): 25–26. Describes Wilson as "misunderstood" and a political "enigma."

3332. "Woodrow Wilson, the Man." *Journal of Education* 79 (April 16, 1914): 427–28. Wilson's first-person reflections on his presidency and personal leadership.

3333. "Woodrow Wilson as a Party Leader." *New Republic* 7 (June 24, 1916): 185–87. Believes that Wilson is not a great President but upholds him as a great party leader.

3334. "Woodrow Wilson: The President's Policies Analyzed." *Nation* 103 (September 14, 1916): 256–58. Praises Wilson's credentials, reveals his political weaknesses, and evaluates his career before becoming President.

3335. "Woodrow Wilson en route to Recovery." *Current Opinion* 75 (August 1923): 154–56. Argues that Wilson is not a stricken man headed for political and personal oblivion.

3336. "Woodrow Wilson: A Valedictory Estimate." *Nation and the Athenaeum* 28 (March 5, 1921): 769–70.

3337. "Woodrow Wilson's Achievement." *Nation and the Athenaeum* 34 (February 9, 1924): 658.

19
Wilson's Associates

A. Family and Friends

Axson, Edward William (1876–1905)
Younger brother of Ellen Axson Wilson, who drowned with his wife and young son near Creighton, Ga.

3338. Biographical sketch, *PWW* 2:372, n. 2.

Axson, Isaac Stockton Keith (1813–1891)
Paternal grandfather of Ellen Axson Wilson and a Presbyterian minister in South Carolina and Georgia.

3339. Papers. Princeton University Library

3340. Biographical sketch, *PWW* 2:547, n. 3.

Axson, Isaac Stockton Keith, II (1867–1935)
Brother of Ellen Axson Wilson; professor of English at Princeton (1899–1913) and elsewhere. He was National Secretary of the American Red Cross (1917–1919).

3341. Biographical sketch, *PWW* 2:386, n. 1.

3342. "The President as Seen by His Brother-in-Law." *Literary Digest* 53 (November 4, 1916): 1197.

Axson, Randolph
Paternal uncle of Ellen Axson Wilson; commission merchant in Savannah.

3343. Biographical sketch, *PWW* 2:557, n. 2.

Axson, Samuel Edward (ca. 1833–1884)
Father of Ellen Axson Wilson, and Presbyterian clergyman in South Carolina and Rome, Georgia.

3344. Papers. Georgia Historical Society collections, Savannah.

3345. Biographical sketch, *PWW* 2:334, n. 3.

Bones, Helen Woodrow (1879–1951)
Wilson's first cousin; daughter of James W. Bones. She became Ellen Axson Wilson's personal secretary shortly after President Wilson entered the White House in 1913.

3346. Biographical sketch, *PWW* 1:650, n. 6.

Bones, James W.
Maternal uncle by marriage of Wilson; father of Helen Woodrow Bones; and commission merchant of Rome, Ga.

3347. Biographical sketch, *PWW* 1:39, n. 4.

3348. Leuchtenburg, William E. "James W. Bones." *DAB* 22:49–53.

Bridges, Robert (1858–1941)
Classmate and friend of Wilson at Princeton who became an author, poet, journalist, and editor of *Scribner's Magazine*.

3349. Papers. Dickinson College Library, Carlisle, Pa., and University of South Carolina Thomas Cooper Library, Columbia.

3350. Biographical sketch, *PWW* 1:285, n. 1.

3351. Bridges, Robert. *The Spirit of Man: An Anthology in English and French from the Philosophers and Poets*. New York: Longmans, Green and Co., 1916.

3352. Stanford, Donald E. "Robert Bridges." *DLB* 98:40–52.

Elliott, Margaret Randolph Axson (b. 1881)
Younger sister of Ellen Axson Wilson, who married Edward Elliott, Professor of Politics at Princeton.

3353. Biographical sketch, *PWW* 2:417, n. 1.

Howe, Annie Josephine Wilson (1853–1916)
Wilson's second oldest sister, who married George Howe.

3354. Biographical sketch, *PWW* 1:4, n. 6.

Howe, George, Jr., M.D.
Husband of Wilson's sister, Annie Josephine Wilson, and a physician in Columbia, S.C.

3355. Biographical sketch, *PWW* 1:4, n. 6; 1:39, n. 8.

Hulbert, Mary Allen (Peck) (1863–1939)
Close friend of Wilson.

3356. Hulbert, Mary Allen. *The Story of Mrs. Peck: An Autobiography*. New York: Minton, Balch, and Co., 1933.

3357. ———. *The Woodrow Wilson I Knew*. Chicago: Liberty, 1919.

McAdoo, Eleanor Randolph Wilson (1889–1967)
Wilson's youngest daughter, and wife of William Gibbs McAdoo.

3358. Biographical sketch, *PWW* 6:407, n. 1.

McCosh, Rev. James (1811–1894)
Author, clergyman, and President of Princeton (1868–1888).

3359. McCosh, James. *The Life of James McCosh*, ed. William M. Sloane. New York: Charles Scribner's Sons, 1896.

3360. Biographical sketch, *PWW* 1:133, n. 4.

3361. Hibben, James Grier. "James McCosh." *DAB* 11:615–17.

3362. Hoeveler, J. David. *James McCosh and the Scottish Intellectual Tradition: From Glasgow to Princeton*. Princeton: Princeton University Press, 1981.

Sayre, Francis Bowes (1885–1972)
Married Jessie Woodrow Wilson, Wilson's second daughter, in 1913 and was a professor at Harvard Law School (1917–1934). Later entered government service, both in domestic and foreign affairs.

3363. Papers. *Library of Congress, Manuscript Division*.

3364. Oral history. The Oral History Collection, Columbia University.

3365. Biographical sketch, *PWW* 28:20, n. 1.

3366. Sayre, Francis Bowes. *Glad Adventure*. New York: Macmillan Co., 1957.

Sayre, Jessie Woodrow Wilson (1887–1933)
Wilson's second daughter, who married Francis Bowes Sayre.

3367. Biographical sketch, *PWW* 5:565, n. 1.

Sheldon, Edward Wright (1858–1934)
Princeton classmate of Wilson and later trustee of the university; also banker, corporation lawyer, and philanthropist.

3368. Biographical sketch, *PWW* 1:241, n. 7.

Toy, Nancy Saunders (1836–1919)
Friend of Wilson and wife of Crawford Howell Toy, the Hancock Professor of Hebrew at Harvard.

3369. Biographical sketch, *PWW* 8:615, n. 1.

3370. Toy, Mrs. Crawford H. "Second Visit to the White House," diary, January 3, 1915. In the R.S. Baker Collection, Library of Congress.

Wilson, Edith (Bolling) Galt (1872–1961)
Wilson's second wife, who married him in 1915.

3371. Papers. *Library of Congress, Manuscript Division.*

3372. Biographical sketch, *PWW* 32:424, n. 1.

3373. Giblin, James. *Edith Wilson: The Woman Who Ran the United States.* New York: Viking Press, 1992.

3374. Hatch, Alden. *Edith Bolling Wilson: First Lady Extraordinary.* New York: Dodd, Mead, and Co., 1961.

3375. Ross, Ishbel. *Power with Grace: The Life of Mrs. Woodrow Wilson.* New York: G.P. Putman and Sons, 1975.

3376. Shachtman, Tom. "Edith (Bolling) Galt Wilson." *DAB* Supp. 7: 795–96.

Wilson, Ellen Louise Axson (1860–1914)
Wilson's first wife, born in Savannah, Ga., who was married to him from 1885 until her death.

3377. Saunders, Frances Wright. *Ellen Axson Wilson: First Lady Caught Between Two Worlds.* Chapel Hill: University of North Carolina Press, 1985.

Wilson, Janet E. ("Jessie") Woodrow (1830–1888)
Wilson's mother.

3378. Biographical sketch, *PWW* 1:4, n. 2.

3379. Faber, Doris. *The Mothers of American Presidents*, 81–89. New York: New American Library, 1968.

Wilson, Joseph Ruggles (1822–1903)
Wilson's father. Also a Presbyterian minister and seminary professor.

3380. Papers. Historical Foundation, Montreat, N.C.

3381. Biographical sketch, *PWW* 1:3–4, n. 1.

3382. McNeilly, J. H. "The Rev. Joseph R. Wilson, D.D." *The Southern Presbyterian* 47 (May 18, 1899): 4.

Wilson, Margaret (1886–1944)
Wilson's oldest daughter.

Woodrow, James (1828–1907)
Wilson's first cousin, and also a Presbyterian clergyman and educator.

3383. Papers. South Caroliniana Library, University of South Carolina.

3384. Biographical sketch, *PWW* 1:576, n. 2.

3385. Balmer, Randell Herbert, and John R. Fitzmier. *The Presbyterians*, 249–51. Westport: Greenwood Press, 1993.

3386. Pomfret, John Edwin. "James Woodrow." *DAB* 20:495–96.

3387. Woodrow, Marion Woodville, ed. *Dr. James Woodrow as Seen by His Friends*. Columbia, S.C.: R. L. Bryan Co., 1909.

Woodrow, Thomas (1793–1877)
Wilson's grandfather, a Presbyterian minister who moved to America with his family in 1836–1837, and lived mostly in Ohio.

3388. Papers. University of Oklahoma Library.

3389. Biographical sketch, *PWW* 1:4, n. 3.

B. Academic Colleagues and Associates

Adams, Herbert Baxter (1850–1901)
Johns Hopkins University professor (1878–1900); organized and promoted the study of history and influenced Wilson's scholarship.

3390. Papers. Johns Hopkins University Library.

3391. Biographical sketch, *PWW* 2:391, n. 1.

3392. Bassett, John Spencer. "Herbert Baxter Adams." *DAB* 1:69–71.

3393. Cunningham, Raymond J. "Herbert Baxter Adams." *DLB* 47:28– 34.

3394. Vincent, John M. "Herbert B. Adams." In *American Masters of Social Science*, ed. Howard W. Odum, 99–127. New York: Henry Holt and Co., 1927.

Cleveland, Grover (1837–1908)
President of the United States (1885–1889, 1893–1897) who later became a lecturer at Princeton and a Princeton trustee (1901–1908).

3395. Papers. *Library of Congress, Manuscript Division*; Buffalo and Erie County Historical Society collections; Detroit Public Library, Burton Historical Collection.

3396. Cleveland, Grover. *Letters 1850–1908*, ed. Allan Nevins. New York: Houghton Mifflin Co., 1933.

3397. ———. *Writings and Speeches*, ed. G. F. Parker. New York: Cassell Publishing Co., 1892.

3398. Nevins, Allan. *Grover Cleveland: A Study in Courage*. New York: Dodd, Mead and Co., 1932.

3399. Paxson, Frederic Logan. "Grover Cleveland." *DAB* 4:205–12.

318 Woodrow Wilson: A Bibliography

3400. Welch, Richard E. *The Presidencies of Grover Cleveland.* Lawrence: University Press of Kansas, 1988.

Cram, Ralph Adams (1863–1942)
Supervising architect to Princeton University during Wilson's tenure and later; also architect for the graduate school in 1913. Designed a number of noteworthy churches and educational buildings elsewhere.

3401. Papers. American Academy of Arts and Letters, New York.

3402. Cram, Ralph Adams. *My Life in Architecture.* Boston: Little, Brown and Co., 1936.

3403. Doumato, Lamia. *Ralph Adams Cram.* Monticello, Ill.: Vance Bibliographies, 1982.

3404. Whitehall, Walter Muir. "Ralph Adams Cram." *DAB* 23:194–97.

Dabney, Richard Heath (1860–1947)
Professor of History at the University of Virginia; Dean of its graduate school.

3405. Biographical Sketch, *PWW* 1:685, n. 1.

Daniels, Winthrop More (1867–1944)
Professor of Political Economy at Princeton (1892–1911); member of the Board of Public Utility Commissioners of New Jersey during Wilson's governorship; member of the Interstate Commerce Commission during his presidency.

3406. Biographical sketch, *PWW* 7:205, n. 3.

3407. Kirkland, Edward C. "Winthrop More Daniels." *DAB* Supp. 3: 211–13.

Dodge, Cleveland Hoadley (1860–1926)
Princeton classmate of Wilson who was later vice-president of the Phelps Dodge Corporation and trustee of Princeton.

3408. Biographical sketch, *PWW* 1:210, n. 3.

3409. Daniel, Robert Leslie. "The Friendship of Woodrow Wilson and Cleveland Hoadley Dodge." *Mid-America* 43 (July 1961): 182–96.

Eliot, Charles William (1834–1926)
Educator and President of Harvard (1869–1909) who also supported Wilson during World War I and the League of Nations.

3410. Papers. Harvard University Archives.

3411. Hawkins, Hugh. "Charles W. Eliot, 1869–1909." *Journal of American History* 51 (1964): 191.

3412. James, Henry. *Charles W. Eliot: President of Harvard University, 1869–1909.* 2 vols. Boston: Houghton Mifflin Co., 1930.

3413. Neilson, W. A. *Charles W. Eliot: The Man and His Beliefs*. 2 vols. New York: Harper & Brothers, 1926.

3414. Perry, Ralph Barton. "Charles William Eliot." *DAB* 6:71–78.

Ely, Richard Theodore (1854–1943)
Economics professor at Johns Hopkins (1881–1892) and subsequently at other universities.

3415. Papers. Louisiana State University Library.

3416. Biographical sketch, *PWW* 2:448, n. 1.

3417. Ely, Richard T. *Ground Under Our Feet: An Autobiography*. New York: Macmillan Co., 1938.

3418. Rader, Benjamin G. *Academic Mind and Reform: The Influence of Richard T. Ely in American Life*. Lexington: University of Kentucky Press, 1966.

3419. Schlabach, Theron F. "Richard Theodore Ely." *DAB* 23:248–51.

Fine, Henry Buchard (1858–1928)
Undergraduate with Wilson at Princeton and later Princeton mathematics professor and Dean.

3420. Biographical sketch, *PWW* 7:223, n. 3.

3421. Leitch, Alexander. *Princeton Companion*, 177–80. Princeton: Princeton University Press, 1978.

3422. Magie, William Francis. "Henry Buchard Fine." *DAB* 6:386–87.

Gilman, Daniel Coit (1831–1908)
President of the Johns Hopkins University.

3423. Papers. Johns Hopkins University Library; Milton S. Eisenhower Library, Baltimore; University of California general collection, Berkeley.

3424. Flexner, Abraham. *Daniel Coit Gilman: Creator of the American Type of University*. New York: Harcourt, Brace, & Co., 1946.

3425. Mitchell, Samuel Chiles. "Daniel Coit Gilman." *DAB* 7:299–303.

Harper, George McLean (1863–1947)
Princeton professor of language and literature (1889–1932).

3426. Papers. Princeton University Library.

3427. Biographical sketch, *PWW* 3:572, n. 1.

3428. Leitch, Alexander. *Princeton Companion*, 240–42. Princeton: Princeton University Press, 1978.

Hart, Albert Bushnell (1854–1943)
Professor of history and government at Harvard and editor of several series, including *Epochs of American History*, to which Wilson contributed a volume.

3429. Papers. Duke University Library; New York Public Library. [*Washington Bicentennial Commission Papers, 1900–33* in Massachusetts State Library.]

3430. Biographical sketch, *PWW* 5:473, n. 1.

3431. Hickson, Shirley A. "Albert Bushnell Hart." *DLB* 17:198–207.

3432. Morison, Samuel Eliot. "Albert Bushnell Hart." *DAB* Supp. 3: 335–38.

Haskins, Charles Hart (1870–1937)
History professor at Johns Hopkins and Harvard, a leading medievalist, and Dean of Harvard's Graduate School of Arts and Sciences.

3433. Papers. Princeton University Library.

3434. Biographical sketch, *PWW* 6:118, n. 1.

3435. Stayer, Joseph R. "Charles Hart Haskins." *DAB* 22:289–91.

Hibben, Jenny Davidson (1864–1933)
Wife of John Grier Hibben and close friend of Wilson.

3436. Biographical sketch, *PWW* 9:125, n. 1.

Hibben, John Grier (1861–1933)
Presbyterian minister, Princeton professor (1891–1912) and President (1912–1932).

3437. Biographical sketch, *PWW* 9:125, n. 1.

3438. Leitch, Alexander. *Princeton Companion*, 251–55. Princeton: Princeton University Press, 1978.

3439. Spaeth, J. Duncan. "John Grier Hibben." *DAB* 21:398–401.

Jacobus, Melancthon Williams (1855–1937)
Professor of New Testament exegesis and criticism and Dean of the Hartford Theological Seminary in Connecticut.

3440. Papers. Hartford Seminary Foundation, Case Memorial Library.

3441. Biographical sketch, *PWW* 12:400, n. 2.

McAlpin, Charles Williston (1866–1942)
Philanthropist and first Secretary of Princeton (1901–1914).

3442. Biographical sketch, *PWW* 12:160, n. 1.

McCormick, Cyrus Hall, Jr. (1859–1936)
   Princeton classmate of Wilson, President and Chairman of the Board of International Harvester Co., and Trustee of Princeton (1889–1936).

3443. Papers. State Historical Society of Wisconsin, The McCormick Collection.

3444. Biographical sketch, *PWW* 5:767, n. 3.

3445. Kellar, Lucile O'Conner. "Cyrus Hall McCormick, Jr." *DAB* 22:402–404.

Patton, Rev. Francis Landey (1843–1932)
   Presbyterian clergyman and theologian; President of Princeton University (1888–1902) and of the Princeton Theological Seminary (1902–1913).

3446. Papers. In the Nancy Fowler McCormick Collection of the Fowler Collection, State Historical Society of Wisconsin.

3447. Biographical sketch, *PWW* 3:114, n. 3.

3448. Balmer, Randell Herbert, and John R. Fitzmier. *The Presbyterians*, 202–30. Westport, Conn.: Greenwood Press, 1993.

3449. Harper, George M. "Francis Landey Patton." *DAB* 14:315–16.

3450. Kerr, Hugh Thomson. "Patton of Princeton: A Profile." *Princeton Seminary Bulletin* n.s. 9 (1988): 50–70.

3451. Leitch, Alexander. *Princeton Companion*, 354–57. Princeton: Princeton University Press, 1978.

Perry, Bliss (1860–1954)
   Professor of English Literature at Harvard.

3452. Papers. American Academy of Arts and Letters, New York; Harvard University Archives; Houghton Library, Harvard University.

3453. Biographical sketch, *PWW* 8:179, n. 3.

3454. Perry, Bliss. *And Gladly Teach: Reminiscences by Bliss Perry*. Boston: Houghton, Mifflin, 1935.

3455. ———. *Praise of Folly and Other Papers*. New York: Houghton Mifflin Co., 1923.

3456. Whitehall, Walter Muir. "Bliss Perry." *DAB* Supp. 5:541–42.

Pyne, Moses Taylor (1855–1921)
   New York City lawyer and financier who was a trustee and vigorous supporter of Princeton for 36 years.

3457. Leitch, Alexander. *Princeton Companion*, 399–401. Princeton: Princeton University Press, 1978.

Reid, Edith Gittings
Correspondent of Wilson and member of a prominent Baltimore family, who was also wife of a Johns Hopkins professor of geological physics and geology.

3458. Biographical sketch, *PWW* 8:509, n. 1.

3459. Reid, Edith Gittings. "Recollection of President Wilson." *English Review* 27 (August 1918): 129–32.

3460. ———. *Woodrow Wilson: The Caricature, the Myth, and the Man.* New York: Oxford University Press, 1934.

Renick, Edward Ireland (1852–1900)
Law school classmate and lawyer with whom Wilson shared offices in Atlanta (1882–1883).

3461. Biographical sketch, *PWW* 2:97, n. 1.

Shaw, Albert (1857–1947)
Attended Johns Hopkins with Wilson, later became the founder and editor of the *Review of Reviews*, and edited the first collection of Wilson's public papers.

3462. Papers. New York Public Library, Rare Books and Manuscripts Division.

3463. Biographical sketch, *PWW* 3:214, n. 1.

3464. Graybar, Lloyd J. "Albert Shaw." *DAB* Supp. 4:738–39.

Turner, Frederick Jackson (1861–1932)
Professor of History at Harvard (1910–1924) and noted historian of the American frontier who was a long time friend of Wilson.

3465. Papers. University of Illinois, Illinois Historical Survey collections; the Houghton Library of the Harvard College Library.

3466. Biographical sketch, *PWW* 6:58, n. 1.

3467. Billington, Ray Allen. *Frederick Jackson Turner: Historian, Scholar, Teacher.* New York: Oxford University Press, 1973.

3468. Burnette, O. Lawrence, Jr., comp. *Wisconsin Witness to Frederick Jackson Turner: A Collection of Essays on the Historian and the Thesis.* Madison: State Historical Society of Wisconsin, 1961.

3469. Paxson, Frederic Logan. "Frederick Jackson Turner." *DAB* 19: 62–64.

3470. Turner, Frederick Jackson. *The Early Writings of Frederick Jackson Turner*, comp. Everett E. Edwards. Madison: University of Wisconsin Press, 1938.

3471. ———. *The Historical World of Frederick Jackson Turner, with Selections from His Correspondence*, ed. Wilbur R. Jacobs. New Haven: Yale University Press, 1968.

3472. Turner, Frederick Jackson, and Alice F. P. Hooper. *"Dear Lady"*: *Letters of Frederick Jackson Turner and Alice Forbes Perkins Hooper, 1910–1932*, ed. Ray A. Billington and Walter Muir Whitehall. San Marino, Calif.: Huntington Library, 1970.

West, Andrew Fleming (1853–1943)
Professor of Latin at Princeton (1883–1928), and Dean of the Graduate School at Princeton (1901–1928).

3473. Biographical sketch, *PWW* 6:529, n. 3.

3474. Leitch, Alexander. *Princeton Companion*, 501–504. Princeton: Princeton University Press, 1978.

3475. Veysey, Laurence R. "Andrew Fleming West." *DAB* Supp. 3:809–811.

C. Vice President, Cabinet Members, and Members of the Administration

Baker, Newton Diehl (1871–1937)
Student with Wilson at Johns Hopkins; Mayor of Cleveland; and Secretary of War (1916–1921).

3476. Papers. Case Western Reserve University Archives and Western Reserve Historical Society, Cleveland. Also *Library of Congress, Manuscript Division*, and New York Public Library.

3477. Beaver, Daniel R. *Newton D. Baker and the American War Effort, 1917–1919*. Lincoln: University of Nebraska Press, 1966.

3478. Cramer, Clarence H. *Newton D. Baker: A Biography*. Cleveland: World Publishing Co., 1961.

3479. Morison, Elting E. "Newton Diehl Baker." *DAB* 22:17–19.

3480. Palmer, Frederick C. *Newton D. Baker: America at War*. 2 vols. New York: Dodd, Mead & Co., 1931.

Bryan, William Jennings (1860–1925)
Congressman from Nebraska; frequent Democratic candidate for President; and Secretary of State under Wilson (1913–1915).

3481. Papers. Nebraska State Historical Society collections; Occidental College Library; Rutherford B. Hayes Library, Fremont, Ohio; *Library of Congress, Manuscript Division*; Yale University Library.

3482. Ashby, LeRoy. *William Jennings Bryan: Champion of Democracy*. Boston: Twayne Publishers, 1987.

3483. Bassett, John Spencer. "William Jennings Bryan." *DAB* 3:191–97.

3484. Bryan, William Jennings. *The Memoirs of William Jennings Bryan*, ed. Mary B. Bryan. Philadelphia: The John C. Winston Co., 1925.

3485. ———. *William Jennings Bryan: Selections*, ed. Ray Ginger. Indianapolis: Bobbs-Merrill, 1967.

3486. Cherney, Tobert W. *A Righteous Cause: The Life of William Jennings Bryan*. Boston: Little, Brown, 1985.

3487. Clements, Kendrick A. *William Jennings Bryan: Missionary Isolationist*. Knoxville: University of Tennessee Press, 1982.

3488. Coletta, Paolo E. *William Jennings Bryan: Political Evangelist, 1860–1908*. 3 vols. Lincoln: University of Nebraska Press, 1964–1969.

3489. Springen, Donald K. *William Jennings Bryan: Orator of Small-town America*. Westport, Conn.: Greenwood Press, 1991.

Burleson, Albert Sidney (1863–1937)
    United States representative from Texas and Postmaster General (1913–1921).

3490. Papers. *Library of Congress, Manuscript Division*, and University of Texas Library, Texas Archives, Austin.

3491. Anderson, Adrian. "President Wilson's Politician: Albert Sidney Burleson of Texas." *Southwestern History Quarterly* 77, no. 3 (1974): 339–54.

3492. Blum, John Morton. "Albert Sidney Burleson." *DAB* 22:74–75.

Colby, Bainbridge (1869–1950)
    Replaced Robert Lansing as Secretary of State in 1920 and formed a brief law partnership with Wilson after Wilson's presidency.

3493. Papers. *Library of Congress, Manuscript Division*.

3494. Colby, Bainbridge. *The Close of Woodrow Wilson's Administration and the Final Years*. New York: Kennerly, 1930.

3495. Novick, Joel R. "Bainbridge Colby, Profile in Progressivism." Ph.D. diss., New York University, 1970.

3496. Smith, Daniel Malloy. *Aftermath of War: Bainbridge Colby and Wilsonian Diplomacy 1920–1921*. Philadelphia: American Philosophical Society, 1970.

3497. ———. "Bainbridge Colby." *DAB* 24:170–71.

Crane, Charles Richard (1858–1939)
    Manufacturer, who became finance chairman of Wilson's 1912 presidential campaign; a member of the President's Special Diplomatic Commission to Russia (1917); and American minister to China (1920–1921.)

3498. Papers. In possession of his son, John O. Crane of New York City and Woods Hole, Mass.

3499. Brodie, Donald M. "Charles Richard Crane." *DAB* 22:128–30.

3500. "Charles Richard Crane." *Who Was Who in America*, 1:272. Chicago: A.N. Marquis, 1942.

3501. Findling, John E. *Dictionary of American Diplomatic History*, 136–37, 2nd ed. rev. and expanded. Westport, Conn.: Greenwood Press, 1989.

Creel, George (1876–1953)
Author, editor, and Chairman of the United States Committee on Public Information under Wilson.

3502. Papers. *Library of Congress, Manuscript Division.*

3503. Creel, George C. *Rebel at Large: Recollections of Fifty Crowded Years*. New York: G. P. Putnam's Sons, 1947.

3504. Francke, Warren T. "George Creel." *DLB* 25:64–73.

3505. Leonard, Thomas C. "George Creel." *DAB* 25:141–43.

Daniels, Josephus (1862–1948)
Journalist; Secretary of the Navy (1913–1921).

3506. Papers. *Library of Congress, Manuscript Division.*

3507. Cronon, Edmund David. "Joseph Daniels." *DAB* Supp. 4:215–18.

3508. Daniels, Josephus P. *The Cabinet Diaries of Josephus Daniels, 1913–1921*, ed. Edmund David Cronon. Lincoln: University of Nebraska Press, 1963.

3509. ———. *Shirt-Sleeve Diplomat*. Chapel Hill: University of North Carolina Press, 1947.

3510. Morrison, Joseph L. *Josephus Daniels: The small-d Democrat*. Chapel Hill: University of North Carolina Press, 1966.

Davis, John William (1873–1955)
Solicitor General of the United States (1913–1918), Ambassador to Great Britain (1918–1921), and an advisor at the Paris Peace Conference. Also the Democratic presidential candidate in 1924.

3511. Papers. Yale University Library; Georgetown University Library, Special Collections Division, Washington, D.C.

3512. Harbaugh, William Henry. "John William Davis." *DAB* Supp. 5:155–56.

3513. ———. *Lawyer's Lawyer: The Life of John W. Davis*. New York: Oxford University Press, 1973.

3514. Huntley, Theodore A. *John W. Davis*. New York: Duffield, 1924.

Davis, Norman Hezekiah (1878–1944)
Financial advisor to the American commission at the Paris Peace Conference;

member of the Reparations Commission; and fervent supporter of the League of Nations. Wilson appointed him Under Secretary of State in 1920.

3515. Papers. *Library of Congress, Manuscript Division.*

3516. Whiteman, Harold B., Jr. "Norman Hezekiah Davis." *DAB* Supp. 3:218–19.

Elkins, Abram Isaac (1867–1947)
Succeeded Henry Morgenthau as Ambassador to Turkey (1916– 1919); directed relief work for a number of agencies during World War I; in 1920, was designated by Wilson as American representative in the first arbitration commission appointed by the League of Nations.

3517. "Elkins, Abram Isaac." In *The National Cyclopedia of American Biography*, 38:47. New York: James T. White & Co., 1926.

Garfield, Henry (Harry) Augustus 1863–1942)
Son of President James A. Garfield and professor of politics at Princeton (1903–1908); President of Williams College (1908–1934), and the of United States Fuel Administration.

3518. Papers. *Library of Congress, Manuscript Division.*

3519. Biographical sketch, *PWW* 14:488, n. 1.

3520. Rudolph, Frederick. "Henry Augustus Garfield." *DAB* Supp. 3: 292–94.

Garrison, Lindley Miller (1864–1932)
Secretary of War under Wilson (1913–1916).

3521. Papers. Princeton University Library; New Jersey Historical Society.

3522. McKee, Oliver, Jr. "Lindley Miller Garrison." *DAB* 21:335–37.

Gerard, James Watson (1867–1951)
Lawyer, financier, and Ambassador to Germany (1913–1917).

3523. Papers. University of Montana Library.

3524. Oral history. Columbia University Oral History Collection.

3525. Barthold, Theodore Richard. "Assignment to Berlin: The Embassy of James W. Gerard, 1913–1917," Ph.D. diss., Temple University, 1981.

3526. Gerard, James Watson. *My First Eighty-Three Years in America.* Garden City, N.Y.: Doubleday & Co., 1951.

3527. ———. *My Four Years in Germany.* London: Hodder and Stoughton, 1917.

3528. Thompson, John A., "James Watson Gerard." *DAB* Supp. 5:241–42.

Gregory, Thomas Watt (1861–1933)
Wilson's Attorney General (1914–1919) and member of Wilson's Second Industrial Conference (1919–1920).

3529. Papers. *Library of Congress, Manuscript Division.*

3530. Anders, E. "Thomas Watt Gregory and the survival of his Progressive Faith." *Southwest History Quarterly* 93 (July 1989): 1–24.

3531. Mallison, A. G. "Thomas Watt Gregory." *DAB* 21:358–60.

Grew, Joseph Clark (1880–1965)
First Secretary of the Embassy at Berlin under James W. Gerard (1912–1916) and Secretary-General of the American commission to negotiate peace in 1919. Ambassador to Japan (1931–1941).

3532. Papers. Houghton Library of the Harvard College Library.

3533. Grew, Joseph Clark. *Turbulent Era: A Diplomatic Record of Forty Years, 1904–1945.* 2 vols. Boston: Houghton Mifflin Co., 1925.

3534. Bennett, Edward. "Joseph Clark Grew." *DAB* Supp. 7:302–303.

3535. ———. *Ten Years in Japan.* New York: Hammond & Co., 1944.

3536. Heinrichs, Waldo H. *American Ambassador: Joseph C. Grew.* Boston: Little, Brown, 1966.

Guthrie, George Wilkins (1848–1917)
Mayor of Pittsburgh (1906–1909) and Ambassador to Japan under Wilson.

3537. Frederick, John H. "George Wilkins Guthrie." *DAB* 8:60.

Hapgood, Norman (1868–1937)
Drama critic, editor, author, and American envoy to Denmark in 1919.

3538. Filler, Louis. "Norman Hapgood." *DAB* 22:280–82.

3539. Hapgood, Norman. *The Changing Years: Reminiscences of Norman Hapgood.* New York: Farrar & Rinehart, 1930.

3540. Marcaccio, Michael D. *Hapgoods: Three Earnest Brothers.* Charlottesville: University Press of Virginia, 1977.

Hoover, Herbert Clark (1874–1964)
Various posts in the Wilson administration coordinating war relief efforts, Secretary of Commerce, and President of the United States (1928–1932).

3541. Papers. Hoover Institution on War, Revolution and Peace, Stanford University; State Historical Society of Wisconsin Collections; Herbert Hoover Presidential Library, West Branch, Iowa; *Library of Congress, Manuscript Division.*

3542. Brandes, Joseph. "Herbert Clark Hoover." *DAB* Supp. 7:357–64.

3543. Burner, David. *Herbert Hoover: A Public Life.* New York: Alfred A. Knopf, 1979.

3544. Gelfand, Lawrence E., ed. *Herbert Hoover, the Great War, and Its Aftermath, 1914–1923*. Iowa City: University of Iowa Press, 1979.

3545. Hoover, Herbert Clark. *Memoirs*. 3 vols. New York: Macmillan Co., 1951–1952.

3546. ———. *State Papers*, ed. W.S. Myers. 2 vols. Garden City, N.Y.: Doubleday and Doran & Co., 1934.

3547. Nash, George H. *The Life of Herbert Hoover*. 2 vols. New York: W.W. Norton, 1983–1988.

3548. Nye, Frank. *Doors of Opportunity: The Life and Legacy of Herbert Hoover*. West Branch, Iowa: Hoover Presidential Library and Association, 1988.

Houston, David Franklin (1866–1940)
   Texas educator, Secretary of Agriculture (1913–1920) and Secretary of the Treasury (1920–1921).

3549. Papers. Houghton Library of Harvard College.

3550. Houston, David F. *Eight Years with Wilson's Cabinet, 1913 to 1920: With a Personal Estimate of the President*. 2 vols. Garden City, N.Y.: Doubleday, Page & Co., 1926.

3551. ———. "Eight Years With Wilson, 1913–1921." *The World's Work* 51 (February 1926): 360, 468–87, 580–600; 52 (October 1926): 22–40, 151–63, 279–95, 399–412, 539–52, 657–69.

3552. Link, Arthur S. "David Franklin Houston." *DAB* 22:321–22.

Hurley, Edward Nash (1864–1933)
   Manufacturer, financier, and chairman of the United States Shipping Board Emergency Fleet Corporation.

3553. Papers. University of Notre Dame Archives.

3554. Hurley, Edward Nash. *The Bridge to France*. Philadelphia: J. B. Lippincott & Co., 1927.

3555. Paullin, Charles O. "Edward Nash Hurley." *DAB* 21:446–47.

Johnson, Robert Underwood (1853–1937)
   Author, editor, and Ambassador to Italy.

3556. Papers. American Academy of Arts and Letters Library, New York; Columbia University Libraries; Bancroft Library, University of California, Berkeley; Hugh M. Morris Library, University of Delaware; New York Public Library; Duke University Libraries.

3557. Johnson, Robert Underwood. *Remembered Yesterday*. Boston: Little, Brown and Co., 1923.

3558. Starr, Louis M. "Robert Underwood Johnson." *DAB* 22:348–49.

Lamont, Thomas William (1870–1948)
Chairman of the Board of J. P. Morgan and Company and representative of the United States Treasury on the American Commission to Negotiate Peace in 1919.

3559. Papers. Harvard University, Graduate School of Business Administration, Baker Library.

3560. Carosso, Vincent P. "Thomas William Lamont." *DAB* Supp. 4: 469–71.

3561. Lamont, Thomas W. *Across World Frontiers*. Cambridge: Harvard University Press, 1951.

Lane, Franklin Knight (1864–1921)
Secretary of the Interior (1913–1920).

3562. Papers. Bancroft Library, University of California, Berkeley.

3563. Lane, Franklin Knight. *The Letters of Franklin K. Lane, Personal and Political*, ed. Anne Wintermute Lane and Louise Herrick Wall. New York: Houghton Mifflin Co., 1922.

3564. McKee, Oliver, Jr. "Franklin Knight Lane." *DAB* 10:572–73.

3565. Olsen, Keith. *Biography of a Progressive: Franklin K. Lane, 1864–1921*. Westport, Conn: Greenwood Press, 1979.

3566. "Wilson in the Armistice Crisis: Letters of Franklin K. Lane." *Literary Digest* 75 (November 18, 1922): 46–48.

Lansing, Robert (1864–1928)
Wilson's Secretary of State (1915–1920).

3567. Papers. Princeton University Library; *Library of Congress, Manuscript Division*.

3568. Hartig, Thomas. *Robert Lansing: An Interpretive Biography*. New York: Arno Press, 1982.

3569. Lansing, Robert. *War Memoirs of Robert Lansing*. London: Rich and Cowan, 1935.

3570. Pinci, A. R. "Our Foreign Relations: An Exclusive 1916 and Still Timely Interview with Robert Lansing, Secretary of State, Unexplainedly Suppressed by President Wilson." *Daughters of the American Revolution Magazine* 93 (January 1959): 9–12.

3571. Pratt, Julius William. "Robert Lansing." *DAB* 10:609–611.

3572. U.S. Department of State. *Papers Relating to the Foreign Relations of the U.S., The Lansing Papers, 1914–1920*. 2 vols. Washington, D.C.: United States Government Printing Office, 1939.

Lord, Robert Howard (1885–1954)
Harvard European history professor who became a technical advisor to the American Commission to Negotiate Peace in 1919 and a member of the postwar mission to Poland.

3573. Biographical sketch, *PWW* 53:357, n. 1.

Marshall, Thomas Riley (1854–1925)
Vice president of the United States under Wilson.

3574. Papers. Indiana State Library.

3575. "A Gallery of Vice Presidents." *American Heritage* 15 (August 1964): 78–80.

3576. Barzman, Sol. *Mad Men and Geniuses: The Vice President of the United States,* 189–95. Chicago: Follett, 1974.

3577. Hicks, John Donald. "Thomas Riley Marshall." *DAB* 12:330–31.

3578. Marshall, Thomas Riley. *Recollections of Thomas R. Marshall: A Hoosier Salad.* Indianapolis: Bobbs-Merrill, 1925.

3579. Thomas, Charles M. *Thomas Riley Marshall: Hoosier Statesman.* Oxford, Ohio: The Mississippi Valley Press, 1939.

3580. Vexler, Robert I., ed. *The Vice-Presidents and Cabinet Members: Biographies Arranged Chronologically by Administrations,* 2:468–534. Dobbs Ferry, N.Y.: Oceana Publications, 1975.

McAdoo, William Gibbs (1863–1941)
An early backer of Wilson who became his son-in-law; also Secretary of the Treasury (1913–1918), Director General of the Railroads, and United States Senator from California.

3581. Papers. Bancroft Library, University of California, Berkeley; University of California Library, Los Angeles; *Library of Congress, Manuscript Division.*

3582. Broesamle, John J. *William Gibbs McAdoo: A Passion for Change, 1863–1917.* Port Washington, N.Y.: Kennikat Press, 1973.

3583. Graham, Otis L., Jr. "William Gibbs McAdoo." *DAB* Supp. 3: 479–82.

3584. McAdoo, William Gibbs. *Crowded Years: The Reminiscences of William G. McAdoo.* Boston: Jonathan Cape, 1931.

McReynolds, James Clark (1862–1946)
United States Attorney General (1913–1914) and Supreme Court Justice (1914–1941).

3585. Papers. University of Virginia Library.

3586. Abraham, Henry Julian. *Justices and Presidents; a Political History of Appointments to the Supreme Court,* 175–78. New York: Oxford University Press, 1985.

3587. Bond, James Edward. *I Dissent; The Legacy of Chief Justice James Clark McReynolds.* Fairfax, Va.: George Mason University Press, 1992.

3588. Leuchtenburg, William E. "James Clark McReynolds." *DAB* Supp. 4:536–38.

Meredith, Edwin Thomas (1876–1928)
   Secretary of Agriculture (1913–1920) and founder of the Meredith Publishing Company in Des Moines.

3589. Papers. University of Iowa Libraries.

3590. Dethloff, H. C. "Edwin T. Meredith and the Interrregnum." *Agricultural History* 64 (Spring 1990): 182–90.

3591. Schmidt, Louis Bernard. "Edwin Thomas Meredith." *DAB* 12: 547–48.

Mezes, Sidney Edward (1863–1931)
   College president and Executive Director of the Territorial Section of the Paris Peace Conference.

3592. Papers. Columbia University Libraries.

3593. Bander, Ingram. "Sidney Edward Mezes and The Inquiry." *Journal of Modern History* 11 (1939): 199–202.

3594. Brownson, Carleton L. "Sidney Edward Mezes." *DAB* 12:588–89.

Miller, David Hunter (1875–1961)
   International lawyer, participant in the World War I peace negotiations, and instrumental in the formulation of the League of Nations Covenant.

3595. Papers. *Library of Congress, Manuscript Division;* University of Washington Library, Seattle.

3596. Harrison, Richard A. "David Hunter Miller." *DAB* Supp. 7: 536–37.

3597. Miller, David Hunter. *My Diary at the Conference of Paris.* 21 vols. New York: Appeal Printing Co., 1924.

3598. _____. *The Drafting of the Covenant.* 2 vols. New York: G.P. Putnam's Sons, 1928.

Morgenthau, Henry, Sr. (1856–1946)
   Businessman, Ambassador to Turkey, and delegate to a number of international conferences.

3599. Papers. *Library of Congress, Manuscript Division.*

3600. Heilbroner, Robert L. "Henry Morgenthau." *DAB* Supp. 4:602–605.

3601. Morgenthau, Henry, Sr. *All in a Life-time*. Garden City, N.Y.: Doubleday, Page and Co., 1922.

3602. ———. *Ambassador Morgenthau's Story*. Garden City, N.Y.: Doubleday, Page and Co., 1918.

3603. ———. *Mostly Morgenthau: A Family History*. New York: Ticknor and Fields, 1991.

Morris, Roland Sletor (1874–1945)
Professor of International Law at the University of Pennsylvania who served in Japan (1917–1921) and on special missions to Siberia (1918–1919).

3604. Papers. *Library of Congress, Manuscript Division*.

Page, Thomas Nelson (1853–1922)
Author, lawyer, and Ambassador to Italy (1913–1919).

3605. Gross, Theodore L. *Thomas Nelson Page*. New Haven, Conn.: College and University Press, 1967.

3606. Nelson, John Herbert. "Thomas Nelson Page." *DAB* 14:141–42.

3607. Page, Thomas Nelson. *Memoir of Thomas Nelson Page*, ed. Henry Field. Miami, Fla.: Field Research Projects, 1978.

Page, Walter Hines (1855–1919)
Journalist and early backer of Wilson, and Ambassador to Great Britain.

3608. Papers. Houghton Library of the Harvard College Library; *Library of Congress, Manuscript Division*.

3609. Cooper, John Milton, Jr. *Walter Hines Page: The Southerner as American, 1855–1918*. Chapel Hill: University of North Carolina Press, 1977.

3610. Meneely, A. Howard. "Walter Hines Page." *DAB* 14:142–44.

3611. Page, Walter Hines. *The Life and Letters of Walter Page*, ed. Burton Jesse Hendrick. 3 vols. Garden City, N.Y.: Doubleday, Page & Co., 1922–1925.

Palmer, Alexander Mitchell (1872–1936)
United States Representative from Pennsylvania, Judge of the United States Court of Claims, and United States Attorney General under Wilson (1919–1921).

3612. Papers. *Library of Congress, Manuscript Division*.

3613. Coben, Stanley. *A. Mitchell Palmer: Politician*. New York: Columbia University Press, 1963.

3614. Murray, Robert K. "Alexander Mitchell Palmer." *DAB* 22:510–12.

Payne, John Barton (1855–1935)
President of the Chicago Law Institute, Cook County Superior Court judge, and Secretary of the Interior under Wilson (1920–1921).

3615. Papers. Earl Gregg Swem Library, the College of William and Mary.

3616. McKee, Oliver, Jr. "John Barton Payne." *DAB* 21:594–95.

Polk, Frank Lyon (1871–1943)
Counselor (second ranking officer) and chief legal officer in the State Department (1915–1920), who became Acting Secretary of State (1918–1919), and who directed the American peace delegation following World War I.

3617. Papers. Yale University Library.

3618. Gelfard, Lawrence E. "Frank Lyon Polk." *DAB* Supp. 3:605–606.

Redfield, William Cox (1858–1932)
United States Representative from New York, and Secretary of Commerce (1913–1919).

3619. Papers. *Library of Congress, Manuscript Division.*

3620. Meneely, A. Howard. "William Cox Redfield." *DAB* 15:442–43.

3621. Redfield, William Cox. *Dependent America.* New York: Houghton Mifflin, 1926.

3622. ———. "From Congress to Cabinet: Experiences and Impressions of Public Life in Washington." *Outlook* 134 (June 20, 1923): 223–29.

3623. ———. With Congress and Cabinet. Garden City, N.Y.: Doubleday, Page and Co., 1924.

Reinsch, Samuel Paul (1869–1923)
United States Minister to China (1913–1919), and 1920 candidate for United States Senator from Wisconsin.

3624. Papers. State Historical Society of Wisconsin collections.

3625. Kirk, Grayson L. "Samuel Paul Reinsch." *DAB* 15:491–92.

3626. Pugach, Noel. *Paul S. Reinsch: Open Door Diplomat in Action.* Millwood, N.Y.: K.T.O. Press, 1979.

3627. Reinsch, Samuel Paul. *An American Diplomat in China.* Garden City, N.Y.: Doubleday, Page & Co., 1922.

Roosevelt, Franklin Delano (1882–1945)
Assistant Secretary of the Navy under Josephus Daniels (1913–1920); later Governor of New York (1929–1933) and President of the United States (1933–1945).

3628. Papers. Franklin D. Roosevelt Library, Hyde Park, N.Y.; Hudson River Valley and Dutchess County (N.Y.) Manuscript Collection, 1630–1941, in F.D.R. Library; Naval and Maine Manuscript Collection, 1730–1942, in F.D.R. Library; Jacob J. Podell Collection, 1896–1943, in Columbia University Library; American Jewish Archives, Cincinnati; *Library of Congress, Manuscript Division.*

3629. Oral history. Franklin D. Roosevelt, oral history interviews concerning, 1947–1971, in F.D.R. Library, Hyde Park.

3630. Abbott, Philip. *The Exemplary Presidency: Franklin D. Roosevelt and the American Political Tradition.* Amherst: University of Massachusetts Press, 1990.

3631. Alsop, Joseph. *F.D.R., 1882–1945: A Centenary Remembrance.* New York: Viking Press, 1982.

3632. Burns, James MacGregor. *Roosevelt.* 2 vols. New York: Harcourt, Brace, Jovanovich, 1956–1970.

3633. Davis, Kenneth S. *F.D.R.: A History.* 4 vols. New York: G.P. Putnam's Sons and Random House, 1972–1994.

3634. Freidel, Frank Burt. *Franklin D. Roosevelt.* 4 vols. Boston: Little, Brown and Co., 1952–1973.

3635. ———. "Franklin D. Roosevelt." *DAB* Supp. 3:641–67.

3636. Leuchtenburg, William E. *Franklin D. Roosevelt and the New Deal, 1932–1940.* New York: Harper and Row, 1963.

3637. Maney, Patrick J. *The Roosevelt Presence: A Biography of FDR.* New York: Twayne, 1992.

3638. Nash, Gerald D., ed. *Franklin Delano Roosevelt.* Englewood Cliffs, N.J.: Prentice-Hall, 1967.

3639. Roosevelt, Franklin D. *The Public Papers and Addresses of Franklin D. Roosevelt,* comp. Samuel Rosenman. 13 vols. New York: Random House and Macmillan Co., 1938–1950.

3640. Rosenbaum, Herbert D., and Elizabeth Bartelme. *Franklin D. Roosevelt: The Man, the Myth, the Era, 1882–1945.* Westport, Conn.: Greewood Press, 1987.

3641. Schlesinger, Arthur M., Jr. *The Age of Roosevelt.* 3 vols. Boston: Houghton Mifflin, 1957–1960.

Sharp, William Graves (1859–1922)
    Lawyer and manufacturer who became a congressman from Ohio (1908–1914) and Ambassador to France (1914–1919).

3642. Sharp, William Graves. *The War Memoirs of William Graves Sharp, American Ambassador to France, 1914–1919.* London: Constable, 1931.

3643. Spaulding, E. Wilder. "William Graves Sharp." *DAB* 17:25.

Wallace, Hugh Campbell (1863–1931)
   Prominent campaigner for, and influential advisor to Wilson, who was Wilson's frequent emissary to Europe and Ambassador to France (1919–1921).

3644. Thomson, Irving L. "Hugh Campbell Wallace." *DAB* 19:371–72.

White, Henry (1850–1927)
   Republican career diplomat who became a commissioner to the Paris Peace Conference.

3645. Papers. *Library of Congress, Manuscript Division*; Columbia University Libraries.

3646. Auchincloss, Louis. *The Vanderbilt Era: Profiles of a Gilded Age*, 71–80. New York: Charles Scribner's Sons, 1989.

3647. Nevins, Allan. *Henry White: Thirty Years of American Diplomacy*. New York: Harper & Brothers, 1930.

3648. ⸺. "Henry White." *DAB* 20:102–103.

Whitlock, Brand (1869–1934)
   Mayor of Toledo (1905–1912) who became United States minister and ambassador to Belgium (1913–1922).

3649. Papers. *Library of Congress, Manuscript Division*; American Academy of Arts and Letters Library, New York; Toledo-Lucas Public Library; Hoover Institution of War, Revolution and Peace, Stanford University.

3650. Anderson, David D. "Brand Whitlock." *DLB* 12:451–55.

3651. Dwight, Harrison G. "Brand Whitlock." *DAB* 20:137–38.

3652. Whitlock, Brand. *Belgium: A Personal Narrative*. New York: D. Appleton and Co., 1919.

3653. ⸺. *Forty Years of It*. New York: D. Appleton and Co., 1914.

3654. ⸺. *The Letters and Journal of Brand Whitlock*, ed. Allan Nevins. 2 vols. New York: Appleton Century, 1936.

Wilson, William Bauchop (1862–1934)
   United States Senator from Pennsylvania and Secretary of Labor (1913–1921).

3655. Papers. Historical Society of Pennsylvania collections, Philadelphia.

3656. Babson, Roger W. *W. B. Wilson and the Department of Labor*. New York: Brentano's, 1919.

3657. Bowden, Witt. "William Bauchop Wilson." *DAB* 20:348–49.

3658. Clarke, Wilhelm. "William B. Wilson: The First Secretary of Labor." Ph.D. diss., Johns Hopkins University, 1967.

D. Advisors and White House Staff

Baker, Ray Stannard (1870–1946)
    Director of the press bureau of the American Commission to Negotiate Peace at Paris; Wilson's biographer.

3659. Papers. *Library of Congress, Manuscript Division*; American Academy of Arts and Letters Library, New York; Jones Library, Amherst, Mass.; Princeton University Library.

3660. Baker, Ray Stannard. *American Chronicle: The Autobiography of Ray Stannard Baker.* New York: Charles Scribner's Sons, 1945.

3661. Bannister, Robert C., Jr. "Ray Stannard Baker." *DAB* 24:46–48.

3662. ———. *Ray Stannard Baker: The Mind and Thought of a Progressive.* New Haven: Yale University Press, 1965.

3663. Semonche, John E. *Ray Stannard Baker: A Quest for Democracy in Modern America, 1870–1918.* Chapel Hill: University of North Carolina Press, 1969.

3664. "Where Were You on the Night of March 6, 1925? Ray Stannard Baker Finishes Woodrow Wilson's Biography." *Saturday Evening Post* 212 (January 13, 1940): 26.

3665. "Wilson's Letters: Windup of the Ray Stannard Baker Series Tells White House Story of 1918." *Newsweek* 13 (June 26, 1939): 34–35.

Baruch, Bernard Mannes (1870–1965)
    Chairman of the United States War Industries Board in 1918; economic advisor for the American Commission to Negotiate Peace at the Versailles Conference in 1919.

3666. Papers. Princeton University Library.

3667. Baruch, Bernard Mannes. *Baruch: My Own Story.* 2 vols. New York: Henry Holt and Co., 1957–1960.

3668. Cuff, Robert D. "Bernard Mannes Baruch." *DAB* 27:34–37.

3669. Grant, James. *Bernard M. Baruch: The Adventures of a Wall Street Legend.* New York: Simon & Schuster, 1983.

3670. Schwarz, Jordan A. *The Speculator: Bernard M. Baruch in Washington, 1917–1965.* Chapel Hill: University of North Carolina Press, 1981.

Brandeis, Louis Dembitz (1856–1941)
    Advisor to Wilson; an Associate Justice of the United States Supreme Court (1916–1939).

3671. Papers. University of Louisville, Law Library; American Jewish Archives, Cincinnati, Ohio; Yivo Institute for Jewish Research, New York City; Zionist Archives and Library, New York City; Harvard Law School Library; Brandeis University, Goldfarb Library.

3672. Brandeis, Louis Dembitz. *Letters of Louis D. Brandeis*, eds. Melvin Urofsky and David W. Levy. 5 vols. Albany: State University of New York Press, 1971–1978.

3673. Brandeis, Louis Dembitz, and Felix Frankfurter. *"Half Brother, Half Son"*: *The Letters of Louis D. Brandeis to Felix Frankfurter*, ed. Melvin Urofsky and David W. Levy. Norman: University of Oklahoma Press, 1991.

3674. Dawson, Nelson L., ed. *Brandeis and America*. Lexington: University Press of Kentucky, 1989.

3675. Freund, Paul A. "Louis Dembitz Brandeis." *DAB* 23:93–100.

3676. Mason, Alpheus T. *Brandeis: A Free Man's Life*. New York: The Viking Press, 1946.

3677. Strum, Philippa. *Louis D. Brandeis: Justice for the People*. Cambridge: Harvard University Press, 1984.

3678. Urofsky, Melvin I. *A Mind of One Piece: Brandeis and American Reform*. New York: Charles Scribner's Sons, 1971.

3679. ———. *Louis D. Brandeis and the Progressive Tradition*. Boston: Little, Brown, and Co., 1981.

Close, Gilbert Fairchild (1881–1952)
    Secretary to Wilson after World War I, who accompanied Wilson to the Paris Peace Conference. Former secretary to Josephus Daniels.

3680. Biographical sketch, *PWW* 49:5, n. 1.

Fosdick, Raymond Blaine (1883–)
    Lawyer and public official. Under Secretary General of the League of Nations, 1918–1920.

3681. Papers. Princeton University Library

3682. Liestmann, Daniel. "Raymond Blaine Fosdick." *DAB* Supp. 9: 287–88.

Grayson, Admiral Cary T. (1879–1938)
    Personal physician to Presidents Theodore Roosevelt, Taft, and Wilson. He

helped control Wilson's affairs after the President's stroke in 1919 and refused to declare him incapacitated.

3683. Papers. Princeton University Library.

3684. Link, Arthur S. "Dr. Grayson's Predicament." *Proceedings of the American Philosophical Society* 138 (December 1994): 487–94.

Hale, William Bayard (1869–1924)
    Editor of a number of major American journals who also edited **354** in 1913 and was Wilson's special agent in Mexico (1913–1914).

3685. Rosewater, Victor. "William Bayard Hale." *DAB* 8:112–13.

Harvey, George Brinton McClellan (1864–1928)
    Reporter, editor, author, major player in Wilson's political ascent, and Ambassador to Great Britain (1921–1923), who ultimately broke with Wilson and the Democratic Party.

3686. Papers. Duke University Libraries.

3687. Biographical sketch, *PWW* 11:369–70, n. 2.

3688. Harvey, George Brinton McClellan. *The Power of Tolerance and Other Speeches*. New York: Harper & Brothers, 1911.

3689. Johnson, William Fletcher. *George Harvey: A "Passionate Patriot."* Boston: Houghton Mifflin Co., 1929.

3690. Meneely, A. Howard. "George Brinton McClellan Harvey." *DAB* 8:372–73.

3691. Russell, Francis. *President Makers of the Twentieth Century; from Mark Hanna to Joseph P. Kennedy*, 131–85. Boston: Little, Brown and Co., 1976.

Hines, Walker Downer (1870–1934)
    Assistant Director General of Railways (1919–1920), and arbitrator of local and international shipping questions on the Danube River (1920–1921).

3692. Papers. Hoover Institution on War, Revolution, and Peace, Stanford University.

3693. Parmeler, Julius H. "Walker Downer Hines." *DAB* 21:406–407.

House, Edward Mandell (1858–1938)
    Advisor to Wilson and a commissioner to the Paris Peace Conference.

3694. Papers. *Library of Congress, Manuscript Division*; Sterling Memorial Library, Yale University.

3695. Creel, George C. "Break between Wilson and Colonel House." *Collier's National Weekly* 77 (May 22, 1926): 7–8.

3696. ———— . *The Intimate Papers of Colonel House, Arranged as a Narrative*, ed. Charles Seymour. 4 vols. Boston: Houghton Mifflin Co., 1926–1928.

3697. House, Edward Mandell. "End of a Friendship: With Memorandum by E.M. House." *American Heritage* 14 (August 1963): 4–9.

3698. Macfarlane, Peter Clark. "President's Silent Partner." *Collier's National Weekly* 51 (May 3, 1913): 7–8.

3699. Richardson, Rupert N. *Colonel Edward M. House: The Texas Years, 1858–1912*. Abilene, Tex.: Hardin-Simmons Publications, 1964.

3700. Seymour, Charles. "Edward Mandell House." *DAB* 22:319–21.

3701. Smith, Arthur Douglas Howdon. "A Collector of Friendships." *Saturday Evening Post* 199 (July 17, August 28, 1926): 12–13+, 25+.

3702. ———— . *Mr. House of Texas*. New York: Funk & Wagnalls Co., 1940.

Johnson, Douglas Wilson (1878–1944)
   Geologist and geographer and a specialist with the American Delegation to the Paris Peace Conference.

3703. Judson, Sheldon. "Douglas Wilson Johnson." *DAB* Supp. 3:389–90.

Kerney, James (1873–1934)
   New Jersey editor and civil service commissioner (1908–1911) who opposed Wilson's nomination for governor in 1910 but later became a friend and counselor to him. In 1918, Wilson appointed him director of the American Committee on Public Information, with headquarters in Paris.

3704. Meneely, A. Howard. "James Kerney." *DAB* 21:466–67.

McCombs, William Frank (1875–1921)
   A student of Wilson at Princeton and one of his early supporters.

3705. Biographical sketch, *PWW* 21:108, n. 1.

3706. Lyons, Maurice F. *William F. McCombs, The President Maker*. Cincinnati: Bancroft Co., 1922.

McCormick, Vance Criswell (1872–1946)
   Publisher, Chairman of the War Trade Board in 1918, and advisor to Wilson at the Paris Peace Conference.

3707. Papers. Yale University Library.

Swem, Charles Lee (1893–1956)
   Wilson's personal stenographer (1912–1921), whose transcripts and shorthand notes of campaign speeches and press conferences still survive.

3708. Papers. The Charles L. Swem Collection, Princeton University Library.

3709. Biographical sketch, *PWW* 25:xi.

Tumulty, Joseph Patrick (1879–1954)
Private Secretary to Wilson during his presidency.

3710. Papers. *Library of Congress, Manuscript Division.*

3711. Biographical sketch, *PWW* 21:19, n. 6.

3712. Blum, John Morton. *Joe Tumulty and the Wilson Era.* Boston: Houghton Mifflin, 1951

3713. ———. "Joseph Patrick Tumulty." *DAB* Supp. 5:696–98.

E. Members of Congress

Alexander, Joshua Willis (1852–1936)
Missouri congressman (1907–1919) and Secretary of Commerce (1919–1921).

Borah, William Edgar (1865–1940)
Republican Senator from Idaho (1907–1940), and foreign policy foe of Wilson.

3714. Papers. Idaho State Historical Society, Manuscript Division; *Library of Congress, Manuscript Division.*

3715. Johnson, Claudius O. *Borah of Idaho.* Seattle: University of Washington Press, 1967.

3716. Maddox, Robert James. *William E. Borah and American Foreign Policy.* Baton Rouge: Louisiana State University Press, 1969.

Clark, James Beauchamp ("Champ") (1850–1921)
Congressman from Missouri (1893–1895, 1897–1921) and Speaker of the United States House of Representatives (1911–1919). Narrowly lost the presidential nomination to Wilson on the forty-sixth ballot at the 1912 Democratic Convention.

3717. Papers. Bethany College Library, West Virginia.

3718. Clark, Champ. *My Quarter Century of American Politics.* 2 vols. New York: Harper & Brothers, 1920.

3719. Hollister, Wilfred R., and Harry Norman. *Five Famous Missourians.* Kansas City, Mo.: Hudson-Kimberly Publishing Co., 1900.

Cox, James Middleton (1870–1957)
Journalist, congressman, Governor of Ohio, and presidential candidate in 1920.

3720. Papers. Ohio Historical Society collections, Columbus; Wright State University, Greater Miami Valley Research Center, University Library, Dayton.

3721. Allen, Michael Patrick. *The Founding Fortunes, A New Anatomy of the Superrich Families in America.* New York: Truman Talley Books, 1987.

3722. Cox, James Middleton. *Journey Through My Years.* New York: Simon and Schuster, 1946.

3723. Smith, Daniel Malloy. "James Middleton Cox." *DAB* 26:128–30.

Glass, Carter (1858–1946)
Congressman, United States Senator, and Secretary of the Treasury (1918–1920).

3724. Papers. University of Virginia Library; *Library of Congress, Manuscript Division.*

3725. Glass, Carter. *An Adventure in Constructive Finance.* Garden City, N.Y.: Doubleday, Page & Co., 1927.

3726. Pulley, Raymond H. "Carter Glass." *DAB* Supp. 4:330–32.

3727. Smith, Rixey, and Norman Beasley. *Carter Glass: A Biography.* New York: Longmans, Green and Co., 1939.

Gore, Thomas Pryor (1870–1949)
Lawyer and United States Senator from Oklahoma.

3728. Papers. University of Oklahoma Library; Western History Collections, Bizzell Memorial Library, Norman, Okla.

3729. Billington, Monroe L. "Thomas Pryor Gore." *DAB* Supp. 4:337–39.

3730. ———. *Thomas P. Gore: Blind Senator from Oklahoma.* Lawrence: University of Kansas Press, 1967.

Hitchcock, Gilbert Monell (1859–1934)
United States Senator from Nebraska and Chairman of the Senate Committee on Foreign Relations.

3731. Papers. *Library of Congress, Manuscript Division.*

3732. Sellers, J. L. "Gilbert Monell Hitchcock." *DAB* 21:410–11.

Johnson, Hiram Warren (1866–1945)
Governor and Senator from California.

3733. Papers. Bancroft Library, University of California-Berkeley; University of Oregon Library.

3734. Fitzpatrick, John J., III. "Senator Hiram W. Johnson: A Life History, 1866–1945." Ph.D. diss., University of California, Berkeley, 1975.

3735. Johnson, Hiram. *The Diary Letters of Hiram Johnson, 1917–1945*, ed. Robert E. Burke. 7 vols. New York: Garland, 1983.

3736. Mowry, George Edwin. "Hiram Warren Johnson." *DAB* Supp. 3:393–98.

3737. Olin, Spencer C., Jr. *California's Prodigal Sons: Hiram Johnson and the Progressives, 1911–1917.* Berkeley: University of California Press, 1968.

3738. Weatherson, Michael A., and Hal Bochin. *Hiram Johnson: A Bio-Bibliography.* Westport: Greenwood Press, 1988.

Kitchin, Claude (1869–1923)
United States Representative from North Carolina, Chairman of the House Ways and Means Committee, and Majority Leader of the House of Representatives.

3739. Papers. University of North Carolina Library, Southern Historical Collection, Chapel Hill.

3740. Arnett, Alex Mathews. *Claude Kitchin and the Wilson War Policies.* Boston: Little, Brown and Co., 1937.

3741. Goebel, Julius. "Claude Kitchin." *DAB* 10:439–40.

3742. Ingle, Homer L. "Pilgrimmage to Reform: A Life of Claude Kitchin." Ph.D. diss., University of Wisconsin, 1967.

La Follette, Robert Marion (1855–1925)
Wisconsin Governor and United States Senator.

3743. Papers. State Historical Society of Wisconsin Collections. *Library of Congress, Manuscript Division.*

3744. Burgchardt, Carl R. *Robert M. La Follette, Sr.: The Voice of Conscience.* Westport, Conn.: Greenwood Press, 1992.

3745. La Follette, Belle Case, and Fola La Follette. *Robert M. La Follette, June 14, 1855–June 18, 1925.* New York: Macmillan Co., 1953.

3746. La Follette, Robert Marion. *Autobiography: A Personal Narrative of Political Experiences.* Madison, Wis.: The Robert M. La Follette Co., 1913.

3747. Paxson, Frederic Logan. "Robert Marion La Follette." *DAB* 10:541–46.

3748. Thelen, David P. *Robert M. La Follette and the Insurgent Spirit.* Boston: Little Brown & Co., 1976.

Lodge, Henry Cabot (1850–1924)
Republican Senator from Massachusetts and chairman of the Senate Foreign Relations Committee during the fight over the League of Nations.

3749. Papers. American Academy of Arts and Letters Library, New York; Syracuse University Library; *Library of Congress, Manuscripts Division*; Massachusetts Historical Society.

3750. Garraty, John Arthur. *Henry Cabot Lodge: A Biography.* New York: Alfred A. Knopf, 1953.

3751. Lodge, Henry Cabot. *Early Memoirs.* New York: Charles Scribner's Sons, 1913.

3752. ———. *War Addresses, 1915–1917.* Boston: Houghton Mifflin Co., 1917.

3753. "Lodge Attack on Wilson." *Literary Digest* 87 (November 7, 1925): 12–13.

3754. Munro, William Bennett. "Henry Cabot Lodge." *DAB* 11:346–49.

3755. Widenor, William C. *Henry Cabot Lodge and the Search for an American Foreign Policy.* Berkeley: University of California Press, 1980.

Norris, George William (1861–1944)
   Republican Senator from Nebraska (1912–1943) who voted against both United States entry into World War I and the League of Nations.

3756. Papers. *Library of Congress, Manuscript Division.*

3757. Lowitt, Richard. "George William Norris." *DAB* Supp. 3:557–61.

3758. ———. *George W. Norris.* 3 vols. Urbana: University of Illinois Press, 1978.

3759. Norris, George W. *Fighting Liberal: The Autobiography of George W. Norris.* New York: Macmillan Co., 1945.

3760. *Norris from Nebraska.* Norris Foundation, 1991.

Root, Elihu (1845–1937)
   Republican Senator from New York (1909–1915) and leading member of the Senate Foreign Relations Committee who in 1917 was appointed head of a mission to Russia by Wilson. He was a leading supporter of the League of Nations.

3761. Papers. *Library of Congress, Manuscript Division;* American Academy of Arts and Letters, New York; the New York Public Library.

3762. Jessup, Philip C. *Elihu Root.* 2 vols. New York: Dodd, Mead & Co., 1938.

3763. ———. "Elihu Root." *DAB* 22:577–82.

3764. Leopold, Richard William. *Elihu Root and the Conservative Tradition.* Boston: Little, Brown, 1954.

Underwood, Oscar Wilder (1862–1929)
   United States Representative and Senator from Alabama.

3765. Papers. Alabama Department of Archives and History; University of Virginia Alderman Library, Manuscripts Department.

3766. Biographical sketch, *PWW* 22:95, n. 1.

3767. Dabney, Virginius. "Oscar Wilder Underwood." *DAB* 19:117–19.

3768. Johnson, Evans C. *Oscar W. Underwood: A Political Biography.* Southern Biography Series. Baton Rouge: Louisiana State University Press, 1980.

3769. Underwood, O. W. *Drifting Sands of Party Politics.* New York: The Century Co., 1928.

Westermann, William Linn (1873–1954)
Professor of History at Columbia and specialist in the Near and Middle East who attended the Paris Peace Conference.

3770. Papers. Columbia University Libraries; the Hoover Institution on War, Revolution and Peace, Stanford University.

3771. Brown, Truesdell S. "William Linn Westermann." *DAB* Supp. 5: 735–36.

F. Military Leaders

Benson, William Shepherd (1855–1932)
Chief of Naval Operations; member of the American War Commission appointed by Wilson to confer with the Allied Powers in Europe; naval advisor to the American Commission to Negotiate Peace; and Chairman of the United States Shipping Board.

3772. Papers. *Library of Congress, Manuscript Division.*

3773. Paullin, Charles O. "William Shepherd Benson." *DAB* 21:70–71.

Bliss, Tasker Howard (1853–1930)
Army Chief of Staff during World War I and a commissioner to the Paris Peace Conference following the war.

3774. Papers. *Library of Congress, Manuscript Division.*

3775. Palmer, Frederick C. *Bliss: Peacemaker: The Life and Letters of General Tasker Howard Bliss.* New York: Dodd, Mead & Co., 1934.

3776. ———. "Tasker Howard Bliss." *DAB* 21:88–90.

3777. Trask, David F. *General Tasker Howard Bliss and "Sessions of the World,"* *1919.* Philadelphia: American Philosophical Society, 1966.

Johnson, Hugh Samuel (1882–1942)
Member of John J. Pershing's expedition to Mexico in 1916 and of the War Industries Board in 1918; appointed chief of military purchase and supply during the war mobilization; originated the selective service plan.

3778. Johnson, Hugh S. *The Blue Eagle from Egg to Earth.* Garden City, N.Y.: Doubleday, Doran, 1935.

3779. Leuchtenburg, William E. "Hugh Samuel Johnson." *DAB* Supp. 3:398–400.

3780. Ohl, John K. "'Old Iron Pants': The Wartime Career of General Hugh S. Johnson, 1917–1918." Ph.D. diss., University of Cincinnati, 1971.

Pershing, John Joseph (1860–1948)
Army officer, Commander of the expedition to Mexico in 1916, and Commander-in-Chief of the American Expeditionary Forces in World War I.

3781. Papers. National Archives, Washington, D.C.; Nebraska State Historical Society, Lincoln; *Library of Congress, Manuscript Division.*

3782. Pershing, John J. *Final Report of General John J. Pershing.* Washington, D.C.: United States Government Printing Office, 1919.

3783. ———. *My Experiences in the World War.* 2 vols. New York: Frederick A. Stokes Co., 1931.

3784. Smythe, Donald. *Pershing: General of the Armies.* Bloomington: Indiana University Press, 1986.

3785. Vandiver, Frank E. "John Joseph Pershing." *DAB* Supp. 4:653–58.

3786. ———. *Black Jack: The Life and Times of John J. Pershing.* 2 vols. College Station, Tex.: Texas A & M University Press, 1977.

Wood, Leonard (1860–1927)
Army physician, Military Governor of Cuba, and Chief of Staff of the Army (1910–1914) who was passed over as commander of the American expeditionary force in World War I in favor of John J. Pershing. Became the 1920 Republican presidential candidate and Governor General of the Philippines (1921–1927).

3787. Papers. *Library of Congress, Manuscript Division*; New York Public Library.

3788. Betts, Thomas Thomas. "Leonard Wood." *DAB* 20:467–69.

3789. Hagedorn, Hermann. *Leonard Wood: A Biography.* 2 vols. New York: Harper and Brothers, 1931.

3790. Lane, Jack C. *Armed Progressive: General Leonard Wood.* San Rafael, Calif.: Presidio Press, 1978.

G. Other Leaders

Carnegie, Andrew (1835–1919)
Philanthropist and founder of Carnegie Steel Co.

3791. Papers. *Library of Congress, Manuscript Division*; New York Public Library; Pennsylvania State University Library, University Park.

3792. Carnegie, Andrew. *Autobiography*, ed. J. C. Van Dyke. Boston: Houghton Mifflin Co., 1920.

3793. ———. *Gospel of Wealth and Other Essays (1889)*, ed. Edward C. Kirkland. Cambridge: Belknap Press of Harvard University Press, 1962.

3794. Hendrick, Burton Jesse. "Andrew Carnegie." *DAB* 3:499–506.

3795. ———. *The Life of Andrew Carnegie*. 2 vols. Garden City, N.Y.: Doubleday, Doran & Co., 1932.

3796. Swetnam, George. *Andrew Carnegie*. Boston: Twayne Publishers, 1980.

3797. Wall, Joseph Frazier. *Andrew Carnegie*. New York: Oxford University Press, 1970.

Croly, Herbert David (1869–1930)
Founder and Editor of the *New Republic*, and major progressive writer who was both admirer and critic of Wilson. The two corresponded but probably never met.

3798. Croly, Herbert David. *The Promise of American Life*. New York: Macmillan Co., 1909.

3799. Levy, David W. *Herbert Croly of the New Republic: The Life and Thought of an American Progressive*. Princeton: Princeton University Press, 1985.

3800. Villard, Oswald Garrison. "Herbert David Croly." *DAB* 21:209–10.

Du Bois, William Edward Burghardt (1868–1963)
Educator and author. Leader in Pan-African movement.

3801. Papers. University of Massachusetts at Amherst Library.

3802. Oral history. Columbia University Library.

3803. Du Bois, W.E.B. *The Correspondence of W.E.B. Du Bois*, ed. Herbert Aptheker. 3 vols. Amherst: University of Massachusetts Press, 1973–1978.

3804. Lewis, David Levering. *W.E.B. Du Bois: Biography of a Race, 1868–1919*. New York: Henry Holt & Co., 1993.

3805. Marable, Manning. *W.E.B. Du Bois: Black Radical Democrat*. Boston: Twayne, 1986.

3806. McDonnell, Robert W. *Papers of W.E.B. Du Bois, 1803 (1877–1963) 1979: A Guide*. Sanford, N.C.: Microfilming Corp. of America, 1981

3807. Rampersad, Arnold. "William Edward Burghardt Du Bois." *DAB* Supp. 7:200–205.

3808. Rudwick, Elliot M. *W.E.B. Du Bois: Voice of the Black Protest Movement*. Champaign: University of Illinois Press, 1982.

Francis, David Rowland (1850–1927)
Governor of Mississippi and Ambassador to Russia.

3809. Papers. Missouri Historical Society collections, St. Louis.

3810. Francis, David R. *Russia from the American Embassy, 1916–1918*. New York: Arno Press, 1970.

3811. _____. *David R. Francis: His Recollections and Letters*. n.p.: n.p., 1928.

3812. Kohlenberg, Gilbert C. "David Rowland Francis: American Businessman in Russia." *Mid-America* 40 (1958): 195–217.

3813. Stevens, Walter B. "David Rowland Francis." *DAB* 6:577–78.

Gompers, Samuel (1850–1924)
American labor leader and first president of the American Federation of Labor.

3814. Papers. New York Public Library.

3815. Commons, John R. "Samuel Gompers." *DAB* 7:369–73.

3816. Gompers, Samuel. *Seventy Years of Life and Labor: An Autobiography*. 2 vols. New York: E.P. Dutton & Co., 1925.

3817. Livesay, Harold C. *Samuel Gompers and Organized Labor in America*. Library of American Biography. Boston: Little, Brown and Co., 1978.

3818. Mandell, Bernard. *Samuel Gompers: A Biography*. Yellow Springs, Ohio: Antioch Press, 1963.

Holt, Hamilton Bowen (1872–1951)
Journalist, editor, and President of Rollins College.

3819. Papers. Rollins College Library; Mills Memorial Library, Winter Park, Florida.

3820. Biographical sketch, *PWW* 11:348, n. 1.

3821. Kuehl, Warren F. *Hamilton Holt: Journalist, Internationalist, Educator*. Gainesville: University of Florida Press, 1960.

3822. _____. "Hamilton Bowen Holt." *DAB* Supp. 5:307–309.

Hudspeth, Robert Stephen (1862–1929)
New Jersey Democratic leader and member of the Democratic National Committee.

3823. Biographical sketch, *PWW* 20:563, n. 2.

Hughes, Charles Evans (1862–1948)
Associate Justice of the United States Supreme Court (1910–1916), Republican candidate for President in 1916, Secretary of State (1921–1925), and Chief Justice (1930–1941).

3824. Papers. *Library of Congress, Manuscript Division*; Brown University Library; Syracuse University Library; Colgate University Archives.

3825. Blodgett, Geoffrey. "Charles Evans Hughes." *DAB* Supp. 4:403–408.

3826. Hughes, Charles Evans. *The Autobiographical Notes of Charles Evans Hughes*, ed. Daniel J. Danelski and Joseph S. Tulchin. Cambridge: Harvard University Press, 1973.

3827. Perkins, Dexter. *Charles Evans Hughes and American Democratic Statesmanship*. Boston: Little, Brown, 1956.

Hughes, William (1872–1918)
Lawyer, New Jersey congressman (1903–1905), Senator (1913–1918).

Lippmann, Walter (1889–1974)
Author, journalist, and political commentator.

3828. Papers. American Academy of Arts and Letters Library, New York; Yale University Library.

3829. Hoogenboom, Lynn. "Walter Lippman." *DAB* Supp. 9:503–506.

3830. Lippmann, Walter. *Public Philosopher: Selected Letters of Walter Lippmann*, ed. John Morton Blum. New York: Ticknor & Fields, 1985.

3831. Steel, Ronald. *Walter Lippmann and the American Century*. Boston: Little, Brown and Co., 1980.

Martine, James Edgar (1849–1925)
Elected United States Senator from New Jersey in 1911 over James Smith, Jr., with Wilson's support.

Murphy, Charles F. (1858–1924)
Tammany Hall leader.

3832. Moley, Raymond. "Charles F. Murphy." *DAB* 13:346–47.

3833. Weiss, Nancy J. *Charles Francis Murphy, 1858–1924: Respectability and Responsibility in Tammany Politics*. Northampton, Mass.: Smith College, 1968.

Nugent, James Richard (1864–1911)
Assistant to James Smith, Jr., United States Senator and Democratic boss of New Jersey.

3834. Duplicate entry omitted.

3835. Biographical sketch, *PWW* 20:215, n. 1.

Roosevelt, Theodore (1858–1919)
Republican President of the United States (1901–1909), who was also the unsuccessful 1912 Progressive Party candidate for President.

3836. Papers. William L. Clements Library, Division of Manuscripts, Ann Arbor, Mich.; University of Virginia Library; American Academy of Arts and Letters Library, New York; University of Chicago Library; *Library of Congress, Manuscript Division*; Colorado College Library; Columbia University Libraries.

3837. Oral history. Theodore Roosevelt Association, Oral History Collection, Columbia University Libraries.

3838. Blum, John Morton. *The Republican Roosevelt.* 2d ed. Cambridge: Harvard University Press, 1977.

3839. Chessman, G. Wallace. *Governor Theodore Roosevelt: The Albany Apprenticeship, 1898–1900.* Cambridge: Harvard University Press, 1965.

3840. Gable, John A., and Cornelius A. van Minnen. *The Many-Sided Theodore Roosevelt: American Renaissance Man.* Middelberg, Netherlands: Roosevelt Study Center, 1986.

3841. Gould, Lewis L. *The Presidency of Theodore Roosevelt.* Lawrence: University Press of Kansas, 1991.

3842. Lodge, Henry Cabot, ed. *Selections from the Correspondence of Theodore Roosevelt and Henry Cabot Lodge, 1884–1918.* 2 vols. New York: Charles Scribner's Sons, 1925.

3843. Miller, Nathan. *Theodore Roosevelt: A Life.* New York: W.W. Morrow, 1992.

3844. Morris, Edmund. *The Rise of Theodore Roosevelt.* New York: Coward, McCann & Geoghegan, 1979.

3845. Mowry, George Edwin. *Theodore Roosevelt and the Progressive Movement.* Madison: The University of Wisconsin Press, 1946.

3846. Paxson, Frederic Logan. "Theodore Roosevelt." *DAB* 16:135–44.

3847. Roosevelt, Theodore. *An Autobiography.* New York: Charles Scribner's Sons, 1913.

3848. ———. *The Letters of Theodore Roosevelt,* ed. Elting E. Morison and John M. Blum. 8 vols. Cambridge: Harvard University Press, 1951–1954.

3849. ———. *Theodore Roosevelt and His Times, Shown in His Own Letters,* ed. Joseph B. Bishop. 2 vols. New York: Charles Scribner's Sons, 1920.

3850. ———. *The Works of Theodore Roosevelt, Memorial Edition,* ed. Hermann Hagedorn. 20 vols. New York: Charles Scribner's Sons, 1924–25.

3851. ———. *The Writings of Theodore Roosevelt,* ed. William Henry Harbaugh. Indianapolis: Bobbs-Merrill, 1967.

Shaw, Anna Howard (1847–1919)
Reformer, physician, minister, suffragist and advocate of the League of Nations who was chaired the women's committee of the Council of National Defense in 1917.

3852. Papers. The Radcliffe Women's Archives, Radcliffe College, Cambridge, Mass.

3853. Gray, Dorothy. *Women of the West*, 121–27. Millbrae, Calif.: Les Femmes Publishers, 1976.

3854. Harper, Ida Husted. "Anna Howard Shaw." *DAB* 17:35–37.

3855. Shaw, Anna H. *The Story of a Pioneer*. New York: Harper and Brothers, 1915.

Smith, James, Jr. (1851–1927)
    United States Senator and Democratic boss of New Jersey.

3856. Biographical sketch, *Who's Who in America* 14 (1926–27): 1768.

3857. Meneely, A. Howard. "James Smith, Jr." *DAB* 17:285–86.

Taft, William Howard (1857–1930)
    Republican President of the United States (1909–1913) who was defeated by Wilson in 1912, and went on to become Chief Justice in 1921.

3858. Papers. *Library of Congress, Manuscript Division*; Cincinnati Historical Society collections; Ohio Historical Society collections, Columbus; American Jewish Historical Society collections, Waltham, Mass.

3859. Anderson, Donald F. *William Howard Taft: A Conservative Conception of the Presidency*. Ithaca, N.Y.: Cornell University Press, 1973.

3860. Coleta, Paolo E. *The Presidency of William Howard Taft*. Lawrence: University of Kansas Press, 1973.

3861. ———. *William Howard Taft: A Bibliography*. Westport, Conn.: Meckler, 1989.

3862. Mason, Alpheus T. *William Howard Taft: Chief Justice*. New York: Simon and Schuster, 1965.

3863. Pringle, Henry Fowles. *The Life and Times of William Howard Taft: A Biography*. 2 vols. New York: Farrar and Rinehart, 1939.

3864. ———. "William Howard Taft." *DAB* 18:266–72.

Wittpenn, Henry Otto
    Mayor of Jersey City and progressive Democrat who announced his candidacy for Governor of New Jersey in 1910.

3865. Biographical sketch, *PWW* 20:577, n. 1–2.

H. Foreign Leaders

Balfour, Arthur James Balfour, 1st Earl of (1848–1930)
    Prime Minister of England (1902–1905), and British Foreign Secretary (1916–1919). Also author of the World War I Balfour Declaration, which asserted British approval of Zionism.

3866. Papers. Public Record Office of the British Foreign Office records. Also British Museum and British Library, London.

3867. Balfour, Arthur. *Chapters of Autobiography*, ed. Blanche E. C. Dugdale. London: Cassell and Co., 1930.

3868. Cecil, Algernon. "Arthur James Balfour." *DNB*. Supp. 1920–1930:41–56.

3869. Dugdale, Blanche Elizabeth Campbell. *Arthur James Balfour, First Earl of Balfour*. 2 vols. New York: G. P. Putnam's Sons, 1937.

3870. Mackay, Ruddock F. Balfour. *Intellectual Statesman*. Cambridge: Oxford University Press, 1985.

3871. Salisbury, Robert Cecil, 1st Earl of, and Arthur Balfour. *Salisbury-Balfour Correspondence: Letters Exchanged between the Third Marquess of Salisbury and His Nephew Arthur James Balfour, 1869–1892*. Hertfordshire Record Society, 1988.

Bernstorff, Count Johann Heinrich Graf von (1862–1939)
    German Ambassador to the United States from 1908 until America's declaration of war against Germany in 1917.

3872. Bernstorff, Johann Heinrich, Graf von. *My Three Years in America*. London: Skeffington and Son, Ltd., 1920.

3873. ———. *Memoirs of Count Bernstorff*, trans. Eric Sutton. New York: Random House, 1936.

3874. Doerries, Reinhard R. *Imperial Challenge: Ambassador Count Bernstorff and German American Relations 1908–1917*, trans. Christa D. Shannon. Chapel Hill: University of North Carolina Press, 1978.

Bethmann Hollweg, Theobald (Theodor Friedrich Alfred) (1856– 1921)
    German Imperial Chancellor before and during World War I, until he was forced to resign in July 1917.

3875. Hildebrand, Klaus. *Bethmann Hollweg: Der Kanzler ohne Eigenschaften?* Dusseldorf, 1970.

Carranza, Venustiano (1859–1920)
    First President (1915–1920) of the new Mexican Republic after the overthrow of the dictator, Porfirio Diaz. He helped keep Mexico neutral during World War I.

3876. Alexander, Robert J., ed. *Biographical Dictionary of Latin American and Caribbean Political Leaders*, 98–99. Westport, Conn.: Greenwood Press, 1988.

3877. Richmond, D. W. "Venustiano Carranza: Archive." *Hispanic American Historical Review* 56 (May 1976): 290–94.

Cecil, Lord Robert (1864–1958)
    British statesman and one of the major architects of the 1919 League of Nations

Covenant. Full title is Cecil (of Chelwood), Edgar Algernon Robert Gascoyne-Cecil, 1st Viscount.

3878. Papers. British Library; Oxford University, Bodleian Library; British Foreign Office records, Public Record Office.

3879. Cecil, Robert. *A Great Experiment: An Autobiography*. New York: Oxford University Press, 1941. London: Jonathan Cape, 1941.

3880. ———. *All the Way*. London: Hodder and Stoughton, 1949.

3881. Noel-Baker, Philip. "Edgar Algernon Robert Gascoyne-Cecil." *DNB* Supp. 1951–1960:199–201.

3882. Thompson, John A. "Lord Cecil and the Historians." *Historical Journal* 24 (September 1981): 709–15.

Chinda, Viscount Sutemi (1856–1929)
    Japanese Ambassador to the United States, delegate to the 1919 Paris Peace Conference.

Clemenceau, Georges (1841–1929)
    Premier of France (1906–1909, 1917–1920); also presided over the 1919 Paris Peace Conference.

3883. Bruun, Geoffrey. *Clemenceau*. Cambridge: Harvard University Press, 1943.

3884. Clemenceau, Georges Eugene Benjamin. *Grandeur and Misery of Victory*, trans. F. M. Atkinson. New York: Harcourt Brace, 1930.

3885. Ellis, Jack D. *Early Life of Georges Clemenceau, 1841–1893*. Lawrence: Regents Press of Kansas, 1980.

3886. Jackson, John Hampden. *Clemenceau and the Third Republic*. New York: Macmillan Co., 1948.

Foch, Ferdinand (1851–1929)
    Field Marshal of France and commander of Allied forces during the last months of World War I.

3887. Beaufre, A. "Marshal Ferdinand Foch." In *War Lords: Military Commanders of the Twentieth Century*, ed. Sir Michael Carver, 122–33. Boston: Little, Brown, 1976.

3888. Churchill, Sir Winston Spencer. *Great Contemporaries*. New York: G. P. Putnam's Sons, 1937.

3889. Foch, Ferdinand. *The Memoirs of Marshal Foch*, trans. T. Bentley Mott. New York: Doubleday, Doran and Co., 1931.

3890. L'Hopital, Commandant. *Foch, L'Armistice et la Paix*. Paris, 1938.

3891. Liddell Hart, Sir Basil Henry. *Foch: The Man of Orleans*. Boston: Little, Brown and Co., 1932.

Grey, Sir Edward (1862–1933)
Also called First Viscount Grey of Fallodon. British Foreign Secretary (1905–1916), who also came to the United States in 1919 on a special mission to promote American membership in the League of Nations.

3892. Papers. Public Records Office, Britain.

3893. Grey, Edward. *Twenty-five Years, 1892–1916*. 2 vols. New York: Frederick A. Stokes Co., 1925.

3894. Robbins, Keith. *Sir Edward Grey: A Biography of Lord Grey of Fallodon*. London: Cassell & Co., Ltd., 1971.

3895. Trevelyan, George Macaulay. "Sir Edward Grey." *DNB* Supp. 1931–1940:366–75.

Huerta, Victoriano (1854–1916)
President of Mexico (1913–1914) after joining a revolt against former dictator Porfirio Diaz. Venustiano Carranza led a revolution against Huerta, and Wilson seized Veracruz allowing arms to reach the revolutionaries. Huerta fled to Spain.

3896. Grieb, Kenneth J. *The United States and Huerta*. Lincoln: University of Nebraska Press, 1969.

Jusserand, Jean Jules (1855–1932)
Scholar, and French Ambassador to the United States (1902– 1925) who helped secure American entry into World War I.

3897. Papers. French Foreign Ministry Archives.

Lloyd George, David (1863–1945)
British Prime Minister (1916–1922), surrounded by a long parliamentary career (1890–1945).

3898. Papers. House of Lords Record Office.

3899. Constantine, Stephen. *Lloyd George*. New York: Routledge, 1992.

3900. Jones, Thomas. "David Lloyd George." *DNB* Supp. 1941–1950: 515–529.

3901. Pugh, Martin. *Lloyd George*. New York: Longmans Green and Co., 1988.

3902. Stevenson, Frances. *Lloyd George: A Diary by Frances Stevenson*, ed. Alan John Percivale Taylor. London: Hutchinson, 1971.

3903. Lloyd George, David. *Memoirs of the Peace Conference*. 2 vols. New Haven: Yale University Press, 1939.

3904. _____. *The War Memoirs of David Lloyd George*. 6 vols. London: Ivor Nicholson and Watson, 1933–1936.

Orlando, Vittorio Emanuele (1860–1952)
Prime Minister of Italy (1917–1919), who led the Italian delegation to the Paris Peace Conference.

3905. Papers. Duke University Library; University of Virginia Alderman Library; College of William and Mary, Swein Library; American Academy of Arts and Letters Library, New York.

3906. Orlando, Vittorio Emanuele. *Memorie*, ed. Rudolfo Mosca. Milan: Rizzoli, 1960.

Smuts, Jan Christiaan (1870–1950)
South African statesman, soldier, philosopher, and Prime Minister (1919–1924, 1939–1948) who campaigned against the Germans in Africa during World War I and who supported the League of Nations thereafter.

3907. Ingham, Kenneth. *Jan Christiaan Smuts: The Conscience of a South African.* New York: St. Martin's Press, 1986.

3908. Keppel-Jones, Arthur Mervyn. "Jan Christiaan Smuts." *DAB* Supp. 1941–1950: 797–804.

3909. Smuts, Jan Christiaan. *Jan Christiaan Smuts.* New York: W.W. Morrow, 1952.

3910. ———. *The League of Nations: A Practical Suggestion.* New York: Hodder and Stoughton, 1918.

3911. ———. *Plans for a Better World: Speeches of Field-Marshall J.C. Smuts.* London: Hodder and Stoughton, 1942.

3912. ———. *Selections from the Smuts Papers*, ed. W. K. Hancock and J. Van der Poel. 4 vols. Cambridge: University Press, 1966–1973.

3913. ———. *The Thoughts of General Smuts, Compiled by His Private Secretary, P.B. Blankenberg.* Cape Town: Juta, 1951.

Sonnino, Baron Sidney (1847–1922)
Italian foreign minister (1914–1919) who successfully promoted his country's entrance into World War I.

Spring-Rice, Sir Cecil Arthur (1859–1918)
British ambassador to the United States (1913–1918).

3914. Papers. British Foreign Office records, Public Record Office.

3915. Chiral, Valentine. "Sir Cecil Arthur Spring-Rice." *DNB* Supp. 1912–1921:504–506.

3916. Gwynn, Stephen Lucius, ed. *The Letters and Friendships of Sir Cecil Spring-Rice, a Record.* 2 vols. New York: Houghton Mifflin Co., 1929.

Villa, Francisco (*Pancho*) (1878–1923)
  Guerrilla leader in Mexico who during 1913–1914 combined forces with Venustiano Carranza in his revolt against Victoriano Huerta. Later he broke with Carranza.

3917. Duplicate entry omitted.

3918. Harris, Larry A. *Pancho Villa: Strong Man of the Revolution.* Silver City, N.M.: High-Lonesome Books, 1989.

20
Post-Presidential Career, 1921–1924

3919. Archer, Mary Urban. "Woodrow Wilson: The Post-Presidential Years." Ph.D. diss., Saint Louis University, 1963. A discussion of his limited political influence, his ideas about America, and the postwar order.

3920. "Armistice Day 1923 and the Radio Message of Woodrow Wilson to the Nation." *Pan American Magazine* 36 (November 1923): 206–8. After quoting Wilson's message verbatim, the editors express the hope that the people of the United States might yet "be counted on the side of a closer international cooperation."

3921. Clapper, Olive Ewing. *Washington Tapestry*, 49–55. New York: McGraw-Hill Book Co., 1946. Includes a short section on Wilson's last years.

3922. Clark, James C. *Faded Glory: Presidents out of Power*, 115–20. New York: Praeger, 1985. Argues that Wilson was discouraged by the rejection of the League and by his own unpopularity.

3923. Creel, George C. "Woodrow Wilson's Last Years." *Saturday Evening Post* 203 (January 10, 1931): 10–11+. The postwar years of Wilson's presidency, including an interview with him about negotiating the peace treaty.

3924. Cunningham, Homer F. *The Presidents' Last Years: George Washington to Lyndon Johnson*, 198–209. Jefferson, N.C.: McFarland & Co., 1989. Describes Wilson's post-presidential years.

3925. Keister, Kim. "The House on 'S' Street." *Historic Preservation* 44, no. 6 (November/December 1992): 58–66, 90–92. What Wilson's final residence reveals about his character.

3926. Kerney, James. "Last Talks with Woodrow Wilson." *Saturday Evening Post* 196 (March 29, 1924): 3–4+. Impressions of Wilson gained from interviews with him near the end of his life.

3927. Martin, Asa Earl. *After the White House*, 408–24. State College: Pennsylvania Valley Publishers, 1951. Covers Wilson's activities from 1920–1924.

3928. Pinci, A. R. "Woodrow Wilson's Ford Boom." *Forum* 78 (August 1927): 181–89. [Also published in *Literary Digest* 94 (August 6, 1927): 60–62.] Discusses Wilson's effort to groom Henry Ford for the 1924 presidential election.

3929. "The Presidency in 1924?" *Forum* 70 (December 1923): 2222– 24. Advances Wilson as a candidate for President.

3930. "When a President Leaves Office." *U.S. News and World Report* 82 (January 24, 1977): 29. Describes Wilson's retirement as being brief and unsatisfying.

21

Death

See also entries under "Contemporary Profiles and Assessments Following Wilson's Death"

3931. Brewster, Eugene V., comp. *The Passing of Woodrow Wilson, Being Excerpts from Various Newspapers and Magazines Gathered . . . at the Time of the Death of Woodrow Wilson.* Brooklyn: Brewster Publications, 1924.

3932. "Death of Woodrow Wilson." *Current History Magazine of the New York Times* 19 (March 1924): 887–95. Includes tributes to Wilson by national and world leaders.

3933. Farmer, Robert, and associates. "The Will of Woodrow Wilson." *Last Will and Testament,* 175–76. New York: Arco, 1968. Reprint of Wilson's 1924 will.

3934. Finley, John Huston. "Obituary Notices of Members Deceased. Woodrow Wilson." *American Philosophical Society Proceedings* 63 (1924): 3–11. Warm tribute by a student and Princeton faculty colleague.

3935. Grier, Sydney C. [Gregg, pseud.]. "Tribute." *Southern Workman* 53 (March 1924): 96a–96b. A tribute taken from a talk to the student body of Hampton Institute.

3936. Johnson, Theodore Richard. "The Memorialization of Woodrow Wilson." Ph.D. diss., George Washington University, 1979. A study of memorials to Wilson from 1921 to 1971 with the theme of Wilson as tragic hero.

3937. U.S. Congress. Senate. Committee on Rules and Administration. *Woodrow Wilson Memorial Commission: Report to Accompany S.J. Res. 51 (87th Cong. 1st sess., 1961).* Washington, D.C.: Government Printing Office, 1961, S. Rept. 751.

3938. *Wills of the United States Presidents,* 174–77. New York: Communication Channels, 1976.

22

Wilson as Public Speaker

3939. Balcer, Charles L. "Woodrow Wilson's Columbian Exposition Speech—'A Liberal Education.'" *Communication Education* 32 (July 1983): 330–38. Analyzes the background and various aspects of Wilson's speech.

3940. Brooks, George Edward. "A Rhetorical Comparison of Woodrow Wilson and Franklin D. Roosevelt, Based upon Aristotelian Criteria." Ph.D. diss., Ohio State University, 1945.

3941. Canby, Henry Seidel. "Man of Letters (Woodrow Wilson)." In *Definitions: Essays in Contemporary Criticism*, 2nd ser., 175–78. New York: Harcourt, Brace, and Co., 1922–24. Contends that Wilson's greatest strengths were his power over words and his ability to express his ideas eloquently.

3942. Carpenter, Ronald H. "Woodrow Wilson as Speechwriter for George Creel: Presidential Style in Discourse as an Index of Personality." *Presidential Studies Quarterly* 19, no. 1 (Winter 1989): 117–26. Refutes James Barber's assertion that the form and style of Wilson's speeches reveal negative dimensions of his personality and argues that they show Wilson to be a master of rhetoric.

3943. Carpenter, Ronald H., et al. "Style in Discourse as a Predictor of Political Personality for Mr. Carter and Other Twentieth Century Presidents: Testing the Barber Paradigm." *Presidential Studies Quarterly* 8 (Winter 1978): 67–78. Examines James D. Barber's classification of Wilson's personality as "active-negative," meaning he applied great energy to his activities in a compulsive desire to escape reality.

3944. Craig, Hardin. "Woodrow Wilson as an Orator." *Quarterly Journal of Speech* 38 (April 1952): 145–48. Reminisces about Wilson's Princeton speeches.

3945. "Dangers of the Epigram." *Literary Digest* 62 (July 12, 1919): 31. Cautions Wilson in his role as phrasemaker.

3946. DeYoung, Harry Rine. "A Study of the Religious Speaking of Woodrow Wilson." Ph.D. diss., Wayne State University, 1965. An examination of the style of some of Wilson's speeches on religion and the impact of those speeches on his public career.

3947. Francesconi, Robert Albert. "A Burkeian Analysis of Selected Speeches of Woodrow Wilson and Henry Cabot Lodge on the League of Nations." Ph.D. diss., Bowling Green State University, 1975. Examines the rhetoric employed by Wilson and Lodge to make their cases for and against the League of Nations, concluding that the chances of reaching a compromise on the issue were remote.

3948. Graham, Gladys Murphy. "Concerning the Speech Power of Woodrow Wilson." *Quarterly Journal of Speech Education* 13 (November 1927): 412–24. Examines a number of works on Wilson's power as an orator, concluding that his deep convictions set his speeches apart from the common rhetoric of other leaders.

3949. Grim, Patricia Ann. "From Strict Neutrality to the Fourteen Points: Woodrow Wilson's Communication Strategies in World War One." Ph.D. diss., University of Pittsburgh, 1983. Stresses his ability to use imagery and to inspire people through moral exhortation.

3950. Heckscher, August. "Wilson—Style in Leadership." *Confluence: An International Forum* 5, no. 4 (Winter 1957): 332–40. Defines Wilson's leadership in terms of his oratorical style.

3951. Henderlider, Clair. "An Evaluation of the Persuasive Techniques of Woodrow Wilson in His League of Nations Speeches, September 4–25, 1919." Ph.D. diss., University of Iowa, 1946.

3952. "If It Wasn't for the Honor of the Thing." *American Heritage* 15 (August 1964): 112. A selection of presidential quotes, including Wilson's quip, "The President should be like an athlete, mother, and early Christian."

3953. "If the President Would Only Be Natural." *Literary Digest* 62 (August 9, 1919): 46–50. Contains a humorous mock speech recommended to Wilson to make his efforts on behalf of the League of Nations successful, poking fun at the formality of his speeches.

3954. Jones, Edgar DeWitt. "Woodrow Wilson." In *Lords of Speech*, 233–48. Chicago: Willett, Clark Co., 1937. [Also published under title *Masters of Speech*, 233–48. Grand Rapids, Mich.: Baker Book House, 1975.] Argues that Wilson was a master rhetorician and that he left as his legacy some of the greatest speeches to be given by an American President.

3955. "Lincoln, Roosevelt, and Wilson." *Literary Digest* 53 (September 23, 1916): 744–45. Compares the three speaking styles.

3956. McDiarmid, John. "Presidential Inaugural Addresses." *Public Opinion Quarterly* 1 (July 1937): 79–82. Statistics on the language and symbols used in inaugural addresses.

3957. McEdwards, Mary G. "Woodrow Wilson: His Stylistic Progression." *Western Speech* 26 (Winter 1962): 28–38. Says change in Wilson's manner of thinking, from early campaigner to mature advocate of structures for world peace, is documented by change in his rhetorical style.

3958. McKean, Dayton David. "Notes on Woodrow Wilson's Speeches." *Quarterly Journal of Speech* 16 (April 1930): 176–84. An analysis of two of Wilson's speeches, the "First Inaugural" and the "Lawyer and the Community."

3959. ———. "Woodrow Wilson." In *History and Criticism of American Public Address*, ed. William Norwood Brigance. McGraw-Hill Series in Speech, 2. New York: McGraw-Hill and Co., 1943. An analysis of Wilson's evolution as a public speaker.

3960. Motter, Thomas Hubbard Vail. "Woodrow Wilson and the Power of Words." *Princeton University Library Chronicle* 17, no. 3 (Spring 1956): 163–72. Examines Wilson as an orator and writer based on examination of several Wilson manuscripts in the Princeton Libraries.

3961. Osborn, George Coleman. "Woodrow Wilson as a Speaker." *Southern Speech Journal* 22 (Winter 1956): 61–72. Examines Wilson's speech-writing techniques and believes that he spoke with the power of authority, the conviction of the evangelist, and the zeal of a crusader.

3962. Paget, Edwin H. "Woodrow Wilson: International Rhetorician." *Quarterly Journal of Speech* 15 (February 1929): 15– 24. Believes Wilson was essentially a politician, a molder of public opinion who, although not reared in the ways of practical politics, longed for a public career.

3963. Patchin, Robert Halsey. "Wilson His Own Stenographer." *Harper's Weekly* 58 (January 31, 1914): 22–23. Describes Wilson's habit of composing a message in shorthand before transcribing it on his own typewriter.

3964. Runion, Howard L. "An Objective Study of the Speech Style of Woodrow Wilson." Ph.D. diss., University of Michigan, 1936. Analysis of 50 Wilson speeches, noting his frequent use of metaphors and rhetorical questions.

3965. Scarr, Lew. "Now Hear This: Birth of the Public Address System." *American Mercury* 84 (June 1957): 135–36. Concerns the first amplified presidential speech by Wilson at Balboa Stadium in San Diego, on September 19, 1919.

3966. Shepherd, Gerald A. "When the President Spoke at Balboa Stadium." *Journal of San Diego History* 32, no. 2 (1986): 92–102. Discusses a speech given by Wilson regarding his League proposal which was attended by about fifty-thousand people and was the first electrically amplified presidential address.

3967. Tulis, Jeffrey K. *The Rhetorical Presidency*, 117–61. Princeton: Princeton University Press, 1987. Analyzes popular rhetoric as a principal tool of twentieth-century Presidents. A section focuses on both visionary and policy-oriented speeches by Wilson and their limitations in his campaign for the League of Nations.

3968. Turner, Henry Andrew, Jr. "Woodrow Wilson and Public Opinion." *Public Opinion Quarterly* 21 (Winter 1957–58): 505–20. How Wilson attempted to gain public support for his policies, focusing on his efforts to become a more skilled writer and orator.

3969. "The Voice That Failed." *Time* 41 (May 10, 1943): 70. The first attempted presidential radio broadcast on July 4, 1919, delivered from Wilson's liner to convoying ships as he returned from the Peace Conference.

3970. Wescott, John W. *Woodrow Wilson's Eloquence*. Camden, N.J.: I. F. Huntzinger Co., 1922. Explicates the nature and function of eloquence by using two of Wescott's speeches which nominated Wilson for the presidency in 1912 and 1916.

3971. Williams, Mark Wayne. "Preaching Presidents." *Homiletic Review* 108 (August 1934): 90–96. Lists the religious references and psalms in Wilson's two inaugural addresses.

3972. Wilson, John Fletcher. "Rhetorical Echoes of a Wilsonian Idea." *Quarterly Journal of Speech* 43 (October 1957): 271–77. Compares Wilson's speeches on world peace with those of Franklin D. Roosevelt, Harry S. Truman, and Adlai E. Stevenson.

23
Wilson's Personal Life

A. Family and Friends

3973. Antrim, Doron Kemp. "Our Musical Presidents." *Etude* 58 (May 1940): 299+. Includes the not-widely-known fact that Wilson had a beautiful tenor singing voice and was an active member of the glee clubs at Princeton and Johns Hopkins.

3974. Axson, Stockton. *Brother Woodrow: A Memoir of Woodrow Wilson by Stockton Axson*, ed. Arthur S. Link. Papers of Woodrow Wilson. Supplementary Volume. Princeton: Princeton University Press, 1993. A fond but frank memoir by Wilson's brother-in-law and close friend, who highlights his successes and failures as President of Princeton.

3975. _____. *The Private Life of President Wilson, by the Brother of His First Wife*. Boston: A. T. Bliss and Co., 1916. A memoir by Wilson's brother-in-law.

3976. _____. "Woodrow Wilson." In *Library of Southern Literature*, ed. Edwin Anderson Alderman and Joel Chandler Harris. 27: Atlanta: Martin and Hoyt Co., 1910. A biographical sketch.

3977. _____. *Woodrow Wilson, the Man, as Seen by One of His Family*. Woodbury, N.J.: Daily Times, 1916. [Originally published in *New York Times Sunday Magazine*, October 8, 1916.] Recollections by Wilson's brother-in-law.

3978. _____. "Woodrow Wilson as Man of Letters—Three Public Lectures Delivered at the Rice Institute on February 18, 25, and March 4, 1934." *Rice Institute Pamphlet* 22 (1935): 195–270. Insightful analyses by Wilson's brother-in-law, who was intimate with Wilson and his family.

3979. Axson, Stockton, ed. "Material on Woodrow Wilson Prepared by Dr. Stockton Axson with Occasional Assistance of Admiral Cary T. Grayson." Mss. Mudd Library, Princeton University.

3980. Brownlow, Louis. "Wilson's Personal Relations." In **1075**, 80–111. Anecdotal description of his several encounters with Wilson.

3981. Butterfield, Roger. "The Camera Comes to the White House." *American Heritage* 15 (August 1964): 33–48. A photo-essay containing three pictures from the Wilson era—one photo of sheep grazing on the White House lawn in an effort to conserve manpower and two photos of Wilson's daughters.

3982. Clark, Melville Antone. "I Played the Harp for Wilson." *Christian Science Monitor Weekly Magazine Section* (May 19, 1945): 6. Reminiscence of a concert given at the White House.

3983. Colman, Edna M. *White House Gossip, from Andrew Johnson to Calvin Coolidge*, 340–77. New York: Doubleday, Page, and Co., 1927. Anecdotes relating to the Wilson presidency.

3984. Cross, Wilbur, and Ann Novotny. *White House Weddings*, 167– 215. New York: D. McKay Co., 1967. The weddings of Wilson's two daughters and his own remarriage in 1915.

3985. Cutler, Charles L., Jr. "'My Dear Mrs. Peck.'" *American History Illustrated* 6, no. 3 (1971): 4–9, 46–48. Deals with Wilson's relationship with Mary Allen Hulbert Peck.

3986. Davis, Parke Hill. "What Woodrow Wilson Did for American Foot-Ball." *St. Nicholas* 40 (November 1912): 13–19. Credits Wilson—as player, coach, and counselor—with helping convert English rugby into an American collegiate game.

3987. Durant, John. "Scholarly Sportsman." *Sports Illustrated* 17 (July 16, 1962): M4. States that, although Wilson's poor health kept him from enjoying many sports, he loved to play golf and to attend major league basketball and football games.

3988. _____. *Sports of Our Presidents*, 84–87. New York: Hastings House Publishers, 1964. A brief look at Wilson's athletic interests and pursuits, especially baseball, football, and golf.

3989. Elliot, Margaret Randolph Axson. *My Aunt Louisa and Woodrow Wilson*. Chapel Hill: University of North Carolina Press, 1944. Recollections of the Wilson family and of Wilson as husband and father, written by his first wife's sister.

3990. Fosdick, Raymond Blaine. "Woodrow Wilson among His Friends." *Harper's Magazine* 213 (December 1956): 57–63. An admiring portrait of Wilson as a warm, personable man who tried to save the world for future generations.

3991. Fredericks, Vic. *The Wit and Wisdom of the Presidents*. New York: Frederick Fell, 1966. Some Wilson quotations scattered throughout.

3992. Furman, Bess. *White House Profile: A Social History of the White House, Its Occupants and Its Festivities*, 287–300. Indianapolis: Bobbs-Merrill Co., 1951.

3993. Helm, Edith Benham. *The Captains and the Kings*. New York: G. P. Putnam and Sons, 1954. An autobiographical work that includes recollections of her life as social secretary to the Wilsons.

3994. Herring, Pendleton. "Woodrow Wilson: A President's Reading." *Historic Preservation* 27, no. 3 (1975): 38–42. A survey of Wilson's attempt to assemble a collection of excellent literature.

3995. Hoover, Irwin Hood (Ike). *Forty-two Years in the White House*. Boston: Houghton Mifflin Co., 1934. A memoir by the White House usher.

3996. Hosford, Hester Eloise. "New Ladies of the White House." *Independent* 73 (November 21, 1912): 1159–65. Wilson's immediate and extended family.

3997. Hurd, Charles. "To Save the World." In *The White House, A Biography: The Story of the White House, Its Occupants, Its Place in History*, 259–78. New York: Harper & Brothers, 1940. Portrays the White House as a living entity that both reflects and directs changes in the country. Includes a section on the years 1916–1919.

3998. Iovine, Julie V. "The Impeccable Gardener." *American Heritage* 37, no. 4 (1986): 66–77. Concerns Beatrix Farrand, who designed gardens for many wealthy Americans, including Mrs. Wilson.

3999. Jaffray, Elizabeth. *Secrets of the White House*. New York: Cosmopolitan Book Corporation, 1927. Memoirs by a White House housekeeper.

4000. Jeffries, Ona Griffin. *In and Out of the White House: From Washington to the Eisenhowers*, 297–310. New York: Wilfred Funk, 1960. Brief discussion of the social life of Wilson and his family in the White House.

4001. Jensen, Amy LaFollette. *The White House and Its Thirty-Three Families*, 201–13. New York: McGraw-Hill Publishing Co., 1962. An account of the life of the Wilsons in the White House, illustrated with fourteen photographs.

4002. Jones, Cranston. *Homes of the American Presidents*, 174–79. New York: McGraw-Hill Publishing Co., 1962. Describes a number of Wilson's homes, with photographs.

4003. Kern, Ellyn R. *Where the American Presidents Lived*, 54–56. Indianapolis: Cottontail Publications, 1982. Chronological list of Wilson's residences, from his first home to his last. Photograph and sketch included.

4004. Klapthor, Margaret Brown. *Official White House China: 1789 to the Present*. Washington, D.C.: Smithsonian Institution Press, 1975. Examines the presidential china settings, including those used during the Wilson presidency.

4005. Lindop, Edmund, and Joseph Jares. *White House Sportsmen*, 4–9, 86–88. Boston: Houghton Mifflin Co., 1964. Wilson's achievements as football coach and amateur golfer.

4006. Luce, Clare Booth. "All for the Love of a Lady." *McCall's* 91 (October 1963): 197–98. This compilation of "scandals" includes stories of unsuccessful attempts by Wilson's opponents to charge him with improper relations with Mary Allen Hulbert Peck, social reformer and feminist J. Borden Harriman, and Edith Bolling Galt.

4007. "Mary Allen Hulbert Tells of Her Proud Friendship with Woodrow Wilson." *Current Opinion* 78 (February 1925): 158–60. This article disputes the Peck myth whereby Wilson and Hulbert (maiden name Peck) had an illicit love affair.

4008. McAdoo, Eleanor Randolph Wilson. "The Wilsons." *Saturday Evening Post* November 14, 1936: 5–7+; November 21, 1936: 14–15+; November 28, 1936: 16–17+; December 5, 1936: 18–19+; December 12, 1936: 12–13+; December 19, 1936: 20–21+; December 26, 1936: 16–17+; January 2, 1937: 26+; January 9, 1937: 27+; January 16, 1937: 23+. Reminiscences by Wilson's daughter of his days as governor, the 1912 Democratic Convention, the inauguration, the first days in the White House, his dealings with Congress, and family life.

4009. McAdoo, Eleanor Randolph Wilson, in collaboration with Margaret Y. Gaffey. *The Woodrow Wilsons.* New York: Macmillan Co., 1937. Affectionate memoir by Wilson's daughter, covering their family life to the death of her mother.

4010. Parks, Lillian Rogers, with Frances Spatz Leighton. *My Thirty Years Backstairs at the White House.* New York: Fleet Publishing Co., 1961. A housekeeper's inside view of White House life.

4011. Saunders, Frances Wright. "Love and Guilt: Woodrow Wilson and Mary Hulbert." *American Heritage* 30, no. 3 (April 1979): 68–77. Using previously restricted correspondence between Wilson and Mrs. Peck, Saunders discusses their relationship, the death of Ellen Axson Wilson, and Wilson's marriage to Edith Bolling Galt.

4012. Seuling, Barbara. *The Last Cow on the White House Lawn and Other Little-Known Facts about the Presidency*, 56–59. Garden City, N.Y.: Doubleday and Co., 1978.

4013. Smith, Ira R. T., with Joe Alex Morris. *"Dear Mr. President . . ." The Story of Fifty Years in the White House Mail Room*, 90–107. New York: Julian Messner, 1949. The mail handler's impressions of the Wilson years.

4014. Smith, Marie. *Entertaining in the White House.* Washington, D.C.: Acropolis Press, 1967. One chapter on the Wilson presidency.

4015. Starling, Edmund William. *Starling of the White House: The Story of the Man Whose Secret Service Detail Guarded Five Presidents from Woodrow Wilson to Franklin D. Roosevelt, as Told to Thomas Sugrue*, 30–164. New York: Simon & Schuster, 1946. [Excerpts in *Life* 20 (February 18, 1946): 102–4.] A memoir by the head of the Secret Service unit.

4016. Sullivan, Michael John. *Presidential Passions: The Love Affairs of America's Presidents—from Washington and Jefferson to Kennedy and Johnson*, 230–36. New York: Shapolsky Publishers, 1991. Describes Wilson's first and second marriages and his alleged affair with Mrs. Peck.

4017. Thackwell, Helen Welles. "Woodrow Wilson and My Mother." *Princeton University Library Chronicle* 12 (Autumn 1950): 6–18. Woodrow Wilson's early love of his first cousin, Harriet Augusta Woodrow, their correspondence, and their decision not to marry.

4018. Truman, Margaret. *White House Pets*, 134–38. New York: David McKay Co., 1969. Brief treatment of the Wilson years by President Truman's daughter.

4019. Van Steenwyck, Elizabeth. *Presidents at Home*, 81–85. New York: Julian Messner, 1980. Brief descriptions of Wilson's various residences. Includes pictures of his birthplace and final home.

4020. Van Zandt, Roland. "Wilsonian Summers in Rural New England." *Saturday Review* 52 (March 8, 1969): 50–53. Wilson's 1913–1915 vacations at Cornish, New Hampshire.

4021. White, William Allen. "The Husband and Father." In **1038**, 129–36. Discusses the effects of Wilson's years in the White House on his family.

B. Personality and Health

4022. Adelman, Kimberly A., and Howard S. Adelman. "Rodin, Patton, Edison, Wilson, Einstein: Were They Really Learning Disabled?" *Journal of Learning Disabilities* 20 (May 1987): 270–79. Addresses posthumous diagnoses of Wilson and others.

4023. Adler, Bill, ed. *Presidential Wit from Washington to Johnson*, 101–14. New York: Trident Press, 1966. Humorous quotations by Wilson.

4024. Ambrosius, Lloyd E. "Woodrow Wilson's Health and the Treaty Fight." *International History Review* 9 (February 1987): 73–84. Concludes that even though Wilson's poor health weakened his leadership on behalf of the treaty, other factors at home and abroad contributed even more to its failures.

4025. Annin, Robert Edwards. *Woodrow Wilson: A Character Study*. New York: Dodd, Mead, and Co., 1924. Contemporary attempt at psychobiography.

4026. "Anomaly at the White House." *Review* 2 (April 3, 1920): 319–20. Looks at the unusual and negative effects Wilson's illness had on his ability to lead the country.

4027. Barber, James David. *The Presidential Character: Predicting Performance in the White House*, 43–48. Englewood Cliffs, N.J.: Prentice-Hall, 1972. Psychological interpretations of Wilson's political behavior.

4028. Boller, Paul F., Jr. *Presidential Anecdotes*, 217–28. New York: Oxford University Press, 1981. Looks at the religious, social, and political attributes that helped shape Wilson's diverse personality.

4029. Brooks, William E. "Woodrow Wilson: Study in Personality." *Century Magazine* 118 (August 1929): 410–20. Examines inconsistencies in Wilson's personality.

4030. Cocks, Geoffrey, and Travis Crosby, eds. *Readings in the Method of Psychology, Psychoanalysis, and History*. New Haven: Yale University Press, 1987. Includes several essays on Wilson and psychohistory.

4031. Cooper, Nancy. "Presidents as Patients." *Newsweek* 106 (July 22, 1985): 18–19. Wilson's incapacity from his October 1919 stroke is among the presidential illnesses described.

4032. Creel, George C. "Woodrow Wilson, the Man Behind the President." *Saturday Evening Post* 203 (March 28, 1931): 37+. Attempts to dispel the myths that Wilson was a cold and unfeeling man.

4033. Crispell, Kenneth R., and Carlos F. Gomez. "Woodrow Wilson: Strokes, Versailles, and the Pathology of Politics." In *Hidden Illness in the White House*. Durham, N.C.: Duke University Press, 1988. Describes Wilson's life-long bouts with various illnesses.

4034. Dabney, Virginius. "The Human Being." In **1038**, 15–34. A personal friend of Wilson describes him as a complicated man, stern in his public appearance yet jubilant and affectionate in private.

4035. ———. "The Human Side of Woodrow Wilson." *Virginia Quarterly Review* 32 (Autumn 1956): 508–23. Sketches the contrasts in Wilson's personality and the effects of his stroke on his personality and relationships.

4036. Dulles, Allen Welsh. "A Foreign Affairs Scholar Views the Real Woodrow Wilson." *Look* 30 (December 13, 1966): 50. In responding to **4040**, a former student of Wilson creates a much more flattering portrait of him as a professor and as President.

4037. Fabricant, Noah Daniel. "The Presidential Disability of Woodrow Wilson." In *13 Famous Patients*, 76–95. Philadelphia: Chilton Co., 1960. Includes a "medical profile" of Wilson.

4038. Feerick, John D. *From Failing Hands: The Story of Presidents' Succession*. New York: Fordham University Press, 1965. Chapter 13 contains a brief discussion of the circumstances surrounding Wilson's illness in 1919–1920.

4039. Feerick, Robert H. *Ill-Advised: Presidential Health and Public Trust*. Columbia: University of Missouri Press, 1992. Believes that because of a history of strokes and arteriosclerosis Wilson never should have been nominated in 1912.

4040. Freud, Sigmund, and William C. Bullitt. *Thomas Woodrow Wilson, Twenty-eighth President of the United States: A Psychological Study.* Boston: Houghton, Mifflin, 1967. [Excerpts in *Look* 30 (December 13, 1966): 36–38.] A highly publicized interpretation by Freud, who never met Wilson, and Bullitt, a disillusioned Wilsonian. Freud's role as author was minimal.

4041. _____. "Woodrow Wilson." *Encounter* 28, no. 160 (January 1967): 3–24; no. 161 (February 1967): 3–24. A two-part psychological study of Wilson.

4042. Garraty, John Arthur. "Woodrow Wilson: A Study in Personality." *South Atlantic Quarterly* 56, no. 2 (April 1957): 176–85. Argues that Wilson had difficulty relating to friends and associates and took refuge in his home and family.

4043. George, Alexander L. "Power as a Compensatory Value for Political Leaders." *Journal of Social Issues* 24, no. 3 (July 1968): 29–50. Singles out Wilson as an example of Harold Lasswell's hypothesis that power-seeking compensates for low self-esteem.

4044. George, Alexander L., and Juliette L. George. "Dr. Weinstein's Interpretation of Woodrow Wilson: Some Preliminary Observations." *Psychohistory Review* 8 (1979): 71–72. Concerns Weinstein's theories about Wilson's medical problems.

4045. _____. *Woodrow Wilson and Colonel House: A Personality Study.* New York: John Day Co., 1956. Argues that Wilson waged a lifelong battle against his father's domineering influence by trying to control people and events.

4046. _____. "Woodrow Wilson and Colonel House: Research Note." In *Varieties of Psychohistory*, ed. George M. Kren and Leon H. Rappoport, 111–119. New York: Springer Publications, 1976. Asserts that Wilson's public actions were largely determined by certain personality needs.

4047. George, Juliette L. "Telephone Interview of Alfred Stengel, Jr." (October 17, 1980), possession of Juliette George. Unpublished interview of the son of Alfred Stengel, the internist whom Wilson consulted.

4048. George, Juliette L., and Alexander L. George. "Woodrow Wilson and Colonel House: A Reply to Weinstein, Anderson, and Link." *Political Science Quarterly* 96, no. 4 (Winter 1981–82): 641–65. The Georges' response to critiques of their thesis in **4045**.

4049. George, Juliette L., Michael F. Marmor, and Alexander L. George. "Issues in Wilson Scholarship: References to Early 'Strokes' in the *Papers of Woodrow Wilson.*" *Journal of American History* 70, no. 4 (March 1984): 845–53. An argument against the Weinstein thesis that Wilson suffered strokes prior to his election as President.

4050. Gilbert, Robert E. "Death and the American President." *Politico* (in Italian) 42 (1977): 719–41. A statistical study.

4051. _____. *The Mortal Presidency: Illness and Anguish in the White House.* New York: Basic Books, 1992. Believes that Wilson's stroke and death interrupted a career that would have been far from over.

4052. Graff, Henry F. "A Heartbeat Away." *American Heritage* 15 (August 1964): 81–87. Describes Wilson's paralysis (1919–1920) and the fear that Vice President Marshall might become President.

4053. Grayson, Cary Travers. "Memories of Woodrow Wilson." *Atlantic Monthly* 204 (November 1959): 65–74. An excerpt from Grayson's memoir covering Wilson in Paris and his subsequent illness.

4054. _____. *Woodrow Wilson: An Intimate Memoir.* New York: Holt, Rinehart, and Winston, 1960. Memoir by Wilson's personal physician.

4055. Hale, William Bayard. *The Story of a Style.* New York: B.W. Heubsch, 1920. Hostile psychoanalytic examination of Wilson's spoken and written style.

4056. Hale, William Harlan. "President Wilson, Dr. Freud, and the Story of a Style." *The Reporter* 18 (June 26, 1958): 28–30. Discusses his father, William Bayard Hale, whose **4055** was an amateur psychoanalytic study of Wilson published in 1920, as well as his father's correspondence with Sigmund Freud on the subject.

4057. Harris, Irving D. "The Psychologies of Presidents." *History of Childhood Quarterly* 3 (1976): 337–50. A study of several Presidents and the impact of their personalities on political policy-making.

4058. Hoffs, Joshua A. "Comments on Psychoanalytic Biography, with Special Reference to Freud's Interest in Woodrow Wilson." *Psychoanalytic Review* 56 (1969): 402–14. A critique of **4040** and a defense of psychobiography as a method.

4059. Hofman, J., and A. Stam. "De Psychoanalyse in Dienst van een Diplomaat, Freud als Co-auteur van W.C. Bullitt." [Psychoanalysis in the Service of a Diplomat, Freud as a Co-Author with W.C. Bullitt]. *Tijdschrift voor Psychiatrie* 24 (1982): 125–134.

4060. Hoover, Irwin Hood (Ike). "The Facts about President Wilson's Illness." I.H. Hoover Papers. Washington, D.C.: Library of Congress.

4061. _____. "The Illness of Woodrow Wilson." *Saturday Evening Post* 207 (July 21, 1934): 23+. Challenges the notion that Wilson had always been an "unwell man" prior to his collapse.

4062. Kerney, James. "Government by Proxy: When President Wilson Lay Ill." *Century Magazine* 111 (February 1926): 481–86. Discusses the breakdown of leadership.

4063. Laukhuff, Perry. "The Price of Woodrow Wilson's Illness." *Virginia Quarterly Review* 32 (Autumn 1956): 598–610. Deals with constitutional problems.

4064. Lewis, Thomas T. "Alternative Psychological Interpretations of Woodrow Wilson." *Mid-America* 65, no. 2 (April-July 1983): 71–85. A historiographical review of the literature.

4065. Link, Arthur S. "The Case for Woodrow Wilson." *Harper's Magazine* 234 (April 1967): 85–93. [Also published in **1155**, 140–54.] Critical response to **4040**.

4066. ———. "Enigma of Woodrow Wilson." *American Mercury* 65 (September 1947): 303–13. Discusses the many contradictions in Wilson's character and presidency.

4067. ———. "A President Disabled." *Constitution* 4, no. 2 (Spring-Summer 1992): 5–15. Details the stroke and the resulting constitutional crisis.

4068. Maddox, Robert James. "Mrs. Wilson and the Presidency." *American History Illustrated* 7, no. 10 (1973): 36–44. Argues that Mrs. Wilson became de facto President after Wilson's stroke in 1919.

4069. Marmor, Michael F. "Wilson, Strokes, and Zebras." *New England Journal of Medicine* 307 (August 26, 1982): 528–35. An overview of Wilson's medical history, attempting to evaluate Edwin Weinstein's conclusion that Wilson suffered a series of strokes as early as 1896.

4070. Marx, Rudolph. *Health of the Presidents*, 309–22. New York: G.P. Putnam's Sons, 1961. A physician's description of Wilson's health, with special attention to his strokes.

4071. Monroe, Robert T. "Comments on 'Woodrow Wilson's Neurological Illness' by Dr. E. A. Weinstein." In The Arthur Walworth Papers. New Haven: Yale University Library, 1971.

4072. Moses, John B., and Wilbur Cross. "The Presidency in Limbo: The Tragedy of Wilson." In *Presidential Courage*, 131–67. New York: W. W. Norton, 1980. Describes the impact of Wilson's disability.

4073. Mowat, Robert Balmain. "College Presidents and College Professors." In *Americans in England*, 258–75. Boston: Houghton, Mifflin Co., 1935. Wilson found great comfort and peace of mind through his visits to the English countryside.

4074. Osborn, George Coleman. "Pass Christian, the Winter White House, Christmas, 1913." *Journal of Mississippi History* 22 (January 1960): 1–26. Pertains to Wilson's vacation in the small Gulf Coast town to recuperate from influenza, December 1913–January 1914.

4075. Park, Bert Edward. *The Impact of Illness on World Leaders*, 3–76, 331–42. Philadelphia: University of Pennsylvania Press, 1986. Wilson's health before and after his 1919 stroke and its effect on the subtle changes in his behavior. An appendix weighs possible medical causes for Wilson's declining health.

4076. _____. "The Impact of Wilson's Neurologic Disease During the Paris Peace Conference." In *PWW* 58:611–630. Explains that the primary sources in *PWW* vols. 51–59 suggest that in 1918–1919 Wilson suffered greatly from hypertensive cerebrovascular disease.

4077. Pitkin, Walter Boughton. "In a Great Man's Shoes." *Reader's Digest* 37 (October 1940): 89–93. Wilson's foot ailment.

4078. Post, Jerrold M. "Woodrow Wilson Re-Examined: The Mind-Body Controversy Redux and Other Disputations." *Political Psychology* 4 (June 1983): 289–312. Reevaluates the psychological and physiological influences on Wilson's behavior, and takes note of his relationship with both parents.

4079. "Presidents as Patients: Aides Sometimes Lie about Their Boss's Condition." *Newsweek* 106 (July 22, 1985): 18–19. Describes the fact that many members of Wilson's administration were kept in the dark about the President's condition, and that Wilson had to be talked out of running for the presidency again in 1920.

4080. Riccards, Michael P. "The Presidency: In Sickness and in Health." *Presidential Studies Quarterly* 7 (1977): 215–31. Includes the effects of disease on Wilson's decision-making.

4081. Rieff, Philip. "14 Points on Wilson." *Encounter* (Great Britain) 28, no. 163 (1967): 84–89. A review article of **4040**.

4082. Rogin, Michael Paul. "Max Weber and Woodrow Wilson: The Iron Cage in Germany and America." *Polity* 3, no. 4 (Summer 1971): 557–75. A review essay prompted by the publication of two books on Max Weber and **4045**.

4083. Roos, C. A. "Physicians to the Presidents, and Their Patients: A Bibliography." *Medical Library Association Bulletin* 49 (July 1961): 350–52. Lists the physicians who attended Wilson during his presidency.

4084. Ross, Dorothy. "Woodrow Wilson and the Case for Psychohistory." *Journal of American History* 69, no. 3 (December 1982): 659–68. A discussion of **373** as part of an argument for the validity of psychohistory as a method.

4085. Runyan, William McKinley. *Life Histories and Psychobiography*, 62–64, 195–97. New York: Oxford University Press, 1982. Comments on psychobiographical methods as applied to Wilson.

4086. Shannon, David A. "Woodrow Wilson's Youth and Personality." *Pacific Northwest Quarterly* 58, no. 4 (1967): 205–7. A review contrasting the first two volumes of *PWW* with **4040**.

4087. Smith, Don. *Peculiarities of the Presidents: Strange and Intimate Facts Not Found in History.* 4th ed., 12, 15, 18, 20, 48, 56, 59, 89. Van Wert, Ohio: Wilkinson Printing Co., 1938. Includes eight entries for "peculiarities" of Wilson, unusual characteristics or events.

4088. "Suffering in Secrecy: Past Leaders Hid Illnesses." *Time* 126 (July 22, 1985): 27. Explains that Wilson's deteriorating condition was carefully kept from the public, that Wilson was never hospitalized, and that Mrs. Wilson restricted all but the most necessary visits.

4089. Toole, James F. "Some Observations on Wilson's Neurologic Illness." In *PWW* 58:635–38. Princeton: Princeton University Press, 1988. Argues that the medical evidence demonstrates chronic hypertension and "recurrent cerebrovascular events" in Wilson over a period of years. To what extent, if any, it affected his behavior is still open to question.

4090. Tuchman, Barbara Wertheim. "Can History Use Freud? The Case of Woodrow Wilson." *Atlantic Monthly* 219 (February 1967): 39–44. A critique of **4040**.

4091. Tucker, Robert C. "The Georges' Wilson Reexamined: An Essay on Psychobiography." *American Political Science Review* 71 (June 1977): 606–18. Compares **4045** with theories of Karen Horney.

4092. "Two Presidents Disabled in Office." *U.S. News and World Report* 43 (December 6, 1957): 39. Says that Wilson's and James Garfield's physical disabilities did not stop them from exercising presidential powers.

4093. Weinstein, Edwin A. "Denial of Presidential Disability: A Case Study of Woodrow Wilson." *Psychiatry* 30 (November 1967): 376–91. Attempts to correlate "organic" and "psychological" factors in Wilson's behavior after his 1919 stroke.

4094. _____. "Politics and Health: The Neurological History of Woodrow Wilson." *Trends in NeuroSciences* 5 (January 1982): 7–9. Examines Wilson's everchanging states of mental and physical health in relation to the major political events in his life.

4095. _____. "Woodrow Wilson's Neurological Illness." *Journal of American History* 57 (September 1970): 324–51. The author outlines his theory of Wilson's multiple strokes.

4096. _____. "Woodrow Wilson's Neuropsychological Impairment and the Paris Peace Conference." In *PWW* 58:630–35. Diagnoses Wilson's condition, even before his 1919 strokes, as multi-infarct dementia.

4097. Weinstein, Edwin A., James William Anderson, and Arthur S. Link. "Woodrow Wilson's Political Personality: A Reappraisal." *Political Science Quarterly* 93 (Winter 1978–79): 585–98. A critique of **4045** which evaluates Wilson's personality by examining his childhood and the Princeton graduate college controversy.

4098. "Wilson's Neurologic Illness at Paris." In *PWW* 58:607–40. Includes **4076**, **4089**, and **4096**. Also contains an editorial introduction and commentary.

4099. Wold, Karl Christian. *Mr. President, How Is Your Health?*, 175–79. St. Paul: Bruce Publishing Co., 1948. Brief account of Wilson's medical history, beginning in childhood.

C. Religion

4100. Alley, Robert S. *So Help Me God: Religion in the Presidency, Wilson to Nixon*, 33–42. Richmond, Va.: John Knox Press, 1972. A brief analysis of Wilson's Presbyterian faith.

4101. Athearn, Clarence Royalty. "Woodrow Wilson's Philosophy." *Methodist Review* 112 (September 1929): 683–88. Describes the importance of religion in Wilson's role as a statesman.

4102. Blythe, Samuel George. "Strange Case of Dr. Wilson and Mr. Wilson." *Saturday Evening Post* 193 (February 5, 1921): 3–4. An assessment of Wilson's Presbyterian background.

4103. Bonnell, John Sutherland. *Presidential Profiles: Religion in the Life of American Presidents*, 180–85. Philadelphia: Westminster Press, 1971. Biographical sketch upholding Wilson as one of the greatest statesmen and patriots in American history.

4104. Copeland, Arthur. "Woodrow Wilson's Opinion of John Wesley." *Methodist Review* 97 (September 1915): 728–30. Summary of an address, entitled "John Wesley's Place in History," by the Princeton President at the Wesley Bicentennial in Middletown, Conn., June 30, 1903.

4105. Curti, Merle Eugene. "Woodrow Wilson's Concept of Human Nature." *Midwest Journal of Political Science* 1 (May 1957): 1–19. Focuses on the religious roots of Wilson's moral principles.

4106. Fuller, Edmund, and David E. Green. "Panorama of Past Presidents: Priests of the National Religion." In *God in the White House: The Faiths of American Presidents*, 35–58. New York: Crown Publishers, 1968. Cites Wilson as possibly the most "God-centered" President to date.

4107. Hampton, Vernon B. *Religious Background of the White House*, 90–101, 187–95. Boston: Christopher Publishing House, 1932. Contains biographical sketches of Woodrow Wilson and Ellen Axson Wilson, with an emphasis on the influence of their faith.

4108. Hampton, William Judson. *The Religion of the Presidents*, 88–91. Somerville, N.J.: Press of the Unionist-Gazette Association, 1925. Describes Wilson as a committed Christian.

4109. Howard, Herbert Roscoe. "The Social Philosophy of Woodrow Wilson." Ph.D. diss., Southern Baptist Theological Seminary, 1944. Examines the influence of Christianity on the development of Wilson's social philosophy and progressivism.

4110. Hunter, Stanley A., ed. *The Religious Ideals of a President*. Allahabad, India: Allahabad Mission Press, 1914. Some selections by Wilson on religious matters.

4111. Isely, Bliss. *The Presidents: Men of Faith.* Rev. ed., 211– 17. Natick, Mass: W. A. Wilde Co., 1961. A brief biographical sketch examining Wilson's religious and academic background.

4112. Johnson, Gerald White. "Wilson the Man." *Virginia Quarterly Review* 32 (Autumn 1956): 494–507. Stresses the importance of Wilson's Presbyterianism in understanding his political views.

4113. Karcher, Joseph T. *A New Appraisal of Woodrow Wilson.* New York: Pamphlet Distributing Co., 1943. Brief and highly laudatory interpretation of Wilson as a Christian.

4114. Lewis, Frank Bell. *Woodrow Wilson's Heritage of Faith.* Staunton: Woodrow Wilson Centennial Commission of Virginia, 1956. Examines Wilson's religious heritage, and looks at its influence on his presidency.

4115. Link, Arthur S. "A Portrait of Wilson." *Virginia Quarterly Review* 32 (Autumn 1956): 524–40. A biographical sketch, emphasizing Wilson's religious beliefs.

4116. _____ . "Woodrow Wilson: Christian in Government." *Christianity Today* 8 (July 3, 1964): 6–10. An essay on Wilson's Christian faith and how it affected his presidency.

4117. _____ . "Woodrow Wilson and the Life of Faith." *Presbyterian Life* 16 (March 1, 1963): 8–15. An examination of Wilson's religious thought.

4118. _____ . "Woodrow Wilson: Presbyterian in Government." In *Calvinism and the Political Order: Essays Prepared for the Woodrow Wilson Lectureship of the National Presbyterian Center, Washington, D.C.,* ed. George Laird Hunt, 157–74. Philadelphia: Westminster Press, 1965. An essay outlining the influence of Presbyterianism on Wilson's politics.

4119. _____ . "Woodrow Wilson and His Presbyterian Inheritance." In *Essays in Scotch-Irish History,* ed. E. R. Green, 1–17. New York: Humanities Press, 1969. [Also published in **1155**, 3–20.] Examines the influences of Wilson's Scotch-Irish heritage, family, and religion on his character and political philosophy.

4120. Mathisen, Robert R. "Evangelicals and the Age of Reform, 1870–1930: An Assessment." *Fides et Historia* 16 (Spring-Summer 1984): 74–85. Response. Jack Barlow, 86–89. Reviews the literature on this subject, and includes a discussion of Wilson's thinking about the role of the church in saving individuals and reforming society.

4121. McCollister, John. *So Help Me God: The Faith of America's Presidents,* 135–37. Louisville: Westminster/John Knox Press, 1991. Emphasizes Wilson's belief in Divine Providence.

4122. Mulder, John M. "'A Gospel of Order': Woodrow Wilson's Religion and Politics." In **1083**, 223–47. A reexamination of Wilson's religious and political thought.

4123. _____. "Wilson the Preacher: The 1905 Baccalaureate Sermon." *Journal of Presbyterian History* 51, no. 3 (Fall 1973): 267–84. Examines Wilson's emphasis on his religious faith and its application in his baccalaureate sermon at Princeton. Includes text of sermon.

4124. Osborn, George Coleman. "Religious Cross Currents of the Wilson Administration." *Journal of Mississippi History* 2 (1940): 136–46. A study of anti-Catholic sentiments expressed during the Wilson presidency in general, and against Wilson's secretary, Joseph Tumulty, in particular.

4125. "The President on Religious Education." *Literary Digest* 48 (June 13, 1914): 1438–39. Lengthy excerpts of a speech by Wilson on the importance of religious influences.

4126. "President Wilson and Others Seek to Revitalize the Country Church." *Current Opinion* 60 (February 1916): 112–13. Asserts that Wilson stressed the social value of church organization by which the whole community could cooperatively benefit.

4127. "Religious Utterances of the President-Elect." *Literary Digest* 45 (December 7, 1912): 1067–68. Sampling of Wilson's speeches which show his basic religious beliefs.

4128. Rogal, Samuel J. "Methodism on the Hustings: Woodrow Wilson and 'John Wesley's Place in History.'" *Perkins School of Theology: Journal* 38 (Spring 1985): 9–18. Examines a speech by Wilson, in which he compared his own times with the 18th century and his role with that of John Wesley.

4129. Salisbury, Dorothy Cleaveland. "Religion as the Leaders of This Nation Reveal It." *Daughters of the American Revolution Magazine* 106 (May 1972): 540–44, 550. Considers Wilson among ten American leaders who have demonstrated religious convictions.

4130. Schulte Nordholt, Jan Willem. "De Religie van Woodrow Wilson." [The Religion of Woodrow Wilson]. *Tijdschrift voor Geschiedenis* (Netherlands) 98, no. 1 (1985): 43–55. Argues for the power of religion in both shaping and distorting Wilson's understanding of politics.

4131. Soper, David Wesley. "Woodrow Wilson and the Christian Tradition." Ph.D. diss., Drew Divinity School, 1945. Uses Wilson as the model to introduce his theory of the authentic link between Christianity and world politics.

4132. _____. "Woodrow Wilson's Concept of Personality." *Personalist: An International Review of Philosophy, Religion, and Literature* 32 (October 1951):

368–80. Says Wilson understood human personality as the true index to the nature of ultimate reality which is moral rather than biological.

4133. Taylor, James Henry. *Woodrow Wilson in Church: His Membership in the Congregation of the Central Presbyterian Church, Washington, D.C., 1913–1924.* Charleston, S.C.: The Author, 1952. A sympathetic recollection by Wilson's pastor.

4134. Vivian, James F. "The Pan-American Mass, 1909–1914: A Rejected Contribution to Thanksgiving Day." *Church History* 51 (September 1982): 321–33. Describes the effect of an interview with the Rt. Rev. Msgr. William T. Russell in 1912 on Wilson's withdrawal of support for the annual Christian Inter-American Festival.

4135. Wallace, Archer. *Religious Faith of Great Men*, 193–217. New York: Round Table Press, 1934. Chapter includes a brief section discussing Wilson's deeply felt religious convictions.

D. Wilson's Wives: Ellen Axson Wilson and Edith Bolling Galt Wilson

See also entries for each under Wilson's Associates

4136. Anthony, Carl Sferrazza. *First Ladies: The Saga of the Presidents' Wives and Their Power, 1789–1961*, 1:343–49, 350–81. New York: W. W. Morrow, 1990–91. Analyzes the influence of Ellen Axson Wilson and Edith Bolling Wilson on the President.

4137. Barzman, Sol. *The First Ladies*, 246–64. New York: Cowles Book Co., 1970. Details Ellen Axson Wilson's 31–year relationship with Wilson and her seventeen months as an active and progressive First Lady. Also describes Edith Bolling Wilson's close relationship with the President and chronicles the active life she continued to lead for nearly four decades following Wilson's death.

4138. Boller, Paul F., Jr. "The Wilson Wives: Ellen Axson Wilson (1860–1914) and Edith Bolling Wilson (1872–1961)." In *Presidential Wives*, 219–41. New York: Oxford University Press, 1988. Brief essay on Wilson's relations with women and his two wives in particular.

4139. Brown, Margaret W. *The Dresses of the First Ladies of the White House*, 118–25. Washington, D.C.: Smithsonian Institution, 1952. Biographical sketches of Ellen Axson Wilson and Edith Bolling Galt Wilson and photographs of their dresses.

4140. Caroli, Betty Boyd. *First Ladies*, 134–52. New York: Oxford University Press, 1987. Portrays Ellen Axson Wilson and Edith Bolling Galt Wilson and their relationships with Wilson against a backdrop of change in America, particularly woman suffrage.

4141. Ewart, Andrew. "Woodrow Wilson and Edith Bolling." In *Great Lovers*, 257–76. New York: Hart, 1968. Includes numerous photographs, correspondence, and excerpts from her 1939 memoirs.

4142. Funderbunk, Charles. *Presidents and Politics: The Limits of Power*. Monterey, Calif.: Brooks Cole Publishing Co., 1982. Discusses how, after Wilson's crippling stroke in the fall of 1919, his wife Edith Bolling Wilson became chief of staff, if not acting President.

4143. Gerlinger, Irene Hazard. *Mistresses of the White House: Narrator's Tale of a Pageant of First Ladies*, 89–91. Freeport, N.Y.: Books for Libraries Press, 1948. Ellen Axson Wilson and Edith Bolling Galt Wilson are profiled approvingly.

4144. Hay, Peter. *All the Presidents' Ladies: Anecdotes of the Women behind the Men in the White House*. New York: Viking Press, 1988. Arranged by category, with anecdotes about the Wilsons scattered throughout.

4145. Healy, Diana Dixon. *America's First Ladies: Private Lives of the Presidential Wives*, 144–50, 151–58. New York: Athenuem Press, 1988. Includes insights into the lives of Ellen Axson Wilson and Edith Bolling Wilson.

4146. Hoover, Irwin Hood (Ike). "Courtship and Marriage of a President." *Saturday Evening Post* 206 (June 23, 1934): 14–15+. Discusses Wilson's marriage to Edith Bolling Galt.

4147. James, Edith. "Edith Bolling Wilson: A Documentary View." In *Clio Was a Woman: Studies in the History of American Women*, ed. Mabel E. Deutrich and Virginia C. Purdy, 234–40. Washington: Howard University Press, 1980. An analysis of Mrs. Wilson's letters in order to understand the pressures on the wife of the President.

4148. Jensen, Amy La Follette. "The President's Lady." *American Heritage* 15 (August 1964): 55–61. Features portraits of Edith Bolling Wilson.

4149. Klapthor, Margaret Brown. *The First Ladies*, 62–65. Washington: White House Historical Association, 1975. Brief biographical sketches of Wilson's two wives, as well as portraits of both women.

4150. La Carruba, Michael A. *Presidents and Wives: Portraits, Facts*, 40. Washington, D.C.: Historic Publications, 1959. Brief biographical sketch of Wilson and his two wives.

4151. Mayer, Arno J. "America's First Ladies." *Newsweek* 94 (November 5, 1979): 49. Describes the importance of Edith Bolling Galt Wilson in Wilson's presidency and her crucial role after Wilson's 1919 stroke.

4152. McAdoo, Eleanor Randolph Wilson. "The Courtship of Woodrow Wilson: Excerpts from *The Priceless Gift*." *American Heritage* 13, no. 6 (October 1962): 28–31, 67–75. Excerpts from Wilson's letters to Ellen Axson Wilson.

4153. McAdoo, Eleanor Randolph Wilson, ed. *The Priceless Gift: The Love Letters of Woodrow Wilson and Ellen Axson Wilson.* New York: McGraw-Hill and Co., 1962. A selective and expurgated collection of letters between Wilson and Ellen Axson Wilson, assembled by their daughter.

4154. Means, Marianne. *The Women in the White House: Their Lives, Times, and Influence of Twelve Notable First Ladies,* 135–64. New York: Random House, 1963. Edith Bolling Galt Wilson is profiled in a chapter covering her courtship by the President, their marriage, and her conduct during the President's illness in 1919.

4155. Miller, Hope Ridings. *Scandals in the Highest Office,* 169– 99. New York: Random House, 1973. Explores Wilson's romance with Edith Bolling Galt and his alleged affair with Mrs. Peck.

4156. Osborn, George Coleman. "The Romance of Woodrow Wilson and Ellen Axson." *North Carolina Historical Review* 39 (Winter 1962): 32–57. Details the correspondence and courtship leading to their marriage on June 24, 1885.

4157. "The Other Presidents." *Good Housekeeping* 94 (February 1932): 18–21+. Wives of Presidents from Wilson to Hoover by "A Well-known Woman Politician."

4158. Phifer, Gregg. "Edith Bolling Wilson: Gatekeeper Extraordinary." *Speech Monographs* 38, no. 4 (November 1971): 277–89. Focuses on Mrs. Wilson's role in shielding Wilson and filtering communications.

4159. Randolph, Mary. *Presidents and First Ladies,* 41, 222–28. New York: D. Appleton Century Co., 1936. The social life of the White House from Theodore Roosevelt to Franklin D. Roosevelt, written by a frequent White House guest.

4160. Ross, George Edward. *Know Your Presidents and Their Wives,* 56–57. Chicago: Rand McNally, 1960. Sketch of Wilson and his two wives.

4161. Saunders, Frances Wright. "'Dearest Ones:' Edith Bolling Wilson's Letters From Paris, 1918–1919." *Virginia Cavalcade* 37 (Autumn 1987): 52–67. Reprints selections from her letters to her family describing state visits, official functions, and travels with Wilson during the Paris Peace Conference.

4162. Seale, William. *The President's House: A History,* 2:767– 835. Washington: White House Historical Association, 1986. Two chapters deal with the Wilson residency, one with Ellen Axson Wilson and the other with Edith Bolling Wilson.

4163. Shachtman, Tom. *Edith and Woodrow: A Presidential Romance.* New York: G. P. Putnam's Sons, 1981. A biographical study of the second Mrs. Wilson and her contribution to Wilson's presidency.

4164. Tribble, Edwin, ed. *A President in Love: The Courtship Letters of Woodrow Wilson and Edith Bolling Galt.* Boston: Houghton, Mifflin Co., 1981. Selections from 250 letters exchanged in 1915.

4165. Waldrup, Carole Chandler. *Presidents' Wives: The Lives of 44 American Women of Strength*, 231–51. Jefferson, N.C.: McFarland & Co., 1989. Biographical sketches of the wives of the Presidents, including Ellen Axson Wilson and Edith Bolling Wilson.

4166. Weaver, Judith L. "Edith Bolling Wilson as First Lady: A Study in the Power of Personality, 1919–1920." *Presidential Studies Quarterly* 15, no. 1 (1985): 51–76. Analyzes Mrs. Wilson's critical role after Wilson's stroke in 1919.

4167. "When Woodrow Wilson Came A-Courting Down in Georgia." *Literary Digest* 76 (February 17, 1923): 48–50. Excerpt from a book on Rome, Georgia, by George M. Battes Jr., dealing with Wilson's courtship of Ellen Louise Axson.

4168. "Wife's Story." *Time* 33 (March 20, 1939): 16. Summary of **4171**, discussing politics and personal stories from the White House years.

4169. Wilson, Edith Bolling Galt. "As I Saw It: Autobiography." *Saturday Evening Post* December 24, 1938: 12–13+; December 31, 1938: 20–21+; January 7, 1939: 16–17+; January 14, 1939: 16–17+; January 21, 1939: 18–19+; January 28, 1939: 20–21+; February 11, 1939: 29+; February 18, 1939: 14–15+; February 25, 1939: 20–21+; March 4, 1939: 25+. A serialized version of Mrs. Wilson's autobiography.

4170. ———. "Letters from Ellen Axson Wilson to Anna Harris of Rome, Georgia, 1885–1912." *Georgia Historical Quarterly* 38 (December 1954): 369–94. Letters describe an inspiring teacher, a devoted husband, a considerate father, an entertaining lecturer, a capable administrator, and a successful politician.

4171. ———. *My Memoir*. Indianapolis: Bobbs-Merrill, 1939. Her recollections of Wilson from their courtship until his death.

4172. ———. "When Woodrow Was Ill." *Saturday Evening Post* 248 (July 1976): 58. Describes Edith Bolling Wilson's protection of Wilson after his stroke but maintains she never made any decisions for him.

24

Iconography and Media Materials

4173. Barclay, McKee. "Wilson among the Cartoonists." *Collier's National Weekly* 53 (March 28, 1914): 17. Cartoonists' efforts to draw Wilson.

4174. Blaidsell, T. C., Jr., et al. *The American Presidency in Political Cartoons: 1776–1976.* Lake City, Utah: Peregrine Smith, 1976. Classic cartoons, mainly by foreign cartoonists.

4175. "Builders of America: Picture Biography." *Scholastic* 42 (May 3, 1943): 14.

4176. Campbell, Craig W. *Reel America and World War I: A Comprehensive Filmography and History of Motion Pictures in the United States, 1914–1920.* Jefferson, N.C.: McFarland, 1985. Wilson's use and appreciation of film technology.

4177. Chase, Joseph Cummings. "Famous Sitters." *Saturday Evening Post* 200 (August 27, 1927): 16–17. Describes painting Wilson's portrait.

4178. Collins, Herbert Ridgeway. *Presidents on Wheels.* Washington: Acropolis Books, 1971.

4179. Crichton, Kyle Samuel. "Mr. Zanuck Bets Five Million." *Collier's National Weekly* 114 (July 22, 1944): 18–19+. The making of a movie on Wilson's life.

4180. Davidson, Jo. "Portrait Bust by Jo Davidson." *American Magazine of Art* 11 (November 1920): 470.

4181. Durant, John, and Alice Durant. *Pictorial History of American Presidents.* 5th rev. ed., 224–35, 350. South Brunswick, N.J.: A. S. Barnes, 1969.

4182. Easterwood, Birch D. *Pen Renderings of the Presidents,* 62–63. New York: Vantage Press, 1968.

4183. Editors of *News Front*. *Contest for Power: The Exciting Pictorial Story of the American Presidential Elections, the Personalities, the Issues, the Turning Points in U.S. Political History from 1778 to the Present*. New York: Year, 1968.

4184. *Exhibit to Mark the Centennial of the Birth of Woodrow Wilson at Staunton, Virginia, December 18, 1856*. New York: Woodrow Wilson Foundation, 1956. [In portfolio.]

4185. Freidel, Frank. *The Presidents of the United States of America*. 5th ed., 60–61. Washington, D.C.: White House Historical Association, 1973, 1982. Short biographical sketch of Wilson. Includes a portrait painted by Sir William Orpen.

4186. Gilder, Rosamond. "Time and the Rivals: 'In Time to Come.'" *Theatre Arts* 26 (March 1942): 149–50. A review of **4191**, a play based on Wilson's life as America's last war President. The reviewer argues that the impact of the play is rendered even more powerful as the United States enters into another world conflict.

4187. Golterman, Guy. *The Book of the Presidents: A Gallery of Famous Portraits of the Presidents of the United States*. Rev. ed. St. Louis: n.p., 1956.

4188. Johnson, Gerald White. *Woodrow Wilson: The Unforgettable Figure Who Has Returned to Haunt Us*. A Look Picture Book. New York: Harper & Brothers, 1944. A pictorial biography.

4189. Kennett, Teresa. *Thirty-Seven Personal Portraits of the Presidents of the United States of America*. Richmond, Calif.: Brombacher Books, 1975.

4190. Knock, Thomas J. "History with Lightning: The Forgotten Film *Wilson*." *American Quarterly* 28 (Winter 1976): 523–43. Discusses **4209** and **4216**.

4191. Koch, Howard. *In Time to Come: A Play about Woodrow Wilson*. Rev. ed. New York: Dramatists Play Service, [1942]. Begins in April 1917, and ends in 1921.

4192. Koch, Howard, and John Huston. "In Time to Come." *Scholastic* 40 (February 23, 1942): 17–19+. Drama, abridged.

4193. Leff, Leonard J., and Jerold Simmons. "Wilson: Hollywood Propaganda for World Peace." *History Journal of Film, Radio and Television* (Great Britain) 3, no. 1 (1983): 3–18. Traces the making of the 1944 film biography of Wilson and its reception in the United States and abroad.

4194. Leisch, Kenneth W., et al., eds. *American Heritage Pictorial History of the Presidents of the United States*, 683–721. New York: American Heritage Publishing Co., 1968.

4195. Littell, Philip. "Sargent's Wilson at the Metropolitan Museum." In *Books and Things*, 3–4. New York: Harcourt, Brace and House, 1919. Concerns a portrait of Wilson painted by John Singer Sargent.

4196. Lorant, Stefan. *The Glorious Burden: The American Presidency*, 509–45. New York: Harper & Row, 1968. [Formerly published as **4197**.]

4197. _____. _The Presidency: A Pictorial History of Presidential Elections from Washington to Truman_, 501–33. New York: Macmillan Co., 1951. Two chapters on Wilson and includes a number of political cartoons.

4198. Pach, Alfred. _Portraits of Our Presidents: The Pach Collection_. New York: Hastings House, 1943. Brief pictorial collection.

4199. Pachter, Marc. _A Gallery of Presidents_. Washington, D.C.: Smithsonian Institution, 1968. Contains a portrait of Wilson and a brief biography.

4200. Post, Robert C., ed. _Every Four Years_. Washington: Smithsonian Exposition Books, 1980.

4201. Potts, E. Daniel, comp. _List of Motion Pictures and Sound Recordings Relating to Presidential Inaugurations_, 3–4. Washington: National Archives, 1960. A bibliography of films and recordings, including the inaugurations of 1913 and 1917.

4202. "The President's Portrait for Dublin." _Literary Digest_ 55 (July 14, 1917): 27. Announces that a portrait of Wilson, commissioned by the National Art Gallery of Ireland, is to be painted by John Singer Sargent.

4203. Purdy, Virginia G. _Presidential Portraits_. Washington, D.C.: Published for the National Portrait Gallery by the Smithsonian Institution Press, 1968.

4204. Reinfeld, Don. _Picture Book of the Presidents_, 50–51. New York: Sterling Publishing Co., 1961.

4205. Sann, Paul. _The Lawless Decade: A Pictoral History of a Great American Transition: From the World War I Armistice and Prohibition to Repeal and the New Deal_. New York: Crown Publishers Inc., 1957. Explains that although Wilson made an earnest appeal to Americans, his League plan was rejected by the nation.

4206. Saunders, Frances Wright. "'No Pale, Cold Scholar': John Singer Sargent's Portrait of Woodrow Wilson." _Virginia Cavalcade_ 30, no. 2 (1980): 52–59. Describes the commissioning by the National Gallery of Ireland of a portrait of Wilson by Sargent.

4207. "Screen Biography." _New York Times Magazine_ June 18, 1944: 18–19. Discusses scenes from **4216**, including some of the most important moments in his life.

4208. Trotti, Lamar. "Wilson." Screenplay [S. L.]: Twentieth Century-Fox, 1943. See **4216**.

4209. Twentieth Century Fox. _Wilson: The Road to War_. Dir. by Henry King. 24 min, 1 reel. Wilmette, Ill.: Films Inc., [1976?]. Motion picture. Excerpts from **4216**. Documentary footage with commentary, focusing on events which led Wilson from his neutrality policy to a declaration of war against Germany in 1917.

4210. ———. *Woodrow Wilson: Spokesman for Tomorrow.* 27 min, 16 mm. Caravel Films: McGraw-Hill Book Co., 1956. Motion picture.

4211. Whitney, David C. *The Graphic Story of the American Presidents*, 175–89. Chicago: J. G. Ferguson Publishing Co., 1968. Includes an in-depth biography of Wilson; and compares Wilson with Abraham Lincoln.

4212. Wilson, Fred Taylor. *Pen Pictures of the Presidents.* Nashville: Southwestern Co., 1937. A comprehensive collection.

4213. "Wilson on the Screen." *New York Times Magazine* March 26, 1944: 16–17. Describes production costs, starring roles, and number of filmed hours for **4216**, which covers Wilson's career from the presidency of Princeton to his death.

4214. "Without Benefit of Hollywood." *New Republic* 37 (February 20, 1924): 326. Comments on a motion picture about Wilson.

4215. "Woodrow Wilson Is Hero of Broadway Play about the League of Nations." *Life* 12 (February 2, 1942): 33–34+. Brief review of **4191**, a play on Wilson's life. Accompanied by numerous photographs of the production.

4216. Zanuck, Darryl. *Wilson.* Dir. by Henry King, written by Lamar Trotti. Motion Picture. Twentieth Century Fox, 1944. Shows the warm and human as well as the political and intellectual characteristics of Wilson, played by Alexander Knox. The picture points out the value of Wilson's ideal of an association of nations to ensure world peace.

Author Index

Subject Index

Numbers in the index refer to entry numbers, not page numbers.

Bibliographies of the
Presidents of the United States

Series Editor: Mary Ellen McElligott

About the Compilers

JOHN M. MULDER is President and Professor of Historical Theology at Louisville Presbyterian Theological Seminary.

ERNEST M. WHITE was Emeritus Professor of Bibliography and Research and Librarian at Louisville Presbyterian Theological Seminary.

ETHEL S. WHITE is a former part-time American history instructor at the University of Louisville.

ISBN 0-313-28185-8

90000>

EAN

9 780313 281853

HARDCOVER BAR CODE